[WHY YOU VOTE

>> POLITICAL VIEWS OF 18–25-YEAR-OLDS]

We should do whatever it takes to protect the environment	**77%**	
Voting gives people like me some say about how government runs things	**72%**	
Illegal immigrants should have the chance to stay	**70%**	
I disapprove of the Iraq war policy	**69%**	
The U.S. relies too much on the military to defeat terrorism	**67%**	
Homosexuality is a way of life that should be accepted by society	**58%**	
Government is not usually inefficient and wasteful	**64%**	
Voting can bring about social change	**56%**	
I feel guilty for not voting	**50%**	
I am registered to vote	**49%**	
It's my duty as a citizen to always vote	**42%**	

SOURCE: Pew Research Center: "How Young People View Their Lives, Futures, and Politics: A Portrait of Generation Next," January 9, 2007.

AM GOV 2009

VICE PRESIDENT & EDITOR IN CHIEF **Michael Ryan**
EDITORIAL DIRECTOR **Beth Mejia**
SPONSORING EDITOR **Mark Georgiev**
MARKETING MANAGER **Bill Minick**
DIRECTOR OF DEVELOPMENT **Nancy Crochiere**
DEVELOPMENT EDITOR **Diane Culhane**
EDITORIAL COORDINATOR **Briana Porco**
EDITING, DESIGN, AND PRODUCTION MANAGER **Melissa Williams**
COVER DESIGN **Preston Thomas**
INTERIOR DESIGN **Pam Verros, Laurie Entringer, Hassan Herz**
ART MANAGER **Robin Mouat**
ILLUSTRATION **Robin Mouat, Rennie Evans, John & Judy Waller, Ayelet Arbel**
PHOTO RESEARCH **Emily Tietz, Editorial Image, LLC**
SENIOR MANUFACTURING SUPERVISOR **Rich DeVitto**
LEAD MEDIA PROJECT MANAGER **Ron Nelms**
SUPPLEMENTS **Southern Editorial**
CREATIVE AND PRODUCTION ASSISTANCE **Jasmin Tokatlian, Rachel Castillo**
COMPOSITION **TBH Typecast, Inc.**
PRINTING **Quebecor World**

AM GOV

BRIEF CONTENTS

BELLE PLAINE 5.7 MI
E. UNION 3.3M
CARVER 7.8M
CHASKA 10.6MI
CUSTER SD 600 MI
SAN FRANCISCO
TOWN HALL 1 MI.
VOTE TODAY

CONTENTS

4 CIVIL LIBERTIES: EXPANDING CITIZENS' RIGHTS 65

Drug Testing vs. Students' Rights

13 BUREAUCRACY: CITIZENS AS OWNERS AND CONSUMERS 317

Katrina and the Slow Federal Bureaucratic Response

15 PUBLIC POLICY: RESPONDING TO CITIZENS 363
American Dream or Nightmare?

FOREIGN AND DEFENSE POLICY: PROTECTING AMERICAN INTERESTS IN THE WORLD 385

Intelligence: Getting It Right

to bring you exclusive commentary on events from the past year.

National Journal — Youth Vote

GENERATION 'WE'
The Awakened Giant

During the first presidential campaign of the new millennium, Harvard students Erin Ashwell and Trevor Dryer, like their counterparts at colleges across the country, eagerly awaited the thrill of voting in a national election for the first time. Their anticipation was tempered, however, by dismissive talk about the apparent political disaffection of young people and the youth vote's irrelevance in the 2000 elections.

This didn't strike Ashwell and Dryer as the whole story. "In 2000, there was a lot of press about how young people don't vote, don't get involved, don't care about politics," Ashwell recalls. "Trevor and I wanted to know if it was true. It didn't seem right: All of our friends were into community service." Although they were only college sophomores—or perhaps because they were college sophomores—the pair decided to test conventional wisdom. They also sought to shed light on the paradox of a generation of young activists who devoted hours each week to tutoring underprivileged children, volunteering at food banks, and promoting environmental activism—but who couldn't be bothered to register or vote.

Ashwell and Dryer began delving into the attitudes of their fellow collegians via a nationwide survey, a project Harvard continued after they graduated. Over the ensuing years, the poll by the Institute of Politics at the John F. Kennedy School of Government has penetrated more deeply than other surveys, using the Internet and other innovative techniques, such as having undergraduates help formulate the questions.

The survey has drawn a picture of a unique generation. Today's youth are an underrated force in American civic life—difficult to stereotype, with attitudes markedly different from those of their predecessors. College students overwhelmingly favor the partial privatization of Social Security, a conservative Republican position and one at odds with the preferences of older Americans. Yet they are far more supportive of gay marriage, gay adoption, and gays' being allowed to serve openly in the military than any other age

group, views that place them in the vanguard of Democratic liberalism. In many respects, they are available to both major parties and, judging by their weak party affiliation, would be receptive to an independent presidential candidate. The 2006 IOP poll went even further, concluding that the traditional labels

trust the federal government to "do the right thing" all or most of the time. Asked about the motivations of politicians, three-fourths of the respondents said that elected officials "seem to be motivated by selfish reasons." More than 70 percent said that America's political institutions were unconcerned with the desires of

Inside Washington

A stunning 60 percent of college students in the institute's new survey said they had faith in the government to do the right thing all or most of the time, compared with 36 percent in 2000. Fully three-fourths of them expressed "trust" in the military, 69 percent said they trusted the president, and 62 percent said they trusted Congress. Four out of five supported U.S. military action in Afghanistan, and the same number rated terrorism as the top issue facing the United States.

Yet two intriguing elements in the 2001 poll were little noticed at the time. First, the college students' newfound hawkishness did not replace their altruism; it supplemented it. The number participating in community service increased, to 69 percent. The second facet that, in hindsight, seems significant is that in the days just after 9/11, college students' support for a military solution, while quite high, was noticeably lower than that of older voters.

By the spring of 2003, 65 percent of college students supported the war (compared with 78 percent of the entire country), but a trend toward multinationalism—particularly support for the United Nations—was building among the students.

The Millennials were, in Della Volpe's words, "creating a unique political voice of their own." By then, the institute was polling twice a year, and the October survey underscored the point about the students' singular identity. In that poll, college students revealed themselves to be more pro-Bush than their older counterparts but simultaneously more skeptical of the Iraq war. The youth vote in the impending presidential race, it seemed, was up for grabs, and by the time of the April 2004 institute poll, John Kerry had emerged on college campuses as a 10-point favorite.

Inside the Kerry campaign and in groups such as Rock the Vote, the high expectations

Today's youth are an **underrated force in American civic life** *— difficult to stereotype, with attitudes markedly different from those of their predecessors.*

were palpable: The 18-to-24-year-olds were going to lead Democrats back into the White House. But Election Day brought heartburn to liberals, starting with erroneous early exit polls that seemed to presage a big Kerry win and then compounded by a widely distributed news service article (also based on exit polls) asserting that the youth-vote surge had not materialized.

But this interpretation was mistaken. David King, the Harvard professor, whose specialty is analyzing voting patterns, says that exit polls weren't taken near college campuses. Furthermore, Election Night stories confused turnout with vote share. Months later, after the Census Bureau released its supplemental information, it became apparent that the number of voters younger than 25 had jumped 11 points—compared with an increase of 4 points among those 25 and older. "One of the missed angles of the 2004 election is that college-age people drove the increase in voter turnout nationally," Jeanne Shaheen, the institute's current director, said at the time.

In 2002, David W. Nickerson made a name for himself as a graduate student at Yale by writing a thesis showing that young voters were just as susceptible to the blandishments of politicians as anyone else, but that it was three times as costly for a political campaign

to reach them. If one also considers that young voters are more fickle than older ones—studies have shown that they are more likely to change their preferences in midcampaign—only a very stubborn campaign manager would spend money wooing the young. But five years can be a long time in politics, especially when a nation is at war, and most especially when technology is developing rapidly. "That calculus is wrong now," King said. "This is the stock you want to invest in—the young."

What has happened in the meantime? Well, Iraq, and the online YouTube and Facebook, to name three things.

It's common political wisdom that George Allen of Virginia narrowly lost his Senate seat—and the Republican majority along with it—after he was videotaped calling one of Democrat Webb's volunteers a "macaca." What's often forgotten is that Webb's campaign, not knowing quite what to do with the footage, simply posted it on YouTube. The effect was devastating.

King has just finished work on a study in which 56 campaign managers involved in 2006 congressional races were interviewed about their outreach efforts aimed at young voters. The questions ranged from what technology they employed to how many of their staffers were younger than 30. Did they upload to YouTube, make appeals on MySpace, or set up a Facebook page, and raise money online?

King's and Della Volpe's assessment is not that e-mails and podcasts have replaced political volunteers at the grassroots. It's that the new technology has altered Nickerson's cost-benefit analysis. It is now far less expensive to reach young volunteers and voters. But a candidate still must have charisma and a message, and be able to translate high-technology methods into good, old-fashioned ground organizing.

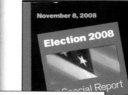

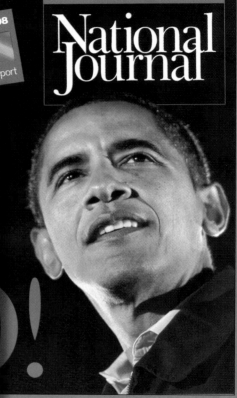

November 8, 2008
Election 2008
Special Report
National Journal

■ **FOR DISCUSSION:** Will Generation We be more involved in politics than previous generations? Will campaigns increasingly use internet technology to successfully mobilize the youth vote, thereby increasing the participation of future generations of young voters? What effect will the presidential election of 2008 have on the participation of tomorrow's college students in the political process?

NATIONAL JOURNAL ARTICLES

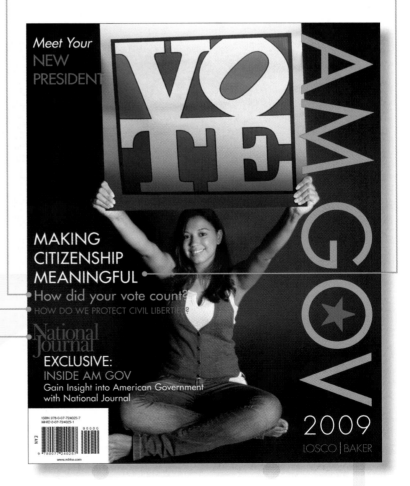

what's inside

1

CITIZENS

MILLENNIALS RISING ▮ Molly Kawahata couldn't wait until she turned eighteen to get involved in politics. "They say I'm a high school student, I can't vote," the seventeen-year-old senior from Gunn High School in Palo Alto, California, told reporters. "But, I work sometimes more than 100 hours plus, because I believe in this candidate." The candidate was Barack Obama. Molly used Facebook to create a network of high school Obama volunteers, parlaying her organizational skills into a leadership role as the national high school director for the campaign. She traveled to Iowa and Nevada with the campaign, and when she was home her bedroom became a makeshift office where she and ten young staffers worked cell phones and laptops to urge people to vote for their candidate.[1]

While Molly's devotion to campaigning may be exceptional, her interest in politics is shared by many of her peers who constitute the Millennial Generation, young people born in the 1980s and 1990s who are attending or about to attend college. More ethnically and racially diverse than previous college generations, Millennials are less cynical, more civic-minded, and politically more engaged than their immediate predecessors in Generation X. In 2008, Millennials showed up in record numbers to vote in primaries across the nation. By the middle of the primary season, turnout among voters between the ages of eighteen and twenty-nine was up an average of 5 percent over 2004;[2] and in many states, like California, it was up over 10 percent from 2000 levels. This is a generation that can make a huge difference in influencing the direction of our political system. By the presidential election of 2016, Millennials will make up nearly 30 percent of all voters.[3] ●◆

HIP IN OUR CHANGING DEMOCRACY

As You READ >>

- What kinds of citizen involvement fuel democracies?
- What ideals fuel American democracy?
- What are some of the changes and challenges facing America today?

Not so long ago, some political observers bemoaned the lack of participation by young people, ascribing the decline in political awareness to a host of factors ranging from careerism to overuse of media. But since 2000, young people seem to have reawakened to the world of politics. In 2004, voter turnout among eighteen- to twenty-four-year-olds increased by 11 percent over 2000. By 2006, UCLA's survey of American freshmen disclosed that 34 percent reported discussing politics frequently in high school, the highest number recorded in the forty-year history of the survey. In January 2007, the Pew Research Center reported 77 percent of Millennials said they were interested in local politics, up 28 percent from 1999; 85 percent reported an interest in keeping up with national affairs.[4]

A variety of reasons have been offered to explain these changes. First, as we will see in Chapter 6, each generation builds a somewhat unique identity based on important events that galvanize attention at an early age. The events of September 11, 2001, may have encouraged young Millennials to pay more attention to world affairs than their predecessors did. Second, political parties, candidates, and interest groups are actively courting young voters and speaking about issues, like the environment, education, and the war, that matter most to them. They are also employing modern technologies, including networking sites, cell phones, and text messaging, to engage young people where they live. This is important, because, as we will see in Chapters 7 and 9, in order for citizens to become actively involved they must believe their participation will make a difference, and they must be asked by political agents to take part in the process. Finally, young people are also using technology to make connections with one another in a manner that helps sustain interest in politics. Facebook, YouTube, and MySpace provide forums for discussion and sharing information that build support and awareness among those with similar views.

Of course, continued interest in politics among the young is not guaranteed. Despite this increased activity, young Americans still vote at lower rates than their older siblings, parents, and grandparents. If political activity among Millennials is to be sustained, candidates must make some headway in fulfilling campaign pledges; political groups and parties must continue their youth mobilization efforts; and a civic culture that encourages engagement must be carefully cultivated. Young people must also make their own commitment to become informed and active partners in our democratic enterprise.

"In a **democracy,** where people rule either directly or through elected leaders, **citizenship** is a two-sided coin: it confers rights and protections on members of the political community, but in return it requires allegiance and involvement. Each of us must weigh the costs and benefits of participation. The benefits may be policies we support; the costs involve our time and attention. Often, involvement will only be achieved with the active encouragement of others.

Molly Kawahata, a high school senior from Palo Alto, California, at work on the Obama campaign.

As you will see throughout this book, citizenship today is in a precarious state. For much of the past half century, the involvement of citizens in their communities has dwindled, voter turnout has remained well below that of other advanced democracies, and the level of trust between citizens and elected national leaders has reached its lowest point in over thirty-five years.[5] We believe that citizenship today is at a crossroads: we can build on recent gains in voter interest and reconstruct the reciprocal bonds of trust between citizen and government, or we can watch these bonds continue to fray. We can either begin finding solutions to the pressing problems that endanger our future or watch these problems continue to worsen. There are some signs that your generation is ready to open a dialogue about how to construct a more vibrant democracy that works for all citizens. That is the central hope of this book, and the actions of young people like Molly Kawahata are its inspiration. ✦

POLITICS, POWER, AND PARTICIPATION

Politics is the process by which we choose government officials and make decisions about public policy. In a democracy, citizens play a primary role in this process, but it is a role they must choose to play. Americans are not forced to leave the pleasures and obligations of private life to engage in political or community service. Yet, the vitality of our social and political institutions depends on our willingness as citizens to step outside of our private lives and to work with others voluntarily in making our neighborhoods safe, our communities strong, and our government work effectively for all. It depends on our readiness to join the collective or **civic life** of the community. By deciding to work on a presidential campaign rather than watch TV, Molly Kawahata chose to engage in a political rather than a private activity and to participate in the civic life of the country.

Civic life includes institutions of **government**—the body or bodies charged with making official policies for its citizens. But it also includes **civil society**, which refers to the broad array of voluntary associations that bring citizens together to deal with community and social issues of common concern. These organizations might include the Key Club, which conducts community service activities, or your campus environmental club that promotes recycling. Voluntary associations build what is called **so-cial capital**, bonds of trust and reciprocity between citizens that form the glue holding societies together. Citizens participate in government by acts like voting, attending political meetings, and campaigning for candidates they support for office. They participate in the actions of civil society when they volunteer or contribute to a good cause.

If associations build social capital and give rise to civic and political involvement, then is it better to have more voluntary associations? Some social scientists regard the number and kind of voluntary associations sustained in society as a sign of a nation's well-being.[6] That is why some of them, like Harvard's Robert Putnam, worry about what they see as a decline in civic activities ranging from attendance at school board meetings to meeting with one's neighbors. Critics have challenged Putnam's findings, noting that participation in new forms of civic activity like soccer leagues has replaced older associations and that young people have turned to electronic networking rather than face-to-face encounters in building social capital.[7]

Even if we were to agree that social capital and membership in the kind and number of voluntary associations that help create and sustain it has declined, does it matter? The simple answer is—it depends. It depends on how one envisions a citizen's relationship to government. Democratic governments extol the virtues of citizen participation and depend on citizen involvement as a source of legitimacy. Your authors

democracy Form of government in which the people rule either directly or through elected leaders.

citizenship Status conferring rights and protections to members of the political community but, in return, requiring allegiance and involvement.

politics The process by which we choose government officials and make decisions about public policy.

civic life Participation in the collective life of the community.

government The body (or bodies) charged with making official policies for citizens.

civil society The broad array of voluntary associations that bring citizens together to deal with community and social issues of common concern.

social capital Bonds of trust and reciprocity between citizens that form the glue that holds modern societies together.

Citizen Activities in a Democratic Society

PRIVATE LIFE	CIVIC LIFE	
Individual activity	Civic engagement activities	
	Nonpolitical activities	Political participation
Family School Work	Recycling Fellowship meetings Service activities	Voting Attending political meetings Political campaigning
Cultivates personal relationships, serves individual needs—e.g., getting an education, earning a living	Provides community services and acts as a training ground for political participation	Fulfills demands of democratic citizenship

Functions

direct democracy Form of government in which decisions about public policy extends to the entire citizenry.

representative democracy Form of government in which popular decision making is restricted to electing or appointing the public officials who make public policy.

majority rule The requirement that electoral majorities determine who is elected to office and that majorities in power determine our laws and how they are administered.

minority rights Protections beyond the reach of majority control guaranteed to all citizens.

political power The ability to get things done by controlling or influencing the institutions of government.

believe there is ample reason for optimism about the future of civic life in America; but, as we will see, civic involvement is not evenly spread across the entire population. This has serious consequences for ensuring an equal voice for all citizens. There is vast room for improvement, and we will highlight some promising avenues in the chapters that follow.

Types of Government

Governments may take a variety of forms, but a key distinction between them is how widely power is shared among the citizens. In a monarchy or dictatorship, a single person exercises absolute power. By contrast, in a **direct democracy**, political decision making extends to the entire citizenry. Some ancient Greek city-states, for example, made decisions about the use of power in open-air assemblies involving thousands of citizens. Only free males, however, were counted as citizens. Few modern nations employ direct democracy; most free nations prefer instead to restrict popular decision making to electing or appointing officials who make public policy. This type of government is properly called a **representative democracy**. Citizens in a representative democracy hold public officials accountable through periodic elections and the rule of law. America's representative democracy is characterized by **majority rule** and protections for **minority rights**. Electoral majorities determine who is elected to office, and majorities in power determine our laws and how they are administered. However, certain rights, like freedom of speech and religion, are beyond the reach of majority control. We will

The right of the president and Congress to wage war, as they did after the attacks of 9/11, is explicitly granted in the Constitution.

discuss these features of our political system in more detail in Chapter 2.

Political Power

The legitimate use of force and political power by a representative government rests upon either explicit contracts establishing the relationship between governors and the governed—such as the U.S. Constitution—or upon certain shared values and standards that citizens have come to accept over time. Although citizens may not agree with specific government policies, they will support as legitimate, or lawful, policies founded upon accepted contracts and standards. For example, many Americans opposed the U.S. invasion of Iraq following the terrorist attacks of September 11, 2001, but few disputed the right of the president and Congress to wage war.

Even in democratic societies, questions frequently arise about who exercises real **political power** by influencing or controlling the institutions of government. One school of thought, the **ruling elite theory**, argues that wealthy and well-educated citizens exercise a disproportionate amount of influence over political decision making, despite the existence of institutions that encourage widespread participation. These individuals are more likely to have access to government officials or to become government officials themselves. They are also more informed about political issues and more interested in the outcome of these issues. The wealthy have a vested interest, for example, in reducing the amount of taxes they pay and creating favorable political and economic conditions for their investments. Some versions of ruling elite theory, however, suggest that elites actually are an important force for social advancement.[8] Empirical studies demonstrate that wealthier and better-educated citizens show a greater commitment to values such as fair play, diversity, and respect for civil liberties than those with less income or education. They are also more alert to threats to basic democratic values and more likely to insist on enforcement of individual rights.

A competing theory called **pluralism** asserts that various groups and coalitions constantly vie for government fa-

The reluctance of the government to withdraw from Iraq, despite the broad backing of the public for withdrawal, is an example of elite dominance.

vor and the ability to exercise political power, but none enjoys long-term dominance.[9] In this view, groups that get their way today may be on the losing end tomorrow.

For example, supporters of school vouchers for private religious schools may be successful in securing funding for their cause from the legislature one day, only to see the courts invalidate the measure tomorrow, as happened in 2006 when the Florida Supreme Court struck down the state's voucher program. In order to maximize their chances of success, like-minded citizens organize into interest groups that employ a wide array of tactics from supporting candidates who promise to advance their cause to developing sophisticated public relations campaigns to rally support (see Chapter 8). As long as the rules guiding interest group competition are fair and fairly enforced, no one group will dominate political decision making.

In practice, modern American government is characterized by elements of each of these theories. Elite dominance tends to prevail in decisions about foreign policy. For example, although large majorities of Americans favor some sort of troop withdrawal from Iraq, the government has been reluctant to take this step. Pluralistic group competition, on the other hand, is more evident in matters of personal choice such as abortion. Both supporters and opponents of legalized abortion, for instance, have had notable successes in advancing their agendas in the political arena. In this book, we are most concerned about increasing participation in ways that bring us closer to achieving genuinely pluralistic outcomes. Some sectors of the American population already participate at very high levels and can be sure their voices are heard, if not always heeded. Others are barely heard at all; we will identify ways throughout the book to increase their volume.

Interest groups support politicians who they believe will advance their cause.

Participation and Democracy

Active citizens who are willing to take part in government by voicing their opinions, running for elective office, and voting have always been essential to the success of democracy. The Greek philosopher Aristotle (384–322 B.C.E.) felt that citizens should not simply sit back and enjoy the benefits of society; they must also take responsibility for its operation. Modern thinkers have generally concurred. British philosopher John Locke (1632–1704) argued that the power of the government comes from the consent of its citizens and that consent is only possible when the citizenry is informed and engaged. Political theorist John Stuart Mill

ruling elite theory View positing that wealthy and well-educated citizens exercise a disproportionate amount of influence over political decision making.

pluralism View positing that various groups and coalitions constantly vie for government favor and the ability to exercise political power but none enjoys long-term dominance.

global Perspectives

Declining Social Trust Around the World—Is This the Beginning of a New Generation of Critical Citizens?

Many established democracies have undergone a long-term decline in public confidence about government and fear a growing disconnect between citizens and the state.[1] Both Europe and America seem to have experienced "a flight from politics, or what the Germans call *Politikverdrossenheit*: a weakness about its debates, disbelief about its claims, skepticism about its results, cynicism about its practitioners."[2]

The figure at right compares the results of surveys of more than twenty thousand citizens across twenty countries conducted in 2004 and 2005 by the World Economic Forum, an independent international research and advocacy organization. The survey asked respondents how much they trusted various national institutions "to operate in the best interests of our society." Of the institutions examined, national governments lost the most ground in fifteen of the nations for which data were made available.

Political scientist Pippa Norris believes widespread cynicism about government signals the emergence of a new type of "critical citizen, dissatisfied democrats who adhere strongly to democratic values but who find existing structures of representative government invented in the eighteenth and nineteenth centuries to be wanting. . . ."[3] These critical citizens "seek more direct and meaningful ways to participate. They believe the forms of governance in the nation-state need to evolve to allow more opportunities for citizen decision making than an election for government every few years."[4] Norris finds, for example, that young citizens around the world are more responsive to nontraditional means of participation like demonstrations or product boycotts than more traditional methods like voting since these alternate approaches promote a greater sense of social solidarity.

[1] Pippa Norris, "Introduction: The Growth of Critical Citizens," in Pippa Norris, ed., *Critical Citizens: Global Support for Democratic Government* (New York: Oxford University Press, 1999), p. 6. See also Ronald Inglehart, *Modernization and Postmodernization: Cultural, Economic and Political Change in 43 Societies* (Princeton, N.J.: Princeton University Press, 1977). [2] Charles Maier, quoted in Norris, p. 6. [3] Norris, p. 27. [4] Norris, p. 27.

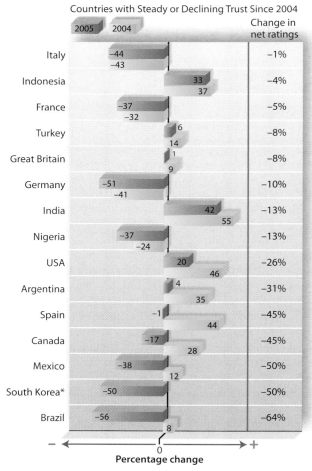

Trust in National Governments
Countries with Steady or Declining Trust Since 2004

	2005	2004	Change in net ratings
Italy	−44	−43	−1%
Indonesia	33	37	−4%
France	−37	−32	−5%
Turkey	6	14	−8%
Great Britain	1	9	−8%
Germany	−51	−41	−10%
India	42	55	−13%
Nigeria	−37	−24	−13%
USA	20	46	−26%
Argentina	4	35	−31%
Spain	−1	44	−45%
Canada	−17	28	−45%
Mexico	−38	12	−50%
South Korea*	−50		−50%
Brazil	−56	8	−64%

− ←—————— 0 ——————→ +
Percentage change

*Percentage change based on 2002 value

Source: World Economic Forum, "Trust in Governments, Corporations, and Global Institutions Continues to Decline." Results accessed on June 19, 2006, at http://www.weforum.org.

---

initiative Procedure that enables citizens to place proposals for laws and amendments directly on the ballot for voter approval.

(1806–1873) believed that even when citizens are content with their government, active participation is necessary to ensure that principles like liberty and free speech don't fade from lack of use. Thomas Jefferson (1743–1826), in his more radical moments, called for periodic citizen uprisings to reinvigorate the spirit of democracy. Much of American history confirms the importance of citizen participation. Throughout our nation's history, many Americans fought long and

hard to gain the opportunity to participate in democratic practices that were previously closed to them.

Many states provide expanded opportunities for citizen participation. **Initiative**, available in twenty-four states, enables citizens to draft laws and constitutional amendments for voter approval if the sponsors of the measure gather enough signatures. Similarly, twenty-four states allow for **popular referendum**, which allows citizens to approve or repeal measures already acted upon by legislative bodies. **Legislative referendum** is another form of referendum, available in all fifty states, that requires legis-

lative bodies to secure voter approval for some measures such as changes to a state's constitution. Finally, eighteen states permit **recall** in which citizens can remove and replace a public official before the end of a term. Arnold Schwarzenegger was first catapulted into the governor's mansion in California as a result of the recall of former Democratic governor, Gray Davis.

A free society relies heavily upon the voluntary activities of free individuals outside of government as well. Our nation accomplishes many of its social needs through the work of charitable organizations, religious congregations, and professional groups. Thousands of charities and foundations provide money and personnel for programs ranging from support for the arts to sheltering the homeless. Volunteers power these organizations by devoting their time and energy to improve the quality of life in our communities. As we will see, these organizations also serve as training grounds for developing the skills we need to become full and active participants in our nation's political system. Free democratic societies depend on the readiness of individuals like Molly Kawahata to take the time to get involved. They demand the willingness of citizens to work with others. They rely on the leadership skills of citizens to help find acceptable solutions to common problems. They also require adopting a set of principles or ideals that extol the worth and contributions of citizens.

John Locke (1632–1704) argued that the power of the government comes from the consent of its citizens.

AMERICAN POLITICAL IDEALS

Ideas, values, and beliefs about how governments should operate are known as **ideologies**. Lib-

Hot or Not?

Does government do too many things better left to businesses and individuals?

eral democracy, the ideology that guided the American experience, reveres individual rights and expresses faith in popular control of government. It rests upon three essential notions: natural rights, the formation of a social contract by consent of the governed, and majority rule. Its most influential advocate was John Locke. A physician by training, Locke became involved in the politics of Whig radicals who challenged the authority of the British Stuart monarchy in the late seventeenth century. These radicals, who favored placing more power into the hands of an elected Parliament, succeeded in pulling off a bloodless revolution in 1688.

Locke speculates that humans at one time probably had little need for authority because there was little competition for resources—nature provided more than enough for everyone. When a person appropriated unclaimed resources, those resources became his or her property, which no one else was entitled to claim. Over time, however, populations grew, creating competition for diminishing resources. Conflicts over ownership of property led to the need for a neutral arbiter to settle disputes peacefully. That arbiter was government. Locke believed that free and equal persons willingly entered into social contracts to establish governments in order to avoid the "incommodities" of war and conflict with others. On our own, we have a limited capacity to protect our life, liberty, and property. If we band together in government, we come to each other's aid in the protection of these natural rights.

In his *Second Treatise of Government,* Locke articulated the underlying philosophy of liberal democracy.[10] He argued that humans are born naturally free and equal; no one is born subject to another's will and no one can control another without that person's consent. People place themselves under the control of a government because of the mutual advantages it offers its citizens. Under such an arrangement, majority

popular referendum A device that allows citizens to approve or repeal measures already acted on by legislative bodies.

legislative referendum Ballot measure aimed at securing voter approval for some legislative acts, such as changes to a state's constitution.

recall Procedure whereby citizens can remove and replace a public official before the end of a term.

ideology Ideas, values, and beliefs about how governments should operate.

liberal democracy Ideology stressing individual rights and expressing faith in popular control of government.

The People in Your Neighborhood Most Likely Look Like You

Composition of Neighborhoods by Racial and Ethnic Groups June 6–25, 2005			
	% of non-Hispanic whites who say there are "many" of each group in area	% of blacks who say there are "many" of each group in area	% of Hispanics who say there are "many" of each group in area
Whites	86%	45%	52%
Blacks	28%	66%	32%
Hispanics	32%	26%	61%
Asians	12%	6%	13%
Recent immigrants	14%	18%	30%

Source: Who Are the People in Your Neighborhood? Gallup Organization, July 12, 2005.

rule provides a reasonable basis for making decisions. In this way, each member of the community has an equal voice in decision making, and decisions reflect the consensus of most citizens. Governments, however, derive authority from the consent of those who form them, and they hold our allegiance only if they protect our life, liberty, and property better than we could on our own. If government becomes a threat to citizens' rights, the social contract fails and the people have the option of dissolving it and beginning anew.

The authors of our Declaration of Independence drew heavily on the ideas of Locke in drafting that document and making the case for independence from British rule. Ideas alone, however, do not make history; they must be advanced by proponents with the skills and determination to see them achieved. American history offers many examples of individuals who worked tirelessly to expand opportunities for **political participation** to an increasingly diverse citizenry.

THE CHANGING FACE OF THE AMERICAN CITIZENRY

As we seek ways to increase the engagement of today's citizens, we must be aware that our citizenry is rapidly becoming older and more diverse. At the same time, the gap between those with substantial resources and those with

few is increasing. Forces of globalization are intensifying these divisions.

Growing Diversity

When the U.S. Constitution was ratified at the end of the eighteenth century, more than four million white Europeans and their descendants lived in the United States. (This figure does not include Native Americans, as estimates of their total population during this period vary greatly; nor does it include over a half million black slaves and an estimated sixty thousand free blacks.) Today the U.S. population is over three hundred million, drawn from all corners of the world. Hispanic Americans are the nation's fastest-growing minority group, now comprising over 13 percent of the population. African Americans are a close second at about 12 percent, and Asian Americans represent about 4 percent of the population. Despite the progress these groups have made in securing civil rights, many are still not well integrated into American civic life.

Fifty years ago, just over a third of all Americans lived in the suburbs; today that figure is about 55 percent. Suburbs, however, tend to be lacking in political and ethnic diversity. As the *Report of the American Political Science Association's Standing Committee on Civic Education and Engagement* emphasized in 2004, "Across the patchwork of suburban jurisdictions, individual suburbs are likely to be characterized not by integration and diversity, but by residential segregation and homogeneity."[11]

The data presented above support this finding. Whites, Hispanics, and African Americans tend to live predominantly among members of their own racial and ethnic groups. This type of segregation breeds distrust, particularly at the local level. It also breeds distrust and a lack of cooperation in addressing social problems.

The past few decades have also witnessed a greater openness about sexual preferences that has produced a more politically active gay and lesbian community. In recent years, same sex partners have pressed for the same rights as those afforded married couples. Action by the Supreme Judicial Court of Massachusetts to legalize gay marriage early in 2004 drew a firestorm of reaction. Eleven states placed referenda banning gay marriages on their ballots in that same year, and all of the measures passed. The battle by gays for the right to the same protections as mar-

> **"TODAY THE COUNTRY** has gone a long way toward an appearance of classlessness. . . . Social diversity has erased many of the old markers."

ried couples is likely to continue in a nation increasingly polarized over the role of government in personal choice. In general, young Americans are more accepting of racial, ethnic, and gender differences than their elders.[12]

Growing Older

The elderly population is expected to double by 2050, when one in five Americans will be over age sixty-five (see "The Graying of America"). The aging of the population poses some special problems. The Social Security and Medicare Boards of Trustees project substantial shortfalls for Social Security and Medicare as fewer able-bodied working-age adults work to support the needs of the growing number of elderly Americans. How will we meet this growing need for financial support and medical services? No doubt the elderly, who vote in much higher numbers than young people, will exert political pressure to keep or even increase their benefits. How will the younger generation respond? Given the enormity of the coming elder boom, will young people still be willing to support generous government programs that provide for the needs of elderly Americans?

The GRAYING of America

Source: U.S. Census Bureau, 1995.

Average Annual Growth Rate (Percent) of the Elderly Population: 1950–2030

3
2.5
2
1.5
1
.5
0

1950–1970   1970–1990   1990–2010   2010–2030

Growing Apart

When the U.S. Constitution was written, **social class** divisions among Americans were much more visible than they are today. They manifested themselves through distinctions in dress, social stature, and political power. For example, while workmen wore functional clothing of washable unbleached linen, gentlemen regularly sported wool coats and jackets, donning powdered "whigs" on special occasions. More than two centuries later, class divisions are not so obvious. According to a recent inquiry into class in America, "Today the country has gone a long way toward an appearance of classlessness. . . . Americans of all sorts are awash in luxuries that would have dazzled their grandparents. Social diversity has erased many of the old markers."[13]

In a world where even the wealthy wear jeans and sweat suits, it is increasingly difficult to tell someone's status by looking at his or her clothes. At the same time, easily available credit and the flattening of prices for technology have given many Americans access to high-end consumer items. Most of you reading this chapter probably own a cell phone, DVD player, or laptop computer. In 2006, there were an estimated 195 million cell phone users in the United States, over eight times the number of users in the 1990s. Even the vacation cruise business now caters to people of moderate income.

Yet economic divisions have not disappeared. By some measures, the gap between rich and poor is growing. Be-

> **political participation** Taking part in activities like voting or running for office aimed at influencing the policies or leadership of government.
>
> **social class** The perceived combination of wealth, income, education, and occupation that contribute to one's status and power in society.

The availability of cheap labor in some foreign countries has prompted many employers to transfer jobs overseas, resulting in fewer job opportunities for American workers.

tween 1979 and 2001, for example, the income of the wealthiest 1 percent of American households rose by 139 percent after taxes, compared with a 17 percent rise for the middle class and a 9 percent rise for the poorest one-fifth of the population.[14] Census figures indicate that in 2005, the richest fifth of the population shared over 50 percent of the nation's income while the poorest fifth had a 3.4 percent share. Moreover, several recent studies show that social mobility has stagnated over the past forty years. A study prepared for *The New York Times* reported that 40 percent of American families remained in the same income range from the 1970s to the 1990s.[15] Another researcher

finds that a person born into the richest fifth of families is over five times as likely to end up at the top as someone born in the bottom fifth.[16]

Throughout much of the twentieth century, many working-class Americans could count on a career in one of the nation's skilled industries like steel or auto manufacturing. Labor unions organized workers in these fields, enhancing their job security and income and propelling them into the middle classes. Over the past thirty years, however, employers have transferred many of these jobs overseas where they can employ cheaper labor. The pace of job loss in these fields seems to be quickening. Between March 1998 and May 2003, 2.9 million jobs were eliminated in U.S. manufacturing industries.[17] Increasingly, the well-paying jobs of the future for American citizens will emphasize high levels of financial acumen, technological

Projected Growth in Employment by Education or Training Category, 2000–2010

Percentage projected growth in employment, 2000–2010

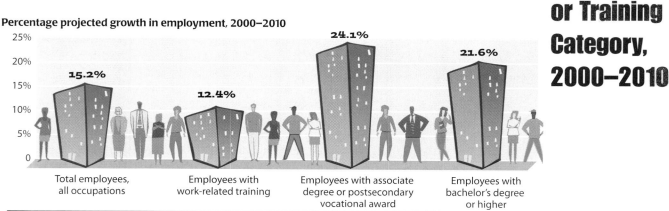

- Total employees, all occupations — 15.2%
- Employees with work-related training — 12.4%
- Employees with associate degree or postsecondary vocational award — 24.1%
- Employees with bachelor's degree or higher — 21.6%

Source: U.S. Department of Labor, Bureau of Labor Statistics.

Reasons for Not Voting, 18–24-Year-Olds

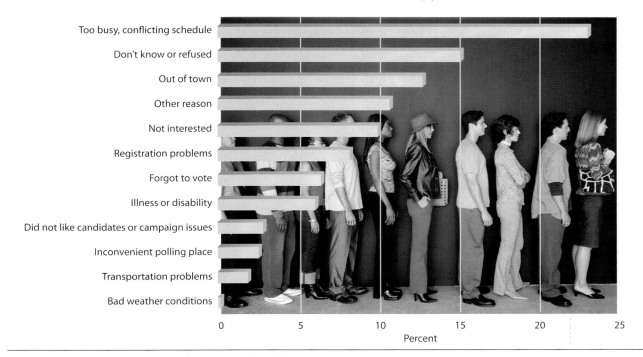

Too busy, conflicting schedule
Don't know or refused
Out of town
Other reason
Not interested
Registration problems
Forgot to vote
Illness or disability
Did not like candidates or campaign issues
Inconvenient polling place
Transportation problems
Bad weather conditions

0   5   10   15   20   25
Percent

Source: U.S. Census Bureau, Current Population Survey, May 25, 2005.

proficiency, and creativity. This shift places great emphasis on access to education for career advancement and financial security. At the same time, however, the cost of a college education is skyrocketing while government resources to help students cover those costs are shrinking.

Social class adds an additional dimension to our consideration of civic engagement. We will see in forthcoming chapters that political activity is not spread evenly across all social classes. Those who vote, run for office, contribute to political campaigns, and engage in a wide array of political and civic activities are disproportionately individuals with more wealth. As a result, the wealthy are more likely to be heard by political actors in the corridors of power.

THE FUTURE OF CITIZENSHIP

A number of ideas are surfacing about how we might alter and improve the civic engagement and political participation of American citizens today. Some states now require students to perform community service in order to graduate from high school. More colleges and universities are turning to student **service learning programs** as a legitimate educational experience. Will service learning eventually reconstruct the social capital that many believe will reinvigorate political participation? Or will it contribute to

a growing sense that political solutions to social problems are futile?

Perhaps changes in our election process and voter mobilization will help. See the figure above for reasons why young people don't vote. Participation improves when government agencies become more open, when participation is made more accessible, and when a range of political and nonpolitical associations mobilize citizens to take action. For

service learning programs Agencies that help connect volunteers with organizations in need of help.

personal is Political

Which factor do you think is most significant in recruiting college student volunteers?

(a) The student's own initiative in approaching an organization

(b) Being asked

(c) Some other way

In this study, 42.7% chose (a); 39.2% chose (b); and 14.6% chose (c).

Source: Karlo Barrios Marcelo, *College Experience and Volunteering*, Center for Information and Research on Civic Learning and Engagement, July 2007, p. 4.

Much of the 9th Ward, once home to many working-class blacks, experienced catastrophic flooding from Hurricane Katrina. Several websites, including Katrinahousing.org, were initiated to aid the victims.

example, declaring Election Day a legal holiday might encourage more people to get to the polls. Perhaps, as voters in the state of Oregon already can, citizens will be able to vote completely by mail—or, in the future, on-line. The political parties are intensifying their efforts to get out the vote. Data from the National Election Studies show an 8 percent increase in voter contact by the major parties in 2004 over the previous presidential election in 2000.[18] Candidates, too, are redoubling their efforts to reach out to young voters by addressing the issues they care about most, like the environment and education, and by toning down the divisive rhetoric that turns off many young people.

civic engagement Involvement in any activity aimed at influencing the collective well-being of the community.

Political communication is undergoing a sea change that promises to have a dramatic impact on **civic engagement** as well. Community groups are finding new and innovative ways to use the Internet to engage citizens in community efforts ranging from recycling and community beautification to economic development and locating housing for those in need. This was particularly useful in the wake of Hurricane Katrina when several websites, including Katrinahousing.org, helped victims find shelter. Political leaders have already had dramatic success using the Internet both as a fundraising device and as a vehicle for involving citizens in political dialogue. Blogging is changing the way Americans get news about current events, although its long-term

impact is uncertain. Virtually all of the 2008 presidential candidates mounted impressive websites with feedback and blogging features. Hillary Clinton solicited votes on-line for a campaign theme song. And Barack Obama used his website to raise record amounts of money from small

Find out how your civic engagement level measures against that of students from around the country. Take the Civic Engagement Quiz from the Center for Information and Research on Civic Learning and Engagement. It is available on the center's website at **www.civicyouth.org**. You can score yourself and compare your level of activity to a national sample of students from around the country.

get involved!

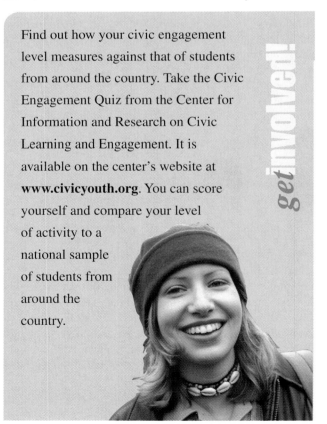

contributors. In 2008, candidates employed a host of new technologies, from text messaging to web networking, to meet young people where they live.

We will discuss many of these ideas and more throughout the course of this text. The most important ideas for improving civic engagement may not yet have been discovered. That is where you come in. As you consider your place in the social fabric of America, we hope you will share your ideas with your class, your community, and your political leaders. In the process, you will be helping to shape the way our democracy functions and fulfilling your role as citizen.

For REVIEW >>

1. What kinds of civic involvement fuel democracies?
   - Democracies thrive on citizen involvement both in government through the ballot box and through voluntary associations that attempt to improve the quality of our lives.
2. What ideals fuel American democracy?
   - American democracy gets its inspiration from the liberal democratic views of John Locke and rests on three essential notions: natural rights, the formulation of a social contract by the consent of the governed, and majority rule.
3. What are some of the changes and challenges facing America today?
   - We are growing more diverse, older, and subject to continuing class divisions.

GENERATION 'WE'

The Awakened Giant

During the first presidential campaign of the new millennium, Harvard students Erin Ashwell and Trevor Dryer, like their counterparts at colleges across the country, eagerly awaited the thrill of voting in a national election for the first time. Their anticipation was tempered, however, by dismissive talk about the apparent political disaffection of young people and the youth vote's irrelevance in the 2000 elections.

This didn't strike Ashwell and Dryer as the whole story. "In 2000, there was a lot of press about how young people don't vote, don't get involved, don't care about politics," Ashwell recalls. "Trevor and I wanted to know if it was true. It didn't seem right: All of our friends were into community service." Although they were only college sophomores—or perhaps because they were college sophomores—the pair decided to test conventional wisdom. They also sought to shed light on the paradox of a generation of young activists who devoted hours each week to tutoring underprivileged children, volunteering at food banks, and promoting environmental activism—but who couldn't be bothered to register or vote.

Ashwell and Dryer began delving into the attitudes of their fellow collegians via a nationwide survey, a project Harvard continued after they graduated. Over the ensuing years, the poll by the Institute of Politics at the John F. Kennedy School of Government has penetrated more deeply than other surveys, using the Internet and other innovative techniques, such as having undergraduates help formulate the questions.

The survey has drawn a picture of a unique generation. Today's youth are an underrated force in American civic life—difficult to stereotype, with attitudes markedly different from those of their predecessors. College students overwhelmingly favor the partial privatization of Social Security, a conservative Republican position and one at odds with the preferences of older Americans. Yet they are far more supportive of gay marriage, gay adoption, and gays' being allowed to serve openly in the military than any other age group, views that place them in the vanguard of Democratic liberalism. In many respects, they are available to both major parties and, judging by their weak party affiliation, would be receptive to an independent presidential candidate. The 2006 IOP poll went even further, concluding that the traditional labels of "liberal" and "conservative" don't adequately capture the complexity of college students' attitudes. One in four college students identify themselves as "religious centrists," a stance that indicates deep concern over the moral direction of the country—and that encompasses issues such as environmental protection, universal health care, and free trade.

Today's college students are not isolationist, but they are the furthest thing from unilateralists. The Institute of Politics poll shows that college students are twice as likely as older Americans to favor a United Nations solution to a foreign crisis than a plan conceived in Washington.

These young people are so little understood that many of the 2006 congressional campaigns ignored them utterly, although candidates who did paid a price for their inattention. Social scientists can't even agree on what to call this generation. Some label those ages 18 to 29 "Generation Y," to distinguish them from the Generation X-ers who preceded them. Others call them "Millennials." The Pew Research Center calls them simply "Generation Next." They are certainly not the "Me Generation." Harvard professor David C. King, research director at the Institute of Politics, calls them "Generation We." Is that an exaggeration?

Released in April 2000, "Attitudes Toward Public Service: A National Survey of College Undergraduates" found that although 59.5 percent of the students surveyed had participated in active community service in the previous 12 months, only 16 percent had signed on to a government, political, or issue-oriented organization and only 6.5 percent had volunteered for any kind of political campaign. The students' attitudes toward government ranged from cynicism to antipathy: Almost two-thirds of them said they didn't trust the federal government to "do the right thing" all or most of the time. Asked about the motivations of politicians, three-fourths of the respondents said that elected officials "seem to be motivated by selfish reasons." More than 70 percent said that America's political institutions were unconcerned with the desires of college students.

A study by the National Association of Secretaries of State, moreover, showed that turnout among young voters in the 1996 presidential election was the lowest on record, and hinted at an even worse performance in 2000. Eight years of Bill Clinton's White House, a contentiously partisan Congress, and a scandal-mongering media had produced nearly the opposite effect that Clinton's boyhood hero JFK had had on the nation's young people. "They were just turned off to politics," pollster John Della Volpe says. "Community service was something they could get their hands on. You could feed a hungry person or teach a struggling high school kid his math problem, and it was tangible. Political success was more ephemeral. We'd get these responses in the focus groups: 'What difference does it make who the president is? It's just some old white guy.' To them, politics wasn't ever cool, and it wasn't very fun."

The dismal forecast for November 2000 came true. According to the Census Bureau's supplemental information (available several months after each election), the turnout among voters ages 18 to 24 stayed at the all-time-low 1996 figure of 36 percent—and turnout among 18-to-21-year-olds fell below 30 percent for the first time.

Then the planes hit.

On September 11, 2001, former Sen. David Pryor of Arkansas was director of the Institute of Politics. Acting on gut instinct, he ginned up the poll again. The results this time couldn't have been more different. "The attacks of 9/11 totally changed the way the Millennial Generation thinks about politics," Della Volpe says today. "Overnight, their attitudes were more like the Greatest Generation."

A stunning 60 percent of college students in the institute's new survey said they had faith in the government to do the right thing all or most of the time, compared with 36 percent in 2000. Fully three-fourths of them expressed "trust" in the military, 69 percent said they trusted the president, and 62 percent said they trusted Congress. Four out of five supported U.S. military action in Afghanistan, and the same number rated terrorism as the top issue facing the United States.

Yet two intriguing elements in the 2001 poll were little noticed at the time. First, the college students' newfound hawkishness did not replace their altruism; it supplemented it. The number participating in community service increased, to 69 percent. The second facet that, in hindsight, seems significant is that in the days just after 9/11, college students' support for a military solution, while quite high, was noticeably lower than that of older voters.

By the spring of 2003, 65 percent of college students supported the war (compared with 78 percent of the entire country), but a trend toward multinationalism—particularly support for the United Nations—was building among the students.

The Millennials were, in Della Volpe's words, "creating a unique political voice of their own." By then, the institute was polling twice a year, and the October survey underscored the point about the students' singular identity. In that poll, college students revealed themselves to be more pro-Bush than their older counterparts but simultaneously more skeptical of the Iraq war. The youth vote in the impending presidential race, it seemed, was up for grabs, and by the time of the April 2004 institute poll, John Kerry had emerged on college campuses as a 10-point favorite.

Inside the Kerry campaign and in groups such as Rock the Vote, the high expectations

Today's youth are an **underrated force in American civic life**—difficult to stereotype, with attitudes markedly different from those of their predecessors.

were palpable: The 18-to-24-year-olds were going to lead Democrats back into the White House. But Election Day brought heartburn to liberals, starting with erroneous early exit polls that seemed to presage a big Kerry win and then compounded by a widely distributed news service article (also based on exit polls) asserting that the youth-vote surge had not materialized.

But this interpretation was mistaken. David King, the Harvard professor, whose specialty is analyzing voting patterns, says that exit polls weren't taken near college campuses. Furthermore, Election Night stories confused turnout with vote share. Months later, after the Census Bureau released its supplemental information, it became apparent that the number of voters younger than 25 had jumped 11 points—compared with an increase of 4 points among those 25 and older. "One of the missed angles of the 2004 election is that college-age people drove the increase in voter turnout nationally," Jeanne Shaheen, the institute's current director, said at the time.

In 2002, David W. Nickerson made a name for himself as a graduate student at Yale by writing a thesis showing that young voters were just as susceptible to the blandishments of politicians as anyone else, but that it was three times as costly for a political campaign

to reach them. If one also considers that young voters are more fickle than older ones—studies have shown that they are more likely to change their preferences in midcampaign—only a very stubborn campaign manager would spend money wooing the young. But five years can be a long time in politics, especially when a nation is at war, and most especially when technology is developing rapidly. "That calculus is wrong now," King said. "This is the stock you want to invest in—the young."

What has happened in the meantime? Well, Iraq, and the online YouTube and Facebook, to name three things.

It's common political wisdom that George Allen of Virginia narrowly lost his Senate seat—and the Republican majority along with it—after he was videotaped calling one of Democrat Webb's volunteers a "macaca." What's often forgotten is that Webb's campaign, not knowing quite what to do with the footage, simply posted it on YouTube. The effect was devastating.

King has just finished work on a study in which 56 campaign managers involved in 2006 congressional races were interviewed about their outreach efforts aimed at young voters. The questions ranged from what technology they employed to how many of their staffers were younger than 30. Did they upload to YouTube, make appeals on MySpace, or set up a Facebook page, and raise money online?

King's and Della Volpe's assessment is not that e-mails and podcasts have replaced political volunteers at the grassroots. It's that the new technology has altered Nickerson's cost-benefit analysis. It is now far less expensive to reach young volunteers and voters. But a candidate still must have charisma and a message, and be able to translate high-technology methods into good, old-fashioned ground organizing.

FOR DISCUSSION: Will Generation We be more involved in politics than previous generations?
Will campaigns increasingly use internet technology to successfully mobilize the youth vote, thereby increasing the participation of future generations of young voters?
What effect will the presidential election of 2008 have on the participation of tomorrow's college students in the political process?

2

THE CONST

THE FOUNDATION OF CITIZENS' RIGHTS

TAXATION WITHOUT REPRESENTATION: THE BATTLE CONTINUES ▌ More than 220 years after the United States secured its independence from England, some Americans are still rallying behind the revolutionary slogan "taxation without representation is tyranny." As amazing as it might seem, taxpayers in one American city are still fighting for voting representation in Congress. Even more surprising is the fact that the city is our nation's capital—Washington, D.C.—whose residents pay more taxes to the federal government than forty-eight of the fifty states.[1]

The District of Columbia was created in 1801 as a protected federal zone in which the national government could operate outside the influence and control of individual states. Because Congress did not consider it a state, citizens of the District of Columbia were denied the right to elect representatives to Congress or to vote for a president of the United States. Residents could not even elect local officials until 1871, and Congress revoked that right three years later; commissioners appointed by the president ran the city for the next century.

In 1961, city residents finally won approval for a constitutional amendment allowing them to vote in presidential elections. ➥

TUTION

- What factors contributed to the need for a Constitutional Convention?
- What are the basic principles that inform our Constitution?
- In what ways does constitutional change occur?

In December 1973, Congress authorized "home rule," leading to a locally elected mayor and city council.[2] Congress restored the District of Columbia's voice in the House of Representatives in 1970, but representative Eleanor Holmes Norton still does not have a vote. In 2007, the House of Representatives passed a bill to make the D.C. delegate a voting member. The bill never made it into law. That same year, a Senate committee adopted a resolution denying the District of Columbia the same representation in the U.S. Senate accorded every other state. In passionate testimony during Senate hearings on the legislation, D.C. mayor Adrian Fenty argued, "The Framers of the Constitution did not intend to deprive residents of the nation's capital of their fundamental right to vote. It goes beyond good sense that our lack of democracy continues more than two hundred years later."[3]

The District of Columbia, created as a protected federal zone in 1801, does not have a voting representative in Congress.

> "The Framers of the Constitution did not intend to deprive residents of the nation's capital of their fundamental right to vote."

The fight for the D.C. vote illustrates several features of our constitutional system. First, there is the deep-seated idea that democratic government is based on the consent of the governed and that the right to vote represents the essence of consent. Second, it illustrates the sometimes labyrinthine nature of our constitutional system, whose structure of separation of powers and checks and balances provides citizens both opportunities and hurdles in advancing their causes. In this chapter, we will examine the framework of American government and the rights it guarantees. We will review the odds the Founders overcame to establish these rights for themselves—and not for some others—and how they developed an institutional framework that was flexible enough to incorporate changes that expanded those rights. We will also look at obstacles that continue to stand in the way of full participation by all segments in our society.

Jamestown, Virginia, founded in 1607, failed as a mining town but became a training ground for self-rule.

THE FOUNDATIONS OF AMERICAN DEMOCRACY

During the first 150 years of English settlement in America, the colonists gave little thought to independence. They focused on survival, which included developing and nurturing institutions of local self-government. Only when the British government looked to the colonies for financial support did relations between the Crown and the colonies sour and, aided by the agitation of radicals, deteriorate to the point of revolution.

Early Colonization

The first permanent British colony in North America was Jamestown, founded in 1607 by the Virginia Company of London for the purpose of developing trade and mining gold. In order to regulate and protect the colony, the settlers formed a government consisting of a president and seven-member council. By 1619, colonists created an assembly known as the House of Burgesses, the nation's first legislative body. Composed of representatives elected from among the settlers, it imbued the settlers with an ardor for self-rule. Unfortunately for the company, there was no gold, and harsh conditions coupled with conflicts with na-

tive populations hampered trade. The Crown took control of the failing colony in 1624, replacing the president with a royal governor. The House of Burgesses, however, survived the king's efforts to abolish it.

A year after the House of Burgesses was created, forty-one religious dissenters called Puritans established a permanent settlement in the area of modern-day Plymouth, Massachusetts. The Puritans rejected attempts by both the Catholic pope and the king of England to dictate religious doctrine or belief. Because of this stance, they found themselves barred from many professional positions that required membership in the official Church of England. Despairing of reform from within the church, they chose to establish foreign religious outposts of their own. Although they came to America to flee religious persecution, the Puritans themselves were intolerant of dissent. Soon,

Did You Know?

. . . That in Puritan Massachusetts the only people allowed to vote were men who had been accepted as members of Puritan congregations—and that all residents of the colony were required to attend religious services, whether or not they had been accepted as congregation members?

some settlers began to challenge Puritan orthodoxy. Faced with execution or expulsion, dissidents migrated to form their own colonies; Rhode Island, for example, grew from breakaway settlements founded by former Massachusetts residents.

By 1732, thirteen British colonies dotted the eastern coast of North America, reflecting a variety of religious and political points of view as well as a wealth of nationalities. Each colony developed its own fledgling institutions of government, which despite their differences reflected a commitment to self-rule, popular consent, and respect for law.

Economic Distress

British policies limited economic progress in the colonies. The Crown saw its colonies primarily as suppliers of raw materials such as cotton, tobacco, and furs to manufacturers in Britain. There these resources were made into finished goods such as clothing, tools, and furniture, many of which were then exported back to the colonies for sale. The colonists were required to trade exclusively with Britain, which meant that all finished goods exported to the colonies—regardless of their source—first passed through England. The goods were loaded on British ships and taxed before sale, making non-British products more expensive for colonists and preventing genuine competition. For years, colonists skirted these limits through tactics such as smuggling and piracy. Colonial governors, whose salaries often depended on approval by local assemblies, largely ignored these widespread practices.

The Seven Years' War (1756–1763) brought home dramatically to Britain the costs of protecting their North American colonies from France and its Native American allies, while maintaining a vast empire elsewhere in the world. The British sought to defray costs by imposing taxes on sugar and stamps, producing protests that led them to repeal the stamp tax. Parliament responded with the Townshend Acts, which imposed taxes on a wide variety of important colonial staples. As dissent grew, many colonial legislatures urged a boycott of British goods. Pamphlets like Samuel Adams's *The Rights of Colonists* stoked the flames of popular anger. The British then inadvertently helped the dissenters' cause by passing several more increasingly hated duties, including a tax on tea. In 1773, Boston radicals protested by storming East India Company ships moored in Boston Harbor, dumping their cargoes of tea into the harbor. Parliament punished the city for the "Boston Tea Party" with actions that included blockading the harbor and forcing colonists to quarter British troops in their homes.

Tensions between Britain and her colonies were reaching a breaking point. Seeking a way to ease these tensions, representatives of every colony except Georgia met in Philadelphia in September 1774 for the first Continental Congress. They approved a declaration of grievances and urged a boycott of British goods. Although hopeful of restoring good relations with Britain, the colonists strengthened their local militias and left open the possibility of another meeting should tensions not ease. Just seven months later, all of the colonies sent representatives to a second Continental Congress in Philadelphia. This gathering produced a more radical agenda that included marshaling military forces under General George Washington and a plan for financing the war effort by borrowing funds and issuing bonds. Even as preparations were being readied, colonial forces and British troops clashed in April 1775. The convention also produced the Articles of Confederation, a constitution of sorts that consolidated the colonies loosely under a common rule. Ongoing efforts to solve the confrontation between Britain and the colonies proved futile and, in 1776, Congress appointed a committee to prepare a formal declaration asserting independence.

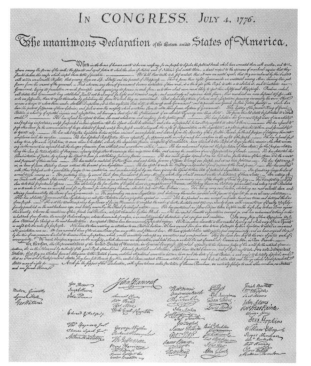

The Declaration of Independence served not only to declare war against Britain, but to assert the equality of men and the right to "life, liberty, and the pursuit of happiness."

sovereign Independent.

Declaration of Independence

Although the Declaration of Independence consists mainly of a list of grievances against England's King George III, it is most important for its embodiment of John Locke's philosophy of natural rights, discussed in Chapter 1. The declaration forcefully asserts the equality of men and the inalienable rights of "life, liberty, and the pursuit of happiness," a phrase that euphemistically expresses an inherent right to own private property. It asserts that these rights are not granted by humans, but by God, and that they must be defended by government for enjoyment by each of its members.

When a government can no longer defend these rights—or when it actively threatens them—the people have the right to alter or abolish that government and replace it with another that is better able to do so.

The Declaration of Independence inspires awe and respect and has been adopted by advocates of liberty the world over. It is not, however, a perfect affirmation of human rights; but we need to see it in the context of the times. Notice that it reserves these rights to men. That term was not then used as a surrogate for humanity; it referred specifically to males. Only property owners of sufficient means were allowed to participate in the political process, and very few female colonists owned enough property to qualify. The signers also clearly did not agree that *all* men were created equal. Many of the signers owned slaves, and some of those who helped draft the declaration forced Jefferson to remove from the document language attacking the institution of slavery.

The Declaration of Independence served not only as a declaration of war with Britain but also as a tool to rally support from a population that lacked consensus about separation from Britain. About one-third of Americans chose to fight for independence from the Crown; another third, it is estimated, were loyal to the king and Parliament; the remainder were too busy scratching a living from the harsh frontier environment to take much interest in politics. Thomas Paine's pamphlet *Common Sense,* published the same year as the declaration, was just as significant for mustering popular support for independence. The pamphlet sold a half million copies, 120,000 within the first three months of publication. By this time, however, the propaganda war had given way to a shooting war with the battles at Lexington and Concord the previous year.

THE BIRTH OF A NATION

In the prelude to the War for Independence, the colonies reconstituted themselves as states and developed governing constitutions, but no similar governing document ex-

isted for the new nation as a whole. The Second Continental Congress drafted the Articles of Confederation to serve that purpose, and it performed that function adequately during the Revolution. Shortly thereafter, however, the flaws of this document became apparent to colonial leaders, who made plans to replace it.

The Articles of Confederation: A Document Whose Time Had Come and Gone

The Articles of Confederation created a single national assembly, or Congress, in which each state possessed one vote. Congress and its various committees coordinated national affairs during the Revolution. This arrangement, however, was inadequate to address the country's myriad postwar economic and security problems. Consequently, colonial leaders began to search for a new national governing structure.

The Articles of Confederation recognized the colonies as **sovereign** or independent units, which limited the ability of the central government to respond to collective problems quickly and with a single voice. This led to three pressing economic problems: the lack of a common national currency, lack of control of interstate commerce, and an inability to collect federal taxes. The first two problems were

In 1786, Daniel Shays led debt-ridden farmers in armed insurrection in Massachusetts, prompting the nation's new leaders to question the viability of the Articles of Confederation as a governing document.

closely linked. As a sovereign entity, each state issued its own currency, while reserving the right to impose duties on goods imported from the others. Both of these practices hindered trade and limited the growth of interstate markets.

bicameral Composed of two houses.

unicameral One-house legislature.

The government's inability to collect taxes concerned leaders who envisioned the new nation emerging as an international economic power. The Continental Congress planned to pay off the debt it amassed during the Revolution by assessing each colony a portion of the war's total cost. States would collect money to pay for the assessments by imposing taxes on their own subjects. Collection, however, proved slow and unreliable; no state fully met its obligations and the nation's poor credit precipitated economic hardship for many. Higher interest rates prevented business expansion and increased the cost of foreign and domestic goods. Lack of financial capital also limited the national government's ability to defend its borders and to improve interstate commerce by building roads and canals. Strengthening of the powers of the central government seemed to be the solution to all three of these economic problems.

High prices for imported commodities, combined with increased taxes imposed by hard-pressed states, drove many people into debt. Small farmers were especially hard

Thomas Jefferson and the members of the Declaration Committee present the Declaration of Independence to the Second Continental Congress.

hit, and the number of people imprisoned for failure to pay debts burgeoned. In 1786, dissidents known as Regulators roamed western Massachusetts demanding debt relief for small farmers. In late summer, a group of Regulators led by Daniel Shays, himself a farmer, captured a cache of weapons from the Springfield armory. The state militia, sent to quell the disturbance, switched sides, adding fuel to the rebellion. The national government was powerless to intervene because it lacked the authority to raise or deploy a standing army. Eventually, representatives of the state's banking interests hired an army of mercenaries to attack the Regulators. It was not until February 1787 that the rebellion was quashed and Shays's followers dispersed into surrounding states. Incidents such as Shays's Rebellion convinced state leaders of their essential vulnerability and of the need for a strong central government.

The Road to Philadelphia

Although state leaders recognized the need for a stronger central government, assembling a group to reform the Articles of Confederation took some doing. In September 1786, representatives from five states (Delaware, New Jersey, New York, Pennsylvania, and Virginia) met in Annapolis, Maryland, to discuss the weaknesses of the articles. Alexander Hamilton and James Madison proposed a more inclusive meeting of delegates from every state to be held the following year in Philadelphia. Congress scheduled a meeting to commence May 14, 1787, for the "express purpose of revis-

ing the Articles of Confederation." Although calls for reform had been met by a lukewarm reception in the past, Shays's Rebellion gave the states a new sense of urgency.

It was not until May 25 that a sufficient number of delegates arrived to permit a formal discussion of reform. The fifty-five delegates represented every state except Rhode Island, which refused to send a delegation for fear that the assembly would ignore the plight of debtors, who made up a substantial portion of the state's population. Judging from external appearances, Rhode Island had reason for concern. Of the fifty-five delegates, almost all were wealthy and well educated. All were white males, six owned plantations, and about a third owned slaves. More than half were lawyers and most had held leadership positions in their states. Each represented the accepted notion of a politician in an age of deference, where wealth and community standing were understood to be requirements for leadership. Nowhere was this principle of elite deference more clearly demonstrated than in the selection of George Washington, the wealthy Virginia planter and Revolutionary War hero, as the convention's president.

The delegates, however, were by no means unified in their ideas about government or about advancing the interests of any particular economic group. All understood that citizens in their home states would closely scrutinize their actions. Each county had interests and concerns that it wanted the delegate from that colony to champion. Producing a workable compromise in such a situation was an extremely difficult task, but the delegates were marked by outstanding political acumen. Grasping the sensitivity of the issues they had come to discuss, they pledged to conduct deliberations in secrecy—behind closed doors and windows—despite the sweltering heat and humidity of the Philadelphia summer. They also understood the art of compromise, and that the time had come to exercise it. The delegates were neither the demigods Jefferson called them nor a crafty elite plotting their own fortunes as some historians have suggested.[4] Political scientist John P. Roche aptly describes them as a group of extremely talented democratic politicians seeking practical answers to practical problems confronting them.[5]

Did You Know?

. . . That the members of the Philadelphia Constitutional Convention were so concerned that they be free to discuss possible changes in the Articles of Confederation without pressure from public opinion that they nailed shut the windows of their meeting room in Independence Hall (in the middle of a very hot summer)!

A New Constitution Is Born

Several delegates came prepared with their own plans for the shape of the national government. Edmund Randolph formally presented Virginia's plan, largely a creation of his colleague James Madison, calling for a **bicameral**, or two-house, legislature. Members of the lower house would be chosen by popular election, and they would in turn select the members of the upper house.[6] Talk of proportional representation in both legislative chambers made delegates from small states uncomfortable. They feared that more populous states such as Virginia, Pennsylvania, and Massa-

James Madison (1751–1836) came to Philadelphia with a blueprint for change and is known as the Father of the Constitution.

chusetts would dominate the legislature. On June 15, William Paterson presented the New Jersey Plan, which was more to the liking of the small states. He proposed a **unicameral**, or one-house, legislature, maintaining the equal state representation established under the Articles of Confederation, but granting Congress additional powers over trade and security. The plan would also establish a plural executive body and a federal judiciary, both chosen by Congress, to enforce national law in the states when necessary.

On June 19, delegates rejected the New Jersey Plan, signaling their desire to create a completely new form of government. By June 21, they settled on support for a bicameral legislature, but the debate—like the weather—was hot. Some delegates withdrew from the convention, never to return. On July 16, Roger Sherman from Connecticut found a solution to the question of congressional representation. His committee called for seats in the lower body to be allocated based on population, while in the upper chamber each state would have an equal vote. At first, both large- and small-state delegates continued to jockey for more favorable terms. The introduction of the requirement that money bills originate in the lower house secured passage of the agreement, known as the **Great Compromise**, by a single vote.

> **Great Compromise**
> Agreement at the Constitutional Convention splitting the legislature into two bodies—one apportioned by population, the other assigning each state two members.

Slavery was the most divisive issue at the Philadelphia Convention, and the compromise agreed upon planted the seeds for civil war.

Regional Tensions

Thorny issues remained, the most important of which touched on the institution of slavery. While the southern economy had become extremely dependent on slaves, the northern states were developing a commercial and manufacturing economy in which slave labor was not as profitable as paid labor. Many northerners opposed slavery on economic, as well as moral and religious, grounds. Some states, such as Rhode Island, had abolished slavery completely or enfranchised free blacks who owned property.

The immediate problem that concerned delegates was the question of how to count slaves for purposes of congressional representation. Should they be treated as inhabitants or simply as property? If they were inhabitants, each would count as a person for determining a state's representation in Congress. This would give southern states a disproportionate amount of political influence relative to the North. At the same time, however, the law required states to pay federal taxes based on population. Under this formula, counting slaves as inhabitants would require southerners to pay more in taxes.

Uncomfortable with either option, southern delegates resurrected an earlier proposal to base representation on the whole number of free citizens and three-fifths of all others, excluding Indians, who did not pay taxes. "All others" clearly referred to slaves. This accommodation, called the "three-fifths compromise," won the day and secured agreement among the delegates. A related issue

dividing regional delegates was the return of runaway slaves. Southern delegates demanded and received a constitutional provision directing states to return fugitive slaves to their owners.

Trade also proved to be a source of friction between states. Delegates from colonies with large trade and mercantile interests insisted that Congress must have the power to regulate commerce in ways that made their goods more competitive with foreign markets. Meanwhile, delegates from agricultural states—particularly those employing slaves—feared that such power would result in Congress taxing agricultural exports to the detriment of their own economies. They also feared that Congress would use its commerce power to halt the importation of slaves and moved to prohibit Congress from taking such action. A number of delegates raised both moral and practical objections to barring congressional regulation of slavery. Luther Martin, an attorney and planter representing Maryland, objected that slavery was inconsistent with the principles of the Revolution, while George Mason, an outspoken delegate from Virginia, argued that "the infernal traffic" in slaves was hampering the nation's economic development.[7] Once again the delegates reached a compromise, permitting congressional regulation of commerce in principle but prohibiting taxes on exports and permitting the importation of slaves until 1808.

A number of unrelated issues that had arisen over the course of the summer had been assigned to committee for consideration. Among these was the provision that states would set their own requirements for voting. This was a

. . . DELEGATES WERE RELUCTANT to support the new agreement until Benjamin Franklin urged them to "doubt a little of their own infallibility and put their name to the instrument."

concession to the fact that qualifications differed from state to state, especially with regard to the types and amounts of property that each required. Although land was considered the standard for southern states, property in northern states assumed a variety of forms. Delegates were wary about the impact any new government might have on property use and wanted to ensure that the dominant property interests in their states at the time would control the ballot box. Committees also wrangled with issues ranging from presidential selection to the jurisdiction of the courts.

Most of the delegates had doubts about various provisions in the final document; some doubted it would survive ratification. To bolster its chances of passage, the delegates determined that the document would take effect whenever nine states had ratified it. This decision was taken to ensure that Rhode Island—a fiercely independent colony—could not sabotage the committee's work by itself. One of the most ingenious features of the document was the incorporation of a process for change, allowing parts of the document to be altered while preserving the structure of government as a whole. Even with these precautions, delegates were reluctant to support the new agreement until Benjamin Franklin urged them to "doubt a little of their own infallibility and put their name to the instrument." Forty-two of the original fifty-five delegates remained at the closing of the convention on September 17, and

enshrines the principles of liberal democracy buttressed with protections achieved through the separation of powers, checks and balances, and federalism.

Liberal Democratic Principles

It is no accident that the Constitution begins with the words "We the People." This is a dramatic expression of citizen consent that expresses the principle at the heart of the document—the belief that humans create governments

> "IN FRAMING A GOVERNMENT which is to be administered by men over men, the great difficulty lies in this: you must first enable the government to control the governed; and in the next place, oblige it to control itself."

thirty-nine signed the document. Three men who played prominent roles in the convention declined to sign, fearing adverse political reaction back home: George Mason and Edmund Randolph of Virginia and Elbridge Gerry of Massachusetts. Their reluctance to sign prefigured the coming battle over ratification.

by their own consent and that once created, governments must be compelled to limit their reach. Madison eloquently captures this philosophy in *The Federalist* No. 51:

> In framing a government which is to be administered by men over men, the great difficulty lies in this: you must first enable the government to control the governed; and in the next place, oblige it to control itself.[9]

CONSTITUTIONAL PRINCIPLES

The Constitution has been called a patchwork document "sewn together under the pressure of time and events by a group of extremely talented democratic politicians,"[8] but this does not mean it lacks vision and principle. Most notably, the United States Constitution

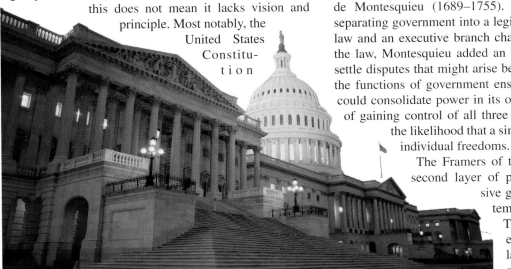

Separation of Powers and Checks and Balances

To limit the reach of the government, the Framers incorporated into the Constitution the principles of separation of powers and checks and balances. The first principle stems from John Locke and the French philosopher Baron de Montesquieu (1689–1755). While Locke proposed separating government into a legislative branch that made law and an executive branch charged with implementing the law, Montesquieu added an independent judiciary to settle disputes that might arise between the two. Dividing the functions of government ensured that no one branch could consolidate power in its own hands. The difficulty of gaining control of all three branches also decreased the likelihood that a single group might threaten individual freedoms.

The Framers of the Constitution added a second layer of protection against excessive government power: a system of checks and balances. This involves providing each branch with overlapping powers so that no one branch could exercise complete control of any function of government.

For example, the Constitution grants Congress principal responsibility for making laws, but allows the president to check this power by vetoing legislation. Congress, however, has the ability to override the veto of a president who stands in the way of needed legislative change. In turn, the courts can check the power of the other branches by challenging the constitutionality of laws passed with the consent of the legislature and the executive branch. To balance the power of the courts, the president can attempt to alter their composition through his or her power of appointment. For its part, Congress can exercise power by withholding funds from the courts or by proposing legislative changes or amendments to circumvent the court decisions.

Although this system may seem to be a prescription for stalemate, it is intended to prevent the arbitrary use of power and to give leaders sufficient time to forge consensus on divisive issues. When faced with a sense of urgency, however, the system can respond expeditiously, such as when Congress and the president quickly approved a mea-

sure in 2008 to save troubled financial institutions involved in risky mortgages whose failure would have worsened an already faltering economy.

Federalism

Although the Framers acknowledged the problems of governing a confederation of autonomous states, they also were aware of the people's fear of putting political power in the hands of a remote national government. To address this concern, the Framers established a form of power sharing between the states and the national government called federalism. Under a federal system, some powers—such as the power to declare war—are properly controlled by the national government, while others—such as the ability to create cities and towns—are reserved to the states. We will see in Chapter 3 that the division of power is actually more fluid than this distinction would

System of Checks and Balances

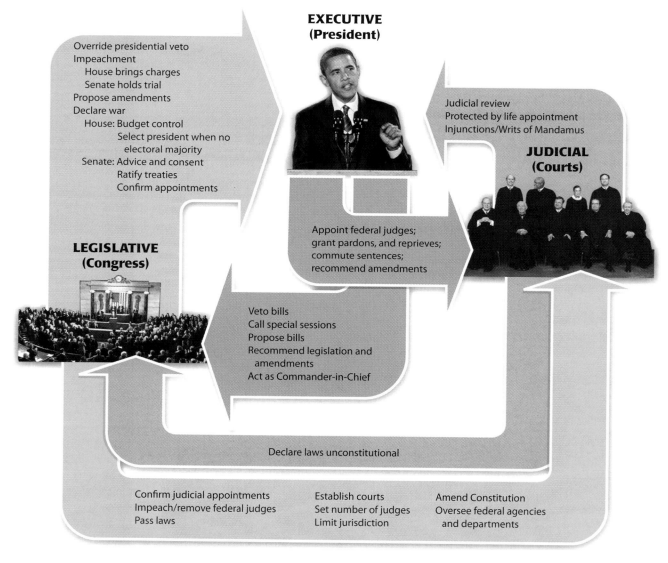

EXECUTIVE (President)

Override presidential veto
Impeachment
 House brings charges
 Senate holds trial
Propose amendments
Declare war
 House: Budget control
  Select president when no
   electoral majority
 Senate: Advice and consent
  Ratify treaties
  Confirm appointments

Judicial review
Protected by life appointment
Injunctions/Writs of Mandamus

JUDICIAL (Courts)

LEGISLATIVE (Congress)

Appoint federal judges;
grant pardons, and reprieves;
commute sentences;
recommend amendments

Veto bills
Call special sessions
Propose bills
Recommend legislation and
 amendments
Act as Commander-in-Chief

Declare laws unconstitutional

Confirm judicial appointments
Impeach/remove federal judges
Pass laws

Establish courts
Set number of judges
Limit jurisdiction

Amend Constitution
Oversee federal agencies
 and departments

While our system of checks and balances seems like a prescription for stalemate, Congress and the president can act with dispatch in times of crisis as they did in bailing out financial institutions in the wake of the recent home mortgage crisis.

imply. Nevertheless, federalism was meant to protect citizens by preventing government from exercising power outside its intended sphere. According to Madison, this division of power works hand in hand with separation of powers to secure individual liberty:

> In the compound Republic of America, the power surrendered by the people is first divided between two distinct governments, and then the portion allotted to each subdivided among distinct and separate departments. Hence a double security arises to the rights of the people. The different governments will control each other; at the same time that each will be controlled by itself.[10]

CONSTITUTIONAL CONSTRUCTION

The U.S. Constitution is a relatively brief document—just 4,608 words that occupy four sheets of parchment. It consists of a preamble and seven articles, each divided into sections, prescribing the powers and limits of various units of government. The preamble expresses the liberal democratic principles upon which the nation was founded and outlines the purposes to which the new government was dedicated. Preambles have become a typical feature of national constitutions following the American example.

Article I establishes a bicameral legislature. It specifies procedures for the election of House and Senate members, their qualifications for office, apportionment of representatives among the states, filling vacancies, and selecting officers. It outlines the House's role in the impeachment of federal officials and the Senate's role in their trial. The legislative powers of Congress are established, including the authority to make those laws necessary and proper for carrying out provisions of any other laws it passes. This provision is sometimes called the **elastic clause** because of the effect it has had on expanding congressional authority. Article I specifies that revenue bills must originate in the lower House and denies to the states many powers granted to the federal legislature.

Article II establishes the executive branch, including the offices of president and vice president. It deals with issues such as qualifications for the office of president, the method of election, succession of the vice president to the office of president in case of a vacancy, the president's salary, and the oath of office. It establishes the powers of the president as commander-in-chief, outlines his authority in negotiating treaties, grants him the power to fill vacancies when the Senate is not in session, and specifies additional duties of the office. One section provides for impeachment as the ultimate check on the authority of federal officials.

Article III establishes the judicial branch, creating the Supreme Court and authorizing Congress to create additional federal courts. It sets the terms of appointment and removal of all federal judges. It specifies the types of cases to be heard in federal courts and how cases will come before the Supreme Court. One section also presents the legal definition of treason.

Article IV discusses the relations among the states and compels them to recognize the legitimacy of each other's duly executed laws and to grant citizens of other states equal protection under the law. It provides for extradition of persons charged with crimes and the return of runaway slaves—a provision abolished by passage of the Thirteenth Amendment ending slavery. It discusses the admission of new states and provides for federal jurisdiction over federal lands such as state parks. It guarantees that all states shall have a republican form of government that, like the national government, derives from the consent of the people. This article also promises the states federal protection from foreign invasion.

> **elastic clause** Provision of Article I of the Constitution authorizing Congress to make those laws necessary and proper for carrying out the other laws it passes.

The remaining articles deal with a variety of miscellaneous issues. Article V details provisions for amending the Constitution (see discussion of the amendment process that follows). The federal government assumes responsibility

The Constitution holds public officials accountable for their actions, including the president, who can be impeached for "high crimes and misdemeanors." Bill Clinton, shown on screen during his impeachment trial, was eventually acquitted.

for the federal debt in Article VI, which also contains the **supremacy clause** that gives federal law precedence over state law. This article also specifies that members of Congress shall swear allegiance to the U.S. Constitution without reference to religious affiliation. Article VII discusses ratification of the Constitution, a process that—as we will see—faced considerable hurdles.

THE FIGHT FOR RATIFICATION

The delegates left Philadelphia hopeful that their work would bear fruit but by no means overconfident. Even before the convention adjourned on September 17, outside observers voiced suspicions about the motives of the delegates who had shrouded themselves in secrecy for so many months. Even some

supremacy clause Provision of Article VI stipulating that the federal government, in exercising any of the powers enumerated in the Constitution, must prevail over any conflicting or inconsistent state exercise of power.

of those who had a hand in creating the document were disgruntled. Some delegates refused to sign the document because it lacked a bill of rights. This provision, common in most state constitutions, defined individual freedoms and protections that were beyond the reach of the government. Tired and impatient to return home, most of the delegates were unwilling to tackle yet another potentially divisive issue. Supporters of the new constitution, called **Federalists**, believed the document sufficiently limited the power of federal bodies, making a bill of rights unnecessary. As it turned out, the delegates' failure to add specific protection for individual rights proved a major stumbling block to ratification.

Antifederalist Opposition

Opponents of the new document, known as **Antifederalists**, were drawn from various quarters and expressed concerns over a range of issues. Many farmers opposed creation of a new national currency, fearing that it might lower prices for their commodities or enable the very wealthy to buy up their land. Debtors saw the national government as a collection agency for wealthy lenders. Small-town residents distrusted the urban, legal, and commercial elite whose members had crafted the document. Others were angry that the delegates ignored their charge to reform the Articles of Confederation and instead created a whole new governing document. As one historian put it:

[T]he average man on the street (or farm) . . . likened [the Constitutional Convention] to an instance where a group of carpenters had been called upon to add a dormer, a walk-in closet, and a pantry, and then, without permission of the absentee owner, decided to tear down the farmhouse and build a new one from scratch.[11]

Philosophically, Antifederalists worried that the new country was so large that only a strong central government could maintain order and unity, a prospect that threatened the very existence of the states. They reminded their opponents that ancient philosophers believed democracies were only possible in small states and that large nations required the rule of a monarch or even a despot. Antifederalists argued that senators served for too long and represented excessively large territories and worried that these factors would cause senators to lose touch with the electorate. They were concerned about the role a standing army would play in enforcing federal law (and collecting federal taxes) within the states. And they worried about the lack of a written bill of rights to protect the freedoms the revolutionaries fought to achieve. Patrick Henry, whose passion-

well versed in history, but I will submit to your recollection, whether liberty has been destroyed most often by the licentiousness of the people, or by the tyranny of rulers. I imagine, sir, you will find the balance on the side of tyranny.[12]

The Battle in the States

The Constitution found support in commercial centers, western territories that desired protection from foreign powers and Native Americans, among land speculators and plantation owners, and in the smaller states that gained equal representation with big states in the proposed Senate. Five states quickly ratified the document by unanimous or lopsided votes, albeit at times by the use of questionable procedures. In Pennsylvania, for example, two Antifederalist delegates were forcibly removed from a local saloon and returned to the assembly hall in order to obtain a quorum, after which the convention ratified the document.

In Massachusetts, the nation's most populous state, a

"[T]HE AVERAGE MAN on the street (or farm) . . . likened [the Constitutional Convention] to an instance where a group of carpenters had been called upon to add a dormer, a walk-in closet, and a pantry, and then, without permission of the absentee owner, decided to tear down the farmhouse and build a new one from scratch."

Trial by jury is guaranteed by the Sixth Amendment to the U.S. Constitution.
....

ate oratory had advanced the revolutionary cause, spoke with equal passion about the lack of written protections:

> How does your trial by jury stand? In civil cases gone—not sufficiently secured in criminal—this best privilege is gone. But we are told that we need not fear; because those in power, being our representatives, will not abuse the power we put in their hands. . . . I am not

showdown loomed as legislators debated ratification for three weeks without resolution. When some Federalists floated the suggestion that Governor John Hancock might serve in the nation's first administration, Hancock swung his support in favor of ratification. To secure his support, however, he demanded that the final document include amendments protecting many of the individual rights guaranteed in Massachusetts's state constitution.

With Massachusetts on board, supporters of ratification turned their attention to two more large and important states: Virginia and New York. Virginia had a sizable Antifederalist contingent, but it also boasted supporters of the document who ranked among the most respected and influential figures in the nation, including Madison, Jefferson, and Washington. Despite a sometimes bitter debate, a promise to amend the document to protect certain individual rights secured ratification by a ten-vote margin on June 25, 1788.

Federalists Supporters of the Constitution and its strong central government.

Antifederalists Opponents of the ratification of the Constitution.

STATE	ORDER OF RATIFICATION	DATE OF RATIFICATION	VOTE
Delaware	1	December 7, 1787	30–0
Pennsylvania	2	December 12, 1787	46–23
New Jersey	3	December 18, 1787	38–0
Georgia	4	January 2, 1788	26–0
Connecticut	5	January 9, 1788	128–40
Massachusetts	6	February 6, 1788	187–168
Maryland	7	April 26, 1788	63–11
South Carolina	8	May 23, 1788	149–73
New Hampshire	9	June 21, 1788	57–47
Virginia	10	June 25, 1788	89–79
New York	11	July 26, 1788	30–27
North Carolina	12	November 21, 1789	194–77
Rhode Island	13	May 29, 1790	34–32

Ratification of the Constitution

Winning ratification in New York proved more difficult, and Federalists exerted great energy there to sway public opinion. In October 1787, James Madison, Alexander Hamilton, and John Jay published the first in a series of eighty-five articles, which came to be known as *The Federalist,* in the New York press extolling the virtues of the new Constitution and attempting to quell opponents' anxieties about the proposed national government. Intended primarily as a propaganda weapon in the Federalist drive to secure ratification, modern scholars hail the *Federalist Papers* for its insightful analysis of the principles of American government.

In *The Federalist,* Madison warns that **factions**—distinct groups most often driven by economic motives—threaten the unity of the new Republic by placing their own interests above those of the nation as a whole. The cure for factionalism, Madison claims, is precisely the type of republican government found in the Constitution. He argued that the size of the new nation, rather than being a threat to citizens, actually serves to protect them. A faction that dominates a single state will find it much more difficult to dominate national politics in a large union. Even large and influential factions will have difficulty controlling large districts such as those proposed in the new republic, where elected representatives are under pressure to weigh the wishes of the diverse interests they represent. Madison also believed that "unworthy" candidates "who practice the vicious arts" of factionalism have more difficulty gaining electoral majorities in large republics than they do in other types of government.[13]

faction Group—most often driven by economic motives—that places its own good above the good of the nation as a whole.

Despite Madison's eloquent arguments, ratification met substantial opposition that included New York governor George Clinton. Undaunted, Alexander Hamilton issued a dire warning to his fellow delegates: "Of course, you know . . . that if you refuse to ratify then New York City will secede from the state and ratify by itself, and where will the Empire State be without its crown jewel?"[14] Faced with the prospect of the state's political breakup, New York delegates ratified the Constitution by a vote of 30 to 27. Shortly thereafter, enough remaining states fell in line to ensure passage. Reluctant Rhode Island conceded the reality of the new regime by ratifying the Constitution in 1790, after the new government was already up and running.

Making Good on a Promise

Once elected to the new Congress, Madison determined to make good on the Federalists' pledge to incorporate additional amendments. Massachusetts had proposed as many as twenty-nine amendments, but Madison moved to submit only seventeen for approval by the states; Congress approved just twelve. The first ten, which constitute our Bill of Rights, were adopted by the states by 1791.

The first three amendments emphasize political liberties including freedom of speech, freedom of religion, freedom of the press, freedom of assembly, the right to bear arms, and protection against being forced to quarter troops in peacetime. The next five outline the basic rights that constitute due process of law, designed to protect innocent citizens accused of crimes. The Ninth and Tenth Amendments deal with federal-state relations and specify that rights and powers not explicitly granted to the federal government in the Constitution remain in the hands of the people and the states.

Although the Bill of Rights protected citizens from acts of the national government, it did not restrict states from depriving their own citizens of some of these same freedoms. In 1833 (*Barrons v. Baltimore*), the Supreme Court ruled that the Bill of Rights applied only to the national government since it was fear of the powers of the national government that provoked Antifederalists to call for these additional protections. As a result, states were not constrained by government limitations imposed by the Bill of Rights or by the Supreme Court's interpretation of those rights. Citizens in many states did not enjoy protections against unreasonable government searches or the right to an attorney or to a speedy trial. Even states that did recognize these rights did not apply them equally to all citizens. In many places, minority populations lacked these basic protections. However, the ratification of the Fourteenth Amendment in 1868 provided a vehicle whereby many of the rights enumerated in the Bill of Rights could be applied to the states. You will learn more about the fight for "incorporating" these rights in Chapter 4.

Madison's Eleventh Amendment, which failed to gain approval at the time, was finally passed more than two hundred years later. It prohibits members of Congress from receiving pay raises during the same session in which they are voted. In 1982, an undergraduate at the University of Texas at Austin, Gregory Watson, discovered that

Freedoms Guaranteed by the Bill of Rights

First Amendment	Prohibits Congress from establishing religion and restricting its free exercise; also prohibits Congress from abridging freedoms of speech, press, assembly, and petition
Second Amendment	Guarantees the people the right to bear arms
Third Amendment	Prohibits enforced quartering of soldiers in times of peace and allows for the regulation of such practices in time of war
Fourth Amendment	Protects against unreasonable searches and seizures
Fifth Amendment	Prescribes the use of grand juries, protects against being tried in the same court twice for the same offense, protects against self-incrimination, prescribes due process and compensation for property taken for public use
Sixth Amendment	Guarantees speedy and public trial in criminal procedures, trial by impartial jury, the right to be informed of charges and the right to face accusers, the right to obtain witnesses and to secure counsel for defense
Seventh Amendment	Guarantees the right to a jury trial in civil cases
Eighth Amendment	Prohibits excessive bail as well as cruel and unusual punishment
Ninth Amendment	Mandates that those rights not explicitly listed are reserved for the people
Tenth Amendment	Mandates that those powers not delegated to the national government are retained by states and the people

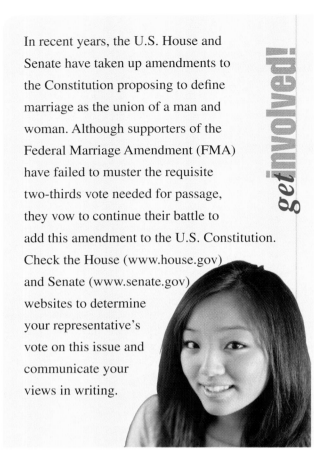

get involved!

In recent years, the U.S. House and Senate have taken up amendments to the Constitution proposing to define marriage as the union of a man and woman. Although supporters of the Federal Marriage Amendment (FMA) have failed to muster the requisite two-thirds vote needed for passage, they vow to continue their battle to add this amendment to the U.S. Constitution. Check the House (www.house.gov) and Senate (www.senate.gov) websites to determine your representative's vote on this issue and communicate your views in writing.

no time limit had been placed on the ratification of early amendments, so Madison's proposal was still eligible for adoption. Watson mounted a one-man ratification drive targeting strategic states whose ratification was not yet secured. In May 1992, the measure received legislative approval in Alabama, putting it over the top and making it the Twenty-seventh Amendment. Madison's proposed Twelfth Amendment, limiting the size of Congress, will experience no such revival, however. When Congress certified the ratification of the Twenty-seventh Amendment, it cancelled other long-standing proposed amendments, including Madison's unsuccessful twelfth proposal.

CONSTITUTIONAL CHANGE

One of the reasons the United States Constitution has endured for as long as it has is that the Framers made provisions for change. Although the amendment process is the most familiar way to alter the document, it is by no means the only one—in fact, it has been used sparingly. Our governmental structure—with its checks and balances, judicial review, and federalism—facilitates more subtle adaptation to accommodate changes to the social, political, and cultural landscape.

Amending the Constitution

The Framers proposed two methods for submitting amendments. Under the first method, an amendment that is introduced to Congress and approved by a two-thirds vote of both houses may be submitted to the states for ratification. This method has been used to initiate every existing amendment. Alternately, if requested by two-thirds of the state legislatures, Congress may call a national convention at which amendments may be proposed. In the 1980s, supporters of an amendment requiring the federal government to balance its budget annually tried this rarely used tactic but failed to gain sufficient support to mount a convention. Some scholars worry that, like the original meeting in 1787, such a convention could wander beyond its original mandate. Presumably, the delegates could propose a whole series of changes—even a new constitution.

Amendments passed by the Congress must still be ratified by three-quarters of the states to become part of the Constitution. This can happen either by approval of the legislatures in those states or by ratifying conventions held in the states. State legislatures have ratified every amendment except the Twenty-first, which repealed the Eighteenth Amendment prohibiting the manufacture and sale of alcoholic beverages in the United States. The ratification process originally had no fixed time limit, which is why

Methods for Proposing and Ratifying Amendments

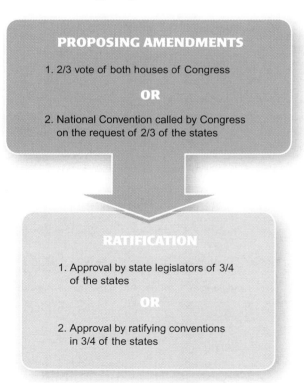

PROPOSING AMENDMENTS

1. 2/3 vote of both houses of Congress

OR

2. National Convention called by Congress on the request of 2/3 of the states

RATIFICATION

1. Approval by state legislators of 3/4 of the states

OR

2. Approval by ratifying conventions in 3/4 of the states

Recent Unsuccessful Attempts to Amend the Constitution

110th Congress (2007–2008)	• To repeal the Sixteenth Amendment (permitting taxing of income) • To prohibit flag desecration • To ensure the right to a clean, safe, and sustainable environment • To establish term limits for Congress • To make English the official language of the United States
109th Congress (2005–2006)	• To specifically permit prayer at school meetings and ceremonies • To allow non-natural-born citizens to run for president if they have been a citizen for twenty years • To specifically allow Congress to regulate the amount of personal funds a candidate to public office can expend in a campaign • To ensure that apportionment of representatives is set by counting only citizens • To make the filibuster in the Senate a part of the Constitution • To provide for continuity of government in case of a catastrophic event
108th Congress (2003–2004)	• To lower the age of representatives and senators from twenty-five and thirty, respectively, to age twenty-one • To ensure that citizens of U.S. territories and commonwealths can vote in presidential elections

one of Madison's amendments remained viable for 203 years. In the early twentieth century, however, Congress began placing time limits on the ratification effort, usually seven years. Congress occasionally allows extensions, as it did in 1982 when it allotted an additional three years for states to consider the Equal Rights Amendment. Despite the extension, the amendment barring discrimination on the basis of sex fell three states short of ratification.

Although the Framers designed the Constitution to be adaptable to change, they did not want change to come easily. They ensured that anyone who wished to amend the Constitution would need to build broad popular support for their proposals. The track record of amendment attempts illustrates the difficulty of the task. Of the more than ten thousand amendments proposed since 1789, only thirty-three made it to the states for ratification and only twenty-seven became part of the Constitution. The table above lists some recent proposed amendments that didn't make it—or, at least, not so far.

Institutional Adaptation

For the Constitution to remain viable, it must be able to adapt to changing times and deal with matters that its authors could hardly have anticipated. The individuals who crafted the Fourth Amendment did not envision the government electronically monitoring the conversations of suspected terrorists, nor did they consider the need to regulate fundraising by political parties when they penned the First

Amendment. Formal parties did not even exist at the time, and the Framers generally viewed them with disdain.

The Constitution is also flexible enough to survive the recurring power struggles among competing branches of government. For example, although the Constitution grants Congress the power to declare war, presidents have repeatedly asserted broad power over the military, greatly expanding the constitutional role of commander-in-chief. In fact, although the United States has been involved in hundreds of armed conflicts, Congress has only formally declared war five times.[15] This reflects, in part, the changing nature of warfare. Compared to the present day, eighteenth-century weapons were crude and communications were extremely slow; national leaders had more time to respond to military threats. The pace and destructiveness of modern warfare has produced a tendency to defer to presidential authority in matters of war and peace, and presidents have not been shy about wielding such authority.

Congress, too, has expanded

The president is commander-in-chief of the armed forces, but Congress is entrusted with the power to declare war.

its powers by the way it has interpreted the language of the Constitution. For example, in the mid–twentieth century, Congress used its power to regulate interstate commerce in a way never imagined a century before to achieve a host of goals unrelated to trade or business. By prohibiting businesses that transport goods and services across state lines from practicing discrimination, Congress advanced the cause of racial integration. Prior to the Civil War, such use of this power was unthinkable.

The Constitution has also withstood substantial changes in the relationship between the states and the federal government. In 1787, the states were independent entities that jealously guarded their power from federal encroachment. Although states can still set policies for residents within their borders, the federal government often uses its budgetary power to compel them to adopt national standards. In the 1980s, for example, Congress voted to withhold federal highway funds from states that failed to adopt a minimum drinking age of twenty-one. Again, these actions reflect adaptation to changing circumstances; variations in drinking ages may have made more sense before interstate highways essentially obliterated the borders between states.

Judicial Review

The decisions of the Supreme Court have effected greater changes to our system of government than any other actions save constitutional amendments. Most Americans take for granted the Court's role as final arbiter in interpreting the Constitution. However, the Constitution does not explicitly grant that power; instead, the Court assumed it in the 1803 case of *Marbury v. Madison.* In his opinion, Chief Justice John Marshall claimed for the Court authority for **judicial review**, the power to rule on the constitutionality of laws or other acts of government. Most scholars agree that the Framers assumed the Supreme Court would have this power, as did the British courts with which they were familiar. Alexander Hamilton even wrote in *The Federalist* No. 78:

judicial review Power granted to the Supreme Court to rule on the constitutionality of a law.

> The interpretation of the laws is the proper and peculiar province of the courts. A constitution is, in fact, and must be regarded by the judges as, a fundamental law. It therefore belongs to them to ascertain its meaning as well as the meaning of any particular act proceeding from the legislative body.[16]

Nevertheless, the Court sometimes endures severe criticism when it exercises this power. In its highly controversial ruling *Roe v. Wade,* the Court ruled that state laws making abortions illegal violated a woman's constitutional right to privacy. Although privacy is not explicitly mentioned in the Constitution, the Court ruled it could be inferred from the Ninth Amendment and the due process clause of the Fourteenth Amendment. Justice Harry Blackmun wrote: "The right to privacy . . . is broad enough to

The First Amendment protects our rights to assemble peaceably and to petition the government for redress of grievances.

encompass a woman's decision whether or not to terminate her pregnancy."[17] More than three and a half decades later, the ruling still arouses heated emotional opposition and political debate. Abortion opponents have been successful in persuading state legislatures to place funding and consent restrictions on the right to obtain an abortion, and they continue to promote a constitutional amendment to reverse *Roe v. Wade.* You will learn more about this in Chapter 4.

Expanding the Franchise

At the time of its writing, the Constitution granted the vote only to propertied, white, adult males. Yet despite placing severe limits on the franchise, it offered a process for expanding individual rights and a structure that enabled citizens to effect change. Property qualifications for voting fell first in the western territories, repealed by settlers attracted by free land and eager to form new social and political networks.[18] This experience taught astute eastern politicians that they could increase their base of popular support by expanding the franchise to those without property. By the middle of the nineteenth century, property qualifications for voting had crumbled across the nation.

Women and African Americans found voting barriers much more difficult to overcome. Prominent women such

PARTICIPATION today

Tracy Westen, CEO of the Center for Governmental Studies in Los Angeles, a nonprofit organization that helps clients use Internet technology in tracking government policies to advocate for policy preferences, argues that direct electronic democracy may be closer than we think. Although he does not believe it will be possible for citizens to vote on every single issue facing government, he does believe the e-voters of the future will be able to establish their preferences directly on the broad issues facing the polity. "Voters might initiate, circulate, and vote on electronic ballot initiatives addressing the 'hot ticket' issues of the day," he argues. "Legislators and legislative bodies will respond with modifications, corrections, and follow-up actions."*

Citing California as a model, he believes a type of direct electronic democracy can be set up quite easily. The first step is to draft a ballot initiative to allow advocates of future initiatives to circulate and collect signatures online to qualify ballot measures. Proponents would then need to pass a second initiative to develop a secure method for voting via the Internet. Aware of the potential for abuse, Westen argues that the next step would be to create an electronic system of checks and balances. These measures might include requiring a supermajority (e.g., 60 percent) to pass ballot measures, or conducting multiple votes over an extended period of time before a measure takes effect.

*The full text of Westen's article is available online at www.netcaucus.org/books/egov2001/pdf/edemoc.pdf (Accessed April 20, 2008).

as Abigail Adams spoke for women's rights from the time of the revolution, but women only secured the vote with passage of the Nineteenth Amendment in 1920 after decades of political protest. The nation had to endure a civil war before African Americans won their freedom with the Thirteenth Amendment and black males won the franchise with the Fifteenth Amendment. It took African Americans a further century of litigation, protest, and political campaigning to secure the full promise of the franchise through civil rights legislation in the 1960s. In 1971, the Twenty-sixth Amendment broadened the franchise even further, granting eighteen-year-olds the vote.

Although most legal barriers to voting are gone, issues of motivation, mobilization, and resources, which disproportionately affect those at the lower end of the income spectrum, remain. We will examine these in later chapters.

A strong voice for equal rights, Abigail Adams (1744–1818) cautioned her husband, the second president of the United States, to "remember the ladies."

THE CONSTITUTION AND CIVIC ENGAGEMENT TODAY

Hot or Not?

Should the government be given greater authority to wiretap telephones in the war against terrorism?

In 2004, Congress passed legislation requiring public institutions that receive federal funds to set aside September 17, the anniversary of the signing of the Constitution, as Constitution and Citizenship Day.[19] On this day, educators are required to conduct programs designed to commemorate the legacy of our founding document. Americans, however, don't need a special day to remind them of their Constitutional heritage; millions practice it every day. We celebrate the U.S. Constitution every time we write our senators and representatives about some important issue, read press accounts of current events, attend religious services, donate money to a political cause or candidate, engage in political debate in the classroom, or make a do-

nation to an interest group—all of these activities reflect fundamental rights enshrined in our Constitution.

Yet, we should remember that rights are never totally secure. They face continuing challenges and must adapt to meet changing times. Since the 9/11 terrorist attacks, many rights have been curbed in the interest of security. In some cases, such as the baggage searches and other intrusions of personal privacy that air travelers must endure, Americans generally take these inconveniences in stride. Most feel that the need for security outweighs issues of personal privacy in such situations. Other measures the government has taken in the name of security are far more controversial. For example, Congress has given the executive branch the right to monitor international phone calls

Recent acts of terrorism are redefining the boundary between civil liberties and national security.

and Internet traffic without obtaining a warrant, and with less judicial oversight than was required in the past. The Federal Bureau of Investigation (FBI) may obtain any citizen's library records if it suspects the records are relevant to an investigation, even if the person whose records they subpoena is not a terrorist suspect. Should the government assume such broad powers and make them a permanent feature of the American political system? Does government need such powers to protect its citizens—or are such powers unwarranted intrusions into our personal lives that go beyond the requirements of genuine security?

These are questions for citizens of your generation to face, just as the founding generation faced questions dealing with the right of government to quarter soldiers in their homes or to shut down town meetings held without the prior approval of royal governors. There are plenty of ways you can get involved in exploring such issues and making your voice heard. You can join one of the many interest groups that focus their efforts on this issue and that can offer detailed information and analysis. You can hold university or community forums to solicit the views of your classmates and neighbors. You can meet with law enforcement officials and legal scholars to get their views. These are rights that your generation has inherited and are yours to keep as long as you stay involved. Thomas Jefferson's famous aphorism "the price of freedom is eternal vigilance" applies no less today than it did in his own day.

For REVIEW >>

1. What factors contributed to the need for a constitutional convention?
   - After the Revolution, colonists found the Articles of Confederation too weak to help them pay their war debt, control interstate commerce, and put down local rebellions like the one fomented by Daniel Shays in Massachusetts.

2. What are the basic principles that inform our Constitution?
   - The basic principles of the Constitution are separation of powers, checks and balances, and a division of power between the states and the national government known as federalism.

3. In what ways does constitutional change occur?
   - The Constitution can be changed through amendment; through the actions of political leaders who stretch its meaning to adapt to social, political, and economic change; and by court interpretation.

National Journal

IS JUDICIAL REVIEW OBSOLETE?

The big Supreme Court decision that the Second Amendment protects an individual right to keep a loaded handgun for self-defense at home is the high-water mark of the "original meaning" approach to constitutional interpretation championed by Justice Antonin Scalia and many other conservatives. At the same time, the decision may show "originalism" to be a false promise.

Scalia's 64-page opinion for the five-justice majority was a tour de force of originalist analysis. Without pausing to ask whether gun rights is good policy, Scalia parsed the Second Amendment's 27 words one by one while consulting 18th-century dictionaries, early American history, the 1689 English Bill of Rights, 19th-century treatises, and other historical material.

And even the lead dissent for the Court's four liberals—who are accustomed to deep-sixing original meaning on issues ranging from the death penalty to abortion, gay rights, and many others—all but conceded that this case should turn mainly on the original meaning of the 217-year-old Second Amendment. They had little choice, given the unusual absence of binding precedent.

But in another sense, the case, *District of Columbia v. Heller* belies the two great advantages that originalism has been touted as having over the liberals' "living Constitution" approach. Originalism is supposed to supply first principles that will prevent justices from merely voting their policy preferences and to foster what Judge Robert Bork once called "deference to democratic choice." But the gun case suggests that originalism does neither.

First, even though all nine justices claimed to be following original meaning, they split angrily along liberal-conservative lines perfectly matching their apparent policy preferences, with the four conservatives (plus swing-voting Anthony Kennedy) voting for gun rights and the four liberals against.

These eight justices cleaved in *exactly* the same way—with Kennedy tipping the balance from case to case—in the decision the same day striking down a campaign finance provision designed to handicap rich, self-funded political candidates; decisions earlier in 2008 barring the death penalty for raping a child and striking down the elected branches' restrictions on judicial review of Guantánamo detainees' petitions for release; and past decisions on abortion, affirmative action, gay rights, religion, and more.

This pattern does not mean that the justices are *insincerely* using legal doctrines as a cover for politically driven votes. Rather, it shows that ascertaining the original meaning of provisions drafted more than 200 years

"A well-regulated militia, being necessary to the security of a free state, the right of the people to keep and bear arms, shall not be infringed."

And even if there is a clear right answer, the voting pattern suggests that conservative and liberal justices will never agree on what it is. More broadly, even when there is no dispute as to original meaning, it is often intolerable to liberals and conservatives alike. For example, no constitutional provision or amendment was ever designed to prohibit the federal government from discriminating based on race (or sex). This has not stopped conservatives from voting to strike down federal racial preferences for minorities (by seeking to extend liberal precedents) any more than

> If originalism **does not deliver on its promises** to channel judicial discretion and constrain judicial usurpations of elected officials' power, what good is it?

ago, in a very different society, is often a subjective process on which reasonable people disagree—and often reach conclusions driven consciously or subconsciously by their policy preferences. And some of us have trouble coming to confident conclusions either way.

Scalia's argument for striking down the District of Columbia's gun laws—the strictest in the country—was persuasive. But so were the dissents by liberal Justices John Paul Stevens and Stephen Breyer. Scalia and the two dissenters all made cogent arguments while papering over weaknesses in their positions. Scalia may have won on points. But more study might tip an observer the other way.

The reason is that the justices' exhaustive analyses of the text and relevant history do not definitively resolve the ambiguity inherent in the amendment's curious wording:

it stopped liberals from striking down the federal laws that once discriminated against women.

Second, the notion that originalists would defer more to democratic choices than would the loosey-goosey liberals has come to ring a bit hollow. The originalists began with a compelling critique of the liberals' invention of new constitutional rights to strike down all state abortion and death-penalty laws, among others. But the current conservative justices have hardly been models of judicial restraint.

They have used highly debatable interpretations of original meaning to sweep aside a raft of democratically adopted laws. These include federal laws regulating campaign money and imposing monetary liability on states. And in 2007's 5-4 decision striking down two local school-integration laws, the

conservative majority came close to imposing a "colorblind Constitution" vision of equal protection that may be good policy but which is hard to find in the 14th Amendment's original meaning.

In the gun case, as Justice Breyer argued, "the majority's decision threatens severely to limit the ability of more knowledgeable, democratically elected officials to deal with gun-related problems." (Of course, Breyer's solicitude for elected officials disappears when the issue is whether they should be able to execute rapists of children or ban an especially grisly abortion method.)

If originalism does not deliver on its promises to channel judicial discretion and constrain judicial usurpations of elected officials' power, what good is it?

Indeed, it seems almost perverse to be assessing what gun controls to allow based not on examining how best to save lives but on seeking to read the minds of the men who ratified the Bill of Rights well over 200 years ago.

The originalist approach seems especially odd when it comes down to arguing over such matters as whether 18th-century lawyers agreed (as Scalia contends) that "a prefatory clause does not limit or expand the scope of the operative clause" and whether (as Stevens contends) the phrase "'bear arms' most naturally conveys a military meaning" and "the Second Amendment does not protect a 'right to keep and to bear arms,' but rather 'a right to keep and bear arms'" (emphasis in original). The justices may as well have tried reading the entrails of dead hamsters.

Is the answer to embrace liberals' "living Constitution" jurisprudence, which roughly

Indeed, not one of the nine justices seems to have a modest understanding of his or her powers to set national policy in the name of enforcing the Constitution.

translates to reading into the 18th-century document whichever meaning and values the justices consider most fundamental?

By no means. Rather, in the many cases in which nothing close to consensus about the meaning of the Constitution is attainable, the justices should leave the lawmaking to elected officials.

Now it seems that the originalist view of the Constitution is indeed incapable of telling today's judges what to do—not, at least, with any consistency from one judge to the next. So is judicial review itself obsolete?

Not quite. Judicial review remains valuable, perhaps indispensable, because it helps provide the stability and protection for liberty inherent in our tripartite separation of powers, with the legislative, executive, and judicial branches serving as the three legs of a stool and with each potent enough to check abuses and excesses by the others.

The June 12 decision rebuffing President Bush's (and Congress's) denial of fair hearings to Guantánamo detainees proclaiming their innocence is a case in point. But the broad wording of Kennedy's majority opinion, joined by the four liberals, went too far by flirting with a hubristic vision of unprecedented judicial power to intrude deeply into the conduct of foreign wars.

Indeed, not one of the nine justices seems to have a modest understanding of his or her powers to set national policy in the name of enforcing the Constitution. But the other branches, and most voters, seem content with raw judicial policy-making—except when they don't like the policies. For better or worse, what Scalia has called "the imperial judiciary"—sometimes liberal, sometimes conservative—seems here to stay.

Given this, the best way to restrain judicial imperialism may be for the president and the Senate to worry less about whether prospective justices are liberal or conservative and more about whether they have a healthy sense of their own fallibility.

■ **FOR DISCUSSION:** Do the intentions of the Constitution's framers still matter in considering issues like gun control? When they're ambiguous, how would you attempt to deduce what those intentions were?

Do you think the constitution is a "living document" or are you an "originalist"?

Should the 2nd Amendment be read to mean that every individual has a right to a firearm? Where should that protection begin and end?

3

FEDERALISM

CITIZENSHIP AND THE DISPERSAL OF POWER

CALIFORNIA GOES ITS OWN WAY ▮ As of April 2008, 178 nations had signed the Kyoto Protocol pledging to attain legally binding targets to reduce greenhouse gases. The one notable exception is the United States. Concerned about the economic impact of the treaty and upset that the treaty granted China a short-term exemption from meeting emissions standards, the U.S. Senate never voted on the protocol. The federal government's refusal to endorse the agreement, however, did not prevent some states from taking matters into their own hands. In September 2006, California governor Arnold Schwarzenegger signed a bill that establishes the world's first comprehensive program to reduce greenhouse gases. The bill requires the California Air Resources Board (CARB) to develop regulations and market-based incentives to reduce carbon emissions to 1990 levels by the year 2020 and to achieve an 80 percent reduction below 1990 levels by 2050. At the ceremony marking the event, the governor commented, "This is something we owe our children and our grandchildren. We simply must do everything in our power to slow down global warming before it's too late."[1] In December 2007, the Environmental Protection Agency (EPA) threw a monkey wrench into California's plans by refusing to grant a waiver that would have allowed the state to set more stringent tailpipe emissions than the rest of the nation, a key provision of its plan to cut greenhouse gases. Nevertheless, the California governor has vowed to press forward with other measures.

Since 2001, almost half of the states and well over one hundred cities and towns across America have taken action to curb the emission of greenhouse gases linked to global warming and climate change. Salt Lake City, for example, has launched a variety of initiatives, including the use of more energy-efficient lighting, wind power purchases, LED traffic signal upgrades, alternative fuel use, cogeneration, and methane capture, that have helped the city eliminate the equivalent of over twenty-three thousand tons of carbon dioxide emissions.[2] According to David Danner, the energy advisor for Washington governor Gary Locke, the states are taking action to fill the vacuum that has been left by the federal government. "We hope to see the problem addressed at the federal level," Mr. Danner said, "but we're not waiting around."[3]

State and municipal authorities can pursue reforms stymied at the national level because of a feature of the American political system known as **federalism**. Federalism disperses authority among different levels of government, providing citizens various platforms for political participation. This chapter focuses primarily on government at the national and state levels, but the nation's governmental structure is much more complex. In addition to the federal and state governments, the United States is composed of 3,034 county governments, 19,429 municipal governments, 16,504 township governments, and 48,000 special and school district governments. Most of these governments have some taxing authority, and all conduct legal and fiscal transactions with other units of government.[4] Relationships among these various levels of government continually evolve to reflect the changing political and financial currents of the day, potentially affecting the lives of millions of citizens. ❖

As You READ >>

- How is power dispersed in American federalism?
- How have the powers of the national and state governments evolved over the nation's history?
- What three factors mold nation-state relations today?

THE DIVISION OF POWER

Following the American Revolution, the nation's Framers faced the problem of organizing a rapidly growing nation whose citizens cherished local rule. While history furnished ideas for power sharing within the national government—such as separation of powers and checks and balances—it offered few workable models for nation-state relations. The individuals who framed the Constitution were forced to devise their own solution—a historic innovation called federalism.

Prevailing Models for Dispersing Power

Prior to the Constitutional Convention, two models of intergovernmental relations predominated throughout the world: unitary and confederated (see figure below). Un-

Diagrams of Unitary and Confederated Forms of Government

Unitary Government

Confederation

Arrows represent the flow of decisions and resources.

 Central   State   Local

California has taken a leading role in attempting to curb the emission of greenhouse gasses from sources like automobiles that clog the state's congested freeways.

Great Britain has a unitary form of government in which most authority is exercised by officials at the national level.

der a unitary form, all power resides in the central government, which makes the laws. State or local governments act primarily as local vehicles to implement national laws. Many of the Framers found this kind of distant government unacceptable and considered it a threat to personal liberty. This form of government characterized the British system against which the colonies rebelled and persists in many nations today, including England and France.

In a confederation, states and localities retain sovereign power, yielding to the central government only limited authority as needed. This form of government—which characterized the government under the Articles of Confederation—was also clearly unacceptable, leading the Framers to call a convention in Philadelphia to address its shortcomings. Confederations are, for the most part, relics of the past. Very few modern nations employ this form of government, because it slows the central government's ability to act. A confederacy does, however, characterize some intergovernmental organizations that include nation-states as members, such as the United Nations.

The Federalist Solution

Even opponents of a strong national government understood that only a more "energetic" central power could remedy the defects contained in the Articles of Confederation. These included a lack of control over interstate commerce and the absence of a national currency, which seriously limited the development of national markets. Most significantly, however, the national government lacked central taxing power, making it impossible to raise money to repay the substantial debts it accumulated during the Revolution. The Continental Congress could assess each state for taxes, but it had no power to enforce collection. The delegates to the Constitutional Convention faced the problem of providing the central government with enough power to function effectively, but not so much that it dominated the states. Federalism was their solution.

In a federal system, four main attributes characterize power arrangements among levels of government:

1. **Enumerated powers** are specifically granted to the national government. Article I in the U.S. Constitution expressly authorizes most of these powers. Section 8 of Article I, known as the elastic clause, implies that the national government exercises additional powers by authorizing Congress to make "all laws which shall be necessary and proper for carrying into execution the foregoing powers." These powers to implement constitutionally enumerated functions are known as **implied powers**. The national government also exercises inherent powers characteristic of any sovereign nation such as the power to wage war and conduct international trade.

2. **Reserved powers** are granted specifically to the states. The Constitution places certain limits upon national power, and the Tenth Amendment reserves to the states or to the people all powers not specifically granted to the national government. Many actions states take with regard to protecting the health and welfare of their residents issue from their **police powers**.

3. **Concurrent powers** are shared jointly by the federal and state governments.

4. **Prohibited powers** are denied to either or both levels of government. The table on page 44 lists examples of major powers in each category.

Many supporters felt that a federal system not only was more practical but also served as

federalism Power-sharing arrangement between the national and state governments in which some powers are granted to the national government alone, some powers are reserved to the states, some powers are held concurrently, and other powers are prohibited to either or both levels of government.

enumerated powers Powers specifically allocated to the national government alone.

implied powers Powers necessary to carry out constitutionally enumerated functions of government.

reserved powers Powers constitutionally allocated to the states.

police powers Authority states utilize to protect the health and welfare of their residents.

concurrent powers Powers shared by both state and national governments.

prohibited powers Powers denied one or both levels of government.

Attributes of U.S. Federalism

Powers of National Government	Powers Reserved to State Governments	Concurrent Powers
Make war	Regulate intrastate commerce	Tax and Spend
Coin money	Protect health and safety	Borrow money
	Pass laws	Establish courts
	Charter local governments	Charter banks and corporations
	Regulate voting	
	Establish schools	
Admit new states		
Regulate interstate commerce		
Establish post offices		
Raise army and navy		
Establish uniform naturalization laws		
Fix standard weights and measures		

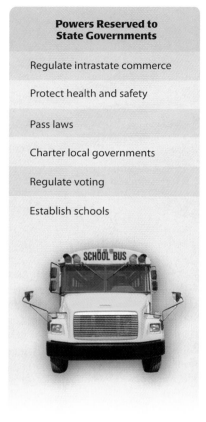
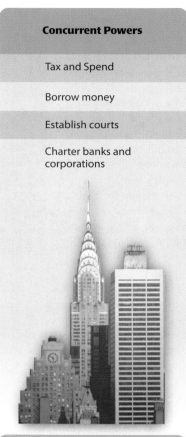

Powers Prohibited National Government	Powers Prohibited States	Powers Prohibited National and State
Capitation tax	Make treaties	Ex post facto laws
Taxing state exports	Impairment of contracts	Bills of attainder
Preferential treatment for ports	Taxing exports	
Granting titles of nobility	Make war	

an additional guarantee of individual freedoms. Madison argued that the federal system offered a dual protection of citizens' rights. In *The Federalist* No. 51, he writes:

> In the compound Republic of America, the power surrendered by the people is first divided between two distinct governments, and then the portion allotted to each subdivided among separate departments. Hence a double security arises to the rights of the people. The different governments will control each other, at the same time that each will be controlled by itself.[5]

For Federalists such as Madison, federalism protected individual freedom, encouraged participation in national affairs, and enhanced public security.

Antifederalists, however, remained suspicious of the power of the national government. They found particularly worrisome the supremacy clause in Article VI, which declared federal law supreme in instances when national and state laws collided. Despite the addition of a bill of rights explicitly limiting the federal government's ability to encroach on the rights of individuals and states, Antifederalists remained uncomfortable with the federal arrangement well into the formative years of the new republic. They warned that the new federal system would unravel the bonds of citizenship that they believed flourished only in small, homogeneous communities.[6] To some extent, the debate over which conditions best foster citizen participation—small, like-minded communities, or larger, more

arguing that a national bank favored northern industry over southern farming and represented unfair competition for state financial institutions. Congress authorized a twenty-year charter for the bank in 1791, setting in motion a schism between supporters of Hamilton and supporters of Jefferson that led to the growth of the nation's first political parties.

The election of Federalist candidate John Adams in 1796 increased tensions between the two groups. In 1798, Adams pushed through Congress the Alien and Sedition Laws, intended to stifle political opposition to his foreign policy. In response, Jefferson, Madison, and their allies developed the new philosophy of **nullification**, which proclaimed that states had

> **nullification** Doctrine that asserted the right of states to disregard federal actions with which they disagreed.

the authority to declare national acts unenforceable within their borders. Although both the Virginia and Kentucky state legislatures passed resolutions affirming the doctrine of nullification in 1798, Jefferson ignored the doctrine after he won the presidency in 1800. Several decades later, southern secessionists resurrected his nullification philosophy as the nation moved toward civil war.[7]

Congress neglected to renew the charter of the First Bank of the United States, which expired in 1811. How-

diverse ones—persists. It seems clear, however, that a federal system is well suited to a country such as the United States, where regional interests must seek accommodation with broader national goals.

THE EVOLUTION OF INTERGOVERNMENTAL RELATIONS

Although the Constitution provides ground rules for the federal allocation of power, the balance of power among various levels of government has not remained static. It has ebbed and flowed over the course of the past two and a quarter centuries, making federalism a dynamic force in our nation's history.

The National Government Asserts Itself: 1789–1832

In the early days of the new republic, former colonial allies heatedly disagreed about how much power the Constitution granted the federal government. The Constitution left all sorts of questions regarding national and state power unanswered, including the meaning of terms and phrases such as *commerce* or *necessary and proper*. Federalists in the new government, such as the treasury secretary, Alexander Hamilton, advocated exercising strong national authority in the arena of finance and commerce, urging President Washington to support his plans for a national bank that would finance the construction of canals and roads. Secretary of State Thomas Jefferson opposed Hamilton's plan,

Alexander Hamilton (1757–1804) championed a strong federal government with the power to take the lead in the nation's economic development (left). Thomas Jefferson (1743–1826) broke with Hamilton, arguing that a national bank favored northern industry over southern farming (right).

Marshall argued that taxation by the states had the potential to destroy federal institutions and undermine the supremacy of national law.

Marshall's ruling set the stage for an expansion of national power at a time when economic production and commerce were burgeoning. Inevitably, questions soon arose regarding the national government's powers to regulate commerce. In 1824, the Marshall court heard its first case to test those powers, *Gibbons v. Ogden*. The case involved a conflict between two steamboat operators, Thomas Gibbons of New Jersey and Aaron Ogden of New York. Both men received rights to operate off the coast of New York and New Jersey: Ogden from the state of New York, and Gibbons by an act of Congress. A lower court upheld Ogden's claim, ruling that the state of New York had the right to regulate commerce with neighboring states, regardless of any concurrent national power over commerce. Gibbons appealed the case to the U.S. Supreme Court.

In *Gibbons v. Ogden*, the Marshall Court upheld the supremacy of the national government in regulating commerce, not simply in intercoastal waterways but also within states when commerce between or among states was involved. Marshall also defined the term *commerce* loosely, applying it to goods as well as to passengers. This definition significantly expanded the power of Congress and the president to oversee the economic development of the new nation in areas previously considered the preserve of states. Advocates for a strong federal role in matters ranging from education to welfare would later use the same logic to support their efforts.

ever, it established a second Bank of the United States in 1816, once again raising the ire of state banking interests. Maryland reacted by enacting a tax on operations at the bank's Baltimore branch, hoping to drive it out of business. The bank's clerk, James McCulloch, refused to collect the tax, arguing that a state could not tax an institution created by the national government. After losing his battle in state court, McCulloch appealed his case to the U.S. Supreme Court, where John Marshall, a longtime Federalist supporter, presided as chief justice.

Marshall's court was asked to decide two issues: (1) Did the national government have the authority to establish a national bank, and (2) if so, could a state tax the bank's operations within its borders? In his landmark decision, *McCulloch v. Maryland* (1819), Marshall ruled against state interests on both issues. He found congressional authority to establish the bank under the "necessary and proper clause" of Article I:

> The government which has a right to do an act, and has imposed on it the duty of performing that act, must, according to the dictates of reason, be allowed to select the means. . . . To its enumeration of powers is added that of making "all laws which shall be necessary and proper for carrying into execution the foregoing powers, and all other powers vested by this constitution, in the government of the United States, or in any department thereof."[8]

dual federalism Approach to federal-state relationships that envisions each level of government as distinct and authoritative within its own sphere of action.

Marshall relied on the supremacy clause to deny states the power to tax a federal institution:

> The result is a conviction that the States have no power, by taxation or otherwise, to retard, impede, burden, or in any manner control, the operations of the constitutional laws enacted by Congress to carry into execution the powers vested in the general government. This is, we think, the unavoidable consequence of that supremacy which the constitution has declared.[9]

Dual Federalism, Disunion, and War: 1832–1865

Nation-state relations in the period preceding the Civil War were dominated by a philosophy of **dual federalism**. Dual federalism holds that the powers of the state and national governments are distinct and autonomous in their own domains. Levels of government are likened to layers in a cake that sit atop each other but do not intermingle. This viewpoint gave rise to disputes over the powers of each level of government, especially with regard to finances and the thorny issue of slavery.

Marshall's strong stance regarding the scope of federal power created resentment among southern farmers and financiers, who feared northern economic dominance. President Andrew Jackson's administration further inflamed these fears by enforcing a tariff on imported goods that protected northern manufacturers, causing some southerners to threaten secession. Jackson's vice president, South Carolinian John C. Calhoun, resigned over the matter in 1832 and justified his home state's opposition to the tariff by citing the Jeffersonian concept of nullification. Jackson adroitly solved the crisis by lowering the tariff, but talk of nullification continued as a debate over slavery took center stage in national politics.

While fear of northern dominance and support for the doctrine of nullification fueled southern passions, the Supreme Court's ruling in *Dred Scott v. Sandford* in 1857 inflamed abolitionist sentiment in the North.[10] Applying the perspective of dual federalism to bolster the power of the states, Chief Justice Roger B. Taney rejected the authority of Congress to outlaw slavery in the states and accelerated the momentum toward civil war. Republican candidate Abraham Lincoln's victory over a divided Democratic Party in the presidential election of 1860 brought the legal stalemate over slavery to an end as seven southern states seceded. Over the next four years, the United States and the Confederacy fought a bloody civil war to resolve not only the issue of slavery but also disputes over the future of our federal system that rhetoric alone could not settle.

After the Confederate surrender in 1865, Congress passed three new constitutional amendments as part of its proposed reconstruction program. The Thirteenth Amendment ended slavery. The Fourteenth Amendment guaranteed to former slaves basic rights under the U.S. Constitution. Further, it asserts that no state shall "deprive any person of life, liberty, or property, without due process of law; nor deny to any person within its jurisdiction the equal protection of the laws." The Fifteenth Amendment gave black males the vote. Of all the Civil War amendments, the Fourteenth has gen-

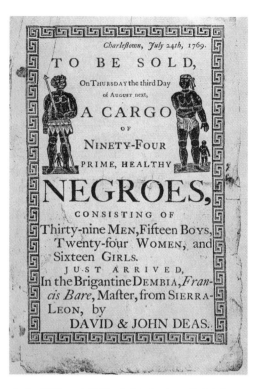

In the 1830s and 1840s, abolitionists intensified their efforts to combat the institution of slavery.

erated the most controversy and continues to define many debates surrounding federalism today.

Federalism in the Age of Commerce: 1865–1932

With the end of the Civil War and the principle of union firmly established, the nation moved into an era of unprecedented economic change and growth. Millions of rural farm workers joined large numbers of immigrants from foreign lands moving into the growing cities. The dangerous working conditions in many urban factories produced calls among reformers for government intervention to improve the lot of American workers. During this era, however, the Supreme Court consistently refused to allow the federal government to intervene in the right of states to issue licenses and to regulate commerce within their borders, and rejected limits on businesses to contract for the services of employees.

In *Hammer v. Dagenhart* (1918), for example, the Supreme Court overturned federal efforts to end child labor. Associate Justice William R. Day, citing the Tenth Amendment, asserted that regulation of production was not expressly delegated to the national government and therefore was reserved to the states and to the people.[11]

The Court delivered a blow to federal efforts to restrain the growth of corporate trusts or monopolies in *U.S. v. E. C. Knight Co.* (1895).[12] The E. C. Knight Company controlled over 98 percent of the sugar refining business in the nation and sought authority for contracts to control even more. The 1890 Sherman Antitrust Act, however, sought

Failing to secure the help of the federal government, reformers during the Progressive Era turned to the states in their quest to end child labor.

to use the federal government's interstate commerce power to limit such monopolization of the market. In *U.S. v. E. C. Knight Co.*, a majority of the justices ruled that manufacturing is not commerce but an intrastate activity subject to state control. The Court argued that the activities of the company only incidentally and indirectly affected interstate commerce.

The Court was even reluctant to uphold a state's power to limit business activity within its borders. In *Lochner v. New York* (1905), the Court overturned a New York state law limiting the number of hours a baker could work. The state legislature had passed the bill on the grounds that extensive exposure to flour dust was detrimental to the health of employees, and that the state had the duty to protect the health of its citizens. The Supreme Court disagreed, arguing that the law interfered with the rights of both the employee and the employer to enter freely into contract, a freedom guaranteed by the Fourteenth Amendment.[13] Justice Oliver Wendell Holmes, Jr., issued a stinging dissent that would later impact Court deliberations concerning the states' policing powers.

Progressives during this period fought unfavorable Court rulings by increasing pressure on local lawmakers.

Citizen reform groups, many headed by women such as labor rights advocate Mother Jones (See "Portrait of an Activist"), conducted marches and confronted political leaders with demands to end child labor, to improve working conditions for women, and to limit the influence of big business on the political process. The success of interest groups at the state level put pressure on federal lawmakers, producing a number of reforms that again reshaped the face of federalism. Perhaps most significant among these changes were constitutional amendments permitting the federal government to tax personal income (Sixteenth Amendment), the direct election of senators (Seventeenth Amendment), and the expansion of the voting franchise to women (Nineteenth Amendment). These amendments focused attention on the powers of the national government as an agent of change.

The Progressive Movement helped swing the pendulum in the direction of increased federal power. President Theodore Roosevelt championed mine safety and meat inspection laws, signed the Pure Food and Drug Act into law in 1906, and expanded efforts to protect the nation's forests. Woodrow Wilson later extended federal powers over commerce by pushing for the Federal Trade Commission and

Mary Harris Jones, known as Mother Jones, led a "Children's Crusade" in 1903, marching from Kensington, Pennsylvania, to Oyster Bay, New York, to confront President Theodore Roosevelt at his summer home with a demand to end child labor.

of a textile mill where the children and their parents were striking—to confront President Theodore Roosevelt at his summer home at Oyster Bay. Along the way, she stopped to make speeches in which she asked the children to show the stumps of fingers, hands, or limbs they had lost while working in the dangerous mills.

Although Roosevelt refused to see her or pursue national legislation outlawing child labor, Jones returned to Pennsylvania and continued her fight. Her efforts first bore fruit at the state level. In 1904, only fourteen states forbade employment of children under the age of fourteen in factories; by 1929, nearly every state outlawed the practice. In 1904, only two states maintained an eight-hour workday for children under age sixteen in factories; by 1929, twenty-nine states did.[*]

Change in the states led to progress at the national level. In 1936, Congress passed the Walsh-Healey act, which prevented the use of child labor by companies engaging in business with the federal government. In 1938, the Fair Labor Standards Act became law, prohibiting the interstate shipment of goods made by companies employing minors.

PORTRAIT OF AN ACTIVIST

Mother Jones and the March to Oyster Bay

It must have been a strange sight to see the sixty-six-year-old woman with a band of scrawny children, accompanied by fifes and drums, marching through the streets of New York. Mother Jones, as this Irish immigrant was known, had marched from Kensington, Pennsylvania—site

* Walter Trattner, *Crusade for the Children: A History of the National Child Labor Committee and Reform in America* (Chicago: Quadrangle, 1970), p. 184.

Did You Know?

. . . That Supreme Court Justice Oliver Wendell Holmes, Jr.—usually celebrated for his progressive rulings and dissents—in 1927 upheld Virginia's right to sterilize "feebleminded" Carrie Buck with these brusque and chilling words: "Three generations of imbeciles are enough"?

the Clayton Antitrust Act of 1914. Although subsequent Court actions weakened some of these measures, by the time of the New Deal, the tide was clearly moving in the direction of greater federal authority.

The New Deal and the Growth of National Power: 1932–1937

Economic, not political, developments triggered the most dramatic increase in federal authority, as the prosperity of the early twentieth century gave way to the Great Depression of the 1930s. In response to the national crisis, President Franklin Roosevelt's administration created programs of economic regulation and development in areas that

President Franklin D. Roosevelt (1933–1945) proposed a New Deal with numerous federal programs designed to address Depression Era insecurities.

had previously been the states' domain, including health, welfare, labor relations, and agriculture. Programs for social and employment security, a federal works project, a national program for rural electrification, and regulation of the banking and securities industries all increased federal participation in American life. Although federally operated, many of these programs required state participation involving financial and human resources. The public reacted positively to Roosevelt's so-called New Deal initiatives, providing him with a landslide re-election victory in 1936. The Supreme Court's reaction was not as enthusiastic.

In a series of cases, the Court struck down key pieces of New Deal legislation, with Chief Justice Charles Evans Hughes and his conservative allies on the bench usually prevailing by a 5 to 4 vote. In 1935, the Court invalidated the National Industry Recovery Act in the case of *Schechter v. U.S.*[14] The Court ruled that the act, which empowered the president to regulate the hours, wages, and minimum ages of industrial employees, was an unconstitutional delegation of legislative authority from Congress to the president. In *U.S. v. Butler*, the Court invalidated portions of the Agricultural Adjustment Act, which rewarded some farmers for reducing production of certain commodities in order to reduce surpluses that drove down prices. The Court declared that such federal activities intruded into state and individual decisions protected by the Tenth Amendment.[15]

Anticipating more bad news from the Court, Roosevelt proposed a Court reorganization plan that would add one new judge for each sitting justice over the age of seventy. Although Roosevelt pitched the plan as a way to lighten the workload of elderly justices, he actually intended to

Linda Brown of Topeka, Kansas, asked the Supreme Court to allow her to attend a local school that only allowed white children, helping to end segregation in Brown v. Board of Education.

use it to pack the court with justices of his own choosing who would produce decisions more to his liking. The plan proved unnecessary, however, when the Court began to decide subsequent decisions in the president's favor. Many historians credit the Court's change in course to Justice Owen Roberts, who altered his previously hostile stance toward New Deal legislation. His "switch in time saved nine," preventing a confrontation over possible expansion of the Court beyond nine members.

Cooperative Federalism: 1937–1960

After 1937, Court opposition to New Deal legislation waned and **cooperative federalism** became the dominant model for state-federal relations. This approach emphasizes federal-state partnerships as the primary means for solving public policy problems. It marries the federal government's financial advantage in tax collection with the states' ability to target services to local populations. The federal government typically sets minimum standards for benefits such as welfare or medical care and funds a portion of the costs. States have some flexibility in enhancing federal benefits and delivering services, but they must also contribute to funding the program. Cooperative federalism still characterizes federal-state relations today in areas including health, welfare, the environment, education, and highway safety.

Such cooperative arrangements eased power struggles between federal and state governments and allowed the different units of government to reach mutual accommodations on a host of issues. The term *marble cake federalism* is sometimes used to describe the blending of federal guidelines with state administration and implementation that characterized much social policy from the 1930s to the early 1960s.

Creative Federalism: 1960s–1970s

Linda Brown of Topeka, Kansas, just wanted to be able to attend her local elementary school like African American children in other states such as New York or California. When the local school board denied her admission to the all-white school and shuttled Linda to a separate school for black children, her family sued for admission. When her case and several others found their way to the Supreme Court in 1954, Chief Justice Earl Warren found for a unanimous Court that the state of Kansas had denied Linda the equal protection of the law guaranteed by the Fourteenth Amendment.[16] The case reversed an earlier 1897 "separate but equal" ruling allowing the states to practice racial segregation as long as they provided relatively equal accommodations for each race. In *Brown v. Board of Education*, the Court insisted that separate "is inherently unequal" and, in subsequent cases, demanded that states tear down the barriers to equal citizenship with "all deliberate speed."

The decision sparked a revolution in citizen rights and federalism. It cast a spotlight on the sometimes parochial side of state and local politics, one that seemed to sacrifice the rights of those without a voice at the state capitols. It likewise gave hope to those who had been discriminated against by state law that the national government would insist that every state accord all of its citizens the same rights under the law. In a flurry of subsequent decisions, the Court made it clear that states must conform to national standards regarding citizen rights. It also affirmed that it would interpret the Fourteenth Amendment's "due process" and "equal protection" clauses to effect national standards in areas ranging from abortion[17] to criminal prosecution[18] to voting.[19]

The Civil Rights Movement of the 1950s and 1960s produced not only new federal programs but also a model of **creative federalism** that sought to eradicate racial and economic injustice by targeting money directly at citizen groups and local governments. Some programs offered assistance directly to local populations, completely bypassing the states. Others allowed the federal government to take over certain operations in states that failed to adopt federal standards within a specific period of time. Many federal projects required states and localities to conform

of reduced federal expenditures as they had to assume a greater share of the cost of government programs. This was particularly problematic for states because most of them, unlike the national government, are required to balance their budgets every year. To the added dismay of many state officials, devolution did not stop the federal government from imposing new national standards. Reagan him-

IN *BROWN V. BOARD OF EDUCATION,* the Court insisted that separate "is inherently unequal" and demanded that states tear down the barriers to equal citizenship with "all deliberate speed."

to national standards regarding discrimination and employment law to qualify for funding. To qualify for federal money to build roads or bridges, for example, states might be required to set aside money for hiring minority-owned contractors. In 1972, Richard Nixon sought to disentangle the federal government from aid to the states. He proposed a program called **revenue sharing** that funneled money directly to states and local governments on the basis of formulas that combined population figures with levels of demonstrated need. The expansive nature of these programs and qualifications spawned a reaction that changed the nature of the federal-state partnership once again.

New Federalism and the Devolution of Power: 1980–Present

The election of Ronald Reagan in 1980 brought still further changes to federalism that limited the role of the federal government. Reagan favored a model of smaller government, known as **devolution**, which returned power to states and localities. To achieve this end, he called for cutting federal programs and reducing federal regulations that had made compliance with federal programs so burdensome to state officials. He also reduced federal expenditures for many existing programs and ended revenue sharing. Although pleased with reduced regulation, states soon felt the impact

President Ronald Reagan (1981–1989) sought a "devolution" of political power with states playing a more active role in governing.

self fought to bring about a uniform national drinking age of twenty-one. To accomplish this goal, Reagan disbursed federal highway funds only to states that agreed to raise their drinking age, thus achieving by incentive what he could not easily accomplish by law.

The pace of devolution accelerated in the 1990s, as all three branches of government seemed willing to cede power to the states. In 1995, Congress passed legislation requiring the federal government to provide detailed justification for programs that require states to spend more than a certain amount of money. The following year, President Bill Clinton supported welfare reform legislation that expanded the options available to states for administering welfare policy. In 1995, the Court signaled its willingness to put the brakes on federal authority by refusing to interpret the commerce clause as allowing the national government to restrict the possession of handguns within a thousand feet of a school. The Court said such activity had nothing to do with commerce.[20] More recently, the Court has strengthened state immunity from federal background checks for handgun buyers[21] and relaxed standards for compliance with federal antidiscrimination laws in such areas as age[22] and disability.[23]

Some observers of these trends fear a reversal of hardwon rights guaranteed by the Fourteenth Amendment. They worry that the nation will return to an era of patchwork rights where some jurisdictions offer more protections than others or, even worse, that the states will institute a more restrictive environment for individual rights that favors the wishes of legislative majorities. Even with recent devolution activities, however,

cooperative federalism Federal-state relationship characteristic of the post–New Deal era that stressed state and federal partnership in addressing social problems.

creative federalism Federal-state relationship that sought to involve local populations and cities directly in addressing urban problems during the 1960s and 1970s.

revenue sharing A grant program begun in 1972 and ended in 1987 that funneled money directly to states and local governments on the basis of formulas that combined population figures with levels of demonstrated need.

devolution A movement to grant states greater authority over the local operation of federal programs and local use of federal funds that gained momentum in the 1980s.

Did You Know?

... That Connecticut, which has consistently scored near the top in academic performance, sued the federal government for forcing the state to weaken its educational standards? Connecticut officials claimed that the federal No Child Left Behind Act would force the state to spend $41.6 million to give a "dumbed-down" federal test to children in grades 3, 5, and 7 instead of the state's own more rigorous test currently administered to students in grades 4, 6, 8, and 10.

Federally mandated testing in schools has created controversy over whether the federal government or local school boards should control what students are required to learn.
....

the national government's financial re-sources allow it to retain a strong hand in steering the future course of federalism by providing states with financial incentives to adopt uniform policies.

Even support-ers of devolution don't want to aban-don federal leader-ship completely. For-mer president George W. Bush championed the federal govern-ment's role in setting national testing stan-dards for the nation's public schools in his signature leg-islation, the No Child Left Behind Act. He also voiced support for an amendment to the U.S. Constitution prohibiting gay mar-

riages in order to prevent states from granting marriage rights to gay couples. It is clear that ongoing changes in the evolution of federalism continue to alter the political landscape.

Hot or Not?

Should "No Child Left Behind" be abolished?

FEDERAL-STATE RELATIONS

We have already discussed the broad outlines of federal-state relations from a historic perspective, not-ing the political currents that have characterized the relative powers of each level of government. We now turn our attention to the means by which these relationships continue to be redefined fiscally, politically, and legally.

Fiscal Relations

Although national and state governments have concurrent powers to tax and spend, the federal government collects far more tax revenue

Categorical grants allow lawmakers to obtain federal funds for their home districts or states, making them popular with their constituents.

than do the states—nearly three-fifths of all tax revenues—and spends almost twice as much as state and local governments combined. Much spending goes directly to individuals in the form of income security through programs such as Social Security and Medicare for the elderly and Medicaid, a program that helps finance health care for the poor. Many other programs, however, are funded through grants in aid, which account for about 17 percent of the federal budget. Nearly 90 percent of these grants go directly to state governments, accounting for almost 30 percent of all state revenues.[24] In turn, much of the money spent by local governments comes from state grants.

Grants in aid are as old as the republic, but their use became more widespread during the middle of the nineteenth century. One of the most successful aid programs was the Morrill Act of 1862, which granted land to states for building public universities specializing in agriculture, mechanics, and military science. Early in the twentieth century, the federal government increased the amount it appropriated for grants to the states, as it assumed greater responsibility for interstate transportation as well as for the health and welfare of its citizens. Grants programs further expanded during the New Deal to address state needs arising from the Great Depression, and again in the 1960s as the federal government earmarked more funding for local programs to revitalize urban life and to reduce poverty.[25]

The federal government employs several types of grant programs: categorical, block, special project, and formula grants. Some types of grants give the donor more authority in specifying how the money is spent. Other types provide the recipient with more choices.

Categorical Grants The largest class of federal grants consists of **categorical grants**, reserved for special purposes such as flood assistance or water projects. These grants sometimes require the receiving government to provide matching funds and may include additional provisions to ensure the funds are spent in a manner Congress approves. Such funds, for example, cannot be allocated in a way that discriminates on the basis of the race, ethnicity, or gender of those receiving government services.

> **categorical grants** Federal programs that provide funds for specific programs such as flood assistance.

Federal authorities sometimes use categorical grants to enforce state and local compliance with federal policy

Federal Grants to States and Localities, 2009 (Estimated)

Energy
General government
Justice
Veterans' benefits
Social security
Income security
Natural resources & environment
Agriculture
Commerce & housing
Transportation
Community & regional development
Health
Education, training, employment, social services

Source: Office of Management and Budget, "Aid to State and Local Governments," *Budget of the United States, Fiscal Year 2009*. Accessed online at www.whitehouse.gov on October 20, 2008.

preferences, even in areas where the national government lacks jurisdiction. This was the case with the Reagan administration's use of federal highway funds to entice states to raise their drinking ages from eighteen to twenty-one.

The federal government currently sponsors over 750 categorical grant programs designed to help states and local governments solve problems they cannot tackle with their own resources.[26] Critics claim that these programs impose burdensome requirements on recipients and create a bewildering array of overlapping programs that lack coordination.

Block Grants Originally devised in 1966, **block grants** combine funding purposes of several categorical grants into one broader category, allowing greater flexibility in how the money is spent.[27] A block grant for public health, for example, may combine previous grants that allocated funds for eradicating individual illnesses. Block grants allow the recipient government to decide how to spend its resources and relieve it of the need to apply for grants from several different agencies. Unlike many categorical grants, however, block grants place a cap on federal funds. Critics of block grants claim that federal policymakers often have no way of knowing how the money is spent or whether target programs meet the needs for which the money is allocated.[28]

Ronald Reagan combined seventy-seven categorical programs into just nine block grants in 1981 as part of his commitment to devolving federal power.[29] Congress slowed the move toward block funding in subsequent years but embraced it as a centerpiece of welfare reform in 1996.

block grants Federal programs that provide funds for broad categories of assistance such as health care or law enforcement.

program grants Federal programs that provide funds for very narrow purposes and contain clear time frames for completion—e.g., construction of a portion of highway.

formula grants Federal programs that use mathematical calculations or demographic factors to allocate funds to states or localities.

Other Federal Grants Other grant programs exist to address a variety of needs. **Program grants** have narrow purposes like categorical grants but are limited to specific time periods. Often, they reflect congressional interest in finding novel approaches to addressing particular needs. For example, the Department of Homeland Security makes money available for protecting ports and transportation systems. **Formula grants** allocate money to state or local governments according to needs calculated in a predetermined manner. For example, schools receive subsidies for free lunch programs based on the number of students from families at or just above the established poverty level.

Political Relations

The interests of political actors at the national, state, and local levels are often at odds for a number of reasons. Policymakers at each level face a different constellation of legal, social, and political pressures that can affect their fortunes at the polls. As a result, it is not unusual for them to differ over how best to fund government programs. As noted, some types of grants—categorical grants, in particular—give the federal government more authority over the recipient government. Categorical grants continue to be popular with Congress. They enable lawmakers to take credit for creating programs and for steering federal funds to their home districts or states. In addition, they provide strict accountability for the use of federal money. Some programs funded in this way also create grateful constituents who receive ongoing benefits that are protected by law. Lawmakers who depended on minority voters for electoral support, for example, often champion categorical grants, which can include provisions for affirmative action hiring or for minority participation.

By contrast, many state and local officials favor the decentralization, experimentation, and flexibility associated with block grants. They argue that local officials know

THE FEDERAL GOVERNMENT currently sponsors over 750 categorical grant programs designed to help states and local governments solve problems they cannot tackle with their own resources.

Prior to this time, categorical grants provided assistance to families living in poverty, guaranteeing funding to recipients as long as they were in need. The new legislation called for block grants that allowed the states to vary the amount and time for which recipients qualified for assistance. This new approach allows states to adjust requirements to local needs but creates a degree of variation that is sometimes confusing to recipients and difficult for policymakers to monitor.

best how to address local problems and that they should be free to experiment to find solutions that work best for their own citizens. Members of local government have a stake in maximizing the flow of federal dollars and minimizing the cost of compliance to taxpayers. With block grants, they may be able to devote more dollars to pressing needs without raising taxes. They may even be able to subsidize purely state and local functions by the infusion of federal funds with few strings attached. Congress, however, has curbed the growth of block grants, and studies show that

Some programs, like the No Child Left Behind Act, establish federal mandates but do not supply all the money necessary to carry them out.

of such groups existed prior to 1900; by the mid-1980s, that number had mushroomed to more than one hundred.[33]

It must also be realized that some types of policies are more likely to be promoted and more likely to be successful if they are undertaken by one level of government rather than another.[34] For example, the national government is better equipped than state and local governments to address problems that spill across geographic boundaries like air pollution or that involve the infusion of substantial resources like aid to the poor. State and local governments are better at addressing issues that require pinpoint targeting of resources like economic development for cities or education reform.

the administration of block grants is uneven. Some states with a highly professional bureaucracy have successfully addressed social problems with block grants, while other states have lagged behind.[30]

State and local officials are also concerned about the growing use of **federal mandates**—federally imposed requirements on state and local governments ranging from election reform to water treatment. They are especially anxious about **unfunded mandates**, which are requirements that Congress passes without providing funds to carry them out. In 1995, Congress passed the Unfunded Mandates Reform Act to stem the tide of such mandates. The act requires the Congressional Budget Office to flag legislation that costs state governments or private sector bodies within the states more than $50 million for compliance. The bill's sponsors hoped that members of Congress would be unwilling to pass legislation that clearly increased the costs passed along to their home states. Although a Congressional Budget Office review found that this tactic substantially reduced the growth of unfunded mandates, such mandates persist.[31] The No Child Left Behind Act, for example, required states to adopt rigorous testing of students in a variety of subjects but failed to provide full funding for its implementation. The National Council of State Legislatures estimates that the act has cost the states about $27 billion in unreimbursed expenditures since its inception.[32]

Debates over federal funding have spurred the growth of **intergovernmental lobbies** to advance the interests of various state and local governing bodies. The National Governor's Association is perhaps the oldest of these, tracing its roots to the administration of Theodore Roosevelt. The U.S. Conference of Mayors also lobbies actively at the state and national levels for programs that address urban problems. Other lobbying groups represent professional bureaucrats and administrators responsible for the daily operation of government programs. Only a handful

Constitutional Issues

One sign that the balance of power is swinging in the direction of the states is the increasing attention the courts have given to the Tenth and Eleventh Amendments. In the 1976 case *National League of Cities v. Usery,* the Supreme Court invalidated a federal law that extended the minimum wage to almost all state and local employees. The majority argued that the Tenth Amendment prohibited the national government from dictating what states can pay their employees.[35] The Court moved again during the 1990s to limit congressional power over the states in a series of cases citing the Tenth Amendment. In 1992, for example, the Court said Congress could not require the state of New York to dispose of low-level radioactive waste at its own expense in order to meet federal mandates just because the private party that generated it could not find suitable alternate means for disposal. Citing the Tenth Amendment, Justice Sandra Day O'Connor said the law "would 'commandeer' state governments into the service of federal regulatory purposes, and would for this reason be inconsistent with the

federal mandates Federal requirements imposed on state and local governments, often as a condition for receiving grants.

unfunded mandates Requirements imposed on state and local governments for which the federal government provides no funds for compliance.

intergovernmental lobbies Professional advocacy groups representing various state and local governing bodies.

Constitution's division of authority between federal and state governments."[36] Several years later, the Court invalidated a provision of the Brady Handgun Act requiring the chief law-enforcing officers in the states to run background checks on handgun purchasers. The Court once again held it unconstitutional to enlist the state in enforcing federal law.[37] However, in 2005, the Court ruled against California in striking down a state law permitting the possession and use of marijuana for medical purposes, holding that Congress's authority to control the trafficking of controlled substances trumped the state's Tenth Amendment rights.[38]

Several cases in the late 1990s also cited the Eleventh Amendment in upholding state sovereignty. In these cases, the state was found to be immune from lawsuits brought by its own citizens whether filed in federal court or within the state's own court system. For example, in *Alden v. Maine*, probation officers sued the state for failure to pay overtime in violation of federal law. Citing the Eleventh Amendment, the court ruled the states are immune from such suits. Writing for the majority, Justice Anthony Kennedy held:

> Federalism requires that Congress accord States the respect and dignity due them as residuary sovereigns and joint participants in the Nation's governance. Immunity from suit in federal courts is not enough to preserve that dignity, for the indignity of subjecting a non-consenting State to the coercive process of judicial tribunals at the instance of private parties exists regardless of the forum.[39]

More recently, the Court has issued mixed judgments on Eleventh Amendment protections for the states. While the Court upheld Florida's claim of immunity from lawsuits by rejecting a suit brought by state university employees claiming age discrimination,[40] it affirmed the right of a disabled man to sue the state of Tennessee for not complying with portions of the federal Americans with Disabilities Act by providing elevator access to a state courtroom.[41] In 2008, a divided court in *District of Columbia v. Heller* rejected a strict gun control law in the District of Columbia, arguing that the Constitution provides federal protection for an individual's right to bear arms. This set the stage for

In 2008, the Supreme Court affirmed an individual citizen's Second Amendment right to bear arms, setting up future judicial challenges over the legality of gun bans in major cities across the country.

additional challenges by states and localities that seek to limit access to handguns within their borders.

INTERSTATE RELATIONS

To function well, our federal system requires not simply coordination between the national and state governments but across state boundaries and even among localities within the states. The Framers provided some guidance for interstate relations in the Constitution, but the contours of interstate cooperation and competition continue to evolve.

Cooperation and Competition

The **full faith and credit** provision of the U.S. Constitution directs states to recognize legal judgments in lawsuits that are valid in another state. An individual who owes a sum of money to a creditor in Pennsylvania cannot escape his obligation by fleeing over the border into Delaware. Delaware is required to recognize the judgment and enforce it if the creditor pursues him. Recognizing that not all interstate relations would be amicable, however, the Framers provided that states with legal disputes may take their cases directly to the Supreme Court. One current issue that touches upon this provision is gay marriage. If one state recognizes gay partners as legally married with all the rights and benefits that accrue to married couples, must a state that outlaws gay marriage grant the same recognition to the couple if they move within its borders?

Section 2 of Article IV provides that the citizens of each state shall be entitled to all the same **privileges and immunities** of citizens of the several states. This wording is ambiguous, however, and litigants often have asked the courts to interpret its meaning. The Supreme Court has ruled that states may not discriminate against nonresidents when it comes to fundamental rights like freedom to make a living and access to the political and legal processes of the state. However, states can treat nonresidents differently in a number of other areas. For example, nonresident workers may pay different tax rates than residents, and nonresident students may pay higher tuition and fees at state schools.[42]

Cooperation among states is often fostered by the use of **interstate compacts**, a device that is given explicit approval "with the consent of Congress" in the Constitution (Article I, Section 10). Such compacts may involve agreements to share environmental responsibility for waterways that cross their borders or to develop transportation authorities across borders with the power to collect fares and distribute revenues. Of course, not all states see eye to eye when it comes to the use of resources that cross borders. Disagreements can result in political conflict or even liti-

The establishment of same-sex marriage laws in some states begs the question of whether other states must recognize these unions when gay couples move.

gation before the Supreme Court. In 2007, Illinois residents and political leaders forced an Indiana oil refinery to back down from its plans to release higher levels of waste products into Lake Michigan along the lakeshore both states share. Indiana had given permission for the increased waste disposal but was saved from litigation and continued political turmoil when the refinery itself decided to withdraw its request.

Recent years have witnessed increased competition among states as they vie for business investment. Despite growing burdens faced by many states as a result of economic stagnation, increased costs for education and welfare, and federal mandates, states have been reluctant to raise taxes for fear they will scare off potential investors or lose businesses already planted within their borders. Competition has grown particularly fierce over foreign investments that make up a larger portion of American business operations as globalization picks up steam. States find themselves in escalating bidding wars by offering companies tax breaks and other incentives. It is estimated that in 1980, "landing a new Nissan plant cost Tennessee $11,000 per job created. In 1985, recruiting the Saturn Corporation cost the state $26,000 per job. In 1992, it cost South Caro-

lina more than $68,000 per job to bring in a BMW plant, and the estimates range from $150,000 to $200,000 per job for the Mercedes Benz plant in Alabama" that began operating in 1997.[43]

Innovation in the States

In his dissent in the case of *New State Ice Company v. Liebmann* (1932), Justice Louis Brandeis argued that the state of Oklahoma should have the authority to determine which businesses serve the public interest and therefore should be required to obtain state licenses. This was a legitimate way for them, he felt, to protect public health and safety. His dissent is most famous, however, for his faith in the power of states to innovate within our federal system:

> To stay experimentation in things social and economic is a grave responsibility. Denial of the right to experiment may be

full faith and credit
Constitutional provision requiring each state to recognize legal transactions authorized in other states.

privileges and immunities
Constitutional phrase interpreted to refer to fundamental rights, such as freedom to make a living, and access to the political and legal processes of the state.

interstate compacts
Cooperative agreements made between states, subject to congressional approval, to address mutual problems.

States have engaged in bidding wars by offering tax breaks and other incentives to win foreign investors.

fraught with serious consequences to the Nation. It is one of the happy incidents of the federal system that a single courageous State may, if its citizens choose, serve as a laboratory; and try novel social and economic experiments without risk to the rest of the country.[44]

American history is replete with examples of public policy innovation by states that served as a catalyst for widespread change. In 1898, South Dakota passed a law granting voters the right to initiate all forms of legislation. States throughout the Midwest quickly adopted the measure, as did many western states. More recently, welfare reform initiatives that originated in Wisconsin in the early 1990s served as a model for national legislation in 1996. Health care for low-income populations has also improved as a result of state initiatives in recent years. Massachusetts passed a law mandating the purchase of health-care insurance in 2006, and several other states are moving to adopt their own versions of universal coverage. But the spread of innovations has been spotty.

Just how extensive is innovation and diffusion in the American federal system? The question is hard to answer because innovation is difficult to measure. Nevertheless, several studies cast light on the matter. In a pathbreaking study published in 1969, political scientist Jack L. Walker studied the spread of innovations in eighty-eight public policy areas ranging from corrections to welfare from 1870 to the mid-1960s.[45] Walker found that larger, wealthier states whose urban populations are well represented in the state legislature are most likely to innovate and to more rapidly adopt ideas pioneered in other states. New York, Massachusetts, and California consistently scored near the top in state innovation.

Stronger competition between parties seems to have increased state innovation after 1930. Presumably, competition makes the parties less complacent and more likely to innovate in order to bring new voters to their cause. Walker also found greater innovation in states with more professional legislatures and state bureaucracies. Regional competition also increases innovation; states adjacent to innovators are themselves more likely to innovate. Finally, he found that the changes in mass communication and technology allowed for more rapid and widespread adoption of new initiatives. More recent studies have found that innovation is related to a state's level of economic development and the availability of policy entrepreneurs—what we might call legislative risk takers—who are willing to spend considerable personal effort in advancing new ideas.[46]

Walker and others have confirmed that federal grants-in-aid significantly shorten the time of diffusion, especially among states that typically are slower to embrace innovation.[47] Some states are willing to innovate consistently, but the federal government must prod others into action.

States as Innovators in Low-Income Health Coverage

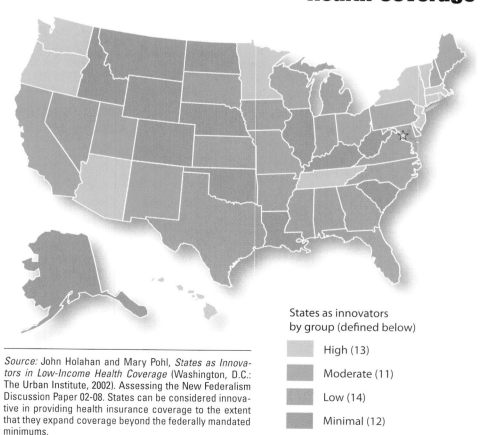

States as innovators by group (defined below)

High (13)

Moderate (11)

Low (14)

Minimal (12)

Source: John Holahan and Mary Pohl, *States as Innovators in Low-Income Health Coverage* (Washington, D.C.: The Urban Institute, 2002). Assessing the New Federalism Discussion Paper 02-08. States can be considered innovative in providing health insurance coverage to the extent that they expand coverage beyond the federally mandated minimums.

Average Time for Diffusion of Innovations (in Years)

Time Period	All Adoptions	First 20 Adoptions
1870–1899	52	23
1900–1929	40	20
1930–1966	26	18

Source: Jack L. Walker, "The Diffusion of Innovations Among the American States," *American Political Science Review* 63, September 1969, 895.

Just as some levels of government are better equipped to handle certain functions than others, each level of government also provides a unique combination of opportunities and challenges for citizen participation. Let us turn to this topic now.

FEDERALISM AND CIVIC ENGAGEMENT TODAY

Because federalism diffuses power across many competing power centers, it multiplies the number of opportunities for citizen political participation. Few of us may have the opportunity to shape national policies directly as members of the U.S. House or Senate, but many opportunities exist for citizen political involvement at the state and local level as elected officials or as volunteer members of boards, associations, and neighborhood councils. These positions afford citizens the opportunity for intensive direct participation in policymaking and implementation and serve as training grounds for those who wish to take the national political stage.

Participation at each level of government is also laden with its own pitfalls and challenges. It may be easier to devise solutions for states and localities, since local populations are more homogeneous and share some of the same regional values and traditions.[48] Of course, entrenched traditions that are difficult to overcome may also hinder progress. For example, many states have passed referenda to ban gay marriages and to bar social services for illegal immigrants.

Although participation in the national political arena requires patience in negotiating among competing interests and respect for a wide diversity of values and traditions, measures calling for the expansion of rights are often more easily accommodated at the national level. Interests that may be in the minority in an individual state may be able to generate the critical collective mass at the national level

necessary to overcome local or regional opposition. The Civil Rights Movement demonstrated the strength numerical minorities can amass at the national level.

A group of political scientists studying the opportunities and challenges of federalism for civic engagement summarized the matter as follows:

> Active citizenship seems to flourish most naturally at the local level and in smaller communities. This does not mean that those who favor civic engagement should abandon wider and more inclusive goals or that those who favor diversity and inclusion should abandon local institutions. It does mean, however, that these two dilemmas—of scale and diversity—pose difficult political challenges.[49]

get involved!

Ballot initiatives have become increasingly popular devices for ensuring popular participation in setting the legislative agendas in many states. You can check on the most recent ballot initiatives in your state by examining the list maintained by Project Vote Smart at http://votesmart.org/index.htm. If you are interested in placing an item on the ballot, you can contact your state secretary of state for information about the requirements. Most states require a certain number of signatures on a petition and sometimes charge a nominal filing fee.

With over a half million elective offices in the United States, 96 percent of which are at the local level of government, opportunities for political involvement abound.

Our discussion in this section echoes the debate that raged between Federalists and Antifederalists during the ratification of the U.S. Constitution. Federalists argued for the benefits of combining local and regional interests in a national policy, while Antifederalists were concerned that national politics would lack the unity of purpose and intensity

it requires that we participate in governmental decisions at multiple levels and understand the challenges of participating at each level. Alexis de Tocqueville took note of this when he toured America in the 1830s:

> But when one examines the Constitution of the United States, the best of all known federal constitutions, it is frightening to see how much diverse knowledge and discernment it assumes on the part of the governed. The government of the Union rests almost entirely on legal fictions. The Union is an ideal no-

"THE GOVERNMENT OF THE UNION rests almost entirely on legal fictions. The Union is an ideal notion which exists, so to say, only in men's minds and whose extent and limits can only be discerned by the understanding."

of citizen involvement present at the state and local levels. U.S. history shows that federalism is flexible enough to accommodate both perspectives, and both viewpoints often have been useful in charting our nation's course.

While a federal system such as ours—with many layers of government—provides added security for citizen rights,

tion which exists, so to say, only in men's minds and whose extent and limits can only be discerned by the understanding.[50]

How much more daunting must it be for busy citizens to fulfill the obligations of citizenship in our federal republic today!

1. How is power dispersed in American federalism?
   - American federalism grants some powers to the national government while reserving others to the states. It allows some powers to be shared jointly while prohibiting both levels of government from exercising others.

2. How have the powers of the national and state governments evolved over the nation's history?
   - Federalism has produced periodic shifts in the relative strength of the national and state governments, sometimes strengthening the national government (e.g., 1937–1960) and sometimes weakening it (e.g., 1865–1932). The current era has been characterized by the devolution of power to the states and localities.

3. What three factors mold national-state relations today?
   - National-state relations are molded today by fiscal and political relations as well as constitutional and legal controls.

National Journal

Identity Problems

Sen. Lamar Alexander argues that in the post-9/11 world the United States needs a national identification card to help prevent terrorist attacks. But the Tennessee Republican vehemently opposes Real ID, the leading federal program to create fraud-resistant identification cards for tens of millions of Americans.

Alexander is co-sponsoring legislation to repeal key sections of the Real ID Act of 2005, which requires states to follow federal standards in verifying someone's identity before issuing a driver's license. The senator complained to National Journal that the law turns motor vehicle department workers "into little CIA agents" and burdens states with expensive new unfunded mandates. "If the federal government thinks this is such a good idea, the federal government ought to pay for it," he said.

In theory, at least, beefing up identification requirements for travel, work, and voting is quite popular. In the most recent national poll on the subject, Gallup found in 2005 that two-thirds of Americans support the creation of a national ID card. Many countries already require them. Advocates in the U.S. tout such cards as a way to fight terrorism and more-conventional crime, reduce illegal immigration, prevent election fraud, and curb identity theft.

In practice, however, efforts to outfit virtually all Americans with more-reliable identification have been fraught with headaches and controversy. And Alexander is far from alone in crying foul.

For example, the Real ID Act has spawned a mini-rebellion at the state level. Ten states have enacted statutes declaring that they will not comply with the federal law.

Invariably, the struggle over IDs bumps up against big, even philosophical, questions: How can identity be proved? Can the government ever really be sure that individuals are who they say they are? If so, at what cost—in terms of lost freedom and privacy, not just dollars and cents?

As Sen. George Voinovich, R-Ohio, noted dryly at a congressional hearing earlier this year, improving American ID security is "easier said than done." It's not a new undertaking. Attempts to expand the federal use of Social Security numbers, a system created in 1935 to make it easier to track and distribute federal retirement benefits, have sometimes failed. President Carter opposed the idea of turning Social Security cards into national identification cards; President Reagan opposed the creation of any form of national ID. But in 2001, the September 11 terrorist attacks heightened the intensity of the national ID debate. All but one of the hijackers had carried some form of ID issued by a government agency in this country, such as a Virginia driver's license. Some of the IDs were fraudulently obtained. The 9/11 commission recommended in 2004 that Congress tighten the security of driver's licenses.

Yet even as ID requirements proliferate, the backlash against them has grown. Some experts argue that there are better, more-direct ways to improve security. Others contend that the only way to create truly fraud-proof IDs is to collect DNA or biometrics from all Americans at birth—a Big Brother scenario that smacks of a surveillance society.

Whatever the ideal model in the long run, America's ID policy is at a crossroads. Americans may eventually embrace a national ID card, as Britons have done recently. Or, U.S. citizens may find themselves carrying multiple smart cards with different uses, as privacy experts prefer. In the meantime, ID wars are breaking out on many fronts.

When officials at the Indiana Bureau of Motor Vehicles set out to check the records of the state's 6.4 million licensed drivers last July, the effort began smoothly. The bureau had just upgraded its computer system and could now verify the Social Security numbers of drivers online, as the Real ID Act would soon require.

The records matched for 97 percent of drivers. In most of the other cases, a simple error—such as a typo or the person's failure to alert the Social Security Administration about a name change—caused a mismatch that was easily corrected. But that still left 34,000 Indiana drivers with records that didn't match. The bureau warned them that their licenses would be revoked if they didn't fix the problem within 30 days. When South Bend lawyer Lyn Leone received a notice, she promptly contacted the American Civil Liberties Union. Leone's Social Security card reads "Mary Lyn Leone." But Leone has been known as Lyn all her life, she says, and she maintains that she has a legal right to go by that name on her driver's license.

"They are basically trying to erase my identity," said Leone, 60, now a plaintiff in an ACLU lawsuit challenging the Indiana Bureau of Motor Vehicles. The licenses of thousands of Indiana drivers could be revoked for similar reasons, said Kenneth Falk, legal director of the Indiana ACLU. "If you are named 'William' but you've always used 'Bill,' and your license is in 'Bill,' you will be terminated."

Although few observers disagree with the basic premise of Real ID—before issuing a driver's license, states should obtain the applicant's identifying documents, such as a birth certificate and proof of legal residency, and verify their authenticity—Indiana's experience spotlights the things that can go wrong when a requirement becomes law with no public debate or hearings. Congress initially set out to bring state officials, privacy experts, and other stakeholders together in what's known as a negotiated rule-making. But in 2005, Real ID Act proponents in the House abruptly attached it to a must-pass appropriations bill funding the Iraq war and tsunami relief.

The Homeland Security Department fielded about 21,000 public comments on Real ID before issuing final regulations in January. By then, state governments were in such an uproar that DHS pushed back its deadline for taking the first steps toward full compliance—from May 11, 2008, to December 31, 2009. The final deadlines for states that pass certain benchmarks will be 2014 for drivers under 50 and 2017 for older ones. The extension averted what would have been a public-relations disaster,

because anyone from a state not issuing Real IDs would have been barred from boarding a plane or entering a federal building.

Both the National Governors Association and the National Conference of State Legislatures have decried Real ID as a massive, unfunded mandate. The law is expected to cost at least $4 billion to implement, according to DHS, but less than $200 million in federal money has been set aside for the changeover. States may use their federal homeland-security money for Real ID, but many governors object.

"It makes our state less homeland-secure," said South Carolina Gov. Mark Sanford, "because while we don't know if we're going to get struck by a terrorist, what we do unquestionably know is that we are going to get struck by another hurricane." In an April 3 letter to members of Congress, the Republican governor called Real ID "the worst piece of legislation I have seen during the 15 years I have been engaged in the political process."

Sen. Daniel Akaka, D-Hawaii, has introduced legislation to repeal Real ID and return to the drawing board by having the negotiations on the issue that were skipped three years ago. Akaka and other critics of Real ID warn that it would create an extraordinary target for hackers and ID thieves: a huge new database loaded with personal information. That's because the states would be forced to link their databases in order to enforce the law's ban on drivers holding licenses from more than one state.

"We believe that this, if ever implemented, is the coming national ID card system," said Tim Sparapani, senior legislative counsel at the ACLU. Bush administration officials strongly disagree. "The notion that there's

Ten states have enacted statutes declaring **that they will not comply** with the federal law.

going to be a national database is just wrong," said Stewart Baker, assistant secretary for policy at DHS. Only "a very narrow" number of state employees will be able to check the databases, and those databases have proven fairly resistant to tampering, he said. Because of the threats posed by terrorism and identity theft, Baker continued, "there's an enthusiasm for good ID that, I think, is going to continue to grow."

Of course, his department's current deadline for final implementation isn't until December 1, 2017, more than 16 years after the 9/11 attacks.

Some experts are convinced that a national, biometric ID card is the answer to the simmering "identity" crisis. "Right now, we are proceeding in hundreds of different ways, for dozens of different IDs, at tremendous expense," said Robert Pastor, co-director of the Center for Democracy and Election Management at American University. It makes more sense to "do it right, once," he maintains.

Pastor's AU colleague Curtis Gans, who heads the university's Center for the Study of the American Electorate, wants to establish a high-level, bipartisan commission to examine the issue of a mandatory biometric government ID. At least theoretically, Americans are receptive, polling shows. Gans is a vigorous advocate: "If we set up this national biometric

ID, we could get rid of identity theft; we could deal with immigration better than the feds; we could provide for success in criminal prosecution and exoneration; we might constructively use it for medical records; we could eliminate the need for physical enumeration in the census. The uses are many and manifold, including the voting process."

But a growing number of scientists and privacy experts insist that requiring a single ID for multiple purposes would actually make Americans less safe. Skeptics liken a national ID to using a skeleton key for one's office, home, and safe deposit box: Lose it—or have it stolen—and you're vulnerable everywhere. The better model, they argue, is using multiple IDs for discrete uses, just as most people carry several keys.

"Uniformity in IDs across the country would create economies of scale" for prying eyes, warns Jim Harper, director of information policy studies at the Cato Institute and author of Identity Crisis: How Identification Is Overused and Misunderstood. "We want to prevent that uniformity. We want to prevent the tools for that surveillance society from being built."

Harper contends, "There's no practical way in a free country to defeat identity fraud." Illegal immigrants, terrorists, and garden-variety criminals forge birth certificates, Social Security cards, and other IDs all too easily, he notes. Reports abound, moreover, of motor vehicle department officials accepting bribes to assist fraud rings.

"Try to prevent it by locking down everybody's ID, and you have to build this cradle-to-grave biometric tracking system," Harper said.

FOR DISCUSSION: Would you support a mandatory biometric ID? Or would you see one as an invasion of your privacy?
Would you rather your state or the Federal Government supply your ID? Why?
Would a Federal ID be a violation of State sovereignty? What arguments might the Federal Government advance in favor of its right to issue one?

4

CIVIL LI

EXPANDING CITIZENS' RIGHTS

DRUG TESTING VS. STUDENTS' RIGHTS ▮

Lindsay Earls recalls the first time she was chosen for a random drug test at Tecumseh High School. At the time, Lindsay was a member of show choir, concert choir, and color guard and captain of the academic team. "They came over the intercom and said, 'Lindsay Earls needs to go to the alumni building,' the place where everyone knew you had to go for drug testing. They might as well have said, 'Lindsay Earls needs to go pee in a cup.' It was terrible."[1]

Lindsay's school district had just instituted a program that required middle school and high school students to undergo drug testing in order to participate in extracurricular activities. The Tecumseh, Oklahoma, school board adopted the program in 1998, after teachers had heard students discussing drugs and subsequently found marijuana in a student's car. Prior to the adoption of the drug-testing program, the district had never cited drugs as a major problem in its schools. Three students, however, tested positive during the first year of ➥

Regret y Abortion

BERTIES

- Why was the incorporation of the Bill of Rights by the Supreme Court important?
- What are the First Amendment rights?
- What are some of the other important civil liberties guaranteed by the Constitution?

Lindsay Earls challenged in court the constitutionality of drug tests for all students engaged in extracurricular activities.

the program, which enjoyed strong community support. The school did not give the test results to law enforcement officials, and the consequences of failing a drug test were limited to participation in extracurricular activities.

Lindsay's parents did not join in the strong community support for the district's drug-testing policy. Her father, a social worker for the juvenile-justice system, asked civil liberties attorneys about the constitutionality of the program. "As an adult, you've got that constitutional right to be free from unreasonable searches; I think that right extends to kids as well," he said.[2] With support from the American Civil Liberties Union, the family decided to litigate. The case worked its way through the courts, reaching the U.S. Supreme Court in June 2002.

Writing for a 5-to-4 majority that ruled against Lindsay, Justice Clarence Thomas concluded that her privacy interest, as protected by the Fourth Amendment's prohibition against "unreasonable searches and seizures," did not exempt her from the Tecumseh policy. Justice Thomas cited the precedent of an earlier case that upheld an Oregon school's testing of all athletes.[3] He argued that schools have a special duty to protect the health and safety of students in their care and that the district's testing policy was a reasonable way to achieve that goal. Requiring the district to show grounds for suspecting individuals before testing them, he asserted, would hinder the school's ability to protect the students in its care. In addition, singling out specific individuals might unfairly target members of unpopular groups and would burden teachers with the task of detecting which students are using drugs. The opinion also stressed that the privacy invasion was minimal and that students who participate in extracurricular activities voluntarily subject themselves to the same intrusions on privacy as do athletes.

The dissenting justices countered that the school's policy was not only unreasonable but also perverse, because it targeted the students least likely to abuse drugs: "It invades the privacy of students who need deterrence least and risks steering students at greater risk for substance abuse away from extracurricular involvement that potentially may palliate drug problems."[4] They also pointed out significant differences between Lindsay's case and the Oregon case. The Oregon school claimed that the athletes were the leaders of a known drug culture, while Tecumseh reported no serious drug problem among any group of students. In addition, unlike many extracurricular activities, athletics can be dangerous, particularly if a competitor is under the influence of drugs. Finally, the Oregon case dealt only with athletics where participants typically undress in a common area. Students in activities such as choir and the academic team have greater expectations of privacy.

Lindsay's response to what she considered a violation of her rights was perfectly appropriate and an excellent example of citizen participation in government. Americans often turn to the courts to protect their rights, and the United States Supreme Court looms large in the lives of citizens due to its role as interpreter of our basic rights. Court decisions have protected citizens from the actions of all governments at every level of American politics and defined the extent of citizens' rights in a wide variety of areas. In this chapter, we will study the nature of those basic rights and freedoms, known as **civil liberties**. ✑

HERITAGE OF RIGHTS AND LIBERTIES

Some of the first settlers in North America declared their dedication to individuality and freedom by setting forth their rights in public documents.[5] As early as 1641, the Massachusetts General Court adopted the "Body of Liberties," which defined the rights of citizens in the Massachusetts Colony. By the time of the American Revolution some 125 years later, each state had its own constitution containing a **bill of rights** that protected a variety of civil liberties. The delegates who met in Philadelphia in 1787 to

Using www.oyez.nwu.edu, listen to the oral argument in a civil liberties case decided in the modern era of personal rights. Which attorney made the best argument before the Court? What questions were asked by the Supreme Court justices during the presentations of the attorneys? What questions would you have asked?

get involved!

create a new governing structure saw no need to add a bill of rights to the new constitution.

The Constitution and Rights

Records of the 1787 deliberations show that the delegates soundly rejected a bill of rights on at least four separate occasions.[6] They did not, however, ignore the subject of individual freedoms. The new constitution forbade the legislature from passing ex post facto laws and bills of attainder. An ex post facto law creates a criminal law and then applies it retroactively to convict persons who committed the behavior before it was a crime. Bills of attainder are legislative pronouncements of guilt that should be left for a court to decide. The delegates also made it difficult for government to deny writs of habeas corpus to accused or convicted persons. Writs of habeas corpus allow individuals to petition judges to assess whether there is sufficient cause to hold an accused person for trial or to imprison a convicted person who may have received an unfair trial. The Federalists opposed adding a bill of rights, however, because they believed that a government founded on the principles of separation of powers and checks and balances would produce a political system free from tyranny. In addition, since the Constitution granted the national government only certain specific powers, the Federalists felt that the states would wield enough power to safeguard the civil liberties of their citizens. Hamilton argued in *The Federalist* No. 84 that a bill of rights was not only unnecessary but also dangerous, because it was foolhardy to list things that the national government had no power to do.[7]

The Federalists successfully prevented the convention from adding a bill of rights to the proposed constitution, but

> **civil liberties** The personal freedoms of individuals that are protected from government intrusion.
>
> **Bill of Rights** The freedoms listed in the first ten amendments to the U.S. Constitution.

> *... That a bill of attainder is a law passed by a legislature that simply declares a person or group of people guilty—usually of treason—without any trial? Bills of attainder were sometimes enacted by the British Parliament and the colonial legislatures.*

Did You Know?

they found public opinion against them when the document went to the states for ratification. After the first five states ratified the document, momentum for a constitution that lacked a bill of rights slowed considerably. Swayed by Anti-federalist rhetoric championing personal freedom, seven of the last eight states approved the document only on the condition that Congress add amendments protecting individual liberties as soon as possible.

selective incorporation The process of applying some of the rights in the Bill of Rights to the states through the due process clause of the Fourteenth Amendment.

The Bill of Rights

After winning a seat in the First Congress, Federalist leader James Madison fulfilled his faction's promise by drafting seventeen new amendments. The Senate rejected five of the proposed amendments, and the states ratified ten of the twelve that Congress sent to them; these amendments became known as the Bill of Rights.[8]

Incorporation

From its adoption, the Bill of Rights stirred controversy concerning how widely it protected the rights it set forth. Did the Constitution protect these rights only from violation by the national government, or did they also protect citizens from the unjust actions of state governments? The Supreme Court first addressed this issue in 1833 in the case of *Barron v. Baltimore*.

John Barron had sued the city of Baltimore for damaging his wharf by dumping sand in the water during road construction. His lawyers argued that the Fifth Amendment's guarantee that "private property cannot be taken for public use, without just compensation" should apply to the states as well as to the national government. Writing the opinion for a unanimous Court, Chief Justice John Marshall limited the application of the Bill of Rights to

The Bill of Rights

First: Free exercise of religion, establishment of religion, free press, free speech, peaceful assembly, right to petition government

Second: Right to keep and bear arms

Third: No quartering of soldiers without owner's consent

Fourth: No unreasonable searches or seizures

Fifth: Grand jury indictment, double jeopardy prohibition, no self-incrimination, due process protection, no seizure of property without just compensation

Sixth: Jury trial in criminal cases, right to speedy and public trial, notice of the nature of the accusation, right to confront witnesses against and call witnesses in favor, right to counsel

Seventh: Jury trial in civil cases

Eighth: No excessive bail, no cruel and unusual punishment

Ninth: Rights not limited by the list of rights in the first eight amendments

Tenth: Powers not delegated to the national government are reserved to the states and the people

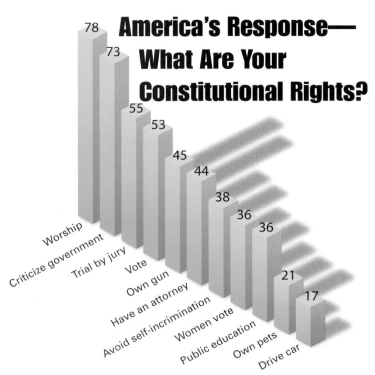

America's Response— What Are Your Constitutional Rights?

78 Worship
73 Criticize government
55 Trial by jury
53 Vote
45 Own gun
44 Have an attorney
38 Avoid self-incrimination
36 Women vote
36 Public education
21 Own pets
17 Drive car

America's answers to "What are your Constitutional rights?"
(in percentages)

Source: McCormick Tribune Freedom Museum, "Americans' Awareness of First Amendment Freedoms," March 1, 2006.

actions of the national government only.[9] He argued that the Antifederalists explicitly called for a bill of rights to protect citizens in their relations with the new national government. He also reasoned that Congress would have clearly stated its desire to have the amendments apply to the states if that had been the goal.

Passage of the Fourteenth Amendment after the Civil War reopened the question of the applicability of the Bill of Rights. That amendment includes the due process clause: "*No state . . . shall deprive a person of life, liberty, or property without due process of law.*"[10] Lawyers argued that if the rights enumerated in the due process clause—life, liberty, and property—were equivalent to the rights in the Bill of Rights, then the states would be bound by the first ten amendments to the U.S. Constitution. At first, proponents of this view met with little success. Ultimately, however, the Court used a process known as **selective incorporation** to conclude that most of the Bill of Rights should apply to the states. Only three of the first ten amendments remain unincorporated: the Second, Third, and Seventh. In addition, the Fifth Amendment right to a grand jury hearing and the Eighth Amendment freedom from excessive bail and fines do not apply to the states.

Selective incorporation greatly enhanced the expansion of rights in the United States because the vast majority of individual actions occur in the states. Most people who exercise their rights of free speech and assembly, for instance, do so in one of the states, unless they carry their protests to Washington, D.C. The process of selective incorporation

also created a uniform definition of our basic rights that is independent of geography. A criminal defendant has the same basic constitutional rights whether he or she lives in Iowa or New York.

The Modern Emphasis on Rights

Selective incorporation helped to usher in an era of greater emphasis on individual rights in which even the most humble citizens claim fundamental protections from government violation. Even so, many citizens today are only dimly aware of their constitutional rights. When asked to name their First Amendment rights besides freedom of speech, a significant number of Americans in a recent survey incorrectly listed the right to vote, to own a gun, to obtain a public education, and even the right to own pets and drive a car. Sadly, more respondents correctly named multiple characters on *The Simpsons* television program than multiple rights in the First Amendment.

Knowledge of First Amendment Rights vs. the Simpsons Characters

	1 or more correct	2 or more correct	3 or more correct	4 or more correct	5 correct
Simpsons characters	72	52	43	34	22
First Amendment rights	65	28	8	1	0

Cumulative answers correct (in percentages)

Source: McCormick Tribune Freedom Museum, "Americans' Awareness of First Amendment Freedoms," March 1, 2006.

FREEDOM OF RELIGION

The first two freedoms listed in the Bill of Rights pertain to the exercise of religion. This is unsurprising; many of the early settlers left Europe to escape religious persecution and to establish communities where they could freely practice their own religions. Although many states placed the guarantee of religious freedom in their state constitutions, the delegates who met in Philadelphia to consider a new constitution had differing ideas about the role of religion in the new country. At a particularly difficult point in the deliberations, Benjamin Franklin proposed that the delegates should pray "for the assistance of Heaven, and its blessings on our deliberations."[11] Nearly all the other delegates attacked Franklin's motion, arguing that a prayer session might offend some of the delegates. The original text of the Constitution reflects this reluctance to address the issue of religion, which is mentioned only once in the document. Article VI requires all government officials to take an oath to "support this Constitution; but no religious

Test shall ever be required as a Qualification to any Office or public Trust under the United States."

The First Amendment contains two clauses dealing with religious freedom: "Congress shall make no law respecting an establishment of religion, or prohibiting the free exercise thereof." The second and least complicated provision is the **free exercise clause**, which prohibits the government from interfering with an individual's right to practice his or her religion.[12] The meaning of the **establishment clause** is less clear. At the very least, it prohibits the government from establishing a national religion. Although they address different aspects of religious freedom, the two clauses occasionally come into conflict. Some people may interpret actions such as providing military chaplains or setting aside Sunday as a day of rest as government attempts to establish religion, while the government may see them as attempts to create greater access to practice religion.

Free Exercise Clause

A literal interpretation of the free exercise clause suggests that a group may practice any religion it chooses, but is such an interpretation reasonable? What if the members engage in dangerous practices such as handling poisonous snakes or illegal ones such as taking hallucinogenic drugs? Should the government prohibit religious activities that are dangerous or offensive to a majority of the community?

Historically, American lawmakers and judges have adhered to the so-called belief-action distinction, articulated by President Thomas Jefferson in an 1802 letter to the Danbury Baptist Association: "Religion is a matter which lies solely between man and his God; that he owes account to none other for his faith or his worship; that the legislative powers of the Government reach actions only, and not opinion."[13] Jefferson believed that free exercise of religion is not absolute; government may regulate religious actions. The Supreme Court has supported this position, upholding

The free exercise of religion clause of the First Amendment protects religious beliefs but not all religious activities, such as the handling of poisonous snakes.

Which Should Have More Influence on U.S. Law?

According to . . .	The will of the American people (%)	The Bible (%)	Don't know (%)
White Evangelical	34	60	6
White Mainline	78	16	6
Catholic	72	23	5
Secular	91	7	2
Total	63	32	5

Source: The Pew Forum on Religion and Public Life, "Many Americans Uneasy with Mix of Religion and Politics," 3. August 24, 2006.

the constitutionality of laws affecting religious practices as long as the legislation serves the nonreligious goal of safeguarding the peace, order, and comfort of the community and is not directed at any particular religion.[14] As a result, the Court has sustained laws prohibiting religiously sanctioned polygamy (the practice of taking multiple wives) and use of the drug peyote during religious services.[15] By contrast, the Court invalidated a law that forced a Seventh-day Adventist to work on Saturday—her faith's Sabbath—in order to receive unemployment benefits.[16] The Court also upheld the right of the Amish to withdraw their children from public school before the age of sixteen.[17] The Amish believe the materialism, competition, and peer pressure that characterize secondary education would have a negative effect on their children's religious beliefs, Bible reading, and appreciation of a simple spiritual life.

Congress and Religious Freedom

Congress does not always agree with the way the Court interprets the free exercise clause. In recent years, the legislative branch has shown greater support for freedom of religious expression than has its judicial counterpart. In 1986, for example, the Court ruled that an ordained rabbi, who was a captain in the U.S. Air Force, could not wear his yarmulke (skullcap) while in or out of uniform. Congress reacted by passing a 1987 law that allowed members of the armed forces to "wear an item of religious apparel while in uniform so long as the item is neat and conservative" and does not "interfere with the performance" of military duties.[18]

After the Court outlawed the use of peyote in religious ceremonies, Congress expressed renewed concern over the Court's reasoning in free exercise cases. In 1993, Demo-

cratic senator Ted Kennedy, a Catholic, and Republican senator Orrin Hatch, a Mormon, led congressional passage of the Religious Freedom and Restoration Act (RFRA). Normally staunch ideological opponents, Kennedy and Hatch joined up to champion a law urging the Court to use a more liberal judicial test to interpret the free exercise clause that would result in less interference with an individual's ability to practice his or her religion. The Court, however, ruled the law unconstitutional, arguing that Congress had no power to tell the Court how to interpret the Constitution.[19]

> **free exercise clause** The First Amendment provision intended to protect the practice of one's religion free from government interference.
>
> **establishment clause** The First Amendment prohibition against the government's establishment of a national religion.

Establishment Clause

While free exercise cases involve government intrusion into the practice of religion, establishment clause cases deal with the formal relationship between religion and government. We will see that the United States has usually followed a tradition of attempting to separate church from state, yet there has also been a strong inclination to mix politics and religion. This is not surprising because Americans are a very religious people. A recent poll has shown that 88 percent of the population believe in God, a majority responded that religion is important in their lives and that they pray on a daily basis, and 39 percent attend church at least once a week.[20] As a result, questions like "Should the Bible or the will of the people have more influence on the passage of laws?" become pertinent. (See the table above.)

Barack Obama has received criticism because of the controversial views of the outspoken Reverend Wright, the longtime pastor of Obama's church. Do you believe that attending church regularly implies that you condone the views of your minister?

Polls of church-attending Americans reveal that the clergy discuss a variety of issues such as poverty, abortion, war, laws regarding homosexuals, and stem cell research. Even the Founding Fathers disagreed about the relationship between church and state. Jefferson wrote that the First Amendment built "a wall of separation between Church and State." This is known as the separationist position because it prohibits most if not all forms of government support for religion.

Most scholars contend that a majority of the Founding Fathers disagreed with Jefferson and instead held accommodationist views. Accommodationists argue that the establishment clause forbids the government from showing preference to one religion with respect to another and prohibits the government from establishing a national religion.[21] However, they believe that government may constitutionally support religion as long it does not discriminate against any particular faith.

The ambiguity of the establishment clause led the Supreme Court to develop a test for resolving establishment cases. According to the **Lemon** test, a law must meet

Court cases concerning the establishment clause deal with the relationship between religion and government, including such issues as school prayer and the teaching of religion in public schools.

three conditions in order not to violate the establishment clause:

1. The law must have a secular (nonreligious) purpose.
2. The primary effect of the law must be one that neither advances nor inhibits religion.
3. The law must not foster an excessive government entanglement with religion.

Using the test, the Court struck down a Pennsylvania law that provided direct state financial aid to pay teachers at a religiously affiliated school. The majority ruled that the law created an excessive entanglement between the state government and religion by requiring close government oversight of church matters.[22] Using similar reasoning, the Court upheld a state law granting property tax exemptions to religious organizations. The majority in that case argued that taxing the churches would create an extensive government entanglement.[23]

Most of the establishment clause cases that have reached the Supreme Court in recent years have involved issues

such as the teaching of religion in public schools; religious use of public school facilities and funds; recitation of prayers in public schools; government aid to religiously affiliated schools; and official endorsement of religious displays such as a nativity scene or the Ten Commandments. Some observers see these disputes as examples of conservative Christians imposing their religious views on others. However, many of the nearly 70 percent of Americans who consider themselves to be Christians see them as a reaction to perceived government hostility toward religion, reflected in attempts to remove prayer from schools or religious displays from public buildings.

Religion and Public Schools

Since the Supreme Court ruled government-sponsored school prayer unconstitutional in the early 1960s, the nation's schools have been a leading battleground in the issue of establishment. Battles frequently have erupted over

Who Has Gone Too Far?

Respondents:

	Conservative Christians in imposing their religious values %	Liberals in keeping religion out of government %
Republican	31	87
Conservative	24	90
Moderate/Liberal	46	82
Democrat	59	60
Moderate/Conservative	51	70
Liberal	80	38
Independent	56	65
Total	49	69

Source: The Pew Forum on Religion and Public Life, "Many Americans Uneasy with Mix of Religion and Politics," 1. August 24, 2006.

state laws that attempt to force the curriculum of secular subjects to reflect particular religious beliefs. Such laws often target subjects that discuss the origins of human life. In 1968, the Court struck down a 1928 Arkansas law that made it a crime for any university or public school instructor to "teach the theory or doctrine that mankind ascended or descended from a lower order of animals" or to "adopt or use . . . a textbook that teaches" evolutionary theory.[24] It has also invalidated a Louisiana law that prohibited public schools from teaching evolutionary principles unless theories of "creation science" were also taught.[25]

Today, opponents of evolution are advancing the same argument under the term *intelligent design*. This theory claims that some biological structures such as DNA

codes are so complex that they could not have occurred because of evolution but must be the work of an intelligent designer. Proponents argue that intelligent design should be taught in schools alongside other scientific theories. Public leaders such as President George W. Bush and former Senate majority leader Bill Frist have endorsed the idea.

> **Lemon test** The three-part test for establishment clause cases that a law must pass before it is declared constitutional: it must have a secular purpose; it must neither advance nor inhibit religion; and it must not cause excessive entanglement with religion.

Religious Use of Public School Facilities and Funds

As a matter of fairness and constitutional protection, do religious groups have the same right to use public school buildings as other groups? The Supreme Court answered the question "yes" with respect to public universities, and later also ruled that religious groups should have access to secondary schools.[26] The Court also ruled that the establishment clause does not require schools to refuse religious groups the same right to free expression as secular groups. In the case of *Rosenberger v. University of Virginia* (1995), the Court struck down the University of Virginia's refusal to allow student religious groups access to funds collected by a mandatory fee of $14 from all full-time students. The university had established a student activities fund to which only nonreligious student organizations could apply for money to pay for the costs associated with the printing of their publications. The Court held that the establishment clause did not mandate discrimination against religious expression.

Prayer in School

School prayer is probably the most controversial of the establishment clause issues. Reciting prayers and reading Bible passages have been commonplace practices in public schools throughout our nation's history. Separationists believed such practices violated the establishment clause and embarked upon a plan to have the Supreme Court abolish them. In the case of *Engel v. Vitale* in 1962, the Court declared that compelling students to recite a twenty-two-word prayer written by the New York State Board of Regents violated the First Amendment.[27] Writing for the majority, Justice Hugo Black stated that "a union of government and religion tends to destroy government and degrade religion." The next year, the Court overturned a Pennsylvania law that required school officials to read at least ten verses from the Bible and the Lord's Prayer each day over the loudspeaker.[28]

The Pennsylvania decision was met with public disapproval; only 24 percent of those surveyed at the time agreed with the ruling, and by 2000, that figure still stood at just 38.8 percent.[29] Despite the decision, many school districts in the South continued the practice of reading the Bible in class. In response to public opinion, Congress members have made over 150 unsuccessful attempts to introduce constitutional amendments to return prayer to public classrooms. Supporters of school prayer have also continued to appeal cases to the Supreme Court, with no more success. Since 1992, the Court has struck down a silent prayer law,[30] the participation of clergy at high school graduation ceremonies,[31] and the traditional Texas practice of delivering a public prayer over a public address system before a high school football game.[32] The silent prayer issue may again become a salient one because a 2005 Gallup poll indicated that American adults prefer silent prayers in public schools to spoken prayers by a margin of 69 to 23 percent and 84 percent of teens between the ages of thirteen to seventeen preferred a moment of silence to allow students an opportunity to pray.[33]

Aid to Religious Schools

The Supreme Court has also wrestled with the question of whether government may provide financial aid to religious schools, and if so, how much. In recent years, the Court has moved in an accommodationist direction on this question. Beginning in 1993, it held that a state may pay to provide a sign-language interpreter for a disabled student at a Roman Catholic high school without violating the establishment clause.[34] Four years later, the Court reversed two earlier cases and ruled that public school teachers may give remedial instruction to at-risk students who attend religious schools.[35] In *Mitchell v. Helms* (2000), the Court found federal aid to religious schools for computer resources, educational materials, and library holdings constitutional, again overruling two earlier cases.

In a landmark 2002 case, the Court upheld the constitutionality of providing government vouchers to attend religious schools. The Cleveland school system, reputedly one of the nation's worst, offered parents up to $2,250 in vouchers to attend private schools, either religious or non-

religious. Over 95 percent of the students who used vouchers to private schools enrolled in religious schools. In a 5 to 4 decision, the Court ruled that the program did not violate the establishment clause.[36] The majority argued that the program was neutral in nature and based on private choice rather than government endorsement of a religious school.

Hot or Not?

When you go to a place of worship, do you want your pastor, priest, rabbi, or imam discussing political issues?

Government Endorsement of Religion

How does placing the words "In God We Trust" on our coins and Federal Reserve notes square with the separation between government and religion mandated by the establishment clause? When does government tolerance of religious expression constitute active endorsement of religion? The Court recently has attempted to establish guidelines to determine what kinds of displays are permissible on government property. For example, it has revised the second part of the Lemon test to hold that public display of a nativity scene on government property is unconstitutional if its effect is to endorse religion. Using such a test, they found a nativity scene located in a government building with the words "Glory to God in the Highest" to be a Christian religious display that violated the establishment clause,[37] but not a government-sponsored nativity scene in a private park with a Santa Claus and a banner displaying the number of shopping days until Christmas.[38] Similarly, in a 2005 decision, the Court ruled a monument of the Ten Commandments on the grounds of the Texas Capitol permissible because it was part of a historical exhibit including forty other monuments such as tributes to the Alamo, Confederate veterans, and Korean War veterans.[39] The same year, however, it found the posting of the Ten Commandments inside two Kentucky courthouses an unconstitutional endorsement of religion.[40]

". . . a union of government and religion tends to destroy government and degrade religion."

FREEDOM OF SPEECH

Freedom of speech is essential to a democratic political system. Without the ability to speak about politics, citizens cannot make intelligent judgments about candidates, political parties, and public policies. Freedom of expression is also essential for the intellectual enlightenment of a society and the human race. John Stuart Mill wrote that freedom of speech was the only way to discover the truth. Mill saw a free society as one that traded in a "marketplace of ideas" that would either confirm previous beliefs or provide new perceptions of the truth.[41]

Speech takes several different forms, which are subject to different levels of protection. Sometimes speech consists not of spoken words, but rather an act such as burning a flag or wearing a sign. As with freedom of religion, freedom of speech is not absolute in the United States. The Supreme Court has established boundaries for permissible speech by refusing to protect utterances that are obscene, defamatory, or that constitute what it calls "hate speech."

Political Speech

Political leaders often believe that freedom of speech is less important than considerations such as national security, public order, the right to a fair trial, and public decency. This sometimes produces legislation limiting freedom of speech to serve goals perceived as vital to the nation's interest. Popular opposition to U.S. participation in World War I led Congress to pass the 1917 Espionage Act, which made it a federal crime to obstruct military recruiting, to circulate false statements intending to interfere with the military, or to attempt to cause disloyalty in the military. The government

Even hate groups like the Ku Klux Klan enjoy the protection of free speech as interpreted by the clear and present danger test.

later prosecuted Charles Schenck, the general secretary of the Socialist Party of Philadelphia, under the act for printing and mailing fifteen thousand pamphlets urging draftees to resist conscription. The Supreme Court upheld his conviction but, in doing so, left a broad scope for permissible speech.

In articulating the **clear and present danger test** to determine free speech cases, Justice Oliver Wendell Holmes ruled that Schenck's writings would be constitutionally protected in ordinary times but "the character of every act depends upon the circumstances in which it is done." He compared writing such a pamphlet during wartime to falsely shouting fire in a crowded theater, stating that the context of a speech determines its permissibility. Only words that produce both a clear (obvious) and a present (immediate) danger are prohibited.[42] Justice Louis Brandeis supported Holmes, reasoning that prohibition is an appropriate remedy only for speech that threatens immediate harm. Given time to discover the facts through discussion and education, more speech serves the public interest better than enforced silence.[43]

Following World War I, fear of the new Communist government in Russia and the spread of Communism led to new limits on freedom of speech. At this time, the Supreme Court replaced the clear and present danger test with more restrictive tests such as the **bad tendency test**, which

> **clear and present danger test** Free speech test that only prohibits speech that produces a clear and immediate danger.
>
> **bad tendency test** Free speech test that prohibits speech that could produce a bad outcome, such as violence, no matter how unlikely the possibility the speech could be the cause of such an outcome.

asked, "Do the words have a tendency to bring about something bad or evil?"[44] In 1969, however, the Court returned to the clear and present danger test to protect the right of a Ku Klux Klan leader to make a speech in Ohio.[45] Since that time, the Court has continued to use this more liberal test despite security concerns related to international terrorism and U.S. overseas military actions.

Campaign Speech

Robust protection for political speech is necessary to maintain the open and public nature of our electoral system, but legitimate questions exist about what constitutes political speech, and the extent to which it is protected. Perhaps the most contentious of these is the question of whether money—in the form of campaign contributions—can be considered speech. Campaign contributions allow citizens and interest groups to express their views by supporting and influencing political candidates and parties. They also enable campaigns, candidates, political parties, and their supporters to present views to the electorate. However, are they equivalent to speech and thus deserving of constitutional protection?

Legal challenges to the 1974 Federal Election Campaign Act gave the United States Supreme Court the opportunity to answer those questions. Among its provisions, the act limited the amount of money that individuals and groups could contribute to federal campaigns in a calendar year. It also placed caps on total group and individual expenditures on behalf of a candidate, as well as the amount candidates could spend on their own campaigns. The Court upheld limits on contributions in order to prevent a political quid pro quo system in which government policies might be purchased by the highest bidder. On the other hand, it ruled that restrictions on expenditures violated free speech guarantees because individuals, groups, and candidates alike had the right to vigorously advocate their positions.[46]

The Court's decision led to a dramatic increase in campaign expenditures by individuals, interest groups, candidates, and political parties. Concerned about the escalating costs of campaigns, Congress passed the Bipartisan Campaign Reform Act of 2002. The law bans unlimited contributions to national political parties and places some limits on the expenditures of groups advocating the election or defeat of a particular candidate. In *McConnell v. Federal Election Commission* (2003), the Supreme Court upheld almost all of the provisions of the act, but in the 2007 case of *Federal Election Commission v. Wisconsin Right to Life/ McCain et al. v. Wisconsin Right to Life*, it held that restrictions on television advertisements paid for by corporate or union funds in the weeks before an election amounts to a censorship of commercial speech.

Commercial Speech

On an average day, people hear far more commercial speech than political speech. Companies are trying to sell us count-

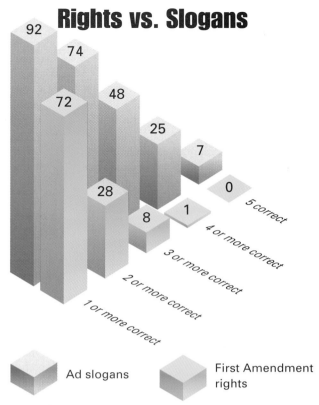

First Amendment Rights vs. Slogans

Ad slogans

First Amendment rights

Number of people who could identify First Amendment rights vs. the number of people who could identify ad slogans

Cumulative correct (in percentages)

Source: McCormick Tribune Freedom Museum, "Americans' Awareness of First Amendment Freedoms," March 1, 2006.

less goods and services on every type of media outlet; it's not surprising that Americans are more familiar with many advertising slogans than with First Amendment rights.

The courts traditionally have viewed commercial speech as being less worthy of free speech protection than political speech because the government has a legitimate interest in protecting consumers from deceptive advertising. If the advertising is not deceptive, however, the Court will protect it. The Supreme Court, for example, has invalidated a Virginia regulation making it unlawful for a pharmacy to advertise the prices of its prescription medications[47] and has supported the constitutional right of lawyers to advertise the prices of routine legal services.[48]

Symbolic Speech

At the time the Bill of Rights was written, political protesters expressed themselves through impassioned speeches and printed publications. Changing technology, however, has multiplied the channels for delivering and receiving political messages that go beyond the spoken or written word. Today, a protest march or a flag burning is more likely to receive media coverage than a forty-five-minute speech or a twenty-page pamphlet. When such activities convey a political message or viewpoint, courts may consider them to be **symbolic speech** worthy of First Amendment protection.

The Supreme Court has ruled that governments may suppress symbolic views if doing so serves an important purpose other than the suppression of unpopular speech. Using that reasoning, it has supported the federal government's authority to ban the burning of draft cards because the cards contain information necessary for the implementation of a military conscription system.[49] On the other hand, it struck down a school ban on the wearing of black armbands to protest the Vietnam War, ruling that the symbolic speech did not negatively affect the school's educational mission.[50] The Court has even held that desecration of the American flag may be considered a form of protected speech. In 1989, the Court invalidated a Texas law that prohibited burning the American flag, arguing that the law's sole purpose was to suppress speech.[51] The decision motivated Congress to pass the Flag Protection Act of 1989, which penalizes anyone who "knowingly mutilates, defaces, physically defiles, burns, maintains on the floor or ground, or tramples upon any flag of the United States." Applying the same reasoning as the Texas case, the Court found that the federal law violated the guarantee of free speech.[52]

Boundaries of Free Speech

The Supreme Court traditionally has given less consideration to speech that is not necessary to stimulate the marketplace of ideas and to preserve the workings of a democratic political systems. For example, the Court has declined to grant First Amendment protection to utterances and writings that are obscene or defamatory. More recently, the Court has added hate speech to the category of unprotected expression.

Obscenity

While the Supreme Court has consistently held that obscenity falls outside the boundaries of free speech, it has struggled to define the meaning of *obscene*. Justice Potter Stewart expressed the difficulty in his famous utterance: "I shall not today attempt to further define [obscenity]. . . . But I know it when I see it."[53] If Justice Stewart were alive today, would he view *Playboy* or Howard Stern's radio program as obscene? The answer depends on the judicial test he used to determine obscenity. Today, the Supreme Court uses the ***Miller* test**, which asks three questions:

symbolic speech Actions meant to convey a political message.

***Miller* test** The current judicial test for obscenity cases that considers community standards, whether the material is patently offensive, and whether the material taken as a whole lacks serious literary, artistic, political, or scientific value.

1. Does the average person, applying contemporary community standards, believe that the dominant theme of the material, taken as a whole, appeals to a prurient interest?
2. Is the material patently offensive?
3. Does the work, taken as a whole, lack serious literary, artistic, political, or scientific value?[54]

If the answer to any of the three questions is no, the Court considers the work not to be obscene.

The Supreme Court has ruled that flag burning may be protected as symbolic free speech.

In 1996, Congress passed the Communications Decency Act (CDA) that prohibited the transmission of any obscene or indecent materials over the Internet to anyone under the age of eighteen. The law did not include an exception for material that has serious literary, artistic, political, or scientific value. In the case of *Reno v. American Civil Liberties Union* (1997), the United States Supreme Court struck down the law, ruling that it was too vague with respect to what materials would be considered "indecent."

In 1998, Congress tried again to limit the transmission of obscene materials in cyberspace with the Child Online Protection Act (COPA). Rather than prohibiting "obscene and indecent" materials, the statute banned any material "harmful to minors." The act applied the "community standards" principle from the *Miller* test to determine what is harmful, but the Court rejected Congress's attempt to regulate the posting of obscene materials on the Internet. It ruled that the "community standards" principle has no application to the Internet because of the unlimited geographic scope of online communications (*Ashcroft v. American Civil Liberties Union,* 2004).

The Child Pornography Prevention Act of 1996 changed tactics, attempting to prohibit "any visual depiction, including any photograph, film, video, picture, or computer or computer-generated image or picture" of children engaging in sexually explicit conduct, including "virtual" child pornography. The Court overturned the law in 2002, ruling that child abuse cannot occur when the children and their sexual acts are computer generated (*Ashcroft v. Free Speech Coalition*).

Defamation

Free speech allows a vigorous exchange of ideas and criticisms that are sometimes hurtful and even mean-spirited. Legislative bodies have placed limits on such comments by allowing a person to sue anyone who makes false statements that injure his or her reputation. **Slander** is a false oral statement that causes injury, whereas **libel** is a written statement that has the same effect. Truth is an absolute defense in a slander or libel suit; a true statement cannot injure or defame.

slander Oral statements that are false and injure another's reputation.

The Court made it much more difficult for public figures to win defamation suits against their critics with its opinion in *New York Times Company v. Sullivan* (1964). In this case, the Court introduced the new **Sullivan rule**, which required that a public official in a libel or slander case not only prove the statements in question are false but also that the defendants wrote or spoke the words with malice. The Court defined *malice* as (1) knowledge the statements were false or (2) reckless disregard for whether the statements were false or not. The Court felt that this higher standard of proof was necessary to avoid self-censorship by critics of public officials, who may not have the ability to guarantee the truth of all their assertions.

Hate Speech

Hate speech involves prejudicial and hostile statements concerning characteristics such as race, ethnicity, sex, sexual orientation, or religion. Many communities and college campuses have adopted laws and policies banning hate speech. Advocates argue that these policies help minorities and women gain equal opportunity to jobs and education by creating less hostile public environments. Opponents of hate speech laws argue that preserving freedom of expression is a more important goal than ensuring civil discourse. Many contend that allowing greater freedom of speech will enhance racial and sexual equality more effectively than placing limits on free speech.[55]

FREEDOM OF THE PRESS

Because both freedom of speech and freedom of the press deal with expression, similar principles underlie each. Both forms of communication are essential to democracy due to their role in transmitting information. As we learned, the Founders knew and stressed the importance of an informed public in creating a successful democracy. The press protections they incorporated into the Constitution reflect those beliefs.

Prior Restraint

The authors of the Constitution and the Bill of Rights agreed with the famous English jurist William Blackstone, who wrote that authors and publishers may only be tried

for legitimate criminal violations once their article is published and their words have entered into the marketplace of ideas. He rejected the notion that government had the right to exercise **prior restraint**, the ability to prevent publication of material to which it objected.[56] The United States Supreme Court embraced this position in the 1931 case of *Near v. Minnesota*, in which it invalidated a Minnesota law intended to prevent publication of material deemed to be malicious, scandalous, and defamatory.

The Court did note, however, that the government's interest in protecting national security, regulating obscenity, or preventing the incitement of violence may justify prior restraint in the most exceptional cases. The Nixon administration cited national security considerations in 1971, when it attempted to restrain *The New York Times* and *The Washington Post* from publishing the "Pentagon Papers," a series of articles about U.S. involvement in Vietnam based on government documents. The Court rejected the administration's argument, ruling that government may not prevent the press from exercising its right to criticize public officials and its duty to inform readers.

The "Pentagon Papers" case seems to have settled the matter of prior restraint, as the Court has heard no further cases of significance in this area. After the terrorist attacks on September 11, 2001, however, the Department of Defense requested that journalists refrain from publishing information that could harm the country's national security. The department also hinted that the government might demand to review stories before publication or broadcast. As of this time, however, the government has censored no articles.

> **libel** Written statements that are false and injure another's reputation.
>
> **Sullivan rule** Standard requiring public officials and public figures in defamation suits to prove that allegedly libelous or slanderous statements are both false and made with malice.
>
> **hate speech** Prejudicial and hostile statements toward another person's innate characteristics such as race and ethnicity.
>
> **prior restraint** A practice that would allow the government to censor a publication before anyone could read or view it.

Government Control of Media Content

The government need not exercise prior restraint to exert control over the media. It can instead exercise control over content by prohibiting the publication of certain information. For example, states often pass laws prohibiting the publication of certain criminal matters in order to protect the victim, the offender, or the fairness of the trial. In *Cox Broadcasting Corporation v. Cohn* (1975), however, the Court ruled that the press has a First Amendment right to report the names of rape victims obtained from judicial records that are open to the public. The Court has also invali-

Under the guarantee of freedom of the press, the media may disclose the names of juvenile offenders although they usually choose not to do so.

dated a state law that prohibits the publication of the identity of juvenile offenders.[57] It has stuck down a trial judge's gag order that prohibited the press from covering a pretrial hearing for fear of prejudicial pretrial publicity.[58]

The government can also influence the media by mandating the publication of certain information, but only with certain limits. In one case, the Court struck down a Florida statute that required newspapers under certain circumstances to print articles written by candidates for political office. In a unanimous decision, the Court ruled that the government has no constitutional authority to order the newspaper to publish an article. To allow such a law would limit the editorial decision-making power of the paper, increase its costs, and perhaps discourage political and electoral coverage.[59]

Traditionally, radio and television have not been as free from government control as the print media. As discussed in Chapter 10, the government decided to license radio and television stations and place more restrictions upon them because of the scarcity of bandwidth. There simply were more persons who wanted to broadcast than there were frequencies to allocate. This scarcity led to the creation of the Federal Communications Commission (FCC) and imposition of such regulations as the fairness doctrine, which required broadcasters to discuss both sides of controversial public issues.

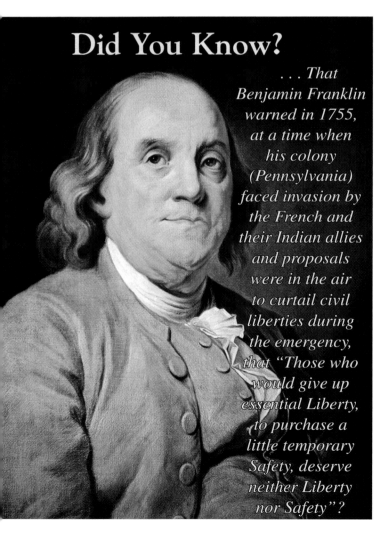

Did You Know?

... That Benjamin Franklin warned in 1755, at a time when his colony (Pennsylvania) faced invasion by the French and their Indian allies and proposals were in the air to curtail civil liberties during the emergency, that "Those who would give up essential Liberty, to purchase a little temporary Safety, deserve neither Liberty nor Safety"?

Special Rights

The media historically have argued for special legal rights to allow them to perform the important function of gathering and reporting the news. In most instances, the United States Supreme Court has looked unfavorably on these claims for special rights. It has not allowed reporters to maintain the confidentiality of their sources if the government can show compelling reasons for requesting their names, such as to advance a criminal investigation.[60] In 2005, the Court refused to review a lower court's decision to imprison *New York Times* reporter Judith Miller for failing to cooperate with a federal investigation. Miller, who wrote an article leaking the name of a CIA operative, refused to tell federal prosecutor Patrick Fitzgerald the name of the person who gave her that information. Miller spent eighty-five days in jail until her source released her from the promise of confidentiality.

Although the media frequently assert a special right of access, the Court has placed a variety of limits on reporters' ability to gather the news. It has found that reporters enjoy no access to county jail inmates that is denied to other individuals.[61] They also have no right to enter a home when police are executing a warrant.[62] The justices also failed to recognize a First Amendment right of the media to attend a closed pretrial hearing in a highly publicized case.[63] The Court ruled differently, however, with respect to a judge's attempt to close a trial to the media and the public. It held in *Richmond Newspapers v. Virginia* (1980) that the media's right to attend trials is implicit in the freedom of the press guarantee.

FREEDOM OF ASSEMBLY AND ASSOCIATION

The First Amendment freedom of assembly is one of the cornerstones of American democracy, granting citizens the right to gather and engage in politics. It is the basis for the formation of interest groups and political parties that attempt to forge public policy and determine who will hold public office. Implied in the freedom of assembly is the right to associate by joining with like-minded individuals to pursue common goals. The freedoms of speech, press, and assembly would be nearly meaningless if one had to do them alone.

Freedom of Assembly

Freedom to assemble is critical for the survival of a democratic political system. Yet this does not mean that people can assemble to advance their own political agenda whenever and wherever they please. The government may have

Right to assembly protects protesters, as long as the assembly is peaceable. This protest in front of the U.S. Marine Corps Recruiting Center in Berkeley reflects anti-Iraq war sentiments.

competing interests that override such freedoms, such as keeping the peace, maintaining order, and protecting the flow of commerce. As a result, governments have the authority to impose "time, place, and manner restrictions" on the conditions of a political gathering.

The freedom of assembly cases that come before the Court typically reflect debate about the significant controversies of the day. During the 1960s, such cases arose from the often emotionally charged civil rights demonstrations in southern cities. In one case, police arrested nearly two hundred African American student demonstrators in South Carolina for refusing orders to disperse after an hour of peaceful protest at the state capitol building. The Supreme Court reversed the conviction, holding that a peaceful demonstration at the seat of state government was the proper way "to petition government for a redress of grievances."[64] In later cases, however, the Court ruled that political assemblies in front of courthouses and jails were not constitutionally protected. The justices feared that protests in front of a courthouse to advocate a certain outcome for a trial could adversely affect the administration of justice and perceptions of the judicial system.[65] The Court ruled out peaceful demonstrations at a jail because jails, unlike state capitol buildings, are not typically open to the public because of security concerns.[66]

In the 1980s, the Court dealt with several cases stemming from confrontations between antiabortion protesters and supporters of a woman's constitutional right to have an abortion. Many states and communities have passed laws to regulate demonstrations outside abortion clinics. The Court upheld the enforcement of noise restrictions and buffer zones around the clinics' entrances and driveways, but not restrictions on signs or buffer zones to the backs and sides of the clinics.[67] The Court has also upheld a Colorado statute in 2000 that prohibited any person from approaching closer than eight feet to a clinic patient for the purpose of distributing literature, displaying a sign, or engaging in oral protest, without the patient's consent.[68]

Freedom of Association

The United States Supreme Court first recognized the implied right of freedom of association when southern states began to restrict the associational rights of civil rights groups. In the 1958 case of *NAACP v. Alabama*, the civil rights group appealed an Alabama law that mandated that the group turn its membership list over to a state agency. The Court struck down the law, arguing that disclosure of the group's membership list in Alabama could lead to economic reprisal, loss of employment, physical coercion, and public hostility against the individual members. Later, the Court recognized the right of the NAACP to use litigation to further its goals by stressing that the First Amendment supports the vigorous advocacy of a group's views.[69]

More recently, private organizations such as business clubs, fraternal organizations, and civic groups have tested their freedom to restrict membership on the basis of race, sex, or sexual orientation. Does freedom of association allow private groups to discriminate? Yes and no. In *Roberts v. United States Jaycees* (1984), the Court found that freedom of association is not an absolute right, nor does it pertain equally to all private organizations. It afforded smaller and more intimate groups—such as a married couple and families—as well as organizations espousing clear political and ideological views, the most protection. It ruled that the First Amendment's protection of larger national organizations such as the Jaycees, which do not express strong ideological views and do not have highly selective membership guidelines, is inferior to the state's interest in combating arbitrary discrimination. The Court reached similar decisions in cases involving the Rotary Club[70] and a private New York men's club.[71] It ruled that the right of a woman to belong and establish informal business contacts outweighs the right of the organization to associate with whomever they want.

By contrast, the Court upheld the right of a private association to prevent gay rights groups from marching in a Saint Patrick's Day parade the association was organizing in Boston.[72] The Court also upheld the right of the Boy Scouts of America to revoke the adult membership of an assistant scoutmaster who at college announced to others that he was gay. The five-person majority agreed with the organization that the retention of a gay member was inconsistent with the values represented by the phrase "morally straight and clean."[73]

RIGHT TO KEEP AND BEAR ARMS

The text of the Second Amendment—"*A well regulated Militia, being necessary to the security of a free State*, the right of the people to keep and bear Arms, shall not be infringed"—has generated significant disagreement and controversy among gun owners and those who favor limits on firearm ownership.[74] Gun control opponents such as the National Rifle Association emphasize the words that are not italicized. They stress that the government owes citizens the right to own guns in order to secure their freedom. Those who favor restrictions on gun ownership stress the italicized words that imply that only persons who are members of a government militia have the right to own firearms. They believe the Second Amendment confers a collective right that only conveys the right to possess a gun to members of a military unit.

For years the meaning of the Second Amendment drew little attention from American courts. In 1939, the Supreme Court agreed with the collective right position when it decided a case that upheld the right of the federal government to require the registration of firearms.[75] By not incorporating the amendment, however, the Court left the states with a great deal of authority to restrict or protect gun ownership. In recent years, states have tended to protect the rights of gun ownership: forty-four state constitutions now include language that recognizes the right to keep and bear arms.

Then in 2008, the Court dramatically changed the meaning of the amendment with its decision in *District of Columbia v. Heller.* Heller, an armed security guard, sued the District after it rejected his application to keep a handgun at home for protection. His application violated a strict 1976 D.C. ordinance that banned the private ownership of all handguns. Rifles and shotguns were allowed if they were kept disassembled or in a trigger lock or some similar device. By a 5 to 4 majority, the Court ruled that the Second Amendment confers an individual right for citizens to keep and bear arms to protect themselves.[76] The Court's decision has spurred a great deal of controversy as well as questions about its policy implications. This is the subject of the "Current Controversy" section at the end of the chapter.

RIGHTS OF THE ACCUSED

The early Americans showed their unhappiness with the British criminal justice system by devoting four of the first eight amendments almost exclusively to the rights granted to accused persons.[77] Remembering the treatment of colonial leaders by their British rulers, the Framers of the Bill of Rights were determined to provide procedural guarantees throughout the criminal justice system to guarantee fairness and justice for the accused. They thus devoted four of the first ten amendments—the Fourth, Fifth, Sixth, and Eighth—to procedural protections for the accused.

The Fourth Amendment: Searches and Seizures

The Fourth Amendment guarantees freedom from "unreasonable searches and seizures," but the only type of search the Constitution mentions is one authorized by a search warrant. To obtain a warrant, police must present

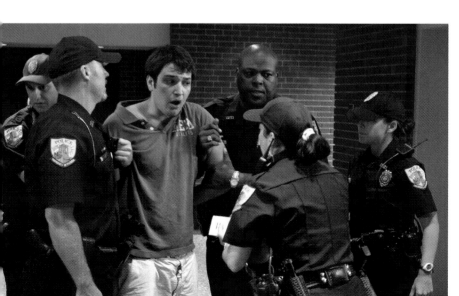

"Don't tase me bro!" What are the rights of a student to interrupt a speech and do the police have the right to use a taser gun to subdue him?

Lock 'em Up

Rate of incarceration in selected nations (per 100,000 people)

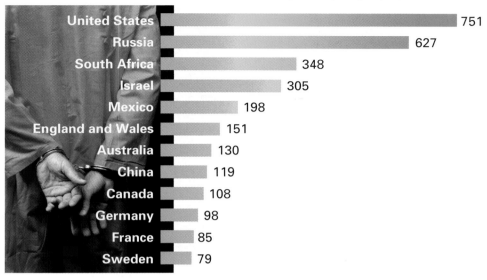

Nation	Rate
United States	751
Russia	627
South Africa	348
Israel	305
Mexico	198
England and Wales	151
Australia	130
China	119
Canada	108
Germany	98
France	85
Sweden	79

Source: International Center for Prison Studies at King's College London; Marc Maner, The Sentencing Project; Bureau of Justice Statistics; Anthony N. Doblo, Center for Criminology, University of Toronto, April 22, 2008.

a neutral judge with an affidavit swearing there is reason to believe that a crime has been committed and that evidence can be found in a specific place. The judge then must determine whether **probable cause** exists to issue the search warrant. Judges usually require the probable cause standard for wiretaps and electronic surveillance as well. Since the passage of the USA Patriot Act in 2001, however, federal agents investigating terrorism can trace e-mail messages with less than probable cause. In late 2005, it came to light that the National Security Agency had been operating a special Collections Program that allowed it to intercept the communications of about fifty-five Americans without a court order. The Bush administration initiated the program by executive order, without congressional authorization.

The Constitution does not preclude the possibility of warrantless searches, it only requires that such searches be reasonable. But what is reasonable? The Supreme Court has recognized several categories of warrantless searches as reasonable:

1. The police may conduct a search at the time of a valid arrest. They may search any area within the suspect's immediate control where he or she might obtain a weapon or conceal evidence.[78]

2. The courts also recognize a search as valid if the police receive permission voluntarily from a person with the authority to do so. In 2001, the Supreme Court ruled that a person on probation gives consent to have his or her property searched if the probation officer has a reasonable suspicion of wrongdoing.[79]

3. Searches without warrants have also been justified when conducted in hot pursuit of a criminal who has just committed a crime, is considered dangerous, and who may destroy evidence if the police must delay a search in order to obtain a warrant.[80]

4. In the case of *Terry v. Ohio* (1968), the Supreme Court approved stop-and-frisk searches in which an experienced police officer believes a suspect is about to commit a crime. The Court reasoned that the police had the power to prevent crimes and that the frisk was necessary to protect the safety of the officer. The Court held in a 2000 case that a young man running from a high-crime area when he saw uniformed police officers created sufficient suspicion to justify such a search.[81]

5. In 1973, the Supreme Court created a new category of warrantless searches known as "loss of evidence searches." In such cases, police may conduct a search if they reasonably suspect that a delay will result in the suspect destroying evidence.[82] In this instance, the Court allowed police to take fingernail scrapings of a murder suspect at the time of the interrogation and before an arrest because of the risk that the evidence could be easily destroyed at a later time.[83] This ruling also forms the legal basis for drug-testing programs such as the one discussed at the beginning of the chapter. However, the Court struck down a hospital-instituted drug-screening program for

> **probable cause** A practical and nontechnical calculation of probabilities that is the basis for securing search warrants.

The police may search open spaces for marijuana plants without a search warrant.

patients that gave results to the police as a requirement for receiving medical care.[84]

6. In considering the constitutionality of warrantless searches, the Court also has taken into consideration the place being searched and the means of the search. For example, it has ruled that the police may search a field for marijuana plants, even though the area is marked with No Trespassing signs.[85] Police may conduct an aerial search for marijuana plants growing in a greenhouse that is missing some of its roof panels.[86] They may not point a thermal imager at a home, however, to detect heat emanating from bulbs used to grow marijuana indoors.[87] The Court has generally given the police greater authority to search automobiles because of their ability to leave the jurisdiction of law enforcement officials, and because of the government's interest in regulating auto traffic and safety. Recently, however, it has not allowed officers at highway checkpoints to look for ordinary criminal wrongdoing such as the possession of illegal drugs.[88]

exclusionary rule The judicial barring of illegally seized evidence from a trial.

***Miranda* rights** The warning police must administer to suspects so that the latter will be aware of their right not to incriminate themselves. The rights include the right to remain silent, the right to know statements will be used against them, and the right to have an attorney for the interrogation.

The Court was also concerned with how to enforce its Fourth Amendment decisions. What sanction could the Court provide to prevent the police from making unreason-able searches? It eventually adopted the **exclusionary rule** that excludes any evidence gathered illegally from consideration at trial, thus removing the incentive for the police to make illegal searches.[89] The Court has allowed some exceptions to the exclusionary rule, for example, when it believes the police are acting in good faith.[90]

The Fifth Amendment: Self-Incrimination

The Fifth Amendment protects the accused against self-incrimination, a right that places limits on police interrogation of criminal suspects. Nevertheless, law enforcement officers frequently employed physical or psychological pressure during private interrogation sessions in order to gain confessions. To remedy this problem, the Court adopted the now familiar ***Miranda* rights**, which require officials to remind suspects of their Fifth Amendment rights. In the 1966 case of *Miranda v. Arizona*, the Court ruled that "prior to any questioning, the person must be warned that he has a right to remain silent, that any statements he does make may be used against him, and that he has a right to the presence of an attorney, either retained or appointed." The warning of silence allows the suspect to make an intelligent constitutional choice concerning self-incrimination. The presence of an attorney guarantees that the right is protected under the intense pressure of a police interrogation. The Court will deny the admissibility of a confession if the police failed to notify the suspect of his or her *Miranda* rights. In 2000, the Court reaffirmed its support of the *Miranda* ruling by declaring unconstitutional a congressional statute mandating a return to a lesser confession standard.[91]

The Sixth Amendment: Right to Counsel

The Sixth Amendment guarantees the accused the right to counsel. At the time the Constitution was written, there were very few attorneys in the United States—most defendants handled their own cases—and criminal law was relatively uncomplicated. As American society became more complex, so did the laws needed to regulate and punish criminal behavior. By the twentieth century, criminal defendants increasingly began to hire attorneys to represent them. Because of the great complexity of modern criminal law, many observers now consider the right to counsel the most important of the rights possessed by the accused. Good legal advice is invaluable at every stage of the criminal justice process; it is no accident that the right to have an attorney is a key element of the *Miranda* warnings.

Although accused criminals had the right to an attorney, nearly 75 percent of them could not afford one. This put most defendants at a significant disadvantage when confronting a government prosecutor. The Supreme Court challenged the constitutionality of this situation under certain circumstances in *Powell v. Alabama* (1932). The year before, police in Alabama arrested nine African American youths, known as "the Scottsboro boys," for allegedly raping two white girls. The jury convicted eight of the nine suspects and sentenced them to death. Upon appeal, the Court ruled that in unusual situations such as these—the defendants were young and uneducated, they were facing the death penalty, and their fate was subject to intense public pressure—the accused were entitled to counsel at the government's expense.[92]

In 1963, the Court expanded the right to counsel for indigent defendants facing felony charges in response to the efforts of Clarence Gideon.[93] Tried and convicted in Florida without the aid of an attorney for the felony crime of breaking and entering, Gideon became a "jailhouse lawyer" by reading law books and filing legal briefs. After many attempts by Gideon, the Supreme Court agreed to hear his case in 1962, and voted that poor defendants did have the right to an attorney when confronting felony charges. Nine years later, the Court expanded its policy by ruling that indigent defendants facing even one day in jail are entitled to legal representation. Such cases may involve complex legal issues, and a guilty verdict leaves the defendant with the stigma of a criminal conviction.[94] Supplying attorneys for all cases can be an expensive proposition for state governments, however. Recognizing this fact, the Court ruled that the state need not supply counsel unless the defendant faces the possibility of jail time if convicted.[95] In a recent case, however, the Court struck down a lower court ruling against a defendant without counsel who received a suspended sentence and two years' probation.

The justices concluded that the state should have provided the defendant with counsel because he faced a possible deprivation of his freedom.[96]

The Sixth Amendment: Trial by Jury

The Sixth Amendment guarantees criminal defendants the right to a jury trial. Although 95 percent of all criminal cases are settled out of court by an informal process known as plea bargaining, the right to a jury trial remains a cornerstone of our criminal justice system. The courts select potential jurors—known as the jury pool, or venire—from government records such as voter registration lists or property tax assessment rolls. In two separate cases, the Supreme Court ruled that jury pools may not exclude blacks or women.[97] The Court has also ruled that prosecutors and defense attorneys may not exclude potential jurors on the basis of race or gender.[98]

At the time the Sixth Amendment was written, the United States employed English trial procedure, in which a twelve-member jury had to reach a unanimous verdict to convict a defendant. By the 1960s, however, many states had reduced the size of juries and made it easier to obtain a conviction. They reasoned that smaller juries and non-unanimous verdicts would save time and money, and result in fewer hung juries. In 1970, the Court upheld the constitutionality of smaller juries in noncapital (not involving the death penalty) cases.[99] Two years later, it held that non-unanimous verdicts in noncapital cases also were constitutional. The Court rejected the assertion that the disagreement of a minority of jurors raised questions of "reasonable doubt" about the verdict.[100]

Executions in the U.S.

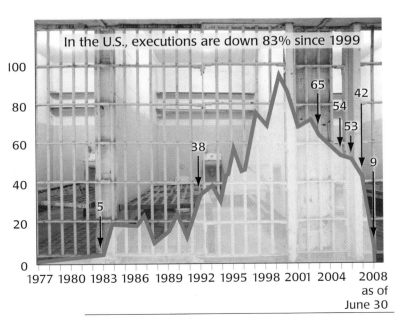

In the U.S., executions are down 83% since 1999

Source: Death Penalty Information Center.

The Supreme Court has ruled that the death penalty is not the type of cruel and unusual punishment that is prohibited by the Eighth Amendment of the Constitution.

The Eighth Amendment: Cruel and Unusual Punishment

The Eighth Amendment's ban on cruel and unusual punishment was probably the Framers' reaction to the barbarous methods of torture and execution practiced in medieval England, such as being stretched on the rack and/or disemboweled. Most of the debate over cruel and unusual punishment in the United States, however, has focused on the death penalty.

The issue received little attention from the Supreme Court until the 1970s. Then, in 1972, a deeply divided Court ruled that the Georgia death penalty was unconstitutional because it led to unacceptable disparities in executions. Blacks who murdered whites were much more likely to receive the death penalty than whites convicted of the same crime.[101] Only two of the justices, however, said

the death penalty was unconstitutional in all circumstances.

Four years later, the Court clarified its position by upholding a new Georgia death penalty statute in **Gregg v. Georgia**.[102] The Court found the law constitutional because it contained adequate safeguards for the defendant. The law prescribed separate phases for trial and sentencing. The trial phase would determine the defendant's guilt or innocence; a verdict of guilty triggered a second phase to consider punishment. The law required jury or judge to consider both aggravating factors and mitigating factors in making a sentencing decision. An aggravating factor is any factor that makes the crime worse, such as murder for hire or felony murder. A mitigating factor is any factor that might excuse the crime to some extent, such as reduced mental capacity on the part of the defendant. The law also provided for an automatic appeal to the state's highest court.

Opponents of the death penalty have been encouraged by recent events. Public support for the death penalty has declined, as has the number of executions and death penalty sentences (see graph on previous page), with the revelation that many innocent persons have been sentenced to death. The declining murder rate has also contributed to a decrease in executions.

In 2000, former governor George Ryan (R-IL) ordered a moratorium on all executions in his state after DNA tests led to the release of thirteen men on death row. Other states are now offering free DNA testing for death row inmates. In 2002, the Supreme Court ruled that the execution of mentally retarded defendants is cruel and unusual punishment; at the time, such executions were legal in twenty states.[103] Three years later, the Court prohibited the death penalty for any defendant who was under the age of eighteen when he or she committed murder.[104] Before the decision, the United States was one of a handful

States Without the Death Penalty

Source: Death Penalty Information Center.

The Death Penalty and Public Opinion

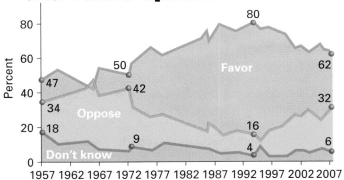

Source: Data from 1995 and earlier are from Gallup; data from 1996 to 2007 are from the Pew Research Center.

of countries, including China, Pakistan, Iran, and Saudi Arabia, which executed juveniles. Despite these rulings, however, the national government and three-fourths of the states still have the death penalty, and the United States is now the only western democracy that uses it.

Opponents of the death penalty were cheered again when the Supreme Court agreed to hear a Kentucky case that challenged the state's administration of the lethal injection method of execution: which chemicals were administered, the training of the personnel, the adequacy of the medical supervision, and the risk of error. The contention of the prisoner was that if the first drug, the barbiturate, was an insufficient anesthetic, the next two drugs that paralyzed the prisoner and stopped the heart could cause excruciating pain without the prisoner being able to move or cry out. Such pain, it was contended, would constitute cruel and unusual punishment. While the Court considered the case, it stayed the execution of the prisoners from states with the lethal injection procedure, and some states voluntarily halted their executions until the Supreme Court rendered its decisions. As a result, only forty-two executions were carried out in 2007 and none in the early part of 2008 until the Court rendered its decision. (See the graph on page 85.)

In April 2008, the Court upheld the Kentucky law.[105] For a 7–2 majority, Chief Justice John Roberts wrote: "Simply because an execution method may result in pain, either by accident or as an inescapable consequence of death, does not establish the sort of 'objectively intolerable risk of harm' that qualifies as cruel and unusual" punishment. Within days of the opinion, states began lifting their execution bans, and by midyear, nine executions had taken place.

The Court ended its term in 2008 by rejecting the death penalty for those convicted of raping a child.[106] A closely divided Court held that with the exception of treason and espionage cases, the death penalty should not be applied when the life of the victim was not taken. Prior to the decision, only five states allowed for the execution of rapists whose victims were children, and the others except for Louisiana applied the penalty only in cases where the defendant had previously been convicted of raping a child. The fact that only five states had such laws and that no prisoner had been executed for the crime for a period of forty-four years led the Court to conclude that a national consensus had been formed on the issue.

Gregg v. Georgia The Supreme Court decision that upheld the death penalty in the United States.

THE RIGHT TO PRIVACY

Although the Constitution does not explicitly mention a right to privacy, the Supreme Court has found an implied constitutional right to privacy and has declared that right to be fundamental.[107] The most controversial applications of the right to privacy have been in cases dealing with the beginning and end of life.

Abortion

Until the 1970s, abortion was not a major political issue. Most states considered it a crime, while including exceptions such as a pregnancy that threatened the health of the mother or one that resulted from rape or incest. That changed after an itinerant circus worker named Norma McCorvey challenged a Texas state law that criminalized

A woman's right to an abortion stems from the 1973 case of Roe v. Wade.

abortion. The pregnant McCorvey already had a child in the care of her mother and did not want to have another; nor did she want to submit to an illegal back-alley abortion. Under the pseudonym Jane Roe, McCorvey ultimately appealed her case to the Supreme Court.[108] In **Roe v. Wade** (1973), the Court concluded that the constitutional right to privacy was broad enough to include the termination of a pregnancy. According to the majority ruling, a woman's right to privacy gives her an absolute right to terminate her pregnancy during the first trimester. In the second trimester, the government can regulate abortions only to protect the health of the mother. It is only in the third trimester that the government's interest in potential life outweighs the privacy interests of the mother, because at that point the fetus is viable and can live outside the womb. Since the passage of *Roe v. Wade*, an estimated one million abortions have been performed every year in the United States.

The *Roe* decision intensified the country's division over the issue of abortion.[109] Antiabortion groups have been unsuccessful in persuading Congress to propose a constitutional amendment banning abortions or the Supreme Court to overturn *Roe*. They have been successful, however, in getting state legislatures (and Congress, to a lesser extent) to adopt abortion restrictions. The Supreme Court

The wrenching story of Terri Schiavo brought the right to die issue to the nation's attention.

has upheld state provisions requiring parental consent for abortions performed on minors, informed consent provisions, and a twenty-four-hour waiting period.[110] It also upheld state bans on the use of public facilities for abortions and has required viability testing at twenty weeks.[111] The justices have also validated the Hyde Amendment, which banned the use of Medicaid funds for poor women who wanted to secure abortions.[112] In the case of *Planned Parenthood of Southeastern Pennsylvania v. Casey* (1992), the Court declared it would not abandon a woman's right to an abortion first articulated in *Roe*, but the Court did dismantle the trimester system, since viability testing can be conducted in the second trimester. In 2007, the Court outlawed a later-term abortion method called intact dilation and extraction, which abortion opponents refer to as "partial birth abortion."[113]

The Right to Die

Longer life expectancies, and modern medicine's ability to prolong the life of terminally ill or comatose patients, have increased Americans' concern with issues regarding the right to die. The Court has ruled that individuals have a constitutional right to die that is derived from their constitutional right to privacy.[114] The problem occurs when

patients have not made clear their wishes in a living will. In such situations, family members may disagree as to the patient's wishes and, in the most unusual of situations, politicians may get involved for a variety of altruistic and self-serving reasons. Such was the case in 2005 of Terri Schiavo, a Florida woman who had been in a vegetative state for over a decade when her husband went to court to have her feeding tube removed. Her parents opposed this decision and asked for custody. Before doctors eventually removed the feeding tube, the Florida state legislature, the Florida governor, Congress, and the president of the United States all attempted to intervene in this most private family issue.

Although the Court defends the right to die, it has not given its approval to assisted suicide. The Supreme Court ruled unanimously in *Washington v. Glucksberg* (1997) that no right to assisted suicide exists in the Constitution. Michigan physician Jack Kevorkian brought sympathetic national attention to the issue by helping terminally ill patients kill themselves quickly and painlessly. The Court, however, has upheld state laws criminalizing assisted suicide, citing the state's interest in preserving human life and protecting the vulnerable group of ill and predominantly elderly patients.

CIVIC ENGAGEMENT AND CONSTITUTIONAL LIBERTIES

Because so many of the political issues facing the nation are settled in the courts, organized interest groups inevitably have fought legal battles and sought judicial support for their views. Lawsuits are especially attractive political instruments for individuals or small groups whose size, limited financial resources, and lack of prestige reduce their influence in the electoral process. Although they may lack the ability to influence the outcome of elections, individuals and smaller groups can make persuasive constitutional and moral arguments to courts. The Jehovah's Witnesses, for instance, have won over 70 percent of their cases before the nation's highest court. As recently as 2002, their legal corporation, the Watchtower Bible and Tract Society, was successful in overturning a city permit requirement for door-to-door religious solicitation.[115]

The Jehovah's Witnesses traditionally go to court to defend the rights of their own members, but some groups sponsor cases on behalf of others. The American Civil Liberties Union (ACLU), for example, waits for a case to arise within its field of concern and then assumes all or part of the function of representing the litigant in court. Founded during the Progressive Era to combat growing militarism, the ACLU is the symbol of a new era of citizenship. It represents those people who believe one or more government policies violate their constitutional rights. They take on cases representing significant constitutional principles such as the privacy issue raised in the case of Lindsay Earls.

In some instances, a group may file a **test case** to challenge the constitutionality of a law. This involves deliberately bringing a case to court to secure a judicial ruling on a constitutional issue. In Chapter 5, we will see how the NAACP used this strategy to advance the cause of civil rights in the courts. The Supreme Court ruling in *Griswold v. Connecticut* (1965), regarding a state ban on advertising or selling contraceptives, was the result of a series of test cases. After a series of unsuccessful test cases, the director of the Connecticut Planned Parenthood League and a physician openly challenged the law by publicly advising married couples on how to use various contraceptive devices. After being arrested and convicted, they appealed the decision to the United States Supreme Court. The Court found the law unconstitutional, in which it recognized a right to privacy.

Organized groups also try to influence the outcome of constitutional liberties cases by filing **amicus curiae**, or "friend of the court," **briefs**. These are legal arguments that provide additional support to the arguments supplied by each side in

Roe v. Wade The Supreme Court case that legalized abortions in the United States during the first two trimesters of a pregnancy.

test case Practice by which a group deliberately brings a case to court in order to secure a judicial ruling on a constitutional issue.

amicus curiae brief Legal briefs filed by organized groups to influence the decision in a Supreme Court case.

get involved!

Using a service like LEXIS-NEXIS, Westlaw, or www.lawcornell.edu, examine the amicus curiae briefs that were submitted for different civil liberties cases. Summarize your arguments for the class and analyze why those particular groups are interested in that particular issue.

the case. When a plaintiff challenges the constitutionality of a state policy before the United States Supreme Court, the state attorney general customarily seeks support from his or her counterparts in other states by asking them to file friend of the court briefs. This strategy backfired in the *Gideon* case, when the Florida attorney general received support from only two states but opposition from twenty-three others. In most constitutional liberties cases, groups from both sides of the issue submit amicus curiae briefs. The more such briefs that are filed with the Supreme Court, the more likely it is to accept a case.[116]

In 1963, the United States Supreme Court recognized that the activities of interest groups in advancing civil liberties issues before the Court were themselves protected by the Bill of Rights. In *NAACP v. Button,* the Court rejected the state of Virginia's attempt to stop the NAACP and other groups from sponsoring lawsuits. The Court ruled that the First Amendment does more than protect abstract discussion; it also protects vigorous advocacy. The justices went on to recognize that the freedoms of speech and association encompass the right to advance issues through the legal system.

Current Controversy

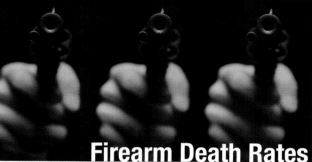

Firearm Death Rates

Firearm death rates per 100,000

United States
Finland
France
Belgium
Austria
Canada
Norway
Italy
Sweden
Australia
Denmark
Germany
Israel
Ireland
Netherlands
Singapore
Japan
Hong Kong

■ Homicides and suicides
▨ Unintentional

0   2   4   6   8   10   12

Source: Jean Lemaire, "The Impact of Firearm Death on Life Expectancies in the U.S.," Wharton School, University of Pennsylvania, June 1, 2005.

Should Handguns Remain an American Right?

When the U.S. Supreme Court declared that the thirty-two-year-old District of Columbia law banning all handguns for its residents was an unconstitutional violation of the Second Amendment, it accelerated rather than ended the legal and political debate concerning the role of guns in American society. Writing for the majority, Justice Antonin Scalia concluded that the Second Amendment protected an individual's right to possess a firearm unconnected to any service in a militia. Citizens possess the right to protect themselves in their own homes. This holding dramatically altered what twenty years earlier had been an almost complete scholarly and judicial consensus that the amendment conferred only a collective right.

What happened? Robert Levy, a senior fellow at the libertarian Cato Institute and lawyer in the case for the plaintiff, cited the fact that liberal law professors such as Laurence Tribe of Harvard University and Sanford Levinson of the University of Texas changed their minds about the amendment's meaning.[117] According to Professor Tribe, "My conclusion came as somewhat of a surprise to me, an unwelcome surprise. I have

always supported as a matter of policy very comprehensive gun control."[118] Professor Levinson also changed the scholarly debate when he published an article in the *Yale Law Journal,* "The Embarrassing Second Amendment," in 1989. According to a spokesman of the leading antigun group, the Brady Center to Prevent Gun Violence, "The Levinson piece was very much a turning point."[119] In addition, the Bush administration reversed a long-standing position of the Justice Department with the individual's-right interpretation of the Second Amendment.

In his dissenting opinion, Justice John Paul Stevens was concerned about the scope of the right recognized by the majority. He wrote: "But a conclusion that the Second Amendment protects an individual right does not tell us anything about the scope of that right. . . . The Second Amendment plainly does not protect the right to use a gun to rob a bank; it is equally clear that it does encompass the right to use weapons for certain military purposes." Governments are now left with the question of what reasonable controls on guns they can impose to protect their citizens.

[**For**
REVIEW >>]

1. Why was the incorporation of the Bill of Rights by the Supreme Court so important?

   • The incorporation of the Bill of Rights protects citizens from civil liberties violations by any level of government and also provides for a uniform definition of these basic rights by the United States Supreme Court.

2. What are the First Amendment rights?

   • The First Amendment rights include freedom of religion, freedom of speech, freedom of the press, freedom of assembly, and freedom of association.

3. What are some of the other important civil liberties guaranteed by the Constitution?

   • The Constitution also guarantees the right to keep and bear arms, various rights of the accused such as protection against self-incrimination and the right to counsel, and the right to privacy.

SURVEILLANCE STANDOFF

From 1985 to 86 the number of registered mobile-phone subscribers in the United States doubled to 500,000. Within two years after that, the number climbed to 1.6 million. By the end of the decade, the cellphone universe had skyrocketed past 4 million.

Organized crime was an early adopter of the mobile phone. In a communications technique presaging that of Islamic terrorists today, members of the Colombian Cali drug cartel operating in New York would briefly use a phone, toss it, and get a new one. To wiretap a mobile device, technicians had to install listening equipment on an "electronic port." But in most switching stations in New York, there were only half a dozen or so ports available at any one time. Federal prosecutors and agents had to stand in line at phone company offices and fight with each other over whose investigation should take priority. Some prosecutors threatened to haul company employees into court on contempt charges so they could explain to a judge why the phone company was unwilling to execute a wiretap order.

Electronic surveillance, once such a dependable, relatively easy craft, was becoming inordinately difficult. FBI Field Agent Jim Kallstrom may have been the first to alert the FBI and the Justice Department to this new reality. The digital revolution generated a constant tension that exists to this day, a push and pull between the federal government in one camp and technology corporations and civil-liberties activists in the other to control the development of the global communications system, and so the balance of power in the Information Age.

This struggle's latest manifestation is the intensely politicized effort to rewrite the Foreign Intelligence Surveillance Act. At issue is nothing less than the government's authority to broadly monitor communications networks to spot terrorists and other national security threats.

Activists and their allies in the business world have been motivated by different but mutually supportive goals: to extend constitutional safeguards to the digital realm, and to keep the government from suffocating technological development with burdensome surveillance laws. Some in those ranks would have liked, and indeed tried, to make the digital network a wiretap-free zone.

But despite the occasionally extreme positions and deeply held convictions of all of these players, the most important laws governing wiretapping, electronic surveillance, and privacy have been the product of negotiation, of people gathering in a room, sitting at a table, and talking—sometimes screaming—until they reached a settlement. The current debate, however, is missing that crucial spirit. It's not entirely clear where or why minds turned so stubborn. But to understand today's political calcification, it helps to recall a simpler time.

In the summer of 1994, the FBI and the Justice Department made a bold play to force the telecom carriers to help them conduct legal wiretaps. They put forth a proposal that would require the companies to build their networks so that law enforcement agents serving a warrant could access them in real time. The legality of wiretapping was not in question. The government wanted legal assurance that it could tap, at any time, and that the industry had an obligation under law to comply with the government's proper authority.

After months of haggling, the Communications Assistance for Law Enforcement Act passed in November 1994. CALEA would let the industry set its own standards to meet the Justice Department's needs. The department could list its surveillance requirements, but the act let companies decide how to build their equipment. Justice won the right to petition the Federal Communications Commission if its officials felt that the companies weren't fulfilling their obligations. But civil-liberties groups also secured the right to challenge the government's requirements in court.

Had the FBI and the Justice Department stopped there, had the government settled for secure access to phone networks, the history of Internet privacy and civil liberties might have turned out differently.

FBI officials knew in 1994 that they were making a mistake by leaving cyberspace out of CALEA. They understood the Internet's potential as a communications device and an intelligence tool—that is, after all, why CALEA's authors exempted "information services."

In early 1995, the Justice Department issued its list of requirements for wiretapping, known as the punch list. Not surprisingly, many telecom executives and their attorneys viewed the demands as unreasonable. Al Gidari, a lawyer representing the wireless industry, was among the first to see the FBI's requirements, during the initial meeting to develop standards for CALEA, which was held that spring in Vancouver, British Columbia. The Justice Department's wish list, he said, amounted to "the Cadillac of wiretaps."

Over the next few years, the Justice Department continued to seek increasingly sophisticated surveillance capabilities, including real-time geographical tracking of mobile phones; the ability to monitor all parties in a conference call regardless of whether they are on hold or participating; and "dialed digit extraction," a record of any numbers that a subject under surveillance punched in during a call, such as a credit card or bank account number. The government got a lot of what it wanted, but not all.

To be sure, criminals' use of new technologies helped drive the law enforcement demands. But telecom carriers worried that the cost of compliance was too high and that the FBI's technical requirements were illegally broad. CALEA, they argued, had forbidden the government from requiring specific system designs or technologies.

Justice, frustrated by its inability to get all the demands on the punch list, finally asked the Federal Communications Commission to step in. In 1997, the Cellular

which then represented mobile carriers, and the Center for Democracy and Technology complained to the commission that the negotiations had deadlocked because of "unreasonable demands by law enforcement for more surveillance features than either CALEA or the wiretap laws allow." The FCC, however, sided with the Justice Department on a host of requirements that privacy groups found overly broad. The tussle dragged on for two more years and ended up in the U.S. Court of Appeals for the District of Columbia Circuit, which overruled the FCC. After the commission took up matters again, it granted some of the FBI's requests, and the CALEA standards were amended.

The level of government surveillance was so low at that time that some questioned why the FBI wanted such multifaceted access at all. In 1994, federal and state authorities were running 1,154 wiretaps nationwide, mostly for drug investigations, at an average cost of $50,000. The government was asking carriers to "design a nuclear rocket ship" for a rarely used tool, Gidari thought. "In [the FBI's] view, there was no limit to the expense the carrier should spare in order to save a life."

CALEA continued to evolve, shaped by the ongoing arguments over the terms of its birth. Activists and carriers thought that the FBI was reneging on its bargain, asking for more than the law allowed. The FBI believed that carriers were stalling when they failed to meet compliance deadlines. As all sides dug in, the meetings on implementation turned bitter.

The government asked those same questions after September 11, 2001. And this time, telecommunications carriers responded. Outside the normal FISA warrant process, which covers intelligence-gathering, carriers opened access to their networks, their customer call data, and their valuable trans-

> **FBI and Justice officials slammed their hands on tables and screamed at carrier representatives,** Gidari recalls. "You're unpatriotic! What do you want to do, help the criminals?"

actional information—the kind that CALEA had intended to exclude. President Bush and his administration believed that the extraordinary nature of the terrorist attacks demanded emergency actions that FISA couldn't accommodate, and the carriers answered the call from law enforcement and intelligence agencies. But government officials also seized on the post-9/11 mentality to change other surveillance laws and procedures, which they believed—just as their predecessors did in 1994—were out of step with technology and reality. About three years after 9/11, officials set their sights on rewriting CALEA.

In August 2004, in response to a petition by the Justice Department, the FBI, and the Drug Enforcement Administration, the FCC expanded CALEA to cover Internet communications, including voice calls and instant messages. The Electronic Frontier Foundation sued, along with industry, civil-liberties, and academic groups. In 2005, the Court of Appeals ruled 2–1 to defer to the FCC's reading of the law.

Many of those who had helped craft CALEA believed that the commission had misread the law and acted on a post-9/11 impulse to give the government more, not less, access to information. But to the FCC, new Internet technologies that operate a lot like telephones blurred the distinction between "information services" and the kinds of technology that CALEA was meant to cover.

After 9/11, law enforcement and intelligence agencies took a variety of measures, apart from wiretaps, to collect and mine potentially valuable information from the Internet. With the cooperation of telecom companies, government accumulated lots of transactional data—including e-mail header information and lists of websites visited by targeted individuals—to support counterterrorism operations. Viewed solely as a reaction to the terrorist attacks of 2001, this kind of collection might seem extraordinary. But through the longer lens of history, the government's steady march into cyberspace is not surprising.

The FISA debate hung on whether companies that assisted warrantless surveillance after 9/11 should have retroactive legal immunity for any laws they may have broken. CALEA has something to say about that, too. The law requires that carriers be able to deliver call identification information to the government remotely. According to Beryl Howell, Sen. Leahy's lead CALEA staffer, that provision was meant to keep government agents from sitting in the phone companies' offices to execute their wiretaps.

It is a basic tenet of wiretapping law, whether for intelligence or law enforcement, that the communications companies act as a buffer between their customers and the government, she says, and that telecom carriers must make their own determination whether official requests should be honored.

FOR DISCUSSION: Will you support wiretaps, warrantless or otherwise, on new technologies like cell-phone and Internet use? Should telecom companies be responsible for protecting their clients' civil liberties? Will we need to rethink the protection of our civil liberties in the information age?

5

CIVIL RIG

FIRST
BAPTIST
CHURCH
of
DEANWOOD

HTS

TOWARD A MORE EQUAL CITIZENRY

THE LITIGIOUS CHEERLEADER ❙ Jennifer Gratz, a senior at Anderson High School in Southlake, Michigan, was the very picture of an all-American girl—blond, pretty, athletic, and socially active. She was a cheerleader, a student government representative, and homecoming queen. Jennifer had always dreamed of attending the University of Michigan as a premed student. Although neither of her parents had attended college, both stressed the importance of hard work, a message Jennifer took to heart. Besides her extracurricular activities, she was a National Honor Society member with a 3.79 grade point average that placed her twelfth in her class of 299 students. She was so confident of being admitted to the Ann Arbor campus that she applied to no other colleges.

Like any other high school senior, Jennifer waited anxiously for her letter of acceptance. One spring day after coming back from cheerleading practice, she saw the envelope from the University of Michigan. Her stomach churned when she realized the envelope was thin. Thin envelopes from universities typically mean rejection or placement on a waiting list. When she found out that the university had not accepted her, Jennifer could hardly believe her fate. She discovered that she had been rejected because of the University of Michigan's affirmative action program for undergraduate admission, which awarded 20 points to every applicant from a designated underrepresented group. Those groups included African Americans, Hispanics, and Native Americans. In order to gain admission, an applicant had to receive 100 of a possible 150 points. The automatic awarding of 20 points to members of certain groups was meant to ensure greater diversity among the student population. By receiving those 20 extra points, minority applicants with grades and extracurricular activities similar to Jennifer's were admitted, and she herself would have been accepted if she had been a member of an underrepresented group. Jennifer's first reaction was "I was discriminated against because of my race."[1] She then turned to her father and asked, "Can we sue them?"[2] ➥

As You READ >>

- How has the Supreme Court's attitude toward the civil rights of African Americans evolved?
- How have other minority groups benefited from the civil rights struggles of African Americans?
- What unique civil rights issues do women face in the United States today?

Jennifer's first reaction was "I was discriminated against because of my race." She then turned to her father and asked, "Can we sue them?"

Conservative interest groups had long believed that affirmative action produces reverse discrimination that punishes qualified white applicants, and their lawyers were looking for cases to advance their claim. One such group, the Center for Individual Rights (CIR), interviewed Jennifer and considered her the ideal litigant. She had no other agenda than to be treated fairly. She was attractive, poised, and confident in her beliefs. Most important, she was female. As one CIR spokesperson put it, "The perception of a man bringing a lawsuit like this is that he's an angry white male and he's bitter. I think the perception of Gratz is that she got a bad break. She doesn't have an ax to grind. She's appealing in a way that maybe not all white males would be."[3]

In 2003, Jennifer's case reached the United States Supreme Court, which found the university's undergraduate admissions program unconstitutional with respect to the equal protection clause of the Fourteenth Amendment. The 6-to-3 majority determined that by automatically awarding 20 points for minority status, the university failed to give the individual consideration to each applicant that equal protection demands. Jennifer won her case, but the wheels of justice turned too slowly for her to live her dream. After being denied admission to the university's Ann Arbor campus, she ended up going to a branch campus in Dearborn and living at home. She still wonders how different her life might have been if she had been able to go away to school on the university's main campus. Jennifer claims that the initial rejection affected her confidence and led her to conclude that she must not be smart enough to be a premed student. She became a mathematics major instead and now works for a vending machine company in California.

Jennifer Gratz challenged the undergraduate admissions program at the University of Michigan after being denied admission to the Ann Arbor campus.

Jennifer's case is instructive with respect to civil rights in the United States. Minority groups historically have faced great obstacles to achieving equality in the United States and have turned to the Supreme Court seeking justice. African Americans endured the degradation of slavery, segregation, and poverty in their quest for equality. The Supreme Court ultimately responded positively to their legal arguments by the way it reinterpreted equality. This interpretation, in turn, mobilized civil rights advocates who fought for other disadvantaged groups, such as Native Americans, Hispanic Americans, Asian Americans, the disabled, seniors, gay and lesbian groups, and women. Jennifer believed that earlier decisions made to protect the equality rights of these minority groups made her a victim of reverse discrimination. The story of disadvantaged groups' struggle for equality, and the impact it has had on the nation, is the subject of this chapter. ◄

AFRICAN AMERICANS AND CIVIL RIGHTS

Whereas civil liberties focus on the personal freedoms guaranteed individuals in the Bill of Rights, **civil rights** concern the protection of persons in historically disadvantaged groups from discriminatory actions. Civil rights constitute a positive action by government to guarantee that every person, regardless of his or her group identity, is treated as an equal member of society.[4] Yet despite espousing equality as one of the nation's core values, the United States has often failed to make that value a reality for millions of Americans. Many groups of Americans have had to struggle for equal rights.

Most people associate the quest for civil rights in the United States with the struggles of African Americans. American blacks were among the first groups to agitate for civil rights, and no other group has had to overcome comparable obstacles to equality: slavery, segregation, and discrimination in voting, housing, and employment. Their battle for equality has served as a road map for other mistreated groups in terms of both inspiration and tactics.

Slavery

When the delegates to the constitutional convention met in Philadelphia in 1787, slavery had existed in North America for nearly 170 years. By this time, the owners of large southern plantations relied heavily on slave labor to produce their cash crops. As a result, the southern delegates to the convention made it clear that they would never sacrifice slavery in order to achieve a new constitution. Although some northern delegates, such as Gouverneur Morris, denounced slavery, powerful southern opposition prevented any attempt to abolish slavery via the new constitution. In the end, each state was left to decide for itself whether to permit slavery.

> **civil rights** Protection of historically disadvantaged groups from infringement of their equality rights by discriminatory action.

The attempts by the nation's early leaders to prevent the issue of slavery from dividing the country were short-lived. As the nation's population moved westward in the early 1800s, northern and southern representatives faced a dilemma regarding the admission of new states to the Union. Would such states have free or slave status? The issue came to a head in 1820, when Missouri applied for admission to

Division of Free and Slave States After the Missouri Compromise

Free states and territories in 1820

Slave states and territories in 1820

Closed to slavery by the Missouri Compromise

Missouri Compromise Line (36°30')

Except for Missouri, new territories and states closed to slavery north of this line

Source: Alan Brinkley: *American History,* 2007, McGraw-Hill.

the Union as a slave state. Northern senators opposed Missouri's admission, which would give the states with slavery a majority of seats in the Senate. The Missouri Compromise temporarily settled this divisive issue by granting Missouri admission as a slave state and allowing Maine to enter the Union at the same time as a free state. The compromise also banned the admission of any slave states from the Northwest Territory above 36 degrees, 30 minutes north latitude, with the exception of Missouri. Unfortunately, the issue of slavery became even more volatile with the continued westward migration of settlers.

Dred Scott

At this explosive point in American history, the Supreme Court heard the *Dred Scott* case in 1857.[5] Scott was a slave whose owner held him in bondage while in the free state of Illinois and the free federal territory of Minnesota. Scott sued for his freedom, arguing that he was emancipated as soon as his owner took him into free territory. The Court, however, rejected Scott's argument, noting that African Americans had long been treated as an inferior race that was unfit to associate with whites in either social or political relations. As a result, they had no rights and thus could justly be reduced to slavery to be bought and sold as ordinary articles of merchandise. Hence, slaves could never be citizens and bring lawsuits to the courts. Chief Justice Roger Taney interpreted the Constitution to be consistent with this view. Taney's opinion went further, arguing that Congress lacked the authority to ban slavery in the Western territories because doing so violated the due process rights of slave owners to own property under the Fifth Amendment. The decision dealt a

Dred Scott was a slave who asked for his freedom in the federal courts and lost when the Supreme Court in 1857 ruled that slaves had no constitutional rights.

swift blow to Scott's freedom and the country's antislavery forces. It invalidated the Missouri Compromise and helped set the stage for the Civil War by removing any possibility for Congress to resolve the divisive issue of slavery in a manner that satisfied all Americans.

The Civil War and Reconstruction

The Civil War and the Reconstruction Period marked the end of slavery and the first great advance of civil rights in the United States. In 1862, at the height of the war, President Lincoln issued the Emancipation Proclamation. This executive order freed all the slaves in states that were still in rebellion as of January 1, 1863. Since the Emancipation Proclamation freed only those slaves living in the South, the complete abolition of slavery did not occur until the adoption of the **Thirteenth Amendment** in 1865. It provided that "neither slavery nor involuntary servitude" shall exist within the United States except as a punishment for the commission of a crime.

However, the passage of the Thirteenth Amendment did not ensure equality for African Americans. The eleven states of the former confederacy failed to ratify the **Fourteenth Amendment**, which provided all persons with the privileges and immunities of national citizenship, guaranteed equal protection under the laws of any state, and safeguarded due process to protect one's life, liberty, and property from state government interference. This led Congress to institute the Reconstruction Program, which was designed to prevent the mistreatment of former slaves in the South. Reconstruction legislation dissolved the state governments in the South and partitioned them into five military districts. These new governments enfranchised blacks and disqualified many white voters who had fought against the Union in the Civil War. Under such pressure, southern legislators ratified the Fourteenth Amendment in 1868. Two years later, the **Fifteenth Amendment** gave former slaves the right to vote.

Soon afterward, however, a partisan political deal at the highest levels of government dashed the hopes and aspirations of the former slaves. In the presidential campaign of 1876, electoral votes in three states were in dis-

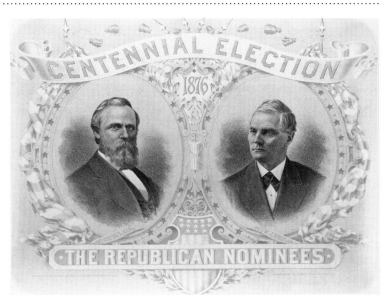

Samuel Tilden was the Democratic presidential candidate who won the popular vote in 1876, but the contested election was awarded to the Republican candidate, Rutherford B. Hayes, when the Republicans agreed to end Reconstruction in the South.

pute, making the election too close to call. Both Republican Rutherford B. Hayes and Democrat Samuel Tilden claimed victory. Congress established a bipartisan commission to determine the victor, but behind the scenes, the Republican Party forged a plan to retain control of the White House. It promised Democratic representatives from southern states that a Republican administration would withdraw federal troops from the South and provide funds to rebuild the area. The Democrats accepted the deal and the commission declared Hayes the winner, bringing the Reconstruction period to an end. The former slaves were once again at the mercy of their former oppressors.

Segregation

The constitutional amendments and the various civil rights laws of the Civil War era were of little value unless the federal government enforced them. Sadly, once federal troops pulled out of the South, most Northern whites lost interest in civil rights, and the former slave states went back to business as usual. This included segregated living, enforced by **Jim Crow laws** that required whites and African Americans to use separate hotels, separate restrooms, separate drinking fountains, and even separate cemeteries.[6] The laws also prohibited interracial marriage. Any violation of the segregation code could lead to violent reprisals by the Ku Klux Klan.

On June 7, 1892, Homer Plessy bought a ticket in New Orleans and boarded a train headed for Covington, Louisiana. He took a seat in the white

The Plessy decision ushered in the worst period of civil rights violations since the abolition of slavery.

coach, even though he later described himself as "seven-eights Caucasian and one-eighth African blood."[7] When Plessy refused to comply with the conductor's order to move, he was arrested for violating the new state of Louisiana's segregation law requiring railroads to carry blacks in separate cars. Plessy's arrest, however, was no accident, but the result of months of planning by the black community in New Orleans in cooperation with railroad officials (who otherwise would not have known Plessy's race). That event on a warm Louisiana day would culminate in a U.S. Supreme Court ruling that defined the status of civil rights in the country for decades to come.

> **Fifteenth Amendment** Civil War amendment that extended suffrage to former male slaves.
>
> **Jim Crow laws** Legislation in the South that mandated racial segregation in public facilities such as restaurants and restrooms.

Plessy appealed his conviction to the United States Supreme Court, where his attorney argued that racial segregation on train cars perpetuated the notion of black inferiority that accompanied the institution of slavery. Since the law did not apply to "nurses attending the children of the other race," he reasoned that this legal exception was made because whites were willing to endure blacks who had a clearly dependent status. As a result, he concluded, the law violated the spirit and intent of the Thirteenth Amendment that ended slavery and the Fourteenth Amendment that promised equal protection under the law.

In May 1896, the Supreme Court handed down its decision supporting the Louisiana law and Plessy's conviction.

Segregation in the South included separate restrooms for both races.

This case established the "separate but equal" doctrine that would dominate U.S. Supreme Court decisions for another fifty-eight years. Under this doctrine, the government considered segregated facilities legal as long as they were equal. In reality, the Court tolerated segregation even when the facilities were clearly unequal. The Plessy decision ushered in the worst period of civil rights violations since the abolition of slavery.

Voting Barriers

The end of Reconstruction, and subsequent Supreme Court decisions, provided southerners with an incentive to discriminate against African Americans and led to a pervasive attempt to deny blacks their rights under the Fifteenth Amendment. Southern officials argued that the amendment did not guarantee African Americans the right to vote but, rather, prohibited states from denying the right to vote on the basis of race or color. This led them to construct so-called "racially neutral" laws to prevent African Americans

from voting. Poll taxes, literacy tests, property qualifications, and even the notorious grandfather clause—a rule that an African American could not vote if his grandfather slave had not voted—could be used to exclude any voter who failed to meet the specific requirement.[8] In practice, these devices were used by white election officials to keep African Americans from voting; most African Americans were too poor to pay poll taxes or to own property and were not educated enough to pass a literacy test, and none of them had grandfathers who had been allowed to vote.

NAACP

African Americans watched with despair as the walls of segregation rose around them. Their hopes for equality that had been based on the Civil War amendments and civil rights laws were nearly gone. In 1909, the publisher of the *New York Evening Post,* who was the grandson of the famous abolitionist William Lloyd Garrison, called a conference to discuss the problem of "the Negro." The group soon evolved into the National Association for the Advancement of Colored People (NAACP).

By the 1930s, the leaders of the NAACP decided to test the constitutionality of *Plessy v. Ferguson* in the federal courts. Lacking the political clout to accomplish legislative change, they believed the federal courts in time might rule that the separate but equal doctrine was a barrier to any hope of equality for African Americans. The NAACP sponsored test cases as forums in which to present sociological data and statistics that provided the courts with evidence of discrimination. The organization decided to concentrate on the field of education, beginning with cases of segregation in graduate and professional schools. Because so few African Americans had attained such advanced educational levels, the NAACP reasoned that whites would be less threatened by such minor changes. They also reasoned that the courts would be more inclined to rule in their favor, because there was little chance that the government would have to implement the decision. Only later did they challenge the segregation of elementary and high schools, which would affect millions of students and the social mores of the country.[9]

The NAACP enjoyed several victories following this strategy, including successfully challenging the exclusion of an African American student from a state law school. The group later paved the way for the Court to declare unconstitutional the establishment of a segregated Texas law school for African Americans only.[10] The NAACP successfully argued that an African American student who was isolated in a segregated state graduate school was denied an equal education.[11]

Modern Era of Civil Rights

The success of the NAACP before the United States Supreme Court ushered in an era of a more equal citizenry. In each of the higher education cases mentioned, the Court decided that the plaintiffs had been denied the opportunity for an equal education. In other words, the facilities were separate but they were not equal. After 1950, the NAACP concluded it was time to change the plan of attack. It decided to pressure the Court to overrule the Plessy decision on the grounds that separate facilities, even if equal, were unconstitutional because segregation *itself* was unconstitutional under the equal protection clause of the Fourteenth

Did You Know?

. . . That the NAACP (National Association for the Advancement of Colored People) was formed by a group of black and white progressives at a meeting at Niagara Falls—on the Canadian side of the border, because on the U.S. side no hotel would rent rooms to blacks?

Amendment. The organization was now ready to challenge legal segregation in the nation's primary and secondary public schools.

Brown v. Board of Education The Brown case actually related to five separate cases brought against local school districts in Delaware, South Carolina, Virginia, the District of Columbia, and Kansas. The plaintiffs in each case challenged the legality of their districts' separate but equal laws. The new chief justice, Earl Warren, wrote the opinion for the unanimous Court striking down the separate but equal laws. Warren acknowledged that the original intent of the Framers of the Fourteenth Amendment was unclear, but argued, "We must consider public education in the light of its full development and its present place in American life throughout the Nation." He reasoned that modern public education was essential for full political participation because it opens up life opportunities and provides the basis for intelligent citizenship. Warren's opinion also confirmed the wisdom of the NAACP's tactic of relying on psychological and sociological studies in its brief, given the lack of legal precedents to support its cause. The unanimous Court held that to separate children from others because of their race generates within them a feeling of inferiority "that may affect their hearts and minds in a way very unlikely ever to be undone."

de jure segregation
Segregation mandated by law or decreed by government officials.

de facto segregation
Segregation that occurs because of past economic and social conditions such as residential racial patterns.

Because the Brown case dealt only with **de jure segregation**—discrimination by law—it primarily affected the southern states that had passed Jim Crow laws. It did not address **de facto segregation**—racial separation based on factual realities such as segregated housing patterns—which existed throughout the United States. In 1955, the following year, the Court ruled in *Brown II* that the racially segregated school systems must be abandoned "with all deliberate speed."[12] They also determined that federal district judges would enforce the decision, instead of state court judges who were more susceptible to local political pressure. Unfortunately, the phrase *with all deliberate speed* gave the southern states the opportunity to delay desegregation and ultimately to engage in massive resistance to the change.

Federal troops were needed to support the Supreme Court's school integration decision in Brown v. Board of Education.

Southern resistance to public school integration led to federal action on several occasions. In 1957, President Dwight D. Eisenhower sent federal troops to enforce the integration of the school system in Little Rock, Arkansas. Throughout the 1960s, Congress drafted major civil rights legislation to advance the cause of desegregation. Some federal judges ordered students bused to schools in other neighborhoods to achieve racially balanced school districts.[13] By 1995, however, support for direct federal intervention had declined, and the Court announced that it would not look favorably on continued federal control of districts like one in Kansas City that had spent millions of dollars under federal direction to attract white students from the suburbs.[14]

Civil Rights Mobilization

The *Brown* decisions sparked not only southern resistance but also a popular civil rights movement exemplified by people such as Rosa Parks. Parks was a petite woman who worked as a seamstress and served as the NAACP youth council adviser in Montgomery, Alabama. She had been active in NAACP activities such as voter registration drives, but she did not intend to launch a civil rights crusade on the Decem-

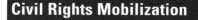

ber afternoon in 1955 when she refused to leave her seat in the front of the bus to make room for a white passenger. Her act of defiance was not only illegal but also dangerous. Montgomery's buses were segregated by law, and African Americans had been beaten and even killed for not obeying bus drivers. Parks later said she did not move because she thought she had the right to be treated the same way as any other passenger on the bus.

Police arrested Parks, who was later convicted of violating the state's segregation law and fined ten dollars. The NAACP responded by distributing handbills urging African Americans to boycott the Montgomery bus system to protest Parks's arrest. Martin Luther King, Jr., a recently arrived minister, emerged as a leader in the yearlong boycott effort. When a lower federal court finally ordered the buses to integrate, the tactic of nonviolent protest had proved its value. Parks received the Congressional Gold Medal in 1999, and upon her death in 2005, political leaders across the nation praised her efforts and character.

The civil rights movement spawned new groups in addition to the NAACP that pursued different strategies to secure equality for African Americans. King formed the Southern Christian Leadership Conference (SCLC), which spurned litigation as a major tactic and instead used nonviolent protest to achieve equality. Whereas the SCLC drew heavily on its base in the southern black community, other groups such as the Student Nonviolent Coordinating

Martin Luther King, Jr., drew national attention to the civil rights movement with his "I Have a Dream" speech in 1963.

Committee (SNCC) were more grassroots in orientation and recruited young people of all races. These new groups organized events (such as boycotts, sit-ins at segregated restaurants, and "freedom rides" pairing civil rights activists with college students) that were designed to draw attention to segregation of public accommodations. Martin Luther King, Jr., became the most famous civil rights leader in the country with his eloquence and courage. He grabbed national attention in August 1963 when he organized a massive march on Washington, D.C. and delivered his famous "I Have a Dream" speech: "I have a dream that my four little children will one day live in a nation where they will not be judged by the color of their skin but by the content of their character. I have a dream today." The march was intended to demonstrate widespread support for President John F. Kennedy's proposal to ban all discrimination in public accommodations, and to argue for an end to discrimination against African Americans in all aspects of life.

Montgomery's buses were segregated by law, and African Americans had been beaten and even killed for not obeying bus drivers.

Civil Rights Legislation

Senior southern Democrats in Congress, supported by conservative Republicans, opposed Kennedy's proposal. Because of their long tenure in Congress, these Democrats held key committee positions that allowed them to dominate both houses of Congress and frustrate the president's plans. Kennedy's assassination on November 22, 1963, changed the political landscape. His successor, Lyndon Johnson, was a Texan who had been a powerful majority leader in the Senate. He knew how to get legislation passed and he knew how to talk to the southern members of Congress. This knowledge, added to the wave of sympathy that accompanied the death of the young president, led Congress to pass the historic **Civil Rights Act of 1964**.[15]

The 1964 Civil Rights Act bars discrimination by public accommodations engaged in interstate commerce. For instance, a hotel that has customers from other states or orders any products from other states cannot refuse to serve customers based on their race.[16] The act also prohibits discrimination in employment on the grounds of race, religion, national origin, or sex. The law established the Equal Employment Opportunity Commission (EEOC) to enforce and monitor bans on employment discrimination and to withhold federal funds from state and local government programs that discriminate against providers or consumers. A year later, Congress passed the **Voting Rights Act of 1965**, which increased voter protections by outlawing literacy tests and by allowing federal officials to enter southern states to register African American voters. This provision enabled hundreds of thousands of African Americans to register to vote in southern states.

Civil Rights Act of 1964
Historic legislation that prohibited racial segregation in public accommodations and racial discrimination in employment, education, and voting.

Voting Rights Act of 1965
Federal legislation that outlawed literacy tests and empowered federal officials to enter southern states to register African American voters; the act dismantled the most significant barriers to African Americans' suffrage rights.

Retrospective

The efforts of those who participated in the civil rights movement dramatically changed the lives of African Americans and their role in civic life. The passage and enforcement of voting laws have resulted in substantial numbers of African Americans winning election to public office since

Household Incomes from 2002 to 2004 Using Average Medians

	Median Income
All races	$ 48,200
Whites	$ 52,000
Blacks	$ 32,060
Native Americans	$ 33,132
Asians	$ 64,200
Hispanics	$ 37,800

Source: U.S. Census Bureau, Washington, D.C., August 28, 2007.

rational basis test Equal protection test used by the Supreme Court that requires a complainant to prove that the use of a classification such as age, gender, or race is not a reasonable means of achieving a legitimate government objective.

intermediate scrutiny test Equal protection test used by the Supreme Court that requires the government to prove that the use of classifications such as age, gender, or race is substantially related to an important government objective.

strict scrutiny test Equal protection test used by the Supreme Court that places the greatest burden of proof on the government to prove that classifications such as age, gender, or race are the least restrictive means to achieve a compelling government goal.

affirmative action Programs that attempt to provide members of disadvantaged groups enhanced opportunities to secure jobs, promotions, and admission to educational institutions.

the 1960s. Although still underrepresented at the national level, even considering the election of Barack Obama, blacks have made considerable advances in state and local government. Today, it is not surprising to find an African American serving as a sheriff in Mississippi or as a mayor in Alabama. Blacks still have a long way to go, however, to achieve full equality in America. The income of the average African American family today is barely two-thirds that of the average white family. African Americans are more likely to be convicted of crimes than whites and are more likely to receive harsher punishments, including the death penalty. Many African Americans still live in segregated neighborhoods, and for them and others, the struggle for civil rights continues.

The struggle for civil rights is the struggle for equality. We have seen how Supreme Court decisions have both hindered and advanced the efforts of African Americans to achieve equality. In the next section, called "Interpreting Equality," we will examine how the Supreme Court interprets equality by creating judicial tests and by determining how to evaluate affirmative action programs.

INTERPRETING EQUALITY

When a disadvantaged group takes a discrimination case to the United States Supreme Court, its success depends on how the Court interprets the word *equality*. The word *equality*, however, appears nowhere in the original Constitution or the Bill of Rights. The Court must, thus, interpret the concept in the context of the Fourteenth Amendment, which guarantees that no state shall deny any person the "equal protection of the laws." In order to interpret equality, the Court has created judicial tests and responded to affirmative action programs.

Judicial Tests

The Court has stated that it prohibits only "invidious discrimination"—that is, discriminatory acts that have no rational basis. But who decides what is rational or reasonable? To answer that question, the Supreme Court constructs judicial tests, specific standards that a government policy must meet in order to be ruled constitutionally permissible. These tests specify which party has the burden of proof. That is, must the party challenging the policy prove that the policy is unconstitutional or must the government prove that the policy is constitutional? Since judicial tests are not part of the Constitution, the Supreme Court has great latitude to decide how and when to use them.

The Supreme Court has constructed three tests for cases arising under the equal protection clause of the Fourteenth Amendment. The oldest of these is known as the **rational basis test**. It considers whether a law that gives preference to one group over another is a reasonable means to achieve a legitimate governmental purpose. The rational basis test sets a high bar by compelling the litigant to prove that the legislature passed an unreasonable law. With this in mind, Justices Douglas and Marshall began to ask for additional tests to protect litigants.[17] In 1976, Justice Brennan authored a new test known as the **intermediate scrutiny test**. It places the burden of proof on the government, and its standards are considered more exacting than the means and ends requirements of the rational basis test. Even before Justice Brennan formulated the intermediate scrutiny test, the Supreme Court adopted the **strict scrutiny test** for racial discrimination cases. This test places the burden of proof on the government to prove that the law serves a compelling government end and that the racial classification law is the "least restrictive means" of achieving that end. Today, the Court uses the rational basis test for discrimination allegations based on economic status, sexual preference, or age; the intermediate scrutiny test for gender discrimination cases; and the strict scrutiny test for racial and ethnic discrimination cases.

Affirmative Action

The quest for civil rights has come to mean more than the elimination of biased behavior toward certain groups. It has also come to mean that government should provide remedies to promote equality. As early as the 1940s, presidents issued executive orders to attempt to expand federal government employment opportunities for African Americans. Since that time, both the government and the private sector have sponsored **affirmative action** programs to ensure equality for historically disadvantaged groups and to eliminate the effects of past discrimination. Affirmative action programs attempt to clear a path to the good life for those whose progress was blocked in the past. Their goals include helping members of disadvantaged groups gain admission to universities, secure employment in all occupational fields, and win promotions once hired.

Affirmative action programs move beyond the traditional notion of equality of opportunity to promote the goal of equality of outcome. Instead of aiming to ensure that everyone has the same chance to receive a good education or good job, they strive to ensure that every group in society has the same rate of success in attaining a good education and a good job. In order to secure equal results, affirmative action promotes preferential treatment for members of groups that have suffered from "invidious discrimination." Such programs typically create separate racial classifications and provide members of historically disadvantaged groups with preferential consideration for admission to universities or promotion in the workplace.

Racial Classifications

The Supreme Court responded to this approach for the first time in the case of ***Regents of the University of California v. Bakke*** (1978). In order to increase minority student enrollment, the University of California at Davis developed two admissions programs to fill the one hundred seats in its freshman medical school class. The regular admissions program evaluated candidates on the basis of undergraduate grades, standardized test scores, extracurricular activities, letters of recommendation, and an interview. The special admissions program was reserved for applicants who indicated they were economically or educationally disadvantaged or who were African American, Chicano, Asian, or Native American. Those in the special admissions program were judged on the same factors as the other applicants, but they competed only against each other. Sixteen of the one hundred seats for the entering class were filled from the special admissions program.

In 1973, Allan Bakke, at the age of thirty-three, applied for admission to the University of California at Davis medical school. Bakke was a white male who had graduated with honors from the engineering program at the University of Minnesota, had received a master's degree in engineering from Stanford, had worked for the National Aeronautics and Space Administration, and was a Vietnam veteran. He was denied admission in both 1973 and 1974. Arguing that his qualifications were higher than those admitted under the special admissions program, Bakke sued. He claimed that the university's dual admissions program violated the equal protection clause of the Fourteenth Amendment.

The Supreme Court was deeply divided over this case. Four justices had serious reservations about affirmative action programs, four strongly supported them, and Justice Powell was caught in the middle. Justice Powell sided with the first group in holding that the university had used race to discriminate against Bakke, who should be admitted to the medical school. Powell applied the strict scrutiny test to the university's admission program, concluding that even though a diverse student body is a compelling governmental interest, the use of racial quotas was an impermissible means of achieving that interest. However, he did align with the affirmative action supporters by stating that such programs were permissible if they did not include quotas and used race as just one of many factors in considering admission.

Regents of the University of California v. Bakke The 1978 Supreme Court case that declared unconstitutional the use of racial quotas to achieve a diverse student body but allowed the use of race as one of many factors in admissions decisions.

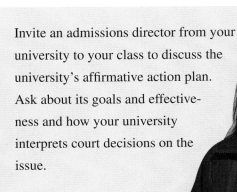

get involved!

Invite an admissions director from your university to your class to discuss the university's affirmative action plan. Ask about its goals and effectiveness and how your university interprets court decisions on the issue.

The *Bakke* case left many questions unanswered. Exactly how could racial classifications be used in university admissions programs? Could racial quotas be used to increase employment opportunities for racial minorities? Could gender classifications be used in affirmative action programs?

The Supreme Court has answered these questions over the past few decades. In 1979, the Court held that an apprenticeship training program at a Kaiser Aluminum and Chemical plant in Louisiana was legal, even though it contained racial quotas.[18] The Court stressed that the company and the United Steelworkers union voluntarily agreed to implement the program and that the plan was temporary in nature. Eight years later, it upheld the use of racial quotas to reverse the effects of long-standing discrimination in the Alabama Department of Public Safety.[19] The Court has also ordered quotas for minority union memberships and added gender as a category to be included in private affirmative action programs.[20]

Current Impact on Education

The Supreme Court reconsidered the constitutionality of affirmative action programs in the 1990s. The court held that federal laws classifying people by race were unconstitutional, even if they were designed to achieve well-meaning

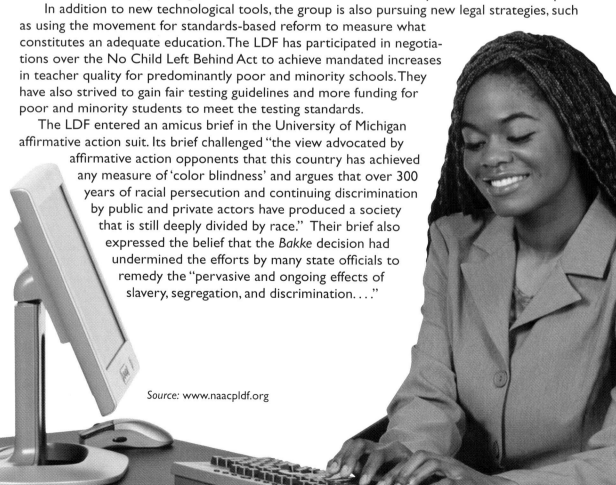

PARTICIPATION today   CIVIL RIGHTS ON THE INTERNET

A half-century after the *Brown* decision, the NAACP Legal Defense and Educational Fund, Inc. (LDF), the organization responsible for civil rights litigation success on behalf of African Americans, is still concerned about education in the United States. Today, the group has moved into cyberspace with a website that includes current issues, amicus briefs filed before the Supreme Court, the announcement of pending cases and case results, and the availability of summer internships.

In addition to new technological tools, the group is also pursuing new legal strategies, such as using the movement for standards-based reform to measure what constitutes an adequate education. The LDF has participated in negotiations over the No Child Left Behind Act to achieve mandated increases in teacher quality for predominantly poor and minority schools. They have also strived to gain fair testing guidelines and more funding for poor and minority students to meet the testing standards.

The LDF entered an amicus brief in the University of Michigan affirmative action suit. Its brief challenged "the view advocated by affirmative action opponents that this country has achieved any measure of 'color blindness' and argues that over 300 years of racial persecution and continuing discrimination by public and private actors have produced a society that is still deeply divided by race." Their brief also expressed the belief that the *Bakke* decision had undermined the efforts by many state officials to remedy the "pervasive and ongoing effects of slavery, segregation, and discrimination. . . ."

Source: www.naacpldf.org

ends.[21] As a result, several states enacted legislation that banned the use of racial preferences in education. In *Hopwood v. Texas* (1996), the Fifth Circuit Court of Appeals held that preferential policies affecting admission to the state universities in Texas, Mississippi, and Louisiana violated the Fourteenth Amendment. The state of California dropped its affirmative action program in light of this ruling. The elimination of these affirmative action programs significantly decreased the proportion of African American and Hispanic students in the California university system. The greatest benefactors of the new race-blind admissions policy were Asian students. The same pattern was evident at the University of Texas, where Asian Americans made up 18 percent of the entry class by the end of the century but only 3 percent of the state's population.[22]

Many believed the Supreme Court would clarify its position on affirmative action when it agreed to hear two appeals challenging affirmative action programs at the University of Michigan. *Gratz v. Bollinger* (2003) challenged the university's undergraduate admissions policies, and *Grutter v. Bollinger* (2003) questioned the admissions policies for the University of Michigan law school. The *Gratz* case overturned the undergraduate admissions program, but the Court reached a different result in the law school case.

The University of Michigan Law School's admissions policy looked beyond test scores and grade point averages

The policy of affirmative action has led to protests of reverse discrimination.

in order to admit a diverse student body. Its goal was to achieve a critical mass of minority students so that they would not feel isolated or feel the need to be spokespersons for their race. The policy did not set quotas for members of underrepresented groups, nor did it award points for minority status. The Court ruled that this admissions policy was narrowly tailored and permitted the individual review of applicants in a nonmechanical way.

The Court clarified its position in 2007 when it held that public school systems could not use voluntary programs designed to integrate schools that take explicit account of a student's race. In outlawing the programs of Louisville, Kentucky, and Seattle, Washington, Chief Justice Roberts wrote for the five-person majority that "the way to stop discrimination on the basis of race is to stop discriminating on the basis of race."[23] The dissenting justices angrily denounced the decision—one that will affect the assignment of students to schools in hundreds of school districts across the United States—as a break from the famous *Brown* decision of 1954.

Hot or Not?

Do you think that affirmative action programs for school admissions should be eliminated?

Continuing Controversy

The constitutionality of affirmative action programs is still uncertain in many areas, and the debate about the wisdom of these policies continues. Opponents of affirmative action programs believe that merit is the only fair way to distribute the benefits of society.[24] They claim that such programs amount to unfair **reverse discrimination** and argue that both the Fourteenth Amendment and the 1964 Civil Rights Act prohibit the use of racial discrimination. They feel that keeping Alan Bakke out of medical school is an example of racial discrimination. Supporters, on the other hand, argue that merit is not always self-evident and may include subjective considerations. They assert not only that affirmative action is necessary to compensate for the effects of past discrimination but also that it benefits the entire community by taking advantage of the talents of all citizens participating in a diverse social, economic, and political environment. Finally, they point to research that indicates that gains for disadvantaged groups come with only small costs to white males.[25] As we will see, these groups include

reverse discrimination
Argument that the use of race as a factor in affirmative action programs constitutes unconstitutional discrimination against the majority population.

not only African Americans but also a wide range of other minorities, and even the largest single segment of the U.S. population—women.

OTHER MINORITY GROUPS

African Americans no longer represent the largest ethnic minority in the United States. The nation's Hispanic and Asian populations, in particular, have grown substantially since 1990. Many of these other minority groups have benefited to varying degrees from the African American struggle to secure equal rights. The victories won by the black civil rights movement gave hope to other minorities that they, too, could work successfully to overcome historical discrimination.

rights. One author has referred to American Indian policy as "genocide-at-law" because it encouraged both the land confiscation and cultural extermination of the native population.[26] The government forcibly resettled the displaced Native Americans onto isolated reservations. In the 1880s, Congress adopted a new strategy of assimilating Native Americans into the mainstream of cultural life. Legislation banned native languages and rituals and required children to attend boarding schools located off the reservation. The federal government did not grant Native Americans citizenship and the right to vote until 1924. It took another twenty-two years after that for Congress to settle financial claims resulting from the confiscation of native lands.

Despite their poor treatment at the hands of the government, Native Americans formed no formal social or political movements to protest their unequal status until the 1960s. At the height of the civil rights movement, however, Native Americans began to mobilize. Indian activists such as Dennis Banks and Russell Means of the American Indian Movement (AIM) drew attention to the plight of Native

ONE AUTHOR has referred to American Indian policy as "genocide-at-law" because it encouraged both the land confiscation and cultural extermination of the native population.

Native Americans

Government policy toward Native Americans has gone from genocide and isolation to assimilation, and finally to citizenship. Congress and the federal courts initially promoted westward expansion at the expense of Indian

Americans. In 1969, Indian activists seized Alcatraz Island in San Francisco to dramatize the loss of Indian lands. Two years later, Dee Brown published the best-selling book, *Bury My Heart at Wounded Knee*,[27] which focused on the 1890 massacre of nearly three hundred Sioux by the United States Cavalry in Wounded Knee, South Dakota. The book helped to mobilize public opinion against the poor treatment of Native Americans in much the same way as Harriet Beecher Stowe's *Uncle Tom's Cabin* did for African Americans a century earlier. In 1973, armed members of AIM held hostages at Wounded Knee for seventy-one days until the national government agreed to consider Indian treaty rights.

Like the NAACP, Native Americans began to use the courts to accomplish their goals, filing hundreds of test cases and forming the Native American Rights Fund (NARF) to finance them. Their victories include the securing of land, hunting and fishing rights, and access to ancient burial grounds and other sacred locations. The 1968 Civil Rights Act included an Indian Bill of Rights, leading one author to conclude that Native Americans have now entered the self-determination phase of their history.[28] Nevertheless, Native Amer-

Population Increases by Race and Ethnicity from 1990 to 2050

Racial or ethnic category	Percent of population in 1990	Percent increase by 2000	Percent increase by 2050 (projection)
White	75.1	5.9	7
Black	12.3	15.6	71
Native American	0.9	26.4	–
Asian	3.6	46.3	213
Hispanic	12.5	57.9	188

Source: www.anthro.palomor.edu.

icans still suffer more than most Americans from ill health, poverty, and poor educational opportunities. Nearly half live on or near a reservation.

An ongoing area of controversy for Native Americans is the continued use of stereotypical and demeaning names and mascots by some professional and collegiate athletic teams. Native Americans have called upon the NFL's Washington Redskins and major league baseball's Atlanta Braves to change their team names. They have also complained about what they consider the offensive caricature of a Native American used as a mascot by baseball's Cleveland Indians. At the college level, the NCAA adopted a new restriction on the use of Native American nicknames, mascots, and logos. Thirty schools have been asked to explain their use of such items under a new appeals system. Some college teams, such as the Florida State Seminoles, the Utah Utes, and the Central Michigan Chippewas, have been allowed to keep their nicknames after deliberations with the NCAA. Other universities continue to appeal.

Hispanic Americans

Hispanic Americans are currently the largest minority group in the United States, making up nearly 13 percent of the country's population. They come primarily from Puerto Rico, Mexico, Cuba, El Salvador, and Honduras. Immigrants from Mexico make up the majority of Hispanics in California, Arizona, Texas, and New Mexico, while large numbers of Caribbean Hispanics populate the states of New York, New Jersey, and Florida.

As with Native Americans, the Hispanic American drive for civil rights began in earnest during the mid-1960s. His-

Hispanic Categories in the United States

Salvadoran 3%
Dominican 2%
Cuban 3.5%
Puerto Rican 9%
All other Hispanic 18.5%
Mexican 64%

Source: Estimated Hispanic Population as of July 1, 2006. U.S. Census Bureau, 2007.

Cities with Large Numbers of Hispanics

City	Number of Hispanics	Hispanic Population (%)
New York	2,160,554	27
Los Angeles	1,719,023	46.5
Chicago	753,644	26
Houston	730,865	37.4
San Antonio	671,394	58.7
Phoenix	449,972	34.1
El Paso	431,875	76.6
Dallas	422,587	35.8
San Diego	310,752	25.4

Source: www.anthro.palomor.edu.

panic leaders carefully observed African American groups and adopted many of the same tactics. Inspired by the NAACP's Legal Defense Fund, Hispanics formed similar organizations, including the Mexican American Legal Defense and Educational Fund (MALDEF). They, too, brought test cases before the courts to realize goals such as implementing bilingual education, increased funding for schools in low-income minority districts, ending employment discrimination against Hispanic Americans, and challenging election rules that diluted Hispanic voting power.

Like other minority groups, Hispanic Americans did not depend exclusively on litigation in their struggle for civil rights. Drawing again on the experiences of African Americans, they staged sit-ins, marches, boycotts, and other related activities to draw attention to their concerns. The best-known Hispanic protest leader, César Chávez, organized strikes by farm workers in the late 1960s and 1970s to attain basic labor rights for migrant workers. Migrants worked long hours for little pay, lived in substandard housing that often lacked plumbing and electricity, and were unwelcome in the local schools. When farm owners refused to bargain with his group, Chavez launched a national boycott of California lettuce and grapes. The boycott was successful as American consumers sided with

Agricultural strikes in the 1960s and 1970s alerted the nation to the harsh economic plight of migrant workers.

the plight of migrant workers. Responding to the pressure, California passed a law giving migrant workers the right to collectively bargain.

Hispanic Americans have clearly benefited from the 1964 Civil Rights Act and other important civil rights legislation first implemented to aid African Americans. For example, a 1968 amendment to the 1964 act funded public school programs that offer English instruction in the language of children for whom English is a second language. In addition, today there are more than five thousand elected Hispanic officials across the United States. The high-profile victory of Antonio Villaraigosa in the 2005 Los Angeles mayoral race signals that this trend is going to continue.

Asian Americans

The first Asian immigrants to this country were Chinese and Japanese laborers who came to the western United States during the late 1800s to build railroads and to work in mines. When the need for railroad laborers declined, Congress passed legislation in 1882 to temporarily halt Chinese immigration. Over the next three decades, the country barred all but a few Asians through a series of informal agreements with Asian governments. In 1921, Congress began to set immigration quotas based on the country of origin. Western European nations were given large quotas and Asian countries very small ones. Only 150 persons of Japanese origin, for instance, could enter the United States annually. In 1930, Congress prohibited immigration from Japan altogether after the Japanese government protested a California law barring anyone of Japanese descent from buying property in the state. Discrimination against Asian immigration did not end until 1965, when Congress adjusted quotas to favor those groups who had previously been targets of discrimination.

World War II marked the darkest chapter in the history of Japanese American civil rights. The Japanese attack on

Many Hispanic Americans shared Governor Bill Richardson of New Mexico's support in endorsing Senator Barack Obama (D-IL) as the 2008 Democratic presidential candidate.

Americans' academic success has not yet been matched by corresponding positions in business management, the professions, or political office; nor have young Asian Americans exhibited high levels of political engagement.

Disabled Americans

After every war over the last century, disabled Americans have lobbied hard for antidiscrimination laws. World War I veterans were largely responsible for the first rehabilitation laws passed in the late 1920s. Following the civil rights campaigns of the 1960s, World War II, Korean War, and Vietnam War veterans saw the success other minority groups were having with respect to civil rights laws and began to work for greater protection for disabled Americans.[29] The 1973 Rehabilitation Act added people with disabilities to the list of Americans who were to be protected from discrimination. The 1975 Education of All Handicapped Children Act entitled all children to a free public education appropriate to their needs. Prior to the legislation, four million disabled students were receiving either no education or one that did not fit their needs.

> **Korematsu v. United States**
> The 1944 Supreme Court decision that upheld the constitutionality of the U.S. government's internment of more than one hundred thousand Americans of Japanese descent during World War II.

The crowning piece of legislation for Americans with disabilities was the 1990 Americans with Disabilities Act (ADA). It guarantees access to public facilities, workplaces, and communication services. No longer can the

During World War II, more than 100,000 Japanese Americans living in the states of California, Oregon, and Washington were placed in internment camps.

Pearl Harbor that brought the United States into the war made Japanese Americans the objects of great fear and hatred, especially on the West Coast. Shortly after Pearl Harbor, Japanese Americans living on the West Coast were subject to nightly curfews. In February 1942, President Franklin D. Roosevelt issued an executive order removing more than one hundred thousand Japanese Americans from their homes in California, Oregon, and Washington and placing them in internment camps for the duration of the war. In *Korematsu v. United States* (1944), the United States Supreme Court ruled the internment was constitutional. Noting the law was based on a racial classification, the Court applied the strict scrutiny test. The Court held, however, that the security of the United States was a compelling governmental interest and that interning Japanese Americans was the least restrictive means to identify potentially disloyal members of the population. Concluding that war involved hardship, the Court ruled the treatment of Japanese Americans was not a civil rights violation. In the late 1980s, Congress expressed its disagreement with this view and granted benefits to former internees.

Asian Americans are the fastest-growing minority group in the United States today, growing from 0.5 percent to over 4 percent of the population in the last half century. They have gained prominent positions in American society and experienced notable academic success based solely on merit. They may still be subject to discrimination, however. Asian

Voting Rates by Ethnic Groups

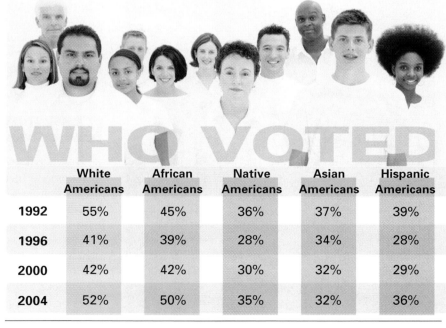

	White Americans	African Americans	Native Americans	Asian Americans	Hispanic Americans
1992	55%	45%	36%	37%	39%
1996	41%	39%	28%	34%	28%
2000	42%	42%	30%	32%	29%
2004	52%	50%	35%	32%	36%

Source: www.civicyouth.org.

stairs, telephones, and buses that kept this minority group out of schools, offices, theaters, and restaurants be used as excuses to deny access. The statute required schools, governments, and businesses to make existing facilities accessible. Wheelchair ramps and grab bars in restrooms have become common sights on the American landscape since 1990. Yet a 2004 survey conducted by *USA Today* of disabled Americans reveals that a majority of them do not believe the law has made a difference in their lives and that four in ten do not expect their quality of life to improve.

Recent Supreme Court rulings have both extended and limited the impact of the ADA. In 1999, the Court ruled that students who require special care at school are entitled to it as long as they do not need a physician to deliver that care.[30] The year before, the Court added persons afflicted with acquired immune deficiency syndrome (AIDS) to the list of those persons protected by the ADA.[31] In contrast, the Court ruled that people with bad eyesight or high blood pressure were not protected, because they can function normally when they wear glasses or take their medicine.[32] Do the 2007 revelations of the dirty facilities, rats, mold-encrusted walls, and poor outpatient treatment for wounded veterans at the Army's Walter Reed Hospital indicate a reduced concern for the handicapped today?

American Seniors

Today, 38 million Americans are sixty-five years of age or older, and that number is likely to double by the year 2025. You will read later about the emergence of "gray power" in

Older Americans continue to work for material and social reasons but they often face discrimination in the workplace.

the political system. The American Association of Retired Persons, for example, has become one of the most powerful interest groups in Washington, D.C., advocating for seniors' rights. Nevertheless, elderly Americans still face various forms of age discrimination such as mandatory retirement rules and cost-cutting measures that target older, higher-paid workers for termination or layoffs. Some professional and graduate schools reject older applicants on the grounds that they will have fewer years to work in their professions upon graduation.

At the height of the civil rights movement in 1967, Congress passed the Age Discrimination in Employment Act (ADEA) that protected workers over the age of forty from age discrimination unless an employer proved that age was a bona fide occupational qualification. The law even applied to an older worker who was replaced by a younger worker who also fell under the protection of ADEA.[33] In 1975, civil rights legislation denied federal funds to any institution discriminating against persons over forty because of their age. Congress amended the ADEA in 1978 to raise the age of mandatory retirement from sixty-five to seventy. In 1986, Congress phased out mandatory retirement for all but a few occupations, such as firefighting.

In dealing with cases of age discrimination, the Supreme Court uses the rational basis test. It has, however, upheld a state law requiring police officers to retire at the age of fifty.[34] In 2000, by contrast, the Court made it easier to win age discrimination cases with circumstantial evidence and inferences drawn from that evidence.[35] In the 2005 case of *Smith v. City of Jackson, Mississippi*, the Court may have also expanded the protection of the ADEA. The Court ruled that a person forty years of age or older can sue if an employer's policies, practices, or other employment actions have a negative effect on older employees, even if unintentional. But in another ruling, the Court, on the basis of the doctrine of sovereign immunity, disallowed age discrimination suits by plaintiffs against any state and local government entities without their consent.[36] Seniors fared better in a 2008 Court decision regarding the federal government. A seven-member majority ruled that federal workers who file claims of age discrimination have the same protections from retaliation as they would in the private sector.[37]

Gay and Lesbian Americans

Some scholars argue that gay and lesbian Americans have had a more difficult time in achieving equality than other minority groups.[38] They must contend with negative stereotyping and **homophobia**. This fear and hatred of homosexuals is deeply rooted in our culture and sometimes finds violent expression. The death of political science student Matthew Shepard is a particularly poignant example. The twenty-one-year-old University of Wyoming student was attacked after attending a meeting for Gay Awareness Week on his campus. After being hit repeatedly in the head with a pistol, and kicked repeatedly in the groin, he was left tied to a fence to die by himself.

Attitudes Toward Gay Rights Depend on Whether the Respondent Knows a Gay or Lesbian Person

homophobia Irrational fear and hatred directed toward persons who are homosexuals.

Gay couples should be able to adopt — 28% / 50%

Gay partners should have social security benefits — 43% / 60%

Gay and lesbian people should serve openly in the military — 48% / 63%

Hate-crime laws should include violence committed against gay and lesbian people — 54% / 69%

Gay partners should have inheritance rights — 50% / 73%

Gay and lesbian people should have equal rights in employment — 77% / 90%

Doesn't know someone gay or lesbian
Knows someone gay or lesbian

Source: www.hrc.org. Oct. 4, 2006.

Although exact numbers are difficult to obtain, millions of Americans identify themselves as homosexual. Homosexuals enjoy higher average incomes and educational levels than other minority groups, but until recently they were

The triggering event of the gay and lesbian rights movement in the United States was a police raid on the Stonewall Inn in New York City on June 27, 1969. The patrons of the popular gay and lesbian bar responded by throwing beer bottles and cans to protest what they viewed as constant police harassment. Stonewall had a galvanizing effect on the gay community. "Gay Power" signs appeared in the city, and gay and lesbian groups such as the Gay Activist Alliance and the Gay Liberation Front began to organize to combat invidious discrimination. Soon hundreds, and then thousands, of state and local organizations sprang up to exert pressure on legislatures, the media, churches, and schools to change laws and public attitudes toward homosexuals.

Gay and lesbian groups have achieved some significant political results at the state and local levels of government. Presently, twelve states and more than two hundred cities have statutes protecting gays and lesbians from discrimination in employment, credit, housing, and public accommodations. In 1996, the United States Supreme Court struck down an amendment to the Colorado state constitution that invalidated state and local laws protecting gays and lesbians. The Court held the Colorado amendment to be in violation of the equal protection clause of the U.S. Constitution.[39]

At the national level, the government has lifted a ban on hiring gay men and lesbians and repealed a law that prohibited gay men and lesbians from immigrating to the United States. President Bill Clinton's attempt to lift the ban on gays in the armed services, however, met resistance from military leaders who viewed homosexuality as incompatible with military service. The resulting "Don't ask, don't tell" compromise policy prevented the military from inquiring about soldiers' sexual orientation but also barred gay and lesbian soldiers from revealing their homosexuality. The new pol-

PRESENTLY, TWELVE STATES and more than two hundred cities have statutes protecting gays and lesbians from discrimination in employment, credit, housing, and public accommodations.

not able to convert these resources into an effective drive for equal rights. Overcoming cultural bias and the strong stance taken by many religious groups against homosexuality has proved to be a daunting task. Most Americans' attitudes about the rights of homosexuals, however, depend on whether they know a gay or lesbian person.

icy has not served gay and lesbian military personnel well. Since the policy went into effect in 1993, over 7,800 gay men and women have been forced out of the military.

Privacy has been an area of particular concern for gay and lesbian civil rights activists. In the 1970s and 1980s, they were successful in reducing the number of states

Gay and lesbian couples continue to face difficulties in winning the right to enter into same-sex marriages.

with antisodomy laws from forty-nine to twenty-four, using both state legislative and judicial strategies. In 1986, however, the United States Supreme Court ruled that antisodomy legislation in the state of Georgia was constitutional. It held that homosexual sex acts were not a fundamental liberty that was protected by the right to privacy in the Fourteenth Amendment.[40] The Court reversed itself seventeen years later in the case of *Lawrence v. Texas* (2003), ruling that the Fourteenth Amendment protects consenting adults engaging in homosexual behavior in the privacy of their homes. On the other hand, the same Court upheld the Boy Scouts' refusal to allow a gay man to serve as a troop leader, based on the premise that such a leader would undermine the organization's "morally straight" values.[41]

One of the most sensitive and controversial issues regarding gay and lesbian rights has been the legalization of same-sex marriages. The issue gained heightened attention in 1993 when the Supreme Court of Hawaii ruled that denying marriage licenses to gay couples might violate the equal protection clause of their state constitution.[42] Other states then began to worry that under the "full faith and credit clause" of the United States Constitution, they might be forced to accept the legality of same-sex marriages performed in Hawaii—or any other state that chose to legalize same-sex marriage. Opponents advocated state laws banning same sex marriages, and a number of states enacted such laws. In 1996, Congress passed the Defense of Marriage Act, which prohibits federal recognition of gay and lesbian couples and allows state governments to ignore same-sex marriages performed in other states.

The issue ignited again in 1999 when the Supreme Court of Vermont ruled that gay couples are entitled to the same benefits of marriage as heterosexual couples.[43] The next year, the Vermont legislature passed a statute permitting homosexual couples to form **civil unions**. The law entitled these couples to receive the same state benefits as married couples, including insurance benefits and inheritance rights. More public attention followed in 2004, when cities such as San Francisco began performing same-sex marriages. Media images of gay and lesbian couples waiting in line to be married spurred opponents to initiate referenda banning same-sex marriages. On the day George Bush was reelected to the presidency in 2004, ballot initiatives banning same-sex marriages passed easily in eleven states. Two years later, voters in seven states passed ballot measures amending their state constitutions to recognize marriage only between a man and a woman. The issue will probably continue to divide the American electorate as it did last year, when the California Supreme Court ruled that same-sex marriages could begin in the state as of June 17. Public opinion is still divided on such marriages and civil unions.

A Majority Supports Civil Unions for Gay Couples

	% Favor	% Oppose	% Don't know
July 2006	54	42	4
July 2005	53	40	7
August 2004	48	45	7
October 2003	45	47	8
East	62	33	5
Midwest	49	48	3
South	46	50	4
West	65	29	6
Total Protestant	43	53	4
White Evangelical	30	66	4
White Mainline	66	30	4
Black Protestant	35	62	3
Total Catholic	63	32	5
White, non-Hispanic	59	36	5
Unaffiliated	78	18	4
Religious attendance			
Weekly or more	36	60	4
Less often	67	29	4

Source: Pew Research Center surveys, 2003–2006.

WOMEN AND CIVIL RIGHTS

The fight for civil rights by women in America differs in many respects from the struggles of the previously discussed minority groups. First, women do not represent a minority in the United States; there are more women than men in the country, and they vote in greater numbers than men. Their struggle for equal rights, therefore, is not based on their small numbers but rather on long-standing historical and cultural assumptions concerning their proper role in society. Second, women began their struggle for civil rights as early as the African American movement but were thwarted by the dominant male culture. In other words, the civil rights movement for African Americans was not so much a template for the woman's movement as a parallel movement to it.

Historically there have been three high points of activity for the pursuit of women's civil rights, followed by years of little visible or public activity. This section will examine those three periods of activity and feature three issues of current concern: workplace and educational fairness, sexual harassment, and women's role in the military.

Women's Mobilization Eras

Although women as early as Abigail Adams discussed the concept of political equality with their prominent husbands, the most active periods of female political mobilization occurred from 1840 to 1875, from 1890 to 1920, and from 1961 to the present.[44]

Early Women's Movement: 1840–1875

The seeds of the early women's movement were planted in 1840 when Lucretia Mott and Elizabeth Cady Stanton accompanied their husbands to London to attend a meeting of the World Anti-Slavery Society. After a long debate, the male participants denied the women the right to participate at the meeting and relegated them to sitting in the balcony as spectators. This rebuff was partially

The suffrage initiative became a broad social movement that led to women getting the right to vote in 1920.

responsible for their determination to work on behalf of women's rights in the United States. Their work was delayed for eight years, however, because both women were raising young children.

The early women's movement was also an outgrowth of religious revivalism.[45] Women who were active in the abolition movement established communication networks among themselves, laying the foundation for the first women's movement in the United States. In 1848, Mott and Stanton organized the first women's rights convention in the small town of Seneca Falls, New York. Over the next twelve years, women's rights groups held seven conventions in different cities. With the outbreak of the Civil War, the movement temporarily suspended its activities to support the Union war effort. After the war, the early feminists learned a cruel political lesson. Despite the critical role they played in abolishing slavery, women were not granted the right to vote in the Fifteenth Amendment. In 1875, the U.S. Supreme Court upheld Missouri's denial of voting rights for women.[46]

> **civil union** Legal recognition by a state of a gay or lesbian relationship; allows gay and lesbian couples to receive the same state benefits as heterosexual married couples.

The Suffrage Movement: 1890–1920

In 1890, women's rights advocates formed the National American Woman Suffrage Association (NAWSA), with Susan B. Anthony as its leader. Rather than trying to seek expanded social, legal, economic, and political rights for women, the new association concentrated primarily on

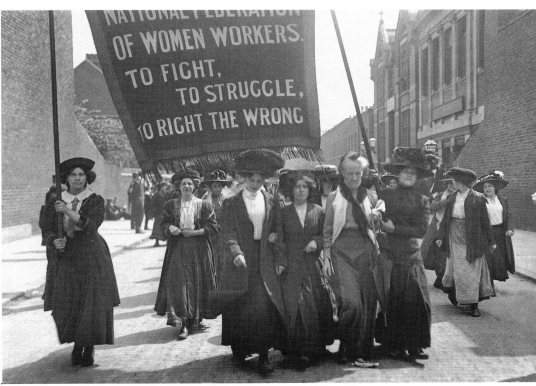

Did You Know?

... *That Susan B. Anthony, one of the pioneers of the woman's rights movement in nineteenth-century America and president of the National American Woman Suffrage Association, was several times arrested from 1872 to 1873 for attempting to vote after the Fifteenth Amendment (which had given the vote to African American men) was ratified?*

securing the vote. Contemporary social trends such as the temperance movement and a concern for the working conditions of women aided the group in its efforts.[47] The tremendous growth of women's clubs in the 1880s and 1890s also invigorated the suffrage movement.[48] Enjoying more free time, white middle-class women joined self-improvement clubs such as reading societies. As women in these clubs became involved in social causes, they soon realized the inferior position shared by all women.

By 1917, the NAWSA boasted over two million members and the suffrage movement had become a broad social movement, guaranteeing its success. A coalition of groups led by NAWSA secured ratification of the Nineteenth Amendment in 1920, guaranteeing women the right to vote. After this historic victory, however, the coalition that made up the suffrage movement soon disintegrated. Winning the vote was the only goal all the participating women's groups shared, and they failed to reach consensus on a post-suffrage agenda. As a result, there was little or-

The initial focus of the second women's movement was the passage of the Equal Rights Amendment, which ultimately failed.

ganized protest for women's rights until the 1960s.

The Second Women's Rights Movement: 1961–Present

The civil rights movement of the 1950s and 1960s attracted many female activists, just as the abolitionist movement had in the nineteenth century. Like their sisters of an earlier era, these activists encountered prejudice and were often treated as second-class citizens by their male activist counterparts. In 1961, the Supreme Court ruled that a jury selection system that virtually excluded women was constitutional because, as the center of home and family life, women should not be burdened with jury duty.[49] This case, and three events that followed in quick succession, initiated the second women's rights movement in the United States.

First, President John F. Kennedy created the President's Commission on the Status of Women in 1961. The commission's 1963 report, *American Women,* documented widespread discrimination against women in all walks of life. That same year, Betty Friedan published her best-selling book *The Feminine Mystique*. Friedan's book challenged women to assert their rights and question the traditional gender assumptions of society. Finally, the 1964 Civil Rights Act prohibited discrimination based not only on race but also on sex. It also created the Equal Employment Opportunity Commission (EEOC) to enforce the antidiscrimination measures. When the EEOC failed to enforce sex discrimination laws, female activists formed

Young Women (18–29) and Men Voters in Presidential Elections

	Women	Men
1992	54%	50%
1996	43%	36%
2000	43%	38%
2004	52%	46%

Source: www.civicyouth.org.

the National Organization for Women (NOW). Like the NAACP, NOW pledged to work within the system by lobbying for a constitutional equal rights amendment and by using the courts to gain equality.

NOW initially focused on the passage of the **Equal Rights Amendment** (ERA), which was first introduced in Congress in 1923 but was never given a hearing. Its wording was simple and straightforward: "Equality of rights under the law shall not be denied or abridged by the United States or by any state on account of sex." Despite intense efforts by women's rights groups, only thirty-five states voted for ratification, three short of the required three-quarters majority. NOW and other allied groups have been more successful in bringing equal protection cases before the United States Supreme Court. Using the intermediate scrutiny test, the Court has prohibited laws that allow women but not men to receive alimony.[50] It has banned single-sex nursing schools.[51] It has also disallowed state prosecutors' use of preemptory challenges to reject either women or men in order to produce a more sympathetic jury.[52] On the other hand, the Court has upheld statutory rape laws that apply only to female victims[53] and draft registration laws that apply only to males.[54]

The modern women's movement has placed more emphasis on involving women in politics. Although women vote more than men, the number of women holding political office is still significantly lower than their share of the population. Yet this trend seems to be changing: in 2006 Nancy Pelosi became the first female speaker of the House; and Hillary Clinton emerged as the nation's first female presidential candidate to lead in national polls. Then, in

August of 2008, Alaska Governor Sarah Palin was chosen by John McCain as his running mate.

Current Issues

By redefining their status in American society, women entered more fully into the public lives of their communities. This move into more public arenas of society gave rise to several issues that are particularly relevant to women's groups of today: workplace and educational equity, sexual harassment, and women's role in the military.

Workplace Equity

American life has changed dramatically since the first debates on the ERA. Very few modern women fit the traditional role of stay-at-home wife and mom. Over seventy million American women are in the workplace—some 60 percent of all adult females in the country—and a majority of those are married. Two-thirds of American mothers who have children below school age work outside the home. Women make up nearly 50 percent of the American civilian workforce, and by 2010 they will constitute the majority.

> **Equal Rights Amendment**
> The proposed constitutional amendment that would have prohibited national and state governments from denying equal rights on the basis of sex.

Congressional legislation to promote fairness in the workplace dates back almost fifty years, to the Equal Pay Act of 1963. The legislation requires equal pay for equal work, regardless of sex. It did not address the fact that some jobs traditionally filled by women (such as nurses and

Although women continue to gain important jobs in the private and public sectors, a gap still exists between the salaries paid to women and men.

secretaries) pay less than jobs tradition-ally held by men (such as construction workers and truck drivers). In 1972, Congress gave the EEOC the power to sue employers suspected of illegal gender discrimination. The 1991 Civil Rights and Women's Equity in Employment Act shifted the burden of proof by requiring employers to demonstrate that their hiring and promotion practices are related to job performance.

Despite these efforts, women still earn less than men earn. When the Equal Pay Act was passed, a female earned, on average, fifty-nine cents for every dollar earned by a male. That figure has increased to seventy-seven cents for every dollar men earn, but a significant gap still exists. Some authors suggest that wage justice can be secured only by adopting a **comparable worth** policy.[55] Such a policy attempts to compare dissimilar jobs in terms of knowledge, effort, skill, responsibility, and working conditions. Jobs that are equivalent in these terms should be compensated equally. Proponents of this approach argue that society historically has devalued jobs traditionally performed by women. They contend that the continued predominance of women in low-paid female-dominated jobs requires a comparable worth solution. Opponents argue that differing pay scales between jobs simply reflect free market economic forces and personal job preferences.

Ratio of Female to Male Earnings

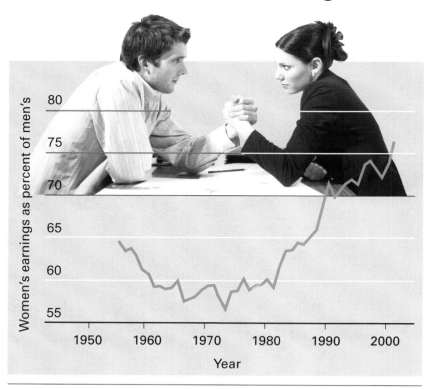

Source: www.census.gov/hhes/income/Listinc/histincb.html.

Income Inequity Between the Sexes

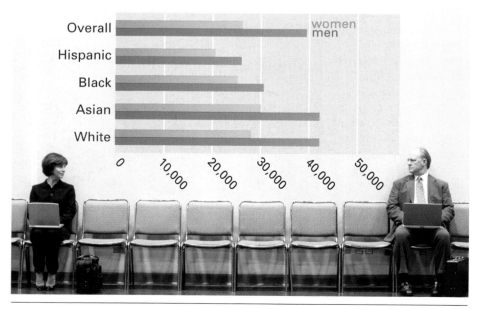

Source: Kelly Rathie, "Male versus Female Earnings—Is the Gender Wage Gap Converging?" *Economic Ltd.*, Spring 2002, vol. 7, no. 1.

Sexual Harassment

With men and women spending more time together in the workplace, **sexual harassment** has become an increasingly important issue for American women. The United States Supreme Court has ruled that sexual harassment qualifies as gender discrimination under Title VII of the 1964 Civil Rights Act if it is so pervasive as to create a hostile or abusive work environment.[56] In 1993, the Court reinforced its position in *Harris v. Forklift Systems.* Under that ruling, plaintiffs are not required to prove the workplace is so hostile as to cause severe psychological injury or prevent them from performing their jobs. The Court emphasized that federal law protects a plaintiff before the harassment leads to serious psychological difficulty.

In two 1998 cases, the Court addressed the employer's responsibility for sexual harassment committed by its managers. In *Faragher v. City of Boca Raton,* the Court ruled that an employer is responsible for a supervisor's sexual harassment of an employee even if the employer is unaware of the sexual harassment. The Supreme Court thus made it easier for employees to win such cases by ruling employers need to take reasonable steps to prevent harassing behavior at the work site. The Court also ruled in 1998 that an employer can be held liable for sexual harassment caused by a supervisor's actions, even though the employee suffered no job-related harm.[57]

Most sexual harassment cases have involved the workplace, but in 1999 the Court turned its attention to sexual harassment in the public schools. The Court determined in *Davis v. Monroe County Board of Education* that a school district was liable for one student harassing another if the school had knowledge of the harassment or was deliberately indifferent to it. The harassment must be so severe, pervasive, and objectively offensive that it deprives the victims of access to the educational opportunities provided by the school. Sexual harassment and sexual abuse against female students at the military service academies have led to congressional and military inquiries, but the Supreme Court has yet to hear a case on the matter.

Women's Role in the Military

Until 1948, women served the military in separate units such as the Women's Army Corps (WACS) and the Nurse Corps. Since that time, the sexes have served together in regular noncombat military units, and women currently make up about 15 percent of the American armed forces. The integration of women into the regular armed forces raises a variety of controversial issues, perhaps the most contentious of which involves women's role in combat. Federal laws and military regulations prevent women from engaging in combat for a variety of reasons, including women's lack of upper body strength, the possibility of capture and rape by enemy forces, and uncertainty about the behavior of men and women thrown together in a combat situation.

Should policies barring women from combat be viewed as sexual discrimination or as a sexual benefit? The realities of modern war undermine many of the traditional ar-

comparable worth The notion that individuals performing different jobs that require the same amount of knowledge, effort, skill, responsibility, and working conditions should receive equal compensation; the proposal would elevate the pay structure of many jobs traditionally performed by women.

sexual harassment The practice of awarding jobs or job benefits in exchange for sexual favors, or the creation of a hostile work or education environment by unwarranted sexual advances or sexual conversation.

Women serving in Iraq face the same dangers as their male counterparts.

guments against women serving in combat. In Iraq, for example, the lack of traditional front lines and the pervasive nature of the threat can produce casualties even among female soldiers not serving in infantry, armor, and Special Forces divisions. More than four times as many female soldiers have died in the Iraq War as in the Vietnam War, which suggests that noncombat policies are no longer protecting women. In light of the record number of female fatalities, some members of the House Armed Services Committee are asking whether current military assignments for women violate the spirit of noncombat policies.

civil rights movement The litigation and mobilization activities of African Americans in the second half of the twentieth century that led to a greater realization of equality for all disadvantaged groups.

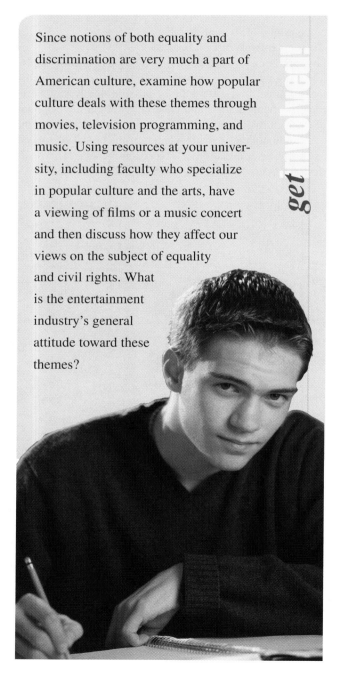

Since notions of both equality and discrimination are very much a part of American culture, examine how popular culture deals with these themes through movies, television programming, and music. Using resources at your university, including faculty who specialize in popular culture and the arts, have a viewing of films or a music concert and then discuss how they affect our views on the subject of equality and civil rights. What is the entertainment industry's general attitude toward these themes?

get involved!

CIVIC ENGAGEMENT AND CIVIL RIGHTS

We have seen in this chapter that the pursuit of civil rights is related to political mobilization. Political mobilization generally is the process by which candidates, parties, activists, interest groups, and social movements induce other people to engage in politics. As we discuss later in the book, people are more likely to engage in politics if they are asked. They are also more likely to participate if they possess such resources as time, skill, knowledge, and self-confidence. Mobilization for the civil rights goals of political, social, and economic equality creates a problem for activists because the people most affected lack many of the resources related to political participation. As a result, initial civil rights activity involves leaders of interest groups and their attempts to influence judicial bodies.

Civil rights activities are often directed toward the United States Supreme Court because deprived groups are seeking constitutional and legal pronouncements of equality. The Supreme Court, as a result, has become known for its policy-legitimizing role in the political system.[58] The interest group leaders in New Orleans sought the intervention of courts to rule that the state's segregation laws were illegitimate. The *Plessy* case was carefully planned even though not ultimately successful. The goal to have the Supreme Court declare the illegitimacy of racist legislation and policies remained the same for African American groups. After its formation, the NAACP pursued a plan of presenting the Court with a series of test cases concerning the segregation policies in graduate and professional schools. The Supreme Court applied the "separate but equal" doctrine of *Plessy v. Ferguson* and found the policies of those schools to be unequal. The NAACP then changed its strategy to challenge the separate but equal doctrine itself and were successful in *Brown v. Board of Education of Topeka*. After the Court ruled that segregated schools should change their policies with "all deliberate speed" in the *Brown II* case, the NAACP issued a directive to all its local branches that detailed procedures for speeding the implementation of the Court decision. The directive advocated such procedures as setting timetables, familiarizing parents with the issue, and (where needed) additional lawsuits.

The success of the NAACP in the *Brown* case soon led to the civil rights movement. The **civil rights movement** was a broad coalition of political, social, and religious groups that engaged in a wide variety of activities with the general goal of securing political, economic, and social equality. A large number of national, regional, and local organizations used sit-ins, freedom rides, boycotts, and lawsuits to further their goals. Extreme pressure was placed on members of Congress to pass the 1964 Civil Rights Act and the 1965 Voting

Rights Act. The movement began to build in the late 1950s, peaked in the mid-1960s, and began to wane by the late 1960s. The movement's decline was related to internal dissension within the movement and the rise of a white southern backlash. As the most important social movement of the twentieth century, however, this civil rights movement served as the model for the activities of many other groups to gain equality.

For REVIEW >>

1. How has the Supreme Court's attitude toward the civil rights of African Americans evolved?
   - The Supreme Court embraced the concept of slavery in *Dred Scott*, later approved of segregation in *Plessy v. Ferguson*, finally recognized the concept of equality in *Brown*, and wrestles today with the issue of affirmative action.

2. How have other minority groups benefited from the civil rights struggles of African Americans?
   - Other minority groups, such as Native Americans, Hispanic Americans, Asian Americans, disabled Americans, American seniors, and gay and lesbian Americans, have used the civil rights tactics of litigation and social protest employed by African Americans as a template for their own struggles for equality.

3. What unique civil rights issues do women face in the United States today?
   - Women, who are not a minority in the United States and who met with less success than African Americans in achieving equality after the Civil War, face the unique civil rights issues of workplace and educational equity, sexual harassment, and their role in the military.

A Tough Sell Gets Tougher

Black Republicans are already considered a contradiction in terms in the African-American community. And the arrival of Barack Obama as the Democratic presidential nominee made selling black voters on the GOP exponentially more difficult.

That hasn't kept a small group of vociferous conservative blacks from trying. They argue that, historically, the GOP is the true home of African-Americans. They posit an unbroken line of civil-rights victories from Abraham Lincoln's Emancipation Proclamation to George W. Bush's Leave No Child Behind initiative, and they object to the Democratic Party's claim to the mantle.

"The Democrat Party has hijacked the civil-rights record of the Republican Party," said Frances Rice, chairwoman of the National Black Republican Association, which boasts 1,000 members in 48 states. "The Democratic Party is the party of slavery, secession, segregation, and now—socialism."

The nimble historical hopscotch behind that claim irks Democratic activists and historians alike, but there's enough truth in it to keep a parlor argument going late into the night. So far, the African-American community has not bought into the story line. President Bush captured only 11 percent of the black vote in the 2004 election, and no Republican African-American lawmakers are serving in Congress.

"My job is difficult whether Barack Obama is standing there or not," said Michael Steele, chairman of GOPAC, the political action committee charged with electing Republicans to state and local offices. Steele was the first African-American lieutenant governor of Maryland and lost a 2006 U.S. Senate bid to Democrat Ben Cardin. He knows well the challenges facing black Republicans, both as candidates and citizens.

"The reality becomes very difficult when the biases toward all things black-Republican are so stark, so personal," Steele said. "People just don't even give you credit for anything."

Shamed Dogan knows these biases firsthand. He is a black Republican campaigning for state representative in Missouri's 88th district. "I tell people I'm running as a Republican and they give me 'The Look'—like they are seeing a unicorn," Dogan said. "If they talked to me for five minutes, they would realize I'm for the betterment of all people, including African-Americans."

African-American Republicans fondly recall the origins of the Grand Old Party, whose creators were fierce abolitionists.

After the Civil War, Southern Democrats returned to Congress and voted against efforts by the then-majority Republicans to pass the 14th and 15th amendments to the Constitution to grant freed slaves U.S. citizenship and full voting rights, respectively. Historians agree: This was largely a group of sullen Southern sympathizers disdainful of Lincoln's Emancipation Proclamation and the 13th Amendment, which abolished slavery. They did all they could to subjugate blacks during Reconstruction and supported local Jim Crow laws that disenfranchised blacks in the former Confederate states for the next century.

"The Democrats [who were] revived in the wake of the Civil War [belonged to] a largely Southern, white-supremacist party," said Yale history professor David Blight.

Not all of the bigotry came from below the Mason-Dixon line. "The Almighty has made the black man inferior, sir," said Rep. Fernando Wood, D-N.Y., in 1865. "By no legislation, by no military power, can you wipe out this distinction."

The so-called radical Republicans battled Democratic President Andrew Johnson and handed him 15 veto overrides, including the Civil Rights Act of 1866 and the Reconstruction Act of 1867.

Republicans remained staunchly pro-civil rights into the 1870s with the help of GOP President Ulysses S. Grant. Together they saw the adoption of the Force Act of 1871 to provide federal oversight of congressional elections, the Ku Klux Klan Act of 1871 to protect blacks from the racial vigilantes, and the Civil Rights Act of 1875. The latter, never fully enforced and ultimately declared unconstitutional in 1883, called for open access to inns, public transportation, and theaters for all races.

Here the litany of pro-black GOP policies stops until passage of the Civil Rights Act of 1964 with the instrumental support of Sen. Everett Dirksen, R-Ill. Not to be overlooked in the effort was the lobbying of Democratic President Lyndon Johnson and Senate Democrats, who wooed Dirksen relentlessly.

"Dirksen did help make the 1964 act possible," said Senate Associate Historian Donald Ritchie. "LBJ made sure Dirksen was on board, front and center," and he was willing to let the senior Republican senator take a large share of the credit in order to close the deal. It worked. The bill passed, and Dirksen appeared on the cover of Time magazine in June 1964.

Last on the checklist for black Republicans is the creation of affirmative action by Assistant Labor Secretary Art Fletcher in 1970 during the Nixon administration. The program, derived from an earlier Johnson administration plan, helped guarantee equal access for women and minorities to public- and private-sector jobs. "We created it," Steele said, "Democrats bastardized it" by letting it become a quota system.

Critics of the rosy recitation of GOP civil-rights accomplishments say the historical take is selective at best and misleading at worst. "Any use of the 'party of Lincoln' rhetoric by the current Republican Party is, frankly, an egregious twisting of history," Blight said. He explains that the original GOP underwent drastic changes from the 1870s into the early 20th century. "They became the party of Big Business interests, imperial expansionism, and ultimately turned their backs decisively on their more egalitarian origins in the Civil War era," Blight said.

The first turning point came during the Great Depression. Until the economic collapse in 1929, most African-Americans voted Republican—if they could vote at all. But blacks began to shift allegiance as President Roosevelt's progressive New Deal created jobs. FDR won 23 percent of the black vote in 1932, a figure that grew to 71 per-

cent in 1936 and stayed high during World War II. President Truman, who ordered the desegregation of the military and aggressively investigated several high-profile lynchings, won 65 percent of the black vote in 1948.

Presidential candidate John F. Kennedy re-established a strong Democratic relationship with the black community through a phone call to Coretta Scott King in 1960, express-ing his concern about the incarceration of her

Sen. Strom Thurmond of South Carolina be-gan the exodus in 1964 by joining the GOP in protest. In 1968, Republican presidential candidate Richard Nixon seized the oppor-tunity to peel off many more disaffected white Democrats with the "Southern strategy" that equated the GOP with "law and order" and "states' rights"—widely regarded as code words for a conservative backlash against civil-rights protections.

capped block grants to states. It also required welfare recipients to enter job-training pro-grams, mandated that states boost child-support enforcement, and limited individual benefits to five years, total. Within three years of enactment, 4.7 million Americans moved off the welfare rolls, and by 2006, caseloads declined 59 percent, according to the Health and Human Services Department.

"We're not against government programs," Steele said. "They need to be suited to the task, not wasteful; and when they've served their purpose, get rid of them."

> "Some Republicans gave up on winning the African-American vote, **looking the other way or trying to benefit from racial polarization**," Mehlman said. "I am here today as the Republican chairman to tell you we were wrong."

husband in the Birmingham, Ala., jail, and subsequent calls for his release. The overture was enough to prompt Martin Luther King Sr., "Daddy King," to publicly renounce the Republican Party and support Kennedy. JFK won the election with the help of 71 percent of black voters.

"What you saw in 1958 to 1964 was more Democratic engagement in the civil-rights movement," said Julianne Malveaux, president of Bennett College for Women in Greensboro, N.C. Although key Republicans ultimately supported the landmark legisla-tion, it was a Democratic Congress and presi-dent that made the 1964 Civil Rights Act and the 1965 Voting Rights Act law, Blight said.

President Johnson garnered an estimated 100 percent of the black vote in 1964 but fa-mously remarked at the time that he feared that Democratic support for civil-rights legislation would cause the party to "lose the South for a generation." It was a historic understatement.

The tactic helped both Nixon and Ronald Reagan win the White House, and it became a staple of modern GOP presidential politics. "Republicans have been more likely to use race as a proxy to signal to [white] people—we've got your backs," Malveaux said.

Steele bitterly regrets the move by his party. "It was a dumb strategy," he said. "It alienated a partner. African-Americans and the GOP had been historically linked since day one."

Black Republicans say that a lot in the con-servative Goldwater/Reagan doctrine strikes chords within the larger African-American community—particularly the admonition to self-sufficiency and frustrations with the wel-fare system that evolved from the Johnson administration's War on Poverty.

Black Republicans laud welfare reform, which congressional conservatives pushed in 1994 and President Clinton ultimately signed into law in 1996. The new system dispensed with open-ended entitlements in favor of

While shrinking the government is a staple of conservative thought, the starve-the-beast rallying cry of the GOP may also quietly alien-ate the black community, Blight says. The federal government ended slavery, gave Afri-can-Americans the vote, and promoted civil rights in the 1860s and 1960s. "If you don't believe in government, you're not going to get many black people to vote for you," he said.

In 2005, the Republican National Com-mittee made a concerted effort to woo back at least a small percentage of the black vote. Then-RNC Chairman Ken Mehlman ap-peared before the NAACP convention in Mil-waukee and offered a striking apology for the Southern strategy. "Some Republicans gave up on winning the African-American vote, looking the other way or trying to benefit from racial polarization," Mehlman said. "I am here today as the Republican chairman to tell you we were wrong."

The contrition strategy failed. Blacks voted 89 percent Democratic in the 2006 elections that cost the GOP control of Congress. Dis-trust of the modern GOP still dominates in the African-American community, and few in it appear willing to countenance black- (or white-) Republican efforts to paint the party in a softer racial light.

■ FOR DISCUSSION: Who do you think deserves the acclaim for the Civil Rights movement? Can one group really even claim credit? Based on your experience of the two political parties today, which one (if either) is doing more to promote the Civil Rights agenda?
What mistakes do you see politicians making today that they might regret the way Ken Mehlman regrets the GOP's callousness to black voters?

6

WHAT'S TO COME

PUBLIC OPINION

LISTENING TO CITIZENS

CHOOSE YOUR WORDS CAREFULLY ▌Barack Obama's 2008 victory over Hillary Clinton for the Democratic Party nomination for president may have come down to the difference between two words: *I* and *we*. While Clinton spent much of the campaign telling voters what she would do for them, Obama was talking about the difference "we" can make.

At least this is the view of George Lakoff, professor of linguistics at the University of California, Berkeley, and co-founder of the Rockridge Institute. The difference between saying "I" and saying "we" is huge, Lakoff explains. "[Obama] understands what it means to connect to people, to listen to them, to understand what their needs and concerns are and that government should be responsive. . . . Hillary is all about policy. It is top-down. It is a rationalist model. It is 'we who understand and know policy who know best.' It is telling people what is best for them."[1]

Lakoff has written several books explaining that voters are not swayed by rational policy arguments but, rather, are moved by a candidate's basic values and the way he or she uses language. Values and language "frame" issues in a way that makes them either more or less palatable for the average voter; they tap into emotions via positive or negative associations, making us either more or less responsive to the message and to the person delivering it.

Lakoff says he learned these lessons from conservative Republicans who pioneered the art of framing during the presidency of Ronald Reagan. He notes, for example, that when discussing the rights of gay and lesbian couples to form legally recognized unions, conservatives use the term "gay marriage" in order to frame the debate in terms of sex. "Framed in that way, the issue of gay marriage will get a lot of negative reaction. But what if you make the issue 'freedom to marry,' or even better, 'the right to marry'? That's a whole different story. Very few people would say they did not support the right to marry [whomever] you choose. But the polls don't ask that question, because the right wing has framed that issue."[2]

One Republican who wouldn't disagree with Lakoff's description of how words frame political debate is Frank Luntz. Luntz, who has done extensive work on language with **focus groups**—small gatherings of individuals used to test ideas before marketing—catapulted into prominence in 1994. In that year, his focus groups produced a series of measures known as the Contract ➥

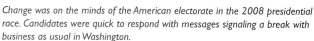

Change was on the minds of the American electorate in the 2008 presidential race. Candidates were quick to respond with messages signaling a break with business as usual in Washington.

with America, which Republicans used to regain control of the House of Representatives for the first time in forty years. He believes that the words a political leader uses can spell the difference between success and failure. In a recent book, Luntz outlined words and phrases he believes will be important for shaping political debate in the twenty-first century, including "imagine," "lifestyle," and "accountability."[3]

Public opinion is an extremely valuable commodity for political leaders and one that they spend a great deal of effort and money attempting to influence. Political leaders and interest groups increasingly have employed marketing strategies such as focus groups to target messages to constituents for both narrow and broad purposes. Ever more sophisticated methods allow pollsters not just to measure opinion but also to attempt to mold it. In today's competitive political climate, citizens must be armed with the ability to distinguish legitimate public sentiment from political contrivance. ◆

UNDERSTANDING PUBLIC OPINION IN THE CONTEXT OF AMERICAN POLITICS

It seems logical that a nation founded on the consent of the governed should recognize and respect the opinions of the people. However, what is less clear is exactly what opinions policymakers should pay attention to, how that opinion is to be gauged, and how political leaders should accommodate it. Should policymakers be more responsive to the opinions of a majority of their constituents, even if ill informed, or to a minority of knowledgeable and better educated civic and business leaders, or **elites**? Over the years, the ways in which opinion has been valued, measured, and utilized have changed dramatically.

The Nature of Public Opinion

Political scientist V. O. Key, Jr., once defined **public opinion** as "those opinions held by private persons which governments find it prudent to heed."[4] Key's definition points out certain essential aspects of public opinion. First, public opinion attaches itself to issues of public, rather than private, concern. Of course, the dividing line between private and public life is fluid and often contentious. Most Americans view sexual behavior as a private matter, but public debate over a woman's right to have an abortion continues unabated.

Second, public opinion sets boundaries on the type and expanse of policy proposals that citizens find acceptable. These boundaries reflect a respect for historical precedent and institutional arrangements, as well as for the political culture that informs our democratic republic.[5] A people's **political culture** is its historically rooted values and beliefs about government. Our political culture emphasizes support for the values of liberty, individualism, equality of opportunity, and private property.[6] Although policy boundaries are flexible, especially with regard to how we practice our dominant values, these values structure the types of solutions that Americans are most willing to support. For example, unlike societies such as Sweden that provide extensive "cradle-to-grave" government services, American political culture supports a far more limited government role in meeting individual needs such as health care and income security. As a result, we provide limited social support for those who demonstrate need, rather than blanket coverage for all citizens.

Third, Key's definition suggests that it might be more important for the government to heed the opinions of some citizens rather than those of others. The public is composed of various groups of individuals, some of whom are more visible to political leaders or more attentive to certain issues at particular times. When considering health-care reform, for example, political leaders will be especially attentive to the views of health-care professionals, such as doctors. Physicians not only have expertise in this matter but are also likely to react intensely to changes that adversely affect their practice, and they can mount substantial opposition to measures they deem ill conceived. Similarly, the elderly, who consume more health-care dollars, are more likely to be attentive to changes in health care than young people, who are more concerned about other issues.

Finally, opinion is different from judgment. Opinions can sometimes reflect momentary feelings based on little reflection. Judgments form slowly over time with the infusion of information and thought. That is why there sometimes appears to be a difference between "overnight polls" that are taken by media outlets in response to events, such as presidential speeches, and long-term support for the policies of the chief executive. Effective leaders understand this difference and are more likely to react to settled judgments than to momentary bursts of opinion.

> **focus groups** Small gatherings of individuals used to test ideas before marketing.
>
> **elites** Individuals in a position of authority, often those with a higher level of education than the population at large.
>
> **public opinion** Opinions held by private individuals that governments find it prudent to heed.
>
> **political culture** The dominant values and beliefs of a political community.

Changes in Assessing and Using Public Opinion

The Framers felt that the opinions of common people were best limited to expression at the ballot box. In *The Federalist* No. 71, Alexander Hamilton wrote:

> The republican principle demands that the deliberative sense of the community should guide the conduct of those to whom they entrust the management of their affairs; but it does not require an unqualified complaisance to every sudden breeze of passion, or to every transient impulse which the people may receive from the arts of men, who flatter their prejudices to betray their interest. . . .[7]

Fear of faction and mob rule caused colonial leaders to be suspicious of popular attitudes. Nevertheless, political leaders were never indifferent to public attitudes. George Washington corresponded with a friend in Virginia, David Stuart, whom he relied on to mingle with ordinary people in order to find out what they thought about presidential actions.[8] And presidents have always spent time "pressing flesh" to engender support and good feelings.

Before the era of scientific polling, political leaders attempted to gauge popular support from a variety of sources. Newspaper reports and editorials provided officials with some measure of information regarding popular attitudes. In the era of the party press (see Chapter 10), however, few reports were objective. From Jackson through Lincoln, it

Public figures seldom pass up the opportunity to "press the flesh" to gain firsthand knowledge of public opinion.

was common for presidents to curry favor with journalists and editors by appointing them to government offices.[9] When the partisan press gave way to the commercial press in the second half of the nineteenth century, politicians paid close attention to opinions conveyed in newspapers printed in their home districts. They also often attempted to influence press coverage of their campaigns. Members of Congress sent newsletters to constituents extolling their skills at representation, and these were often simply reprinted verbatim in local newspapers.

Party leaders in wards and precincts could sometimes predict election results with uncanny accuracy—a result of both their proximity to average citizens and their ability to turn out those who supported their candidate. In some cases, informal polls were conducted by party leaders at political rallies among partisan supporters with predictable results duly reported to cheering crowds.

A variety of ad hoc methods of sampling also produced often surprisingly ac-

Hot or Not?

Should political leaders allow poll results to influence their decisions?

curate portraits of public opinion. Tavern owners placed "poll books" in their establishments where townspeople could register their preferences. **Straw polls**, which sampled opinions from lists of experts, journalists, or subscribers to particular newspapers or consumer services, became popular at the turn of the twentieth century.[10] The *Literary Digest* magazine conducted perhaps the most famous of these polls, mailing millions of ballots to people from across the country from lists generated by automobile registration records and telephone directories. Despite the unscientific nature of its poll, the *Digest* accurately picked presidential winners in 1924, 1928, and 1932. In 1936, the magazine's luck ran out when it predicted an electoral victory for Alf Landon; it went out of the polling business shortly thereafter.[11]

That same year, George Gallup issued his first scientifically designed presidential election poll, based on emerging marketing research techniques. After accurately predicting Franklin D. Roosevelt's win, Gallup's newly created American Institute of Public Opinion quickly became a world leader in survey research, conducting weekly polls for a number of newspapers across the country. Gallup did not intend that politicians should slavishly follow survey results, however, and many did not. In the decades that followed, many political leaders advanced policies well beyond the mainstream of public opinion by advocating bold initiatives in areas such as race relations and civil liberties. For these public opinion leaders, polls provided not so much a road map for political success as a way of gauging how far they could advance reforms before facing serious resistance.

Today, survey research is ubiquitous. Hardly a day goes by when we do not hear about one poll or another regarding almost every aspect of life, from health care to fashion to politics. Survey research can aid in making life more enjoyable and bringing public policies more in line with public sentiment. However, it can also be used to manipulate preferences and behavior. More than ever, citizens must be able to navigate their way through polls and to understand the nature and limits of public opinion in a democracy.

HOW POLITICAL OPINIONS ARE FORMED

Individuals develop opinions about the political world from a host of sources, including family, friends, schools, and the media. We form many of the enduring attitudes, values, and beliefs that shape our opinions early in life through a process called **political socialization**. Even so, we constantly form new opinions and revise old ones as we confront new issues, new people, and new technologies.

The Process of Socialization

Pioneering studies in the 1950s and 1960s demonstrated that children begin forming impressions about the political communities in which they live as early as preschool age.[12] They embrace national symbols, such as the flag, and associate authority figures like police and firefighters with the protective functions of government. Impressions at this stage are fairly positive, although the strength of these sentiments may vary among subcultures and minority populations.[13] Children also develop an awareness of national, racial, and gender differences in early grade school, along with friendly or hostile feelings toward specific groups. Even at this early stage, gender differences seem to appear regarding issues of war and peace, with boys more likely than girls to support military options.[14]

As children approach adolescence, they become more skeptical of political authority, begin differentiating between leaders they like and those they dislike, and learn to distinguish between the major political parties. Much of their awareness remains impressionistic at this stage. It is only with late adolescent maturity that we come to associate issue and party positions with particular ideological viewpoints, such as liberalism or conservatism. Many of the political opinions we develop in youth have sticking power. This is especially true for party identification, but less so concerning specific issues, which are more subject to reformulation over time.[15]

Civic education has a strong impact on increasing knowledge and interest in politics among young adults.[16] Young people who take courses in government, or who engage in student government opportunities in high school, are more likely to be politically active as adults.[17]

Political outlook and behavior can change as we age. Some of the age differences in politics are the result of **life cycle effects**, or changes in our life circumstances. As people age, they accumulate more property and political knowledge. They settle into community life and become

straw poll An unscientific survey of popular views.

political socialization The process by which individuals come to adopt the attitudes, values, beliefs, and opinions of their political culture.

life cycle effects The impact of age-related factors in the formation of political attitudes, opinions, and beliefs.

. . . That George Washington did not, as a little boy, chop down a cherry tree and then confess to his father that he had done it, for "I cannot tell a lie"? The story was invented by a Virginia clergyman known as Parson Mason Locke Weems, as part of a highly successful effort to enshrine Washington as a blameless hero in the American historical memory.

Did You Know?

more aware of their material self-interest. As a result, they are more likely to participate in the political system.

Other age-related differences are not as predictable. Known as **generational effects**, they result from unique issues and events confronting each **cohort**, or generation, at a time when its political identity is being forged.[18] For the generation that grew up in the 1950s and 1960s, the civil rights movement served as a catalyst for civic activism and spurred support for the expansion of individual rights and freedoms. We are likely to see a different worldview among those who came of age politically in the wake of the September 11, 2001, terrorist attacks. For them, the world may seem more dangerous than for those who grew up in previous eras. One indication, for example, is that support for the war in Iraq remained higher among younger Ameri-cans for a longer period of time than for older citizens, even after U.S. efforts began to falter.[19]

Agents of Political Socialization

A number of cultural and institutional forces shape and mold our opinions over a lifetime. Their relative impact on our political maturation depends on when, how long, and how strongly we are exposed to them. Families, for instance, have the greatest impact on political socialization because of our intense interactions with family members during our formative years.[20]

Family Families help to shape our interest in politics, our party affiliation, and the attitudes we hold toward others in society. Our first memories of political events often come from family members expressing their own political viewpoints. For example, many who grew up in Democratic households during the Clinton era recall hearing about economic prosperity and budget surpluses. Children of Republicans at that time are more likely to have heard about the Monica Lewinsky scandal. These early memories carry an emotional weight that we often express in adulthood by adopting the party preferences of our parents.

Parental influence is far wider than partisan affiliation alone. According to a recent study, young people whose parents discuss politics regularly in the home are more likely to exhibit trust in government, feel a greater sense of political efficacy, believe in the importance of voting, and volunteer their time.[21] Three-quarters of young people who grew up with political discussion in the home are registered to vote, compared with only 57 percent of those who grew up in households without political discussion. And children who accompany their parents to the polling place on Election Day are far more likely to develop the habit of voting themselves. It is no wonder that children of politically active families often follow in the footsteps of their parents.

Educational Institutions Early experiences in school tend to encourage support for our political system and its underlying values. Tales about George Washington and the cherry tree, and daily recitation of the Pledge of Allegiance, are intended to build positive feelings toward the government and its leaders. Middle and high school education fills in a little more detail of American history; but it is only in college, when most students are exposed to extensive study of our nation's past, warts and

Voting, like any habit, is most enduring if developed early.

all, that they form their own opinions about our republic. To a greater degree than many others around the world, our educational system emphasizes egalitarian themes and encourages support for equal opportunities. Unlike some European countries, such as Germany, that provide different educational tracks for the college and noncollege bound, American schools tend to provide similar educational paths for all students.

Variations in political attitudes between those who attend college and those who do not reveal important differences that higher education can make. Compared to peers who have some college experience, young adults who do not attend college—or do not intend to go to college—express less trust in government, are more likely to see politics as the business of elites rather than average citizens, are less likely to believe their votes count, and are less likely to believe that political leaders are interested in their problems. Race complicates the picture. African Americans at all levels of education express more pessimism than whites about politics in general and about their ability to bring about meaningful change.[22] This may change as more black leaders like Barack Obama overcome obstacles to seeking high office.

Religious Institutions Americans are among the most religious people in the world, as measured by expressed belief in God and attendance at church services. America's religious preferences are also more diverse than those of any other nation. Eighty-four percent of Americans claim affiliation in one of twenty-one major denominations or in one of the scores of minor church assemblies across the nation. In recent years, increasing numbers of Americans have described themselves as non-Christians or claimed no particular religious belief.[23] Still, the number of those who consider themselves religious and who attend services is quite high. Slightly more females than males consider themselves religious and attend services regularly.

There is little racial integration within denominations. Only nine of the twenty-one largest denominations have black membership of 10 percent or higher, demonstrating the familiar refrain that "Sunday morning service is the most segregated hour in America." Hispanics, by contrast, attend services with white Catholics. The controversy over remarks made by Barack Obama's pastor, the Reverend Jeremiah Wright, during the 2008 presidential campaign shows how race and religion interact. Survey results showed that a clear majority of whites who heard about Wright's sermons say they were personally offended by what he said, whereas most blacks who heard about his sermons say they were not offended.[24]

There are significant differences in party affiliation by denomination. Mormons and evangelical Protestant congregations, including Southern Baptists and Pentecostals, heavily favor the Republican Party. Mainline Protestants such as Episcopalians and Presbyterians are fairly evenly divided

by party. High turnout among conservative evangelicals proved to be a powerful force for Republicans in recent elections. Latino Protestants trend Democratic, while black Protestants are overwhelmingly in the Democratic camp. Although white Catholics have drifted away from the Democratic Party, a plurality still call themselves Democrats. Support for the Democratic Party is far stronger among Latino Catholics. Smaller Christian congregations skew Republican, while Jews and members of minority religions continue a long tradition of support for the Democrats. Among the growing number of those expressing no particular religious affiliations, Democrats outnumber Republicans.

Churches are important training grounds for learning civic skills, as we will see in Chapter 7. They provide opportunities to learn organizing and management skills that can be useful in the political realm. Organizing a church outing or social gathering is not

generational effects The impact of events experienced by a generational cohort on the formation of common political orientations.

cohort The members of one's own generation.

Party Affiliation of Various Religious Groups

% Republican / Lean Republican
% Democrat / Lean Democrat

	% Rep	% Dem
Total	47	47
Mormon	65	22
Evangelical churches	50	34
Mainline churches	41	43
Orthodox	35	50
Catholic	33	48
Jewish	24	66
Unaffiliated	23	55
Buddhist	18	66
Hindu	13	63
Muslim	11	63
Hist. black churches	10	77
Jehovah's Witness	10	15

Source: PEW Forum on Religion and Public Life, U.S. Religious Landscape Survey (Washington, DC, June 2008), p. 85.

much different from helping to plan a political meeting or rally. For the poor and for minorities, churches provide a venue for acquiring civic skills that is often unavailable elsewhere due to limited educational and workplace opportunities.[25]

Voluntary Associations The connection between activity in voluntary associations and political engagement is less clear. For example, although college students support voluntarism in their communities, they do not regularly discuss politics and they express little interest in getting involved politically, with the possible exception of voting.[26] Often, young adults see community activism and political activism as separate domains. Those who are active politically are less likely to volunteer on a weekly basis, and those who volunteer are half as likely to be registered to vote or to take part in political activities.[27] This lack of close connection raises questions about the value of service learning for fostering political engagement. Volunteering also has little impact on increasing a general sense of trust in others, one of the elements of social capital (discussed in Chapter 1) that serves to bind members of the political community together. Instead, it increases trust only of others we perceive to be like ourselves.[28]

Media Because we hold preexisting opinions and points of view, it is difficult to disentangle the effects of media

News and entertainment shows frequently poke fun at national leaders. Does this impact the way we think about politics?

messages from the impact of other socializing agents. Although the media pervade every facet of our lives, most researchers believe the media have a minimal effect on our political views.[29] The source of one's political information, however, does seem to determine how politically informed one is. It should come as no surprise that those who get their news from newspapers (or newspaper websites) seem to be better informed than the almost two-thirds of the American public who rely on television as their major news source.[30] Newspapers provide longer, more detailed coverage of events and issues. Nevertheless, a recent study found that a large percentage of highly knowledgeable Americans turned to *The Daily Show*, *The Colbert Report*, and *The NewsHour with Jim Lehrer* for their news.[31] Of course, it is hard to know whether they are knowledgeable because of these sources or whether they turn to these sources because they are knowledgeable. With the explosion in media outlets available through cable television and the Internet, we also see more self-selection based on one's political point of view. Conservative viewers are more likely to tune to FOX, liberals to CNN and PBS. Conservatives log on to WorldNetDaily, liberals to Daily Kos.

The media may impact our beliefs and attitudes in subtle ways. News and entertainment shows alike, for example, often communicate negative stereotypes about the political process, making it seem inherently corrupt and portraying political leaders as untrustworthy. News programs afford political scandals an inordinate amount of coverage, and late-night comics incessantly poke fun at national leaders. Our views about other races may be influenced by the way television news portrays them. For example, one study found that white viewers exposed to local news coverage of crime on television had more negative attitudes toward African Americans and expressed greater support for punitive measures against those convicted of crime.[32]

GROUP DIFFERENCES IN POLITICAL OPINIONS

We all go through life assembling a variety of group identifications that make a difference in the views we hold. While we can decide to join a fraternity or sorority or play on a softball team, we cannot make choices regarding other aspects of our identity, including race, ethnic background, gender, and area of the country where we are born. The life experiences associated with given group identities generate interesting political differences across America's diverse population.

Racial and Ethnic Identity

African Americans, who make up about 12 percent of the U.S. population, generally are more liberal on domestic political issues than whites. They express much stronger support for government enforcement of civil rights and government action to aid the poor. They favor educational quotas and preferences for blacks in hiring and promotion by a four-to-one margin over white respondents.[33] They also express greater support than whites for a national health-care system and for a more progressive tax system that would redistribute the wealth more equitably among individuals.

Most Hispanic Americans are Catholics and are strongly opposed to abortion. They also desire to preserve their cultural heritage, which is reflected in their support of bilingual education in the public schools. The Hispanic American population is itself quite diverse, however, with each subgroup reflecting the strong influence of its country of origin. Cuban Americans are strongly anticommunist because many families fled to the United States after Fidel Castro assumed power in 1959. Puerto Ricans and Mexican Americans hold opinions similar to African Americans, especially in support of social welfare and antidiscrimination policies.

Asian Americans also display a wide variety of national origins, yet very little research is available about variation of political opinions among these groups.[34] The same is true regarding the views of Native Americans, who are in many ways the least visible ethnic group in America because nearly half live in enclaves known as reservations. A long history of displacement, discrimination, and broken promises by federal authorities has produced high levels of cynicism and distrust of government among Native Americans.

Gender

For many years, social scientists claimed that there were few differences in political attitudes and opinions between males and females. That viewpoint changed when researchers discovered a significant **gender gap** in the 1980 presidential election. Women voted about equally for Ronald Reagan and Jimmy Carter, but men favored Reagan by 19 percentage points. As discussed in other chapters, this gender gap has persisted nearly unabated in both voting behavior and party preference ever since.

Gender differences characterize specific issues as well. As the table below indicates, women are much less likely than men to support policies involving force, violence, and aggression. They are much less likely to support the death penalty, more likely to favor stricter gun control laws, and somewhat less likely to support an increase in military spending. Gender differences also exist concerning attitudes toward health care, good jobs, and helping the poor. Women express more support for government programs in all of these areas than do men. These attitudes may well stem from differences in

gender gap Systematic variation in political opinions that exists between males and females.

Gender Differences in Political Opinions

Opinion Force, Violence and Aggression	Men	Women Percent	Difference
Want stricter gun control laws*	42	60	18
Favor death penalty for those convicted of murder*	76	62	14
Government should spend more on military**	55	40	15
Compassion			
Government should see to good jobs/standard of living***	29	33	4
Federal spending on welfare programs should be increased**	18	27	9
Government should provide health care for sick**	40	47	7
Government definitely or probably should help reduce differences between rich and poor**	19	23	4

* Gallup 2007–8 (See Lydia Said, Shrunken Majority Now Favors Stricter Gun Laws, October 11, 2007. Accessed at www.gallup.com/poll/101731 on April 27, 2008 <http://www.gallup.com/poll/101731%20on%20April%2027>. Frank Newport, Sixty-nine-Percent of Americans Support the Death Penalty. Accessed at www.gallup.com/poll/101863 on April 27 <http://www.gallup.com/poll/101863%20on%20April%2027%202008>.

**ANES 2004.

***GSS 2006.

early socialization. Studies reveal that adults accept or even encourage aggression as part of the socialization of young boys, whereas they discourage such behavior in young girls.[35]

Women also exhibit less interest in and engagement with politics than their male counterparts.[36] A recent study by Verba, Burns, and Schlozman found that these differences persisted even after controlling for occupation, education, and access to political resources.[37] There is one interesting exception to this pattern: political engagement among women is higher in states having a female U.S. senator or a female governor than in states where women do not hold these visible elective offices. Some observers conclude that the lack of political interest among women may be tied to the scarcity of role models.

Variation in Political Culture Among the States

Moralistic Dominant   Individualistic Dominant   Traditionalistic Dominant

Geography

Geography also plays a part in explaining differences in political opinions. Southerners, for example, tend to be somewhat more conservative, are more supportive of our military, and—along with Midwesterners—express greater pride in being an American than those who live in the Northeast or on the West Coast.[38] Some political scientists, such as Daniel Elazar, believe that these differences can be traced to regional or even state-by-state variations in political culture. According to Elazar, three strains of American political culture characterize most states: individualistic, moralistic, and traditionalistic. The remainder of the states are considered hybrids, although scholars believe one of the three major political cultures dominates each.

The *individualistic political culture* emphasizes the concept of limited government instituted primarily for the purposes of safety and security. Government should protect the marketplace but not attempt to impose its own definition of a so-called good society and the costs associated with achieving it. A *moralistic political culture* envisions an active and committed citizenry working in partnership with government to achieve the collective goals of the community. It sees government service as a noble calling demanding the highest level of personal conduct. A *traditionalistic political culture* values established moral principles and accepts a limited role for government in protecting them. It supports a hierarchical view of society in which established elites play a dominant role.[39]

One can argue that changes in communications and transportation have created a more uniform national culture today. We all tend to watch the same TV shows, listen to the same music, and eat at the same fast-food outlets, no matter where we live. Millions of Americans move from one state or region to another each year. Nevertheless, regional variation, as evidenced by differences in ideology and party identification, is very real. As we will see in coming chapters, southern states have become increasingly conservative and Republican, while the Northeast has become more liberal and Democratic. And there are many states undergoing continuing change.

direction The attribute of an individual's opinion that indicates a preference for or against a particular issue.

salience The attribute of an individual's opinion that indicates how central it is to her or his daily concerns.

intensity The attribute of an individual's opinion that measures how strongly it is held.

MEASURING PUBLIC OPINION

Making meaningful assessments about public opinion requires an understanding of the dimensions around which opinions form as well as accurate ways of measuring them. Simply knowing that an individual prefers one candidate over another tells us little about the individual's probable behavior in an upcoming election or the person's reasons for holding that view. Only when pollsters apply systematic methods to measure and sample opinions can the results of a poll give us some measure of confidence about what the public is thinking.

Dimensions of Public Opinion

When legitimate pollsters ask for our views, they usually attempt to peer beneath the surface of our opinions. They seek to know not only what we believe but also how strongly we believe it, how long we have held that view, the grounds on which we base that belief, how important that belief is to us, and what we might be prepared to do about it. Together, these elements make up the various dimensions of public opinion.

The term **direction** refers to an individual's preference with respect to a particular issue. Does the respondent favor the Democrat or the Republican for president? Does he favor or oppose gay marriage? This is the dimension of an opinion that the sponsor of the poll reports most often. **Salience** is the importance we attach to an issue or topic about which we are asked. Conservation may be an issue we are prepared actively to lobby and work to promote, or we may think about the matter only when a pollster asks about it. **Intensity** consists of how strongly an individual holds a particular preference on an issue. This dimension is important because people are more likely to act on opinions they hold intensely.

The term **stability** refers to how consistently an individual maintains a particular preference over time. Americans have had stable views about the death penalty but unstable opinions about foreign policy issues. This is understandable because beliefs about crime and punishment change slowly; our views about foreign policy are tied to changing world events. The dimension of **informational support** tells us how well informed the respondent is regarding an opinion. When a person responds to a multiple-choice question, we have no way of knowing whether he or she is reacting to the question from a basis of knowledge or ignorance. For example, many individuals incorrectly believe that it is a crime to burn the American flag. A person who has little or no information about a subject may readily change his or her opinion when supplied with accurate information.

Types of Polls

Political campaigns employ a wide variety of polls and surveys. Campaigns often conduct **benchmark surveys** at the time a candidate enters a political race. These surveys measure the public's knowl-edge and assessment of the candidate at that point in time. **Trial heat surveys** pair competing candidates and ask citizens whom they would vote for in such a contest. **Tracking polls** supply the most current information on a race by polling on a daily basis. These polls allow campaigns to change their strategies on a moment's notice to respond to the latest changes in public sentiment. Such polls often interview one hundred people a day for four days and then report the totals. On the fifth day, pollsters interview an additional one hundred people whose responses become part of the total, while the one hundred responses from the first day are dropped. Respondents are subsequently added and dropped on a rotating basis for the length of the poll. *USA Today* reports tracking poll results in the presidential contest for several months before the election.

A **push poll**, the most notorious of campaign polls, is really a campaign tactic disguised as a poll. Campaign workers contact voters to provide them with negative information about their opponent and then ask the voters questions about that candidate. The goal is not to secure accurate information but to influence attitudes. Finally, **exit polls** survey voters as they leave polling places. These polls help campaign professionals analyze demographic factors that influence election outcomes. These types of polls generally are accurate but do experience occasional

stability The attribute of an individual's opinion that measures how consistently it is held.

informational support The attribute of an individual's opinion that measures his or her amount of knowledge concerning the issue.

benchmark survey A campaign poll that measures a candidate's strength at the time of entrance into the electoral race.

trial heat survey A campaign poll that measures the popularity of competing candidates in a particular electoral race.

tracking polls Campaign polls that measure candidates' relative strength on a daily basis.

push poll Campaign tactic that attacks an opponent while pretending to be a poll.

exit poll Interviews of voters as they leave the polling place.

get involved!

Conduct an opinion poll of students in your class on an issue confronting your campus. First, try surveying a randomized selection by using a table of random numbers (found in most statistics texts). Then check the results by asking the entire class. (The larger the class, the better.) How closely does the sample track the results of the class as a whole? Before you begin, be sure to pretest the questions so that you can remove any bias or ambiguity.

One of the most embarrassing moments for election pollsters came in 1948 when they predicted Republican Thomas E. Dewey would defeat President Harry Truman. Truman won, but newspapers giving the victory to Dewey had already been printed. Here Truman holds an example.

problems. In the 2000 presidential election, for example, the major media networks initially cited erroneous exit poll results that awarded the state of Florida to Al Gore.

Polling Techniques

To be informed consumers of polls, we need to understand what makes a poll scientific and which techniques differentiate good polls from bad. What makes a poll reliable? What are some of the most common flaws and how can we spot them? What information should we be looking for in order to evaluate poll results? To avoid being misled, we need to know how the poll was conducted, who was surveyed, and what questions respondents were asked.

scientific polls Any poll using proper sampling designs.

sample The individuals whose opinions are actually measured.

population The people whose opinions are being estimated through interviews with samples of group members.

probability sampling A sample design showing that each individual in the population has a known probability of being included in the sample.

Who Is Asked? Selecting the Sample

Scientific polls use the mathematical laws of probability to ensure accuracy. These laws specify that we don't need to count every member of a population as long as we count a representative group within that population in a manner that isn't biased. For example, we don't need to count every

green and red marble in a large container to know their relative proportions. So long as we select marbles in a random manner, a small sample can yield a very close approximation of the proportions in the entire container.

The individuals whose opinions pollsters measure constitute the **sample**. In a national presidential preference poll, the sample is likely to include between one thousand and twelve hundred respondents. The **population** consists of the larger group of people whose opinions the poll attempts to estimate by interviewing the selected sample. In the case of a presidential preference poll, for example, the population might be all citizens of voting age or likely voters throughout the United States.

In measuring our opinions, pollsters try to select samples that accurately represent the broader population from which they are drawn. All good sampling designs use **probability sampling**, in which each individual in the population has a known probability of being selected. One type of probability sampling, **simple random sampling**, gives everyone in a population an equal chance of being interviewed. In a pure random sample of Americans, each person interviewed would have roughly one chance out of three hundred million of being selected. Probability sampling avoids the kind of selection bias that affected the 1936 *Literary Digest* presidential poll. The sample for that poll included only people with automobiles or telephones at a time when a large percentage of potential voters possessed neither of these conveniences. Without using probability sampling, it is impossible for the pollster to know how closely the sample mirrors the overall population.

Simple random sampling, however, is not feasible in a country as vast as the United States. Even census data do not contain a complete and current list of all Americans. As a result, national pollsters use **systematic sampling** as a means of approximating the ideal. They begin with a universe of known telephone numbers, names, or locations. After picking the first number or name at random, they might make additional picks in a predetermined sequence. Some polls randomly select portions of the telephone number and append randomly selected digits to complete the number. As in pure random sampling, the goal is to approximate an equal chance of selection for every individual in the population.

Sampling error refers to a poll's degree of accuracy, usually expressed as a percentage. For example, in a population where every individual has the same chance of being selected, a poll of between one thousand and twelve hundred respondents yields a sampling error of only ±3 percent. That is, the results will deviate no more than three percentage points in either direction from results that would be obtained if every person in the entire population were surveyed. Suppose, for

Hot or Not?

Should pollsters be prohibited from making unsolicited calls to your cell phone?

views of a highly selective portion of the population, since respondents must choose to log on to a particular site to participate.

Perhaps a more daunting challenge confronting pollsters is rapidly changing communication technology that makes it more difficult to reach potential respondents. A growing number of people—especially young people—no longer have land lines and do not list their cell phone numbers. Call screening technology also helps individuals avoid the sometimes prying questions of pollsters. Pollsters are currently testing new techniques to avoid systematically excluding the views of these individuals by, for example, adjusting the sample to reflect the known proportion of various groups in the general population before analyzing the results. The samples are "weighted" by region, party, age, race, religion, and gender. In other words, pollsters know the number of men and women in the population, for example, and use that information to adjust the sample if too many or too few women are in the sample. Fortunately for political pollsters, recent studies show little difference between cell phone and land line respondents on key political measures such as presidential approval, Iraq policy, voter preference, and party affiliation. As one study concludes, analysis of two separate nationwide studies shows that including interviews conducted by cell phone does not substantially change any key survey findings.[40]

simple random sampling Technique of drawing a sample for interview in which all members of the targeted population have the same probability of being selected for interview.

systematic sampling A sample design to ensure that each individual in the population has an equal chance of being chosen after the first name or number is chosen at random.

sampling error The measure of the degree of accuracy of a poll based on the size of the sample.

leading question A question worded to suggest a particular answer desired by the pollster.

example, that a poll of one thousand people shows Candidate A leading Candidate B by a margin of 42 percent to 46 percent. This means that Candidate A's margin among the entire voting population is anywhere from 43 percent to 49 percent, and Candidate B's is anywhere from 39 percent to 45 percent. From that information, the pollster would be wise to conclude that the race is too close to call. Polls that survey fewer individuals have a higher sampling error rate. Polls of just a few hundred are sometimes used when the sponsor lacks the money or time to conduct a larger survey, or when there is an interest in the gross dimensions of opinion and the poll sponsor is willing to accept greater uncertainty about the results.

Until now, pollsters have usually conducted polls in person or on the telephone. This could change with the advent of Internet polling, which is extremely inexpensive and could be conducted by virtually anyone with access to the Web and some simple software. These polls, however, pose significant risks regarding accuracy. Many Internet surveys reflect the

What Is Asked? Paying Attention to the Questions

A reliable poll must not only use good sampling techniques but also ask the kinds of questions that will accurately capture the respondent's true opinions. It should avoid asking **leading questions**, which are phrased in such a way as to produce a predetermined response. In the 1982 Democratic primary race for governor of Ohio, candidate Jerry Springer—who went on to become a televi-

Leading questions skew poll results, as was the case when current TV host Jerry Springer ran for governor in Ohio.

sion personality—was the target of a classic example of a leading question:

> As you may know, in 1974, Jerry Springer, who had gotten married six months earlier, was arrested on a morals charge with three women in a hotel room. He also used a bad check to pay for the women's services and subsequently resigned as mayor of his city. Does this make you much more likely, somewhat more likely, somewhat less likely, or much less likely to support Jerry Springer for governor this year?

Few persons responding to a survey want to admit that they are uninformed about an important or timely subject. As a result, they sometimes respond with **nonattitudes**, or uninformed responses to which they have given little thought. Nonattitudes are considered artificial opinions created by the poll.[41] A poll can at least partially avoid the problem of nonattitudes by screening for the respondent's level of knowledge or interest, and by making it socially acceptable for respondents to say they are unfamiliar with a particular issue or question. Question order is also important. It is easy to imagine that your initial response to a question that asks whether you favor free speech might be affected if it were preceded by a question asking whether you believe the government has a role in limiting the spread of child pornography.

nonattitudes The generation of opinions by a poll that do not exist in reality.

political cynicism The view that government officials look out mostly for themselves.

THE CONTENT OF AMERICAN PUBLIC OPINION

How knowledgeable are Americans about political issues? Do Americans develop their opinions out of confidence and trust in government institutions? Do citizens believe that their opinions matter? Do Americans really believe in the implementation of democratic principles we often uncritically espouse? Let's take a closer look at the content of Americans' attitudes and beliefs.

Political Knowledge

For years, surveys have shown that Americans' political information levels persistently have fallen short of the democratic ideal. The table at right shows that levels of political knowledge changed little from 1989 to 2007. As expected, however, this characterization does not hold for all Americans: those who are well educated, those with higher incomes, and those who are older are quite knowledgeable

about our political system and even about world politics. Education is the strongest single predictor of political knowledge; better informed citizens "hold more opinions, have more stable opinions that are resistant to irrelevant or biased information . . . and have opinions that are more internally consistent with each other and with basic ideological alignments that define American politics."[42]

Some types of political knowledge are more widespread than others. Americans are better informed about institutions and processes of government than they are about people and players in the political arena. For example, they are more likely to know that the speaker of the House is the individual who presides over floor debate in the House of Representatives than the name of the current House speaker, Nancy Pelosi. This makes intuitive sense because political personnel change more frequently, and often with less fanfare, than political institutions.

Americans are generally poorly informed about global affairs. In one recent survey, Gallup found that only two in ten Americans knew that the European Union (EU) is larger than the United States. Even those who claimed to be fairly knowledgeable about the EU were more likely than not to incorrectly estimate the population of the EU relative to the U.S. population. Among those saying they knew a great deal or a fair amount about the EU, only 34

Political Knowledge— Then and Now

Percent who could name. . .	1989 %	2007 %	Diff %
The current vice president	74	69	-5
Their state's governor	74	66	-8
The president of Russia[1]	47	36	-11
Percent who know. . .			
America has a trade deficit	81	68	-13
The party controlling the House	68	76	+8
The chief justice is conservative	30	37	+7
Percent who could identify. . .			
Tom Foley/Nancy Pelosi	14	49	+35
Richard Cheney/Robert Gates	13	21	+8
John Poindexter/Scooter Libby[2]	60	29	-31

[1]President of Russia trend from February 1994

[2]John Poindexter trend from April 1990 at the conclusion of his trial for involvement in the Iran-Contra affair while in the Reagan administration from 1985 to 1986

Source: What Americans Know: 1987–2007, Public Knowledge of Current Affairs Little Changed by News and Information Revolutions (Washington, D.C.: PEW Center for People and the Press, April 15, 2007).

percent correctly said that the EU's population is larger than that of the United States.[43]

The pattern of limited political knowledge has been found to be quite stable over the last fifty years of survey research. The fact that educational levels have increased significantly over that period gives cause for concern since we would expect a more educated populace to be more politically sophisticated. When presented with clear and relevant information, however, Americans prove able to focus on matters of importance. For example, interest in world affairs spiked upward immediately following the September 11, 2001 terrorist attacks. A majority of Americans could identify the Muslim nations cooperating with the American war on terrorism, could name the countries sharing a border with Afghanistan, and knew the name of the new Cabinet office, Homeland Security, created in the wake of the attacks. What's more, attention spurred by the attacks increased the level of interest in politics more generally for most Americans.[44] These results illustrate the fact that political learning is instrumental and reflects self-interest. Americans are able and willing to pay attention and to learn about government when they consider events important and when they are presented with a clear and steady stream of reliable information. Of course, we are prone to pick up erroneous information as well when it is repeatedly touted by authoritative sources. Despite evidence to the contrary, many Americans continue to believe that Iraq played a direct role in the 9/11 attacks, in part because of repeated inferences made by some government officials.

Despite evidence to the contrary, many Americans continue to believe that Iraq played a direct role in the 9/11 attacks.

great deal of confidence in either the leaders of Congress or the executive branch, and only one in three has confidence in the United States Supreme Court.

Trust in Government

Trust in government, just like confidence, has fallen since the late 1960s. Trust consists of the belief that the people who run government genuinely have the best interests of the public in mind. Lack of trust is expressed as **political cynicism**, the view that government officials mostly look out for themselves. Trust in government declined significantly in the wake of the Watergate scandal, in which President Richard Nixon was accused of covering up a break-in into Democratic Party headquarters during his 1972 reelection campaign. Nixon subsequently resigned from office rather than face possible impeachment. Public support for the congenial Ronald Reagan lifted trust briefly and modestly in the 1980s, and it rose temporarily once again following the 9/11 terrorist attacks. Still, as the top figure on the next page demonstrates, trust in government remains low.

The decline in trust in government cuts across all demographic groups and ages. Although young people exemplified somewhat more confidence in government shortly after 9/11, by 2006, their levels of trust in government had fallen to levels comparable to their elders. Perhaps more disturbing is the fact that young people are growing more distrustful of others in general. In a recent study, only 35 percent of

Confidence in Government Institutions

In 1966, a majority of the American public had a great deal of confidence in the people running major companies, medicine, education, the military, and the United States Supreme Court. More than 40 percent had a great deal of confidence in organized religion, Congress, and the executive branch of the federal government. Then, a crisis of confidence in the leadership of major American institutions took place, variously blamed on political scandals, increased partisanship, or negative media coverage of politics.[45] No matter what the cause, confidence in U.S. institutions has never returned to its pre-1966 levels, with the exception of a short-term surge after the September 11 attacks. Today, fewer than one in six Americans has a

Confidence in U.S. Institutions

Percentage with "a great deal" or "quite a lot of confidence"

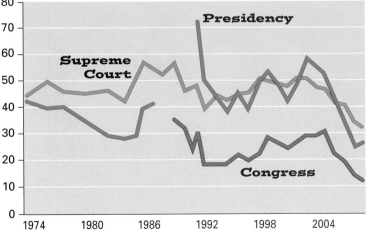

Source: Gallup Organization, Confidence in Congress: Lowest Ever for Any U.S. Institution, June 20, 2008. Accessed at www.gallup.com/poll/108142 on June 20 <http://www.gallup.com/poll/108142%20on%20June%2020>, 2008.

Can You Trust the Government to Do the Right Thing?

Trust in Government Index 1958–2004

Source: *The American National Election Studies*, November 30, 2005.

young adults age fifteen to twenty-five agreed that "most people can be trusted." Sixty percent believed that, as far as trust is concerned, "you can never be too careful."[46] Scholars have linked this decrease in trust to a decline in volunteerism.[47] As troublesome as this trend appears, however, we should not consider it a purely American phenomenon. Scholars have found similar declines in other industrialized countries as well.[48]

Political Efficacy

Political efficacy measures citizens' perception about their capacity to produce a desired outcome. It combines measures of a citizen's level of confidence in his or her own ability to navigate the political landscape (internal political efficacy) and the belief that individual political action does have, or can have, an impact on the political process in general (external political efficacy).[49] External political efficacy is especially important to well-functioning democracies, which are predicated on the notion of citizen self-government.

The long-term trend in external political efficacy is also down, but there is much more variation in this measure over

Do You Believe You Can Affect Political Change?

External political efficacy index 1952–2004

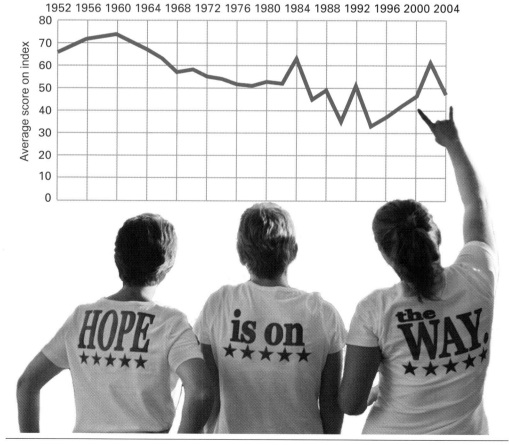

Source: *The American National Election Studies*, November 30, 2005.

time. External efficacy seems more closely tied to political events and issues than do confidence and trust. Levels of efficacy are not substantially different by party affiliation, regardless of which party is in office. As with other measures of attitudes and opinions, however, differences surface when we look at education and income. Those with more of both of these resources exhibit vastly higher levels of efficacy than those with less.

Support for Democratic Values

Our democracy emphasizes not only support for majority rule but also support for the rights of minorities. Tolerance for diverse viewpoints and lifestyles is necessary for the preservation of liberty and equality of opportunity. Nevertheless, pioneering studies on political toleration just following World War II suggested that general support for civil liberties was surprisingly low among average Americans.[50] Of course, this was a period characterized by fear of the threat of communism and a greater willingness to sacrifice liberties for security.[51] Toward the end of the Cold War, tolerance among the general public seems to have improved. Even today, however, Americans are not as supportive of democratic norms as one might hope, given our long tradition of liberty and diversity.

Many political scientists blame institutional factors for a lack of tolerance and support for political liberties. They criticize politicians for exploiting public fears to win votes, as well as the media's failure to engage citizens in a

manner that encourages thoughtful consideration of often conflicting national goals.[52] Timely events also have an impact on support for basic freedoms. In 1987 and 1988, only 29 percent of Americans surveyed believed that it "will be necessary to give up civil liberties to curb terrorism." Following the terrorist attacks in 2001, that number jumped to 44 percent.[53] By 2005, however, the number had fallen again to 33 percent.[54]

Political Ideologies

A **political ideology** is an ordered set of political beliefs.[55] These beliefs usually stem from an individual's philosophy about the nature of society and the role of government. In Chapter 2, we discussed the liberal democratic ideology that informed the origins of our nation. That ideology emphasizes liberty, equal opportunity, private property, and individualism. The dominant ideologies today in America are **liberalism** and **conservatism**. Each borrows elements from our founding values.

Unlike the liberal democracy extolled by the Framers, liberalism today embraces a larger role for government in protecting and ensuring equal opportunity, such as affirmative action. Like its earlier namesake, however, liberalism places a premium on civil liberties and counsels against government intrusion in private matters of personal and moral choice. For example, liberals generally support a woman's right to obtain an abortion. Liberals have a sense of optimism about our ability to improve our lives by changing institutions and patterns of authority.

Historically, political conservatives have believed that human nature is complex, unpredictable, and often immoral. As a result, conservatives tend to be suspicious of change. They place their trust in institutions such as the church and the family and traditional values that have demonstrated a capacity for constraining the excesses of human conduct. Conservatives today support a limited role for government in the private economy and faith in

> **political efficacy** The belief that an individual's actions can have an impact on the political process.
>
> **political ideology** A cohesive set of beliefs that form a general philosophy about the role of government.
>
> **liberalism** Political philosophy that combines a belief in personal freedoms with the belief that the government should intervene in the economy to promote greater equality.
>
> **conservatism** Political philosophy that rests on belief in traditional institutions and a minimal role for government in economic activity.

Public Tolerance for Advocates of Unpopular Positions, 1953–1998

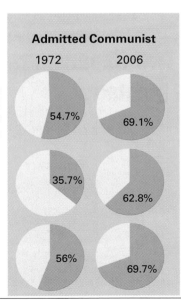
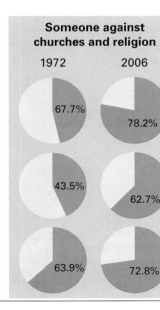

Admitted Communist

Someone against churches and religion

Percent who agree the advocate should be allowed to make a speech — 1972: 54.7%, 2006: 69.1% | 1972: 67.7%, 2006: 78.2%

Percent who agree the advocate should be allowed to teach in college — 1972: 35.7%, 2006: 62.8% | 1972: 43.5%, 2006: 62.7%

Percent who agree the advocate's book should remain in library — 1972: 56%, 2006: 69.7% | 1972: 63.9%, 2006: 72.8%

Source: GSS (various years).

Conservative evangelicals have made support for school prayer a cornerstone of their ideology.

free market mechanisms, both of which are consistent with the values of the Framers. However, conservatives today also support a more interventionist role for government in ensuring the preservation of traditional values and institutions. For example, many conservatives support prayer in public schools.

But ideology is more complex than the simple liberal-conservative dichotomy usually presented in popular culture and the media. Individuals can be liberal on some dimensions, such as support for government programs to help the poor, but conservative on other dimensions, like support for school prayer. Similarly, individuals can express liberal positions on social issues but reject government regulation in the economy, a position usually favored by conservatives.

populist Political philosophy expressing support for equality and for traditional social values.

libertarianism Political philosophy that espouses strong support for individual liberty in both social and economic areas of life.

ideologue One who thinks about politics almost exclusively through the prism of his or her ideological perspective.

The figure at right presents a more sophisticated model of ideological differences across two dimensions. The first dimension is economic, ranging from support for greater equality, even if government intervention is necessary to achieve it, to support for economic liberty where government plays a minor role. The other dimension deals with our views on social issues. On this dimension views range from progressive, for example, support for gay marriage, to traditional, such as the view that marriage should take

place only between a man and a woman. Those in the upper left-hand quadrant are generally considered liberals, and those in the lower right quadrant are conservatives. Those who support greater equality but hold traditional views on social issues are generally known as **populists** (lower left quadrant); those who stress economic liberty and progressive social views follow a political philosophy called **libertarianism**.

Despite ideological leanings, Americans traditionally have been a pragmatic people, more interested in finding solutions to problems than in enforcing ideological purity. Very few Americans are **ideologues**, those who think about politics almost exclusively in ideological terms. About 23 percent of Americans today identify themselves as liberals.

A Two-Dimensional View of Ideology

Economic issues

	Equality	Liberty
Progressive	Liberal	Libertarian
Traditional	Populist	Conservative

Social issues

Are Political Ideologies Inherited?

At least since Plato, political observers have wondered if political views and orientations are inherited. Is there such a thing as a "gene for conservatism" or a "gene for liberalism"? For years, social scientists in the modern era have favored environmental factors over genetic factors. Their explanations stress "nurture" over "nature." Recently, however, studies inquiring into the genetic basis of a variety of behaviors and attitudes have increased.

In 2005, three researchers created quite a stir when they claimed to have found that one's ideology is highly inheritable—that

is, traceable to one's genetic makeup. They studied the attitudes of identical twins (monozygotic twins, who share 100 percent of their genes). They analyzed responses from thousands of twins using a list of terms the researchers believed reflect basic conservative ideas (such as *women's liberation, school prayer, and censorship*). On the basis of positive or negative reactions to these terms, the researchers calculated a total score for conservatism and compared the results for each set of twins. The monozygotic twins they tested were much more likely to have similar responses to these items than

more genetically differentiated fraternal twins, even after environmental similarities and differences were factored in. They further hypothesized that there may be two genetically rooted types of political personalities: one conservative and the other liberal.

Conservative personalities, the researchers say, are characterized by suspicion of out-groups (for example, immigrants), a yearning for strong leadership, a desire for clear moral and behavioral codes, support for swift and severe punishment for violations of this code, and an inherently pessimistic view of human nature. Liberals, by contrast, are relatively tolerant toward out-groups, take a more content-dependent rather than rule-based approach to proper behavior, and are inherently optimistic about human nature.[*]

These findings have been attacked for methodological flaws and for over-simplifying ideological points of view.[†] The original researchers insist, however, that continued refinement of their methodology is only likely to confirm their results and that new DNA technology will improve the measurement of the genetic basis of attitudes in the future.[‡] More than 2,300 years after Plato's death, the "nature debate" is far from dead in political science.

[*] J.R. Alford, C. L. Funk, and J. R. Hibbing, "Are Political Orientations Genetically Transmitted?" *American Political Science Review*, no. 2 (2005): 164-165.

[†] See, for example, Evan Charney, "Genes and Ideologies", *Perspectives on Politics 6, no. 2* (2008): 299-319.

[‡] J.R. Alford, C. L. Funk, and J. R. Hibbing, "Beyond Liberals and Conservatives to Political Genotypes and Phenotypes," *Perspective in Politics 6, no. 2* (2008): 321-328.

The number of Americans who consider themselves conservatives is about 32 percent, a number that has risen in recent years. Only a small percentage are willing to call themselves populists and a somewhat larger but growing percentage consider themselves libertarian.[56] However, over 40 percent reject these labels and call themselves either moderates (26 percent) or undecided (20 percent).[57] White men are the most consistently conservative group in America. Persons under the age of thirty are the most liberal age group, and there are some minor variations within this age category by gender.

PUBLIC OPINION AND PUBLIC POLICY

Democratic theory posits a close relationship between public opinion and the policies generated by the political system. In a well-functioning democracy, we would expect elected leaders to act on the preferences of voters by providing policy solutions acceptable to a majority of citizens.

There are a number of uncertainties that arise in this process, however. First, voters may simply not have clear preferences on a number of issues. For example, although there is widespread support for health-care reform, so many different proposals have circulated that the public has not settled on a particular approach for ensuring coverage. In an environment of uncertainty, public opinion is subject to influence by a variety of forces that frame issues in ways that benefit more narrow interests. In lieu of public mandates, minority interests attempting to control the agenda often subject policymakers to intense political pressure (see Chapter 8).

A second problem complicating the straightforward conversion of public opinion into policy is majority tyranny. What if majority opinion supports policies detrimental to the rights of minorities? The Framers believed that a representative government would act as a filter for public opinion, channeling it in ways that were not destructive to fundamental freedoms and rights. These concerns are not simply hypothetical; elected and appointed leaders sometimes find it necessary to act contrary to public opinion to preserve more fundamental principles. During the 1950s, for example, many southern states refused to abide by Supreme Court opinions ordering the integration of public schools. The Court was attempting to secure minority rights in an atmosphere superheated by opposing public sentiment. In this tense atmosphere, the federal government sent troops to public schools in the South to protect African American students against hostile crowds.

Despite these potential problems, studies reveal a high degree of correspondence between public opinion and public policy. Studies of policymaking from the Progressive Era through the late twentieth century show that changes in public opinion generate responsive policies. Political scientist Eileen Lorenzi McDonagh found that when voters expressed popular support in state referenda for labor reform, women's rights, and prohibition, Congress responded by passing legislation accordingly. House members representing areas where referenda occurred tended to cast roll call votes supporting constituents on these controversial measures.[58]

Benjamin I. Page and Robert Y. Shapiro, in a famous political science study, found similar results when they examined hundreds of national policies between 1935 and 1979. Substantial changes in opinion, they found, were almost always followed by policy change in the same direction: "When there is opinion change of 20 percentage points or more, policy change is congruent an overwhelming 90 percent of the time."[59] The finding is especially impressive when the population considers the policy in question important. Policy change is less certain when the percentage of opinion change in one direction or the other is small, and when there is a high degree of uncertainty among the public about which policy is preferable. These and other studies suggest that policymakers do heed public opinion in forging policy, even though such congruence is not, and need not be, universal in a democratic republic.[60]

There are plenty of counterexamples, of course. For example, although a majority of Americans favored waiting for United Nations approval before attacking Iraq in 2003, President Bush, with the support of Congress, proceeded with the invasion.

PUBLIC OPINION AND CIVIC ENGAGEMENT TODAY

The role that public opinion should play in a democracy remains as highly controversial today as it was when the Framers penned our Constitution. The consent of the governed is the centerpiece of liberal democracy, but how closely should public officials track it? As we have seen, public opinion is often based on low levels of information and little understanding of the complexities of policy options. It is sometimes prone to manipulation by political consultants who seek to frame issues in self-serving ways. Some political scientists believe that public policy is best left in the hands of elites who are better informed, are more knowledgeable about government, and often are more committed to ideals of tolerance and fair play than the population at large. Some even believe that citizens themselves are more comfortable leaving policy decisions in the hands of experts.[61]

There are others, however, who believe that citizens are fully capable of making informed decisions if they

are given the tools. Professors James Fishkin and Robert Lushkin have pioneered a new kind of opinion research that could yet prove an informed and engaged citizenry not only is possible but may be the essential foundation for successful and thoughtful decision making. Called *deliberative polling,* the process begins with a baseline poll of a random, representative sample of the population. A sample of the interviewees are then invited to gather for several days to discuss the issue in question with others. Carefully balanced briefing materials are sent in advance to each of the participants, who then come together to discuss the issues in small, moderated groups. At the conclusion of the discussions, the participants are surveyed again. "I think it's fair to say that the public, in aggregate if you give them a chance, is very wise," Fishkin said. "Policymakers and experts are always surprised at how smart the results are when people get together and focus on an issue. And it's usually some combination of positions that are not entirely predictable beforehand. It's not that they move left or right—they focus on the substance of the issues and come up with some way of dealing with it that often defies stereotypes. It's really inspiring."[62]

Many political scientists remain skeptical about deliberative polling and caution that such forums place citizens in an artificial environment. Nevertheless, political scientists who have studied long-term trends in public opinion reject the tendency to blame the public for inattention, apathy, and ignorance, concluding that "If society provides accurate, helpful information about public policy; if it offers moral leadership, encourages participation, and in a broad sense educates its citizenry, then there is every reason to expect that citizens will rise to the occasion and democracy will flourish."[63]

For REVIEW >>

1. What is public opinion and why is it important?
   - Public opinion consists of those opinions held by private persons that governments find it prudent to heed. In a democracy, public opinion gives elected officials a sense of what citizens want and what they are willing to accept.

2. How is opinion best measured and how do we know these measures are reliable?
   - Opinion is best measured by scientific surveys using random samples in which every member of the population has about the same probability of being selected for interview. The reliability of surveys depends on how well the sample is drawn and on the quality of the questions.

3. What are some of the most basic features of American public opinion today?
   - Americans are not very trusting of their government and have lost confidence in elected leaders and institutions. Most consider themselves neither too liberal nor too conservative, and their knowledge about politics is lower than many political theorists would desire.

National Journal

THE PEOPLE V. WASHINGTON

Alexander Hamilton famously labeled public opinion "a great beast." The notion is that vital matters of state are best left to well-informed professional elites, not to the masses. And if the people don't like an adopted course of action, this reasoning goes, they can always vote out its representatives.

To give the argument its due, it is certainly true that the American public wins no medals for mastery of world geography and the intricacies of foreign politics and culture.

And yet there is a difference between knowledge and judgment. Even in a republic like the United States the unknowledgeable are presumed to possess a capacity, or at least a potential, for good judgment. Otherwise, why permit the average citizen to vote at all?

In early 2007, President Bush informed the nation of his decision to increase the number of U.S. troops in Iraq by about 20,000 as the key element in his new strategy for "a way forward" in the conflict. Bush's plan was based on extensive consultations with foreign-policy and military experts of various stripes, inside and outside the administration. No doubt he received a variety of opinions. But let's consider what "The People" think.

More than five years have passed since the 9/11 attacks, which inaugurated the administration's global war on terrorism and put into play the question of whether to invade Iraq. Over this period, all major polling outfits have been taking the public's pulse at regular intervals on just about every imaginable national security question.

These data indeed tell an interesting story, at odds with certain myths that have taken root about the public's mind-set on Iraq. Perhaps vox populi is a beast. But it is a beast with some fascinating things to say—about its initial attitudes on the Iraq war, about its sentiments as the war has ground on, about what it thinks is "a way forward" on Iraq, and, beyond Iraq, about America's role in the post-9/11 world.

On the eve of the Iraq invasion in March 2003, virtually every major opinion poll showed a solid majority of Americans—64 percent of respondents in the Gallup/CNN/USA Today poll, 59 percent in the Princeton Survey Research Associates/Pew Research Center poll—in favor of taking military action to remove Saddam Hussein from power. From these high numbers, a certain conventional wisdom developed about the public's support for the war.

The saga goes like this: The public backed a war whose rationale was sold, like a product, by the Bush administration and affiliated hucksters and never really challenged by a cowed and gullible news media.

A stream of public opinion surveys suggests . . . that **the federal government is following a misplaced set** of national security priorities.

Team Bush's own pronouncements buttress this story line. In explaining the White House's slow start in the summer of 2002 in putting together a plan to rally the public around the need to confront Saddam, Andy Card, at that point Bush's chief of staff, famously told The New York Times early in September 2002: "From a marketing point of view, you don't introduce new products in August."

According to this plot sequence, public opinion went over to the war camp as a result of the administration's fear-mongering statements about Saddam's weapons of mass destruction capabilities. Just days before the first anniversary of 9/11, on September 8, 2002, then-National Security Adviser Condoleezza Rice said on CNN, "We don't want the smoking gun to be a mushroom cloud."

The problem with this marketing-based account is that it is a myth. In the PSRA/Pew Research Center poll, public support for "military action in Iraq to end Saddam Hussein's rule" was 64 percent in an August 14-25, 2002, survey, before the administration's PR blitz, and at 64 percent in a September 12-14 survey, in the three days following Bush's Ground Zero visit. In the September

26-27 poll, support was 63 percent. Where's the bounce?

In fact, nearly all polls recorded their highest backing for war in the months immediately after the 9/11 attacks, when Washington was not talking much about invading Iraq. In November 2001, public support for military action against Iraq was at 78 percent in the ABC News/Washington Post poll, 77 percent in Fox News/Opinion Dynamics, and 74 percent in Gallup/CNN/USA Today. During the buildup to war that culminated in the invasion 17 months later, those numbers never went higher. This suggests a fierce, if misguided, reaction to the attacks. As everyone now acknowledges, Saddam was not behind 9/11.

Just days after the invasion began on March 20, 2003, 23 percent of respondents said United States had "made a mistake"—that's the key phrase—"in view of the developments since we first sent our troops to Iraq." Because at that starting juncture, virtually no "developments" to speak of had taken place, the 23 percent can be seen as the slice of the people who had already made up their minds about the war. 75 percent said, no, the war was not a mistake. Only 2 percent registered no opinion.

The Gallup consortium kept asking that question. But despite early waves of good news—light casualties, the fall of Baghdad on April 9, Bush's declaration on May 1 of the end of "major combat"—the "mistake" number kept rising. By early October, little more than six months after the invasion, it was already up to 40 percent; and it was 42 percent in the first poll taken after the ballyhooed capture of Saddam in his spider hole in mid-December of that first year of the war. The sensational revelations of the Abu

Ghraib prison torture scandal, in mid-April 2004, did not move the number much.

The "mistake" cohort reached a majority, 54 percent, for the first time in a poll taken on June 21-23, 2004—15 months after the invasion began, and a week after the 9/11 commission found "no credible evidence" of a link between Iraq and Al Qaeda, as the White House had asserted.

In his second inaugural address, Bush declared, "The survival of liberty in our land increasingly depends on the success of liberty in other lands. The best hope for peace in our world is the expansion of freedom in all the world."

In that speech and others, Bush has, in effect, offered both a diagnosis and a prescription for what ails the post-9/11 world. His premise that a freer world is a more placid one may not seem particularly controversial, or even original. Elites generally applauded. The beast, though, was unconvinced.

Eight months later, the Chicago Council on Foreign Relations released a comprehensive poll, "Americans on Promoting Democracy." In that survey, only 26 percent agreed that "when there are more democracies, the world is a safer place." This was not a reaction against democracy per se. Consider this second, more nuanced finding: 68 percent said that "democracy may make life better within a country, but it does not make the world a safer place."

So, broadly speaking, a stream of public opinion surveys suggests, and has been suggesting for several years, that the federal government is following a misplaced set of national security priorities. And while the people are not speaking with a single voice, majorities favor clear positions—and those majorities seem to be not fickle or mercurial but fairly solid.

With respect to Iraq, the balance of opinion, following the logic of accepting the war as a mistake, is clearly in favor of reducing America's involvement in Iraq. In the December 2006 CBS News poll, 57 percent of respondents favored setting a timetable for withdrawing U.S. troops. In the exit poll of midterm election voters, 55 percent said the United States should withdraw some or all troops, and only 17 percent supported "send more." And these beliefs carry some urgency: In Gallup's first poll after the midterms, Republicans, independents, and Democrats, all by very large margins, listed the situation in Iraq as the "top priority" for Washington to address.

These poll numbers are the stuff of front-page news. But they don't tell the whole story. Iraq is the most urgent public priority because it is an active, bleeding mess. But the public does not view Iraq as the key to dealing with America's principal, long-term problems in the world. The people are not saying to Washington, "Disengage from Iraq and then focus on the problems at home."

Americans have said that their No. 1 priority in the war on terrorism is "increasing CIA and FBI efforts to find and capture suspected terrorists," and the second goal was "capturing or killing Osama bin Laden." Even though Washington no longer talks much about getting the devastator of the twin towers, the public has clung to its wrath—and its demand for blood justice.

The Program on International Policy Attitudes posed the broader question, "What kind of foreign policy does the American public want?" In that survey, respondents listed the issues that they believed deserved greater attention from national policy makers. First was "working to reduce U.S. dependence on oil," followed by "port security," and "coordinating with the intelligence and law enforcement agencies of other countries to track and capture members of terrorist groups."

The top priority, reducing U.S. reliance on oil, is a sophisticated choice. Stories about oil dependency are not what lead the evening news, and congressional committee chairmen do not make big splashes with hearings on the subject. "Reducing oil dependency"—a goal that lends itself to quantitative measurement—may sound prosaic compared with "the expansion of freedom in all of the world." No spines tingle at the phrase. But the beast, it seems, is in a mood for prose, not poetry.

The People, to boil things down, think three big things: Washington should disengage from the military conflict in Iraq, take out bin Laden and all other known terrorists who mean America lethal harm, and reduce the nation's dependence on oil.

Two days before the 2006 midterm elections, ABC's George Stephanopoulos noted in an interview with Vice President Dick Cheney, "It seems like the public has turned against" the administration's policy on Iraq. Cheney responded, "It may not be popular with the public. It doesn't matter, in the sense that we have to continue the mission and do what we think is right, and that's exactly what we're doing."

The Iraq debacle is unavoidably calling into question the horse sense of the political establishment. "I would rather be governed by the first 2,000 names in the Boston phone book than by the 2,000 members of the faculty of Harvard University," William F. Buckley Jr. once quipped. Buckley was getting at the idea that ordinary citizens in a democracy can possess a certain collective wisdom. He also once said, less notably, "The best defense against usurpatory government is an assertive citizenry."

FOR DISCUSSION: Has your opinion of the War in Iraq evolved? Did you have a strong opinion when the war was launched? How does it compare to your opinion now?
How much should government listen to polls? Can popular wisdom be trusted to govern something as complex as a war? What are your top three priorities in the War on Terror? How do they compare to the country's?

7

POLITICAL PA

EQUAL OPPORTUNITIES AND UNEQUAL VOICES

PROVING HE'S NOT TOO YOUNG TO BE MAYOR ▌Mayor Casey Durdines has had a busy year. "The toughest issues facing California Bourough right now are public safety, our new sewage project, and encouraging residential, commercial, and industrial development," Mayor Durdines reported in an interview. "All of these issues have their share of challenges associated with them. As mayor, it is my responsibility to deal primarily with public safety concerns, so I place those before anything else. Currently I am in the process of hiring more full-time police officers as well as attempting to start a K9 unit and bicycle unit. Funding is always a concern with a small community so I am also looking for grant money to help fund these and other projects."[1] These are daunting challenges for any mayor, but they are particularly demanding when you are in your early twenties and working on a college degree.

Casey's interest in politics goes way back. His father, a liberal Democrat, engaged Casey in endless debates but often found himself on the losing end. In 2005, Durdines, then the chairman of the campus College Republicans, was encouraged by local party officials to fulfill a longtime dream by announcing his candidacy for mayor. ●◆

RTICIPATION

- What are the basic requirements for political involvement?
- How do political messages from citizens vary?
- Who is most likely to get involved in political activity?

Durdines conducted a vigorous campaign in his solidly Democratic hometown, putting up his own yard signs, knocking on doors, and talking to townspeople at Friday night football games. One of the challenges he faced was convincing voters that he was not too young to be mayor. "I hope to change the opinions of people about my age," he told a reporter. "I care about this community and I have the time to dedicate to it."[2]

Now twenty-three, Casey has graduated from California University of Pennsylvania and has some notable mayoral accomplishments under his belt. "I feel that my greatest accomplishment so far has been restoring and maintaining 24 hour a day, 7 day a week police coverage. This is something that had been lost under the previous administration." But Casey isn't finished. "I'm hoping to have more accomplishments prior to my reelection campaign next year. I am working with the California Borough Recreation Authority to construct a walking trail through a wooded parcel of land owned by the borough. Together we are also working to establish a river kayaking program on the Monongahela River. I am also working with faculty and students from the Art and Design Department at California University of Pennsylvania to assist with beautifying our community through murals and other art projects."

During the past year, Casey has kept in touch with other young mayors, sharing ideas and promoting participation by other young people. "All of us are in our 20s and face similar challenges. Facebook has been a great tool for all of us to share information and ideas. I am currently trying to recruit two people in their 20s to run for local office next year. One has expressed a serious amount of interest in doing so."

Casey's drive might be unusual, but the story of how he became politically active is not. Like other political activists, Casey was exposed to political discussion early in his childhood by family and friends. His school provided access to a political club, the Young Republicans, and he was encouraged to jump into the campaign by local leaders. Of course, it helped that he was well informed, interested, optimistic about making a difference, and ready to heed the call when the opportunity to run for office arose.

In this chapter, we will discuss the nature of political participation, the kinds of opportunities open to Americans to take part in the political process, and the factors generally associated with the likelihood that people will become involved. We will pay special attention to what motivates citizens to vote and to the reasons why many choose not to do so. We will examine the economic and social backgrounds of those who are most likely to participate and consider how this affects the kinds of policies enacted by our elected leaders. Finally, we will explore potential ways to increase citizen participation in the political process. ◄

Casey Durdines was first elected mayor when he was a student at California University of Pennsylvania.

POLITICAL PARTICIPATION: OPPORTUNITIES, COSTS, AND BENEFITS

Free societies thrive on the active participation of citizens in the civic and political life of their communities. They also require equal access to the nation's civic and political institutions so that all who desire to contribute may do so. America, however, did not realize the promise of equal access all at once. Voting restrictions based on property ownership, race, and gender fell away only slowly, and the government did not fully enforce the voting rights of minorities until the mid-1960s.

Civic-minded reformers, working outside the formal channels of government, led the effort to remove many of these obstacles to participation. Nineteenth-century Abolitionists raised political consciousness about the evils of slavery and paved the way for its eventual elimination after the Civil War. At the end of the century, civic-minded Americans who comprised the suffrage movement broke down further barriers to participation, as did civil rights groups in the twentieth century.

Opportunities for Americans to participate in government and civic life have never been greater. Political activities open to us range from voting to attending local school board meetings to running for office to campaigning for candidates to signing petitions. Outside of the arena of government, we can work for changes in our communities by joining with other residents to pressure polluters into conforming with emission control standards or by boycotting manufacturers who don't pay their workforce a living wage or by **BUYcotting**—that is, intentionally supporting with our purchases the products of environmentally friendly companies.

Opportunities alone, however, do not guarantee participation. Personal factors such as income, age, and political socialization play a large part in determining our inclination to participate. In addition, all political and civic activities involve tradeoffs between the cost of involvement and the perceived benefits. Not everyone believes they can afford the costs of participation, and many don't believe the cost is worth the effort. The perspective that choices are based on our individual assessment of costs and benefits is called the **rational actor theory**.

From the perspective of a perfectly rational actor, it is difficult to account for people taking part in some types of political participation at all— voting, for example. One vote has an infinitesimal chance of affecting the election outcome and requires the effort of registering and getting to the polls. If the candidate I vote for loses, I wasted that effort; if the candidate I prefer wins without my vote, I enjoy the benefits with-

> **BUYcotting** Using purchasing decisions to support the products and policies of businesses.
>
> **rational actor theory** The theory that choices are based on our individual assessment of costs and benefits.

Civic-minded reformers can work outside government channels to bring about change. The suffragists staged protests to raise popular support for the right of women to vote.

ity.[3] Still, not everyone believes political participation is worth the price. Perhaps they lack the resources to get involved, feel they are not knowledgeable enough to make an informed decision, or don't believe the candidates offer them a meaningful choice. Perhaps it's simply that no one has asked them for their vote. We will see next that the availability of resources, psychological motivation, and the invitation to get involved all play a part in our calculations of costs and benefits.

out having exerted any effort. The most rational approach might be to use my time in a way that is more lucrative or enjoyable and simply hope my candidate wins. Those who enjoy the benefits from an activity without paying the costs of participation are known as **free riders**. They are a problem in a society that does not force people to participate in the political system in order to receive its benefits.

free riders Those who enjoy the benefits from activities without paying the costs of participation.

Perhaps surprisingly, large numbers of citizens defy this logic every Election Day. For them, preserving democratic opportunities for engagement outweighs the cost of gathering information about issues or candidates and going to the polls. Activists report that they receive more psychological gratification from voting than from any other political activ-

CHARACTERISTICS OF POLITICAL PARTICIPATION

Distinctions between political participation and other forms of civic engagement are not always clear-cut. For example, a charity walk to raise money for AIDS research may not seem like a political activity, yet it raises public awareness of the issue and may pressure political leaders to devote more public funds to the cause. The activities of religious organizations or social clubs may also seem quite removed from politics, but the skills learned in organizing events for these groups are good preparation for political action such as running for office or becoming an advocate for a cause. Alexis de Tocqueville long ago recognized the close relationship between civic and political activity, noting that civic associations pave the way for political ones.[4]

Political participation differs from civic voluntarism, however, in at least two ways. First, people undertake political activities with the intent of directly or indirectly influencing government policy.[5] This includes a wide array of actions, such as voting in elections, working for a party or candidate, or writing a

Attributes of Political Activities

Activity	Capacity for Conveying Information	Variation in Frequency and Strength of Messages Conveyed
Voting	Low	Low
Working on a Campaign	Mixed	High
Contributing to a Campaign	Mixed	High
Contacting an Official	High	Intermediate
Participating in a Protest	High	Intermediate
Performing Informal Community Work (e.g., taking part in a Neighborhood Watch)	High	High
Serving on a Local Board	High	High
Being Affiliated with a Political Organization	Mixed	High
Contributing to a Political Cause	Mixed	High

Source: Adapted from Sidney Verba, Kay Lehman Schlozman, and Henry E. Brady, *Voice and Equality: Civic Voluntarism in American Politics* (Cambridge: Harvard University Press, 1995), 48.

letter to a congressperson in support of specific legislation. Second, political activities have broad legal consequences for the entire community, not merely for members of a private group or organization. When individuals engage in political activities to help elect a member of Congress or to change public policy regarding a military draft system, those activities affect all members of the community if the candidate is elected or the policy is adopted. The winning candidate will represent everyone in the community, and a new draft system would affect all eligible individuals as well as their families and friends.

Not all forms of political participation are identical. Some types convey more information than others, and some communicate more loudly than others. Some forms of participation give all citizens an equal voice, while others give certain members of the community more clout than others. The table on the previous page categorizes the types of political participation open to American citizens according to the amount of information they convey and the amount of variation they permit.[6]

Amount of Information Conveyed

Voting is the hallmark of democratic systems and the most studied form of participation, yet it conveys very limited information. Voters support a political candidate for a variety of reasons, including party affiliation, agreement on issues, personal characteristics, and advertising. Their choice usually depends on a combination of these factors. With such a wide variety of potential motivations, there is no clear way to know precisely what message the voters are sending. For the same reason, voters cannot be sure how the winner will interpret the message they sent at the ballot box.

Other types of political participation convey more explicit messages. For example, working for a candidate, joining a political party, or contributing money to a campaign imparts more information about support than voting alone. Participating in a protest sends a very clear message to politicians; letters to public officials can offer even more detailed information about a constituent's concerns. At an even deeper level, community organizing or service on a local school board enables citizens to help fashion policies that express their preferences. All these activities, however, may also involve higher costs in terms of time or money.

Variation in Frequency and Strength of Messages Conveyed

Effective political communication requires citizens to convey messages frequently and loudly enough so that leaders will pay attention. Some messages can be delivered only once; their variability is low. For example, each citizen may vote once and only once in an election. Other activities permit great variation in frequency, making involve-ment possible as often as time and resources allow. For example, serving on a school board affords an individual multiple opportunities to have his or her messages heard by other decision makers. Campaign donors can contribute at several points during a political campaign, up to the limits allowed by law.

Similarly, some acts of participation speak more loudly to political leaders than others. Conventional political wisdom suggests that candidates pay more attention to donors than to protesters, although the size and timing of the protest may have an impact on the candidacies. Not only can big donors convey their messages more frequently, but they can do so more loudly by the quantity of the dollars they contribute. We should keep in mind that the frequency and strength of the message participants convey are strongly related to the resources they possess.

INGREDIENTS FOR INVOLVEMENT

Why do some citizens become politically active while others remain on the sidelines? Three conditions are necessary for political participation. First, citizens must have the resources to participate. Some types of political activity require time; some require money; many require skill. These resources are not evenly distributed and their acquisition is tied to several factors, as we shall see. Second, participants must be interested in the political process and believe that their actions will make a difference. They must not only see political events as important to their lives but also believe that they can somehow influence the course of those events. Finally, people must be asked to participate. Much as in sports, those not recruited to play the game end up sitting on the sidelines.

Access to Resources

All acts of participation require the expenditure of resources: voting requires time; making cash contributions requires money; organizing a political rally requires time and skill. The type and amount of resources required vary according to the type of political activity. Writing to a member of Congress, for example, requires only basic literacy. For highly educated Americans, this is a relatively simple task, but many Americans lack the confidence in their communication to undertake it. Running for a local school board position requires more varied resources. A candidate must not only communicate effectively but also possess the ability to organize, strategize, and work with others. Conducting even a relatively small political campaign also requires time and money.

The unequal distribution of resources means that some individuals are in a better position to take political action

Resources Necessary for Various Types of Political Activities

Activity	Required Resources
Vote	Time
Campaign Work	Time, Skills
Campaign Contributions	Money
Contact an Official	Time, Skills
Protest	Time
Informal Community Work	Time, Skills
Member of Local Board	Time, Skills
Affiliation with Political Organization	Time, Skills, Money
Contribute to a Political Cause	Money

Time · Money · Skills

Source: Adapted from Sidney Verba, Kay Lehman Schlozman, and Henry E. Brady, *Voice and Equality: Civic Voluntarism in American Politics* (Cambridge: Harvard University Press, 1995), 48.

than others. Politicians may not hear those with few resources as clearly or as loudly as those with more resources. Money is a prime example of a resource that is not equally distributed among citizens. Some individuals can and do donate to a large number of causes and candidates up to the limits permitted by law. Other citizens cannot afford to contribute, so this form of participation is not open to them.

Family Wealth You have probably noticed that the same family names crop up time and time again in positions of political authority. The Bush, Kennedy, and Rockefeller families are legendary not only for their wealth but also for their intergenerational commitment to public service. This is no accident; family wealth confers opportunities that make a difference in the ability to participate in political life. Wealth directly affects the ability to contribute to political fundraising, and it is indirectly related to the possession of other resources, such as the time and skill necessary to engage effectively in other types of political activity. Many upper-income professionals have flexible schedules that allow them time to take part in community and civic projects, whereas few blue-collar workers can take time out of their workday to attend such functions.

As the figure below illustrates, the wealthy are more likely than those in low-income groups to take part in a wide range of political activities, from affiliating with political organizations to sitting on community boards. They are nearly twice as likely to vote than individuals from low-income families. The wealthy are more likely to engage in voluntary activities outside of politics, as well. For example, they are more likely to donate their time and money to charity. Wealth also opens doors to educational opportunities that train individuals in the skills necessary to participate in civic life. These skills include the ability to communicate effectively and to organize individuals to achieve particular goals.

Education No resource predicts political activity better than education.[7] The better educated are more likely to engage in electoral activities, including voting and working for political campaigns, and to participate in community activities such as charity fundraising. Education also has transgenerational effects; parents with high levels of education are more likely to expose their children to what Steven Rosenstone and John Hansen term "social networks that inform them about politics and reward political action."[8] Such children are more likely to hear their parents talking with acquaintances about political issues and to be encouraged to take part in political activities. As a consequence, they are more likely to develop habits of civic involvement than are children of parents with less formal education. Involvement in student government activities also enhances the likelihood of participation in politics, as does exposure to classroom teachers who encourage debate and open discussion.[9]

Religious Affiliation Many less affluent citizens acquire civic skills from the places where they worship. Organizing activities associated with religious institutions provides useful training for political activities such as running a campaign. Religious institutions that open leadership positions to a large number of members often

Political Activity Among High- and Low-Income Groups

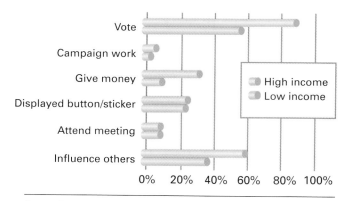

Source: Data from National Election Studies, 2004. High income is the top income quintile; low income is the bottom quintile.

Participation Rates by Race and Gender

Activity	Whites	Blacks	Hispanics	Men	Women
			Percent		
Vote	65	60	47	62	65
Campaign work	8	12	8	9	8
Campaign contribution	25	22	12	27	20
Contact political leader	37	24	17	38	30
Informal community activity	17	19	14	19	16

Source: Table constructed from data presented in Verba et al., 1995, 233 and 255, except for voting data, which come from the U.S. Census Bureau figures for 2004.

provide greater opportunities to learn necessary civic skills than do organizations with strongly hierarchical chains of command. This may explain why Hispanics, who generally attend highly structured Catholic congregations, are less active in civic life than are African American Protestants of similar economic means.[10] Many Protestant denominations allocate considerable authority and responsibility to local church leaders and members of the congregation. Jewish congregations are also organized in a decentralized manner, allowing members of a synagogue many opportunities for involvement and the exercise of leadership skills.

Workplace The workplace also provides opportunities to develop resources such as analytic and communication skills that are useful for political life. Upper-income jobs, however, typically provide more such opportunities than those that pay considerably less. These high-paying jobs often stress human relations skills and provide many opportunities for exercising the organizational talent necessary to engage in politics. They also place individuals within a circle of acquaintances who are likely themselves to be politically active.

By contrast, low-skill jobs that require little formal education provide fewer opportunities for making decisions or leading meetings. Labor unions, however, offer low-skill workers the opportunity to occupy leadership positions, thus providing an alternative forum for civic learning. Union forepersons, for example, must learn to resolve disputes and to represent the rank and file to the management. Unions also promote civic activism by educating members about political issues and urging them to become active in their communities. Unfortunately, steep declines in union jobs over the last quarter century have severely undercut such opportunities for many workers.

Race and Gender Access to resources varies according to race and gender, but these variations likely reflect underlying differences in wealth as well as leadership and educational opportunities. Whites, on average, participate in greater numbers than African Americans in political activities, and Hispanics have lower participation rates than either whites or blacks. However, voting rates among blacks have risen since the passage and enforcement of voting rights laws in the 1960s. In addition, blacks and whites with similar levels of education vote at about the same rates.

> **political engagement**
> Psychological predisposition toward or interest in politics.

Women now vote at higher levels than men, whereas men contribute significantly more money to political leaders and contact political leaders more often than women.[11] Women's political contributions have increased in recent years, but a gap remains, perhaps because women receive lower pay than men with similar jobs. Women may be somewhat less likely to contact political leaders because far fewer leaders are female.

Political Engagement

Personal resources supply the necessary ingredients to take part in government, but they alone cannot explain why some people get involved while others do not. Some people become politically active because they see it as their civic duty or because politics is a vocational interest. These persons display a psychological predisposition toward political involvement called **political engagement**. Others participate only when they feel their political issues touch directly on their vital interests, such as a local ordinance that threatens to close an individual's business. Many simply feel politics has no relevance to their day-to-day lives or problems. People who hold these latter views strongly are unlikely to have the motivation to participate. Cross-cultural studies also show that po-

Political Inactives' Reasons for Their Inactivity

	%
I don't have enough time	39
I should take care of myself and my family before I worry about the community or nation	34
The important things of my life have nothing to do with politics	20
I never thought of being involved	19
Politics is uninteresting and boring	17
Politics can't help with my personal or family problems	17
Politics is too complicated	15
As one individual, I don't feel I can have an impact	15
For what I would get out of it, politics is not worth what I would have to put into it	14
Politics is a dirty business	13
I feel burned out	9
It is not my place	9
I don't like the people	7
It is not my responsibility	6
There are no good causes anymore	6
I might get into trouble	3

Source: Sidney Verba, Kay Lehman Schlozman, and Henry E. Brady. *Voice and Equality: Civic Voluntarism in American Politics* (Cambridge: Harvard University Press, 1995), 129.

litical engagement is affected by the overall level of income inequality within the nation. Where greater income inequality prevails, individuals at the bottom of the income ladder are far less likely to demonstrate an interest in politics, to discuss politics, or to vote.[12] The adjacent table lists several reasons why people choose not to get involved in politics.

Political engagement involves four dimensions or elements: political interest, political efficacy, political information, and strength of party identification.[13] **Political interest** is the level of concern that a politically engaged person has about an election outcome and the candidates' positions on the issues. Politically interested individuals care which candidate will win an election and which position on an issue the government will adopt. As a result, they tend to be more politically active. Political efficacy is the sense of empowerment or satisfaction created by political involvement. This dimension has both internal and external components.[14] **Internal political efficacy** is the confidence individuals have in their ability to understand and participate in the political world. People with high levels of internal political efficacy believe they can comprehend political issues and know how to make themselves heard. **External political efficacy** is an individual's belief that the government will respond to his or her actions. Individuals with high levels of external political efficacy are confident that the government will listen when they speak and respond appropriately. People who lack a sense of political efficacy often regard political activity as intimidating and wasteful.

The third dimension of political engagement is **political information**, the amount of knowledge a person has about political issues, figures, and the workings of the political system. Citizens with more knowledge of the Constitution, political leaders, and the issues of the day are more likely to participate. That is why it is important for young people to acquire sound political education in the schools. A final dimension of political engagement is **strength of party identification**. We will see in Chapter 9 that identification with either the Democratic or Republican Party can predict not only the direction of a person's vote but also whether he or she is likely to vote at all.

It is unclear whether political engagement causes one to become active politically or whether participating in political activity increases one's sense of political engagement. The causal relationship probably runs both ways.

Mobilization

Even an individual with the necessary resources, a high level of interest, and confidence in his or her ability to make a difference is unlikely to get involved unless asked to do so. Through the process of **political mobilization**, a variety of sources alert citizens to opportunities to participate and encourage them to become politically involved. These sources include political parties, elected officials,

Personal contact is one of the most effective ways to mobilize citizens to participate in the political process.

interest groups, candidates for political office, voluntary associations, friends, and neighbors.

Direct mobilization involves contacting citizens personally to invite them to take part in political activities. Examples include door-to-door canvassing, direct mail solicitation, circulation of petitions, requests for money, and letter-writing campaigns. In appealing to citizens, activists are likely to provide either inducements, such as political promises, or assistance, including transportation to the polls. Political parties traditionally played the principal role in mobilizing voters. They would inform voters about when elections were being held and which candidates were running. During the twentieth century, however, the mobilizing role of parties weakened as other institutions, such as the mass media, began delivering political information without the "personal touch" of a local precinct captain or party worker.

Many scholars believe the loss of personal contact in voter mobilization has contributed to a decline in voting. It is easier to ignore an admonition to vote from a television newscaster than to ignore a personal appeal from a neighbor who represents your party of choice. In fact, voter turnout in America peaked during the heyday of political parties at the turn of the twentieth century. During this period, turnout was as high as 80 percent or more, partly because of party efforts to directly touch voters. Political parties energized communities with parades and picnics to generate support and sought out the visible loyalty of citizens by providing their constituents with jobs, government contracts, and other tangible benefits. As we will see in Chapter 9, candidates have begun doing a better job of voter mobilization in the last two presidential elections.

Indirect mobilization occurs when leaders use networks of friends and acquaintances to persuade others to participate. Political leaders know that citizens are far more likely to respond to appeals from a member of their own religious congregation, for example, than from a politician they do not know. As a result, political leaders use the power of organized groups such as professional associations, business groups like the Chamber of Commerce, labor unions, civic associations, and churches to spread enthusiasm for a candidate or a cause.

Where voluntary associations are numerous and strong, their potential impact on political participation should be great. Where such associations are few or weak, political agents have fewer organizations to utilize for recruitment. There is no doubt that the falloff in the number of Americans active in traditional types of voluntary associations has made political mobilization more difficult.

Several factors affect the timing, targets, and method of mobilization. First, political actors—whether through direct or indirect mobilization—are likely to target their efforts at strategic times to enhance the success of their cause. For example, political parties concentrate their activities around primary or general elections.

Second, political actors are more likely to target groups of individuals they believe will respond positively to their

political interest An attribute of political participants that measures one's concern for an election outcome and the positions of the candidates on the issues.

internal political efficacy An individual's self-confidence in his or her ability to understand and participate in politics.

external political efficacy An individual's belief that his or her activities will influence what the government will do or who will win an election.

political information A measure of the amount of political knowledge an individual possesses concerning political issues, political figures, and the workings of the political system.

strength of party identification The degree of loyalty that an individual feels toward a particular political party.

political mobilization Process whereby citizens are alerted to participatory opportunities and encouraged to become involved.

direct mobilization Process by which citizens are contacted personally to take part in political activities.

indirect mobilization Process by which political leaders use networks of friends and acquaintances to activate political participation.

Political leaders use community groups and organizations to help spread their message.

message. Local party activists rarely try to convert supporters from the opposition party. This is also true for those who engage in indirect mobilization, such as political advocacy groups. They usually address their appeals to upper-income, highly educated individuals who have been willing in the past to write letters, to donate money, or to make phone calls in support of their cause.

Finally, the cost of the action being requested affects mobilization. Signing a petition involves little effort. Voting requires a bit more. Writing a thoughtful letter to a member of Congress can require more time, energy, and skill. People are likely to consider responding to invitations if the requests do not come too often, if there is a realistic chance of success, if they consider the outcome important, and if participation does not conflict with other important demands on their time.

VOTING

Voting is a unique political activity for a variety of reasons. As we noted earlier, a rational actor may well see very little reason to vote, based on the perceived costs and benefits. And because voting conveys little information, even those who vote have no idea whether a candidate will respond to their needs. Nevertheless, tens of millions of Americans vote regularly in national elections. For many of them, voting confers the psychological benefit of satisfying one's civic responsibilities and promotes candidates and issues important to their interests.

Who Votes? Who Doesn't?

Clearly resources make a difference in voting. Voter turnout increases directly with employment status and wealth, level of education, and age. Females now vote at a greater rate than males, reversing a long-standing trend. White Americans vote more often than African Americans but, as noted earlier, this difference vanishes when one controls for education. Regional differences also exist; both coasts have higher voting rates than the interior of the country.

Turnout generally increases with age but declines again for the most elderly in the population. Young people between the ages of eighteen and twenty-four have the lowest voting turnout. Some of this is the result of maturation. Young people take some time to adjust to their status as adult citizens, develop independent roots in their communities, establish themselves in careers and families, and develop an interest in how government policy affects their lives. Younger citizens are often not able to shoulder the costs of participation,

as we discuss next. Voting turnout among youth not only is lower than it is for other age groups but, until most recently, has been dropping since eighteen-year-olds first exercised the franchise in the 1972 presidential election.

Only a fifth of those surveyed between the ages of eighteen and twenty-four see voting as a responsibility. About a third see it as a choice (34 percent) or a right (31 percent). Fewer than 10 percent consider voting a duty. Many do not vote, because they do not believe government is responsive

Who Votes?

Total Voting

61.2%*

Percentage who reported having voted in 2004	
Race and Ethnicity	
White	65.4
Black	60.0
Asian	44.1
Hispanic (of any race)	47.2
Gender	
Men	62.1
Women	65.4
Age	
18 to 24 years	46.7
25 to 34 years	55.7
35 to 44 years	64.0
45 to 54 years	68.7
55 to 64 years	72.8
65 to 74 years	73.3
75 years and over	68.5
Employment Status	
Employed	65.9
Unemployed	51.4
Educational Attainment	
Less than 9th grade	38.8
9th to 12th grade, no diploma	39.8
High school graduate or GED	56.4
Some college or associate degree	68.9
Bachelor's degree	77.5
Advanced degree	84.2
Income	
Lowest fifth	56
Second fifth	68
Third fifth	82
Fourth fifth	90
Highest fifth	89
Region	
Northeast	64.1
Midwest	61.0
South	61.0
West	64.0

* 2008 Preliminary estimate of Voter Eligible Population.

Source: U.S. Census Bureau, *Voting and Registration in the Election of November 2004,* Washington, D.C., November 8, 2005; except for income, which came from National Election Study, 2004. Figures are for voting age population.

Voter Turnout in Presidential Elections, 1972–2008*

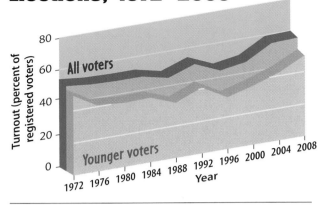

* 2008 Preliminary estimate of Voter Eligible Population.

Source: Center for Information and Research on Civic Learning and Education.

those who have met all criteria for voting, including registration. When we use this latter measure, we get a slightly higher turnout rate. Nevertheless, it is the first measure that is usually cited by newspapers, most scholars, and the U.S. Census Bureau. Either way, two facts stand out. From about 1960 to 1992, turnout in presidential elections declined. After a spike in 1992, it dipped again, only to rebound in 2004 and 2008. A second undisputed feature is that American turnout compares unfavorably to rates in other democracies, although some European countries have begun to experience turnout declines as well. Four factors are primarily responsible for our poor turnout compared to other nations. First, Americans must register to vote either in person or by mail, and they must reregister if they move or fail to vote in a certain number of consecutive elections. By contrast, some countries use a civil registry system that automatically registers every eligible resident. Denmark, for example, uses a computerized national civil registry to produce a voter list. The government issues each citizen a number, somewhat like our social security numbers, for

to their needs. Only 53 percent of young people feel the government and elections address the concerns of young people. Only 48 percent say political leaders pay at least some attention to people like them.[15] Nevertheless, voting among the young is experiencing a resurgence. Turnout among young people increased in 2008 from four years earlier as did participation by older voters. However, the 1 percent increase in the youth share of the vote was smaller than many had anticipated in light of the interest generated by the campaign.

Factors Influencing Voter Turnout

When measuring voter turnout, some scholars say that we should look at all voting age citizens—that is, citizens eighteen years of age or older. The rationale is that this represents the true potential pool of individuals who could cast votes if they took the time to register and come to the polls on election day. Others claim that we should examine only the pool of eligible voters—

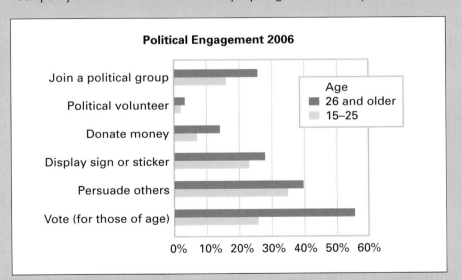

personal **is Political**

What kind of political involvement would you find most appealing?

- Voting (for those of age)
- Joining a political organization
- Volunteering for a candidate or party
- Persuading others to vote a certain way
- Donating money
- Displaying a sign or bumper sticker

Compare your answers to those of other people, aged fifteen and up.

Political Engagement 2006

Age
- 26 and older
- 15–25

Source: Mark Hugo Lopez, Peter Levine, Deborah Both, Abby Kiesa, Emily Kirby, and Karlo Marcelo, *The 2006 Civic and Political Health of the Nation: A Detailed Look at How Youth Participate in Politics and Communities* (College Park, MD: Center for Information and Research on Civic Learning and Engagement, October 26), 16.

the delivery of all government services and the payment of taxes. Voters can present the number for identification at the polls throughout the country, no matter where they live. In 2007, some states in this country experimented with a

voter fatigue A tendency to tire of the process of voting as a result of frequent elections.

form of this procedure known as Vote Centers. Preliminary analysis shows a slight increase in turnout. Many countries also require registration only once in a lifetime so that voters remain permanently eligible no matter where or how often they move within the country.

The timing and scheduling of elections also affects turnout. Voting in the United States often takes place on a Tuesday, which means that most Americans must adjust their workday schedules to go to the polls. By contrast,

Average Turnout in National Elections, Western Europe and United States Since 1945

	Average Turnout*
Belgium	92.5
Austria**	90.9
Italy	89.8
Luxembourg	89.7
Iceland**	89.5
Malta	88.2
The Netherlands	86.6
Denmark	86.0
Sweden	85.7
Germany	85.0
Norway	80.4
Greece	79.9
Spain	75.7
Finland**	75.6
United Kingdom	75.2
France**	74.8
Portugal**	73.6
Ireland**	72.6
Switzerland	56.6
United States**	47.2

* Data presented are percent of registered voters, except for the United States, where percent of voting age population is given. This reduces somewhat the rate for the U.S. but does not substantially change the rank order.

** Presidential forms; includes results from both presidential and representational body elections.

Source: European data from International Institute of Democracy and Electoral Assistance; U.S. data from U.S. Census Bureau.

Many nations hold elections on weekends to increase turnout.

some European countries schedule elections on a national holiday to make it easier for voters to show up at the polls. Other nations, including Norway, Japan, Switzerland, and New Zealand, hold elections on weekends.

Our two-party system also helps explain low turnout in the United States. Most other Western democracies have multiparty parliamentary systems that generally represent the interests of particular economic groups within the nation. In Great Britain, for example, the Labour Party has a long tradition of appealing to the working class; the Conservatives (popularly called the Tories), by contrast, make their appeals to the more affluent. The economic orientation of political parties can exert a powerful influence on getting out the vote by convincing voters that their economic interests are taken seriously by political leaders. In America, the major political parties rarely structure their messages primarily around economic divisions, preferring to appeal to the vast middle of the economic and ideological spectrum. (We will discuss this characteristic of American parties at greater length in Chapter 9.) Some researchers believe that the centrist appeal of American parties is partly responsible for the poor turnout of lower-income groups because citizens in these brackets fail to hear candidates addressing their concerns.[16]

The number and frequency of elections is a fourth factor depressing turnout in the United States. The United States holds more primary and general elections at the national,

global Perspectives

Changing Patterns of Political Participation

In today's world, where personal identity and expression are seen as more important than simply voting one's pocketbook, younger people seem less interested in traditional activities like voting or joining organizations and more interested in finding new modes of political self-expression. The table at right, based on data compiled by Ronald Inglehart and Gabriella Catterberg,[1] charts the rise in unconventional political activities like protesting and boycotting in Western industrial democracies over the period from 1974 to 2000. The authors claim the rise in these forms of participation reflects the interest younger people have in more direct methods of expression beyond the simple act of voting.

Although Inglehart and Catterberg find that this pattern does not yet hold for new democracies that are experiencing economic and political uncertainties, they believe that it represents a new reality in the political landscape of advanced democracies.

The authors reject the notion that citizens in advanced democracies are withdrawing from civic action. Instead, they insist, citizens in today's world are increasingly critical of elite decision making and unwilling to join elite institutions; and they are increasingly ready to intervene actively to influence specific decisions. In short, "the nature of citizen politics in advanced democracies has changed."[2]

Percent Increase in Unconventional Participation in Industrialized Democracies
1974–2000

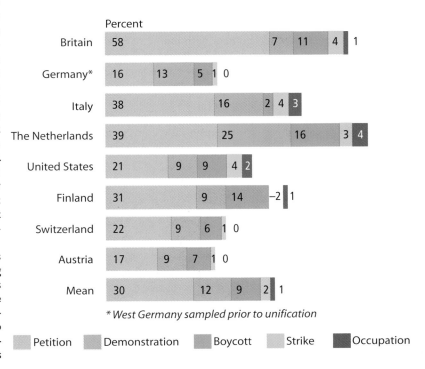

* West Germany sampled prior to unification

Petition Demonstration Boycott Strike Occupation

[1] Ronald Inglehart and Gabriella Catterberg, "Trends in Political Action: The Developmental Trend and the Post-Honeymoon Decline," *International Journal of Comparative Sociology* 43, no. 3–5 (2002): 300–316.
[2] Inglehart and Catterberg, 314.

---

state, and local levels than any other democracy. Unlike many European voters, who go to the polls once every three, four, or five years, American voters in most states are asked to vote in primary and general elections every year, and often more frequently. Special elections may be called to replace candidates who resign or are removed from office. Some states also ask citizens to vote on referenda to approve or reject particular measures ranging from tax increases to special funding for public schools. Many analysts believe the frequency with which Americans are called to vote creates **voter fatigue**, a tendency to tire of the process and refrain from going to the polls.

Finally, the competitiveness of the race affects turnout: the more competitive the race, the more interest it draws. Voters are less likely to show up if the result is clearly predictable. Although competitive races attract more interest

and participation, only about half of the presidential contests since 1952 have been close right up to Election Day, and congressional elections today are rarely competitive (as we will see in Chapter 11).[17]

OTHER FORMS OF POLITICAL PARTICIPATION

Many forms of political participation require citizens to spend more resources than the simple act of voting. Some, such as volunteering to work in a political campaign or writing letters to political leaders, require additional expenditures of time. Others, such as contributing to a candidate or cause, require additional financial resources.

Beyond Voting: Activities That Require More Time

Although U.S. voter turnout compares poorly to that in other democracies, Americans show greater levels of participation in more time-consuming political activities. One study comparing the United States to Austria, the Netherlands, the United Kingdom, and Germany found that Americans ranked first in the amount of time they devoted to campaign work, contact with public officials, and community volunteering.[18] Unlike voting, there is no limit to the number of times one can perform such acts or the amount of time one can devote to them. Some stalwart activists find themselves limited only by the number of hours in the day. Activities that require more time also vary in the amount of information they convey and the level of skill necessary to perform them. Writing a thoughtful letter to a member of Congress and working a candidate's phone bank during a political campaign are two examples of time-intensive activities that convey a high level of information and require a high level of skill and knowledge.

Because time-intensive activities demand a greater level of commitment than voting, we would expect these acts to hold the potential for greater benefits. Some of the benefits may be material. A successful candidate might appoint campaign workers to advisory positions or promote policies that directly benefit them, such as a change in zoning that permits business expansion. Participation also provides psychological rewards such as the opportunity to meet and work with others who share similar views. Activists feel gratified when their work results in the implementation of policies they support.[19] Other, less conventional forms of participation such as petitioning and demonstrating enable the individual to take some direct and personal role in promoting an idea or cause. Many times these are tools used by groups that feel they can find no other way to make their voices heard. Some people find these activities more personally rewarding than anonymous acts

Mike Kostyo meeting with a new campaign volunteer.

PORTRAIT OF AN ACTIVIST

Meet Mike Kostyo

Iowa is where the action is.

This surprised a lot of people when I told them I was moving to Iowa to work on Hillary Clinton's presidential campaign. But Iowa, because it holds the first caucus in the nation, becomes ground zero for presidential politics every four years.

I never planned on doing this. As a college journalism major, I had to keep my political opinions to myself. But I was very passionate about free speech issues, which led to my involvement with the American Civil Liberties Union, which led to advocacy on a number of other issues.

We do all of the things you normally associate with campaigns—walk in parades, attend county council meetings, plan events, facilitate visits from the candidate or surrogates, try to get endorsements, clean the office, etc.—in order to build an organization of support, one by one, that will be there for us on caucus night.

I enjoy it, because it turns politics into a two-way street. It gives the average citizen the opportunity to become closely involved with the political process. Our success depends on the personal relationships we have with voters, which is something you rarely see in national politics.

like voting and more relevant to their everyday lives. And Americans are not alone. The incidence of unconventional activity like protesting seems to be increasing in many developed democracies. Some researchers believe these actions represent an emerging pathway to more meaningful citizen engagement—a pathway that needs further scholarly exploration.[20]

Beyond Voting: Activities That Require More Skill

Voting is a fairly simple act. So is donating money. But some acts of political participation require more sophisticated skills. Political campaigns in America are fueled by thousands of unpaid average citizens who staff phone banks, contact donors, serve as financial consultants or liaisons with the press, coordinate activities with political parties, and organize rallies. Even writing a letter to one's congressperson requires confidence in one's ability to communicate effectively. These activities put us in close contact with our elected leaders, giving us an opportunity to express our views more clearly than the act of voting alone.

Citizens who engage in these activities are not equally drawn from all segments of the political community. The more affluent are more likely to write letters, volunteer for political campaigning, make political contact with elected officials, and work on solving community problems. The affluent often have training in the skills necessary for these more demanding tasks. Nevertheless, as we have seen, religious organizations and labor unions can provide those with fewer resources opportunities to develop these same skills. Often, lower levels of participation by the poor are traceable not to lack of skill but to

lower levels of interest or a lack of confidence in their political efficacy. When political activities require financial commitment, however, the discrepancy in participation between rich and poor is not only greater, it is more difficult to overcome.[21]

Beyond Voting: Activities That Require Money

Contributing money is the political act that has the greatest capacity for variation from individual to individual. Within the limits of the law, contributors can donate as little or as much as they want. However, the clarity of the message conveyed by political donations can vary depending on the identity of the recipient. Contributing to a narrow political cause sends a clear message that one supports the goals established by the group. By comparison, contributing money to a presidential campaign may signal support for a candidate's position on social security reform or for his or her personal leadership abilities. The actual motivation for giving is ambiguous for the recipient.

Campaign contributions continue to come largely from those with greater resources, but the Obama campaign in 2008 demonstrated the potential of the Internet for widening the base of financial support. His campaign raised $1 million a day or more, mostly from donors contributing $250 or less.

Advocacy groups that promote a political agenda outside of the electoral arena, for example, by petitioning administrative agencies and the courts, also need money—often great sums of it. These types of activities

Political leaders and organizations increasingly rely on posh fundraising events to fuel their political campaigns.

are very expensive. As a result, political candidates and advocacy groups must turn to supporters who can afford to contribute to the cause.

Financial giving as a form of participation raises concerns about the type of citizen commitment that today's politicians and activists value most. Some scholars worry that we have entered a period of **checkbook democracy** where little is required of citizens beyond their cash.[22] Campaign strategists and advocacy group professionals in Washington offices plot political operations with little citizen input, contacting the public only for the funds necessary to keep their organizations going. Politicians rarely consult citizens about specific proposals, tactics, or campaign goals. This deprives citizens of opportunities to develop civic skills they might acquire through face-to-face participation. The most worrisome aspect of this trend is the potential for the wealthy to dominate political participation and policymaking, shutting the less well off out of the process.

This portrait of political participation in America is overly bleak. Many campaign organizations and advocacy groups combine citizen action with cash contributions. They alert contributors and noncontributors alike to measures that threaten their interests and mobilize them to take action by contacting elected officials by letter or phone or over the Internet. Many advocacy groups facilitate citizen communication with political leaders by providing contact information or even

direct access through the association's telecommunications network.

Another type of financial activism is on the rise as well: **consumer activism**, the practice of making a political or social statement with one's buying power. Commerce today is dominated by global corporations that reach beyond single continents. Their activities often escape regulation by individual nations. Except for shareholders with major stakes in these companies, individuals have little control over their operation. Nevertheless, some consumers find it useful to make a personal statement about the behavior of these companies or their products through their buying habits. Consumers can register their disapproval for the acts of certain businesses by boycotting their products; they can reward companies they believe are exemplary by BUYcotting. Consumer activism of this sort is surprisingly widespread. Roughly half of the adult population in America reports having used their buying power to either punish or reward companies or products in the past twelve months. These activities seem to be spread across all age levels, although they are more likely to be practiced by Americans with higher incomes and among those who are most attentive to politics.[23]

Hot or Not?

Should BUYcotting, or selectively buying products based on a company's record of social responsibility, be considered a form of political action?

Many people, especially the young, are turning to consumer activism as a means of making political statements.

THE IMPACT OF PARTICIPATION PATTERNS ON POLICY

Does it matter that those at the upper end of the socioeconomic spectrum participate more and have greater contact with political elites than the less advantaged? If the concerns and issues that mobilize the well off are the same as those important to the rest of the population, there should be little cause for concern. However, if the concerns of the two groups differ, then there is reason to believe that politicians are more likely to pay attention to the needs of the wealthy while ignoring those of the poor.

Voting data seem to indicate that the attitudes and preferences of voters and nonvoters are substantially similar.[24] With the possible exception of extremely close elections, like the 2000 presidential contest, increased turnout by the less advantaged would probably not affect the outcome of most elections.[25] Participation that conveys more information to leaders, however, displays a larger gap between the concerns of those who participate most and those who are least politically active. Citizens who depend on government assistance programs such as welfare, food stamps, and income support are far less likely to write letters, take part in community activities, contact political leaders, protest, or contribute time or money to a political campaign. When they do communicate with leaders, they are twice as likely as the advantaged to refer to their basic needs—food, housing, health care, and the like. By contrast, wealthier citizens—who are three times as likely as the disadvantaged to contact elected officials—are more likely to voice concerns about taxes, government spending, and the budget.[26] As a result, leaders hear more from their constituents about taxes and budgets than they hear about government programs that are vital to a large segment of the population.

Economic inequality not only affects the kind of issues political leaders are likely to take up. It also, as one researcher concludes, "stacks the deck of democracy in favor of the richest citizens and, as a result, most everyone else is more likely to conclude that politics is simply not a game worth playing."[27] Differences in access to resources, interest, and mobilization create patterns of political participation in America that result in a much louder voice for those already advantaged. Political scientist Sidney Verba describes the process this way: "Socioeconomic inequality produces inequality in political voice; this in turn fosters policies that favor the already advantaged; and these policies reinforce socioeconomic inequality."[28]

Some observers might argue that this imbalance in political participation is not all bad. After all, the affluent are often better informed and more tolerant of divergent beliefs than are the less well off. One might argue that domination of political discourse by the more affluent will result in more enlightened policies.[29] Democratic governments, however, are supposed to balance the interests of different groups. The balancing act is made more difficult when our political leaders hear disproportionately from one segment of the population.

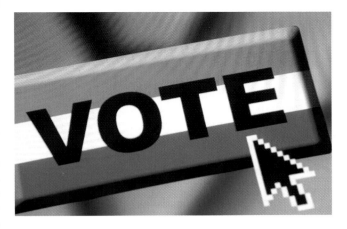

Is electronic voting in our future?

PARTICIPATION AND CIVIC ENGAGEMENT TODAY

Many social scientists believe American democracy is in crisis today largely because its citizens have turned away from political participation.[30] What do such trends as the decline in voter turnout and participation in civic organizations, particularly among the young, indicate about civic engagement today, and what can we do to spark even greater civic interest and involvement in government? Although the challenge is great, changes in current practices can make some forms of participation less costly in terms of time and money, two of the biggest constraints on participation.

> **checkbook democracy** A term that expresses the notion that little is required of citizens beyond their cash.
>
> **consumer activism** The practice of making a political or social statement with one's buying power.

Several proposed reforms, such as keeping polls open longer on Election Day, could greatly reduce the inconvenience associated with the act of voting. In some states, the polls close as early as 6 P.M., disenfranchising many working people and discouraging many young adults—a group that reports the need for greater flexibility in polling hours to accommodate their work and school schedules.[31] Second, many nonvoters say they would be more likely to vote if Election Day were a national holiday or held on a weekend. Making Election Day a holiday would also heighten social awareness of the importance of the activity. Third, all states could adopt same-day registration. This would

Percent Voting in Advanced Industrialized Countries with Compulsory Voting

Country	Under 30	30-44	45-64	65 and Older
Australia (2004)	97%	98%	98%	99%
Belgium (2004)	89%	98%	97%	92%
Greece (2000)	90%	93%	95%	93%
Luxemburg (1999)	91%	93%	95%	86%

Source: Martin P. Wattenberg, *Is Voting for Young People?* (New York: Pearson Education, 2007), 168.

reduce the burden on citizens who frequently move or who want to participate but either are unaware of registration requirements or learn about them too late to comply with cut-off dates. Several states already have same-day voter registration; among these are states like Maine, Wisconsin, and Minnesota, with some of the highest turnout rates in the nation. Other states are actually making the process of voting even more onerous by requiring the presentation of official voter identification, such as a state driver's license, at the polls. Although this may discourage voter fraud (a practice that most believe is negligible), it also has the unintended consequence of discouraging those without official IDs from voting. Recently, the U.S. Supreme Court upheld Indiana's stringent voter ID requirement (*Crawford v. Marion County Election Board*). Finally, new methods of voting—such as Oregon's vote-by-mail experiment or pilot online voting programs in Arizona and Washington—could complement the current procedure of casting a ballot at a polling place. These methods are proving very popular, especially among young people. States experimenting with no excuse early voting found an increase in turnout, with as many as a third of voters taking advantage of this added convenience.

Some scholars suggest that voting rates have dipped too low for such piecemeal solutions. They recommend adopting compulsory voting as a means of reigniting the voting habit.[32] Compulsory voting laws would require eligible citizens to show up at the polls on Election Day or pay a small fine. Data show that such laws in other countries result in high turnout among every age category. However, the idea of making voting a compulsory activity seems utterly out of sync with America's reliance on volunteerism. As a result, this is one solution that may have little future in this country.

Reducing the cost of running for public office may reduce financial barriers to participation by limiting the importance of campaign fundraising. For example, networks could make free television available to political candidates to scale back the largest single cost of campaigning. A system of partial public financing for presidential elections is already in place, and several states are experimenting with public funding of campaigns for state offices (see Chapter 9). Government could make more public funding available to those who wish to run.

Enhancing civic skills to improve participation rates is perhaps the simplest reform to achieve—at least in theory. In this area, educational institutions may be in the best position to increase their efforts and effectiveness. Over the last generation, high schools have reduced by two-thirds the median number of civics and government courses they offer. This represents an abandonment of one of the traditional functions of public schools: training students in the skills necessary to take part in their democratic heritage.[33] Schools could provide more intensive—and more interesting—courses in government. Students show more excitement and interest in politics when they are asked to get involved rather than merely to study a subject from a textbook or listen to lectures. Many schools already offer opportunities to learn by encouraging or requiring students to attend public meetings, talk to government officials, and engage in service learning activities to assist community members in solving local problems. Schools can do more to encourage voting as well. Colleges can hold voter registration drives, help students locate polling places, and assist in disseminating absentee ballots.

In future chapters we will examine how institutional factors like our system of elections (Chapter 9), difficulties in establishing third-party alternatives (Chapter 9), the purposeful drawing of noncompetitive districts (Chapter 11), and the electoral college (Chapter 12) all contribute to voter disillusion and diminish interest in participation. These factors alienate many voters, making them feel that their vote is unnecessary or useless. In fact, Rosenstone and Hansen conclude from their comprehensive study of voting that the "blame" for the long-term decline in citizen involvement rests as much with failures of the political system as with citizens themselves. The authors state the case bluntly: "Citizens did not fail the political system; if anything, the political system failed them."[34] This need not be the case, and in subsequent chapters, we will discuss what changes can be made to reverse this situation.

Hot or Not?

Should voting be made compulsory?

Current Controversy

Do Celebrity Endorsements Matter?

Studies show that celebrities have a limited impact on voter choices. Among the endorsements with the greatest impact are those of state governors, ministers, and local newspapers. Beyond that, voters report that celebrity endorsements have little or no impact on their choices. Here are some of the notable endorsements in the 2008 campaign.

Rap star Jay-Z endorsed Barack Obama.

Red Sox pitcher Curt Schilling supported John McCain.

Whoopi Goldberg endorsed Hillary Clinton after she had first announced support for Obama.

Tom Selleck endorsed John McCain.

George Clooney was an Obama supporter.

Barbara Streisand endorsed Hillary Clinton.

Sylvester Stallone endorsed McCain.

Sean Penn supported Dennis Kucinich.

Madonna endorsed Hillary Clinton.

Oprah Winfrey campaigned for Obama.

Chuck Norris endorsed Mike Huckabee.

There were two exceptions to the limited impact of celebrity endorsements according to voters in 2008: 21 percent of respondents said they would be less likely to vote for a candidate endorsed by conservative talk show host Bill O'Reilly, and 23 percent said that they would be more likely to vote for a candidate endorsed by *The Daily Show* host Jon Stewart.

Source: Pew Center for the People and the Press, *Do Political Endorsements Matter?* September 20, 2007. Accessed at http://people-press.org/reports/display.php3?ReportID=357 on May 22, 2008.

For REVIEW >>

1. What are the basic requirements for political involvement?
   - Political involvement requires access to resources like time, skills, and money, as well as a desire to engage and an invitation to take part in political activities.

2. How do political messages from citizens vary?
   - Political messages vary in the amount of information they convey to leaders, in their frequency, and in the strength of the message conveyed. For example, letters to a member of Congress can convey a stronger and clearer message with more frequency than can the act of voting.

3. Who is most likely to get involved in political activity?
   - Those with higher incomes and more education from families with an interest in politics are most likely to get involved, Religious organizations and labor unions also have an impact on raising participation levels among those with fewer financial and educational resources.

National Journal

Pennsylvania: Voter Participation in a Schizophrenic State

Few states resisted Barack Obama more than Pennsylvania during the Democratic primary season. Partly as a result, few states are more critical to his hopes of winning the White House this fall.

Most of Pennsylvania's recent political developments, from the trend in voter registration to the latest statewide results, tilt toward the Democrats, often sharply. But the one exception to that pattern encourages Republicans: Although Democrats have carried the state in the past four presidential elections, their winning margins have dropped from about 9 percentage points under Bill Clinton in 1992 and 1996 to 4 points under Al Gore in 2000 and to just 2.5 points under John Kerry in 2004. And in John McCain, who polls well nationally among independents, Republicans may have a nominee capable of reversing the Democrats' two-decade advance in the affluent, growing, and once reliably Republican suburbs of Philadelphia—the trend most responsible for the Democratic rise in Pennsylvania.

Add to these factors Obama's weak performance in the April primary, and the state's top Democrats are cautioning the party to expect a tough fight in Pennsylvania. "I still think it's a swing state, and all you have to do is look at the trend lines . . . in presidential politics, it has been getting closer and closer," Democratic Gov. Ed Rendell told National Journal. "And McCain is the best Republican candidate they have fielded presidentially since Ronald Reagan, in the sense that his reputation as a maverick and a moderate . . . holds him in very good stead with the independents and [suburban] Republicans who have been tending to vote Democratic in the last four elections."

Yet the very ferocity of the Keystone State's Democratic presidential primary may have strengthened Obama's chances by spurring a registration surge that has swelled the Democratic lead over the GOP on the voter rolls to nearly 1.1 million, almost double the party's 2004 edge. According to Rendell, that's a record voter-registration advantage for the Democrats, and it dramatizes the extent to which Pennsylvania remains a difficult challenge for McCain, especially amid the intense disillusionment with Bush there. The state is "still in play . . . but the idea that it is evenly divided between McCain and Obama, that it is a 50-50 toss-up, I think that is just wrong," says Ruy Teixeira, an electoral analyst at the liberal Brookings Institution who co-authored a recent comprehensive study of the state's demographic and political trends. "It is a purple state leaning blue, and it may be even bluer than it was in 2004. So it is a real uphill climb for McCain in my view."

In its recent political evolution, Pennsylvania has been a tale of two states. It has simultaneously moved sharply toward the Democrats in the southeast, particularly in the comfortable Philadelphia suburbs, and sharply toward the GOP in the southwest, especially in the largely blue-collar suburbs of Pittsburgh. McCain's challenge is to reverse the first trend and reinforce the second, as well as the GOP's more modest gains in presidential races in hardscrabble northeastern counties around Scranton.

"You can play the chess game almost any way, but the Philly 'burbs, southwestern Pennsylvania, and those counties up there [around Scranton] are basically it," says G. Terry Madonna, a longtime Pennsylvania pollster who is now the director of the Center for Politics and Public Affairs at Franklin and Marshall College. "McCain has to win the [blue-collar] Reagan Democrats in the west and the northeast, and he has to win some independents, independent-minded Republicans, and Democrats in the Philly suburbs."

For generations, the Philadelphia suburbs were the home of prosperous "Main Line" moderate Republicans. But like other socially moderate, white-collar suburbs outside the South, these communities began moving toward the Democrats during Clinton's 1992 race. They have shifted even further in that direction under Bush, who has given the GOP a more Southern and more evangelical face.

In the four suburban counties immediately outside Philadelphia, the change has been profound. From 1920 through 1988, no Democratic presidential nominee won Delaware or Montgomery counties, with the exception of Lyndon Johnson in his 1964 landslide. During that period in Bucks County, the only Democratic winners were Johnson and Franklin D. Roosevelt in 1936. As late as 1988, George H.W. Bush won 60 percent of the vote in all three counties.

But starting with Clinton in 1992, Democrats have now carried that trio of counties in four consecutive elections. And their margins in Delaware and Montgomery have increased each time. "The suburbs are a place that really liked Bush 41 but couldn't relate to Bush 43," said Christopher Nicholas, a Harrisburg-based Republican consultant who ran the successful 2004 re-election campaign of Republican Sen. Arlen Specter. "They liked the Connecticut Yankee and had trouble relating to the Texan."

Over the same period, though, the state's southwest corner—the counties surrounding Pittsburgh, such as Beaver, Washington, and Westmoreland—have moved in the opposite direction. Although Pittsburgh itself has remained solidly Democratic, these counties, much less affluent and less white-collar than the Philadelphia suburbs, have responded favorably to George W. Bush's conservative cultural and national security policies.

On balance, this geographic swap has benefited Pennsylvania Democrats, because their new strongholds are bigger and are gaining population, while some of the increasingly Republican areas are shrinking. "Where population is growing, the Democrats are doing better. Where it is declining, Republicans are doing better," says Teixeira,

the co-author of the Brookings analysis with demographer William Frey.

The conversion of the Philadelphia suburbs and exurbs, in addition to the Democrats' continuing dominance of Pittsburgh and heavily African-American Philadelphia, has provided the party a fragile but perceptible advantage in the state. After the 2000 election, Republicans controlled the governorship, both U.S. Senate seats, a majority of U.S. House seats, and both chambers of the state Legislature.

In 2002, Rendell captured the governorship. In 2006, Democrats re-elected Rendell, won a majority of the state House, ousted four GOP lawmakers to gain a majority of the state's U.S. House delegation, and took a U.S. Senate seat as Democrat Bob Casey routed staunchly conservative GOP Sen. Rick Santorum. The 2006 recoil from the GOP was especially powerful in the four Philadelphia suburban counties, where Democrats defeated two Republican House members and Casey annihilated Santorum by more than175,000 votes. Six years earlier, Santorum had swept those counties by nearly 152,000 votes.

In this period of Democratic advance, the one big exception was Specter's successful 2004 campaign. On the day that Bush lost the state to Kerry, Specter won re-election with nearly 53 percent of the vote. Specter, a moderate who supports abortion rights, built a much different coalition from Bush's, actually running behind him in 29 of Pennsylvania's 67 counties. Nearly all of these were culturally conservative counties either near Pittsburgh or in the heavily rural "T" that extends through the state's center. But Specter, a former Philadelphia district attorney, ran far better than Bush through all of the eastern counties, from Philadelphia north to Scranton and beyond to the New York border. Most important, Specter held down his

the very ferocity of the Keystone State's Democratic presidential primary **may have strengthened Obama's chances** by spurring a registration surge

losses in Philadelphia itself and amassed a nearly 150,000-vote lead in the four suburban Philadelphia counties that decisively rejected Bush.

Running against the first African-American presidential nominee of a major party, McCain has little chance of minimizing the Democratic advantage in Philadelphia as much as Specter did. But, apart from that, the Specter map may be "as good a model as McCain can find," Madonna says.

In fact, Republicans hope that McCain can do better than Specter among culturally conservative voters. "Obama's challenge is, how does he win over the working-class white folks that he didn't win [in the primary]?" says consultant Nicholas. "He is just radically different from their lives, and McCain is not. Military, father in the military, grandfather in the military: That's an arc they can understand. The Obama life story, while very unique and interesting, is not something folks in these little railroad towns can relate to."

Rendell, who openly declared during the primary that some Pennsylvania voters might not be willing to vote for a black presidential candidate, says he thinks that economic anxiety may help Obama perform better than Republicans anticipate in the Scranton and Pittsburgh areas. But to hold the state,

Rendell is mostly counting on Obama's energizing new voters and maintaining the Democratic advantage in the Philadelphia suburbs and Lehigh Valley.

Can Obama defend the Democratic beachheads outside Philadelphia? Since 2004, Democrats have posted substantial voter-registration gains in all four suburban counties, as well as across the Lehigh Valley. But in the Democratic primary, Obama did not run as well in these places as he did in white-collar communities elsewhere: Clinton split the four Philadelphia suburbs with him and swept the Lehigh Valley.

Those results worry Rendell, who was Clinton's highest-profile Pennsylvania supporter. "There is a very strong reservoir of support for Clinton among women [in these counties]," he says. "So . . . we have real work to do in the suburbs." Plus, he adds, McCain's reputation for independence will make him a "tough" competitor for moderate suburban voters.

Rendell says that Obama might win the Philadelphia suburbs "by a smaller margin than Kerry did," but he expects the senator from Illinois to run well enough there to hold Pennsylvania. Republicans hope that Rendell is wrong. Both sides agree that no matter how much ground McCain gains elsewhere, he is unlikely to capture the state unless he can run even with or better than Obama immediately outside of Philadelphia. "All roads end up pointing back to those Philly suburbs," one senior McCain campaign aide said.

Madonna agrees. "You can't just give up about 90,000 votes in the Philadelphia suburbs [as Bush did]," he says. "There are so many votes there that making up that kind of deficit elsewhere is really difficult." Such inescapable math ensures the Philadelphia suburbs a spot high on the list of the places picking the next president.

FOR DISCUSSION: Look up the results of the Presidential Election in Pennsylvania. How well did it conform to the pattern *National Journal* observed?

According to the election, how does geography delineate political preference in your own state?

What strategies would you offer candidates looking to maximize their voter turnout in Pennsylvania?

8

WHAT'S TO COME

INTEREST GROUPS IN AMERICA

IMMIGRATION REFORM: THE INSIDE GAME ▌ In the spring of 2006, two distinctly different groups of immigrants—using two divergent strategies—demonstrated their opposition to proposed legislation imposing tighter border controls. In the streets of Washington, D.C., hundreds of thousands of Hispanic restaurant workers and landscapers took part in a rally to focus public attention on their effort to overhaul immigration practices to include a pathway to citizenship for those who entered the country illegally. At the same time, in the offices of a powerful Washington lobbying firm, Aman Kapoor and a few hundred skilled Indian and Chinese high-tech experts worked with the firm's representatives to advocate for reducing the waiting period for lawful permanent residency papers (green cards) granting the experts the right to continue working at their lucrative positions.[1]

Aman, a computer programmer, used the Internet to mobilize thousands of other Asian high-tech workers who, like him, had been waiting for years to be granted lawful residence in the United States. Together, they founded the organization Immigration Voice (IV) to bring their case before key members of Congress. They turned for help to Quinn Gillespie & Associates LLC, a lobbying firm begun by two extremely well-connected political insiders.

Quinn Gillespie set up a series of meetings between IV members and staffers of key members of congressional committees at the center of immigration reform. The lobbyists encouraged IV members to share their personal stories and to pitch their recommendations as an effort to enhance American competitiveness. The group settled on a list of specific recommendations, which included greater quota flexibility for countries sending large numbers of highly skilled workers to the United States. Immigration Voice persuaded lawmakers to include its measures in the 2007 Immigration Reform Bill, but the bill went down to defeat during the first session of the 110th Congress. Aman knows that success may take some time, and IV is reaching out to other professional lobbying groups for assistance.

Aman's group understood that their cause was viewed somewhat less sympathetically than that of the unskilled immigrants who staged the protest march. For their purposes, Immigration Voice required a focused message aimed at the key lawmakers who would write the fine details of the immigration law. It therefore pursued an **inside strategy**—that is, working directly with ➡◆

As You READ >>

- What are interest groups and what types of interests do they represent?
- Why might someone join an interest group?
- What do interest groups do?

Thousands of Hispanic Americans took to the streets to demonstrate support for immigration reform when Congress considered the matter during the 2007–2008 session.

influential political insiders. By contrast, most Hispanic immigrants who crossed the border to find work do not have the skills, the organizational prowess, or the financial means to chart the same course. One of the few options open to them is the **outside strategy** of taking to the streets in peaceful protest.

In this chapter, we will learn how interest groups organize to exert pressure on the political system to advance their collective interests. We will examine their genesis, the ways they have evolved and adapted to historic change, the kinds of people who join, the reasons why people support them, the strategies and tactics they employ, and their impact on civic engagement and public policy.

ORGANIZED INTERESTS: WHO ARE THEY?

Accomplishing broad yet shared goals is always easier when a number of people pitch in to help. Both joining with neighbors to clean up a community after a storm and banding together with friends to convince your college cafeteria to purchase "free trade" coffee are examples of cooperative action. Group activity is a hallmark of America's volunteer ethic. The same is true in politics. Organized groups are nearly always more effective in attaining common goals than individuals acting alone. The term **interest group** refers to those formally organized associations that seek to influence public policy.[2] In America, it applies to a dizzying array of diverse organizations reflecting the broad spectrum of interests that make up our pluralistic society. They include corporations, labor unions, civil rights groups, professional and trade associations, and probably some of the groups with which you are associated as well.

personal Is Political

Think you don't belong to an organized interest or advocacy group? Think again. Are you a member of any of these groups?

- ❏ American Automobile Association (AAA)
- ❏ Amnesty International
- ❏ American Society for the Prevention of Cruelty to Animals (ASPCA)
- ❏ Defenders of Wildlife
- ❏ 4 H
- ❏ Future Farmers of America
- ❏ Interfaith Alliance
- ❏ Mothers Against Drunk Driving
- ❏ National Audubon Society
- ❏ National Council of Church of Christ in the USA
- ❏ National Rifle Association
- ❏ National Organization for Women
- ❏ Ocean Conservancy
- ❏ Parents Teachers Association (PTA)
- ❏ Sierra Club
- ❏ United Students Against Sweatshops (USAS)
- ❏ Veterans of Foreign Wars
- ❏ Students Take Action Now–Darfur (STAND)

Neighbors or Adversaries?

Theorists from Alexis de Tocqueville to Robert Putnam have praised voluntary associations as training grounds for citizen involvement. De Tocqueville saw collective action as evidence of democracy at work. Putnam extols organized interests for creating social capital, the glue that binds the citizenry so they can achieve collective goals. Not all political theorists, however, share these views. In *The Federalist* No. 10, James Madison warned against factions—groups of individuals, "whether amounting to a majority or minority of the whole, who are united by some common impulse of passion, or of interest, adverse to the rights of other citizens, or to the permanent and aggregate interests of the community."[3] Although opposed to factions, Madison felt that they could not be eliminated since they expressed the innately human drive for self-interest. Instead, he argued, the government must dilute their influence by filtering their views through elected officials and submerging their interests in a sea of competing interests. Only by countering the ambition of such groups with the ambition of others, he believed, could government fashion the compromises necessary to accommodate interests common to all.

inside strategy A plan of action for advancing one's policies by working directly with influential political insiders.

outside strategy A plan of action for advancing one's policies by building popular support for one's cause.

interest group Any formally organized association that seeks to influence public policy.

political movement An organized constellation of groups seeking wide-ranging social change.

Interest groups usually do not intend to work against their communities, but the benefits they seek may result in costs for others. Whether a particular group is a "good neighbor" or an adversary is often in the eye of the beholder.

Distinctive Features

Like the **political movements** of the past that advanced causes such as abolition or civil rights, interest groups seek to use the power of government to protect their concerns. However, although political movements promote wide-ranging social change, interest groups are more narrowly focused on achieving success with regard to specific policies. Where the Women's Movement of the 1960s sought to change Americans' views about the role of women at home and in the workplace, interest groups like the National Organization for Women (NOW) focus on solving specific problems faced by women in a world that has already grown more accepting of the diverse roles women play.

Interest group causes may be purely economic, as in the case of a business seeking tax breaks or a union seeking negotiating clout; they may be ideological, as in the case of those favoring or opposing abortion rights. Some, known

Businessmen often sought favors from President Ulysses S. Grant as he indulged in brandy and cigars in the Willard Hotel lobby in Washington, D.C.

as **public interest groups**, advocate policies they believe promote the good of all Americans, not merely the economic or ideological interests of a few. Environmental groups such as the Sierra Club fall into this category. Some interest groups, such as trade associations and labor unions, have mass memberships; others represent institutions and have no individual membership at all. One example of the latter is the American Council on Education (ACE), a collection of institutions of higher education that promotes policies that benefit colleges and universities.

As with other forms of participation, those who are better educated and better off financially are more active in interest group politics. The wealthy and well-educated belong to more associations, are more likely to be active in these interest groups, and give more money to political causes than those with less education and income. Highly educated professionals are many times more likely to belong to one or more interest groups than those who lack a high school degree. It is also important to note that interest group activity has exploded over the last forty years, even while our nation has experienced a long-term decline in voter turnout. This reflects the fact that interest groups multiply the opportunities for participation by those who are already politically active.[4]

THE ROOTS OF INTEREST GROUP POLITICS IN AMERICA

Political scientists offer a number of reasons for the growth of interest groups. First, there is the ever-present reality that Americans are joiners. Echoing de Tocqueville, historian Arthur M. Schlesinger wrote that our "instinctive resort to collective action" is "one of the strongest taproots of the nation's well-being."[5] Beyond this, interest group growth is tied to forces of change such as technological innovation, war, and the expansion of the role of government.

Interest Groups on the Rise

By the time Alexis de Tocqueville traveled across America in 1831, voluntary associations—including those with explicitly political goals—were already well established. Women, who were excluded from leadership positions in government, organized many groups that provided hu-

manitarian relief to the poor, sick, and disabled. These "auxiliary societies," as they were sometimes called, were formed to combat perceived evils like drunkenness and prostitution.[6] Abolitionist societies were perhaps the most politically influential associations, and many of them organized across class and racial lines to advocate an end to slavery. Women also organized for the right to vote, meeting in Seneca Falls in 1848 to issue a *Declaration of Rights and Sentiments.*

By the mid-nineteenth century, economic change and advances in transportation brought rapid growth in the number of voluntary and political organizations. The development of a national railroad system led the Central Pacific Railroad to send its own representative to Washington in 1861 to protect railroad subsidies and land grants. A number of rural associations arose in reaction to these changes. For example, the Grange, an association of rural farmers, formed in opposition to high rates set by rail carriers for hauling their produce to the nation's largest markets. The origin of the term **lobbying** to describe the practice of influencing public decisions for private purposes dates back to this period. It seems that businessmen often approached President Ulysses S. Grant (1869–1877) to seek favors as he indulged in brandy and cigars while relaxing in the lobby of the Willard Hotel.

By the end of the nineteenth century, the pace of economic development displaced many rural workers, who migrated to cities to compete for dangerous, low-wage jobs in the new industrial economy. Labor organizations, charitable associations, and reform groups arose to lobby for better working conditions, an end to child labor, and safe food and medicines. As the organizing strength of political parties began to decline, interest groups emerged as the great hope for participatory democracy. They became the principal means for expressing popular views and mobilizing support for reform.[7]

World War I created a large pool of veterans who organized to petition the government for benefits in compensa-

A NATION OF JOINERS:
The Case of the National Consumers' League

In 1888, Leonora O'Reilly, a shirtmaker in New York City's garment district sweatshops, made an eloquent appeal to a gathering of wealthy and educated women to do whatever they could to rectify the working conditions of those like herself. In response, those in attendance left their names and addresses, signaling their willingness to answer the call. Over the course of the next several years, an organization emerged to advance the cause of working women, the National Consumers' League. It published a "White List" of stores that treated their workers fairly and urged women to reward these establishments with their business, even if goods were slightly more expensive. The League advocated research and dissemination of information about the manufacture and contents of all family products and urged women to shop selectively.

By 1913, the League had amassed a membership of over 30,000 in local chapters. It later successfully defended an Oregon law limiting the workday for women to ten hours a day. NCL's work culminated in the Fair Labor Standards Act, which created a national minimum wage in 1938. The League continues in existence today, largely as an advocacy group operating out of Washington, D.C., sustained by tax-free contributions (http://www.nclnet.org/welcome.html).

---

tion for their service to country. In 1932, over 30,000 World War I veterans and their families and supporters marched on Washington, D.C. and set up makeshift camps in the capital, demanding redemption of government certificates issued after the war. Although federal troops routed the so-called "Bonus Army" out of their camps, veterans eventually received the cash payments they sought. Their actions paved the way for more generous benefits for future generations of soldiers.

The New Deal spawned hundreds of groups with a stake in federal policies, as did the explosion of government regulation of business and the environment in the 1960s and 1970s. The period following World War II brought increased specialization and professionalization to the workforce at the same time as it saw increases in union affiliation. Membership in the American Bar Association quadrupled during the period from 1945 to 1965. Union membership rose in the postwar period from about 12 percent of the nonagricultural workforce in 1930 to over 30 percent in the 1950s before cascading downward in the last quarter of the twentieth century.[8]

The Advocacy Explosion

In the 1950s and 1960s, the nation experienced a "rights revolution" that had important implications for the evolution of interest group politics in America.[9] African Americans led the way as they sought to dismantle segregationist policies in the South by lobbying the national government to enforce constitutional guarantees. Other groups followed, insisting that government help tear down the barriers of racial, ethnic, and gender exclusion that characterized associational life in earlier eras. Soon, even mainstream interests like those of consumers joined the "rights revolution." The national focus of these reform efforts made it imperative for rights advocates to establish a presence in Washington.

The period witnessed an explosion in Washington-based **advocacy groups**, associations asserting broad public goals but without local chapters and often without any formal membership.[10] Leaders of these groups, often self-appointed and aided by philanthropic organizations and think tanks that supplied financial and intellectual capital, helped forge a new relationship between citizen and leadership. Citizens no longer needed to organize locally, meet with one another, or choose neighborhood leaders. Instead, national leaders would set the agenda, formulate strategies, and lobby public officials for them. All that citizens needed to do was write checks and an occasional letter to a public officeholder. Political engagement became more passive as citizens had their interests managed for them.[11]

The impact of the explosion in advocacy has been mixed. On the one hand, these groups are instrumental in protecting individual rights and in making the products we use safer and more effective. On the other hand, they have contributed to a more passive role for citizens. The period that witnessed a rise in Washington-based advocacy groups also witnessed an overall decline in civic voluntarism. We will return to assess these changes at the end of this chapter.

> **public interest groups** Those advocating policies they believe promote the good of all Americans and not merely the economic or ideological interests of a few.
>
> **lobbying** Tactic for influencing public decisions for private purposes, usually employing personal contact with elected officials.
>
> **advocacy groups** Groups organized around broad public goals but without local chapters and often without formal membership.

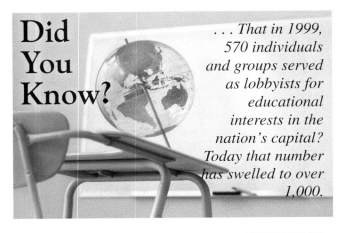

WHOSE INTERESTS ARE REPRESENTED?

The array of interest groups active in American politics is large and wide-ranging. Some groups boast large numbers, others have financial heft, and some are lead by the well-connected with access to power brokers. Each employs the resources it has at its disposal to advance its cause.

Who Has the Numbers?

The single largest sector of the interest group community is composed of trade associations, and of these, business interests predominate.[12] The U.S. Chamber of Commerce, for example, represents thousands of small and medium-size businesses throughout the country, and the National Association of Manufacturers advances the interests of major manufacturing companies. In addition, most large corporations either maintain their own Washington offices or employ Washington-based consultants to represent them.

Professional associations such as the American Chemical Society represent the next largest sector of the Washington interest group community. Labor unions also maintain a strong presence, although union members currently represent less than 13 percent of the labor force. Education is a fast-growing sector, with nearly a thousand individual lobbyists and organized groups such as the American Federation of Teachers practicing in the nation's capital today.

Advocacy groups represent a growing portion of the interest group community.[13] A few of these, including the Children's Defense Fund, promote the interests of those who don't have the resources to advocate for themselves. But an increasing array, such as Common Cause (dedicated to government reform) and Public Citizen (organized to safeguard consumers), cater to more wealthy contributors on whom they rely for support. Numerous single-issue groups also have organized around specific legislative concerns, such as banning handguns or outlawing abortion. The overwhelming majority of organized interests founded since 1960 have been advocacy groups,[14] but they

have a high rate of attrition. Only 33 percent of advocacy organizations active in 1960 existed two decades later. The most successful of the survivors deal with environmental and consumer issues.[15]

Governments themselves also organize for representation in Washington. Virtually every nation in the world maintains a Washington office to oversee its relations with American leaders. So, too, do state and local governments, whose policies are often impacted by federal law. The National Association of Counties, the National League of Cities, and the U.S. Conference of Mayors are but three examples. Even executive branch agencies in the U.S. government hire legislative liaisons to communicate their needs to members of Congress.

Who Has the Money?

Another way to evaluate which interests are best represented is to examine the resources groups expend. The

Education is a fast-growing and powerful sector of the interest group community. Together the American Federation of Teachers (AFT) and the National Education Association (NEA) boast 4.6 million members.

Which Interests Are Best Represented?

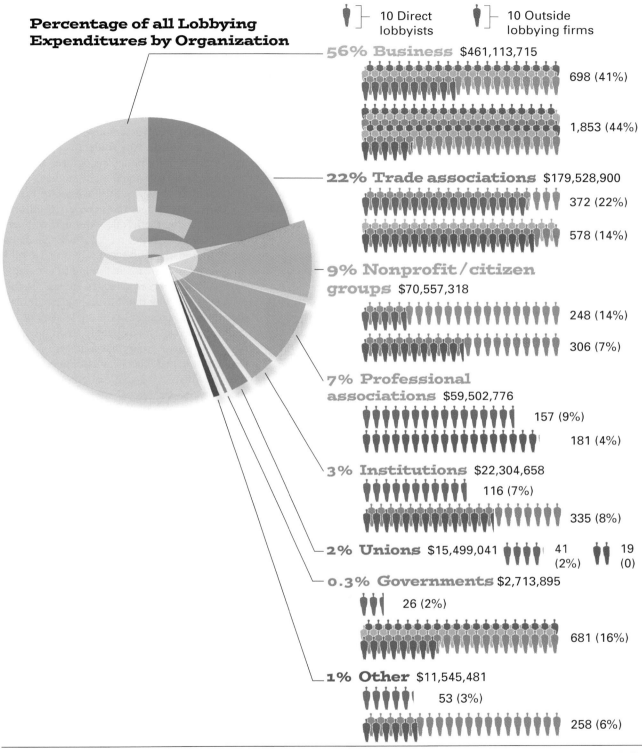

Percentage of all Lobbying Expenditures by Organization

10 Direct lobbyists | 10 Outside lobbying firms

56% Business $461,113,715
698 (41%)
1,853 (44%)

22% Trade associations $179,528,900
372 (22%)
578 (14%)

9% Nonprofit/citizen groups $70,557,318
248 (14%)
306 (7%)

7% Professional associations $59,502,776
157 (9%)
181 (4%)

3% Institutions $22,304,658
116 (7%)
335 (8%)

2% Unions $15,499,041
41 (2%)
19 (0)

0.3% Governments $2,713,895
26 (2%)
681 (16%)

1% Other $11,545,481
53 (3%)
258 (6%)

Source: Compiled from Frank Baumgartner and Beth L. Leech, "Interest Niches and Policy Bandwagons: Patterns of Interest Group Involvement in National Politics," *Journal of Politics* 63, no. 4 (2001), Table 1, 1195, and Table 3, 1197.

figure above provides information on the number of paid professionals—either from within the organization or from outside firms—representing various sectors of the interest group community in Washington. It also lists the total expenditures each made in pleading its case before government. Business groups employ the largest number of paid professionals and spend more than half of all the money spent on lobbying. Over 40 percent of all Washington lobbyists, whether in-house or working as consultants, represent business interests.

Clearly, interest group politics in America has a distinctively upper-class tilt. Many interests at the bottom of the economic spectrum enjoy minimal or no representation at all. There are no lobbyists for the homeless or groups representing Americans without health insurance. Interest group politics, however, is quite fluid; new groups often arise to meet emerging challenges.[16] For example, the northern migration of blacks from the South spawned the birth of organizations like the National Association for the Advancement of Colored People (NAACP) and the National Urban League to champion the cause of equal rights. Similarly, the environmental movement in the 1960s led to the expansion of groups advocating the protection of air and water quality. In addition, existing groups often expand to adopt causes tangential to their mission. For

Environmental activists in the 1960s dramatized their concerns about the nation's unhealthful air quality at public protest rallies.

example, several philanthropic and health advocacy organizations joined forces in 2007 to push for the adoption of wider health insurance coverage for America's uninsured children.

WHY JOIN?

Political strength comes from assembling the resources and voices of many individuals. Any student who has tried to effect changes in university policy recognizes that administrators are more likely to listen if many students work collectively to voice their concerns. Still, the job of bringing students together, getting them to agree to a uniform set of proposals, and having them follow through with letters or petitions or marches is not an easy task. Students who agree with proposed changes may prefer to have others do the hard work of organizing and going to meetings. After all, if proposed changes are successful, even students who don't lift a finger will reap the benefits. Fortunately for the leaders of organized interests, many people are highly motivated to join a group that fights for a cause they support, and others can be enticed by various incentives. A group can employ various incentives to sustain membership and active commitment, and it can add or change incentives as the organization matures.[17]

Material Incentives

Material benefits include anything that can be measured in terms of money, such as goods, special services, and financial incentives. The American Association of Retired Persons (AARP), for instance, began with the goal of providing affordable health care for the elderly but now offers its members discounts in a variety of establishments, guidance in avoiding consumer fraud, organized travel opportunities, auto insurance, low-interest credit cards, and a discounted mail-order pharmacy. Offering these material benefits has helped AARP recruit over 35 million members and become the most powerful organization in America representing the interests of the elderly. Political leaders who seek to change Social Security or Medicare policies recognize the importance of courting this organization if their proposals are to have any chance of passage.

Few organizations can match AARP's clout, but many business associations and unions offer material incentives as well. For example, the U.S. Chamber of Commerce offers member businesses access to health-care plans that are cheaper than plans they could buy on their own. Although the power of unions has waned in recent years, many can still provide members with higher negotiated wages than workers could obtain without a union card.

Solidary Incentives

Human beings are social creatures who enjoy the company of others. Membership in a group whose participants share a common interest can be very pleasurable. It provides the joiner with the likely possibility of friendship and an opportunity for "networking." Again, this is a selective benefit reserved to the members of the group that nonmembers cannot easily share. Members of professional organizations, such as the American Medical Association (AMA), look forward to annual meetings where they can renew friendships, share new ideas, and network. Often, members attending these conventions vote on resolutions outlining the political agendas the organization will pursue over the course of the coming year.

Purposive Incentives

Interest groups offer their members more than discounts and social outings. They offer the opportunity to pursue policy goals that members genuinely support. Members gain a measure of inner satisfaction from knowing that they are trying to change the world rather than just complaining about it. Despite the cynicism that sometimes pervades media reports about those engaged in public life, millions of Americans devote countless hours volunteering in big and small ways to promote causes in which they believe.

For organizations that depend heavily on purposive incentives, the role of the **political entrepreneur** is particularly important in mobilizing support among those who sympathize with the group's goals.[18] Political entrepreneurs develop support for latent causes or projects that have not yet gained widespread popularity. Even groups with passionate views, such as those on both sides of the abortion issue, rely on strong and enterprising leaders to recruit members and to sustain interest and activity.

Assessing Motives

Economist Mancur Olson argued that it is irrational for individuals to join most groups. It is more rational, he wrote, to be a free rider who receives benefits without doing the work or paying dues. We can all enjoy clean air without being a member of an environmental group, and we can earn the latest increase in the minimum wage without car-

The health insurance industry mounted a vigorous television campaign featuring a fictional couple, Harry and Louise, in a successful effort to thwart President Clinton's health-care reform program.

rying a union card. We can remain rationally uninvolved and spend our free time pursuing leisure activities or working at a second job to earn extra money.[19] Olson believes that providing incentives is the only way for membership in interest groups to flourish.

Despite the seeming logic of Olson's view, people often do not make what appears to be the rational choice. Political scientist Jack Walker conducted a study in which interest group leaders ranked the benefit of each type of incentive as an inducement for attracting members. Contrary to rational choice theory, the leaders of all types of groups ranked material benefits to be the least important of all the incentives. The study also found that most groups do not even use such inducements. Instead, leaders of all kinds of groups ranked purposive incentives highest, with solidary incentives close behind.[20] Additional studies have confirmed high levels of purposeful joining, especially among interest group activists.[21] This finding should be surprising only to those who have paid insufficient attention to our history as a "nation of joiners." There is an additional consideration for free riders to ponder. If everyone acted like a free rider, **collective goods**—goods that are not owned privately but benefit all citizens equally, such as clean air—would have no champions, and all of us would suffer the consequences.

> **political entrepreneur** Individual who develops support for latent causes or projects that have not yet gained widespread popularity.
>
> **collective goods** Goods that are not owned privately but benefit all citizens equally, such as clean air.
>
> **strategy** A group's overall plan for achieving its goals.

INTEREST GROUP STRATEGIES

In order to get what they want, interest groups must develop a plan and execute it with a series of specific actions. The overall plan is their **strategy**; the specific actions they

undertake are **tactics**. Strategies and tactics employed by an interest group vary with the nature of the issue under consideration and the kinds of resources the group has available to it.

Generally speaking, strategies can be categorized as inside or outside. Inside strategies emphasize direct personal encounters with public officials to present information or resources that might impact the course of policy. Tactics useful to implement this strategy include lobbying and contributing money to support the election of political candidates favorably disposed to the group's viewpoint. Outside strategies are activities intended to show popular support for one's cause and indirectly to create public pressure on elected officials. Outsiders usually adopt grassroots tactics that include letter-writing, shaping public opinion, and orchestrating protests. (Recall our discussion of these contrasting strategies in the opening vignette.)

tactics Specific actions that groups take to implement strategies.

revolving door Term referring to the back-and-forth movement of individuals between government and interest group employment.

Groups adopt strategies based on the types of issues involved and the resources the group can bring to bear. Some groups have wide-ranging interests that are likely to attract the attention of a large number of Americans. For example, military intervention is an issue that affects almost everyone—from those who fight or lose family members in battle to those who simply oppose the use of their tax dollars in this manner. Both supporters and opponents of the use of military force are likely to employ outside strategies to demonstrate to lawmakers the depth and breadth of public sentiment for their position. Changes in the tax code, on the other hand, are likely to provoke the use of inside strategies by groups whose immediate but narrow interests are most directly affected. The arcane and complicated features of our tax code rarely draw widespread attention, enabling those with an immediate interest and expertise to fashion changes to their liking through direct interaction with lawmakers.

There are times when it makes sense for groups to employ both inside and outside strategies. For example, when the health insurance industry perceived its interests threatened by the health-care plan proposed by President Bill Clinton, it used professional lobbyists to gain the ear of critical lawmakers—an insider's approach. However, it also used the outside strategy of producing a series of television commercials in which fictional middle-class characters, Harry and Louise, raised doubts in the minds of voters and urged them to contact members of Congress to defeat the plan.

Resources useful in advancing a group's cause include money, numbers, prestige, and leadership. Businesses, for example, can generally count on accumulating money to communicate their message, but they cannot often count on large numbers of individuals supporting their cause. Labor unions, on the other hand, try to exert influence by the number of votes they can muster for particular candidates and parties. To be effective, however, a group's members must be dispersed geographically across areas that key lawmakers represent. Sometimes, groups with smaller numbers have an easier time organizing politically since they can maintain greater intensity and cohesiveness. Strong intensity is a characteristic of groups on both sides of the abortion issue in recent years. Prestige is also an important resource; when the American Medical Association speaks on matters of health care, for example, it can be particularly persuasive.

Leadership from a variety of sources—scholars, celebrities, political entrepreneurs, and public officials themselves—can generate momentum around issues previously ignored by the political system. Rachel Carson's controversial 1962 book *Silent Spring* is credited with almost

Rock stars like Bono have been effective in mobilizing support for increasing aid to developing nations.

single-handedly launching the environmental movement. More recently, Irish rock star Bono mobilized global support to fight AIDS and to provide debt relief for poor and developing countries. Since few interest groups have sufficient quantities of all of these resources to dispense at will, each group must carefully assess how best to deploy the strengths it possesses.

LOBBYING AND OTHER TACTICS

Interest groups have many tactics at hand to advance their positions. The table at right reveals the range of tactics many Washington groups say they employ in pleading their causes. In this section, we'll review some of the most notable.

Lobbying

In the early years of our republic, members of Congress had no offices; most lived alone in boardinghouses or hotels. The only way to make contact with them was to wait outside their offices, or in the lobbies of the places where they were staying, in hopes of having a word with them as they came and went. Modern-day lobbyists continue to ply their trade in the hallways of the Capitol, but interest groups have found far more sophisticated ways to increase their clout.

Who Lobbies? Average citizens lobby on behalf of issues they support by writing or calling elected leaders, but lobbying is increasingly the province of permanent and salaried professionals. Sometimes these are interest group staffers who work in Washington or a state capital directly on behalf of the group's membership. Increasingly, they are "hired guns" whose services groups purchase from professional firms specializing in government relations. An estimated 15,000 people work as lobbyists in Washington, D.C., and many are quite well paid.

A good lobbyist needs to be a specialist in a policy area and needs to have thorough knowledge of the political process. For this reason, former government workers are well suited for the job. Individuals who have worked as congressional staff members or in administrative agencies have the kind of policy and political knowledge useful for lobbying. One study reports that 46 former staffers from the powerful House Appropriations Committee, 36 from the Ways and Means Committee, and 34 from the House Energy and Commerce Committee left their congressional jobs since 1998 to work as registered lobbyists.[22] Former members of Congress also make formidable lobbyists, sometimes maintaining virtually unlimited access to the chambers and the congressional gym. Of the 198 lawmakers who left the House of Representatives from 1998 to 2005, 43 percent became lobbyists.[23]

Some refer to the movement between government service and interest group employment as a **revolving door**. The door swings in both directions. Not only do retiring lawmakers and staffers join firms that lobbied them when they were in government, but government agencies often recruit issue specialists from fields that they regulate. Defenders of this practice claim that the revolving door keeps good and knowledgeable people involved in the policy

Exercising Influence: Interest Group Tactics

Tactic	Percent of surveyed groups employing
■ Testifying at hearings	99
■ Contacting government officials directly to present your point of view	98
■ Engaging in informal contacts with officials at conventions, over lunch, etc.	95
■ Presenting research results or technical information	92
■ Sending letters to members of your organization to inform them about activities	92
■ Entering into coalitions with other organizations	90
■ Attempting to shape the implementation of policies	89
■ Talking with people from the press and the media	86
■ Consulting with government officials to plan legislative strategy	85
■ Helping to draft legislation	85
■ Inspiring letter-writing campaigns	84
■ Shaping the government's agenda by raising new issues and calling attention to previously ignored problems	84
■ Mounting grassroots lobbying efforts	80
■ Having influential constituents contact their congressperson's office	80
■ Helping to draft regulations, rules, or guidelines	78
■ Serving on advisory commissions and boards	76
■ Alerting congresspersons to the effects of a bill on their districts	75
■ Filing suit or otherwise engaging in litigation	72
■ Making financial contributions to electoral campaigns	58
■ Doing favors for officials who need assistance	56
■ Attempting to influence appointments to public office	53

Source: Kay Lehman Schlozman and John T. Tierney, "More of the Same: Washington Pressure Group Activity in a Decade of Change," *Journal of Politics* 45 (1983), 357.

process. It develops a cadre of experts, many of whom have spent their lives studying issues under government scrutiny. Critics believe the practice raises ethical concerns, especially when a person leaves a federal government position to join an interest group he or she once helped to regulate. Representative Billy Tauzin (R-LA), for example, left the House of Representatives in 2004 to become the president of the Pharmaceutical Research and Manufacturers Association shortly after writing the Medicare Drug Benefit law that is widely seen as protecting the interests of drug companies that he now represents. There are laws limiting the kinds of access former officials may have once they leave office and specifying the time period during which they are required to abstain from active lobbying.

Lobbying Congress Despite lobbyists' sometimes unsavory reputation, most members of Congress see them as possessors of valuable resources. Two of the most valuable of those resources are information and electoral support, often in the form of campaign contributions.

Members of Congress need information, because they must vote on many highly technical pieces of legislation during the course of a legislative session. Except for the policy areas they know well because of their committee assignments, congresspersons are policy generalists who lack the kind of detailed information that lobbyists can supply. Such information is crucial to legislators because they never know which vote on a bill could become an issue in the next campaign.[24]

To maintain a good relationship with a legislator, the lobbyist must supply credible and reliable information based on accurate research. Since technical information is in short supply, overworked legislators welcome help from interest group advocates in assessing and sometimes even drafting legislation. Lobbyists also contribute political information or cues. They communicate to legislators how a particular piece of legislation will sit with important constituencies back home. Lobbyists may communicate information by testifying at congressional committee hearings. By testifying openly, the interest group can impress its members back home with its status as a Washington player. Such visibility can increase membership and, in turn, the group's potential clout.

Did You Know?

... That the American Medical Association (AMA) conducted one of the most successful special-interest operations in the twentieth century when it blocked President Harry Truman's effort to establish a national insurance system in the 1940s? The AMA printed leaflets that alarmed the public and warned it about the dangers of "socialized medicine" should Truman's proposed expansion of Social Security be enacted. Congress defeated the measure, and no system of national health insurance for the general population has ever been enacted in the United States.

Lobbyists might slant information in order to "make the sale," but they dare not lie. A good lobbyist will even include information damaging to his or her cause from time to time in order to maintain credibility. As one lobbyist put it, "You can't ever afford to lie to a member of Congress because if you lose access to him, you've had it."[25]

Lobbyists need access to members of Congress in order to obtain policy results for their members. Opportunities for access in the policymaking process have increased in recent years since seniority and the powers granted committee chairs have been weakened, making individual members more important. Greater turnover, occasioned by term limits for committee chairs and self-imposed term limits by some individual legislators, has elevated the status of congressional staff members, whose cultivation can be useful in communicating a group's message to lawmakers. Staff contacts are particularly important in the smaller Senate, whose members have greater responsibilities and time commitments.[26]

Even the White House lobbies Congress in order to secure legislation it deems important. The Office of Legislative Affairs in the White House acts as the president's liaison with Congress. This office gives the White House a very powerful means of influencing legislator behavior. For example, the White House may release information beneficial to the cause of members whose support they seek, or the president can accept an invitation to a fundraising event for a member who is up for reelection. Some presidents pay more attention to congressional relations than others. Usually, those who work hard at nurturing support with key members are the ones most likely to gain support for their legislative agendas.

Lobbyists employ several generally recognized rules of thumb to maximize their effectiveness with Congress. They are aware that it is rarely effective to lobby opponents to one's cause in an effort to convert them. It is better to deploy one's resources working with allies in high places, especially members of key committees with jurisdiction in the area of one's interests. It is generally easier to avoid conflicts on big issues and concentrate instead on writing the details to one's advantage. It is easier to defeat a measure than to pass new ones.

Lobbying the Executive Branch Since the beginning of the twentieth century, the federal government has greatly expanded its authority over a wide range of private activities, from regulating pollutants emitted by industries to overseeing fair employment practices. This has provided interest groups with fertile ground for lobbying the cabinet departments and independent agencies of the federal bureaucracy that oversee these activities. Agency administrators and personnel are policymakers just as much as members of Congress. Their task is to write the rules that implement federal legislation. These rules involve a great deal of technical detail, take considerable time to draft, and often are the result of negotiations between bureaucrats and lobbyists for the organizations affected. Some of the rules implementing the Clean Air Act of 1991, for example, took 12 years to draft. Through the Federal Register, a daily compilation of federal regulations and legal notices, executive agencies invite public comment and reactions to proposed rules. This allows organized interests to draft written responses and appear before hearings to present their arguments. Lobbyists who have established good relationships with agency staff members can get an early start on the process by learning, in advance of public disclosure, what new rules are being considered.[27]

If they fail to influence the rulemakers, interest groups can pursue a number of alternative approaches, such as challenging rules they believe to be unfair in the courts. They can also seek favorable treatment by influencing the appointment of agency officials with whom they must deal. This is generally easier if the organization has good contacts with the administration and with key senators who must confirm the appointments of top administrators. Finally, interest group representatives can serve on advisory commissions and boards that meet with executive agencies to provide advice and guidance in areas of agency jurisdiction.[28]

Critics of executive branch lobbying worry that businesses and groups that are regulated by a particular agency often manage to "capture" the agency by exercising too much influence over the rules it writes and implements. For years, many observers believed the airline industry exercised undue influence over the Federal Aviation Administration, which resulted in overly favorable treatment regarding fee arrangements and travel routes. Research into agency capture produced no firm or universal findings, however, and the recent trend to deregulate and open business activity to market forces has weakened support for this viewpoint.[29]

Some critics also worry about what has been described as an **iron triangle**, a decision-making process dominated by interest groups, congressional committees, and executive agencies. In this arrangement, the parties cooperate by advancing each other's goals: Interest groups benefit by winning policy concessions or contracts; members of Congress benefit from electoral support supplied by the interest group; and federal agencies benefit from congressional approval for their administrative proposals.[30] In 1961, President Eisenhower warned about an overly cozy relationship between defense industry lobbyists, the Pentagon, and members of congressional appropriation committees. Most policy observers today agree, however, that the threat from potential "iron triangles" is on the wane,[31] especially because of inroads made by advocacy groups in gaining access to policymakers and in opening records of meetings.[32]

Still, it is not uncommon for small groups of experts to dominate policy creation and implementation. These groups, sometimes called **issue networks**, include lobbyists, members of Congress, bureaucrats, and policy specialists from think tanks and universities. These expert groupings are more open, less formal, and less permanent than iron triangles. Actors come together around immediate issues and disband once the issue is settled. Rather than having a permanent and reciprocally beneficial relationship, their only link is shared interest and expertise in a particular policy area. Issue networks often are open to groups with opposing interests and viewpoints, unlike the iron triangles where policy interests are more uniform.

Regulating Lobbying Activity Concerns about inappropriate lobbying activity date back to the nineteenth century, when bribery in Washington was not uncommon. In

> **iron triangle** A decision-making structure dominated by interest groups, congressional committees, and executive agency personnel who create policies that are mutually beneficial.
>
> **issue networks** Decision-making structure consisting of policy experts, including lobbyists, members of Congress, bureaucrats, and policy specialists from think tanks and universities.

Helping members of Congress raise money for campaigns is a powerful tactic presidents employ in securing support for legislation they favor.

1946, Congress passed the Federal Regulation of Lobbying Act, which attempted to deter the excesses of lobbying through the concept of disclosure. The law required lobbyists to register with the clerk of the House and the secretary of the Senate if they received money used principally to influence legislation before Congress. Despite these provisions, the act did not regulate the *practices* employed by lobbyists to any great extent, and it lacked enforcement. In 1995, Congress passed a new Lobbying Disclosure Act that defined lobbyists more broadly and included those seeking access to the executive branch. It also adopted new rules on gifts and sponsored travel.

A series of high-profile scandals that erupted in 2005 raised corruption as a major issue in the congressional elections of 2006. Super-lobbyist Jack Abramoff went to prison for bilking his Native American clients out of millions of dollars while lobbying on behalf of their gaming interests. So, too, did former Congressman Bob Ney (R-OH), who was convicted of accepting illegal gifts from Abramoff. In unrelated scandals, Congressman Randy "Duke" Cunningham was forced to resign and serve jail time for accepting bribes from defense contractors who sought favors from the Defense Appropriations Subcommittee on which he served, and Representa-

tive William Jefferson (D-LA) was forced to relinquish his position on the House Ways and Means Committee amid reports of bribes after the FBI found $90,000 in cash in his freezer. Reacting to these events, the 110th Congress passed a new round of reforms, the 2007 Honest Leadership and Open Government Act, that included a ban on accepting gifts, meals, or trips from lobbyists. The bill also ended the practice of accepting free or reduced-fare trips on corporate jets, mandated greater disclosure about special pet projects (known as earmarks) that legislators insert into bills on behalf of special interests, and required greater disclosure and tracking of the source of campaign funds exceeding $15,000 that come in "bundles" from members of the same organization. It also required senators and members of the executive branch to wait two years after leaving government service before lobbying Congress; House members must wait one year.

These changes have by no means leveled the playing field for political access; lobbying Congress is a very expensive game that only the best-financed interests can play effectively. According to the Federal Election Commission (FEC), for example, assorted groups spent over $2.8 billion on lobbying in 2007. Just one organization, the U.S. Chamber of Commerce, spent nearly $53 million on federal lobbying in 2007.[33] Nor are these changes likely to allay the suspicions of many Americans who perceive a culture of corruption in Washington. The reforms include loopholes that permit lobbyists to make campaign contributions that the representative or senator can then use to take the lobbyist to dinner to discuss matters of mutual interest. Both major-party presidential candidates, who promised to run campaigns free of special interests, were forced to release campaign staff during the 2008 race because of their lobbying ties. As a result of disclosures such as these, many citizens still find it difficult to distinguish between the few who take advantage of the system and the majority of Washington insiders who try their best to navigate difficult ethical waters while advocating the interests of those they represent.[34]

Hot or Not?

Should Congress ban all gifts from lobbyists to members of Congress or should they allow gifts as long as they are fully disclosed to the public?

Both presidential candidates were stung by revelations of the lobbying ties of campaign aides. Doug Goodyear, John McCain's Republican convention manager, stepped down due to his lobbying ties to the repressive regime in Burma. Jim Johnson (below), Barack Obama's choice to head his vice presidential search team, stepped down because of his ties to a firm involved in the mortgage crisis.

Financing Campaigns

The public perception out there that someone who gives a thousand dollars has influence is laughable. It really is, because that's such chump change today that it doesn't even register on the scale.

Wright Andrews, lobbyist[35]

No one really knows when organized interests started taking over the financing of political campaigns. An early milestone was Marcus A. Hanna's success in raising over $3.5 million for the campaign of Republican William McKinley in 1896 by assessing corporations and banks predetermined

PAC Spending Limits and Regulations

- $5,000 per candidate per election. Elections such as primaries, general elections, and special elections are counted separately.
- $15,000 per political party.
- $5,000 per PAC. PACs are allowed to give to other PACs.
- PACs are not limited in the amount they spend on advertising to support their own issues.
- PACs must register with the FEC within 10 days of formation, providing name and address for the PAC, treasurer's name, and names of any connected organizations.
- Affiliated PACs (those affiliated with other organizations under the same control) are treated as one donor for the purpose of contribution limits.

Source: Federal Elections Commission and Opensecrets.org.

amounts to finance the campaign.[36] Since then, it seems incumbent on organizations that want an elected official's ear to "pony up." For the average individual, $1,000 is hardly "chump change," but some U.S. Senate races cost over $30 million to run. In light of extravagant campaign costs, candidates are in a continuous search for funds, and interest groups stand ready to help.

Financing elections takes place within a web of legal restrictions that have become more complicated and contentious over time. The first regulations date to 1907, when the Tillman Act outlawed contributions directly from corporations. The act was fraught with loopholes, however, and enjoyed little genuine enforcement. It was not until the 1970s that Congress seriously revisited the issue of campaign finance regulation. The Federal Election Campaign Act of 1971 required candidates to disclose the sources of contributions but did little to reform campaign financing beyond reporting. Congress passed more sweeping legislation in 1974, in the wake of the Watergate scandal. The legislation provided for public financing for presidential elections (see Chapter 12) and the creation of the Federal Election Commission to monitor election finances and place limits on contributions by individuals, political parties, and **political action committees** (PACs). PACs are organized financial arms of interest groups that collect and distribute money to candidates for elective office.

Interest groups challenged the law's limits on political contributions by individuals and PACs as a violation of their First Amendment right to free speech. In *Buckley v. Valeo* (1976), the Supreme Court struck down some of the bill's provisions but allowed continued limits on individual and PAC contributions. With caps on the contributions allowed by any given PAC, the number of PACs increased dramatically. PAC growth represents a wide spectrum of political and economic interests, including business, labor, and citizens' groups. Even elected officials maintain so-called **leadership PACs** as a means of financing the campaigns of political allies who they believe will reciprocate with support for their own political ambitions.

Congress revisited the issue of campaign finance in 2002, passing the so-called McCain-Feingold bill, named for its two vocal Senate sponsors, John McCain (R-AZ) and Russell Feingold (D-WI). Although interest groups challenged these reforms in 2003 and again in 2007,[37] the Supreme Court upheld most of the new law's provisions. Much of the reform had to do with limitations on money spent by political parties (see Chapter 9) and on advertising, but the bill also changed the amount of PAC contributions permitted.

Campaign contribution limits are shown in the adjacent figure. It shows the amount of money individuals may give to candidates and PACs, and how much PACs may contribute

> **political action committees (PACs)** Organized financial arms of interest groups used to collect and distribute money to candidates for elective office.
>
> **leadership PACs** Political action committees set up by political leaders as a means to finance the campaigns of political allies whom they believe will reciprocate with support for their own political ambitions.

PAC Expenditures, 1989–2006

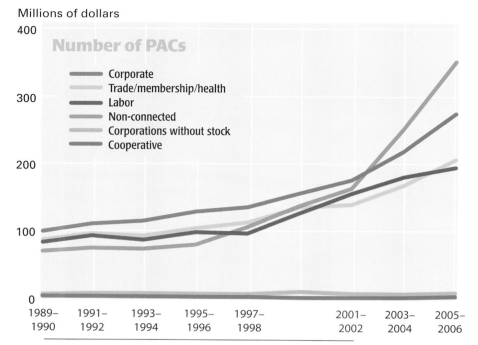

Millions of dollars

Number of PACs

- Corporate
- Trade/membership/health
- Labor
- Non-connected
- Corporations without stock
- Cooperative

400
300
200
100
0

1989–1990 1991–1992 1993–1994 1995–1996 1997–1998 2001–2002 2003–2004 2005–2006

Source: FEC, Summary of PAC Financial Accounting, 1990–2006.

stakes, competitive arena of campaign finance in order to advance the interests they espouse.

Corporate interests are also major players. Corporate interests may be represented by multiple PACs—once through a company PAC itself and then through several additional professional and trade PACS. Business PACs historically have given the largest proportion of their dollars to incumbents. While interests such as business and finance generally favor Republicans, and others (including labor and trial lawyers) generally favor Democrats,[40] party loyalty is not the exclusive hallmark of PAC giving. All but the most ideologically committed groups commonly adjust their spending when party control changes hands.[41] Labor PACs, on the other hand, give more consistently to Democratic candidates. Although labor unions represent less than 10 percent of the total number of PACs, the amount they contribute is impressive. As of May 2008 in the most recent election cycle, labor PACs had already contributed over $31 million to Congressional campaigns, 90 percent of which went to Democratic candidates.[42]

Interest groups also can form tax-exempt organizations, known as **527 groups**, to engage in political activities ranging from grassroots mobilization to sponsoring ads promoting or criticizing a candidate's record on an issue. (Prior to a 2007 Supreme Court ruling, such ads could not mention the candidates by name and could not run for a short period of time prior to Election Day.)[43] These organizations have thus far remained outside the range of government regulation. The top fifty 527 organizations spent a total of more than $182 million on the congressional elections of 2006.

The number and diversity of interests may seem so great, and the amounts spent so large, that one might assume no interests go unheard in the corridors of power. The interests of some groups, however, such as children and the poor, generally go unrepresented. As one-time Senate majority leader Bob Dole said, "There aren't any Poor PACs or Food Stamp PACs or Nutrition PACs or Medicaid PACs."[44]

to candidates and other PACs. The amounts are adjusted for inflation with each election cycle. Keep in mind that interest group members and lobbyists can contribute individually to a candidate and again to PACs that support the candidate. According to the FEC, campaign donations from individual lobbyists to congressional candidates totaled over $18.5 million in 2006. Lobbyists also sometimes serve as treasurers of campaign committees for candidates, thereby elevating the visibility of their group.[38]

As the figure above shows, advocacy groups (non-connected) and business interests dominate the money game. The number of issue groups like the National Rifle Association or the National Organization for Women has increased dramatically in recent years, and so have their contributions. According to one study, citizen groups constituted five of the fastest growing sources of campaign funds when individual contributions and PAC funds are combined.[39] The growth of this sector clearly suggests that civic groups, sometimes responding to requests by entrepreneurial leaders, are not shrinking from engaging in the high

527 groups Tax-exempt organizations set up by interest groups to engage in political activities.

political disadvantage theory View positing that groups are likely to seek remedies in courts if they do not succeed in the electoral process.

grassroots mobilization The practice of organizing citizen support for a group's policy or candidate preferences.

mobilizing the grass tops Mining databases for high-status community leaders for purposes of contacting legislators in key districts regarding sponsoring a group's position.

Accessing the Courts

The courts can play a pivotal role in public policy when they affirm or reject legislative or administrative actions. However, judges cannot be lobbied in the same way that congresspersons and bureaucrats can. One of the most important tactics lobbyists can legally employ, however, is to attempt to control the membership of the courts. Interest groups historically have played a significant role in influencing presidents and senators during the appointment process.

When a group believes that a piece of legislation will cause them harm or raises constitutional concerns, it is the group's right to litigate. Litigation is expensive, however, and groups with abundant financial resources, access to full-time staff attorneys, a wellspring of public support, and a clear issue focus are most likely to undertake it.[45] Some groups file suit in court when they are relatively certain there is little support for their cause in the court of public opinion. This is sometimes known as the **political disadvantage theory**,[46] for which the tobacco industry serves as a prime example. It is far easier to convince a court to reject an industry regulation on legal grounds than to expect sympathy from a public that is increasingly turned off by smoking. Instead of bringing suit themselves, many interest groups file *amicus curiae*, or "friend of the court" briefs outlining their support for the claims of others, especially when the case holds promise to advance their own interests.

Most of the important constitutional cases with broad policy implications decided by the Supreme Court in recent years have taken the form of test cases. These are cases brought by organized interests in an attempt to set new precedents.[47] In the 1950s, for example, the Legal Defense Fund of the National Association for the Advancement of Colored People (NAACP) won numerous court cases supporting equal rights for African Americans.[48] More recently, advocacy groups who agree with the legal claims of environmentalists, women, civil libertarians, or fundamentalist Christians have supported their cases before the Supreme Court.[49] We will return to discuss the role of advocacy groups in the courts in Chapter 14.

Grassroots Mobilization

Grassroots mobilization is the practice of organizing citizens to exert direct pressure on public officials in support of a group's policy preferences. Lawmakers want to be reelected, and they know constituents retain the power to reward or punish them at the polls. As a result, organizations with large member bases and with members spread across a broad swath of congressional districts can be especially effective.[50] The National Education Association (NEA) is one of the larger membership-based grassroots organizations, representing more than 3 million educators. The Christian Coalition is another, with an estimated 1.9 million members. The strength of large organizations like these comes from their ability to mobilize large numbers of citizens into action quickly. Such groups can rouse members to write or call their lawmakers, to work on political campaigns, and to get out the vote on Election Day. Organized groups can provide workers to bring a candidate's message door-to-door, distribute campaign literature, and staff telephone banks. The electioneering efforts of the Christian Coalition helped the Republicans gain control of Congress in 1994, and the strong efforts by organized labor provided Democratic gains in both houses in 2006.

As we know from Chapter 7, those who are better educated and more affluent are more readily mobilized, and their communications are more highly prized by political leaders. Because of this, some public relations firms specialize in mining databases for high-status community leaders to contact legislators in key districts to support the sponsoring group's position. This practice, known as **mobilizing the grass tops**, earns these firms hefty fees for setting up meetings between high-profile constituents and members of Congress.[51] The National Federation of Independent Business (NFIB), for example, regularly communicates by Internet and e-mail with its

Who Gives to Republicans?
Who Gives to Democrats?

Totals by sector

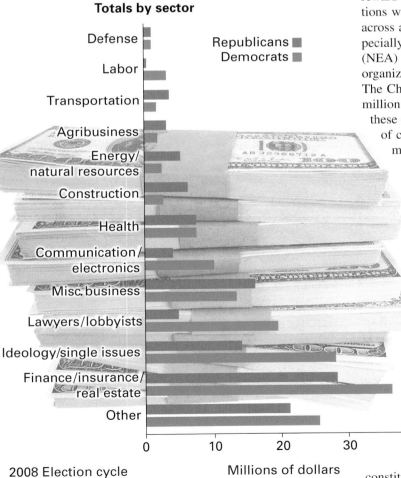

Republicans ■
Democrats ■

2008 Election cycle   Millions of dollars

Source: Opensecrets.org, accessed May 26, 2008 at www.opensecrets.org

In addition to their constituents, what interests do your U.S. representative and senators represent? How much money did they raise in the last election cycle and where did it come from? You can search financial records that reveal this information easily at www.opensecrets .org. The site provides access to the source of both individual and PAC funds. Once you have this data, you can check voting records to discover whether or not they voted for issues supported by major backers.

members to educate and mobilize them.[52] The group maintains phone and fax numbers of its members and information about members' types of businesses, issue positions, political backgrounds, and legislative districts. This kind of data makes it easy for the NFIB to target its message to those members who are most likely to respond to calls for quick mobilization.

Another tactic, known as **astroturf lobbying**, uses deceptive practices and lack of transparency to manufacture grassroots support for an issue important to a particular set of unidentified interests. For example, the Harry and Louise commercials we spoke of earlier were sponsored by a group calling itself the Coalition for Health Insurance Choices (CHIC), a name that implied broad grassroots support. CHIC was, however, merely the name adopted by the true sponsors—all of whom were members of the health insurance industry that believed the reform bill was bad for their

The Christian Coalition distributes voting guides to churches the Sunday before Election Day to inform congregation members about candidate voting records on issues the group considers most important.

★ 2008 Christian Coalition ★
V O T E R GUIDE
PRESIDENTIAL ELECTION

John McCain (R) — ISSUES — Barack Obama (D)

John McCain (R)	ISSUES	Barack Obama (D)
Supports*	Education vouchers that allow parents to choose public or private school for their children	Opposes*
Opposes*	Sex education for children in kindergarten through 12th grade	Supports*
Opposes*	Increase in federal income tax rates	Supports*
Supports*	Appointing judges that will adhere to a strict interpretation of the Constitution	Opposes*
Opposes*	Further restrictions on the right to keep and bear arms	Supports*
Opposes*	Public funding of abortions, (such as govt. health benefits and Planned Parenthood)	Supports*
Supports*	Parental notification for abortions by minors	Opposes*
Supports*	Legislation mandating health care for infants surviving abortions	Opposes*
Opposes*	Granting sexual preference a protected minority status under existing civil rights laws	Supports*
Opposes*	Allowing adoption of children by homosexuals	Supports*
Supports*	Enforcing the 1993 law banning homosexuals in the military	Opposes*
Supports*	Prohibiting public funding for art that is pornographic or anti-religious	Opposes*
Supports*	Tax credits for purchasing private health insurance	Opposes*
Supports*	Allowing federal funding for faith-based charitable organizations	Opposes*
Supports*	Tax credits for investment in renewable sources of energy, (such as wind, solar & biomass)	Supports*
Supports*	Legislation to enact a "cap & trade" system to reduce carbon dioxide emissions	Supports*

www.johnmccain.com   www.barackobama.com

Each candidate was sent a 2008 Federal Issues Survey by mail and/or facsimile machine. When possible, positions of candidates on issues were verified or determined using voting records and/or public statements, articles or campaign literature. An asterisk (*) indicates such information was used to determine positions and sources are available on request.

Paid for and authorized by the Christian Coalition; PO Box 37030 - Washington, DC 20013

The Christian Coalition is a pro-family, citizen action organization. This voter guide is provided for educational purposes only and is not to be construed as an endorsement of any candidate or party.
Please visit our web site at www. cc.org

★ Vote on November 4 ★

★ Vote on November 4 ★

Dear fellow American Christian,

You are holding one of the most powerful tools Christians have ever had to impact our society during elections – the Christian Coalition voter guide. This simple tool has helped educate tens of millions of citizens across this nation as to where candidates for public office stand on key faith and family issues.

I want to assure you that your church or civic group has every right to distribute these non-partisan voter guides, and distributing them poses no threat whatsoever to any organization's tax-exempt status. In fact, Christian Coalition is the only organization whose voter guides are prepared in accordance with IRS approved guidelines for distribution in churches.

I encourage you to help spread this important information to others by making additional copies for distribution. You can make voter guides available in every way possible – in churches, at Christian bookstores, as neighborhood handouts and even outside your local polling station. You can also visit our web site at www.cc.org to find links to this guide which you can forward via email to others. They can then download and print directly from our web site.

Also, please be in prayer for our nation, as we continually need God's hand of mercy and protection.

This is a crucial election and too much is at stake for God's people to sit on the sidelines. Be sure to make your vote count by going to the polls this coming Election Day!

Thank you for the stand you are taking as a Christian citizen and may God bless America!

Sincerely,
Roberta Combs
President, Christian Coalition

★ Please go to www.cc.org and help support our 2008 Voter Guide Project ★

business. After these commercials aired, Congress and legislatures in several states proposed legislation outlawing astroturf lobbying.

Many interest groups build grassroots support for their causes by supplying voters with ratings or scorecards to guide their electoral choices. The Christian Coalition has been particularly adept at this practice, issuing ratings for candidates that have agreed with their issue positions to member churches for distribution on the Sunday prior to election. The liberal group Americans for Democratic Action (ADA) uses a similar rating scheme. The group gives each legislator a score based on the percentage of times he or she voted in favor of the group's position. In the first session of the 110th Congress (2007), the ADA found the average rating for House Republicans to be 16 percent, whereas the Democrats was 92 percent. The ADA also publishes a list of House and Senate "heroes" (100 percent agreement with the group) and "zeros" (0 percent agreement with the group).

> **astroturf lobbying** Using deceptive practices and lack of transparency to manufacture grassroots support for an issue important to a particular set of unidentified interests.

Americans for Democratic Action Ratings for Senators in 110th Congress (2007)

HEROES
100% Agreement with ADA positions

Stabenow (D-MI)
Klobuchar (D-MN)
Casey (D-PA)

ZEROS

Ensign (R-NV)
Burr (R-NC)
DeMint (R-SC)

0% Agreement with ADA positions

Source: Americans for Democratic Action, accessed at http://adaction .org/media/votingrecords/2007.pdf on February 15, 2008.

Coalition Formation

The rapid growth in the number and variety of interest groups over the last thirty years has created a strong incentive for groups to act in concert by forging coalitions. Organized groups benefit from alliances by expanding their access to resources and information, increasing their visibility, and enlarging the scope of their influence. Members of Congress and federal bureaucrats often seek out coalitions because they provide a means for reconciling intergroup differences in a way that facilitates compromise in policy formation.

Coalitions are not always easy to build, because there are risks in joining. Some of the views of coalition partners may be at odds with those of other partners, and smaller groups may fear that their priorities will be submerged beneath those of larger partners. Each group must evaluate the trade-offs of joining a coalition on an issue-by-issue basis.[53] Sometimes, however, issues bring together coalitions of highly unlikely partners. For example, groups as disparate as the liberal American Civil Liberties Union (ACLU) and the conservative Rutherford Institute found common ground in opposing restrictions on civil liberties proposed in the USA Patriot Act following the September 11 attacks.

Protests

Protests have always been a part of the American political landscape. They include nonviolent techniques such as picketing or marches and sit-ins like those used by the civil rights movement under the leadership of Dr. Martin Luther King. They may also involve violence, as in Shays's Rebellion shortly after the American Revolution. Protest is the ultimate form of grassroots activity, because members are asked to be willing to sacrifice their lives and their freedom for the cause. As a result, protest usually accompanies issues that are highly charged emotionally. The 1973 *Roe v. Wade* decision, for example, triggered a significant increase in protest activity that continues to surround the abortion issue to this day.

Although it is protected by the First Amendment, many observers see protest as being outside the mainstream of political activism. As a result, it is a common tactic among those with few resources and little direct access to the centers of power. Protesting might be considered the ultimate outside strategy, reserved for groups with few other visible means for making their voices heard, such as the Hispanic demonstrators we saw at the outset of this chapter. This does not mean, however, that protesters themselves are poor and uneducated. Some studies show that protesters disproportionately come from those with higher levels of income and education.[54]

INTEREST GROUPS AND CITIZEN ENGAGEMENT TODAY

Whereas voluntary associations of earlier eras emphasized local organization and citizen training, interest group politics today is often run by professionals in Washington. This development is the result of important structural changes in the nature of our political system. As Matthew A. Crenson and Benjamin Ginsberg note, "Beginning with the development of its

regulatory capacity at the start of the twentieth century, American government multiplied the mechanisms by which organized interests could achieve their ends without mobilizing their grassroots constituents."[55] Petitioning of executive branch agencies and litigation necessitate the work of skilled professionals, not average citizens. Government and philanthropic foundations multiplied the opportunities for groups to support themselves without relying exclusively on membership contributions. As a result, interest groups increasingly seem to manage interests from above rather than fully involving the citizens they are supposed to represent.[56]

Some warn that these changes in patterns of interest group activity are transforming citizens from "participants" to "mailing lists." Today, entrepreneurial advocacy groups launch campaigns from Washington seeking direct access to lawmakers and the courts without first investing much effort in generating popular support for their positions in towns and neighborhoods.[57] The AARP, for example, has the largest membership base of any American interest group. Yet their 35 million members do not gather in conventions to determine their political agenda. Their leaders contact them by mail. Participation is limited to contributions; the leadership sets the agendas, and groups often bring their issues before courts or administrative boards without needing to demonstrate any broad support for the actions they undertake. Interest groups demand little from members but much from government.

However, interest groups have *always* depended on strong national leadership willing to employ new techniques in mobilizing popular support. Some of the largest grassroots organizations today, such as the NAACP, began as national organizations and later cultivated local

United Students Against Sweatshops and other organizations have mounted effective grassroots campaigns to stop retailers from carrying clothing made by manufacturers employing unfair and unsafe labor conditions.

chapters for support. Advocacy groups continue to play an important role in opening new avenues of expression and preserving constitutional rights for millions of previously disaffected minorities. To a large extent, interest groups have simply adapted their methods to reflect changes in the lifestyles of most Americans. Most Americans have little time to meet with neighborhood associations after a long day of work and after-dinner soccer practice with their children. They cannot monitor the fine points of legislation that may threaten their interests. Organized groups recognize this reality by offering citizens a variety of participatory options; for instance, they encourage check writing and provide help in contacting local representatives. They are even developing hybrid techniques that combine national activation with local action. For example, some groups use the Internet not merely to inform citizens of legislative threats or to solicit funds but also to help local citizens organize meetings in their own communities. These "meet ups" hold the promise of reigniting community activism in the Internet age.

Finally, there is growing interest in global issues that defy national borders and traditional interest group activities. Young Americans are especially interested in global organizations like Greenpeace and Oxfam, and in expanding the frontiers of political action. Many of the organizations that address international issues, such as United Students Against Sweatshops (USAS) and the Global Fund to Fight AIDS, Tuberculosis and Malaria, employ innovative approaches to political participation that include boycotting manufacturers who use sweatshop labor or BUYcotting—selectively purchasing from merchants who donate a portion of their receipts to a good cause.

Nevertheless, interest group politics continues to pose challenges to our voluntaristic ethic. Although citizens are indeed writing more letters and checks, boycotting, and BUYcotting, these actions continue to be taken dispropor-

Find an interest group that addresses the issues that are most important to you and communicate with that group about opportunities for working with it to advance your cause. Does the group have a local chapter? If not, find out how to start one yourself and develop plans for taking your issue to your congressional representative on behalf of the organization.

get involved!

tionately by those who are well off. As a result, groups reflecting the interests of the upper reaches of society are better represented when political decisions are rendered. The pluralism that thrives in a community characterized by numerous interest groups is at risk when the majority of those groups speak with what one political scientist calls "an upper class accent."[58]

For REVIEW >>

1. What are interest groups and what types of interests do they represent?
   - Interest groups are formally organized associations that seek to influence public policy. They represent myriad specific interests, but those representing the wealthy and better educated are more numerous.
2. Why might someone join an interest group?
   - Someone might join an interest group to receive material advantages, such as discounts for products or services, or social support from others with similar backgrounds or interests, or because she or he believes strongly in a cause the group seeks to advance.
3. What do interest groups do?
   - Interest groups try to influence government policies through tactics like lobbying, financing campaigns, filing suits in court, working to create grassroots support, protesting, and forming alliances with others to advance their cause.

National Journal

WHY THEY LOBBY

Thank You for Smoking, the 2005 film based on a novel by Christopher Buckley, follows the life of Nick Naylor, a chief spokesman for Big Tobacco with questionable morals, who makes his living defending the rights of smokers and cigarette-makers and then must deal with how his young son, Joey, views him. Naylor may have been a fictitious character, but Washington has its share of lobbyists arguing for the interests of industries with a perceived darker side.

The cynical response is that career decisions and political give-and-take revolve around money: Greenbacks triumph over ethics. But those who represent socially sensitive industries such as tobacco and alcohol have a lot more to say about why, out of all the potential job opportunities, they chose and often "love" what they do.

They all make it a point to note that the First Amendment sanctions lobbying: "the right of the people . . . to petition the government for a redress of grievances."

Tobacco

In the film, Naylor works for the Academy of Tobacco Studies, which Buckley based on the Tobacco Institute, the industry's former trade association. Andrew Zausner, who has lobbied for tobacco for 30 years, feeds off the challenge. "The more unpopular the client, the better you have to be as a lobbyist," he declares. "Believing in your client's position makes you a more forceful advocate." Although Zausner doesn't want his children to use tobacco, he notes that the "product has been continuously used in the United States before the United States existed" and says that the industry has a legitimate point of view and a constitutional right to express it.

Beau Schuyler lobbies for UST Public Affairs, a subsidiary of the holding company that owns U.S. Smokeless Tobacco and Ste. Michelle Wine Estates. A former congressional aide to two Democratic House members from his native state of North Carolina—in the heart of tobacco country—Schuyler says

that the "opportunity to work internally at one of the oldest continually listed companies on the New York Stock Exchange was just too good to pass up."

Gambling

James Reeder, a lobbyist at Patton Boggs, has spent about half his time over the past decade representing the gambling industry. He insists he didn't seek out this niche, adding, "I tell my grandchildren that gambling is a bad habit . . . and to go fishing."

Shortly after Reeder joined Patton Boggs, a client named Showboat called the firm looking for someone who knew about Louisiana because the company was interested in building a casino there. Reeder happened to be from the Pelican State and was put on the case. He reasoned that Louisiana has always been a home to illegal gambling, and "if the culture of the state supports the industry, [the state] might as well make it legal and reap the benefits and get more tax money."

"Whenever you take on one of these vices like booze or gambling and you just pass a law to say it is illegal," Reeder says, "you end up like in Prohibition, when the mob took over the liquor business."

Reeder excelled at lobbying for the gambling industry even though he avoids games of chance. "I don't gamble, because I am not a good card player," he says. "My friends would die laughing because I would go to offices to talk to clients on gambling and I would never go into a casino." If a lawmaker was morally opposed to gambling, Reeder wouldn't argue with him, he says.

John Pappas began working for the industry as a consultant for the Poker Players Alliance while at Dittus Communications.

Pappas calls poker a game of skill that has a rich history in America. He grew up playing cards with family members and friends, and noted during an interview that he would be playing poker with 20 lawmakers that evening at a charity tournament. "Responsibility in all aspects of life is paramount," he says.

Firearms

Richard Feldman's book, *Ricochet: Confessions of a Gun Lobbyist*, has been gaining the former National Rifle Association employee some attention recently. Feldman says that the gun control issue, like most, is not black and white. Working for the NRA, he says, "was the best job I ever had." The "huge power" he was able to wield "in the middle of major political battles" was more attractive to him at the time than the money he earned.

Feldman says he would sometimes play hardball but "didn't hit below the belt" in his pursuit of the gun industry's objectives. "Lobbying an issue that you have some special passion on (guns) is like waking up every day already having consumed a triple espresso," he said in an e-mail to *National Journal*. "On the other hand, if you can empathize with your client's position regardless of the issue, one can be a more convincing advocate, which I've always viewed as the more critical aspect of truly effective lobbying.

Video Games

Because many video games contain a fair share of gunplay and other violence, Entertainment Software Association President Michael Gallagher has had to address complaints that playing violent games causes psychological harm such as increased aggression.

His group lobbies against "efforts to regulate the content of entertainment media in any form, including proposals to criminalize the sale of certain video games to minors; create uniform, government-sanctioned entertainment rating systems; or regulate the marketing practices of industry."

Gallagher, a former assistant Commerce secretary for communications and information in the Bush administration, calls video games a great form of family entertainment. The titles are responsibly rated, he says, and the gaming consoles have easy-to-use parental controls.

"I have been playing video games all my life," Gallagher says, including with his children. He contends that his industry "leads all forms of media when it comes to disclosure on what's in the game" and says that it works with retailers to "make sure minors can't buy games that are inappropriate for them."

Alcohol

Lobbyists who work for the beer, wine, and spirits industries have to deal with a host of negative images, among them drunk-driving accidents, underage drinking, and the effects of alcohol on health.

Mike Johnson, a lobbyist for the National Beer Wholesalers Association, acknowledges that alcohol is a "socially sensitive product" and says that is why the industry operates under strict government guidelines.

"I am blessed. I get to represent some great family-owned and -operated businesses that are very active in their communities and provide some really great jobs," Johnson says. "I am completely comfortable one day having a conversation with my son about who I work for, because I can tell him what a great job that beer distributors do in ensuring a safe marketplace and in protecting consumers from a lot of the problems we see with alcohol in other places in the world."

Craig Wolf, president of the Wine & Spirits Wholesalers, calls alcohol a "great social lubricant" that "creates great environments." Wolf got involved in wine-industry issues when he was counsel for the Senate Judiciary Committee. As his job there was ending, Wolf was offered the post of general counsel at the association; he took over as president in 2006.

"The key to advocating for a socially sensitive product is doing business responsibility," Wolf says. "We spend more time and resources [on the issue of] responsible consumption of alcohol than all other issues combined."

Distilled Spirits Council President Peter Cressy says, "I was interviewed for this position precisely because the Distilled Council wanted to continue and increase its very serious approach to fighting underage drinking." As chancellor of the University of Massachusetts (Dartmouth), Cressy says, he was active in "fighting binge drinking on campuses." The opportunity to join the council, which has lobbyists in 40 states, gave him the chance to have a national audience, he says. After nine years with the council, Cressy notes, he "has not been disappointed."

Snack Foods

Nicholas Pyle stands at the policy divide where junk food meets America's bulging waistlines. "I love my job," says Pyle, a lobbyist for McKee Foods, the makers of Little Debbie, America's leading snack-cake brand.

Many of the brand's affordable treats contain a dose of sugar, along with corn syrup, partially hydrogenated oil, bleached flour, and artificial flavor. Little Debbie "has been the target of a number of folks out there who want to paint people as a victim of the foods they eat," says Pyle, who is also president of the Independent Bakers Association. Little Debbie is a "wonderful food, great product, wholesome," with a wonderful image, he says. Pyle explains that he and his children enjoy the snacks.

"The big question of obesity is all about personal responsibility and people balancing [snacking] with a healthy and active lifestyle," Pyle insists. He contends that McKee, a family-owned business, doesn't target children in its marketing. "We market to the decision makers in the household," he says, adding that the company doesn't advertise on Saturday morning cartoon shows.

Snack Food Association President and CEO Jim McCarthy says that lobbying is one of his many duties as head of the organization. "Our belief is that all foods fit into the diet," McCarthy says, and "we don't like the term 'junk food.'"

The industry has developed healthier products over the years, McCarthy says, but at "certain times consumers haven't bought these products." He attributes the obesity problem to a lack of exercise and shortcomings in educating people about the need for a balanced diet.

Challenging Stereotypes

No matter what industry they represent, lobbyists interviewed for this article said that a good practitioner of their profession knows all sides of an issue, enabling lawmakers and their staffs to make the best-informed decision.

Although many of the lobbyists acknowledge some familiar situations in *Thank You for Smoking,* they insist that the stereotypes are not altogether fair. "I think people don't understand the importance of lobbying to the system. If I don't explain what we do and I am not here to explain it to people, Congress will make uninformed decisions without understanding the consequences to the industry," a former liquor lobbyist says.

For consumers, the message that lobbyists appear to be sending is that the individual is responsible for making the right choices in life. Yet the profusion of advertising, marketing ploys, political rhetoric, and seemingly conflicting studies can be bewildering. And although the financial incentive is ever-present, lobbyists believe they fill a fundamental role in society and deserve some relief from the negative stereotypes.

FOR DISCUSSION: Would you take a job lobbying for a "sin industry"? What about a job lobbying for an industry or cause you believe in but others do not?

Should we regulate the influence of certain lobbies but not others?

Do you feel the positions put forward by the lobbies mentioned in the article have affected the way you think about their industries?

9

PARTIES

AND POLITICAL CAMPAIGNS

CITIZENS AND THE ELECTORAL PROCESS

FOOD (AND DRINK) FOR THOUGHT: HOW PARTY STRATEGISTS MICROTARGET YOUR VOTE ■ Wine drinkers vote Hillary Clinton. Latte drinkers skew toward Barack Obama. And bourbon is the drink for supporters of John McCain. Dr. Pepper is the choice of Republicans; Democrats prefer Pepsi and Sprite.[1]

These are just some of the discoveries political strategists find useful in planning campaigns for their clients. In recent years, a practice known as *microtargeting* has aided political operatives in identifying potential supporters, designing customized messages, and mobilizing voters to show up on Election Day on the basis of their preferences. It is a practice that strategist Karl Rove utilized very effectively in getting out the vote for George W. Bush in 2004.[2]

Five years ago, Republican Party leaders in Washington pored through reams of data on consumer habits to identify previously inactive Republican supporters and sympathizers. They discovered those who leaned Republican were more likely than Democratic sympathizers to drink Coors beer, drive BMWs, watch college football, and subscribe to Caller ID.[3] This information was fed to local volunteers around the country, who scoured their neighborhoods for individuals who fit the profile. Local get-out-the-vote (GOTV) volunteers then passed information about these individuals to a command center in suburban Virginia, where campaign specialists developed individualized messages for thirty-two subgroups based on voters' specific interests. This approach yielded a fourfold increase in the number of potential Republican voters contacted during the 2004 election over previous presidential election cycles and is widely credited with ➥

National party conventions galvanize the support of partisans and help catapult the party's nominee into the general election campaign.

the nominee selected by the party's candidate for president. In addition to making policy recommendations, the national committees select sites for the presidential nominating conventions. The Democrats chose Denver for their site in 2008, while the Republicans picked Minneapolis–St. Paul. Both parties picked sites in regions of the country where they hoped to pick up additional support for their presidential nominee. The national committees also work to coordinate electoral activities with the staffs for presidential and congressional campaigns.

soft money Money that is outside the federal regulatory framework but raised and spent in a manner suggesting possible intent to affect federal elections.

hard money Campaign money received by candidates or parties that can be used for any purpose.

The national party chair presides over everyday operations of the national headquarters, monitors electoral races throughout the nation, helps set the party agenda and rules, and acts something like a referee when there is a contested primary. Howard Dean, Democratic National Committee chair, had to walk a fine line during the contest between

Hillary Clinton and Barack Obama in 2008. His job was made more difficult when Michigan and Florida violated party rules by advancing their primaries earlier in the year than the party had authorized. Party rules prescribed a loss of all convention delegates as punishment. Dean and members of the Rules Committee for the Democratic National Convention played a critical role in balancing the interests of Clinton, who won both contests, and wanted all of the delegates to count, and Obama, who removed his name from one state's primary, campaigned in neither, and floated the option of seating only half of the states' delegations. Ultimately, the full delegations from both states were seated, but only after Hillary Clinton conceded the nomination to Obama. We will discuss the presidential election in more detail in Chapter 12.

In recent years, fundraising has been one of the primary functions of the national committees. Until 2002, most of these funds took the form of **soft money**, large sums, mostly from wealthy contributors, intended for "party building" activities such as voter registration and running generic issue ads that do not mention specific candidates. In actuality, much of the money went to bolster presidential or congressional nominees in key battleground states. The Bipartisan Campaign Reform Act of 2002 banned parties from raising and spending soft money. However, the act increased contribution limits on **hard money**, donations that candidates or parties can use directly for electoral activities. Even with these new rules in place, the national committees have demonstrated an impressive capacity for collecting large sums of money. Many critics of the campaign reform law believed that it would divert funds away from parties and into the hands of outside groups with a stake in election outcomes. This has clearly not been the case. The parties have adapted well to the ban on soft money, and today they are more significant players in financing presidential and congressional campaigns than they were before the law went into effect.[31] Democrats, who for many years badly trailed Republicans in fundraising, have been somewhat more competitive in raising funds over the past three election cycles (2004, 2006, and 2008).

New Limits on Fundraising Following Bipartisan Campaign Reform Act, 2007–2008

	To each candidate or candidate committee per election	To national party committee per calendar year	To state, district & local party committee per calendar year	To any other political committee per calendar year[1]	Special limits
Individual may give	$2,300*	$28,500*	$10,000 (combined limit)	$5,000	$108,200* overall biennial limit: • $42,700* to all candidates • $65,500* to all PACs and parties[2]
National party committee may give	$5,000	No limit	No limit	$5,000	$39,900* to Senate candidate per campaign[3]
State, district & local party committee may give	$5,000 (combined limit)	No limit	No limit	$5,000 (combined limit)	None
PAC (multicandidate)[4] may give	$5,000	$15,000	$5,000 (combined limit)	$5,000	None
PAC (not multicandidate) may give	$2,300*	$28,500*	$10,000 (combined limit)	$5,000	None
Authorized campaign committee may give	$2,000[5]	No limit	No limit	$5,000	None

* These contribution limits are increased for inflation in odd-numbered years.

1. A contribution earmarked for a candidate through a political committee counts against the original contributor's limit for that candidate. In certain circumstances, the contribution may also count against the contributor's limit to the PAC.

2. No more than $42,700 of this amount may be contributed to state and local party committees and PACs.

3. This limit is shared by the national committee and the Senate campaign committee.

4. A multicandidate committee is a political committee with more than 50 contributors that has been registered for at least 6 months and, with the exception of state party committees, has made contributions to 5 or more candidates for federal office.

5. A federal candidate's authorized committee(s) may contribute no more than $2,000 per election to another federal candidate's authorized committee(s).

Source: Federal Election Commission.

Divergent Views:
Convention Delegates and Voters in 2008

Social issue	% Democratic delegates	% Democratic voters	% All voters	% Republican voters	% Republican delegates
Abortion should be generally available	70	43	33	20	9
Illegal immigrants should be allowed to stay in current jobs and apply for citizenship	68	50	40	26	22
Gay couples should be allowed to legally marry	55	49	34	11	6
Gun control laws should be more strict	62	70	52	32	8
Political ideology					
Liberal	43	48	26	5	—
Moderate	50	34	36	30	26
Conservative	3	16	36	63	72

Source: *New York Times*/CBS Poll of Convention Delegates, Sept. 1, 2008.

The office of the national committee is also an important source of information and expertise. Candidates can tap national committees for the latest polling results and can secure the advice of campaign consultants. The national committee also places candidates in contact with interest groups that will raise additional funds and provide volunteers and campaign workers.

national convention Event held every four years by each political party to formally anoint its presidential candidate and to signal the initiation of the general election campaign.

A close working relationship with interest groups has transformed national parties into "networks of issue-oriented activists," as one political scientist puts it.[32] These groups have pressured the parties to adopt specific positions on divisive issues like abortion, civil rights, and gun control. Changes in party operations have also increased the role of ideological and single-issue activists. For example, beginning in the 1960s, the Democratic Party mandated greater inclusion of women and minorities at its national political conventions, diminishing its reliance on seasoned state and local party officials. Consequently, the Democratic National Committee has moved more to the left, while social conservatives have taken advantage of similar changes to move the Republican Party to the right. The result has been greater polarization of the parties at the national level.

Nowhere is the ideological divide clearer than in the makeup of delegates to the **national convention**, the quadrennial gathering of party members to nominate their party's presidential candidate (see Chapter 12 for details). The convention also approves the **platform**, or statement of issue positions, that the party will nominally espouse for the next four years. In recent years, large blocs of convention delegates have been a veritable who's who of interest group politics. Labor unions and pro-choice activists, for example, constitute a large chunk of Democratic delegates. Members of the Christian Coalition, anti-abortion activists, and business groups dominate the Republican convention. Party platforms often reflect the interests of these select groups. They do not, however, necessarily reflect the views of the average voter, or even those of the average party supporter, as the table at left illustrates. Candidates often run away from some planks in the party platform as they attempt to attract a wider range of voters in the general election. Faced with a strong antiabortion plank in the 1996 Republican platform that he believed would alienate many voters, candidate Bob Dole remarked that he hadn't even read the platform.

Congressional and Senatorial Campaign Committees

Each party maintains organizations to help its candidates win election or reelection to the two national legislative chambers. These committees—the National Republican Congressional Committee (NRCC), the National Republican Senatorial Committee (NRSC), and their Democratic counterparts, the Democratic Congressional Campaign Committee (DCCC) and the Democratic Senatorial Campaign Committee (DSCC)—work with other party committees and with individual candidates to raise and distribute funds, share polling data, and offer expertise about running campaigns.

Not every candidate can count on help from these committees, however. Because resources are limited, Democratic and Republican committee staffs make strategic choices about which candidates are most likely to benefit from assistance. In 2006, DCCC chair Rahm Emanuel (D-IL) and DSCC head Charles Schumer (D-NY) aggressively supported moderate candidates in their successful effort to win back Congress. By 2008, both the DCCC and the DSCC had raised substantially more than their Republican counterparts.

The national parties can give up to $5,000 to individual House candidates and $39,900 to Senate candidates to spend directly on their campaigns. In addition, members from **safe seats**, in which the incumbent faces only limited or token opposition, often make some of their own campaign contributions available to more needy candidates. Candidates can receive additional funds through so-called leadership PACs that are affiliated with party leaders in each chamber. Like all PACs that give to multiple candidates, leadership PACs can contribute up to $5,000 per candidate per election (i.e., $5,000 for a primary election and $5,000 for the general election). Such donations may be instrumental in providing the margin of victory for recipients, and they generate a substantial amount of goodwill for the legislative donor. In the 2006 congressional campaign, House Majority Leader Steny Hoyer (D-MD) contributed $916,000 to the campaigns of fellow Democrats campaigning for House seats in the November elections. John Boehner (R-OH), the minority leader in the House, contributed more than $1 million to fellow Republicans.[33] Halfway through the 2008 congressional campaign, both were on pace to surpass their 2006 contributions.

State Committees

State parties have organizations somewhat parallel to those found at the national level. While each state organization has its own peculiarities, most state parties are headed by state committees—sometimes known as state central committees—drawn from county, congressional district, and municipal party officials and led by a state party chair. State party officers, together with their staffs, concentrate on statewide elective offices such as governor and key state legislative positions. Members of the state committees may meet only once or twice a year to ratify policies generated by national and state leaders. Day-to-day activities remain in the hands of the chairperson.

There is quite a bit of integration of party activities between national and state organizations. For example, national and state parties may share campaign costs for joint appearances and coordinate their advertising efforts. Until soft money was banned in 2002, national parties channeled millions of dollars through state parties for party-building activities such as voter registration drives. Today, state parties often team up with independent organizations tied to national interest groups to organize voter registration around the state. For example, liberal groups such as Americans Coming Together (ACT) and conservative groups like the Club for Growth were actively involved in voter mobilization and issue-ad sponsorship at the state level during recent election cycles. The Democratic and Republican governors associations also actively participate in funding support for state candidates.

State parties have become more professionalized in recent years, with the support and encouragement of the national parties.[34] They have substantially improved their ability to raise money, and they employ some of the same high-tech communication methods used by their national counterparts. For example, state parties have developed clearly targeted mailing lists for use in both fundraising and communicating with constituents about pressing issues. The bulk of their expenditures include political contributions to candidates and local campaign committees for consultants, polling, and advertising—together with funds for administrative expenses like salaries, rent, equipment, and travel. State committees also spend money on media for the entire ticket. Both parties have fairly consistent spending patterns; however, Republicans spend substantially more on fundraising activities.

> **platform** Statement of political principles and campaign promises generated by each party at its national convention.
>
> **safe seats** Legislative districts that regularly remain in the hands of the same candidate or party.

get involved!

Become a delegate to your party's state or national political convention. If you are 18 and registered to vote, you probably qualify. Contact your precinct leader or your party's local office. In some states, you can become a delegate by working directly for a candidate if he or she wins the primary election. In others, delegates have to file their own nominating petitions and are elected directly by the voters. In most states, you can also work closely with your local party to be considered as a delegate from your district. As a delegate, you'll attend the convention in the city selected for the event and have a voice in forging your party's platform as well as in selecting official party candidates for the general election.

Did You Know?

. . . That today's "negative campaigning" is nothing new? In 1884, Democratic presidential candidate Grover Cleveland faced accusations (which he did not deny) of having once fathered an illegitimate child, leading Republicans to shout, "Ma! Ma! Where's my Pa?" The Democrats, who ultimately prevailed in the election, responded, "Gone to the White House. Ha, ha ha!"

Local Party Organizations

Local party units in cities, counties, and towns recruit candidates as well as organize and run campaigns for many local offices, including mayor, sheriff, and county council. They can also be influential in securing local projects and contracts from the state and national government when their party is in power. The higher levels of party organization have an incentive to work with local parties, since the national parties ultimately rely heavily upon local personnel to get out the vote on Election Day. Nevertheless, local party units are not the powerhouses they were in the days of machine politics. Many factors contributed to this decline, including party reform, the replacement of patronage employees by a professionalized government workforce, the growth of government welfare services to replace favors once performed by local party bosses, the development of candidate-centered campaigns, and the rise of the mass media as an independent source for voter information.

precinct The geographic area served by a polling place and organized by local party units.

third party Minor parties that run a slate of their own candidates in opposition to major-party organizations in an election.

splinter parties Political parties that are formed as offshoots of major political parties, usually by dissenters.

Precinct Organizations

The level of organization that comes closest to the voter is usually called the **precinct**. Precincts include the population served by a polling place and can vary markedly in size, depending on population dispersion. Loyal party supporters are elected or appointed at the precinct level to act as liaisons between the voter and the party. Many precinct workers hold political jobs and have a keen interest in the outcome of elections, even though federal laws prevent hiring and firing on the basis of party allegiance. Precinct workers are our neighbors, and they can exert a powerful influence on our voting behavior. They keep us alert regarding local issues and inform us about voting procedures, poll locations, approaching registration deadlines, and candidates running for office. They remind us of our civic duty and even drive us to the polls on Election Day.

Recent campaigns have demonstrated how national and local party organizations can effectively work together to win elections. Parties are actively experimenting with new technologies and new methods that combine information gleaned from large national databases with canvassing provided by local party activists in order to get out the vote. As our opening vignette demonstrated, political parties are not shy about investigating consumer habits of voters and using them to identify potential supporters. Armed with this information, precinct workers, along with local candidate supporters and interest-group volunteers, can design individualized messages to bring to voters' doorsteps. Text messaging, social networking, and peer-to-peer appeals are proving especially useful in mobilizing younger voters. These techniques are reinvigorating local party activity, and their use will be studied to see if they can sustain increased voter turnout. We will describe additional efforts to attract young voters later in this chapter, in the section "Parties, Political Campaigns, and Civic Engagement Today."

Hot or Not?

Do Republican and Democratic parties do an adequate job of representing the American people, or do they do such a poor job that a third major party is needed?

THIRD PARTIES AND INDEPENDENT CANDIDACIES

Minor parties are far from absent in American politics. Perennial **third parties**, as minor parties are sometimes called, include the Libertarians, Socialist Workers, and more recently, the Green Party. Some third parties arise for a year or two and then disappear. This does not mean, however, that our nation has not witnessed important third-party challenges, no matter how short-lived. Usually, third par-

Teddy Roosevelt received 27 percent of the popular vote while running under the mantle of the Bull Moose Party in 1912.

ties and significant independent candidacies arise in periods of great change or crisis. They attract the attention of many who had not previously voted and those who perceive a lack of genuine difference between the major parties. Often they reflect a desire for change in the political direction of the nation.

Some third parties are **splinter parties**,[35] parties that break away from one of the major parties. The Republicans began as a splinter party, breaking away from the Whigs over the issue of slavery in 1852 and eventually supplanting them as the major competitor to the Democrats. Other notable splinter parties included the Populists, who emerged as an offshoot of Democratic politics in 1892; the Bull Moose Party, which nominated former president Teddy Roosevelt in 1912 after he broke with Republicans; the States' Rights and Progressive parties, which split in different ideological directions from the Democrats in 1948; and the American Independent Party, which broke off from the Democrats over civil rights policy in 1968 by nominating Alabama governor George Wallace for president.

Some third parties are **ideological parties** that reflect a commitment to an ideological position different from that of most voters. Socialists committed to government ownership of factories and businesses gathered limited support for their cause during the early twentieth century. More recently, Libertarians, who call for smaller government and the privatization of many government services, have gathered some support, especially among younger voters.

Finally, some independent campaigns outside of the major parties arise around a **single issue or candidate**. Ross Perot's impressive showing in 1992 revealed the potential strength of personal appeal coupled with a compelling issue: fiscal responsibility in the face of mushrooming budget deficits. The Green Party, which advocates environmental reform, has also fielded successful candidates in

a number of state and local elections across the country.

Faced with the substantial obstacles involved in getting on the ballot and the difficulties involved with organizing supporters and amassing sufficient funds to mount a credible campaign—all the while lacking incumbent officeholders to promote programs—it is no wonder that most third-party and independent candidacies fail to persist. Many candidates emerge for one or two election cycles and then disappear because of a lack of resources. Ralph Nader's independent candidacy, for example, fizzled in 2004 after gaining almost 3 percent of the popular vote in 2000. Some independent and third parties continue on as perennial minor players (e.g., the Libertarians or the Greens). Still others are absorbed by a larger party that heeds their message, or adopts their ideology or policy prescriptions. For

ideological parties Minor parties organized around distinct ideological principles.

single-issue or -candidate parties Minor parties arising in electoral response to important issues not addressed by major-party candidates or around a strong personality.

Did You Know?

. . . That the longest-running third party in American history is the Prohibition Party, founded in 1869 and still (barely) functioning? Over the course of its venerable history, several Prohibition Party members have been elected state governors and members of Congress; most recently (in 2001) someone claiming affiliation to the party was elected as a township assessor in rural Pennsylvania, and in 2004 its presidential candidate won 1,894 votes in the two states in which the party was on the ballot.

10

MEDIA

TUNING IN OR TUNING OUT

THE SOCIAL MEDIA GENERATION ▌Digital campaigning as practiced in the presidential campaign of 2008 has had an impact on how citizens, particularly young citizens, interact with the media. In January 2008, for instance, candidate Barack Obama videotaped a response to President Bush's final State of the Union address. His five-minute statement drew little response from media reporters, but the video caught fire on the Internet. Within weeks, it had been viewed more than 1.3 million times, had been linked to by more than five hundred blogs, and had been distributed widely on social networking sites like MySpace and Facebook. More than a month later, Senator Obama made a serious speech about the issue of race in America. This time the broadcast media carried his speech. Some young persons may have first learned of it from the traditional media, but they are more likely to have seen it on YouTube, where it was viewed 3.4 million times within days, or on Facebook, where it became one of its most shared links.

That young persons interested in political campaigns are turning to alternative sources like YouTube and Facebook for news is not startling to those who practice and study politics. What is changing, however, is that these young persons utilize these sources as part of their social networks. They are more than just consumers of the news. They are channels. They send out videos and e-mail links to their social networks. Likewise, they rely on friends and their online connections to get the news. As Lauren Wolf, the president of College Democrats of America, says, "I'd rather read an e-mail from my friend with an attached story than search through a newspaper to find the story."[1] Two-thirds of Web users under the age of thirty indicated they use social networking sites like MySpace and Facebook, and more than a quarter of them get campaign information from the sites.[2] Such sites can also provide users with a sense of connection to presidential candidates. By April 2008, Senator Obama had a million "friends" between the two sites, Senator Clinton had 330,000, and Senator McCain had 140,000. When young persons use Internet sources to receive and transmit political news within their social networks, they are bypassing the professional filter of the media.[3] According to writer Brian Stelter, "In one sense, this social filter is simply a technological version of the oldest tool in politics: word of mouth."[4]

Traditional media are also affected by the Internet in other ways. Internet bloggers create a new type of citizen media that is not afraid to question stories by professional journalists. Many Americans now believe news organizations often fail to get the facts straight. (See the graph on the next page.) In 2008, only 40 percent of Americans had a favorable view of the media.

Even though the traditional media may be bypassed and challenged by citizens today and even though they are viewed unfavorably by a majority of Americans, they are not without ▪➤

- How has media consumption in America changed in recent years?
- What are the major characteristics of mass media in America?
- How do the media cover political campaigns?

significant power. They determine what stories are newsworthy, they often influence what issues should be placed on the national agenda, and they interpret the motives of political officials. Today's media, however, must adapt to declining consumption. They are also facing more competition.

Traditional news outlets aimed to broadcast the news to large numbers of people at once. Today's abundance of media sources has led to "narrowcasting"—that is, targeting news to individuals who choose only programming that really interests them. Today's young people are characterized by declining interest in traditional news sources. This worries some observers, who wonder how the young can fulfill their citizenship responsibilities without getting the news in the same way as their parents and grandparents.

Modern media operate in an environment that allows private ownership with minimal interference by the government. In order to increase its audience and make money for its owners, today's media emphasize entertainment and adversarial journalism more than ever before. They want the news to be lively and edgy, but this style of reporting, especially when applied to politics and government, has an impact on civic engagement. To a great extent, citizens are disengaging from the political system as they tune out the media's information about it. ◆

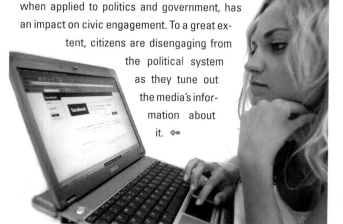

The Perceived Accuracy of the News Media

Stories often inaccurate

Get the facts straight

	July 1985	Feb. 1999	Sept. 2001	Nov. 2001	July 2002	July 2003	June 2005	July 2007
	55	58	57		56	56	56	53
				46				
				45				
	34	37	35		35	36	36	39
	11	5	8	9	9	8	8	8

Percent

Don't know

Source: Pew Research Center, "Internet News Audience Highly Critical of News Organizations," August 9, 2007.

Spreading information and campaigning through online social networking programs have helped candidates reach a new demographic of young voters.

Declining National Network News Viewership

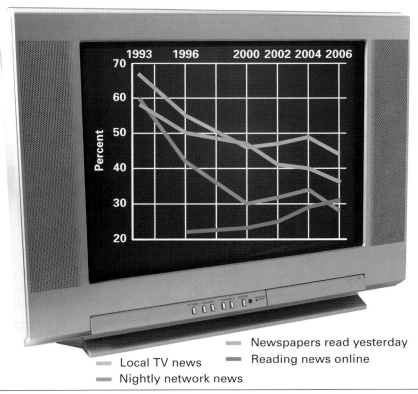

Local TV news
Nightly network news
Newspapers read yesterday
Reading news online

Source: Pew Research Center, "Online Papers Modestly Boost Newspaper Readership," July 30, 2006.

EVOLVING CIVIC LIFE AND MEDIA CHANGES

In the early days of the United States, politics was essentially an oral art conducted in taverns, boardinghouses, legislative chambers, and private parlors.[5] As the nation matured, a mass media developed—first newspapers and then the broadcast media—to keep citizens informed about local and national politics. The changes that the media has undergone over time have had an important impact on how the American people view their government and how that government connects to its citizens.

Early Days

Newspapers in colonial America did not get off to an auspicious start. The first newspaper published in America, *The Publick Occurences, Both Foreign and Domestick*, appeared in Boston in 1690 and included an article on the alleged immoralities of the king of France. Offended by the article, the Massachusetts Bay Colony authorities ordered that no person could print a

newspaper without first applying for a license from the government. Thus, the first American newspaper ended publication after just one edition. America's first regularly published newspaper, *The Boston News-Letter*, debuted in 1704 and appeared weekly until 1776. The paper's local and intercolonial articles included political speeches, official proclamations, crime stories, weather, and obituaries.[6]

By 1775, on the eve of the American Revolution, the colonies boasted forty newspapers that played an important role in promoting discussion of the issues of the day. Such discussion would ultimately threaten the deferential politics that flourished in the hierarchical society of colonial America.[7]

Partisan Press

After the ratification of the U.S. Constitution, political leaders such as John Adams and Thomas Jefferson quickly saw the advantage of having newspapers promote their points of view. By granting newspapers lucrative contracts to print government documents, politicians could ensure the wide dissemination of their words and deeds and secure friendly coverage of their

The Growth of Political News Consumption

Percent of all adults who look online for news or information about the campaign

	Spring 2000	Fall 2000	Spring 2004	Fall 2004	Spring 2008
Total	36	23	31	34	40
On a typical day	3	8	8	10	17

Source: Pew Internet & American Life Project Surveys. Most recent is the Spring 2008 Survey. Margin of error is ±2%.

news articles online at a higher rate than any other age group. They are more likely to get their news from portals like Yahoo.com or MSNBC.com, which stream news headlines with constant twenty-four-hour updates. The sites where people most often get their news online are listed in the table on the previous page. They are also more skeptical of traditional news sources and more likely to seek alternate types of reporting. One report on the use of these new media by young adults concludes, "Young people want a personal level of engagement and want those presenting the news to them to be transparent in their assumptions, biases and history."[15] Overall, the growth of campaign political news consumption online has grown dramatically over the last three presidential election cycles. (See table above.)

We have seen that young persons often bypass the traditional media by setting up social networks. In 2008, a survey found that 10 percent of all Americans have used sites such as Facebook or MySpace for some kind of political activity.[16] (See table at right for leading social network sites.) For young adults in particular, the sites are a major component of their online political experience. Sixty-seven percent of Internet users under the age of 30 have a social-networking profile, and half of these profile owners used social network sites to get or share information about the candidates and the campaign.[17] In 2008, young voters tilted toward the Democrats generally and Senator Obama specifically. Thirty-six percent of online Democrats created social network profiles, compared to 21 percent of Republicans, and Obama supporters were more likely to be Internet users than the Clinton supporters. A 2006 study of teens showed that the trend of social networking will likely continue and grow.[18]

Increased Consumption of Narrowcasting A third trend evident today is the public's affinity for **narrowcasting**, programming that is directed to a small, specific segment of the population. In the early days of radio and television, news was broadcast to millions of Americans at the same time, which meant that most Americans shared the same news experiences; this is no longer the case. If you have access to cable or satellite television, you know about the great variety of channels available to viewers with specific and narrow interests.

Television coverage of the 2004 national party conventions provides an example of political narrowcasting. Republicans, for instance, preferred watching Fox News because of its more conservative slant. Democrats and Independents were more likely to tune to CNN. The way these cable stations chose to present the conventions to their viewing audiences was also revealing. Fox News, CNN, and MSNBC used their primary on-air personalities Bill O'Reilly, Larry King, and Chris Matthews as hosts. Coverage of the conventions followed a talk show format as the hosts chatted with pundits, politicians, other journalists, and entertainers such as Ben Affleck and Bono. They devoted less than 10 percent of their coverage to reporting what was going on at the podium, or where the candidates or the parties stood on specific issues. At least 30 percent of the coverage was spent on ranting, raving, and shouting matches.[19] At one point, Chris Matthews's aggressive style led a guest, former senator Zell Miller, to strike back,

Top 10 Social Networking Sites for May 2008

Site	(Millions of Users)		Growth
	May 2008	May 2007	
MySpace.com	60,676	56,586	7%
Facebook	26,042	14,196	83%
Classmates Online	14,344	11,936	20%
LinkedIn	7,691	3,124	146%
Windows Live Spaces	7,649	8,172	-6%
Reunion.com	7,286	4,011	82%
AOL Hometown	6,564	7,143	-11%
Fixster	4,854	2,851	70%
Club Penguin	4,455	3,196	39%
Imeem	3,157	1,566	102%

Source: Nielsen Online.

Today's media coverage of political conventions emphasizes on-air personalities such as Stephen Colbert of The Colbert Report.

saying he was sorry we no longer lived in a world where he could challenge Matthews to a duel. The 2008 coverage continued to ignore the podium except for one or two speeches per evening.

Narrowcasting has changed the way that citizens receive messages from political leaders. Commenting on the trend of narrowcasting, one author concludes that "the effect of the fragmentation in the audience will be a reduction in the commonality of Americans' political experiences."[20] On the other hand, specialized programming may provide a better fit between public messages and audience needs. At the end of this chapter, we will examine how the changing media landscape affects civic engagement by allowing citizens to utilize a variety of media sources to monitor or graze for information that interests them.

THE MEDIA ENVIRONMENT IN AMERICA

Today's American mass media environment is characterized by several trends that shape the messages we receive about government and, in turn, affect the kinds of citizens we become. These trends include private ownership that is becoming more highly concentrated; some government regulation, particularly of broadcast media outlets; an expansion of entertainment content at the expense of news content; an adversarial style of journalism that attacks politicians and their motives; and a belief by some that the media exhibit political bias.

Private Ownership

Private individuals have always owned the nation's media outlets; most modern Americans would consider any other ownership arrangement odd or even threatening. Yet, the United States is the only advanced industrial nation in the world in which virtually all the major media outlets are privately owned.[21] The only exceptions are the Public Broadcasting System, National Public Radio, and public access channels. In other Western democracies such as France and Denmark, the government owns the media.[22]

> **narrowcasting** Programming targeted to one small sector of the population, made possible by the emergence of cable television and the Internet.

Ownership of U.S. media outlets is becoming more highly concentrated. Large chains such as Knight-Ridder and Gannett own nearly 80 percent of all daily newspapers. Gannett alone owns ninety-nine newspapers—in-

National Journal

New Media as the Message

During Super Bowl broadcasts just days before the Super Tuesday primaries, Barack Obama appeared in a 30-second campaign ad that was unremarkable in its presentation save for three words and a number that appeared midway through the footage of the candidate surrounded by excited crowds. As Obama's long arms reached out to grasp outstretched hands, viewers received an invitation: Text HOPE to 62262.

In an around-the-clock media environment fixated on all things political, Obama has experimented with new tools for communication in a media climate so diffuse that it's difficult for any candidate to shape a message let alone hold it for a few hours. He and his team have exploited the elite media's enthusiasms for the history-making features of his campaign, while also making adroit use of technology to push information to supporters using a network that some describe as "off-line."

The people who sent text messages to the campaign that Sunday were greeted with a request to provide some information about themselves: "Welcome to Obama mobile news and updates. Reply with your ZIP code to get local Obama info."

This 2008 twist on political message delivery seized the power of two communications technologies at once: the ability of television to engage a broad audience using emotion, music, and moving images; and the capacity of text messaging to establish social links that can help transform citizen engagement into political support, one person at a time.

Campaigns understand that the quirky electronic new-media platforms can easily spark coverage or help candidates play defense against rivals. Online news aggregators collect establishment reporting but are willing to be guided by what's popular. Many blogs mix opinion with reporting and analysis. And a handful of cliquish, minutia-obsessed political websites follow hour-by-hour developments in polling, horse race predictions, and he-said/she-said sparring among rival candidates.

YouTube and the social-networking sites Facebook and MySpace did not exist as political forces four years ago, and it's anyone's guess how technology will have altered "news" dissemination and voter persuasion by 2012. It's not ridiculous to imagine computer-generated, three-dimensional hologram "candidates" conversing interactively with individual voters in their living rooms.

Obama's Internet savvy and willingness to spend millions of dollars to forge fast new electronic connections with supporters have helped his campaign to set online fundraising records, and enriched his voter-turnout organizations in key states.

Ari Fleischer, a spokesman for candidate George W. Bush during the 2000 election and later his White House press secretary, said that it's possible to get carried away in the midst of a tight, contested race. "The wonderful thing about all these changes is that you can communicate better and faster, but the enduring factor is that you have to have something to communicate," he cautioned. "You have to connect with the voters on something the voters care about. Substance and character come first, and speed comes second."

Dee Dee Myers, who writes a blog for Vanity Fair and appears as a Democratic political analyst on MSNBC, believes that Obama opponent Hillary Clinton's approach to campaign communications reflects what a twice-successful team was familiar with light-years ago. In the 1990s, the media mix was easier to peg; there was a defined news "cycle" during a 24-hour day; and it was possible to pinpoint the power hitters who controlled political information that influenced voter choices.

"A lot of people who are running Hillary Clinton's campaign came of age during Bill Clinton's campaign, so I think a lot of the approaches that they use, the way they see campaigns and the way they see the world, were defined 16, 18, 20 years ago," Myers said. "The Obama campaign culture was created in 2007, not in 1992."

Obama has demonstrated his ease with traditional news outlets and electronic media, but he has also shown his willingness to use alternative outlets. For instance, he posted a written defense of his controversial pastor, the Rev. Jeremiah Wright, on The Huffington Post a political website, before responding to the establishment press. Appearing on the Huffington site showed deference to his younger constituents, who do everything on the Web.

The public's online reactions to the Wright videos were part of the blowback that convinced the Obama campaign that an important speech about race was necessary. And the candidate's March address in Philadelphia got heavy replay of its own on YouTube and was "rebroadcast" as text and video on the mainstream media—seemingly enough exposure to blunt the intense news-industry dissection of Wright's most objectionable video excerpts. After Obama's damage-control speech, public opinion polls indicated that he held his ground with voters, with 10 primary contests left on the calendar.

Obama's approach to media and message complements his personality, his "change" agenda, and his young, educated, and tech-savvy upper-income supporters. "Obama and Clinton have different audiences, and if Hillary Clinton were just as smart about using the new media, it wouldn't do her as much good," analyst Kathleen Hall Jamieson suggested, "because it's not her natural audience. It's not as if the new media alone is able to persuade an audience and bring them in."

If Internet prowess and the swooning of young people were what it took to get to the White House, former Vermont Gov. Howard Dean or Rep. Ron Paul of Texas would have done better against their opponents. Even wealthy Mitt Romney, who tapped a documentary filmmaker, Michael Kolowich, to create a "Mitt TV" video channel for his campaign, could not overcome GOP reservations that he was inauthentic and squishy on core conservative issues.

In a blog post titled "Ten Lessons From Mitt TV," written after the former Massachusetts governor withdrew from the race, Kolowich predicted, "What we're learning from the use of tactical Web video in the 2008 presidential campaign will inform and inspire marketing and communications well beyond politics in 2008." But how a campaign can win more votes with clever videos of a flawed candidate, he did not say.

New forms of information-sharing for election purposes via the Internet, talk radio, and entertainment TV go back at least to the early 1990s, a period when the networks' news programming had already shed millions of viewers and candidates were jostling to find alternatives. Bill Clinton famously appeared on MTV and on Arsenio Hall's late-night talk show, while President George H.W. Bush, seeking a second term, resisted such exposure, believing that it was unpresidential.

Sixteen years later, presidential contenders know they need websites to present themselves. Some have turned to the Internet first to announce their candidacies. And in 2008, no leading presidential candidate would dream of rejecting an opportunity to appear before today's voter-rich talk-show audiences.

The latest research by political scientists is inconclusive about whether candidates' use of new-media technologies and approaches can or will deliver new political outcomes. Did voters turn thumbs-down when some presidential candidates thought that it was silly to answer debate questions posed via citizen-created YouTube videos, one of which featured a talking snowman? Can candidates woo new voters with personalized e-mail? With e-mail carrying videos? Will voters' opinions be shaped more by political attack ads on TV or passed around in cyberspace,

Anyone using the Internet can become a game-changer.

or by the truth-squading of those same ads by media organizations?

"The big story of this campaign cycle is citizen-generated media," said Diana Owen, a Georgetown University political scientist. Citizen-generated media can be blogs, video, text, recordings, photos, research, pass-around issue papers, Facebook propaganda, text-messaging—virtually anything. Examples this year include the Yes We Can music video that was done for Obama but not by his campaign, and "Obama Girl," the cheeky, scantily clad young woman who appears on BarelyPolitical.com. Owen cautions, however, that these pass-around messages have not yet been transforming; mainly, they've been additives. "What does it take to move the agenda?" she asked. "At this stage, citizen-generated media still has to make it into the mainstream media."

If the diffusion of information and the individualization of political communication on the Internet enlarges participation in the political process, particularly among the 18-to-29-year-olds who year after year always seem to fall short of the turnout forecasts, that expansion could recast the types of candidates and public policies taking center stage.

Keep in mind that social networking on the Web is almost exclusively an interest of young people: 67 percent of those ages 18 to 29 have used the sites, and 27 percent said they used them to get campaign news, Pew has reported.

"This may be an audience in search of a candidacy," Jamieson said. A media era of electronic politics and interactive communications could slice through the establishments of both parties. "It may wipe an entire generation out of politics," Jamieson suggested.

Some 42 percent of adults 29 and younger cite the Internet as a regular source of campaign news for the '08 race. For voters 50 and older, the Internet figure is just 15 percent but even that has doubled since 2004. The people in between also made a big leap in tapping political news on the Internet—up from 16 percent in 2004 to 26 percent now.

Because the coverage surrounding the 2008 race has been especially event-sensitive, anyone using the Internet can become a game-changer. "There's the potential for one blogger, one person with a video camera to have a huge impact," said Amy Mitchell, deputy director of the Project for Excellence in Journalism.

One final thought for 2009: How will the next president be tempted to take advantage of today's communications complexities? Will he use social-networking sites to gin up support for a bill in Congress? Will he stop begging reluctant TV networks to open their prime time to East Room speeches—and instead take every word to YouTube's POTUS channel? Obama pledged in January that if he's elected he will throw open the West Wing to C-SPAN to broadcast his negotiations with "all parties" to get health care legislation.

"We can easily put too much attention on the techniques of delivering a message, rather than focusing on the message itself," warned Martha Joynt Kumar, a Towson University scholar who writes extensively about White House communications. In politics, the new media may have become a message. But in governing, the message is still the message.

FOR DISCUSSION: How did the pervasive use of new media in the 2008 election influence the outcome of the election? How do the ways campaigns have changed their tactics hint at the ways government in general will adapt to the new environment? Will the use of new media ever be more persuasive than the political message itself?

11

WHAT'S TO COME

CONGRESS

DOING THE PEOPLE'S BUSINESS

CAN CONGRESS GET ANYTHING DONE? ▎ It seemed like the time had come to take bold action to combat global warming. Congressional critics who once rejected the notion that humans are causing the temperature of the globe to rise have become a shrinking minority. More importantly, there has been a growing demand by the public that Congress take action. Seventy-one percent say global warming constitutes a serious threat to the planet, and nearly half of all Americans are ready to make major sacrifices to reduce its impact.[1] Nearly two-thirds said they would feel more favorably about their members of Congress if they supported a bill to reduce greenhouse gas emissions.[2] So in June 2008, when a bill sponsored by John Warner (R-VA) and Joe Lieberman (I-CT) made it out of committee and onto the floor of the Senate, there were high hopes that Congress would take the first step toward stemming the globe's rise in temperature. The bill would have required that by 2020 greenhouse gas emissions be cut 18 percent below 2005 levels, and nearly 70 percent by midcentury—a significant reduction but still modest compared to what many scientists say is necessary. So why did the bill fail?

First, there are the parliamentary reasons. In the Senate, a minority can block a bill from coming to a final vote by offering numerous amendments and forcing a three-fifths (supermajority) vote of 60 to close debate. The Senate failed to reach that threshold by 12 votes. Then there are stalling tactics. Opponents called for the clerk to read the entire 492-page document on the floor, a process that took nearly ten hours.

More important, however, are the details of the legislation. Virtually every bill in Congress produces winners and losers. While just about everyone—including energy companies—is in favor of keeping the planet inhabitable, there are serious questions about how we should proceed and who should pay. Most emission-reduction bills that have surfaced, including the Warner-Lieberman bill, call for a "cap and trade" system that would cap the production of heat-trapping gases and force polluters to use permits to emit carbon dioxide. Companies that rely on coal, which generates about half the nation's power, say that the permits should be free so that customers in the Midwest and the Great Plains, where coal is heavily used, are not disproportionately penalized. Power producers that are less dependent on coal say that the emitters of carbon dioxide should have to pay for the permits.[3]

Then there is the question of alternative fuels. Some in Congress favor the increased use of nuclear energy; groups like the Natural Resources Defense Council favor making large investments in alternative technologies like wind power. Still others say conservation is the key. Finally, even though Americans are eager that something be done, most are already hard-pressed to keep up with rising energy costs and their representatives in Congress are hearing plenty of hardship stories. ●◆

- What powers does Congress have?
- What are some factors affecting election to Congress?
- What are the keys to political power in Congress?

In the face of these daunting challenges the Warner-Lieberman bill died on June 6, 2008 when it failed to muster enough support to bring it to a final vote. Democrats, who control the Senate, blamed Republicans for its defeat. But Republicans claimed Democrats ran away from the bill because it would have raised energy prices in an election year.[4]

The fate of the Warner-Lieberman bill illustrates the difficulties Congress faces in making headway on important issues that confront our nation. Members of Congress are pressured by lobbyists, grassroots organizations, the president, party leaders, policy experts, donors, and, of course, their **constituents**—the people who elect them. Building consensus is even more difficult in the age of modern technology. Online grassroots organizations and talk radio hosts can mobilize opponents at a moment's notice. Given these pressures, Americans may be surprised that Congress gets anything done at all. The Framers, however, wouldn't necessarily consider this a bad thing. They deliberately created a system of checks and balances to ensure that change would be difficult without genuine consensus.

In this chapter, we will come to understand why Congress has a difficult time getting the job of lawmaking done and what might be done about it. We will see that the constitutionally mandated structure of Congress, the limits on its powers, and the interplay among Congress, the other governmental branches, and the public affect the politics and performance of the U.S. Congress. First, however, we'll start by looking at the origins of our system of representation. ↩

Some scientists believe that wildfires like those that destroyed thousands of acres of forests in California over the past few years are caused by the spread of dry weather conditions fueled, in part, by global warming.

personal Is Political

Do you happen to know the name of the current Speaker of the U.S. House of Representatives?

Barbara Boxer

Nancy Pelosi

Scooter Libby

Dennis Hastert

Answer: Nancy Pelosi. (78% of Americans answered correctly but only 58% of 18–29-year-olds answered correctly.)

Source: Pew Center for the People and the Press, Public Knowledge Update, accessed September 25, 2007, at http://pewresearch.org/pubs/601/political-knowledge-update.

ORIGIN AND POWERS OF CONGRESS

When the Framers met in Philadelphia to devise a new system of government and draft a constitution, they turned their attention first to the body that would represent citizen interests and make laws. Ten of the thirteen colonies had **bicameral**, or two-chamber, legislatures. The delegates' familiarity with this type of legislative arrangement led to the adoption of a two-chamber Congress despite a call by New Jersey for a **unicameral**, or single-body, legislature. Instead of copying Britain's parliamentary system, however, they created a new presidential form of government with multiple checks and balances.

Some delegates to the Constitutional Convention called for proportional representation in both houses of Congress. Under such an arrangement, the three most populous states—Virginia, Pennsylvania, and Massachusetts—would have commanded almost half the seats in both the upper house (the Senate) and the lower house (the House of Representatives). Luther Martin of Maryland reflected the views of many small-state delegates when he called the plan a "system of slavery which bound hand and foot ten states of the Union and placed them at the mercy of the other three."[5]

After nearly two months of deliberation, the delegates finally reached what scholars refer to as the **Great Compromise**. They agreed to apportion seats equally in the Senate, while apportioning seats in the House according to population. This satisfied the demands of smaller states by giving them an equal voice with larger states in at least one chamber.

The delegates carved out a number of differences between the two houses. The House of Representatives was the "people's house" with its members elected directly by the people. The Senate, however, was designed to safeguard the rights of the states and minorities against mass opinion. As a result, state legislatures elected senators until 1913, when ratification of the Seventeenth Amendment provided for the direct popular election of senators.

Most of the delegates favored short terms of office and frequent elections in order to keep lawmakers on a short leash. James Madison, however, debated that members of Congress needed time to learn and ply the legislative art. A compromise fixed a two-year term for members of the House and a staggered six-year term for senators, with one-third of the Senate coming up for election every two years. In most cases, both houses jointly exercise congressional powers, but some powers reside principally with one or the other body.

In addition to power sharing between the houses, the delegates to the Constitutional Convention also debated which powers to accord to Congress and which to reserve to other branches of government. The following table lists **enumerated powers**, that is, powers the Constitution explicitly grants to Congress. Most notably, Congress has the power to make laws, including those that are "necessary and proper" for carrying out other duties. Over time, Congress has used this phrase, sometimes known as the **elastic clause**, to expand the reach of the federal government. It gives Congress the ability to adapt to changing circumstances unforeseen at the time the Constitution was written. For example, Congress today makes laws establishing agencies and procedures to protect the environment, a consideration that was hardly a worry for the Framers.

constituents The citizens from a state or district that an elected official represents.

bicameral A legislative assembly consisting of two separate houses or chambers.

unicameral Single body legislature.

Great Compromise Name given to the motion presented by the Connecticut delegation to the Constitutional Convention proposing a bicameral legislature with the seats in one house apportioned equally and the seats in the other apportioned by population.

enumerated powers Powers explicitly granted to a branch of government by the Constitution.

elastic clause Term applied to the necessary and proper clause of Article I giving Congress flexibility in deciding the range of its legislative authority.

Major House and Senate Differences

House	Senate
Apportioned on basis of population	Equal representation (2) from each state
Fixed (since 1911) at 435 members	100 members
Two-year terms	Six-year terms (one-third elected every two years)
Members must be at least 25 years of age, 7 years a citizen, and reside in the state from which chosen	Members must be at least 30 years of age, 9 years a citizen, and reside in the state from which chosen
Power to impeach federal officeholders	Power to try federal officeholders who have been impeached
Initiate bills raising revenue	Approve treaties, cabinet-level appointments, and appointments to the Supreme Court
Choose president in case of electoral vote tie (Article II)	Choose vice president in case of tie (Article II)*

*Originally, the Constitution accorded the vice presidency to the runner-up in the presidential election, provided the presidential candidate received a majority of electoral votes. This procedure was altered by the Twelfth Amendment (1804), which provided for separate ballots in the selection of the president and vice president.

Enumerated Powers by Function*

Financial & Economic Powers

Power to levy and collect taxes and duties *(expanded by the Sixteenth Amendment in 1913 to include taxing income)*
Power to borrow money
Power to regulate commerce with foreign nations and among states
Power to coin money
Power to fix standards of weights and measures
Power to punish counterfeiters
Power to grant patents and copyrights
Power to establish uniform laws on bankruptcy
Power to establish post office and post roads

Defense-Related Powers

Power to declare war
Power to raise and support armies
Power to create and maintain the navy
Power to regulate the armed forces
Power to organize the militia (today's National Guard) and to call the militia into national service to defend against rebellion

Checks & Balances

Power to impeach federal officials
Power to establish lower federal courts along with specifying (with some exceptions in the case of the Supreme Court) the kinds of cases each can hear
Power to override presidential veto

Legislative Power

Power to make all laws necessary and proper for carrying out foregoing powers
Power to govern the District of Columbia

---

* Congress also has a role in the process of succession to the office of president should a vacancy occur, a procedure that was clarified and strengthened with the adoption of the Twenty-fifth Amendment in 1967.

Article I of the Constitution also explicitly denies Congress certain powers, including granting of titles of nobility, imposing certain types of taxes, and suspending certain categories of individual rights. Of course, the actions of other branches also limit congressional power. The balance of power between Congress and the executive branch has changed throughout history as each has jockeyed for control over the nation's political agenda. In Chapter 14, we will also see how the judicial branch can limit the power of Congress by challenging the constitutionality of congressional actions.

CIVIC LIFE AND CONGRESSIONAL CHANGE

Congress has responded to changes in American civic life by becoming more open and hospitable to involvement by an increasingly diverse citizenry. Minorities and women, once denied a formal role, are a growing presence in the halls of Congress. Today, Americans enjoy unprecedented access to their representatives and senators through websites, e-mail, telephone, and letter. Thousands of groups representing almost every conceivable interest give citizens the opportunity to amplify their individual voices in pressuring members of Congress to respond to their concerns. Congress now does a great deal of its work in public, with floor sessions and many committee meetings broadcast live on C-SPAN, thus allowing citizens to keep watch over their lawmakers. Access and openness did not come easily or all at once, however. Powerful interests, strong and obstinate leaders in control of legislative procedures, and clashes with other branches of government have all stymied change at one time or another.

Building the Institution

When the first session of the U.S. Congress met in New York City in 1789, many of the members knew each other personally from serving together on other governing bodies, including colonial legislatures. The new Congress moved quickly to create committees, prescribe the powers of leadership, and place limits on floor debate, but most policy initiatives in these early days, including the call for a national bank and the funding of canals for commerce, came from the office of the president.

The elimination of property qualifications for voting led political leaders to mobilize newly enfranchised citizens into political parties. Control of Congress soon became a political contest with the strongest party in each chamber assuming the leadership positions. President Andrew Jackson (1829–1837) used his popularity with voters to assert authority over members of his own party in Congress by rewarding those members who supported his proposed legislation and punishing those who opposed him. Few presidents in subsequent decades would enjoy such power at the expense of Congress.

As Congress admitted additional states to the Union, new and independent Senate leaders emerged to challenge Jackson. Many represented the new Whig party, which attacked the Democrats on the issue of slavery. During this time, the Senate became the preeminent forum for debate on the issues dividing the Union, eclipsing the presidency as the hub for policy formation. Floor debates could be intense—and violent. In 1856, Congressman Preston Brooks of South Carolina assaulted Senator Charles Sumner, an antislavery advocate from Massachusetts, on the Senate floor. Brooks beat Sumner senseless with a walking stick over Sumner's opposition to admitting Kansas to the union as a slave state.[6] Debate and compromise, it seemed, could not bridge the growing divide over slavery. By the time Abraham Lincoln was elected president in 1860, hope for avoiding dissolution of the Union had all but faded. A bloody civil war ended slavery in the United States and opened the way for greater citizen participation by enfranchising all former male slaves.

After the war, southern states elected the first black members of Congress, including thirteen ex-slaves. In the years that followed, Congress reasserted its authority in national affairs. Party leaders such as Speaker of the House Joseph "Uncle Joe" Cannon gained enormous influence, controlling the timing and content of bills brought to the floor and effectively rewarding or punishing fellow members. Partisan power was just as strong in the Senate, which had come to dominate legislative affairs and which many Americans considered a "millionaire's club" that represented only the interests of party bosses and big business trusts.

The Era of Reform

The Progressive Era brought significant changes to Congress. A coalition of Democrats and "insurgent" Republicans wrested control of the House from Speaker Joe Cannon in 1910 and brought the chamber more in line with the growing demand for reform in government. The Seventeenth Amendment (1913) gave voters the power to elect senators directly, taking it out of the hands of local and state party bosses who had dominated the process for decades. Rule changes in both the House and Senate further curtailed the power of party leaders. The Progressive Era also produced a more professional Congress, one in which members were expected to become experts in matters under the jurisdiction of the committees on which they served. Another landmark change came in 1917, when Jeannette Rankin became the first female House member after spearheading a successful drive for women's suffrage in her home state of Montana.

The Resurgent Executive Branch

This shift of power away from Congress became increasingly apparent during the presidencies of Theodore Roosevelt and Woodrow Wilson. With the election of Franklin Delano Roosevelt in 1932, it became a central fact of American political life. With commanding Democratic majorities in both houses, FDR rushed through Congress numerous emergency measures to spur economic recovery during the Great Depression of the 1930s. The first one hundred days of Roosevelt's administration were some of the most prolific in legislative history.

By 1937, however, disputes over the constitutionality of Roosevelt's New Deal legislation led conservative southern Democrats in the House to defect and form an alliance with Republicans. This conservative group created new rules designed to slow or block presidential initiatives. Cracks in Democratic solidarity also led to brief

In 1917, Jeannette Rankin became the first woman to serve in Congress even before women were granted suffrage by the Nineteenth Amendment.

Money and Incumbency: Senate and House Fundraising by Type of Seat*

Fundraising

Senate

Type of Candidate	Total Raised	Number of Candidates	Average Raised
Incumbent	$249,302,835	41	$7,178,118
Challenger	$56,086,015	83	$675,735
Open seat	$32,189,007	27	$1,192,185
Grand total	$382,577,857	151	$2,533,628**

House

Type of Candidate	Total Raised	Number of Candidates	Average Raised
Incumbent	$347,900,124	433	$803,464
Challenger	$88,410,666	482	$183,425
Open seat	$74,552,405	256	$291,220
Grand total	$510,863,195	1,171	$436,262**

* As of June 6, 2008 based on data released by the FEC. Figures include all candidates who have filed reports.

** This number is obtained by multiplying the average raised by the number of candidates in each category and dividing the sum for all categories by the number of candidates.

Source: Center for Responsive Politics. Available online at http://www.opensecrets.org.

Midterm Elections

Midterm elections—those contested in years between presidential elections—draw on average about 15 percent fewer voters than do presidential elections. Scholars have advanced many theories to explain voter drop-off in midterm elections, including election fatigue (i.e., a sense of political exhaustion after the sometimes bruising politics of presidential elections), less media coverage of politics between presidential elections, and voter apathy.

Candidates in midterm elections confront an electoral environment that is somewhat differ-

redistricting The practice of drawing congressional district boundaries to accord with population changes.

reapportionment The periodic reallocation of 435 House seats among the states as population shifts from one region to another.

ent from that of presidential election years. First, only the most committed partisans are likely to vote in midterm races. Voters with weak or no partisan ties are harder to mobilize; only the visibility and media focus of a presidential contest will draw their active involvement. Second, the issues that motivate strong partisans often work against members of the president's party. Midterm voters sometimes use their ballots to register dissatisfaction with the president by voting against members of the same party in congressional races. In 2006, voter disenchantment with the war in Iraq helped to mobilize support against Republicans and contributed to the Democratic takeover of both houses. As a rule, the president's party usually loses seats in midterm elections, as the honeymoon between voters and the president wears off. Even if a sitting president is popular, candidates from the president's party rarely benefit from being on the same ticket, or riding the president's coattails, during these off-year contests.

The table at the top of the next page also illustrates wide variation in the pattern of midterm losses for the president's party. In 1994, Republicans seized control of Congress from the Democrats using the "Contract with America," a pledge to produce quick and dramatic results for the GOP agenda at a time when many Americans appeared tired of gridlock between Congress and the White House. Just four years later, however, Democrats regained seats as voters apparently punished Republicans for impeaching President Bill Clinton over an affair with an intern, Monica Lewinsky. Clinton's economic policies were quite popular with the electorate, and polls showed that most Americans believed his affair with Lewinsky should have remained a private matter. In 2002, President Bush received a similar congressional bonus largely because of support for his handling of the "War on Terror" following the 9/11 attacks. As we saw, however, the unpopular war in Iraq resulted in large losses for the president's party in 2006.

Redistricting

Candidates for the House of Representatives face an additional obstacle in their quest for office: **redistricting**, the

Gains and Losses of Congressional Seats for the Party of the President in Midterm Elections

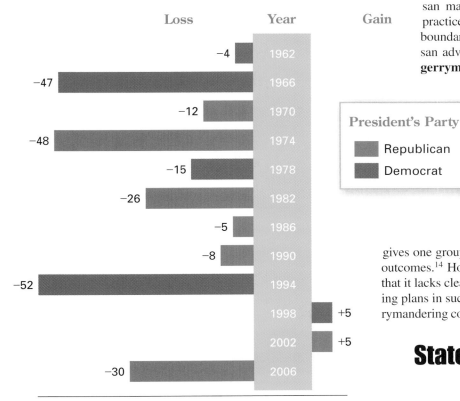

Loss	Year	Gain
−4	1962	
−47	1966	
−12	1970	
−48	1974	
−15	1978	
−26	1982	
−5	1986	
−8	1990	
−52	1994	
	1998	+5
	2002	+5
−30	2006	

President's Party
- Republican
- Democrat

Source: *Congressional Quarterly*, various years.

redraw the boundaries of districts so that each district has relatively equal numbers of voters, a principle sometimes called the "one-person–one-vote" rule. Since political bodies control the process in most states, it is subject to partisan manipulation. The practice of drawing boundaries for partisan advantage is called **gerrymandering**, after the tactics employed by Massachusetts governor Elbridge Gerry in 1812 to create a district that favored Republicans over Federalists. The odd shape of the district inspired one cartoonist to depict it as a creature much like a salamander, and the term *gerrymander* has stuck ever since.

> **gerrymander** Practice of drawing congressional boundaries to the advantage of one party.

A person can bring suit in court under the Fourteenth Amendment to prevent a redistricting plan that gives one group an unfair advantage in affecting election outcomes.[14] However, the Supreme Court has concluded that it lacks clear standards for refereeing among competing plans in such cases.[15] As a consequence, political gerrymandering continues to this day. Party leaders in control

redrawing of the electoral boundaries of the districts they represent. Since people are always moving within and between states, election districts must be adjusted to reflect population changes. The Constitution prescribes **reapportionment**, or reallocation, of seats every ten years based on the latest census data. Supreme Court rulings in the 1960s made it clear that the size of the population within each district must be relatively equal.[12] The Supreme Court also recently ruled that redistricting may take place more often.[13] Because Congress permanently fixed the total number of seats in the House at 435 in 1911, some states gain seats with reapportionment as their states grow while others lose seats. Over the past few decades, states in the Northeast and Midwest generally have lost seats, while southern and western states have made gains.

Once each state knows how many seats it will have, state legislatures

States Gaining and Losing Congressional Seats Following 2000 Census

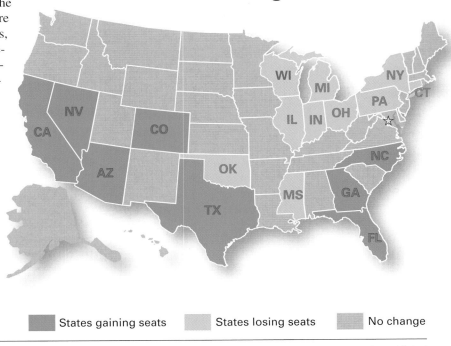

States gaining seats · States losing seats · No change

Source: U.S. Census Bureau, 2000 and 1990 census, www.census.gov; and 1990 census also published in 1990 CPH-2-1, Population and Housing Unit Counts, United States, Table 3.

of state legislative chambers work with demographic and political consultants to fashion districts that consolidate opposition voters into as few districts as possible, while expanding the reach of their own supporters.

In 2003, Texas undertook its second redistricting in a decade, thanks to an effort by state Republicans under the leadership of former House majority leader Tom DeLay. To offset potential congressional midterm losses for his party brought about by gains in other states, DeLay urged Republicans in his home state to redraw the map to corral Democrats into fewer competitive seats. The effort succeeded in electing twenty-one Texas Republicans—more than in any other state—and unseating seven Democrats. The Republican gains in Texas netted the party three additional seats in the 109th Congress. The Supreme Court in 2006 upheld the Texas redistricting plan, excepting one of the districts, which it determined placed Latinos at an electoral disadvantage.[16]

Some critics of Congress blame partisan redistricting for reducing competitiveness in House races. Reformers have called for the creation of nonpartisan commissions to take over the job from politicians with a vested interest in the outcome. Several states have already adopted such reforms. Studies show, however, that partisan redistricting is not entirely to blame for high levels of reelection by incumbents.[17] Demographic changes and the increased polarization of the electorate have led some districts and states to become more politically homogeneous,[18] potentially increasing the number of safe seats. We will revisit this issue at the end of this chapter.

Not all forms of redistricting, however, decrease the appeal of politics for voters. Beginning in the 1990s, the Justice Department supported efforts to create **minority-majority districts**, which are districts formed by fitting together pockets of minority populations to enhance the chances of electing minority candidates. This practice faced a court challenge as being discriminatory after the North Carolina legislature created a bizarrely shaped 165-mile-long majority-minority district that snaked along Interstate 85. The Supreme Court invalidated the district on the grounds

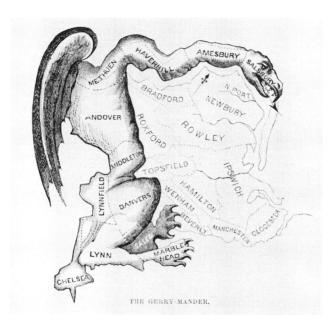

THE GERRY-MANDER.

The odd shape resulting from the partisan redrawing of this Massachusetts district in 1812—largely through the efforts of Governor Elbridge Gerry—inspired one cartoonist to depict it as a creature much like a salamander, giving rise to the term gerrymander.

that race cannot be the sole factor used in redrawing district boundaries. However, it left open the door to other gerrymandered districts where race is one but not the only consideration.

There is some evidence that minority-majority districts increase participation by African Americans and Hispanics without diminishing turnout among whites. Districts where African Americans and Hispanics together constitute a majority report higher turnout among both groups.[19] Nevertheless, by compressing minorities into fewer districts, this form of gerrymandering may also increase the number of districts that elect white representatives who may be less attuned to the needs of minority populations.[20] As a result, racial gerrymandering may actually work against achieving the policies that many minorities support, even as it ensures a higher number of minority members in Congress.

minority-majority district District in which minority members are clustered together, producing a majority of minority voters in the district.

delegate role Theory of representation stressing the lawmaker's role as a tribune of the people who reflects their views on issues of the day.

DOING THE JOB: RESPONSIBILITIES AND BENEFITS

Once elected, members of the House of Representatives and the Senate face a variety of tasks besides their primary function of making laws. They must deal with constituents and represent their interests in government; meet with lobbyists and interest groups; consult with fellow members; and work with policy experts on their staffs. Members receive substantial resources to help them carry out these functions.

Representing the People

One of the oldest issues facing members of Congress is how to interpret their roles as representatives. Should representatives mirror the views of their constituents on all votes, or should they exercise their own judgment on behalf of the citizens who have elected them to make such decisions? A more recent debate has arisen around the question of whether the makeup of Congress should reflect the so-

Not a Model of Diversity

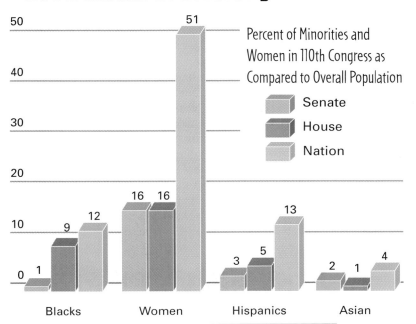

Percent of Minorities and Women in 110th Congress as Compared to Overall Population

Senate
House
Nation

Blacks: 0, 1, 12 / Women: 16, 16, 51 / Hispanics: 9, 3, 5, 13 / Asian: 2, 1, 4

Source: Greg Giroux, "An Old Boys' Club with New Twists," *CQ Weekly Online,* February 26, 2007, 604–608. Accessed online at http://library.cqpress.com on June 14, 2007.

cioeconomic, gender, and racial composition of the nation. If so, is our representative legislature truly representative?

Roles of Representatives Members of Congress typically attempt to balance several roles in representing their constituents. Some assume a **delegate role**, attempting to champion the views of their constituents on crucial issues. However, given the hundreds of votes members must cast annually, it is impossible for them to know their constituents' will on every issue. In fact, their constituents may be indifferent to or uninformed about a number of issues on which members cast ballots. This does not mean that representatives are inattentive to the wishes of their constituents. As we will see, members and their staffs spend a lot of time on constituent communications. Often representatives see themselves as **trustees**, exercising their own judgment on behalf of those they serve. For example, a member of Congress privy to classified information may vote for increased security at airport terminals despite the wishes of an impatient flying public back home.

From a practical standpoint, most members of Congress jockey back and forth between delegate and trustee roles, a practice known as the **politico** role of representation. In some matters, representatives can ill afford to stray too far from constituent wishes. For example, representatives with a substantial number of senior citizens in their districts will not likely vote for cuts in Social Security. Similarly, representatives whose constituents include a high proportion of evangelical Christians are unlikely to vote for Medicaid coverage of abortion procedures. On issues about which their constituents are silent, most members are on their own.

How Representative Are Our Representatives? If the makeup of a "representative" political body must reflect the diversity of the population it represents, then the U.S. Congress is hardly representative. The membership is older, much better educated, more well off financially, and much less ethnically and racially diverse than the U.S. population at large. Some observers have referred to the members of Congress as primarily "pale, male, and stale." The average senator is in their mid-sixties; the average House member is in their mid-fifties. A majority of House and Senate members hold advanced degrees and come from occupations that are more prestigious and generally more lucrative than those held by the general population. Law, elective or appointed government office, and business occupations like sales or banking predominate. They are more likely to belong to one of the many Protestant religious denominations, with far fewer Catholics, Jews, or members of minority religions represented. Minorities are also generally underrepresented compared to their numerical strength in the overall population, and women are grossly underrepresented. However, Congress is becoming more diverse than it once was. More minorities and

trustee Theory of representation stressing the lawmaker's own judgment in legislative decision making.

politico Approach to representation in which the lawmaker vacillates between trustee and delegate roles as he or she deems appropriate.

Nancy Pelosi became the first woman to hold the office of Speaker of the House when the 110th Congress convened in 2007.

women hold leadership positions. Perhaps the most notable of these is Nancy Pelosi, the first woman to hold the position of Speaker of the House beginning in 2007 and continuing in the position during the current session.

Although the electoral qualifications for Congress outlined in the Constitution are very broad and inclusive, the elite historically have made up the bulk of the membership. This longstanding trend reflects past patterns of discrimination, disparities in educational attainment, and difficulty in obtaining the financial resources necessary to make the long and costly run for office. Fortunately, these gaps are closing.

Pay and Perks

Benjamin Franklin proposed that elected government officials go unpaid for their service, but his views did not carry the day. Instead, the Framers provided compensation to be paid from the federal treasury. From 1789 to 1815, members of Congress received $6.00 per day while Congress was in session. Members began receiving a salary in 1815, when they were paid $1,500 per year. Today, the members' annual salary is $169,300; salaries for party leaders are somewhat higher. All members receive retirement and health benefits under the same plans available to other federal employees. Additional benefits of holding office are listed in the figure on the right.

Home-Style Politics

Keeping in touch with constituents is vital both for members' electoral prospects and for the health of representative government. Members pursue a variety of activities to gauge the pulse of the community, such as holding town meetings in their districts, making themselves available to local press for interviews, and keeping close tabs on mail from back home. These "home-style" activities enable members to present themselves to the voters and to explain their actions in Washington.[21]

Representatives often first become aware of important issues confronting constituents through personal communications such as a letter, fax, or phone call. These communications first pass through the hands of staff members, who sift through correspondence, tally support for issues coming up for a vote, and respond to constituents who wrote or called. They also select individual messages for the lawmaker's personal attention. Often, the letters the lawmaker sees come from high-profile constituents whose electoral support is important. Sometimes, they reflect a representative sample of opinion or simply provide a well-articulated perspective. Staff also carefully track mass mailings organized by interest groups—especially those that are active in election-year politics—although these generally have less impact than more personalized communications. E-mail correspondence has increased the workload of staffers, but it has not significantly altered the process for handling communications. According to a survey of 270 congressional offices, about 90 percent of all House and Senate members use e-mail, but they send more than 80 percent of all replies by regular mail.[22]

Much of the mail a member receives involves a direct request for assistance. Staffers in the member's home district are responsible for fulfilling such requests. For example, if a veteran of the war in Iraq has difficulty obtaining a benefit to which he believes he is entitled, a call to the Department of Veterans Affairs from the office of his congressperson usually will resolve the problem. Such requests provide the lawmaker with the opportunity to serve as a constituent ombudsman, or personal liaison between citizen and government agency, and filling them builds support for reelection. Constituent service can turn congressional offices into reelection machines that special-

Perks Aplenty: Benefits for Members of Congress

- Free office space in Washington, D.C., and in the home district
- A staff allowance (in 2007) of $831,252 for each House member and from $1,926,936 to $3,170,602 for clerical/administrative staff for Senators (depending on the population of the state and its distance from the Capitol). In addition, each Senator is authorized $472,677 to appoint up to three legislative assistants
- An expense account for telephone, stationery, and other office expenses
- Reimbursed travel to and from home district based on a formula using distance from Washington
- Routine or emergency medical healthcare available onsite
- Travel allowance and free travel to foreign lands on congressional inquiries
- Extensive franking privileges
- Free access to video and film studios to record messages for constituents
- Free reserved parking at Reagan Washington National and Dulles Airports
- Discounted use of congressional gym
- Free assistance in preparation of income taxes
- Generous pension benefits
- Up to $3,000 tax deduction for living expenses while away from their districts or states
- Participation in Federal Employee Group Life Insurance Program

Source: Congressional Research Service, *Congressional Salaries and Allowances*, August 30, 2007.

Several times a year, members of Congress return to their districts for town meetings. These question-and-answer sessions provide a good opportunity for you to find out what your representative has been up to and to ask questions about issues you feel are important. Members will often list times and locations of their town meetings on their congressional websites. Come equipped with some understanding about your legislator's political affiliation, committee assignments, tenure, and voting record. You can find information about legislation members have sponsored and their voting records at www.house.gov or www.senate.gov.

get involved!

ize in cultivating personal ties between constituents and representatives.[23]

Members initiate contact with constituents by mailing newsletters and questionnaires to let voters know what they are up to, and to solicit opinions about current issues. Increasingly, they are turning to websites to provide constituents with information about the members' legislative activities and to provide contact information for government services. Lawmakers also use news conferences, interviews, and even one-minute speeches on the House floor to state positions on issues they believe will find favor with their constituents. Members usually reserve visits to their home districts to announce federal funding or grants they manage to secure for the region, a practice known as credit claiming.[24] Attention to home-style politics pays off for most members of Congress. Although only a minority of Americans approve of the way Congress as a whole is handling its job,[25] most believe their individual lawmaker is doing just fine—and most of the time they demonstrate their approval by returning the lawmaker to office.

Dealing with Organized Interests

Members of Congress interact frequently with lobbyists, or representatives from interest groups, to their mutual benefit. Because of the help these groups provide in campaigns and elections, they often gain favored access to Congress members and greater support for their causes. In addition to campaign contributions and voter mobilization, lobbyists and interest groups help members by supplying detailed information about the impact of legislation that only groups close to the policy may be in a position to offer. G. William Whitehurst, who represented Virginia for eighteen years as a Republican member of the House, recalls "many instances when I emerged from a meeting with an industry lobbyist better informed and therefore better prepared to vote on legislation that was pending."[26] Whitehurst warned, however, about the volatile situation that results from the ever-increasing number and stridency of groups seeking access to lawmakers who, in turn, rely upon these groups for money and reelection support:

> The result is a cacophony that leads to an unstable legislative arena, where calm, dispassionate, and reasonable discussion is made more difficult.[27]

Lobbyists are especially interested in gaining access to committee chairs and members of committees with jurisdiction over issues important to their clients. Often this has been accomplished by performing favors like providing corporate jets for Congressional travel or by raising funds for re-election campaigns. The often cozy relation between lobbyists and Congress carries with it the potential for sheer corruption. In 2005, the House forced Randy "Duke" Cunningham (R-CA) to resign after he plead guilty to accepting millions of dollars from defense contractors in return for using his position on the Defense Appropriations Subcommittee to steer lucrative contracts to these firms. In the face of public consternation, Congress passed a reform act in 2007 that restricts the amount and kind of gifts and travel lobbyists can provide to members of Congress, requires greater disclosure of lobbyist contributions, and lengthens the period of time in which former members of Congress, staffers, or certain members of the Executive Branch must refrain from lobbying their former colleagues. Additional prosecutions have accompanied this heightened scrutiny.

Lobbyists are frequently given the opportunity to testify before congressional committees when legislation that affects their interests is debated.

Most members of Congress hire student interns to work in their offices both in Washington, D.C., and in their home districts. To apply, contact the office of your representative or senator or log on to their websites, where internship opportunities are usually posted. Interns perform such tasks as answering telephones, running errands, helping answer mail, scheduling meetings, and researching constituent problems. Most internships are unpaid positions, so they are not for everybody. Nevertheless, they are a valuable source of knowledge and provide great contacts for career advancement.

The Committee System

Committees allow members of Congress to scrutinize particular types of legislation in depth, enabling committee members to develop expertise in certain topic areas. The real work of lawmaking occurs in these so-called "little legislatures." There are four basic types of committees: standing, select, joint, and conference.

Standing Committees

These permanent committees, which continue from session to session, have jurisdiction in a variety of subject areas. Committee size varies depending on jurisdiction, with the House average near forty committee members and the Senate about half that number. Standing committees typically feature subcommittees that have expertise in specific areas. For example, the Senate Committee on Foreign Relations consists of seven subcommittees that focus on different geographical regions and topic areas.

ways in which they refer to one another during floor debates. Even during heated arguments, members will usually address each other as "colleagues" or "friends." For years, newcomers refrained from grandstanding to advance their personal careers. Instead, they followed the lead of more senior members to become specialists in the legislative work of their committees and cooperated with their colleagues in producing compromise legislation. The increasing partisan polarization of Congress in recent years has weakened, although not yet extinguished, many of these norms.[29]

A member of the House may sit on as many as two full committees and four subcommittees, although members sitting on the most influential and time-consuming committees, like Appropriations, have fewer assignments. Senators may serve on even more committees, depending on the importance of the committee's role in the legislative process. Since each committee must meet at least once a month, members stay busy familiarizing themselves with bills under consideration and working with committee staff in order to stay on top of their workload.

The majority party controls most of the seats on each committee, including the leadership positions. The distribution of committee seats usually reflects the party makeup of the body as a whole. Subcommittee assignments also reflect party balance and longevity, with party members bidding for available slots on the basis of seniority. Committees that deal with the ethical behavior of members, such as the Committee on Standards of Official Conduct in the House and the Senate's Select Committee on Ethics, are exceptions to these rules, containing equal numbers of Republicans and Democrats.

Both the House and the Senate employ party committees to nominate members for seats on standing committees. For Republicans, the Steering Committee performs this function in the House, and the Committee on Committees does so in the Senate. Democrats employ a Steering Committee in each

KEYS TO POLITICAL POWER

The principal role of the legislative branch is making laws. To help it perform this function more efficiently, Congress divides its workload among smaller bodies called committees, which may be further divided into subcommittees. The process of lawmaking is complex; lawmakers who occupy key positions of authority and understand the intricacies of the legislative process can make a dramatic difference in advancing legislation or stopping it in its tracks.

pork barrel projects Term applied to spending for pet projects of individual members of Congress.

earmarks Funding for specific projects that are added by members of Congress to appropriation bills usually without oversight or public debate.

Committees in the House and Senate in 111th Congress, 2009–2011

House Standing Committees	Senate Standing Committees
Agriculture	Agriculture, Nutrition, and Forestry
Appropriations	Appropriations
Armed Services	Armed Services
Budget	Banking and Housing and Urban Affairs
Education and Labor	Budget
Energy and Commerce	Commerce, Science, and Transportation
Financial Services	Energy and Natural Resources
Foreign Affairs	Environment and Public Works
Homeland Security	Finance
House Administration	Foreign Relations
Judiciary	Health, Education, Labor, and Pensions
Natural Resources	Homeland Security and Government Affairs
Oversight and Government Reform	Judiciary
Rules	Rules and Administration
Science and Technology	Small Business and Entrepreneurship
Small Business	Veterans' Affairs
Standards of Official Conduct	
Transportation and Infrastructure	
Veterans' Affairs	
Ways and Means	

Source: U.S. House of Representatives; U.S. Senate.

chamber. Experienced members receive requested committee appointments more often than do freshman representatives, although seniority is no longer as important as it once was. A freshman's chance of attaining a desired assignment depends on a number of factors, including party, interest and expertise, the size and importance of his or her legislative district, and the member's ties to leadership. Leaders sometimes intervene to ensure that newly elected members from important districts get slots that maximize their public exposure and showcase their talents to constituents back home. Once assigned to a committee, members are expected to develop expertise on the subject of the committee's concern, usually with the aid of policy specialists on the committee staff.

Not all standing committees have equal status or power. Committees dealing with spending and taxes, such as the Appropriations and Ways and Means committees in the House and the Budget Committee in the Senate, are considered the most powerful. These committees can be crucial for serving the reelection needs of members because they approve **pork barrel projects** designed to fund popular ventures in members' districts. Sending federal dollars back to the home district allows members to show that they are making a tangible impact on the lives of constituents.

Many pork projects appear ridiculous to the casual observer. For example, the 2008 budget included $211,509 for olive fruit fly research in Paris, France; $188,000 for the Lobster Institute in Maine; and $49,000 for construction of a National Mule Packers Museum in Bishop, California. A nonpartisan budget watchdog organization estimates that the 2008 budget includes more than $33 of pork per citizen, although some states received much more than others.[30] Most of what is deemed "pork" is inserted in the form of **earmarks**, funding requests for specific projects that are added on to appropriation bills by individual mem-

Subcommittees of the Senate Committee on Foreign Relations

- Subcommittee on Western Hemisphere, Peace Corps, and Narcotics Affairs
- Subcommittee on Near Eastern and South and Central Asian Affairs
- Subcommittee on African Affairs
- Subcommittee on East Asian and Pacific Affairs
- Subcommittee on International Operations and Organizations, Democracy, and Human Rights
- Subcommittee on European Affairs
- Subcommittee on International Development and Foreign Assistance, Economic Affairs, and International Environmental Protection

Top 10 States: Pork per Capita

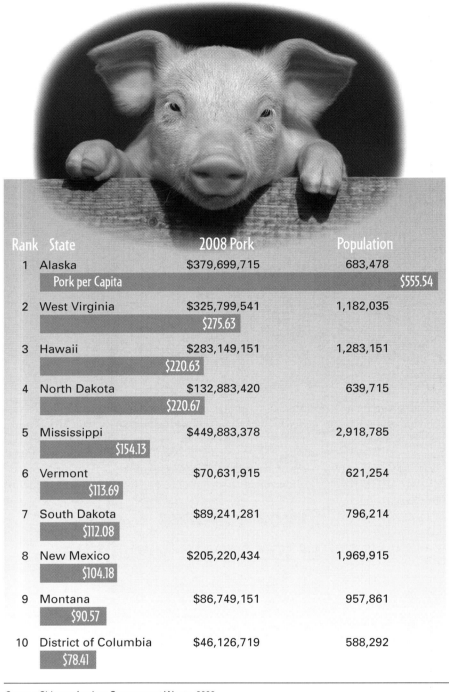

Rank	State	2008 Pork	Population	Pork per Capita
1	Alaska	$379,699,715	683,478	$555.54
2	West Virginia	$325,799,541	1,182,035	$275.63
3	Hawaii	$283,149,151	1,283,151	$220.63
4	North Dakota	$132,883,420	639,715	$220.67
5	Mississippi	$449,883,378	2,918,785	$154.13
6	Vermont	$70,631,915	621,254	$113.69
7	South Dakota	$89,241,281	796,214	$112.08
8	New Mexico	$205,220,434	1,969,915	$104.18
9	Montana	$86,749,151	957,861	$90.57
10	District of Columbia	$46,126,719	588,292	$78.41

Source: Citizens Against Government Waste, 2008.

measure did not pass, Congress has restrained its appetite for these projects. The $17 billion spent on earmarks in fiscal year 2008 was $12 billion less than the record $29 billion spent in 2006. Despite their sometimes controversial nature, pork projects mean real money for constituent groups back home and bragging rights for the members who secure them. This explains why a new form of "soft earmark" has arisen in which congressional committees recommend a specific project to an agency they are funding instead of explicitly authorizing it. Most agencies receiving these "suggestions" are likely to take them seriously.

In the House, the Committee on Rules is of special importance because of the role it plays in fashioning the terms for debate and amendment of bills coming to the floor. Often these rules mean the difference between passage and defeat, and the majority party guards its control of procedures by assigning two-thirds of the members to this body. The Rules Committee also may initiate legislation on its own; Congress gives immediate consideration to measures the Rules Committee brings to the floor.

Select Committees The leadership of each house usually appoints select committees for a limited period to handle matters that do not routinely fit into areas of standing committee jurisdiction. For example, the House or Senate may create a committee to investigate official misconduct or inquire into unique events or problems. The activity of select committees usually culminates with official reports that the members may or may not use to generate legislation to be considered by other committees.

Some select committees act more like permanent standing committees. For example, the House Permanent Select Committee on Intelligence, first created in 1977, continues to hold hearings on various aspects of intelligence gathering and threats to national security. The most recent addition to the constellation of select committees is the House Select Committee on Energy Independence and Global

bers, usually without oversight or public debate. In 2007, Congress, faced with mounting criticism of such spending in the media, passed legislation lowering the ceiling on such projects and calling for open disclosure on the Internet of the names of the members who have sponsored them. In 2008, House Republicans attempted unsuccessfully to call a moratorium on all earmarks for one year. Although the

Warming. Established in 2007 by Speaker Nancy Pelosi, the committee does not pass legislation. Instead, it organizes hearings, issues reports, and holds briefings to raise awareness about threats to the environment.

Joint Committees Joint committees include members from both houses and can be either temporary or permanent. Most do not handle legislation, but monitor and report on activities of government agencies. For example, the Joint Committee on Taxation reviews tax policy and the operation of the Internal Revenue Service. Party leaders in each house appoint the members of joint committees.

Conference Committees Before sending legislation to the president for approval, the House and Senate must pass identical versions of the same law. When conflicting versions emerge, the leadership in each house selects members for a conference committee that attempts to resolve differences. Only after both the House and the Senate approve the conference reports of these committees can legislation move to the president's desk. When a single party controls both houses of Congress, conference committees concentrate mainly on accommodating the wishes of majority-party members in both chambers. In such cases, the opposition can reliably complain about being excluded.

Party

The majority party—the one with more elected members—controls the chamber. The majority party determines the organizational structure, the composition of internal bodies such as committees and subcommittees, positions of leadership, and the flow of the legislation itself. The minority party plays a role, but its impact is small by comparison, especially if the majority party also controls the White House. Currently, the Democrats have a clear majority in the House. Democrats also control the Senate and in 2008 increased their numbers to just shy of the margin needed to completely control floor debate. Independent representatives and senators must caucus with one or the other party.

When Republicans took control of the House after the 1994 midterm elections, they made sweeping changes in the committee system. These included imposing term limits for committee chairs, changing committee jurisdictions, limiting the number of subcommittees, reducing the number of staff assignments, and strengthening the role of party leaders. By contrast, when control of the Senate shifted to the GOP in the 1980s after years of Democratic

domination, Senate Republicans imposed fewer changes than did their counterparts in the House. Although the Democrats regained control of both Houses in 2006, they made few organizational changes.

Changes in party composition in both chambers since the 1980s reflect the changes in the electorate. The Democrats thus have fewer members representing moderate and conservative constituencies, giving them as a group a more liberal tilt. Similarly, Republicans have tilted toward greater conservatism by picking up strength among traditionally conservative constituencies in the South.

Just as a closely divided electorate has produced divisive partisan campaigns, a closely divided Congress has produced a highly charged partisan environment in both chambers. One indicator of the intensity of partisan conflict is party unity, or the extent to which mem-

> ### Did You Know?
> . . . That the term pork barrel *legislation refers to the practice of plantation owners taking salt pork from barrels to give to their slaves as a treat.*

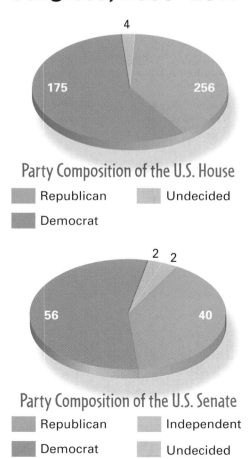

Party Control of the 111th Congress, 2009–2011

4
175   256

Party Composition of the U.S. House

■ Republican   ■ Undecided
■ Democrat

2 2
56   40

Party Composition of the U.S. Senate

■ Republican   ■ Independent
■ Democrat   ■ Undecided

bers of each party vote together and in opposition to members of the other party. Since the early 1990s, members have increasingly tended to vote along party lines, making it more difficult for moderate members of each party to reach bipartisan consensus. House Democrats were more unified than ever in 2007, voting with their party's majority 92 percent of the time, on average. In the Senate, Democrats' average party unity score of 87 percent was just short of their all-time high of 89 percent in 1999 and 2001. Republican Party unity in the House and Senate peaked in 2003 at 91 percent and has since fallen slightly below.[31]

Speaker of the House The most powerful leader of the House of Representatives.

majority leader Leader of the majority party in each house, responsible for marshaling support for the party's agenda.

minority leader Leader of the minority party in each house, responsible for marshaling support for the party's agenda.

With fewer moderates on both sides of the aisle, traditional civility and decorum sometimes break down, making it more difficult to forge the kind of bipartisan consensus necessary to deal with controversial problems such as Social Security reform. When the Democrats took control in 2007, they promised greater openness and flexibility in the rules of debate to allow an opportunity for the parties to work together. Although the session may have started out with good intentions, decorum broke down by midsummer, and studies showed the flexibility promised by Democrats had all but evaporated.[32] Partisan bickering in Congress turns many Americans away from politics and may reduce civic involvement. Not everyone is dissatisfied with this situation, however. Surveys show that voters whose party controls the majority are much more satisfied with the institution than are voters from the minority party or independents.[33]

Getting legislation passed is sometimes made more difficult in times of divided government when one party controls one or both houses of Congress and the other party controls the White House. Divided government has become more frequent in recent decades. We have experienced divided government during eighteen of the last twenty-seven sessions of Congress (1955–2009). Some political scientists believe that about the same amount of legislation passes under divided government as under unified government, when the same party controls both branches, and that divided government forces parties to reach across the aisle to get things done.[34] There have been some notable legislative successes in periods of divided rule. For example, President Clinton worked with Republicans after they took over control of Congress in 1994 to pass landmark welfare reform. President George W. Bush worked across party lines with Senator Ted Kennedy (D-MA) to produce the No Child Left Behind Act. Voters often tell pollsters that they prefer divided government because it acts as an additional check on legislative excess. However, divided government slows down the legislative process, and may dilute legislation as a result of efforts to achieve consensus.[35] It may also result in the failure to enact important legislation—especially when the legislation is initiated by Congress and opposed by the sitting president of the opposition party.[36]

Position

Parties control leadership positions in both houses, and the majority party always controls the most important offices. The majority party always has more seats on every committee than the minority party, based roughly on the proportion of seats each party controls in the chamber. Every committee chair is likewise always a member of the majority party. In addition, the majority party controls the top leadership positions responsible for the scheduling and flow of the legislative process. Just as Congress itself has adopted a more partisan outlook in recent years, so too have its leaders. Leaders are increasingly chosen for their ability to frame issues along party lines, for their skill in controlling the legislative agenda, and for their ability to raise funds for fellow party members.[37]

House Leadership The most powerful leader in the lower chamber is the **Speaker of the House**. The majority party selects one of its members to be Speaker, subject to approval by the entire House membership. The Speaker refers bills to committees for consideration and appoints members of the majority party to sit on some of the most powerful House committees, as well as all members of select and conference committees. Some of the most significant appointments are to the Committee on Rules, which sets conditions for debate. Rules can be an important source of power. Rules that extend debate can be an invitation to compromise; rules that limit debate may silence dissent. The Speaker schedules legislation for floor consideration and may choose to preside over sessions of the body, although this is frequently delegated to another member of the majority party. The Speaker helps control

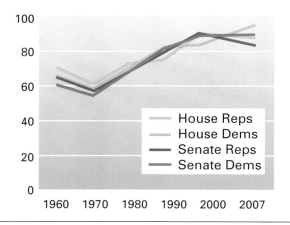

Soaring Partisanship in Congress

Legend:
— House Reps
— House Dems
— Senate Reps
— Senate Dems

Source: Congressional Quarterly Weekly, January 14, 2008, 148.

Congressional Leaders

HOUSE

**Speaker of
the House**
Nancy Pelosi (D-CA)

Majority Leader
Steny Hoyer (D-MD)

Majority Whip
James Clyburn (D-SC)

Minority Leader
John Boehner (R-OH)

Minority Whip
Roy Blunt (R-MO)

SENATE

**Vice President of
the United States**
Joseph Biden (D-DE)

President Pro Tempore
Robert Byrd (D-WV)

Majority Leader
Harry Reid (D-NV)

Minority Leader
Mitch McConnell (R-KY)

the flow of debate and exercises wide discretion in interpreting and applying parliamentary rules. As the one individual with a commanding view of the entire legislative process, the Speaker is in a position to know the status of all legislation at all times and has the ability to influence its course. Although the Speaker is entitled to debate and vote on all legislation, she or he normally only votes on matters of great importance or when his or her vote would be decisive.

The House has a long history of Speakers who have wielded considerable authority, such as "Uncle Joe" Cannon, who dictated House policy at the turn of the last century. Sam Rayburn (D-TX) served as Speaker three times from 1940 to 1961, with two interruptions of service when Republicans controlled the chamber. Rayburn won notoriety and respect for using his command of House rules to win passage of civil rights reform despite the opposition of southern Democrats. Newt Gingrich, who served from 1995 to 1999, engineered the modern resurgence of the Republican Party in Congress. The current occupant, Nancy Pelosi (D-CA), is the first woman to hold the position.

Members of the majority party elect a **majority leader**, who assists the Speaker in setting the legislative agenda in the House. The majority leader works to generate support for the positions of party leaders, acts as a spokesperson for the party's legislative program, helps shepherd the party's legislation through the lawmaking process, and assists in scheduling floor action and the flow of debate. Majority leaders can enforce voting discipline among party members by influencing appointments to important committees, by responding to staffing requests, and by lending support to a member's legislation. Of course, the majority leader can also withhold favors from a member who fails to support the party's legislative agenda. Tom DeLay (R-

TX), who assumed the position of majority leader in 2002, earned the nickname "The Hammer" because of his power in enforcing discipline among party members. He resigned from the House in 2006 following a felony indictment for violating campaign finance rules.

The minority party also selects a leader to advance its own agenda in the legislative process. This is not an easy job when the opposition holds the levers of power. Nevertheless, the **minority leader** can speak out on issues important to members, put pressure on majority-party leaders to hold hearings on controversial issues, and organize floor debate among minority-party members. The majority party may consult the minority leader on scheduling and developing procedures for floor debate, but the minority rarely has an equal voice in negotiations.

Each party also employs elected **whips**, assistant party leaders, who are responsible for building support for a party's agenda and ensuring that members are present and prepared to vote as their parties prefer. Whips also help negotiate agreements among members to trade votes so that each benefits from the actions of the other, a practice known as **logrolling**.

> **whips** Assistant party leaders in each house whose jobs include ensuring that party members are present for floor votes and prepared to vote as the party prefers.
>
> **logrolling** The practice of trading votes to the mutual advantage of members.

Senate Leadership The leadership structure in the Senate is similar to that of the House, with only a few differences at the very top. The Constitution specifies that the vice president of the United States serve as the president of the Senate, with the authority to preside over the body and to vote in case of a tie. Beyond this, the vice president

THE FUNCTIONS OF CONGRESS

Lawmaking is the preeminent function of Congress, but the body also exercises the powers to declare war, to monitor the actions of the executive agencies it creates, to impeach and try federal officials, and to fund the federal government through the budget process. In addition, the Senate ratifies treaties and confirms presidential appointments.

markup Committee sessions in which members review contents of legislation line by line.

pocket veto Automatic veto achieved when a bill sits unsigned on a president's desk for ten days when Congress is out of session.

Lawmaking

Former congressman Lee Hamilton (D-IN) blanches when he sees diagrams illustrating how laws are made. "How boring! How sterile!" he complains. Indeed, what diagrams miss are the intricacies of interpersonal relations necessary to win support for one's cause.

You don't just have an idea, draft it in bill form, and drop it in the House hopper or file it at the Senate desk. Developing the idea is very much a political process—listening to the needs and desires of people and then trying to translate it into a specific legislative proposal. Even the earliest stages of drafting a bill involve much maneuvering. The member needs to consult with col-

Formal Procedure: How a Bill Becomes Law

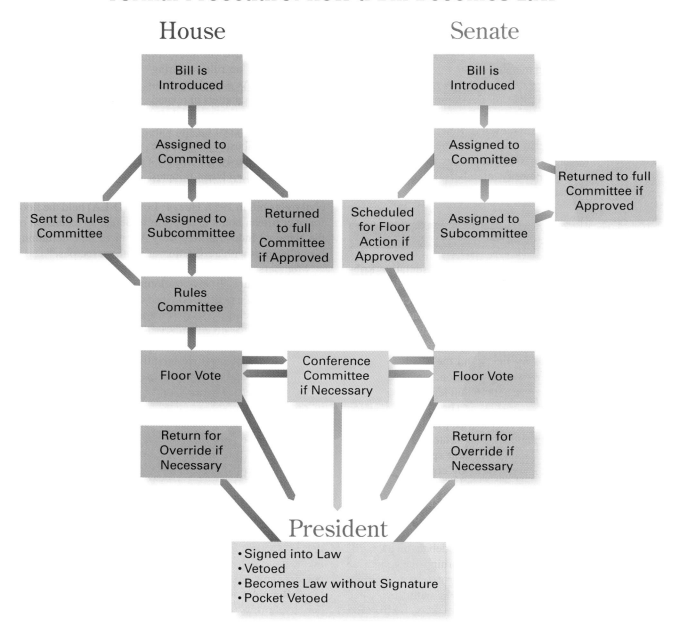

House / Senate

Bill is Introduced

Assigned to Committee

Sent to Rules Committee · Assigned to Subcommittee · Returned to full Committee if Approved · Scheduled for Floor Action if Approved · Assigned to Subcommittee · Returned to full Committee if Approved

Rules Committee

Floor Vote · Conference Committee if Necessary · Floor Vote

Return for Override if Necessary · Return for Override if Necessary

President
• Signed into Law
• Vetoed
• Becomes Law without Signature
• Pocket Vetoed

leagues, experts, and interest groups to refine and sharpen the idea; gauge the political impact and viability of the proposal (especially with constituents); determine how to formulate the idea so it appeals to a majority of colleagues; study how it differs from and improves upon related proposals introduced in the past; decide how broadly or narrowly to draft it (to avoid it being sent to too many committees); and decide how to draft it so it gets sent to a sympathetic rather than an unsympathetic committee.[41]

approves to the full committee, which may amend the bill and subject it to a process known as **markup**, which involves reviewing and approving its language. The mortality rate for bills in committee is very high, approximately 90 percent, with most bills failing to gain sufficient support of party leaders to warrant further action.

In the House, bills approved by committees proceed to the Rules Committee, whose members prescribe procedures for debate and amendment on the floor. The Rules

"YOU DON'T JUST HAVE AN IDEA, draft it in bill form, and drop it in the House hopper or file it at the Senate desk. Developing the idea is very much a political process—listening to the needs and desires of people and then trying to translate it into a specific legislative proposal."

With this caveat in mind, we nevertheless can sketch the formal course a bill must take in wending its way through the legislative chambers.

Bills must pass both houses to be eligible for presidential action. Much legislation today actually originates in the White House. In such cases, the president engages faithful party colleagues in the House or Senate to introduce the bill. With the exception of revenue bills that must originate in the House of Representatives, all bills can be initially introduced into either chamber. The procedures in each body parallel one another with a few significant differences.

Once introduced, the leadership assigns the bill to one or more standing committees, depending on jurisdiction. If the bill involves more than one committee's jurisdiction, the leader may partition it so that different committees address portions of the bill related to their own jurisdiction. Once in committee, the chair can assign the bill to a subcommittee for more detailed analysis and consideration. A bill dealing with new technology for use by first responders sent to the Committee on Homeland Security, may, for example, subsequently be directed by the committee chair to the Subcommittee on Emergency Preparedness, Science, and Technology for consideration.

Generally, subcommittees will request investigations and reports from various executive branch offices impacted by the legislation. The committee can call witnesses to testify about the impact of the bill. In the previous example, the committee may call administrators from the Department of Homeland Security to testify about which technologies they believe to be the most useful in tackling terrorist threats. Representatives of various interest groups with a stake in the legislation are also likely to get a chance to voice their views. Most committees hold open hearings; some, like Appropriations, must do so by law.

At the conclusion of its investigation, the subcommittee votes to determine whether to send the bill through the rest of the process or to table it—that is, leave it to die without further action. The subcommittee sends each bill it

Committee also schedules the bill for consideration by the entire body; the legislation must receive the support of a majority of members present for passage. There is no parallel committee in the Senate that sets rules on a bill-by-bill basis. Instead, the Senate leadership will ask for unanimous consent regarding debate limits that the majority leader previously worked out with interested senators from both parties. If the full Senate does not grant consent, unlimited debate with the possibility of filibuster governs floor action. Votes in each house require a simple majority for passage, with two exceptions: treaty approval—which occurs only in the Senate—requires a two-thirds vote, and overriding a presidential veto requires two-thirds approval by both houses.

If differences exist between House and Senate versions of a bill, the leadership of each house will appoint members to a conference committee, usually composed of members from both parties on the relevant House and Senate committees. If the conference committee can resolve the differences, the measure returns to the floor of both bodies for final approval.

Bills that pass both houses of Congress then proceed to the White House, where the president can take one of several actions:

- Sign the bill into law.
- Veto the bill, in which case both houses will need to secure a two-thirds vote to override the veto.
- Allow the bill to become law without the president's signature simply by failing to take action within ten days. This tends to occur when the president does not support the legislation but recognizes that it has enough support for a veto override.
- Exercise a **pocket veto** by letting the bill sit unsigned for ten days when there are fewer than ten days left in the legislative session. Since many bills do not pass until the end of a session, the potential for pocket veto is substantial.

States presides over the trial, during which witnesses offer testimony and undergo examination and cross-examination just as in a court of law. Removal from office requires a two-thirds majority. Congress has impeached seventeen federal officials, most of them federal judges. Neither of the presidents who faced impeachment was removed from office. We will discuss presidential impeachments in more detail in Chapter 12.

oversight Congressional authority to monitor the actions and budgets of executive agencies it creates.

legislative veto Device, declared unconstitutional in 1983, allowing Congress to rescind rules promulgated by an executive agency.

congressional review Congressional action, requiring approval by both houses and the president, that can stop implementation of executive branch regulations.

signing statements Documents presidents append to legislation indicating their particular interpretation of its contents.

Oversight

Congress also provides **oversight**, or close scrutiny, of the federal agencies and programs it creates and of the actions of the other branches of government. Oversight is not an enumerated power, but it is implied by the system of checks and balances. Congress exercises its power of oversight through a wide variety of activities and mechanisms.

Congress conducts investigations to examine policy implementation or to scrutinize the activities of government personnel and officeholders. Congress has the power to subpoena witnesses to testify under oath, although witnesses can, of course, refuse to testify under rights granted by the Fifth Amendment. Live television and radio broadcasts of congressional investigations provide citizens with the opportunity to see exactly how their elected representa-

President Bush cited executive privilege in shielding his former White House counsel, Harriet Miers, from testifying before Congress as it investigated allegations of political interference in hiring attorneys at the Justice Department. Congress responded by issuing a subpoena, one of its options in exercising oversight responsibility.

tives protect their interests. This opportunity for civic engagement is not without its risks, however; live broadcast also allows lawmakers to exploit the hearings to gain publicity for themselves.

The executive branch often resists congressional oversight, arguing for autonomy in matters under its principal jurisdiction. The administration of President George W. Bush has been especially reluctant to allow congressional scrutiny, denying Congress access to papers and documents dealing with matters ranging from energy policy to conduct of the war in Iraq to the firing of U.S. attorneys. It has also exercised what it calls "executive privilege" in refusing to permit members of the administration to testify before Congress as when the President sought to prevent the testimoney of former White House counsel Harriet Miers regarding the allegedly political firing of U.S. attorneys. Of course, the executive branch can avoid oversight more easily when the president's party controls both houses of Congress. The number of oversight hearings soared to more than 600 in the first half of 2007, when the Democrats took control of Congress. By contrast, the Republican-controlled 109th Congress held fewer than two-thirds that number during its entire two-year term.[46]

Congressional committees also exercise oversight by monitoring budgets and holding hearings on the authorization of programs run by executive agencies. The authorization of budgets is potentially Congress's most powerful tool for influencing an agency's operations. Often, however, this power is quite fragmented. For example, no fewer than seventy-nine committees and subcommittees exercise some kind of oversight of the Department of Homeland Security and its many programs. Such fragmentation makes genuine oversight difficult, creating many opportunities for interest groups and specialists within the agencies to secure their funding objectives.

Congress can also create special commissions and task forces to evaluate policies. Such oversight activities can serve as a warning to agencies that lawmakers are displeased with their performance. They also send the message to constituents that members of Congress are doing their jobs. Until 1983, Congress could also repeal or prevent enforcement of agency rules developed by the executive branch, a provision known as the **legislative veto**. Although the Supreme Court ruled that this power was an unconstitutional infringement on the powers of the executive branch,[47] there have been examples of its continuation, and it survives so long as the president does not challenge Congress's use of the device.[48]

Similar to the legislative veto, the power of **congressional review** permits Congress to nullify agency regulations after sixty days by passage of a joint resolution by both houses and approval by the president. In 2001, Congress used its power of congressional review to nullify a rule proposed in the waning days of the Clinton administration that would have forced employers to conduct ergonomic assessments of their workplaces to minimize worker fatigue and injury.

In our system of checks and balances, moves by either the legislative or the executive branch to control policy often spawn responses by the other branch. In order to evade oversight, or to circumvent portions of legislation that they believe infringe on presidential prerogatives, presidents have taken to issuing **signing statements**. These controversial statements explain how the president chooses to interpret the legislation he signs, and sometimes explain why he will ignore certain provisions he finds objectionable. Critics of signing statements argue that presidents who utilize them are violating the Constitution by essentially rewriting the laws that Congress has passed. We will discuss these in more detail in Chapter 12.

Budgeting

While the president makes recommendations regarding the administration's budget priorities, the Constitution gives Congress alone the authority to decide how the money is spent. In addition, it specifies that all bills to raise revenues must originate in the House of Representatives.

The budgeting process begins when the president sends Congress a proposed budget (usually after the annual State of the Union message in January or February). A special independent agency, the Congressional Budget Office, then reviews all spending proposals and makes detailed estimates of expenditures needed to accomplish the president's policy objectives. Budget committees in both houses consult with executive agency representatives and develop a **budget resolution** that projects income and sets spending ceilings for various programs. Both houses must pass the budget resolution by April 15 of each year, but it does not require a presidential signature. The figures in the resolution guide the remainder of the budget process.

The Appropriations Committees in each house send portions of the resolution to the subcommittees with authority over the various federal agencies requesting funds. These legislative committees authorize spending to fit within prescribed targets. Spending requests are then returned to the Appropriations Committee in each house for approval. More than two-thirds of the expenditures are nondiscretionary—that is, they go to fund ongoing commitments and operations like Medicare or Social Security. Most of the intense debates occur over the roughly 30 percent of the budget allotted for discretionary or new spending programs. If the need arises, Congress can change funding targets for various programs to stay within the budget guidelines. This amending process is known as **reconciliation**.

Final passage of spending bills is supposed to occur just prior to the beginning of the government's fiscal year, the yearly budgeting period that begins on October 1. Often, however, Congress does not meet the deadline and must pass **continuing resolutions** that allow agencies to operate at the previous year's funding levels until the new budget is passed. In recent years, as Congress has failed to pass a budget on time, it has resorted to passing an omnibus bill that folds spending for all programs into a single bill.

budget resolution Early step in budgeting process in which both houses of Congress set spending goals.

reconciliation Process of amending spending bills to meet budget targets.

continuing resolution Vehicle for funding government operations at the previous year's levels of support when a new budget is delayed.

Advice and Consent

The Constitution accords additional powers to the U.S. Senate under the category of "advice and consent." The first of these is the power to approve treaties negotiated by the president, which requires a two-thirds vote. The second is confirmation by simple majority of presidential appointments, ambassadors, other "public Ministers and Consuls, Judges of the Supreme Court, and all other Officers of the United States." The Framers saw the Senate's power of advice and consent as a way for Congress to check presidential power. The use of the Senate for this purpose—rather than the House—ensured that the interests of both large and small states would be respected, because each state has equal representation in the Senate.

Ever since George Washington visited the Senate in 1789 to confer with members about a series of agreements negotiated with Native American tribes, presidents have employed a number of tactics to win Senate support for treaties. Some presidents have involved senators in the negotiation process itself, as William McKinley did in negotiating a peace treaty with Spain in 1898. Woodrow Wilson, on the other hand, paid a price for his failure to include senators in negotiations for the Treaty of Versailles, which ended World War I. The Senate twice refused to ratify the treaty. More recently, presidents have conferred with Senate leaders during the negotiating process. This approach worked particularly well for Ronald Reagan in winning approval for an arms control treaty in 1987.

Hot or Not?

Does Congress have a responsibility to fund the troops in battle even if a majority of Americans oppose the war?

Did You Know?

. . . That when President George Washington went to the Senate to ask for its "advice and consent" regarding a treaty, the senators made it very clear that they would deliberate by themselves, without presidential participation? Since that time, no president has attempted to take part personally in any Senate proceedings.

Woodrow Wilson paid a price for his failure to include senators in negotiations for the Treaty of Versailles ending World War I. The Senate twice refused to ratify it.

The Senate generally has been reluctant to reject treaties, approving more than fifteen thousand while turning down just twenty-one.[49] Still, presidents frequently are reluctant to subject their international negotiations to Senate scrutiny. Some have circumvented the process by adopting executive agreements with other nations that carry the same force of law as treaties but do not require Senate approval. We will discuss the increasing use of these agreements in Chapter 12.

Today, the Senate is asked to confirm thousands of civilian and military nominations during each two-year session of Congress. While it confirms the vast majority of these in blocks, controversial nominees do engender significant debate. This is particularly true with respect to Supreme Court nominees, who enjoy lifetime appointments. We will discuss these at length in Chapter 14. Much of the controversy over Senate approval of presidential appointments centers around the proper meaning of "advice and consent." Some scholars and senators believe Congress should reject presidential appointees only if the nominee is deficient in competence or character. Others believe the Senate should have the discretion to deny appointment for any reason whatsoever, including disagreements over policy or political perspective.

CIVIC ENGAGEMENT AND CONGRESS TODAY

Although Congress today reflects the nation's changing currents of partisan affiliation, it appears poorly equipped to find broad-based solutions to problems Americans deem important, such as controlling discretionary spending, balancing the budget, reforming the tax system, and providing affordable health care for all. The skillful use of pork barrel projects and casework may ensure the loyalty of some voters, but the public expresses general dissatisfaction with the institution of Congress as a whole for its inability to solve social problems. Many citizens believe Congress is inefficient, laggard, and unresponsive, and that it has lost touch with the public.[50] Over the past decade, the number of Americans expressing trust in Congress has rarely exceeded a third of the population; and in 2008, that number plummeted to just 12 percent.[51] Fewer than half of eligible voters turn out for midterm congressional elections.

These attitudes are, in part, understandable reactions to the political dynamics of the institution today. In a closely divided Congress, bipartisan consensus takes a backseat to partisan politics as members of each party seek to please groups most important to their electoral success. Debate becomes shriller. Compromise and reconciliation of differences become more difficult to achieve. Each party pursues the politics of winning at any cost.[52] Gerrymandering, the high cost of campaigning, and incumbent privileges keep turnover low. Voters are turned off. A number of reforms could help change this picture.

First, since competitive elections tend to increase citizen interest and turnout, we could change practices that protect incumbents to level the playing field for challengers. Campaign spending reform would help to increase competition since most money flows to incumbents. Spending reform might range from allowing all candidates free media time to public financing for congressional contests much like that available for presidential candidates. Of course, spending reform would also decrease the perception of corruption among the public.

Nonpartisan redistricting might help as well. Officials should monitor experiments in states such as Arizona and constituents' views on national problems and seek consensus-based solutions.

Ultimately, making lawmakers more attentive to long-standing problems that citizens want resolved will require greater initiative and engagement by citizens themselves. While over 90 percent of Americans believe it is their duty to communicate with their representatives in Congress, only one-fifth have actually contacted their House member or one of their senators.[55] We already know from Chapter 7 that those who do communicate are not representative of the public at large. Instead, they represent the higher social and economic tiers of the population. As a result, lawmakers hear quite a lot about the concerns of the well-to-do but very little from the poor, children, or the uninsured.

We also need to place more attention on civic education beyond the ballot box. Students should learn not just the value of voting but also the value of following up with elected officials to check on their political investment. Don't assume that your vote communicates any information about your issue preferences. The only sure way for lawmakers to know what you think is for you to let them hear directly from you. Members of Congress do pay attention to constituents; after all, they are doing our business.

Montana that use nonpartisan redistricting commissions to draw Congressional boundaries to determine their impact on competitiveness. The current practice of partisan gerrymandering can discourage supporters of candidates who have little chance of winning against an entrenched incumbent within a secure district.[53] The current process also contributes to a lack of confidence in the legislative process, leading some commentators to conclude that citizens no longer pick their lawmakers—instead, lawmakers pick their constituents.[54]

Finally, greater use of national forums and the creative employment of new technologies could keep constituents and lawmakers in closer communication. As expanded availability of the Internet shrinks the digital divide, legislators could host electronic town meetings to gauge their

For REVIEW >>

1. What powers does Congress have?
   - Congress has enumerated powers in the areas of lawmaking, budgeting, and defense as well as implied powers granted by the elastic clause of the Constitution. The Senate has the additional powers of ratifying treaties and approving presidential appointments. The House can impeach federal officials; the Senate tries them.

2. What are some factors affecting election to Congress?
   - Factors affecting election to Congress include resources; incumbency; past performance; whether the election occurs in a presidential year when turnout is higher; and in the House, redistricting.

3. What are the keys to political power in Congress?
   - Political power in Congress flows from the committee system, party control, control of key positions of leadership, and command of parliamentary procedures.

National Journal

A Rookie Congressmen: Savvy, Minus the Seniority

Freshman Rep. Peter Welch, D-Vt., knew immediately who was calling when he picked up the phone in his congressional office a few days before last year's August recess. "Pee-tah," bellowed Sen. Bernie Sanders, I-Vt., "I need your help."

Sanders was asking his successor in the House to perform a daunting task—and with less than 24 hours' notice. He wanted Welch to add to the House version of a sweeping energy bill a Sanders amendment that encouraged universities to support energy-efficiency projects. The Senate had approved the proposal—which was of great interest to environmentally friendly Vermont—but House committees had dropped it. To help Sanders, Welch would have to bump up against Energy and Commerce Committee Chairman John Dingell, D-Mich., the dean of the House who is not accustomed to taking suggestions from the Senate, let alone from a newcomer in his own chamber.

"I had to get Chairman Dingell to be agreeable," Welch recounted in a recent interview. "He agreed that I could call his committee staff, though they objected [to adding Sanders's amendment] because they wanted more leverage in the conference committee with the Senate." Ultimately, Welch used the parliamentary leverage of the Rules Committee, on which he sits, to get the provision inserted into the House-passed package, and it was part of the broader energy bill enacted in December. He explained that the feat was possible because "I had built some relationship at the Rules Committee with Mr. Dingell, who is a very gracious man."

At a time when many freshman House Democrats are worrying about a tough re-election campaign—or are still trying to find their way around the Capitol—Welch acts like a veteran. He has drawn on his background as a lawyer who served two lengthy stretches in the Vermont Senate, including eight years as

president pro tem, to comfortably maneuver through Washington's legislative channels. He has already taken on substantial energy and environmental issues and procurement reforms that Speaker Nancy Pelosi, D-Calif., and committee chairmen have highlighted in their agenda.

"He's very smart, and he takes the initiative," Oversight and Government Reform Committee Chairman Henry Waxman, D-Calif., said of Welch. "He speaks with a great deal of authority. He has a very bright future."

A veteran House Democratic leadership aide added, "It's like [Welch] has been here for years. He is connected in every way. . . .

they described as an unintentional error, Welch said, "I don't totally trust the administration to get it right, and I'm skeptical of their explanation that this was, quote, a mistake."

Despite the administration's opposition, the House passed Welch's legislation by voice vote. Rep. Tom Davis, R-Va., the ranking member on the Oversight Committee, said he enjoyed working with Welch, and he praised the freshman's handling of the bill, including his willingness to accept some technical changes. "He is thoughtful, nice, and earnest," said a GOP aide who has watched Welch in action. "He clearly wants to learn and has respect for others' views."

At a time when many freshman House Democrats are worrying about a tough re-election campaign— or are still trying to find their way around the Capitol—Welch acts like a veteran.

He's always looking for something to do. He knows that it will help him to be involved."

Involved indeed. When Democrats regained control of Congress, they decided that as an inducement to serve on the Rules Committee, they would permit its members to serve on another prominent House committee as well. Welch used the opportunity to join Waxman's Oversight panel, which has wide-ranging investigative authority. The two have worked together on numerous issues.

Welch's influence was apparent, when the House passed his bill to close a potential loophole on government contracts. He initiated the measure after learning that the Justice Department had published a proposed regulation in November that would have exempted overseas contracts from federal reporting requirements. Even though Bush administration officials later acknowledged and fixed what

Welch, who recalls with nostalgia the less partisan tone of the Vermont Senate, said, "My goal is to protect taxpayers. And I have more confidence that will happen when there is bipartisan agreement." Although he succeeded a socialist, Sanders, in the House, Welch takes a more pragmatic, middle-of-the-road approach. His score in National Journal's 2007 vote ratings made him the 77th-most-liberal House member, while Sanders was the fourth-most-liberal senator.

Top Democrats took notice of Welch soon after he arrived in Washington. Only a few weeks after he was sworn in, he announced that he had become the first House member to make his congressional office carbon-neutral. By providing financial support for renewable-energy projects in Vermont, he said, he was offsetting the greenhouse-gas emissions generated by his D.C. office.

After Welch discussed his actions with Pelosi aides and with Dan Beard, the House's chief administrative officer, Pelosi and other Democratic leaders announced a "greening the Capitol" initiative last June to make Congress carbon-neutral. "Peter Welch has been a leader on this issue," Pelosi said in unveiling the plan. "The House must lead by example, and Congressman Welch exemplifies this key model."

Welch has been out front on two other major energy and environmental policy initiatives. Working with co-sponsors from California, he took the lead in September in urging the Environmental Protection Agency to grant California a waiver for its stricter tailpipe-emissions standards. That issue has generated significant attention in Vermont and other states that have adopted the California standard; Vermont's attorney general spearheaded a lawsuit against EPA after Administrator Stephen Johnson rejected the application.

More recently, Welch has provided talking points to party leaders to support their call for the president to stop filling the Strategic Petroleum Reserve, because of soaring gasoline prices. With Democratic Caucus Chairman Rahm Emanuel, D-Ill., and Rep. Edward Markey, D-Mass., who chairs the Select Committee on Energy Independence and Global Warming, Welch filed a bill in February to suspend purchases for the reserve. "We should stop paying record prices to top off a reserve that is nearly full," Welch said at the time. History shows that the result will be lower oil and gas prices."

In advocating his energy proposals, Welch has cited the onerous burden of high fuel prices on his home state and what he has called the "Enron loophole" that has allowed energy speculators to "rip off" his constituents who struggle to heat their homes each winter. "My work is all about Vermont," he said.

At the Rules Committee, Welch has managed 17 House rules, which govern floor deliberations on legislation by, for instance, setting the length of debate and the amendments allowed. The panel has long been viewed as a "leadership arm" where politically secure members perform vital housekeeping tasks on behalf of majority-party leaders. Given the leadership's increasingly centralized control, entrepreneurial panel members can be highly productive, as long as their efforts are politically attuned. As the leadership aide noted, the Rules Committee freshmen are "very valuable to the speaker."

While some might find it surprising that a freshman would exert influence at the committee, which was once the bastion of more-senior members, a notable generational shift has taken place on the panel. Rules Chairwoman Louise Slaughter, D-N.Y., is the only Democratic member who served there before the party lost its majority in 1994. Of the panel's eight other Democrats, four are freshmen, two joined the House after 2002, and the two others have served a bit more than a decade.

Republicans started the move toward putting junior lawmakers on Rules when they took control in 1995, although only one GOP member was then a freshman. Perhaps the GOP's most significant internal change at Rules came in 2005, when four veteran members departed to join Ways and Means, Energy and Commerce, and other more-influential House panels. Asked about the exodus from the supposedly prestigious panel, Rep. Deborah Pryce, R-Ohio, said at the time that sitting on the Rules Committee limits members because they "don't get involved as much in the substance" of legislation.

Some committee veterans have viewed these moves with dismay as a downgrading of the panel's influence. "The result is good for individual members, but it distracts from the prestige that the Rules Committee once had," said Don Wolfensberger, a former GOP chief of staff at Rules who is now director of the Congress Project at the Woodrow Wilson International Center for Scholars.

So far, the Rules Committee has clearly been "good" for Welch. But he is modest in refusing to discuss his prospects for advancing in the House. "This is a target-rich environment," he said. "I am philosophical. We work hard, and things will take care of themselves."

He reacted with mock horror to the suggestion that he might be in line to succeed either of his home-state senators, each of whom is several years older than he. "That gets me in trouble," Welch said. "I am very, very friendly with Patrick [Leahy] and Bernie. We have an excellent working relationship. . . . Patrick's seniority has been very helpful to me." In particular, Leahy, who chairs the Judiciary Committee, has told Welch that he enthusiastically supports his contractor-abuse measure and wants to secure Senate passage.

Although Welch noted, "I am old for a freshman," he said his age adds to his comfort level. "I am settled and I don't look at other rungs on the ladder." The death in 2004 of his wife, Joan Smith—who was a dean at the University of Vermont—after a long struggle with cancer "gave me perspective," he added. "She was from Chicago and she loved politics. She would love Congress." Welch appears to be drawing pleasure for the two of them.

FOR DISCUSSION: Will the informal legislative system in which seniority rules and influence are traded back and forth remain an inevitable aspect of Congress?

Will future newcomers to Congress experience similar difficulties in getting things done?

How would you navigate the complicated hierarchy of the House of Representatives to serve your constituents and push your agenda?

THE PRE

POWER AND PARADOX

POLITICAL CAPITAL: NOW YOU SEE IT, NOW YOU DON'T ▌ In 2004, George W. Bush captured three million more popular votes than his opponent, becoming the first president in sixteen years to win a majority of both popular and electoral votes. He also was the first in a long time who seemed to have **coattails**, as his Republican Party added four Senate seats and three House seats to its majorities in Congress. One could thus understand the exuberance he displayed at a press conference the day after his victory. "I earned capital in this campaign, political capital, and now I intend to spend it," Bush told reporters. "It is my style. When you win, there is . . . a feeling that the people have spoken and embraced your point of view." Bush added, "And that's what I intend to tell Congress, that I made it clear what I intend to do as the president; now let's work."[1]

The president wasted little time. Within weeks, he presented an ambitious second-term agenda to Congress and the American people. Bush called on Congress to make permanent the tax cuts he had secured during his first term, pushed forward with the unpopular ➡️

SIDENCY

of *Bush v. Gore* ended the recount process in Florida and gave the victory to Bush.

The 2000 election was just the most recent, and perhaps the most disturbing, example of the problems that can arise within our presidential election system. Anomalies such as these have caused some critics to wonder whether the Electoral College has outlived its usefulness and whether it has a dampening impact on political engagement today. Recent Gallup polls show that over 60 percent of the American people would support an amendment to replace the institution with the direct election of the president.[8]

battleground state
Competitive state where neither party holds an overwhelming edge.

express powers Powers granted to the president by the Constitution.

Electoral College Strategy Because the Electoral College, not the popular vote, determines the victor, candidates must devise a strategy to ensure that they gather the 270 electoral votes they need to win. This means candidates must determine which states are crucial for their success and plan their campaigns accordingly. First, each party must secure its "base" states, those that reliably vote for that party in general elections. Candidates rarely spend significant time or other resources in their opponents' strongholds. In recent elections, political observers referred to Republican base states as "red" states and Democratic base states as "blue" states. Red states are generally less populated but more numerous and are spread across the South and Midwest. The more heavily populated blue states are concentrated along the West Coast and in the Upper Midwest and Northeast.

Second, candidates must pick and choose **battleground states**—competitive states—where neither side has a major advantage—where they feel they have the best hope of success. As campaigns carefully piece together strategies that focus on the precise combination of states necessary to reach the 270-vote mark, both candidates will be eyeing the battleground states. The number of contested states today has fallen well below the twenty-four considered up for grabs in 1960 and the twenty-two considered swing states in 1992. Some studies have shown that the shrinking battleground map can have damaging effects on political engagement, because turnout tends to be lower in noncompetitive states.[9]

In 2008, both Barack Obama and John McCain set out to change the electoral map by expanding the number of battleground states and trying to pick up states traditionally won by the opposing party. Obama campaigned hard in formerly Republican territory in Colorado, Nevada, North Carolina, and Virginia. McCain turned his attention to the Democratic-leaning states of Michigan, Minnesota, and Pennsylvania. Both candidates continued to pay close atention to Ohio and Florida, where recent presidential contests had been won or lost.

Each candidate went into the fall campaign with strengths and weaknesses at a time when the mounting financial crisis generated voter anxiety. McCain was favored by voters who cited experience and readiness to lead in times of crisis. Obama showed support among voters who believed he understood middle class needs for health care reform and economic security. Surveys of those who watched the three presidential debates believed that Obama did a better job and improved his image as a thoughtful leader. Some McCain supporters, however, faulted McCain for choosing a running mate they believed was unready to assume the presidency if the need arose. On the Democratic side, there was worry about a "Bradley Effect," a term referencing a candidate for governor of California whose lead in the polls evaporated on Election Day, apparently because many white voters told pollsters what they thought the pollsters wanted to hear instead of their real voting intentions.

Obama had two very big advantages over McCain. First, since he did not accept public financing, he could continue to raise and spend virtually unlimited sums of money. In September, he broke all previous records by taking in over $150 million. By contrast, McCain was limited to the publicly provided sum of $84 million for the general election campaign, although he could also count on the Republican National Committee to spend on his behalf. Nevertheless, Obama's fundraising advantage allowed him to pour millions into advertising. For example, according to the Federal Election Commission, Obama and Democratic party committees that supported his effort spent nearly $105 million from October 1 to October 15 alone. McCain and Republican party entities, by contrast, spent just over $25 million. Obama's media buys included spending in traditional

The Shrinking Battleground

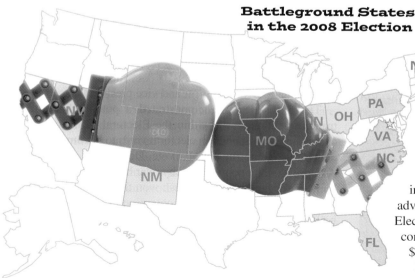

**Battleground States
in the 2008 Election**

Republican strongholds like Indiana, forcing McCain to spread his scarce resources thin just to maintain visibility. In late October, Obama bought half-hour slots on prime time network TV (at a total cost of over $4 million) to present his closing arguments. Neither campaign received substantial ad support from outside groups like 527 organizations, partly because of bad publicity and fines levied in earlier campaigns, but also because both McCain and Obama discouraged such spending on their behalf.

Secondly, the Obama campaign built a formidable ground operation during the long primary season that it resurrected in September and relied upon heavily in the final weeks of the campaign. More than 700 offices were opened in battleground states, operated by paid staff who organized thousands of volunteers neighborhood by neighborhood. Unlike John Kerry, who in 2004 relied on outside groups to get out the vote, Obama utilized locally recruited citizens to canvass their own neighborhoods—an approach that has shown to be far more effective. While Republicans had employed the same techniques in 2004 and again in 2008, the Obama effort dwarfed those of their Republican counterparts. In addition, Obama made effecrive use of new technologies by collecting the e-mail addresses and cell phone numbers of thousands of young people who attended his campaign events and then sending them periodic messages about how they could help.

Perhaps the most important advantage for Obama, however, was the financial crisis and quickly deteriorating state of the U.S. economy. Obama could point to McCain's record of support for Republican initiatives which many believed contributed to the crisis. The Republican candidate faced an almost insurmountable hurdle being associated with the policies of a very unpopular president.

PRESIDENTIAL POWER

The American presidency has evolved into the most powerful post in the world. Effectively exercising this awesome power requires the ability to diagnose problems, assert priorities, work cooperatively with others, recruit support from other decision makers, shepherd policies through a giant bureaucracy, and communicate effectively to the public. The

Presidential powers are both real and ceremonial. The nation looks to the president for leadership in times of crisis.

potential for failure is high, particularly when opponents place roadblocks in the president's path. It is no wonder that Franklin D. Roosevelt, considered to be the architect of the modern presidency, once called the presidency a lonely job. "If you are president," he once commented to an advisor, "you'll be looking at the door over there and knowing that practically everybody that walks through it wants something out of you."

As we discussed earlier, the Framers were wary of executive power. As a result, the Constitution gives presidents few **express powers**, or explicit grants of authority, and constrains them through a system of checks and balances. Congress can also cede powers to the executive that enable the president to enforce laws. Modern presidents use these **delegated powers** to enact a great deal of legislation. When Congress authorizes a clean air law, for example, it does not specify the quantity of pollutants smokestacks may release into the atmosphere. Instead, it delegates to the executive branch the authority to make rules specifying such matters.

The president may also exercise **discretionary powers** associated with carrying out official duties. Presidents have used their discretionary power to claim extensive authority, especially during times of war or national emergency. After the September 11, 2001, terrorist attacks, President Bush issued a number of directives in the name of national security to protect the homeland. For example, he authorized the CIA to engage in political assassination of named terrorists, effectively lifting a 25-year ban on such activities. And he authorized the Treasury Department to freeze assets of alleged terrorists.[10] The president must learn how best to use this mix of express, delegated, and discretionary powers in fulfilling the various roles of the office.

> **delegated powers** Powers ceded by Congress to the president.
>
> **discretionary powers** Powers the president assumes, giving him greater authority and flexibility in performing the duties of office.

Chief Executive

As the nation's chief executive officer, the president oversees a vast bureaucracy that administers countless programs on which millions of Americans depend. Virtually every citizen has an interest in the efficient operation of the federal agencies the president oversees. Yet the scope of the federal government is so vast that a single person cannot hope to personally manage all of its affairs. The president exercises the power of appointment to hire people to run the day-to-day operations of government and to assist in broader duties, such as budgeting and law enforcement. The president may also issue executive orders to achieve policy goals in the absence of legislation, a long-standing yet controversial practice.

Appointment Even our earliest presidents appointed a substantial number of persons to government jobs. George Washington filled over one thousand positions from customs collector to surveyor, usually on the basis of statements attesting to the candidate's good character and moral virtue.[11]

The president is free to choose the leaders for top administrative posts, known as the cabinet, but must seek the **advice and consent** of the Senate for their approval. Senate committees subject nominees to extensive screening and hearing procedures before the entire body votes on confirmation. The president sometimes personally introduces nominees to senators or solicits suggestions from powerful Senate leaders. The Senate has rejected few presidential nominees in the modern era. Senators are reluctant to reject the president's preferred choice for a post unless they believe the nominee is genuinely unfit for service. When the Senate does block a nominee, the president may respond by waiting until Congress goes into recess and then appointing the nominee without Senate approval. Such **recess appointments** are effective only until the end of the next Senate session. President Bush used this tactic in 2005 to appoint his choice for U.N. Ambassador, John Bolton, whose sharp criticism of the world body prompted a Senate filibuster. Bolton withdrew his name from consideration when Congress reconvened, rather than face intense scrutiny by the new, Democratic-controlled Senate.

Presidential selection and Senate confirmation of court nominees have been somewhat more controversial, especially in recent years. We will discuss this process more extensively in Chapter 14. The Constitution grants department heads and other government officers the power to make lower-level agency appointments, but a staggering number—between 50,000 and 100,000—are subject to Senate approval, although most of these are routine low-level appointments handled in large batches.[12]

Budgeting Although the Constitution gives Congress the power to control the purse strings, presidents have taken the initiative in proposing and implementing budgetary priorities. Before 1921, each federal agency submitted a separate budget request directly to the House of Representatives. To impose order on this chaotic process, Congress passed the Budget and Accounting Act of 1921, which required the president to coordinate the budget and submit to Congress annual estimates of program costs. The Office of Management and Budget (OMB, originally the Bureau of the Budget) assists the president in generating budget requests and monitoring expenditures. The OMB reviews agency requests, clears policy recommendations, ensures that agency expenditures and policies conform to the president's priorities, and guides the president's agenda through Washington's bureaucratic maze.[13]

The increased budgetary authority of the executive branch has given presidents immense power to control the political agenda but has also generated heated battles with Congress, which must authorize spending. Until 1974, for example, the president could rein in congressional spending by **impoundment**, or withholding of funds. Responding to what it considered the Nixon administration's overtly partisan use of this tool, Congress placed severe limits on the president's authority to withhold funds already appropriated. Several presidents have sought the power to exercise a **line item veto**, the authority to slice individual programs from budgets passed by Congress. Governors in most states already have such authority. However, the Supreme Court held that enacting such a change in presidential power requires a constitutional amendment, a lengthy and politically difficult process.[14]

Law Enforcement Under the Constitution, Congress makes the laws, the president enforces the laws, and the courts interpret them and have a say over how executive departments enforce them. Traditionally, law enforcement has been the province of state and local government, but as the federal government has grown and assumed greater responsibilities, the federal executive has played an ever-larger role in law enforcement. Today, executive agencies enforce not only criminal laws but also laws affecting public health, business regulation, and civil rights, among a host of other areas.

The executive branch attempted to strengthen and centralize its control over federal law enforcement in the wake of the 2001 terrorist attacks. A congressional commission

advice and consent Process by which the president seeks Senate approval of certain political appointees.

recess appointment Political appointment made by the president when Congress is out of session.

impoundment Presidential refusal to expend funds appropriated by Congress.

line item veto Power, enjoyed by state governors, to reject a portion of a bill, usually a budget appropriation.

Washington filled over one thousand positions . . . usually on the basis of statements attesting to the candidate's good character and moral virtue.

investigating the attacks found that existing criminal law made it difficult, and sometimes impossible, for federal law enforcement agencies to share pertinent information regarding ongoing terrorist investigations. The commission proposed a number of steps to break down interagency barriers. These included creating a National Terrorism Center to coordinate intelligence about potential terrorist attacks and establishing a new Office of the Director of

issued by President George W. Bush (Executive Order 13440, issued in July 2007) exempts captured Taliban, Al Qaeda, and foreign fighters in Iraq from protections of the Third Geneva Convention and authorizes the CIA to use interrogation techniques more severe than those used by military personnel. Some members of Congress object that the order would allow the use of "waterboarding," or simulated drowning, which some claim amounts to torture. The courts

Lincoln reacted to the Confederate attack on Fort Sumter by . . . suspending habeus corpus, and trying civilians in military courts. . . .

National Intelligence to oversee intelligence from a variety of agencies.[15] More controversially, changes in the surveillance of domestic citizens passed under the USA Patriot Act allowed the government to seek records of library and video store rentals by "persons of interest" without their knowledge. Congress passed the legislation in 2001 and reauthorized it in 2006, revising some sections that civil liberties activists found particularly objectionable.

In addition to the power to enforce the law, the president also holds the power to pardon convicted criminals. This power can be far-reaching, as demonstrated by President Gerald Ford's decision to pardon Richard Nixon after the Watergate scandal. More recently, President Bush commuted a portion of the sentence requiring prison time for vice presidential aide Lewis "Scooter" Libby, who was convicted of lying to a grand jury about a news leak regarding a CIA operative. The action drew criticism from Democrats. Despite the controversial nature of the pardon power, the Constitution does not limit it or require that the president share it with any other branch.

Executive Orders A president may issue **executive orders**, decrees with the force of law but not requiring legislative approval, for a variety of reasons. Although the Constitution does not define these orders, presidents have construed them as lawful instruments for carrying out constitutionally defined executive duties. The president issues executive orders most frequently to establish executive branch agencies, modify bureaucratic rules or actions, change decision-making procedures, or give substance and force to statutes.[16] Presidents also use them during times of crisis to carry out actions deemed essential to national security. Woodrow Wilson, for example, issued nearly two thousand such decrees during World War I.

Many of these orders are mundane, dealing with bureaucratic organization. Others are used to mollify interest groups. Bill Clinton used Executive Order (EO) 12836 to strengthen assurances for minority and union labor in federal hiring that had been weakened during the previous Bush administration. George W. Bush, who succeeded Clinton as president, used Executive Order 13201 to countermand Clinton's EO 12836 in response to complaints by some business groups.

Some executive orders break new legal ground and are highly controversial. One of the over 250 executive orders

see executive orders as a legitimate executive tool, but their use remains controversial. James Madison believed that executive orders threatened the separation of powers by allowing presidents to make their own laws. Nevertheless, Congress can pass laws limiting discretionary presidential action, and public opinion can limit the lengths to which a president will go before incurring the voters' wrath.

Commander in Chief

The Framers understood that the president must have the power to defend the nation and command the troops in times of conflict, but they disagreed about giving the president the power to make war. They compromised by permitting the chief executive to act to repel invasions but not to initiate war.[17] Article II, Section 2 of the Constitution reflects this compromise but has sowed confusion because of its ambiguity.

Although Congress has the constitutional power to declare war (see Chapter 11), it has done so formally only five times.[18] In most of the conflicts in which the nation has been involved, the president has asserted the authority to act in response to a perceived crisis. Abraham Lincoln, for example, reacted to the Confederate attack on Fort Sumter by raising troops, imposing naval blockades on southern ports, suspending habeas corpus, and trying civilians in military courts—acts that extend presidential power beyond constitutional limits. He failed to convene Congress for months and received support for his actions only retroactively. He agonized over the dilemma but concluded that "measures otherwise unconstitutional might become lawful by becoming indispensable to the preservation of the nation."[19]

Presidents usually can count on wide public support during times of war or when U.S. interests are attacked, a phenomenon known as **rallying around the flag**. The public is willing to give the president a free hand for only a limited time, however. For example, Americans expressed strong support for President George W. Bush's retaliatory attack on Afghanistan after the September 11, 2001, terror-

> **executive order** A decree with the force of law but not requiring legislative approval.
>
> **rallying around the flag** Sense of patriotism engendered by dramatic national events such as the September 11, 2001, terrorist attacks.

ist attacks. He met with more resistance, however, in the lead-up to the war in Iraq. The revelation that Iraq had no weapons of mass destruction—compounded by mounting U.S. casualties—led to a precipitous drop in public support for the operation.

During times of crisis, the president may assume **emergency powers** to protect the nation, but their use is controversial and has led to conflicts over the preservation of civil liberties. Following the U.S. invasion of Afghanistan in 2002, President Bush declared that military tribunals, not civilian courts, would try all **enemy combatants** captured in battle, whether or not they were members of a national army. Prisoners were not allowed to hear the charges against them and had no access to attorneys. The Supreme Court in 2004 (*Hamdi v. Rumsfeld*) responded to a petition filed on behalf of a prisoner of American descent by holding that the prisoner was entitled to consult with an attorney and to contest his imprisonment before a neutral decision maker. In a companion case, *Rasul v. Bush*, the Court held that foreign-born detainees can also challenge their detention in U.S. courts.

After these decisions, the administration set up military review boards where detainees could challenge their enemy combatant status, and Congress approved the procedures with passage of the Detainee Treatment Act of 2005, which also stripped detainees of access to federal courts to review their cases. Once again, the Supreme Court, in *Hamdan v. Rumsfeld* (2006), ruled against administration actions, arguing that the military commissions violated international law and that the Detainee Treatment Act did not cover pending cases. The administration could not proceed without additional congressional authorization. In response to *Hamdan*, Congress quickly passed the Military Commissions Act of 2006, which stripped federal district courts of their authority to hear any detainee challenges, *including those that had already been filed.* The law also set up a process by which detainees would be tried before commissions that could consider hearsay evidence and evidence obtained through coercion. Once again, the Supreme Court, in *Boumediene v. Bush* (2008), rejected these procedures, ruling that Guantanamo detainees have a constitutional right under habeas corpus to go to court to challenge their detention. If Congress intends to suspend

emergency powers Wide-ranging powers a president may exercise during times of crisis, or those powers permitted the president by Congress for a limited time.

enemy combatant Enemy fighter captured on the field of battle whether or not a member of an army.

extraordinary rendition The practice of secretly abducting terror suspects and transporting them to detention camps in undisclosed locations.

The practice of holding enemy combatants for years without trial at Guantanamo Bay prison has stirred controversy over the president's use of emergency powers.

habeas corpus—something the Constitution does allow it to do—it must provide the accused with a more adequate substitute than the one provided in the Military Commission Act. Writing for the majority, Justice Anthony Kennedy said, "The laws and Constitution are designed to survive, and remain in force, in extraordinary times." In a stinging dissent, Justice Antonin Scalia argued that providing detainees with access to the courts "will almost certainly cause more Americans to be killed."[20] The rights of detainees still have not been firmly established, only their right to challenge their status. No doubt the matter of how to treat individuals captured in the nation's war on terrorism will continue to be fought out in the courts in coming years.

Another controversial practice employed in connection with the war on terrorism was **extraordinary rendition**, or secretly abducting terrorist suspects and transporting them to detention camps in undisclosed locations. Critics assert that the United States deprives these suspects of due process and that interrogators at the camps torture them. The controversies these measures raise about presidential powers in wartime are unlikely to be resolved any time soon.

Chief Diplomat

The Constitution directs the president to share with the Senate responsibility for making treaties and with Congress the conduct of diplomacy. Historically, however, the president has taken the lead and Congress has then reacted to that decision. Among the tools of foreign policy at the president's disposal are diplomatic recognition, presidential doctrines, executive agreements, and summit meetings. **Diplomatic recognition** of foreign officials by a president, an extension of the Constitution's authorization to receive ambassadors and other public officials (Article II, Section 3), can elevate the world status of a nation and entitle it to certain benefits, such as expanded trade. Often, recognition is contentious, especially when it involves former enemies. The United States did not recognize the Republic of Vietnam, for example, until 1995, more than twenty years after the termination of hostilities.

Presidential doctrines are formal statements that outline the goals or purposes of American foreign policy and the actions the United States is prepared to take in advancing these goals. Presidential doctrines have a venerable history. Perhaps the most famous is the Monroe Doctrine, issued by President James Monroe in 1823 in response to colonial expansion by European powers. The Monroe Doctrine has become a foundation on which other presidents have built to define America's interests and role in the world. It asserts the intention of the United States to resist any attempt by a European power to interfere in the affairs of any country in the Western Hemisphere not already a colony. Theodore Roosevelt added the Roosevelt Corollary in 1904, announcing our nation's intention to act as this hemisphere's policeman if needed to protect neighbor nations. The Roosevelt Corollary was used to justify U.S. intervention in Latin America. President Harry Truman offered the Truman Doctrine as the foreign policy credo of the Cold War, calling for the United States to support free people who are resisting subjugation anywhere in the world. Presidents Eisenhower, Nixon, Carter, and Reagan issued similar doctrines asserting our right to defend other regions of the world, including the Middle East and the Persian Gulf.

In the wake of the September 11, 2001, terrorist attacks, George W. Bush declared a doctrine of preemptive self-defense. According to the highly controversial **Bush Doctrine**, the nation's right of self-defense entitles the United States to attack an enemy it feels presents an imminent threat to national security, even if the enemy has not attacked first. In 2003, the Bush administration utilized this doctrine to justify invading Iraq, arguing that its weapons of mass destruction constituted

> **diplomatic recognition** Presidential power to offer official privileges to foreign governments.
>
> **presidential doctrine** Formal statement that outlines the goals and purposes of American foreign policy and the actions to take to advance these goals.
>
> **Bush Doctrine** Foreign policy position advanced by George W. Bush asserting the U.S. government's right to authorize preemptive attacks against potential aggressors.

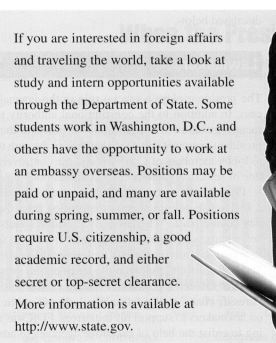

If you are interested in foreign affairs and traveling the world, take a look at study and intern opportunities available through the Department of State. Some students work in Washington, D.C., and others have the opportunity to work at an embassy overseas. Positions may be paid or unpaid, and many are available during spring, summer, or fall. Positions require U.S. citizenship, a good academic record, and either secret or top-secret clearance. More information is available at http://www.state.gov.

get involved!

13

BUREAU

CITIZENS AS OWNERS AND CONSUMERS

KATRINA AND THE SLOW FEDERAL BUREAUCRATIC RESPONSE ▌ In late August 2005, Hurricane Katrina—the nation's worst natural disaster in over a century—struck the Gulf Coast. Water driven by Katrina's high winds overtopped or broke three levees protecting New Orleans and poured into the city's neighborhoods. Thousands of residents, mostly African American and poor, were unable to evacuate. Many escaped the rising water by climbing on their roofs and awaiting rescue. Hundreds lost their lives.

The mayor opened the city's sports arena, the Superdome, to provide a safe haven from the storm, but it soon became a nightmare for the refugees. The air conditioning and lights failed; the facility lost running water and the toilets overflowed. At least two rapes occurred, as anarchy reigned inside and outside the famous facility. Looting was rampant and in some outrageous instances, the police joined in the plunder.

Colonel Tim Tarchick of the Air Force Reserve Command contacted several federal agencies, including the Federal Emergency Management Agency (FEMA), to get permission to fly rescue helicopters into the disaster zone as soon as the storm abated. FEMA, the national agency assigned to handle disasters, told Tarchick that it could ➥

UCRACY

As You READ >>

- What is the federal bureaucracy?
- Who are federal bureaucrats and what do they do?
- What are the sources and limits of bureaucratic power?

The national government's problems involving its response to Hurricane Katrina included FEMA's slow provision of trailers for refugees that later were proven to be unsafe once they were delivered.

Hot or Not?

Does the federal government do a good job of responding to natural disasters?

not authorize his mission. After more than a day, the Defense Department finally gave him clearance to rescue hundreds of people from rooftops.[1]

The director of FEMA, Michael Brown, became the lightning rod for agency criticism after his remarks to the media left the impression that he was ignorant of the situation in New Orleans. Public disapproval of Brown increased after the revelation that he lacked any training in emergency relief and that he owed his appointment to political cronyism. Although President Bush initially praised Brown's performance, he soon called Brown out of the disaster area.[2] Brown resigned three days later, but the incident seriously weakened the president's standing with the public.

The slow response to Katrina undermined the president's claim that he was the best person to lead the nation in times of crisis. When the hurricane struck, Bush was just completing a five-week vacation, raising questions about how engaged he was. The president made several trips to New Orleans and announced a federal government plan to send $62.3 billion to the tattered Gulf Coast area, but the damage was already done. By late 2005, Bush's approval rating had fallen to 38 percent.

The plight of the hurricane victims and their treatment by the government did not improve over time. First, those made homeless by Katrina had to wait months—and sometimes years—for FEMA to supply them with trailers for temporary housing. Compounding the injury, the walls and cabinets of the trailers were made from formaldehyde-containing particleboard. Many residents began reporting respiratory problems resembling those associated with formaldehyde poisoning. Formaldehyde can cause lung problems, exacerbate asthma, and pose a risk of cancer. An oversight hearing conducted by the House Committee and Government Reform Committee later revealed that FEMA attorneys in 2006 had recommended against testing the trailers for fear of the agency's incurring legal liability.

The national government's response to the Katrina disaster highlights several realities. First, our expectations about the national government have grown immensely. Early citizens expected the government to collect taxes, deliver the mail, and little else—certainly not to rescue them from natural disasters. Second, a large and complex bureaucracy provides the government services that affect the lives of many citizens. The bureaucracy includes all the offices and people who work in the executive branch of government. They interact with Americans more than elected government officials do, and these interactions often lead to complaints about discourtesy, inefficiency, and even dishonesty among government bureaucrats. Finally, the president is ultimately responsible for the conduct of the bureaucracy, and he and other lawmakers have some control mechanisms to influence its behavior.

Federal **bureaucrats** today exercise a great deal of power through their ability to make rules that determine how the government implements laws, as well as their authority to mediate disputes. The increased significance of the bureaucracy reflects political life in the twenty-first century. For interest groups, bureaucracy has become a target of lobbying in an effort to shape agency policies for private benefit. For public officials, bureaucracy is often a convenient scapegoat when policies go awry. For citizens, bureaucracy is increasingly treated like a business that is expected to provide reliable service even while keeping costs, and the taxes that fund them, low. Some scholars worry that we are becoming a nation that treats government like just another provider of services, rather than a nation of citizens who own the government and use it for public purposes. ◄►

BUREAUCRATIC CHANGES AND EVOLVING CIVIC LIFE

The bureaucracy has changed dramatically both in size and in the manner in which government agencies are staffed. During the 1790s, fewer people worked for the national government than worked at President Washington's Mount Vernon home.[3] The Framers presumed that the tasks of the

The greatest surge in federal bureaucratic growth occurred in response to the Great Depression of the 1930s.

national government would be rather limited, so they did not envision the need for a large bureaucracy. By 1800, there were still fewer than three thousand civilian employees working for the federal government.

Growth of Bureaucracy

The federal bureaucracy began to expand rapidly following the Civil War, and the pace of growth accelerated during the latter part of the nineteenth century as various groups began to lobby Congress for the promo-

bureaucrats The civilian employees of the national government who are responsible for implementing federal laws.

14

THE COURTS

JUDICIAL POWER IN A DEMOCRATIC SETTING

SELECTION OF A CHIEF JUSTICE ∎ As the United States Supreme Court neared the end of its term in late June 2005, it notified the White House to expect word of a Court retirement. The news was not surprising, because for weeks many observers had been anticipating the retirement of the ailing Chief Justice, William Rehnquist. However, when the president opened a sealed envelope the next day from the Supreme Court's chief marshal, he found out that Associate Justice Sandra Day O'Connor was retiring—not the chief justice. O'Connor informed the president she would remain on the Court until the Senate approved a replacement.

O'Connor's retirement presented President George W. Bush with a defining moment to change the course of Supreme Court decision making for decades to come. The closely divided Court had not experienced a vacancy for eleven years, the longest time between vacancies in the history of the nine-member tribunal. Having waited a period of four and a half years for the opportunity to name a new justice, the president and his staff already had a list of possible successors. There was much speculation that more women were being added to the list so that a woman could be selected to replace the first female Supreme Court justice in the nation's history. First Lady, Laura Bush, said, "I would really like him to name another woman," in an interview on the *Today* show.

Less than three weeks after the announcement of the vacancy, President Bush nominated Judge John Roberts, Jr., of the federal appeals court of the D.C. Circuit. The White House then immediately began a campaign to sell the nomination to the United States Senate and the American public. The formal announcement was made from the White House during prime time for maximum exposure. Administration officials went on various news programs to underscore the brilliance and good nature of the nominee. Liberal and conservative interests weighed in with their views of Roberts, as did hundreds of bloggers.

Amid the furor, fate intervened when Chief Justice Rehnquist died on September 4, 2005. Now the president had an additional vacancy to fill. He quickly nominated Roberts as chief justice and decided to fill the O'Connor seat only after Roberts was confirmed. The new nomination meant that Roberts was neither replacing a woman nor a swing justice. These facts, in addition to Roberts's record, led to an easy Senate confirmation. The president then named Harriet Miers, a ➥

- What is the nature of the judicial process?
- How are Supreme Court justices selected?
- What is the nature of Supreme Court decision making?

White House lawyer and friend of the Bush family, to replace Sandra Day O'Connor. Her nomination went much less smoothly. Mounting criticism, particularly from conservative groups, forced her to withdraw her name, and Bush nominated federal appeals judge Samuel Alito to replace O'Connor. The Senate ultimately confirmed Alito by a vote of 58 to 42.

It is not surprising that the Roberts nomination garnered so much attention among politicians and political interest groups. The Supreme Court has become a powerful national institution that defines the basic freedoms American citizens enjoy. It is the institution most likely to determine the extent of the personal rights that have become a focus of modern American democracy. Members of the Supreme Court exercise considerable political power, but they do so in a different manner than members of Congress, the president, and bureaucrats. Their ability to affect the lives of citizens has heightened public interest in their selection and in the ways they make decisions. Their prominence has also created new opportunities for citizens to interact with the Court. ◄•

Today, nominees to the Supreme Court, like Samuel Alito (shown here), must testify before the Senate Judiciary Committee before being confirmed by the Senate.

NATIONAL COURT STRUCTURE

The national court structure first began to take on its present look with the passage of the Judiciary Act of 1789. The Constitution provided for just the Supreme Court and "such inferior courts as the Congress may from time to time ordain and establish." Once the Constitution was ratified, the Congress moved quickly to establish a complete national judiciary, including trial courts and other appellate courts. At this time, each state government already had its own system of courts. The existence of one national court system and separate court systems in each of the states is known as a **dual court system**. Citizens of any state are subject to the jurisdiction of both state courts and national courts.

The first bill introduced in the Senate dealt with the unresolved issue of national inferior courts. After considerable debate, Congress passed the law that led to the foundation of the current judicial system. It created a three-tier system of national courts. At the base were 13 district courts, each presided over by a single distinct judge. In the middle were circuit courts located in every district. Each circuit court was composed of two Supreme Court justices and one district judge. The country was divided into an Eastern, a Middle, and a Southern Circuit. Two justices were assigned to each circuit and traveled to the various courts located within that circuit. At the top of the national structure was the Supreme Court, consisting of a chief justice and five associate justices.

Currently there is a division of responsibilities between the national court system and the state court systems. Most cases that begin in a state court system are resolved in that system. The only way a case can move from a state court system to the national system is by an appeal from the state's highest court to the United States Supreme Court. Appeals may not move in the opposite direction. A case that begins in the national court system will be resolved in that system. For the most part, state and national courts have separate jurisdiction. A few cases, such as diversity suits (civil cases that involve parties from different states) brought for amounts greater than $75,000, may be initiated in either system. Once the case is initiated, however, it must stay in that system except for a possible appeal from the state system to the United States Supreme Court. See the figure below showing the American dual court structure.

> **dual court system** System under which U.S. citizens are subject to the jurisdiction of both national and state courts.

District Courts

Today, the national court system includes ninety-four U.S. district courts. Each state contains at least one district court, and no district court crosses state lines. U.S. district courts are trial courts; they represent the entryway to the national court system. District courts typically deal with cases involving the violation of federal labor, civil rights, Social Security, truth-in-lending, federal crimes, and anti-

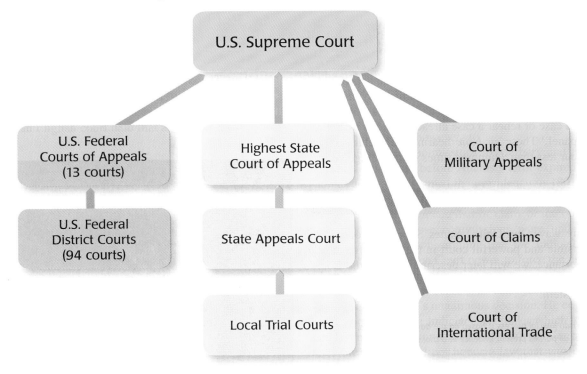

Diagram of the U.S. Court System

- U.S. Supreme Court
  - U.S. Federal Courts of Appeals (13 courts)
    - U.S. Federal District Courts (94 courts)
  - Highest State Court of Appeals
    - State Appeals Court
      - Local Trial Courts
  - Court of Military Appeals
  - Court of Claims
  - Court of International Trade

to the Constitution, it had no power to force Jefferson to honor the appointment. Marshall ruled that the Court had a duty to declare laws null and void if they conflicted with the Constitution, establishing the precedent of Court oversight on congressional statutes.

class action suit Lawsuit in which one or more persons sue on behalf of a larger set of people claiming the same injury.

jurisdiction The power of a court to hear and decide cases.

justiciability The doctrine that excludes certain cases from judicial consideration because of the party bringing the lawsuit or the nature of the subject matter.

original jurisdiction The power of a court to hear and decide a case first.

appellate jurisdiction The power of a court to receive cases from trial courts for the purpose of reviewing whether the legal procedures were properly followed.

standing Proof that a party has suffered harm or been threatened with harm by the circumstances surrounding a lawsuit.

political questions Issues determined by the Supreme Court to be better resolved by Congress or the president.

Civil and Criminal Law

The two basic types of law under the American judicial system are civil law and criminal law. Civil law involves disputes between private parties over such matters as contracts, personal injuries, family law, and the buying and selling of property. The parties may be individuals, business corporations, or governments acting in a private capacity. Criminal law involves the prosecution of individuals who commit acts that are prohibited by the government.

The party who initiates a civil case is the *plaintiff*. The person against whom the lawsuit is brought is the *defendant*. Some types of civil law use the terms *petitioner* and *respondent* instead. Some civil cases may have multiple plaintiffs, multiple defendants, or both. In some situations, plaintiffs may bring a case known as a **class action suit**, in which one or more persons sue on behalf of a larger set of people who share the same situation. The Supreme Court writes the rules that determine how easy or how difficult it is to qualify for a class action suit. The party that initiates criminal cases is the government. The government is the plaintiff in criminal cases, because the government considers crime to be a violation of the interests of society as a whole, not just those of an individual or group.

Judicial Requirements

The judicial requirements of **jurisdiction** and **justiciability** limit the types of cases that a particular court can hear. Jurisdiction is the power of the court to hear and decide cases. The Constitution grants the United States Supreme Court **original jurisdiction** in cases involving ambassadors or states suing other states, and **appellate jurisdiction** in cases involving federal law, cases involving citizens from one state suing citizens from another state (diversity suits), or cases in which the federal government is a litigant.

Justiciability is a less precise term than *jurisdiction*. Chief Justice Earl Warren once referred to [justiciability] as one of "the most amorphous [concepts] in the entire domain of public law."[4] Basically, it means that a court can exclude certain cases from judicial consideration because of the identity of the party bringing the lawsuit or the subject of the lawsuit. For a lawsuit to meet the standard of justiciability, the party bringing the case must have **standing**. That is, the defendant's actions must either harm the plaintiff or threaten the plaintiff with harm. In other words, a litigant must demonstrate a personal stake in the outcome of the case. The Court can make litigation more available to citizens by relaxing

Julia Roberts's movie role as Erin Brockovich demonstrated how courts encourage civic engagement through litigation by allowing class action suits.

May It Please the Court

Access to the United States Supreme Court

Jurisdiction	**The power of the U.S. Supreme Court to hear the particular types of cases.**
Federal questions	A lawsuit that involves a federal statute, treaty, or the United States Constitution.
Federal party	A lawsuit in which the federal government is either the plaintiff or defendant.
Diversity of citizenship	A civil lawsuit that involves parties from different states in which the dollar amount exceeds $75,000.
Justiciability	**The exclusion of certain lawsuits to the party bringing the case or the subject of the lawsuit.**
Standing	The party bringing the lawsuit must have suffered real harm.
Mootness	The controversy is no longer alive by the time it reaches the Court.
Political question	The Court will not resolve cases more properly resolved by Congress or the president.
Class Action Suits	**The ability of a litigant to bring a lawsuit on behalf of a larger set of people who share the same situation.**
Amicus curiae briefs	**Interest groups can submit their views to the Court even though they are not parties to the lawsuit.**

the standards of standing. The Supreme Court has ruled, for instance, that federal taxpayers have standing to challenge the constitutionality of federal programs if they can show that a specific expenditure of tax monies violates the Constitution.[5]

The federal courts also will not hear cases that involve **political questions**. The Supreme Court has acknowledged that other branches of the federal government are better equipped to address this class of constitutional issues. The concept, however, is flexible; at one time, the Court said the issue of political reapportionment was a political question,[6] but it later reversed itself in *Baker v. Carr*.[7] A summary of the principles that permit access to the Supreme Court are presented in the table above.

Real Cases and Controversies

When trial judges confront legal questions in the context of a case, they or a jury must first determine the facts of the case, which are not always self-evident. The judicial process in the United States uses the adversary system to ascertain the truth, in which two opposing parties both present their own interpretation of the facts. An impartial third party, a judge or jury, has the responsibility of choosing between the two alternative versions of the facts. When Supreme Court justices receive a case, lower courts have already determined the facts. The job of the Supreme Court justices is to match the facts with the relevant law. When determining the law, the Court may interpret the meaning of a constitutional provision or a statutory provision. Either process allows the justices more discretion than might be imagined, because the meaning of these provisions is often subject to a variety of interpretations.

litigious Marked by a tendency to file lawsuits.

America is a **litigious** society that increasingly looks to the courts to resolve its disputes.[8] Americans file more lawsuits per capita than the citizens of Japan, Italy, Spain, Germany, and Sweden, but about the same as counterparts in England and Denmark.[9] As more cases are filed in the courts, the Supreme Court has more opportunity to choose which cases to hear on appeal. Congress also has made the courts more accessible to Americans with the passage of legislation that makes it easier to pay for litigation. The 1964 Civil Rights Act allows private citizens who file discrimination claims to collect their attorney's fees from the defendant if they win. Other legislation makes it easier for victims of gender bias and consumer fraud to press their claims in court. Ultimately, however, lower court decisions may be subject to Supreme Court review, and they must clear this hurdle to remain in force.

CHANGING NATURE OF THE SUPREME COURT

The United States had no national judiciary under the Articles of Confederation.[10] It was not until the nation adopted the Constitution in 1787 that the Supreme Court came into existence as an independent and permanent court.[11] At the time, it was the object of much popular suspicion from citizens who feared the power of a national court. Alexander Hamilton was quick to assure readers, in the *The Federalist* No. 78, that the new Supreme Court would be the "least dangerous branch" of the new national government. Without the power of the purse to appropriate money, or the power of the sword to enforce the law, the Court would prove no threat to the other branches of government, Hamilton reasoned.[12]

The Early Court

The Supreme Court first met on Monday, February 1, 1790, in the Royal Exchange Building located in what is today New York City's Wall Street district. Things began slowly for the justices, elegantly clad in the black and scarlet robes of English tradition: they had no cases to hear that first year.[13] Due to its perceived weakness in the new national government and its small workload, the early Court lacked status. Many men turned down presidential nominations to the Court, and others, including inaugural Chief Justice John Jay, soon left for positions they thought carried more respect.

Marbury v. Madison marked a watershed in the history of the Supreme Court. By establishing the principle of ju-

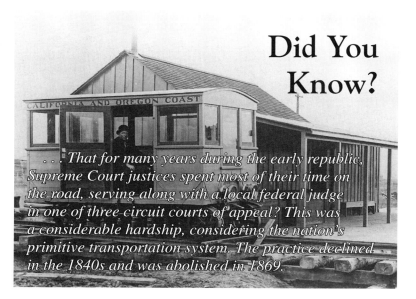

Did You Know?

. . . That for many years during the early republic, Supreme Court justices spent most of their time on the road, serving along with a local federal judge in one of three circuit courts of appeal? This was a considerable hardship, considering the nation's primitive transportation system. The practice declined in the 1840s and was abolished in 1869.

dicial review, the Marshall Court placed the Court squarely in the mainstream of American government and made it a force to reckon with. The Marshall Court's rulings, however, tended to affirm policies that supported the aims of the national government, contributing to a generally congenial relationship among the three branches of government.

Marshall's successor, Roger Taney, used the Court's power in quite a different fashion. Under Taney, the Court tilted much more dramatically toward protecting state power from incursion by the federal government. The Taney Court often found itself at odds with the other branches of the federal government. When the Taney Court decided to hear the *Dred Scott* case (discussed at length in Chapter 5), it caused nearly irreparable damage to the institution. By declaring the Missouri Compromise unconstitutional, the Court provided slave owners with a major political victory and incurred the wrath of abolitionists and the Republican Party. When Republican president Abraham Lincoln took office in 1861, his first inaugural address criticized the Supreme Court in some of the most scathing language ever uttered by a president about another branch of government. Congressional Republicans followed these remarks by attempting to weaken the Court through manipulating the number of justices for political advantage.[14] They also removed some of the Court's appellate jurisdiction.[15]

President Eisenhower called the nomination of liberal Chief Justice Earl Warren one of his two biggest mistakes as president.

The Court, Business, and Social Welfare

The Court would face peril again some eighty years later when the laissez-faire economic philosophy of most of its members conflicted with Franklin Roosevelt's activist program to combat the Great Depression. When the Court declared eight of the ten legislative proposals of the New Deal unconstitutional in 1935 and 1936, the president introduced his "Court-Packing Plan." He proposed that for every Supreme Court Justice who had reached the age of seventy and chose not to retire, the president could nominate an additional judge to help with the workload. The real purpose of the proposal had nothing to do with helping elderly justices. The Court was typically voting 6 to 3 to invalidate New Deal programs. Five of the six justices voting against the president were at least seventy years of age. If Roosevelt were able to appoint new justices for all those who did not retire, he could turn a 6-to-3 deficit into a 9-to-6 victory. Believing the bill violated the judicial independence of the Supreme Court, however, Congress narrowly defeated its passage. Two members of the Supreme Court understood the politics of the moment and the long-term implications for the Court as an institution. Chief Justice Charles Evans Hughes and Justice Owen Roberts changed their positions and began consistently to uphold New Deal attempts to regulate the economy. Statutes were now surviving on 5-to-4 votes. The two justices understood how close their beloved institution had come to losing its independence.

The Court and Personal Rights

Since its retreat during the New Deal, the Court has fundamentally changed its emphasis regarding the nature of the cases it hears. Today the Court's emphasis in the area of constitutional law is civil liberties and civil rights. This modern era of support for rights is most identified with the leadership of Earl Warren, who became chief justice in 1953. The Court's direction, however, did not change dramatically under the leadership of Warren Burger or William Rehnquist. Whether the Roberts Court will continue this trend supporting civil liberties and civil rights issues remains to be seen.

SUPREME COURT DECISION MAKING

The modern Supreme Court bears little resemblance to the institution that first convened in 1790. Today, the Court meets on a regular basis and turns away work. Its annual term begins on the first Monday in October and continues until late June or early July of the following year. Through-

The current Supreme Court justices: Back row from left: Stephen Breyer, Clarence Thomas, Ruth Bader Ginsburg, Samuel Alito; front row: Anthony Kennedy, John Paul Stevens, Chief Justice John Roberts, Antonin Scalia, and David Souter.

out the term, the schedule alternates between two weeks of sittings and two weeks of recess. During the *sittings*, the justices hear case arguments and announce decisions. During the *recess*, they have time to think, research, and write opinions.

The Supreme Court now functions as nine small and independent law firms, each with a justice as the senior partner aided by three to four law clerks.[16] The justices spend little time interacting with each other, and such interactions are almost impersonal. As one law clerk observed, "Justices don't think that much about what other justices are doing. They spend little time with them and rarely see each other. They often come in and sit by themselves day after day without really talking to any of the other justices."[17] Most of the communication among them takes the form of a written Memorandum to the Conference (MTTC), and much of it is done by the law clerks. Clerks also provide valuable service to the justices they serve by reviewing petitions from potential appellants and writing the legal opinions explaining the outcomes of cases. All Supreme Court clerks come from top law schools, and many of them clerk in a lower federal court for a year or two before coming to the Supreme Court.

writ of certiorari Order issued by a superior court to one of inferior jurisdiction demanding the record of a particular case.

Rule of Four Requirement that a minimum of four justices must vote to review a lower court case by issuing a writ of certiorari.

In this section, we will examine how the Supreme Court chooses which cases it will hear, how it decides these cases, and then how it justifies its decisions. Once the Court makes and justifies its decisions, others must implement them. We will explore how the Court can help in this process. Finally, we will analyze what factors best explain why Supreme Court justices behave as they do.

Agenda Decisions

The Supreme Court has almost complete discretion in deciding what cases to review. Since 1988, nearly all cases that have made it to the nation's highest court arrived there on a petition for a **writ of certiorari**. *Certiorari* is a legal term that means literally "to be informed." If the Court grants such a writ, the lower court will send a record of the case to the Court for purposes of review. In a typical year, the court receives more than nine thousand petitions for writs of certiorari but accepts fewer than one hundred for full hearing and decision. Each office takes one-eighth of the petitions at random to summarize and share with the other chambers in a pool memo (Justice Stevens does not participate in this arrangement, and his clerks read all the petitions). Clerks perform the initial substantive review of these petitions, "marking up" the memo based on the interests and values of the individual justices and concluding with a recommendation to grant or deny.

The chief justice plays a special role in the agenda-setting process. Several times during the term, the chief justice prepares a "discuss list" consisting of the forty to fifty cases he believes the Court should consider at the next meeting of the justices. On Friday afternoons during the sittings, the justices gather in conference to review the discuss list. At these private meetings, the justices decide whether to grant or deny certiorari. According to the **Rule of Four**, if at least four of the justices vote to grant certiorari, the Court will hear the case and notify the parties.

One scholar asserts that the Court will deny certiorari when (1) the case is frivolous; (2) the case is too fact bound; (3) insufficient evidence is presented in the briefs; (4) the case involves an issue the justices want to avoid; (5) the legal issue has not percolated enough in the lower courts; (6) the briefs contain disputed facts; (7) a better case is in the pipeline; or (8) the case will fragment the Court.[18] The question still remains as to which cases the justices will vote to hear. The Court itself wrote Rule 10 to govern the process. It specifies that the Court will accept cases that have been decided differently by the various federal circuits, cases that conflict with Supreme Court precedents, and state cases that conflict with federal decisions. Based on interviews with justices and law clerks, one author concluded that the justices follow Rule 10, stating that conflict in the federal circuits is "without a doubt, one of the most important things to all the justices. All of them are disposed to resolve conflicts when they exist and want to know if a particular case poses a conflict."[19]

The Court, however, does not accept all such cases with conflicts because there are too many of them.[20] The subject of the case often determines whether it gets a hearing. During the Vinson and Warren Court eras (1946–1969), the Court was more likely to accept cases dealing with labor relations, civil rights and civil liberties, and federalism.[21] As we saw in Chapter 4, the Court is also more likely to hear a case for which supporters have submitted *amicus curiae*, or "friend of the court" briefs. The solicitor general, who is responsible for handling most Supreme Court appeals on behalf of the federal government, appears as a party or a friend of the court in more than 50 percent of the cases the Court hears each term. The influence of the office is so great that it has a suite of offices within the Supreme Court building and its occupant is referred to as the "tenth justice."[22] Because of this special

The Supreme Court decided the outcome of the Bush-Gore 2000 presidential election when it did not allow a recount of the contested Florida ballots.

relationship, the Court accepts some 70 to 80 percent of cases the solicitor general's office brings before it, compared to less than 5 percent for all other petitioners.[23]

Voting Decisions

Attorneys arguing cases before the Court have thirty minutes to present their legal arguments, a rule that is strictly enforced. A flashing white light signals when the attorney has but five minutes remaining; when the light turns red, time has elapsed and the attorney must stop immediately at that time—even in midsentence. Although attorneys often prepare for weeks, or even months, for their appearance before the Supreme Court, there is no guarantee that they will be able to present all of their arguments. The members of the Court may interrupt at any time with probing questions that can befuddle a lawyer who is not on top of his or her game. An attorney cannot possibly anticipate all the questions the justices may ask, but the experienced ones are able to use these questions to emphasize the points they want to make.

Late on Wednesday afternoons after hearing oral arguments, and all day on Fridays when the Court is sitting, the justices meet in conference to decide the cases just argued. Since 1836, the justices have begun the conference session with a round of handshaking. It serves as a subtle reminder that they remain colleagues even though they may soon be engaged in a heated exchange of views. The associate justice with the least seniority acts as both official stenographer and doorkeeper.

By tradition, the chief justice presides over the conference and has the task of allowing adequate discussion, while at the same time moving the Court efficiently through its docket of cases. The chief justice speaks first, followed by the eight associate justices in order of seniority. At one time, justices tried to change the minds of others with their comments, but the purpose of the conference session is now just to discover consensus.[24] The individual justices vote at the same time they discuss the case. At this point, however, the individual votes are still tentative and subject to change. The Court will not deliver

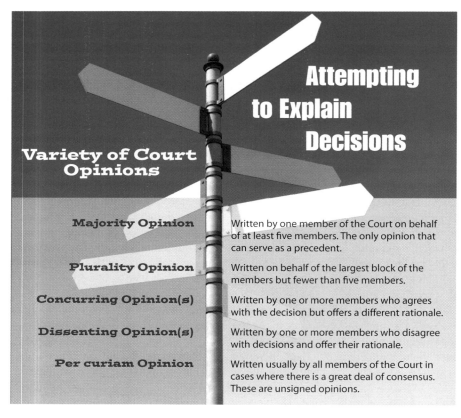

Variety of Court Opinions

Attempting to Explain Decisions

Majority Opinion — Written by one member of the Court on behalf of at least five members. The only opinion that can serve as a precedent.

Plurality Opinion — Written on behalf of the largest block of the members but fewer than five members.

Concurring Opinion(s) — Written by one or more members who agrees with the decision but offers a different rationale.

Dissenting Opinion(s) — Written by one or more members who disagree with decisions and offer their rationale.

Per curiam Opinion — Written usually by all members of the Court in cases where there is a great deal of consensus. These are unsigned opinions.

a final vote until the completion of the next stage of the process.

Explaining Decisions

After the members of the Court cast their initial votes concerning a case **decision**, their next task is to explain their votes by writing **opinions**. Whereas the decision indicates which litigant the Court supports and by how large a margin, the opinion explains the reasons behind the decision. Only one justice writes the opinion for the Court, but other justices have the option of writing additional opinions. The chief justice decides who will write the opinion if he or she is in the majority on the initial vote in a case. If not, the most senior associate justice in the majority assigns the task.

When John Marshall was chief justice of the Supreme Court, the Court's decision was most often explained in just one opinion. Today, the members of the Court are more likely to be fragmented in their reasoning as well as in their votes. As a result, four different types of opinions may accompany any particular decision. A **majority opinion** is written by one member of the Court on behalf of at least five mem-

decision The indication of which litigant the court supports and by how large a margin.

opinions The written arguments explaining the reasons behind a decision.

majority opinion An opinion written by a justice who represents a majority of the court.

concurring opinion An opinion written by one or more of the justices who agree with the decision but for different reasons than those stated in the majority opinion.

bers of the Court; the reasoning in the opinion can serve as a precedent for future cases. A **concurring opinion** is one written by a justice who agrees with the decision, but offers a different rationale for the Court's finding. A **plurality opinion** is one that is written on behalf of the largest bloc of the justices, but less than a majority, who agree on the reasons supporting the court's decision. A plurality opinion does not serve as a precedent for future cases. Finally, a **dissenting opinion** is one that is written by one or more justices who disagree with the case decision and the opinion of the majority or plurality of the Court. Occasionally, the Court will submit a **per curiam opinion** to explain its reasoning in a case. These are unsigned opinions that represent the view of the Court in a case where there is a great deal of consensus, or in a case where time is a critical factor. The Court issued a per curiam opinion in the case of *Bush v. Gore* (2000). Justices may dissent from such opinions but rarely do so.

The combination of opinions that finally accompany the decision in a particular case is the result of negotiations that begin after one of the jurists in the majority receives the assignment to write the Court's opinion. According to political scientist David O'Brien, "Writing opinions is the justice's most difficult and time-consuming task."[25] Since the original conference vote is not final, a dissenting opinion occasionally becomes the majority opinion, and vice versa. In 1970, for instance, the Court voted 5 to 3 in conference to deny famous boxer Muhammad Ali's conscientious objector claim for refusing induction into the Army. After two months of negotiation, however, the Court ruled for Ali.[26] Ultimately, the bargaining ends, the final votes are recorded in a conference meeting, and the opinions are printed and made public.

Implementing Decisions

Once the Supreme Court has reached its final decision in a case, the decision has to be implemented. Implementation consists of how judicial decisions are enforced on the parties to the lawsuit, as well as how and whether the decisions are translated into general public policies. With respect to the litigants, if the Supreme Court affirms a lower court decision, the lower court then enforces its original decision. If the Supreme Court reverses the lower court ruling, the original decision is void. Often, the Supreme Court remands a case—sends it back to the court that originally heard it—with instructions to retry it under proceedings consistent with the Court's opinion. After the Supreme Court ruling in *Miranda v. Arizona* (see Chapter 4), the trial court retried Miranda, but the prosecution was not allowed to use his confession. Even so, the lower court once again found the defendant guilty.

Turning Supreme Court decisions into general public policy is a more difficult process. The Court alone cannot enforce its decisions; it must depend on other public officials to do so who may not always desire to cooperate. When upset with a Supreme Court ruling, President Andrew Jackson is reported to have said, "John Marshall has made his decision; now let him enforce it." In other words, implementation is not an automatic process.

Two political scientists have written that the implementation of a Supreme Court decision depends on several elements.[27] First, there is the *interpreting population,* made up largely of judges and lawyers, who must correctly understand and reflect the intent of the decision in subsequent decisions. Lower judges usually follow the rulings of the Supreme Court, but sometimes they circumvent rulings to pursue their own policy preferences.[28] The federal district court judges in the South, for example, circumvented the *Brown v. Board of Education* decision (see Chapter 5) for years.[29] The second element in the process is the *implementing population,* such as school administrators who implement prayer in school decisions or police departments that implement search and seizure decisions. Finally, a *consumer population* must be aware of these new rights if they are to exercise them. Suspects who are about to be interrogated are the consumers of the *Miranda* decision, and women who want abortions are the consumers of the *Roe v. Wade* decision. The Supreme Court must hope that other actors will respect its moral authority and legal expertise enough to implement its policies. The Court can help itself, however, by writing clear opinions.

Understanding Decisions

Scholars today look to a variety of nonlegal factors to understand Supreme Court decisions. Some of these factors are external to the individual justices and comprise the political environment, such as Congress, the president, and public opinion. Other factors, including ideology, perception of their role, and the ability to negotiate with colleagues on the bench, originate with the individual justices.

External Factors When making decisions, the Supreme Court is aware of the many checks the Constitution provides Congress over the behavior of the Court. If Congress is unhappy with a Supreme Court decision, it can propose a constitutional amendment to overturn the decision. The Eleventh, Fourteenth, Sixteenth, and Twenty-Sixth Amendments were all passed in response to congressional unhappiness with a Court decision. Congress can also threaten to modify the Court's appellate jurisdiction. If Congress believes the Court has interpreted one of their laws or their legislative intent erroneously, Congress can rewrite the law. In 1993, for example, Congress enacted the Religious Freedom Restoration Act because members believed a Court decision was too restrictive of religious liberty.[30] The Rehnquist Court responded, however, by declaring the law unconstitutional.[31] At other times, the Court clearly responds to congressional wishes, such as when it began to declare New Deal legislation constitutional. Congress can also express its displeasure with Court decisions by withholding funds necessary for implementation of a decision and by careful Senate scrutiny of future Court nominees.

Presidents exercise control over the Supreme Court by filling vacancies on the Court with nominees who share their beliefs. As chief executive, the president also often plays a key role in implementing Supreme Court decisions that have broad policy ramifications. If President

> **plurality opinion** An opinion that is written on behalf of the largest bloc of the justices, representing less than a majority, who agree on the reasons supporting the court's decision.
>
> **dissenting opinion** An opinion written by one or more justices who disagree with a decision.
>
> **per curiam opinion** An unsigned opinion of the Supreme Court that usually signals a high degree of consensus.

President Lyndon B. Johnson nominated the first African American to the U.S. Supreme Court, Thurgood Marshall.

Eisenhower had not called out the troops to enforce school integration in Little Rock, Arkansas, the implementation of *Brown v. Board of Education* (1954) might have been hopelessly stalled. Presidents also appoint the solicitor general, who has an important relationship with the Court.

Since the American public does not directly elect Supreme Court justices, the justices do not have to worry about constantly analyzing public opinion polls or running for reelection. This does not mean, however, that public opinion has no effect on the Court's behavior. After all, the justices work and live among the rest of us, and social trends influence their attitudes as well. Since popularly elected officials must nominate and approve Supreme Court justices, the justices' views usually reflect those of the majority of Americans. Justices who have been on the Court for a long time may reflect political views that are no longer in vogue, but even they know that a decision at odds with public opinion will produce a backlash and even resistance to obeying the law. There are even times when the Court clearly follows public opinion in making decisions. In its 2002 ruling that executing mentally retarded criminals constitutes cruel and unusual punishment, the Court noted "powerful evidence that today our society views mentally retarded offenders as categorically less culpable than the average criminal."[32]

Internal Factors Supreme Court justices do not magically rid themselves of all their attitudes and political biases so that they can function as neutral judges. In fact, the president chooses nominees—and the Senate confirms them—largely on doctrinal qualifications. Therefore, it is reasonable to assume that justices often follow their own policy preferences when making legal decisions. Justices with a liberal ideology typically support civil liberties and civil rights claims, back the government in economic regulation cases, and vote for national regulation in federalism cases. Conservatives, of course, cast votes in the opposite direction. Knowledge of the justices' ideology can lead to accurate predictions of their voting patterns. For instance, conservative justices Antonin Scalia and Clarence Thomas vote together much of the time, in opposition to liberal justices Ruth Bader Ginsburg and Stephen Breyer. Not all cases, however, can be analyzed neatly on a liberal versus conservative basis.

Other studies emphasize that a single justice can accomplish little because a majority of justices must reach the same conclusion to render a decision, and a majority must agree on a single opinion in order to set a precedent.

judicial activism The belief that the Supreme Court should make policy and vigorously review the policies of other branches.

judicial restraint The belief that the Supreme Court should not become involved in questioning the operations and policies of the elected branches unless absolutely necessary.

Therefore, a single justice must work strategically in order to advance his or her goals.[33] Such strategic behavior manifests itself in the number of times justices change their votes and revise their opinions. Studies have shown that between the initial vote in conference and the official announcement of the decision, at least one vote switch occurs more than 50 percent of the time.[34] Also, in almost every case, some justice will revise an opinion to please his or her colleagues.[35] It is not unusual for a justice to revise an opinion ten times in order to hold the original majority.

Individual justices also hold their own views as to the proper role of a good judge and of the Court. Some justices subscribe to a philosophy of **judicial activism**, arguing that the Court should make public policy and vigorously review the policies of the other branches. Others, convinced that the belief the Court should not become involved in questioning the operations and policies of the elected branches unless absolutely necessary, believe in **judicial restraint**.

Hot or Not?

Did the Supreme Court do the right thing in establishing a woman's right to an abortion?

SUPREME COURT SELECTION

One hundred and ten individuals have served on the Supreme Court. Most have been wealthy, white males between the ages of forty-one and sixty, with Protestant backgrounds. Although the Constitution is silent with regard to qualifications, all have been lawyers and many were federal judges, were state judges, or had their own legal practice just prior to nomination. Seven had served as attorney general, and several others had held other high executive offices such as secretary of state. Eight had served in Congress; three had been state governors. Their number has even included a former president, William Howard Taft. Let's now examine the process by which these men and (a few) women have risen to the most powerful court in the land.

Nomination

Unlike other appointments, presidents are intimately involved in the selection of Supreme Court nominees. The retirement or death of a sitting justice gives the president a chance to make a lasting impact on the direction of U.S. legal and political practices. The president fills openings for associate justices from a wide pool of candidates, as we will discuss shortly. When the chief justice position becomes vacant, however, the president may select the

United States Supreme Court Chief Justices

Name	Party	Term
John Jay	Federalist	1789–1795
Oliver Ellsworth	Federalist	1796–1800
John Marshall	Federalist	1801–1835
Roger Taney	Democrat	1836–1864
Salmon Chase	Republican	1864–1873
Morrison Waite	Republican	1874–1888
Melville Fuller	Democrat	1888–1910
Edward White*	Democrat	1910–1921
William H. Taft	Republican	1921–1930
Charles Hughes	Republican	1930–1941
Harlan Stone*	Republican	1941–1946
Fred Vinson	Democrat	1946–1953
Earl Warren	Republican	1953–1969
Warren Burger	Republican	1969–1986
William Rehnquist*	Republican	1986–2005
John Roberts	Republican	2005–

*Appointed chief justice while serving as an associate justice.

new chief justice from among the sitting associate justices. In most cases, however, presidents have chosen someone from outside the Court to fill the position. Only three of the sixteen chief justices came from among sitting associate justices. When a president chooses a sitting associate justice to be the new chief justice, an opening is created for a new associate justice.

Presidents play the major role in selecting Supreme Court nominees, although other individuals and groups also influence the selection process. Over half of all nominees have been personal friends of the president, which suggests that presidential advisors play a lesser role in shaping the president's choice. Interest groups close to the administration may participate privately in the selection process, or at least receive consideration of their views. Conservative interest groups and columnists, for example, sank the nomination of Harriet Miers, whom President Bush originally selected to replace Sandra Day O'Connor, claiming that Miers was not conservative enough. The American Bar Association (ABA) plays a unique role in the nomination process by assigning nominees a rating of "well qualified," "qualified," "not opposed," or "not qualified." These ratings signal to the public the ABA's assessment of a nominee's legal qualifications. The Reagan administration did not work with the ABA in choosing its nominees, and

George W. Bush announced early in his presidency that he would use the more conservative Federalist Society to investigate his nominees to the federal bench.

To further ensure that damaging information regarding a candidate does not surface and affect the credibility of the president who makes the nomination, the FBI has played an increasingly important role in the selection process. Candidates who survive an initial screening process fill out questionnaires that include information about their personal lives. FBI agents thoroughly examine the potential nominee's life to make sure that there are no skeletons in the closet. The examinations, however, do not always turn up every potentially damaging fact about a nominee. The Reagan administration, for instance, withdrew the nomination of Douglas Ginsburg when the media verified that Ginsberg had smoked marijuana as a youth and as a member of the Harvard University law faculty.

Nomination Criteria

Political scientists disagree about which criteria presidents use when choosing a Supreme Court nominee. Some argue that the relatively high caliber of appointments over time demonstrates that presidents rely primarily on merit and do not want to be embarrassed by choosing unqualified nominees.[36] Others stress that the politics inherent in the selection process outweighs any concern for merit.[37] Herbert Hoover's nomination of Benjamin Cardozo in 1932 shows that the truth lies somewhere between these extremes. Cardozo, a Democrat, was the chief judge of the New York Court of Appeals and author of the universally praised book *The Nature of the Judicial Process*. He was "a man widely regarded as one of America's most brilliant jurists," who enjoyed great support from the legal community and the United States Senate.[38] The Republican Hoover drew considerable praise when he crossed party lines to nominate Cardozo. Although it was a merit selection, it was also a political maneuver by the president. At the time, Hoover's administration was struggling to respond to the Great Depression, and he may have seen

15

1443

FORECL

PUBLIC

RESPONDING TO CITIZENS

AMERICAN DREAM OR NIGHTMARE? ▮

Their stories became all too familiar in the last two years. Stories like that of Kue McIntyre, thirty-three, a single mother of three who fought unsuccessfully to avoid losing her row house in the Belair-Edison neighborhood of Baltimore. "When I bought my house, it was the American Dream," she recalls.[1] Two years ago, she took out a sub-prime loan (loans that offer adjustable interest rates to consumers with low credit scores) to purchase a brick row house for $125,000. Her initial payments were $841 a month. When her adjustable interest rate shot up—from 8.35 percent to 13.25 percent—she had difficulty paying her bills. The mortgage lender suggested she consolidate her other debts and pay them down first. Kue followed that advice, but when she lost her job, she had no reserves. This caused her to miss her mortgage payments, and her house went into foreclosure.

Kue is among a growing number of Americans for whom the American Dream has become a nightmare. People lost their homes at a record-breaking rate in the first quarter of 2008, according to the Mortgage Banker's Association. Both foreclosure and delinquency rates surpassed previously recorded highs going back to 1979.[2] Not all areas of the nation experienced the same amount of pain, however. Florida, California, Nevada, and Arizona, where prices became ●◆

POLICY

As You READ

>>

- What is public policy?
- What are the principal stages of the public policy process?
- How can we explain policy outcomes?

highly inflated in the 1990s, were worst hit. Now prices have fallen sharply, leaving many borrowers owing more on their mortgages than their homes are worth.

Many actors had a hand in creating the credit crisis that hit America in the past few years: homebuyers who bought more house than they could afford; speculators who flipped houses (bought and sold them in rapid succession) in an effort to turn a quick profit, thereby inflating market prices; unscrupulous mortgage brokers who looked the other way in approving loans for people with poor credit; investment bankers who sold these mortgages to investors as secure instruments; and credit rating agencies that failed to give investors accurate advice about the quality of the mortgages they were buying. When the housing bubble began to burst, the economic fallout extended well beyond these original players. Credit became tighter for everyone, and the resulting housing glut caused real estate prices to fall and the building trades to lay off workers. The Federal Reserve (discussed later in this chapter) cut interest rates to keep credit flowing, but this also caused the dollar to lose value in international markets, making everything Americans buy—including oil—more expensive. As the economic fallout spread throughout the economy, Americans looked to the government for help.

The federal government took a number of steps designed to stem the bleeding: President Bush called upon lenders to freeze mortgage rates for some homeowners with adjustable rates and encouraged lenders to work with borrowers to renegotiate terms so that buyers could stay in their homes. The Federal Reserve made aggressive interest rate cuts to keep credit flowing, and the Fed chairman engineered a buyout of Bear Sterns, one of the largest holders of subprime loans. Regulation of lending practices was strengthened. Congress passed a plan to help borrowers refinance loans if their lenders agree to forgive a portion of their debt. And the Justice Department brought indictments against a number of real estate brokers and investment managers for fraud. Still, continued instability caused some of the largest financial institutions to fail and others had to be rescued by the government.

Taken together, these actions may help stabilize credit markets, but they come to late for Kue.

Stories like Kue's demonstrate several valuable lessons about public policy in America. First, public policies arise in response to the tangible problems of real individuals. Second, social and economic problems that begin in one sector often spill over into others and eventually affect nearly every American. Even if you had no involvement with real estate in recent years, you felt the impact of the credit crisis

Kue McIntyre, like many Americans in recent years, watched her dream of home ownership turn into a nightmare as the subprime mortgage crisis led to the worst financial meltdown since the Great Depression.

when you paid higher rates for a loan to purchase a car, when your dollars bought less on your overseas travels, and when you paid more to fill up the tank at the gas station. Finally, when government decides it must take action, it must balance the interests of a wide variety of players, some with a much larger stake in the outcome than others, and some of whom exert more political clout than others. Let's take a look at how public policy is made. ⟵•

THE NATURE AND SCOPE OF PUBLIC POLICY

Public policy pervades our lives; it is impossible to go through the day without being affected by programs issuing from federal, state, and local governments. If you go to a university, even a private one, you may participate in student loan programs, Pell grants, and work-study opportunities that pay at least the federally mandated minimum wage. If you attend a public university, the state bears the largest share of the cost of your education, and a host of state laws and programs affect everything on campus from curriculum to traffic safety. When you shower, you use water regulated by a host of federal, state, and local laws. The wastewater from your shower is treated by local governmental authorities following federal guidelines. In return for these services, you pay taxes to all of these governmental units.

Simply put, **public policy** is anything the government chooses to do or not to do.[3] This can include tangible actions, such as providing student grants or imposing taxes, as well as symbolic gestures, such as creating a legal holiday to commemorate the birthday of Martin Luther King, Jr. Governments as-

Crises such as a terrorist assault on our nation require immediate action as well as long-range planning.
....

sert policy even when they fail to act. As we discussed in Chapter 3, the Senate's failure to ratify the Kyoto Protocol on controlling greenhouse gases communicated the U.S. government's decision to pursue unilateral strategies for addressing the issue.

POLICY MAKING AND EVALUATION

A host of actors, including both government officials and private citizens, shape the policymaking process. Their options are limited by a number of factors, including the availability of resources and political control of the instruments of power (e.g., which party controls the Congress and the presidency). Tradition and public opinion serve as additional constraints. For example,

> **public policy** Anything the government chooses to do or not to do.

even if it were possible to eliminate poverty by placing limits on how much property an individual could own, few Americans would agree to such a policy. It simply is not part of the American tradition, nor does it reflect the guiding ideology of either major political party. The process sometimes moves very slowly, at other times with great speed. With these caveats in mind, let us review the basic stages in the policymaking process.

Problem Recognition

The first step in policymaking is identifying and defining the problem as something the government can and should do something about. Some problems are easy to identify, such as the threat to homeland security signaled by the attacks on the World Trade Towers in New York on September 11, 2001. The threat was clear and visible; the government stood ready to respond. In other cases, we may only dimly and gradually perceive a problem and government's role in addressing it. For example, even though some scientists have long warned that greenhouse gas emissions caused by human activity are producing climate change, many lawmakers remained reluctant until recently to involve government in devising solutions.

Agenda Setting

After identifying a problem, we need to determine how important it is and how urgent it is for us to act. Problems such as a terrorist assault on our nation require immediate action as well as long-range planning. Following the 9/11 attacks, the government took immediate steps including securing airports and seaports and issuing alerts about threat levels; but various government actors also began exploring longer-range plans to enhance domestic security.

Competing political actors often have different agendas in jockeying for national attention. The president commands the national spotlight when he speaks, but so do members of Congress and interest groups—all of whom can sound alarms about problems they want confronted and how we should address them. After 9/11, the president proposed new restrictions on travel by foreign citizens and enhanced the investigative tools to root out terrorist cells; members of Congress and civil liberties groups voiced concern over freedom of movement and privacy.

Policy Formation

The next step is to review possible solutions and select those most likely to be successful. Potential solutions come from a variety of sources, including scholars and think tanks, politicians, interest groups, and even average citizens who suggest ideas to lawmakers. In most cases, experts within government agencies present their own ideas to Congress and members of the executive branch.

Following 9/11, there was no shortage of ideas about how to enhance our security. Think tanks like the liberal Brookings Institution and the conservative American Enterprise Institute issued competing ideas on an assortment of measures, including how we should employ and train airport security. Members of Congress

proposed the creation of a new cabinet-level department to coordinate terror response among a host of existing agencies. President Bush at first resisted this measure, but at the urging of fellow Republicans, he eventually embraced the idea of creating the Department of Homeland Security.

Policy Adoption and Implementation

Elected leaders are responsible for choosing which of the available policy options to adopt and how to put them into effect. At the federal level, this generally means passing laws in Congress with the support of the president and then utilizing the federal bureaucracy to implement them. Late in 2002, Congress passed and the president signed a bill creating the Department of Homeland Security. By March 1, 2003, Tom Ridge, the agency's first secretary, began the task of uniting twenty-two agencies that were formerly in the Departments of Agriculture, Commerce, Defense, Energy, Health and Human Services, Justice, Transportation, and Treasury.

As we discussed in Chapter 13, government bureaucracies usually carry out the task of executing policy. In carrying out its functions, Homeland Security had to formulate new rules and procedures for integrating formerly separate administrative divisions, coordinating and assessing intelligence from multiple sources, delivering emergency aid to areas of the country that might require assistance, and communicating with the public regarding threats to national security. For example, early on, the department devised color-coded warnings to reflect threat levels. In implementing policies, officials must be sensitive to the effects policies may have on multiple constituencies, including their own employees. The Bush administration ran into opposition from federal employees to a plan calling for the removal of some civil service protections for job security and advancement for those individuals assigned to the new agency. Eventually, differences were resolved, although some employment protections were relaxed.

The courts play a role in the policy process as well. Provisions of the USA Patriot Act, passed quickly after 9/11, came under attack by civil liberties groups that sought to

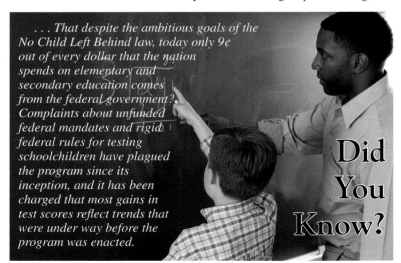

. . . That despite the ambitious goals of the No Child Left Behind law, today only 9¢ out of every dollar that the nation spends on elementary and secondary education comes from the federal government? Complaints about unfunded federal mandates and rigid federal rules for testing schoolchildren have plagued the program since its inception, and it has been charged that most gains in test scores reflect trends that were under way before the program was enacted.

Did You Know?

overturn some of its provisions in court. In 2004, a federal court struck down a provision that allowed the government to obtain sensitive consumer records from businesses and Internet providers without a warrant. In an effort to accommodate some of the concerns of civil libertarians, the act was revised by Congress in 2006, and some of the more restrictive provisions were altered. It was not until June 2008—nearly seven years after 9/11—that Congress and the White House worked out a deal permitting limited surveillance (including emergency wiretaps without court orders) on American targets if it is determined that important national security information would otherwise be lost, and immunity for telecommunication companies that took part in earlier warrantless wiretaps at the reqest of the president.

Policy Evaluation

Ideally, once policies are in place, the government assesses their impact to determine their continued utility. Once again, bureaucracies play a vital role by collecting statistics and conducting studies to measure the progress of these policies in solving problems. The president and Congress use this information to reauthorize programs and to make changes to fine-tune their impact. Political factors may be as important as objective measures of success in the decision whether to continue, change, or abandon a

Colleges and universities have complained that immigration restrictions imposed after 9/11 made it more difficult for foreign students to obtain visas to study here.

policy. Each policy has a constituency that supports it and individuals who benefit from its operation—whether or not it works as intended. Because all of these factors are difficult to balance, it is not surprising that most policymaking involves incremental rather than wholesale change.

Policies often have unintended consequences that are not always apparent at the time they are adopted. For example, in the wake of 9/11, the Immigration and Naturalization Service (INS) made it more difficult for foreign visitors to obtain visas to enter the United States. Colleges and universities complained that this policy unfairly penalized foreign students enrolling at their campuses, and some businesses argued that this policy made it more difficult to hire specialists needed to keep their operations competitive. Since then, the INS has made the restrictions less burdensome for students and foreign workers from some nations. Policymakers can minimize unintended consequences by carrying on conversations about proposed policies with constituencies that may be impacted by the policy decision. As policies are evaluated and changes adopted, they continue to recycle through the policymaking process. Rarely does policymaking produce a finished product that escapes revisiting.

Explaining Policy Outcomes

Whether or not government adopts a policy depends largely on the costs the policy imposes and the benefits it confers. How the policy allocates costs and benefits plays a significant role in determining whether the policy is adopted, how well it is accepted, and how easily it can be

the cap, or overall level of pollution for the industry as a whole. This more flexible approach gives lagging companies more time to bring their plants into compliance, while rewarding with cash those companies that already have achieved lower levels of pollution. Although industry insiders prefer this new approach, critics charge that the market-based trading of pollution credits undermines efforts to bring all polluters into uniform compliance. They also claim that the EPA does not set targets low enough to adequately address the rising threat posed by global warming. Some elements of command and control have been maintained, however. For example, Congress in 2007 increased mandatory fuel efficiency standards for automakers for the first time in thirty-two years, boosting required mileage efficiency to a fleet average of 35 miles per gallon by 2020. In April 2008, President Bush sped up the implementation of this new law, requiring the auto companies to deliver average fuel efficiency for cars and trucks of 31.5 miles per gallon by 2015. The president and Congress also agreed to mandate an increase in the production of homegrown fuels such as ethanol and a ban on the sale of inefficient incandescent light bulbs by 2012.

Environmental Protection in a Global Context

Policymakers have also been engaged in efforts to stem the tide of pollution on a worldwide scale to stave off the threat of global warming, thought to be a by-product of the use of fossil fuels. International treaties have met with vary-

Few public officials now question the reality of global warning, but there are widely divergent views about what, if anything, we should do about it.

ing degrees of success. Under the auspices of the United Nations, the 1992 Rio Treaty was negotiated; in it 154 nations pledged voluntarily to reduce the emission of greenhouse gases (carbon dioxide, methane, and several other industrial pollutants) in an effort to stem climate change. In 1997, industrialized nations negotiated a follow-up treaty, the Kyoto Protocol, which committed signatories to achieve reductions in greenhouse gases below 1990 levels by the year 2012. Although it was strongly supported by the Clinton administration, President George W. Bush rejected the agreement as a drain on the economy, preferring to call on industries to develop voluntary guidelines. Other member nations warn that without an enforceable agreement that includes America, the single largest user of fossil fuels per capita, the potential for natural disasters will increase, including the incidence of flooding and drought along with a rise in sea level in coastal areas. (See Global Perspective Box.)

Resistance to the scientific evidence of global warming seems to be weakening within the halls of Congress. Although there continue to be serious debates about who should pay the costs for a greener planet, consensus is growing about the need to attack the problem, as we saw in the opening vignette in Chapter 11. In the waning months of his administration, President Bush also took up the cause of global warming, calling for an end to increases in emissions by 2025. The candidates nominated by both parties in the 2008 presidential election vowed to make climate change a priority in the next administration.

As we saw in Chapter 3, some states and even localities have taken measures on their own to reduce carbon emis-

Greenhouse Gas Polluters

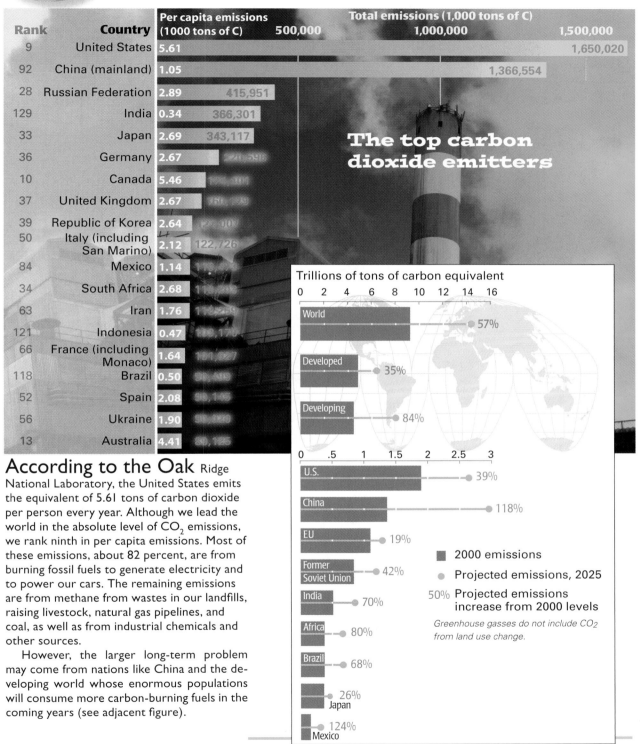

Rank	Country	Per capita emissions (1000 tons of C)	Total emissions (1,000 tons of C)
9	United States	5.61	1,650,020
92	China (mainland)	1.05	1,366,554
28	Russian Federation	2.89	415,951
129	India	0.34	366,301
33	Japan	2.69	343,117
36	Germany	2.67	
10	Canada	5.46	
37	United Kingdom	2.67	
39	Republic of Korea	2.64	
50	Italy (including San Marino)	2.12	122,726
84	Mexico	1.14	
34	South Africa	2.68	
63	Iran	1.76	
121	Indonesia	0.47	
66	France (including Monaco)	1.64	
118	Brazil	0.50	
52	Spain	2.08	
56	Ukraine	1.90	
13	Australia	4.41	

The top carbon dioxide emitters

Trillions of tons of carbon equivalent

- World — 57%
- Developed — 35%
- Developing — 84%
- U.S. — 39%
- China — 118%
- EU — 19%
- Former Soviet Union — 42%
- India — 70%
- Africa — 80%
- Brazil — 68%
- Japan — 26%
- Mexico — 124%

■ 2000 emissions
● Projected emissions, 2025
50% Projected emissions increase from 2000 levels

Greenhouse gasses do not include CO2 from land use change.

According to the Oak Ridge

National Laboratory, the United States emits the equivalent of 5.61 tons of carbon dioxide per person every year. Although we lead the world in the absolute level of CO_2 emissions, we rank ninth in per capita emissions. Most of these emissions, about 82 percent, are from burning fossil fuels to generate electricity and to power our cars. The remaining emissions are from methane from wastes in our landfills, raising livestock, natural gas pipelines, and coal, as well as from industrial chemicals and other sources.

However, the larger long-term problem may come from nations like China and the developing world whose enormous populations will consume more carbon-burning fuels in the coming years (see adjacent figure).

Sources: Top figure: Marland, G., T.A. Boden, and R.J. Andres. 2004. Global, Regional, and National CO₂ Emissions. In *Trends: A Compendium of Data on Global Change.* Carbon Dioxide Information Analysis Center, Oak Ridge National Laboratory, U.S. Department of Energy, Oak Ridge, Tenn., U.S.A. (available online at http://cdiac.esd.ornl.gov/trends/emis/tre_coun.htm). Bottom figure: Kevin A. Baumert, Tim Herzog, and Jonathan Pershing, *Navigating the Numbers: Greenhouse Gas Data and International Climate Policy,* Washington, D.C.: World Resources Institute, 18.

Who Are the Poor?

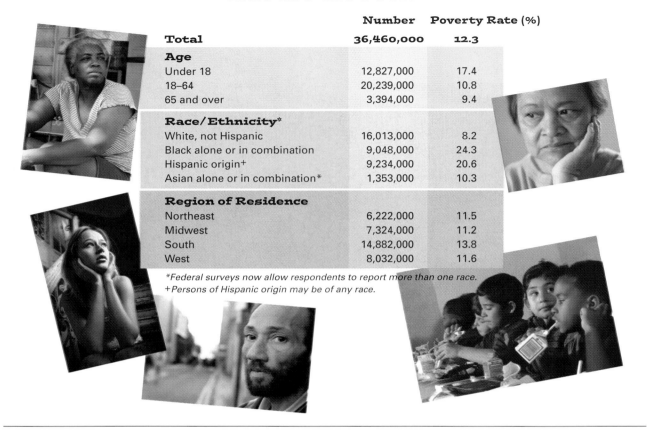

	Number	Poverty Rate (%)
Total	36,460,000	12.3
Age		
Under 18	12,827,000	17.4
18–64	20,239,000	10.8
65 and over	3,394,000	9.4
Race/Ethnicity*		
White, not Hispanic	16,013,000	8.2
Black alone or in combination	9,048,000	24.3
Hispanic origin+	9,234,000	20.6
Asian alone or in combination*	1,353,000	10.3
Region of Residence		
Northeast	6,222,000	11.5
Midwest	7,324,000	11.2
South	14,882,000	13.8
West	8,032,000	11.6

*Federal surveys now allow respondents to report more than one race.
+Persons of Hispanic origin may be of any race.

Source: U.S. Census, *Income, Poverty, and Health Insurance Coverage in the United States: 2006,* 60–233.

sions. Some states, such as Vermont, have passed legislation mandating a 30 percent reduction in carbon dioxide emissions from cars and trucks by 2016. Late in 2007, a federal judge upheld the law in a suit brought by American automakers, explaining that he believed the industry had sufficient technological skill to meet the challenge.[6] Should the Vermont statute pass muster in the Supreme Court, it could set in motion a movement that catapults the states farther ahead of the national government in the battle against global warming.

Helping the Poor

The "social safety net," designed to protect the health and welfare of American citizens, offers an example of a dramatic change in government policy over time. Prior to the turn of the twentieth century, few laws protected American workers, and private charitable organizations provided virtually all relief to the poor. The dangerous conditions in early twentieth-century factories gave rise to the first laws against child labor, laws improving sanitation, and laws favorable to the formation of labor unions as a means to increase wages. All of these initiatives, first enacted for the most part by the states, played a part in relieving poverty among urban populations.

The widespread unemployment and financial panic triggered by the Great Depression of the 1930s forced the federal government to take a more central role in alleviating suffering. Many programs now basic to American society, such as unemployment compensation and Social Security, emerged as part of the massive Social Security Act of 1935. Unemployment compensation, financed through a combination of employer contributions and federal and state funding, provides temporary

In 2006, about 37 million Americans lived below the poverty threshold of $20,614 a year for a family of four.

The Escalating Share of Mandatory Spending

Type of Spending as a Share of Total Outlays

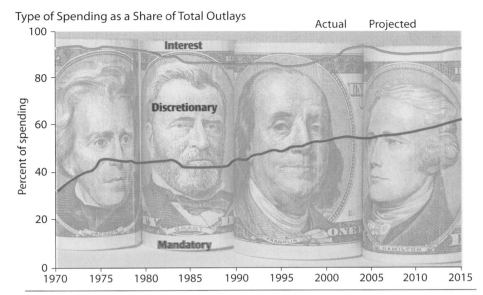

Actual   Projected

Source: Congressional Budget Office.

from them, account for approximately 40 percent of the federal budget. Their expenditure is mandatory because they represent a promise made to those who are eligible to receive benefits, and that proportion of the population grows as the country ages. On our current budget trajectory, this will leave little for discretionary programs in other areas the government seeks to pursue. As a result, the debate over the future of Social Security is highly charged. Attempts to reform the program present political hazards to those who try, as President George W. Bush found out when he took on the issue in 2005 and faced mounting opposition. Nevertheless, political leaders seeking electoral advantage continue to propose additional benefits for the elderly. In 2003, Congress enacted a Medicare Prescription Drug Plan that the Office of Management and Budget estimates may cost as much as $42 billion over the next decade.[9]

and partial wage replacement for those who have been involuntarily laid off from their jobs. Another provision of the act, known as the Supplemental Security Income Program (SSI), provides supplemental income to those who are blind, aged, or disabled. The major provision of the act, the Federal Old-Age and Survivors Insurance Trust Fund (currently known as Social Security), provided retirement income to the elderly, financed by employer and employee contributions. In 1965, the government added health-care coverage for the elderly through a program known as Medicare, financed again through a combination of employer and employee contributions. This was followed shortly thereafter by a companion program for the poor called Medicaid. The government designed these programs to attack the major causes of widespread poverty: unemployment, disability, and old age.

These programs have had considerable success in reducing poverty, especially among the elderly. Whereas the poverty level in the 1950s stood at about 30 percent, by the 1970s it had fallen to about 11 percent.[7] Since then, there have been marginal increases and declines based on a number of factors, including the amount of funds available for antipoverty programs and the state of the U.S. economy. In 2006, approximately 12.3 percent of Americans, about 37 million, lived below the poverty threshold of $20,614 a year for a family of four.[8] The highest percentage of poverty occurs among children, minorities, and urban populations. Even so, in absolute numbers, there are more white adults between the ages of eighteen and sixty-four living in poverty than any other single group.

The problem with social safety net programs is their burgeoning cost. These programs, known as **entitlements** because anyone who qualifies is entitled to receive benefits

Welfare Reform The biggest changes in antipoverty policy have come in the form of public assistance programs—generally known as **welfare**. From the New Deal until the mid-1990s, the principal program for poor families was Aid to Families with Dependent Children (AFDC). This entitlement program provided payments to families with children who either had no income or earned below the annually adjusted standard poverty level established by the Bureau of Labor. Responding to complaints that AFDC generated welfare dependency and thwarted self-sufficiency, Congress passed a reform measure in 1996 that ended welfare's status as an entitlement. Under the new program, Temporary Assistance to Needy Families (TANF), the federal government provides block grants (see Chapter 3) to the states, which decide work requirements, payment levels, and time limits within guidelines set by Congress. These guidelines specify that the state must cap continuous cash benefits at two years and lifetime benefits at five years. The following year, Congress passed amendments to the program to ensure that cash payments under TANF did not go below previous AFDC benefit levels.

Scholars debate the overall success of welfare reform. One study shows that those who fared best after welfare reform found additional government programs—food stamps, job counseling, child care, and various state-sponsored medical programs for children—to supple-

entitlements Programs promising aid without time limit to anyone who qualifies.

welfare Term characterizing the wide variety of social programs developed during the New Deal to help the poor, unemployed, disabled, and elderly.

ment their TANF income.[10] As states struggle to control poverty, they may have difficulty in sustaining funding for programs, especially medical programs, that have proved critical to the success of welfare reform. State officials are also concerned about the growing number of working families who are poor but do not qualify for many government programs. The U.S. Census Bureau reports that almost one in six American families has at least one working member living in poverty. Many of the workers in these families are the most vulnerable to changes in the workforce generated by recession and the outsourcing of jobs associated with globalization.

Unlike Social Security, where both costs and benefits are widely dispersed, programs for the poor provide concentrated benefits that are secured only through well-organized pressure. But the poor lack the political clout to advance their programs. They are not as active politically as are the elderly. Although a variety of interest groups such as the Children's Defense Fund exist to speak for the poor, interests that are more vocal and active than America's poor dominate lobbying for government funds.

fiscal policy Taxing and spending policies prescribed by Congress and the president.

recession Period of the business cycle characterized by high levels of unemployment.

Religious groups, which have historically sought to help the poor, recently have become partners with the government in administering federal antipoverty programs. Former President George W. Bush was an advocate of faith-based initiatives providing federal funds to churches and religious organizations that offer food, clothing, shelter, and counseling to the poor in their neighborhoods. Often, these programs provide religious instruction as well, raising questions about the possible blurring of the line between church and state. Religious providers argue that the poor benefit from both the government services and the spiritual instruction, which is available if they wish it.

The lack of affordable health care is a major contributor to economic insecurity among Americans today.

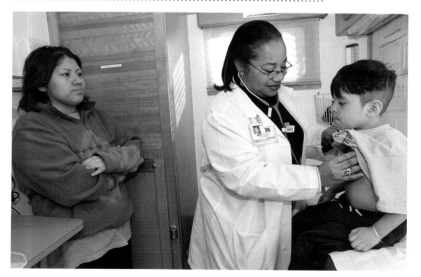

Critics both inside and outside of religious circles worry about entanglements between religion and government.[11]

Health Care and Poverty In recent years, rising health-care costs have become a major threat to the financial security of many Americans. Nearly 47 million Americans, or 16 percent of the population, were without health insurance in 2005. This represents an increase of almost 7 million uninsured people since the year 2000. More than 80 percent of the uninsured come from working families—almost 70 percent from families with one or more full-time workers and 11 percent from families with part-time workers.[12] These individuals often do not qualify for Medicaid but cannot afford to buy their own health insurance. The outsourcing of manufacturing and some service jobs contributes to the problem, as businesses that once provided health-care coverage either reduce or cancel this benefit in order to compete with foreign companies that do not. In most other industrialized nations, government provides universal coverage, thus freeing businesses from shouldering the costs themselves. While national policymakers struggle to deal with this problem, some states have once again jumped in to fill the void. Massachusetts passed a mandatory coverage program, and several others are considering their own versions designed to provide coverage—either privately purchased or provided by government—to cover all or nearly all uninsured individuals. Health-care reform was a major issue in the 2008 presidential campaign, with both the Democratic and Republican candidates presenting the voters with a plan to consider.

ECONOMIC POLICY

The federal government has played a role in economic activity since its inception, collecting taxes, funding the construction of roads and canals, and granting licenses to companies, all in the name of economic development. The Great Depression, however, triggered the most extensive expansion of government activity into the economic realm.

Many factors contributed to the Great Depression. Increases in productivity outpaced wages, leading to a surplus of goods many Americans could not afford. Restrictive international trade practices worsened this situation, as overseas sales by U.S. firms plummeted. Investors overspeculated in the booming stock market of the 1920s, and investors who lost money stopped supplying capital for business expansion. Laid-off workers defaulted on mortgages and cut back on purchases, further depressing business activity and investor confidence. More than a quarter of the labor force was out of work. Banks began to fail as depositors de-

The poor are especially vulnerable when disasters hit. They rely on government programs for assistance.

British economist John Maynard Keynes (1883–1946). Keynes argued that fiscal policy can be used as a discretionary tool to moderate cycles of inflation and unemployment, known as the business cycle. By varying the amount of taxes they levy or spending they authorize, Keynes asserted, governments can control overall economic demand. For example, government can respond to **recessions**—periods of high unemployment and reduced demand—in one of two ways. It can either buy more goods and services itself, thereby putting income into the hands of workers

manded their savings and banks were unable to collect on outstanding loans fast enough to provide liquidity. Food riots were not uncommon, and lines of men, women, and children waiting for help at soup kitchens stretched for blocks.

Franklin Roosevelt's New Deal attempted to prop up the failing economy, reassure financial markets, and provide hope for the legions of unemployed. Although scholars debate the overall economic effectiveness of these policies, they agree that the New Deal marked a significant change in the nature of federal intervention in the economy. Under Roosevelt, the national government took the direct hand in promoting, directing, and regulating economic activity that it maintains today.

Fiscal Policy

Fiscal policy consists of the use of the government's taxing and spending authority to influence the national economy. By virtue of its sheer size, the government's fiscal policies can dramatically affect the direction of the economy. Government regulations, such as those that ensure the quality of food and drugs and protect workers, also affect economic activity.

Tools for Fiscal Policy Fiscal policy is made by the president, who proposes a yearly budget for the U.S. government, and by Congress, which authorizes taxing and spending through a process discussed in Chapter 11. The figure to the right shows the projected 2009 fiscal year budget, illustrating the source of revenue and where the money is spent.

Much of the thinking about the goals and effects of fiscal policy was outlined early in the twentieth century by

Where the Money Comes From and Where It Goes

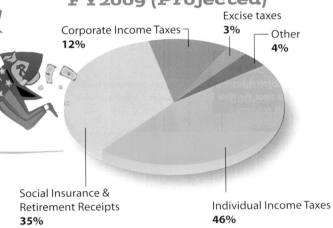

Federal Revenues by Source FY2009 (Projected)

- Corporate Income Taxes **12%**
- Excise taxes **3%**
- Other **4%**
- Social Insurance & Retirement Receipts **35%**
- Individual Income Taxes **46%**

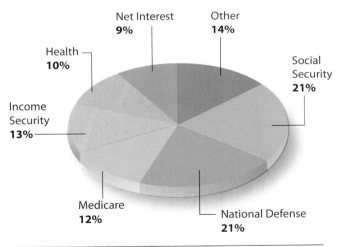

Total Federal Outlays FY2009 (Projected)

- Net Interest **9%**
- Other **14%**
- Health **10%**
- Social Security **21%**
- Income Security **13%**
- Medicare **12%**
- National Defense **21%**

Note: Other includes general science, space, and technology; energy; agriculture; commerce and housing credit; community and regional development; general government; allowances; and undistributed offset requests.

Source: Office of Management and Budget.

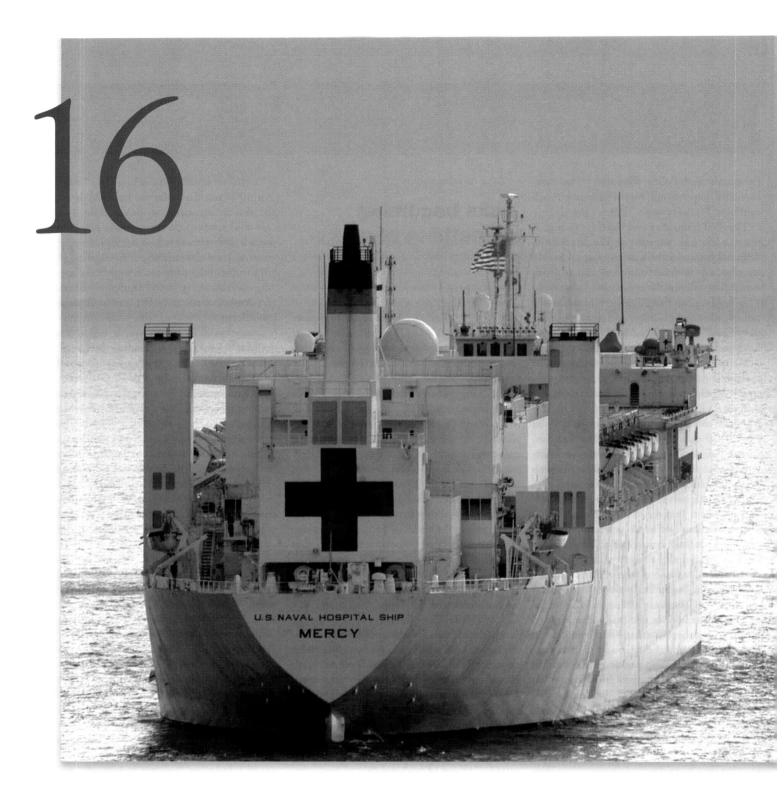

FOREIGN
AND DEFENSE

PROTECTING AMERICAN INTERESTS IN THE WORLD

INTELLIGENCE: GETTING IT RIGHT ▌ In his 2002 State of the Union address, President Bush warned that the West was facing a nuclear threat from an "axis of evil" that included Iraq, Iran, and North Korea. Later that year, he outlined his case against Iraq in a speech: "Saddam Hussein has held numerous meetings with Iraqi nuclear scientists . . . Satellite photographs reveal that Iraq is rebuilding facilities at sites that have been part of its nuclear program in the past. Iraq has attempted to purchase high-strength aluminum tubes and other equipment needed for gas centrifuges, which are used to enrich uranium for nuclear weapons. . . . America must not ignore the threat gathering against us. Facing clear evidence of peril, we cannot wait for the final proof—the smoking gun—that could come in the form of a mushroom cloud."[1]

In subsequent speeches Vice President Dick Cheney, Secretary of State Colin Powell, and National Security Advisor Condoleezza Rice all cited the same intelligence as evidence of the threat posed ➥

POLICY

As You READ >>

- What are the major goals of American foreign policy?
- Who are the principal actors in the foreign-policy-making process?
- What are the tools that foreign-policy makers have at their disposal?

by Iraq's Saddam Hussein. Few members of Congress questioned these assertions, not even those who, because they sit on committees dealing with national security issues, were privy to secret briefings. Although such countries as France and Germany warned that the United States should not take precipitous action against Iraq until the United Nations had completed its inspection of potential nuclear development sites, many other countries were impressed by the intelligence and convinced that Saddam's efforts to stall inspections meant that he had something to hide.

After the invasion, the world soon learned that the U.S. intelligence estimates were wrong. The Iraqi president had dismantled his country's nuclear program after the Gulf War in 1991. Now the rationale for invasion shifted from disarming Saddam to spreading democracy throughout the Middle East. At the same time, questions began to surface about the reliability of U.S. intelligence. How could we have gotten it so wrong? Could we ever again trust the intelligence community to get it right? Should we believe the administration sources who had begun touting intelligence about new nuclear threats in neighboring Iran? While some political observers suspected that the Bush administration had purposely distorted intelligence to justify military action, members of the intelligence community were harboring more profound concerns about their ability to assemble credible information for policymakers.

Secretary of State Colin Powell presented intelligence regarding Iraq's possession of weapons of mass destruction in order to gain United Nations support for the U.S.-led invasion. The intelligence later proved to be faulty.

The failure of U.S. intelligence on Iraq spurred a full-scale reappraisal of intelligence gathering. Key leadership changes were made; the intelligence community was reorganized; greater emphasis was placed on intelligence sharing among the nation's intelligence-gathering agencies; and information was subjected to more intense scrutiny. New rules banned the use of anonymous sources, which had contributed to erroneous assessments of Saddam Hussein's nuclear arsenal. Thomas Fingar, the chairman of the National Intelligence Council (NIC), which reports to the director of national intelligence, demanded that agents submit formal assessments of all intelligence, including the strengths, weaknesses, and credibility of sources. His aim, as one report put it, was "to make estimates more rigorous, shades of judgment starker, politics and guesswork less prominent."[2]

This approach has already produced some surprising results. A National Intelligence Estimate issued by the NIC on Iran's nuclear program in December 2007 stated "with high confidence" that Iran had stopped working on nuclear weapons in the fall of 2003, probably as a result of international pressure. The estimate came as a shock to hawks who had warned that Iran's nuclear capabilities were growing. It remains to be seen whether this estimate is any more reliable than those used to justify the invasion of Iraq. One thing is certain, however. As the director of the Central Intelligence Agency (CIA), General Mike Hayden, puts it: "The long war in which the nation is engaged is an intelligence war—one that will be won or lost with information and ideas, not smart bombs."[3]

In this chapter, we will discuss the foreign policy dilemmas that the United States faces in an increasingly uncertain world. We will examine the institutions charged with assessing risks and formulating policies to protect the American homeland and provide security for U.S. interests in the world. Along the way, we will identify the role that citizens can and must play to protect the ideals we value. ◆

DEFENSE AND FOREIGN POLICY IN HISTORICAL PERSPECTIVE

The world has changed dramatically during your lifetime. Most of you were born about the time of the collapse of the Soviet Union in 1991, which marked the end of the Cold War. Many observers believed that a period of world peace would follow. A bloody war in the Balkans, bombing of the World Trade Center in 1993, attacks on U.S. embassies in Kenya and Tanzania in 1998, and most especially the events of September 11, 2001, shattered that dream and ushered in a period of increased global terrorism. The requirements for defending the nation change dramatically depending on the source and the nature of the enemies it faces. Defense and foreign policies that promoted peace and security during the Cold War may not meet the challenges of the "age of terrorism." New policies must be developed. **Defense policy** generally involves strategic decisions about the scale and use of military force in national security. **Foreign policy** is broader: it deals with the whole array of military, diplomatic, economic, and security exchanges the United States has with foreign nations.

Finding a Place in the World

Alexis de Tocqueville noted that America's prosperity rested in part on its geographic isolation, its defensible borders, and the absence of passion for war:

> The Americans have no neighbors and consequently no great wars, financial crises, invasions, or conquests to fear; they need neither heavy taxes nor a numerous army, nor great generals; they have also hardly anything to fear from something else which is a greater scourge for democratic republics than all these others put together, namely, military glory.[4]

He went on to observe that the foreign policy of early American presidents took advantage of the country's relative isolation and was guided by a defensive posture that steered clear of entangling alliances.[5]

Despite George Washington's admonition in his farewell address to avoid embroilment in the affairs of other nations, it soon became clear that America could not isolate itself from world affairs, especially since much of the North American continent was still in the hands of European nations that involved Americans in their causes when it served their interests. Soon, presidents were called upon to deal with naval skirmishes that interfered with free trade and hostilities with Native Americans that were instigated or exacerbated by foreign powers. Americans soon began to develop an active foreign policy aimed at expanding American territorial frontiers at home and defending American commercial interests abroad against ambitious Europeans.[6]

By the time James Monroe became president in 1817, America's western frontier had already been pushed almost halfway across the continent. Faced with the dual threat of Russian incursions in the Pacific Northwest and European designs on reacquiring recently liberated countries in Central and South America, Monroe presented a new foreign policy to Congress on December 2, 1823. The Monroe Doctrine, as it came to be known, warned that the United States would consider any attempt by European powers to extend their systems to the Western hemisphere as a threat to the nation's peace and safety. In return for European restraint, the United States would refrain from interference in the internal affairs of Europe. In subsequent years, this doctrine—which was never enacted by Congress and had no status in international law—was expanded to ward off European powers and to justify U.S. expansion to the Pacific.

In the second quarter of the nineteenth century, America supplemented its westward territorial expansion with international economic expansion. Diplomatic relations with the rest of the world continued to grow, along with American prestige; but the domestic fight over slavery

defense policy Strategic decisions about the scale and use of military force for national security.

foreign policy Strategies for dealing with foreign nations on a broad array of military, diplomatic, economic, and security issues.

. . . That the Monroe Doctrine was actually the creation of Monroe's secretary of state, John Quincy Adams? Both Monroe and Adams were experienced diplomats, but Adams was the shrewder practitioner of international politics.

Did You Know?

consumed most of the nation's energy, and in 1861 the growing schism between slave states and free states led to the Civil War.

Becoming an International Power

With the Civil War behind it, the United States once again turned its gaze outward. Unlike many European nations, America sought to achieve economic expansion without acquiring political outposts. By the turn of the twentieth century, it was becoming a world power, exercising military might to protect its interests in the Western hemisphere and expanding its influence in the South Pacific. America also began carving out a larger role for itself on the international stage. The Open Door Policy, initiated by John Hay, secretary of state in the administration of President William McKinley, declared that all nations trading with China should have equal privileges and also opposed China's partition by foreign powers.

In 1904, President Theodore Roosevelt issued his Roosevelt Corollary to the Monroe Doctrine, reasserting U.S. opposition to European intervention in this hemisphere but claiming America's right to intervene in the domestic affairs of its neighbors if they proved unable to maintain order and national sovereignty on their own. The corollary was used as a justification for U.S. intervention in a number of Caribbean countries, including Cuba, Haiti, and the Dominican Republic. The United States consolidated its dominance in the hemisphere with the opening of the Panama Canal in 1914.

Eventually, America was dragged into playing an even larger role. Despite President Woodrow Wilson's determination to keep the country out of World War I, the sinking of American merchant vessels by German submarines propelled America to join the fight. After the war, Wilson's efforts to prevent future wars by establishing the League of Nations, one of his Fourteen Points for international cooperation, failed to gain traction

containment American policies designed to limit the expansion of Soviet power around the world during the Cold War.

mutually assured destruction Arms policy followed by the superpowers during the Cold War, in which each side maintained an arsenal of nuclear weapons sufficient to destroy its enemy even after a first strike.

Despite President Woodrow Wilson's determination to keep the country out of World War I, the sinking of American merchant vessels by German submarines propelled America to join the fight.

either at home or abroad, and the Treaty of Versailles he helped negotiate to end the war was not even ratified by the U.S. Senate.

During this period, the involvement of American citizens in the consequences of foreign policy decisions expanded. The military draft initiated in 1917 was seen as a democratic response to the need for military personnel, and wealthier citizens could no longer buy their way out of it. A peacetime draft was instituted just before the United States entered World War II—a commitment that the country had tried to avoid. The Selective Training and Service Act of 1940 required all men between the ages of twenty-one and thirty-five to register with the Selective Service System and to remain available for service regardless of wealth or education. Deferments were available in the case of hardship, and those who opposed war on religious grounds were given the opportunity for alternate service.

The Nuclear Age

After World War II, the United States and the Soviet Union were the world's preeminent powers; both possessed large nuclear arsenals and could dispatch conventional military forces quickly anywhere in the world. In 1947, President Harry Truman issued the Truman Doctrine, declaring the intention of the United States to support free peoples who

Military Costs of Major U.S. Wars

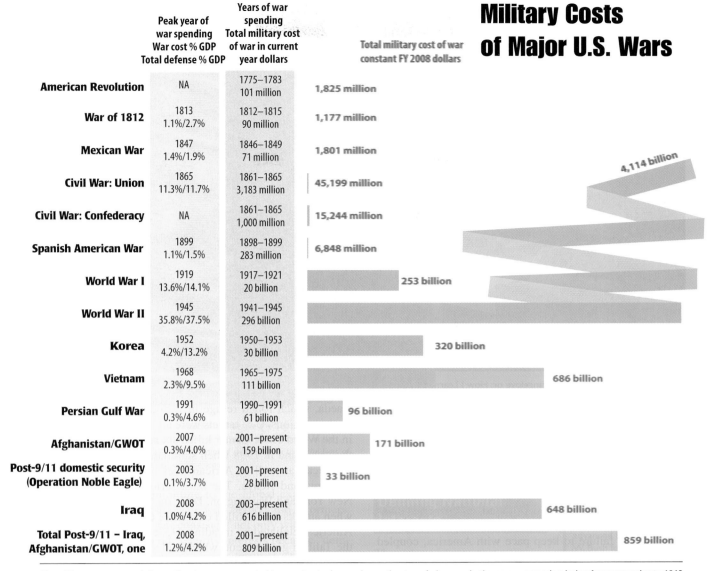

	Peak year of war spending War cost % GDP Total defense % GDP	Years of war spending Total military cost of war in current year dollars	Total military cost of war constant FY 2008 dollars
American Revolution	NA	1775–1783 101 million	1,825 million
War of 1812	1813 1.1%/2.7%	1812–1815 90 million	1,177 million
Mexican War	1847 1.4%/1.9%	1846–1849 71 million	1,801 million
Civil War: Union	1865 11.3%/11.7%	1861–1865 3,183 million	45,199 million
Civil War: Confederacy	NA	1861–1865 1,000 million	15,244 million
Spanish American War	1899 1.1%/1.5%	1898–1899 283 million	6,848 million
World War I	1919 13.6%/14.1%	1917–1921 20 billion	253 billion
World War II	1945 35.8%/37.5%	1941–1945 296 billion	4,114 billion
Korea	1952 4.2%/13.2%	1950–1953 30 billion	320 billion
Vietnam	1968 2.3%/9.5%	1965–1975 111 billion	686 billion
Persian Gulf War	1991 0.3%/4.6%	1990–1991 61 billion	96 billion
Afghanistan/GWOT	2007 0.3%/4.0%	2001–present 159 billion	171 billion
Post-9/11 domestic security (Operation Noble Eagle)	2003 0.1%/3.7%	2001–present 28 billion	33 billion
Iraq	2008 1.0%/4.2%	2003–present 616 billion	648 billion
Total Post-9/11 – Iraq, Afghanistan/GWOT, one	2008 1.2%/4.2%	2001–present 809 billion	859 billion

Note: The current year dollar estimates are converted to constant prices using estimates of changes in the consumer price index for years prior to 1940 and using Office of Management and Budget and Department of Defense estimates of defense inflation for years thereafter. The CPI estimates used here are from a database maintained at Oregon State University. The database periodically updates figures for new official CPI estimates of the U.S. Department of Commerce.

Source: Stephen Daggett, "Cost of U.S. Major Wars," *CRS Report for Congress*, July 24, 2008, 2.

were resisting attempted subjugation by armed minorities or by outside pressures. This doctrine guided the U.S. policy of **containment**, which was used to justify U.S. military intervention in order to stem Communist expansion and led to the United States fighting wars with perceived Soviet surrogates in Vietnam and elsewhere.

Vietnam marked another change in citizen involvement in war. Deferments for those who could afford to go to college led to disenchantment with the way that the Selective Service operated. In response, a draft lottery that limited deferment opportunities was initiated in 1969. In 1973, as the Vietnam War was winding down, the draft was replaced by a system of voluntary military enlistment. Today, the all-volunteer army includes a growing number of women, although they are barred from direct combat roles.

U.S. nuclear policy during the Cold War was informed by a principle of **mutually assured destruction** (MAD), which presumed that neither superpower would be the first to launch a nuclear attack if it understood that such an act would lead to its own certain destruction. The discomfort many Americans felt living under this threat was reflected in the popular culture of the 1960s. Movies such as *Dr. Strangelove or: How I Learned to Stop Worrying and Love the Bomb* poked fun at living in a world of permanent nuclear stalemate.

détente Foreign policy begun in the Nixon administration stressing accommodation with rivals rather than conflict.

A period of **détente** opened in the 1970s when the United States and the Soviet Union attempted to ease tensions by undertaking a number of cooperative actions like forcement Administration (DEA), which are both part of the Justice Department; and other bodies. According to the 9/11 Commission, which investigated the attacks on the World Trade Center and the Pentagon, the failure of the intelligence community to identify and track the perpetrators was due in part to the lack of intelligence sharing among these agencies.[15] Reorganization under the supervision of the Office of the Director of Intelligence was meant to integrate foreign, military, and domestic intelligence in defense of the homeland and of United States interests abroad.

Some civil libertarians fear that the resulting amalgamation of information from domestic and foreign sources may lead to unwarranted spying on U.S. citizens. In fact, in 2002, President Bush signed a secret order authorizing the NSA to eavesdrop on U.S. citizens and foreign nationals in the United States, despite previous legal prohibitions against this practice. The aim of the program was to rapidly monitor the phone calls and other communications of people in the United States believed to have contact with suspected associates of Al Qaeda and other overseas terrorist groups. Techniques employed under the program included the use of data harvesting to monitor and sort through the e-mail, telephone calls, and other communications of hundreds, and perhaps thousands, of people. In 2007, the president signed into law the Protect America Act, which eased restrictions on surveillance of terrorist suspects when one or both parties

Foreign Intelligence Surveillance Act court (FISA court) Secret court housed in the Justice Department and used to oversee requests by federal agencies for surveillance warrants based on suspected espionage or terrorism.

are located overseas. As a result, communications that begin or end in a foreign country may be wiretapped.

In response to claims by critics that these laws gave the executive branch almost unchecked power to snoop on citizens, Congress and the president agreed to a new law in June 2008. The law strengthens the ability of intelligence officials to eavesdrop on foreign targets and allows them to conduct emergency wiretaps without court orders on American targets for a limited time if it is determined that important national security information would otherwise be lost. However, the law limits the use of such wiretaps to terrorism and espionage cases and calls for greater oversight, including advance approval by a secret court created under the Foreign Intelligence Surveillance Act of 1978. The **FISA court** is staffed by eleven judges appointed by the chief justice of the United States to serve seven-year terms. The 2008 legislation also included a controversial provision to extend immunity to telecommunication companies that had acceded to prior administration requests for information about their customers at a time when the transfer of such information was not authorized.

Other Executive Agencies In an era dominated by concerns about global terror and the global economy, virtually no executive agency is without some role in advancing U.S. foreign policy goals. The departments of Commerce and Treasury help expand peaceful trade; the Drug Enforcement Administration (DEA) attempts to interdict drug shipments; the departments of Energy, Defense, and Commerce all monitor the types of technology we transfer to potentially hostile nations; the Department of Health and Human Services provides technical support to nations combating HIV/AIDS. All of these activities advance the national security goal of creating "a more secure and prosperous world that benefits the American people and the world community."[16]

The treatment of Afghan and Iraqi prisoners at Guantanamo Bay led to charges that the administration condoned torture techniques such as waterboarding and undermined U.S. credibility on issues of human rights.

While the Iraq War has drawn antiwar protests, their size and intensity is not as great as those directed against the Vietnam War at a time when young men were faced with a military draft.

During the Bush administration, Vice President Cheney exercised unprecedented power in foreign-policy making by creating additional ad hoc working groups that conducted their own reviews of intelligence and made input directly to the president. He worked closely with an inner circle of lawyers, including his chief of staff, David Addington, to formulate policies on torture and the detainment of enemy combatants.[17]

Congress's Role

Congress can play a key role in foreign and defense policy even if it is sometimes overshadowed by executive branch power. In Chapter 11, we learned that the Framers split authority for national security by authorizing the president to take immediate action to defend against attacks on U.S. interests but reserved to Congress the prerogative to declare war. We also learned that presidents have usually managed to secure authorization from Congress for waging war

Congressional Actions Influencing War Termination

Year	Congressional action
1801	Amended treaty ending quasi-war with France, forced further negotiations
1919	Rejected Versailles Treaty that ended World War I
1919	Tie vote on resolution calling for withdrawal of U.S. troops intervening in Soviet Russia, prompting order for withdrawal within days
1923	Voted on resolution asking for immediate return of U.S. occupation troops from Germany, prompting withdrawal announcement within days
1970	Barred further military operations in Cambodia following U.S. withdrawal
1973	Forced U.S. air combat operations in Southeast Asia to end
1975	Rejected last-minute requests for aid to South Yemen
1993	Wrote into law Clinton administration promise to withdraw troops from Somalia

Source: Adapted from Charles A. Stevenson, *Congress At War: The Politics of Conflict Since 1789* (Dulles, VA: National Defense University Press, 2007), 68.

short of formal declarations. Nevertheless, Congress is not powerless to oppose presidential powers related to defense and security. Congress can cut off funding for war; it can reject presidential requests for authority to commence hostile activities; it can expand or reject presidential requests for foreign aid; and, by holding hearings on presidential policies and procedures, Congress can convey its own preferences. The House Permanent Select Committee on Intelligence and the Senate Select Committee on Intelligence receive briefings from the intelligence community, conduct oversight hearings, and authorize budgets for intelligence operations. In addition, the Senate can reject treaties with other nations. These checks on presidential authority are not merely hypothetical.

Congress has successfully reined in presidential authority on a number of occasions. Nevertheless, in times of international tension, support for presidential authority is sometimes difficult for congressional opponents to overcome. Such was the case in 2007, when a newly elected Democratic Congress repeatedly tried to force an end to the war in Iraq by rejecting the president's call for a military "surge"—the infusion of more than 21,000 additional troops into Iraq to quell the rising tide of violence— and by proposing a redeployment to limit our combat role. President Bush was able to maintain the loyalty of enough members of his own party to block congressional action.

One of Congress's principal foreign policy functions is to provide funding for military, diplomatic, and foreign aid programs. The cost

John Harabedian, Andrew Klaber, and Adam Grogg with schoolchildren in Kitale, Kenya.

PORTRAIT OF AN ACTIVIST

Andrew Klaber

Young people can play an especially important role in spreading soft power, and examples of civic activism across borders abound. One is Andrew Klaber, a twenty-six-year-old Harvard Business School student who, on a summer trip to Thailand, witnessed teenage girls being forced into prostitution. Upon his return to the United States, he started Orphans Against AIDS (www.orphansagainstaids .org/). Orphans Against AIDS pays school-related expenses for children who have been orphaned or otherwise affected by AIDS in poor countries. Andrew and the volunteers that he works with pay for all administrative costs themselves so that every penny raised goes to the children. Nicholas Kristof, who trumpeted the work of Andrew and several other social entrepreneurs in *The New York Times*, feels good about the global civic activism of today's young people: "These are the social entrepreneurs, the 21st-century answer to the student protesters of the 1960s."*

* Nicholas D. Kristof, "The Age of Ambition," *New York Times*, January 27, 2008.

---

can make a positive contribution to the lives of others and enhance the humanitarian reputation of the United States throughout the world.

Each year, **nongovernmental organizations (NGOs)** send volunteers and money all over the world to feed the hungry, alleviate poverty, combat disease, educate the young, and provide expertise to help local populations build civil societies and the infrastructure needed to succeed in development. NGOs are nonprofit, voluntary citizens' groups organized on a local, national, or international level. On the international stage, NGOs perform a variety of service and humanitarian functions, bring citizen concerns to governments, advocate and monitor policies, and encourage political participation. Although some NGOs are partly funded by or housed within larger bodies such as the UN, for the most part governments do not play an active role in their governance or operation.

nongovernmental organizations (NGOs) Nonprofit citizens' groups organized for a variety of charitable and humanitarian purposes on a local, national, or international level.

soft power The ability to persuade others without coercion.

NGOs offer many and varied opportunities for Americans interested in working to help others in foreign lands. Some NGOs are well-known, such as the American Red Cross and Save the Children. Many are associated with religious organizations, such as the Quakers. For instance, the American Friends Service Committee operates the Mexico Summer Project, which brings together youth from diverse communities for seven weeks to live with indigenous peoples in the Sierra Norte de Puebla, Mexico. The project aims to expand social justice and sustainable development in the region.

Such opportunities not only provide direct help to those in need but also spread goodwill. This goodwill is part of **soft power**, the ability to shape the preferences of others without coercion.[30] Soft power is spread through the sharing of American values, customs, and culture. Through civic outreach, we foster cooperation and inspire others to share our concerns for fairness and just outcomes. We motivate others to want the same outcomes that we want. You can read about one such example in this chapter's "Portrait of an Activist."

1. What are the major goals of American foreign policy?
   - Foreign policy seeks to secure the nation's defense and to promote its economic and ideological interests.

2. Who are the principal actors in the foreign-policy-making process?
   - The president plays the primary role in foreign-policy making through executive agencies that include the National Security Council, the Department of State, and the Department of Defense, as well as the intelligence community and other bodies. However, major roles are also played by Congress, nongovernmental agencies like think tanks, and the public.

3. What are the tools that foreign policy makers have at their disposal?
   - Foreign-policy makers employ military power, diplomacy, and foreign aid in advancing U.S. interests. They also seek to forge ties with other nations and with multinational organizations to achieve shared objectives.

■ **FOR DISCUSSION:** Should the MEK, and similar groups hostile to unfriendly nations, remain a terrorist organization? Should America regard the enemies of its enemies as friends, no matter how distasteful? Do the threats of some regimes, such as the theocracy in Iran, require you to compromise and make pragmatic concessions to militant groups trying to overthrow them?

The foregoing Declaration was, by order of Congress, engrossed, and signed by the following members:

JOHN HANCOCK

New Hampshire
Josiah Bartlett
William Whipple
Matthew Thornton

Massachusetts Bay
Samuel Adams
John Adams
Robert Treat Paine
Elbridge Gerry

Rhode Island
Stephen Hopkins
William Ellery

Connecticut
Roger Sherman
Samuel Huntington
William Williams
Oliver Wolcott

New York
William Floyd
Philip Livingston
Francis Lewis
Lewis Morris

New Jersey
Richard Stockton
John Witherspoon
Francis Hopkinson
John Hart
Abraham Clark

Pennsylvania
Robert Morris
Benjamin Rush
Benjamin Franklin
John Morton
George Clymer
James Smith
George Taylor
James Wilson
George Ross

Delaware
Caesar Rodney
George Reed
Thomas M'Kean

Maryland
Samuel Chase
William Paca
Thomas Stone
Charles Carroll, of Carrollton

Virginia
George Wythe
Richard Henry Lee
Thomas Jefferson
Benjamin Harrison
Thomas Nelson, Jr.
Francis Lightfoot Lee
Carter Braxton

North Carolina
William Hooper
Joseph Hewes
John Penn

South Carolina
Edward Rutledge
Thomas Heyward, Jr.
Thomas Lynch, Jr.
Arthur Middleton

Georgia
Button Gwinnett
Lyman Hall
George Walton

Resolved, That copies of the Declaration be sent to the several assemblies, conventions, and committees, or councils of safety, and to the several commanding officers of the continental troops; that it be proclaimed in each of the United States, at the head of the army.

THE CONSTITUTION OF THE UNITED STATES OF AMERICA[1]

We the People of the United States, in Order to form a more perfect Union, establish Justice, insure domestic Tranquility, provide for the common defence, promote the general Welfare, and secure the Blessings of Liberty to ourselves and our Posterity, do ordain and establish this CONSTITUTION for the United States of America.

ARTICLE I

SECTION 1

All legislative Powers herein granted shall be vested in a Congress of the United States, which shall consist of a Senate and House of Representatives.

SECTION 2

The House of Representatives shall be composed of Members chosen every second Year by the People of the several States, and the Electors in each State shall have the Qualifications requisite for Electors of the most numerous Branch of the State Legislature.

No Person shall be a Representative who shall not have attained to the Age of twenty-five Years, and been seven Years a Citizen of the United States, and who shall not, when elected, be an Inhabitant of that State in which he shall be chosen.

[Representatives and direct Taxes[2] shall be apportioned among the several States which may be included within this Union, according to their respective Numbers, which shall be determined by adding to the whole Number of free Persons, including those bound to Service for a Term of Years, and excluding Indians not taxed, three fifths of all other Persons.][3] The actual Enumeration shall be made within three Years after the first Meeting of the Congress of the United States, and within every subsequent Term of ten Years, in such Manner as they shall by Law direct. The Number of Representatives shall not exceed one for every thirty Thousand, but each State shall have at Least one Representative; and until such enumeration shall be made, the State of New Hampshire shall be entitled to chuse three, Massachusetts eight, Rhode-Island and Providence Plantations one, Connecticut five, New York six, New Jersey four, Pennsylvania eight, Delaware one, Maryland six, Virginia ten, North Carolina five, South Carolina five, and Georgia three.

When vacancies happen in the Representation from any State, the Executive Authority thereof shall issue Writs of Election to fill such Vacancies.

The House of Representatives shall chuse their Speaker and other Officers; and shall have the sole Power of Impeachment.

SECTION 3

The Senate of the United States shall be composed of two Senators from each State, chosen by the Legislature thereof, for six Years; and each Senator shall have one Vote.

Immediately after they shall be assembled in Consequence of the first Election, they shall be divided as equally as may be into three Classes. The Seats of the Senators of the first Class shall be vacated at the Expiration of the second Year, of the second Class at the Expiration of the fourth Year, and of the third Class at the Expiration of the sixth Year, so that one-third may be chosen every second Year; and if Vacancies happen by Resignation, or otherwise, during the Recess of the Legislature of any State, the Executive thereof may make temporary Appointments until the next Meeting of the Legislature, which shall then fill such Vacancies.

No Person shall be a Senator who shall not have attained to the Age of thirty Years, and been nine Years a Citizen of the United States, and who shall not, when elected, be an Inhabitant of that State for which he shall be chosen.

The Vice President of the United States shall be President of the Senate, but shall have no vote, unless they be equally divided.

The Senate shall chuse their other Officers, and also a President pro tempore, in the absence of the Vice President, or when he shall exercise the Office of President of the United States.

The Senate shall have the sole Power to try all Impeachments. When sitting for that purpose they shall be on Oath or Affirmation. When the President of the United States is tried, the Chief Justice shall preside: And no person shall be convicted without the Concurrence of two thirds of the Members present.

Judgment in Cases of Impeachment shall not extend further than to removal from Office, and disqualification to hold and enjoy any Office of honor, Trust, or Profit under

[1.] *This version, which follows the original Constitution in capitalization and spelling, was published by the United States Department of the Interior, Office of Education, in 1935.*
[2.] *Altered by the Sixteenth Amendment.*
[3.] *Negated by the Fourteenth Amendment.*

eedings shall be proved, and the Effect thereof.

[5.] *Qualified by the Eleventh Amendment.*

its equal Suffrage in the Senate.

sign and certify, and transmit sealed to the Seat of the Government of the United States, directed to the President of the Senate. The President of the Senate shall, in the Presence of the Senate and House of Representatives, open

ARTICLE VI

All Debts contracted and Engagements entered into, before the Adoption of this Constitution, shall be as valid against the United States under this Constitution, as under the Confederation.

This Constitution, and the Laws of the United States which shall be made in Pursuance thereof; and all Treaties made, or which shall be made, under the Authority of the United States, shall be the supreme Law of the Land; and the Judges in every State shall be bound thereby, any Thing in the Constitution or Laws of any State to the Contrary notwithstanding.

The Senators and Representatives before mentioned, and the Members of the several State Legislatures, and all executive and judicial Officers, both of the United States and of the several States, shall be bound by Oath or Affirmation to support this Constitution; but no religious Tests shall ever be required as a qualification to any Office or public Trust under the United States.

ARTICLE VII

The Ratification of the Conventions of nine States shall be sufficient for the Establishment of this Constitution between the States so ratifying the same.

Done in Convention by the Unanimous Consent of the States present the Seventeenth Day of September in the Year of our Lord one thousand seven hundred and Eighty seven, and of the Independence of the United States of America the Twelfth. In Witness whereof We have hereunto subscribed our Names.[6]

George Washington
President and deputy from Virginia

New Hampshire	Thomas Mifflin
John Langdon	Robert Morris
Nicholas Gilman	George Clymer
	Thomas FitzSimmons
Massachusetts	Jared Ingersoll
Nathaniel Gorham	James Wilson
Rufus King	Gouverneur Morris
Connecticut	*Delaware*
William Samuel Johnson	George Read
Roger Sherman	Gunning Bedford, Jr.
New York	John Dickinson
Alexander Hamilton	Richard Bassett
	Jacob Broom
New Jersey	
William Livingston	*Maryland*
David Brearley	James McHenry
William Paterson	Daniel of St. Thomas
Jonathan Dayton	Jenifer
	Daniel Carroll
Pennsylvania	
Benjamin Franklin	

SECTION 2

The President shall be Commander in Chief of the Army and Navy of the United States, and of the Militia of the

Virginia	*South Carolina*
John Blair	John Rutledge
James Madison, Jr.	Charles Cotesworth
	Pinckney
North Carolina	Charles Pinckney
William Blount	Pierce Butler
Richard Dobbs Spaight	
Hugh Williamson	*Georgia*
	William Few
	Abraham Baldwin

Articles in Addition to, and Amendment of, the Constitution of the United States of America, Proposed by Congress, and Ratified by the Legislatures of the Several States, Pursuant to the Fifth Article of the Original Constitution[7]

AMENDMENT I

Congress shall make no law respecting an establishment of religion, or prohibiting the free exercise thereof; or abridging the freedom of speech, or of the press; or the right of the people peaceably to assemble, and to petition the Government for a redress of grievances.

AMENDMENT II

A well regulated Militia, being necessary to the security of a free State, the right of the people to keep and bear Arms shall not be infringed.

AMENDMENT III

No Soldier shall, in time of peace, be quartered in any house, without the consent of the Owner, nor in time of war, but in a manner to be prescribed by law.

AMENDMENT IV

The right of the people to be secure in their persons, houses, papers, and effects, against unreasonable searches and seizures, shall not be violated, and no Warrants shall issue, but upon probable cause, supported by Oath or affirmation, and particularly describing the place to be searched, and the persons or things to be seized.

AMENDMENT V

No person shall be held to answer for a capital or otherwise infamous crime, unless on a presentment or indictment of a Grand Jury, except in cases arising in the land or naval forces, or in the Militia, when in actual service in time of War or public danger; nor shall any person be subject for the same offence to be twice put in jeopardy of life or limb;

[6] *These are the full names of the signers, which in some cases are not the signatures on the document.*

[7] *This heading appears only in the joint resolution submitting the first ten amendments, which are collectively known as the Bill of Rights. They were ratified on December 15, 1791.*

nor shall be compelled in any criminal case to be a witness against himself, nor be deprived of life, liberty, or property, without due process of law; nor shall private property be taken for public use, without just compensation.

AMENDMENT VI

In all criminal prosecutions, the accused shall enjoy the right to a speedy and public trial, by an impartial jury of the State and district wherein the crime shall have been committed, which district shall have been previously ascertained by law, and to be informed of the nature and cause of the accusation; to be confronted with the witnesses against him; to have compulsory process for obtaining witnesses in his favour, and to have the Assistance of Counsel for his defence.

AMENDMENT VII

In suits at common law, where the value in controversy shall exceed twenty dollars, the right of trial by jury shall be preserved, and no fact tried by a jury, shall be otherwise reexamined in any Court of the United States, than according to the rules of the common law.

AMENDMENT VIII

Excessive bail shall not be required, nor excessive fines imposed, nor cruel and unusual punishments inflicted.

AMENDMENT IX

The enumeration of the Constitution, of certain rights, shall not be construed to deny or disparage others retained by the people.

AMENDMENT X

The powers not delegated to the United States by the Constitution, nor prohibited by it to the States, are reserved to the States respectively, or to the people.

AMENDMENT XI [1795]

The Judicial power of the United States shall not be construed to extend to any suit in law or equity, commenced or prosecuted against one of the United States by Citizens of another State, or by Citizens or Subjects of any Foreign State.

AMENDMENT XII [1804]

The Electors shall meet in their respective States and vote by ballot for President and Vice-President, one of whom, at least, shall not be an inhabitant of the same State with themselves; they shall name in their ballots the person voted for as President, and in distinct ballots the person voted for as Vice-President, and they shall make distinct lists of all persons voted for as President, and of all persons voted for as Vice-President, and of the number of votes for each, which lists they shall sign and certify, and transmit sealed to the seat of the government of the United States, directed to the President of the Senate;—The President of the Senate shall, in the presence of the Senate and House of Representatives, open all the certificates and the votes shall then be counted;—The person having the greatest number of votes for President, shall be the President, if such number be a majority of the whole number of Electors appointed; and if no person have such majority, then from the persons having the highest numbers not exceeding three on the list of those voted for as President, the House of Representatives shall choose immediately, by ballot, the President. But in choosing the President, the votes shall be taken by states, the representation from each state having one vote; a quorum for this purpose shall consist of a member or members from two-thirds of the states, and a majority of all the states shall be necessary to a choice. And if the House of Representatives shall not choose a President whenever the right of choice shall devolve upon them, before the fourth day of March next following, then the Vice-President shall act as President, as in the case of the death or other constitutional disability of the President.—The person having the greatest number of votes as Vice-President, shall be the Vice-President, if such number be a majority of the whole number of Electors appointed, and if no person have a majority, then from the two highest numbers on the list, the Senate shall choose the Vice-President; a quorum for the purpose shall consist of two-thirds of the whole number of Senators, and majority of the whole number shall be necessary to a choice. But no person constitutionally ineligible to the office of President shall be eligible to that of Vice-President of the United States.

AMENDMENT XIII [1865]

SECTION 1

Neither slavery nor involuntary servitude, except as a punishment for crime whereof the party shall have been duly convicted, shall exist within the United States, or any place subject to their jurisdiction.

SECTION 2

Congress shall have power to enforce this article by appropriate legislation.

AMENDMENT XIV [1868]

SECTION 1

All persons born or naturalized in the United States, and subject to the jurisdiction thereof, are citizens of the United States and of the State wherein they reside. No State shall abridge the privileges or immunities of citizens of the United States; nor shall any State deprive any person of life, liberty, or property, without due process of law; nor deny to any person within its jurisdiction the equal protection of the laws.

SECTION 2

Representatives shall be apportioned among the several States according to their respective numbers, counting the whole number of persons in each State, excluding Indians not taxed. But when the right to vote at any election for the choice of electors for President and Vice-President of the United States, Representatives in Congress, the Executive and Judicial officers of a State, or the members of the Legislature thereof, is denied to any of the male inhabitants of such State, being twenty-one years of age, and citizens of the United States, or in any way abridged, except for participation in rebellion, or other crime, the basis of representation therein shall be reduced in the proportion which the number of such male citizens shall bear to the whole number of male citizens twenty-one years of age in such State.

SECTION 3

No person shall be a Senator or Representative in Congress, or elector of President and Vice-President, or hold any office, civil or military, under the United States, or under any State, who, having previously taken an oath, as a member of Congress, or as an officer of the United States, or as a member of any State legislature, or as an executive or judicial officer of any State, to support the Constitution of the United States, shall have engaged in insurrection or rebellion against the same, or given aid or comfort to the enemies thereof. But Congress may by a vote of two-thirds of each House, remove such disability.

SECTION 4

The validity of the public debt of the United States, authorized by law, including debts incurred for payment of pensions and bounties for services in suppressing insurrection or rebellion, shall not be questioned. But neither the United States nor any State shall assume or pay any debts or obligation incurred in aid of insurrection or rebellion against the United States, or any claim for the loss or emancipation of any slave; but all such debts, obligations, and claims shall be held illegal and void.

SECTION 5

The Congress shall have the power to enforce, by appropriate legislation, the provisions of this article.

AMENDMENT XV [1870]

SECTION 1

The right of citizens of the United States to vote shall not be denied or abridged by the United States or by any State on account of race, color, or previous condition of servitude.

SECTION 2

The Congress shall have power to enforce this article by appropriate legislation.

AMENDMENT XVI [1913]

The Congress shall have power to lay and collect taxes on incomes, from whatever source derived, without apportionment among the several States, and without regard to any census or enumeration.

AMENDMENT XVII [1913]

The Senate of the United States shall be composed of two Senators from each State, elected by the people thereof, for six years; and each Senator shall have one vote. The electors in each State shall have the qualifications requisite for electors of the most numerous branch of the State legislatures.

When vacancies happen in the representation of any State in the Senate, the executive authority of such State shall issue writs of election to fill such vacancies: Provided, That the legislature of any State may empower the executive thereof to make temporary appointments until the people fill the vacancies by election as the legislature may direct.

This amendment shall not be so construed as to affect the election or term of any Senator chosen before it becomes valid as part of the Constitution.

AMENDMENT XVIII [1919]

SECTION 1

After one year from the ratification of this article the manufacture, sale, or transportation of intoxicating liquors within, the importation thereof into, or the exportation thereof from the United States and all territory subject to the jurisdiction thereof for beverage purposes is hereby prohibited.

SECTION 2

The Congress and the several States shall have concurrent power to enforce this article by appropriate legislation.

SECTION 3

This article shall be inoperative unless it shall have been ratified as an amendment to the Constitution by the legislatures of the several States, as provided in the Constitution, within seven years from the date of the submission hereof to the States by the Congress.

AMENDMENT XIX [1920]

The right of citizens of the United States to vote shall not be denied or abridged by the United States or by any State on account of sex.

Congress shall have power to enforce this article by appropriate legislation.

AMENDMENT XX [1933]

SECTION 1

The terms of the President and Vice-President shall end at noon on the 20th day of January, and the terms of Senators and Representatives at noon on the 3d day of January, of the years in which such terms would have ended if this article had not been ratified; and the terms of their successors shall then begin.

SECTION 2

The Congress shall assemble at least once in every year, and such meeting shall begin at noon on the 3d day of January, unless they shall by law appoint a different day.

SECTION 3

If, at the time fixed for the beginning of the term of the President, the President elect shall have died, the Vice-President elect shall become President. If a President shall not have been chosen before the time fixed for the beginning of his term or if the President elect shall have failed to qualify, then the Vice-President elect shall act as President until a President shall have qualified; and the Congress may by law provide for the case wherein neither a President elect nor a Vice-President elect shall have qualified, declaring who shall then act as President, or the manner in which one who is to act shall be selected, and such person shall act

accordingly until a President or Vice-President shall have qualified.

SECTION 4

The Congress may by law provide for the case of the death of any of the persons from whom the House of Representatives may choose a President whenever the right of choice shall have devolved upon them, and for the case of the death of any of the persons from whom the Senate may choose a Vice- President whenever the right of choice shall have devolved upon them.

SECTION 5

Sections 1 and 2 shall take effect on the 15th day of October following the ratification of this article.

SECTION 6

This article shall be inoperative unless it shall have been ratified as an amendment to the Constitution by the legislatures of three-fourths of the several States within seven years from the date of its submission.

AMENDMENT XXI [1933]

SECTION 1

The eighteenth article of amendment to the Constitution of the United States is hereby repealed.

SECTION 2

The transportation or importation into any State, Territory, or possession of the United States for delivery or use therein of intoxicating liquors, in violation of the laws thereof, is hereby prohibited.

SECTION 3

This article shall be inoperative unless it shall have been ratified as an amendment to the Constitution by conventions in the several States, as provided in the Constitution, within seven years from the date of the submission hereof to the States by the Congress.

AMENDMENT XXII [1951]

No person shall be elected to the office of the President more than twice, and no person who has held the office of President, or acted as President, for more than two years of a term to which some other person was elected President shall be elected to the office of the President more than once.

But this Article shall not apply to any person holding the office of President when this Article was proposed by the Congress, and shall not prevent any person who may be holding the office of President, or acting as President, during the term within which this Article becomes operative from holding the office of President or acting as President during the remainder of such term.

This article shall be inoperative unless it shall have been ratified as an amendment to the Constitution by the legislatures of three-fourths of the several states within seven years from the date of its submission to the states by the Congress.

AMENDMENT XXIII [1961]

SECTION 1

The District constituting the seat of Government of the United States shall appoint in such manner as the Congress may direct:

A number of electors of President and Vice-President equal to the whole number of Senators and Representatives in Congress to which the District would be entitled if it were a State, but in no event more than the least populous State; they shall be in addition to those appointed by the States, but they shall be considered, for the purposes of the election of President and Vice-President, to be electors appointed by a State; and they shall meet in the District and perform such duties as provided by the twelfth article of amendment.

SECTION 2

The Congress shall have power to enforce this article by appropriate legislation.

AMENDMENT XXIV [1964]

SECTION 1

The right of citizens of the United States to vote in any primary or other election for President or Vice President, for electors for President or Vice President, or for Senator or Representative in Congress, shall not be denied or abridged by the United States or any state by reason of failure to pay any poll tax or other tax.

SECTION 2

The Congress shall have the power to enforce this article by appropriate legislation.

AMENDMENT XXV [1967]

SECTION 1

In case of the removal of the President from office or of his death or resignation, the Vice President shall become President.

SECTION 2

Whenever there is a vacancy in the office of the Vice President, the President shall nominate a Vice President who shall take office upon confirmation by a majority vote of both Houses of Congress.

SECTION 3

Whenever the President transmits to the President Pro Tempore of the Senate and the Speaker of the House of Representatives his written declaration that he is unable to discharge the powers and duties of his office, and until he transmits to them a written declaration to the contrary, such powers and duties shall be discharged by the Vice President as Acting President.

SECTION 4

Whenever the Vice President and a majority of either the principal officers of the executive departments or of such other body as Congress may by law provide, transmit to the President Pro Tempore of the Senate and the Speaker of the House of Representatives their written declaration that the President is unable to discharge the powers and duties of his office, the Vice President shall immediately assume the powers and duties of the office as Acting President.

Thereafter, when the President transmits to the President Pro Tempore of the Senate and the Speaker of the House of Representatives his written declaration that no inability exists, he shall resume the powers and duties of his office unless the Vice President and a majority of either the principal officers of the executive departments or of such other body as Congress may by law provide, transmit within four days to the President Pro Tempore of the Senate and the Speaker of the House of Representatives their written declaration that the President is unable to discharge the powers and duties of his office. Thereupon Congress shall decide the issue, assembling within forty-eight hours for that purpose if not in session. If the Congress, within twenty-one days after receipt of the latter written declaration, or, if Congress is not in session, within twenty-one days after Congress is required to assemble, determines by two-thirds vote of both Houses that the President is unable to discharge the powers and duties of his office, the Vice President shall continue to discharge the same as Acting

President; otherwise, the President shall resume the powers and duties of his office.

AMENDMENT XXVI [1971]

SECTION 1

The right of citizens of the United States, who are eighteen years of age or older, to vote shall not be denied or abridged by the United States or by any State on account of age.

SECTION 2

The Congress shall have the power to enforce this article by appropriate legislation.

AMENDMENT XXVII [1992]

No law varying the compensation for the service of Senators and Representatives shall take effect until an election of Representatives shall have intervened.

FEDERALIST PAPER NO. 10 (JAMES MADISON)

Among the numerous advantages promised by a well-constructed union, none deserves to be more accurately developed than its tendency to break and control the violence of faction. The friend of popular governments never finds himself so much alarmed for their character and fate as when he contemplates their propensity to this dangerous vice. He will not fail, therefore, to set a due value on any plan which, without violating the principles to which he is attached, provides a proper cure for it. The instability, injustice, and confusion introduced into the public councils have, in truth, been the mortal diseases under which popular governments have everywhere perished, as they continue to be the favorite and fruitful topics from which the adversaries to liberty derive their most specious declamations. The valuable improvements made by the American constitutions on the popular models, both ancient and modern, cannot certainly be too much admired; but it would be an unwarrantable partiality to contend that they have as effectually obviated the danger on this side, as was wished and expected. Complaints are everywhere heard from our most considerate and virtuous citizens, equally the friends of public and private faith and of public and personal liberty, that our governments are too unstable, that the public good is disregarded in the conflicts of rival parties, and that measures are too often decided, not according to the rules of justice and the rights of the minor party, but by the superior force of an interested and overbearing majority. However anxiously we may wish that these complaints had no foundation, the evidence of known facts will not permit us to deny that they are in some degree true. It will be found, indeed, on a candid review of our situation, that some of the distresses under which we labor have been erroneously charged on the operation of our governments; but it will be found, at the same time, that other causes will not alone account for many of our heaviest misfortunes; and, particularly, for that prevailing and increasing distrust of public engagements and alarm for private rights which are echoed from one end of the continent to the other. These must be chiefly, if not wholly, effects of the unsteadiness and injustice with which a factious spirit has tainted our public administration.

By a faction I understand a number of citizens, whether amounting to a majority or minority of the whole, who are united and actuated by some common impulse of passion, or of interest, adverse to the rights of other citizens, or to the permanent and aggregate interests of the community.

There are two methods of curing the mischiefs of faction: the one, by removing its causes; the other, by controlling its effects.

There are again two methods of removing the causes of faction: the one, by destroying the liberty which is essential to its existence; the other, by giving to every citizen the same opinions, the same passions, and the same interests.

It could never be more truly said than of the first remedy that it was worse than the disease. Liberty is to faction what air is to fire, an aliment without which it instantly expires. But it could not be a less folly to abolish liberty, which is essential to political life, because it nourishes faction than it would be to wish the annihilation of air, which is essential to animal life, because it imparts to fire its destructive agency.

The second expedient is as impracticable as the first would be unwise. As long as the reason of man continues fallible, and he is at liberty to exercise it, different opinions will be formed. As long as the connection subsists between his reason and his self-love, his opinions and his passions will have a reciprocal influence on each other; and the former will be objects to which the latter will attach themselves. The diversity in the faculties of men, from which the rights of property originate, is not less an insuperable obstacle to a uniformity of interest. The protection of these faculties is the first object of government. From the protection of different and unequal faculties of acquiring property, the possession of different degrees and kinds of property immediately results; and from the influence of these on the sentiments and views of the respective proprietors ensues a division of the society into different interests and parties.

The latent causes of faction are thus sown in the nature of man; and we see them everywhere brought into different degrees of activity, according to the different circumstances of civil society. A zeal for different opinions concerning religion, concerning government, and many other points, as well of speculation as of practice; an attachment to different leaders ambitiously contending for pre-eminence and power; or to persons of other descriptions whose fortunes have been interesting to the human passions, have, in turn, divided mankind into parties, inflamed them with mutual animosity, and rendered them much more disposed to vex and oppress each other than to co-operate for their common good. So strong is this propensity of mankind to fall into mutual animosities that where no substantial occasion presents itself the most frivolous and fanciful distinctions have been sufficient to kindle their unfriendly passions and excite their most violent conflicts. But the most common and durable source of factions has been the various and unequal distribution of property. Those who hold and those who are without property have ever formed distinct interests in society. Those who are creditors, and those who are debtors, fall under a like discrimination. A landed interest, a manufacturing interest, a mercantile interest, a moneyed interest, with many lesser interests, grow up of necessity in civilized nations, and divide them into different classes, actuated by different sentiments and views. The regulation of these various and interfering interests forms the principal task of modern legislation and involves the spirit of party and faction in the necessary and ordinary operations of government.

No man is allowed to be a judge in his own cause, because his interest would certainly bias his judgment, and, not improbably, corrupt his integrity. With equal, nay with greater reason, a body of men are unfit to be both judges and parties at the same time; yet what are many of the most important acts of legislation but so many judicial determinations, not indeed concerning the rights of single persons, but concerning the rights of large bodies of citizens? And what are the different classes of legislators but advocates and parties to the causes which they determine? Is a law proposed concerning private debts? It is a question to which the creditors are parties on one side and the debtors on the other. Justice ought to hold the balance between them. Yet the parties are, and must be, themselves the judges; and the most numerous party, or in other words, the most powerful faction must be expected to prevail. Shall domestic manufacturers be encouraged, and in what degree, by restrictions on foreign manufacturers? [These] are questions which would be differently decided by the landed and the manufacturing classes, and probably by neither with a sole regard to justice and the public good. The apportionment of taxes on the various descriptions of property is an act which seems to require the most exact impartiality; yet there is, perhaps, no legislative act in which greater opportunity and temptation are given to a predominant party to trample on the rules of justice. Every shilling with which they overburden the inferior number is a shilling saved to their own pockets.

It is in vain to say that enlightened statesmen will be able to adjust these clashing interests and render them all subservient to the public good. Enlightened statesmen will not always be at the helm. Nor, in many cases, can such an adjustment be made at all without taking into view indirect and remote considerations, which will rarely prevail over the immediate interest which one party may find in disregarding the rights of another or the good of the whole.

The inference to which we are brought is that the *causes* of faction cannot be removed and that relief is only to be sought in the means of controlling its *effects*.

If a faction consists of less than a majority, relief is supplied by the republican principle, which enables the majority to defeat its sinister views by regular vote. It may clog the administration, it may convulse the society; but it will be unable to execute and mask its violence under the forms of the Constitution. When a majority is included in a faction, the form of popular government, on the other hand, enables it to sacrifice to its ruling passion or interest both the public good and the rights of other citizens. To secure the public good and private rights against the danger of such a faction, and at the same time to preserve the spirit and the form of popular government, is then the great object to which our inquiries are directed. Let me add that it is the great desideratum by which alone this form of government can be rescued from the opprobrium under which it has so long labored and be recommended to the esteem and adoption of mankind.

By what means is this object attainable? Evidently by one of two only. Either the existence of the same passion or interest in a majority at the same time must be prevented, or the majority, having such coexistent passion or interest, must be rendered, by their number and local situation, unable to concert and carry into effect schemes of oppression. If the impulse and the opportunity be suffered to coincide, we well know that neither moral nor religious motives can be relied on as an adequate control. They are not found to be such on the injustice and violence of individuals, and lose their efficacy in proportion to the number combined together, that is, in proportion as their efficacy becomes needful.

From this view of the subject it may be concluded that a pure democracy, by which I mean a society consisting of a small number of citizens, who assemble and administer the government in person, can admit of no cure for the mischiefs of faction. A common passion or interest will, in almost every case, be felt by a majority of the whole, a communication and concert result from the form of government itself; and there is nothing to check the inducements to sacrifice the weaker party or an obnoxious individual. Hence it is that such democracies have ever been spectacles of turbulence and contention; have ever been found incompatible with personal security or the rights of property; and have in general been as short in their lives as they have been violent in their deaths. Theoretic politicians, who have patronized this species of government, have erroneously supposed that by reducing mankind to a perfect equality in their political rights, they would at the same time be perfectly equalized and assimilated in their possessions, their opinions, and their passions.

A republic, by which I mean a government in which the scheme of representation takes place, opens a different prospect and promises the cure for which we are seeking. Let us examine the points in which it varies from pure democracy, and we shall comprehend both the nature of the cure and the efficacy which it must derive from the Union.

The two great points of difference between a democracy and a republic are: first, the delegation of the government, in the latter, to a small number of citizens elected by the rest; secondly, the greater number of citizens and greater sphere of country over which the latter may be extended.

The effect of the first difference is, on the one hand, to refine and enlarge the public views by passing them

occasions it might be perfidiously abused. May not this defect of an absolute negative be supplied by some qualified connection between this weaker department and the weaker branch of the stronger department, by which the latter may be led to support the constitutional rights of the former, without being too much detached from the rights of its own department?

If the principles on which these observations are founded be just, as I persuade myself they are, and they be applied as a criterion to the several State constitutions, and to the federal Constitution, it will be found that if the latter does not perfectly correspond with them, the former are infinitely less able to bear such a test.

There are, moreover, two considerations particularly applicable to the federal system of America, which place that system in a very interesting point of view.

First. In a single republic, all the power surrendered by the people is submitted to the administration of a single government; and the usurpations are guarded against by a division of the government into distinct and separate departments. In the compound republic of America, the power surrendered by the people is first divided between two distinct governments, and then the portion allotted to each subdivided among distinct and separate departments. Hence a double security arises to the rights of the people. The different governments will control each other, at the same time that each will be controlled by itself.

Second. It is of great importance in a republic not only to guard the society against the oppression of its rulers, but to guard one part of the society against the injustice of the other part. Different interests necessarily exist in different classes of citizens. If a majority be united by a common interest, the rights of the minority will be insecure. There are but two methods of providing against this evil: the one by creating a will in the community independent of the majority—that is, of the society itself; the other, by comprehending in the society so many separate descriptions of citizens as will render an unjust combination of a majority of the whole very improbable, if not impracticable. The first method prevails in all governments possessing an hereditary or self-appointed authority. This, at best, is but a precarious security; because a power independent of the society may as well espouse the unjust views of the major as the rightful interests of the minor party, and may possibly be turned against both parties. The second method will be exemplified in the federal republic of the United States. Whilst all authority in it will be derived from and dependent on the society, the society itself will be broken into so many parts, interests and classes of citizens, that the rights of individuals, or of the minority, will be in little danger from interested combinations of the majority. In a free government the security for civil rights must be the same as that for religious rights. It consists in the one case in the multiplicity of interests, and in the other in the multiplicity of sects. The degree of security in both cases will depend on the number of interests and sects; and this may be presumed to depend on the extent of country and number of people comprehended under the same government. This view of the subject must particularly recommend a proper federal system to all the sincere and considerate friends of republican government, since it shows that in exact proportion as the territory of the Union may be formed into more circumscribed Confederacies, or States, oppressive combinations of a majority will be facilitated; the best security, under the republican forms, for the rights of every class of citizen, will be diminished; and consequently the stability and independence of some member of the government, the only other security, must be proportionately increased. Justice is the end of government. It is the end of civil society. It ever has been and ever will be pursued until it be obtained, or until liberty be lost in the pursuit. In a society under the forms of which the stronger faction can readily unite and oppress the weaker, anarchy may as truly be said to reign as in a state of nature, where the weaker individual is not secured against the violence of the stronger; and as, in the latter state, even the stronger individuals are prompted, by the uncertainty of their condition, to submit to a government which may protect the weak as well as themselves; so, in the former state, will the more powerful factions or parties be gradually induced, by a like motive, to wish for a government which will protect all parties, the weaker as well as the more powerful. It can be little doubted that if the State of Rhode Island was separated from the Confederacy and left to itself, the insecurity of rights under the popular form of government within such narrow limits would be displayed by such reiterated oppressions of factious majorities that some power altogether independent of the people would soon be called for by the voice of the very factions whose misrule had proved the necessity of it. In the extended republic of the United States, and among the great variety of interests, parties, and sects which it embraces, a coalition of a majority of the whole society could seldom take place on any other principles than those of justice and the general good; whilst there being thus less danger to a minor from the will of a major party, there must be less pretext, also, to provide for the security of the former, by introducing into the government a will not dependent on the latter, or, in other words, a will independent of the society itself. It is no less certain than it is important, notwithstanding the contrary opinions which have been entertained, that the larger the society, provided it lie within a practicable sphere, the more duly capable it will be of self-government. And happily for the republican cause, the practicable sphere may be carried to a very great extent by a judicious modification and mixture of the federal principle.

Chapter 1: Citizenship in Our Changing Democracy

1. Julia Prodis Sulek, "Young Voters' Interest in Politics Surges," *The Mercury News*, March 28, 2008.

2. Scott Keeter, "Young Voters in the 2008 Presidential Primaries," Report of Pew Center for People and the Press, February 11, 2008. Accessed on April 13, 2008 at http://pewresearch.org/pubs/730/young-voters.

3. Peter Leyden and Ruy Teixeira, The Progressive Politics of the Millennial Generation. Paper prepared for the New Politics Institute, June 21, 2007. Accessed on April 13, 2008 at http://www.newpolitics.net/node/360?full_report=1.

4. Ibid.

5. Jeffrey M. Jones, "Low Trust in Federal Government Rivals Watergate Era Levels," *Gallup Organization Report*, September 26, 2007. Accessed on April 19, 2008 at http://www.gallup.com/poll/28795/Low-Trust-Federal-Government-Rivals-Watergate-Era-Levels.aspx.

6. Robert D. Putnam, *Bowling Alone: The Collapse and Revival of American Community* (New York: Simon and Schuster, 2000).

7. See, for example, C. Everett Ladd, *The Ladd Report* (New York: Free Press, 1999).

8. See, for example, C. Wright Mills, *The Power Elite* (New York: Oxford University Press, 1956); Michael Parenti, *Democracy for the Few,* 7th ed. (Belmont, CA: Wadsworth Publishing, 2001); Gaetano Mosca, *The Ruling Class* (Boston: McGraw-Hill, 1959); see also Peter Bachrach, *The Theory of Democratic Elitism: A Critique* (Boston: Little-Brown, 1967).

9. Robert Dahl, *A Preface to Democratic Theory: How Does Popular Sovereignty Function in America?* (Chicago: University of Chicago Press, 1963).

10. Joseph Losco and Leonard Williams, *Political Theory: Classic and Contemporary Readings,* vol. 2, 2d ed. (Los Angeles: Roxbury Press, 2003).

11. Report of the American Political Science Association's Standing Committee on Civic Education and Engagement, *Democracy at Risk: Renewing the Political Science of Citizenship* (Chicago: American Political Science Meeting, 2004), 69.

12. Michael Olander, Emily Hoban Kirby, and Krista Schmitt. Attitudes of Young People Towards Diversity: Fact Sheet of the Center for Information and Research on Civic Learning and Engagement. February, 2005.

13. Janny Scott and David Leonhardt, "Class in America: Shadowy Lines That Still Divide," *New York Times*, May 15, 2005, 1.

14. Ibid., 18.

15. Study prepared for the *New York Times* by Susan Weber and Andrew Beveridge, reported in Scott and Leonhardt, 16.

16. Study by Thomas Hertz reported in "Ever Higher Society, Ever Harder to Ascend," *The Economist*, Dec. 29, 2004.

17. Robert Scott and Adam Hersh, *Economic Snapshots* (Washington, DC: Economic Policy Institute, June 11, 2003).

18. American National Election Studies summary data available at http://www.electionstudies.org/nesguide/toptable/tab6c_1a.htm, accessed Aug. 23, 2007.

Chapter 2: The Constitution: The Foundation of Citizens' Rights

1. Gerald Prante, "How Much Taxation (Without Representation)?" Accessed online at www.taxfoundation.org on May 25, 2007.

2. Historical information from The DC Voting Rights Movement. Accessed online at http://www.dcvote.org on May 25, 2007.

3. Yolanda Woodlee, "Senate Panel Hears String of Impassioned Appeals," *Washington Post,* May 16, 2007, B04.

4. Charles Beard, *An Economic Interpretation of the Constitution of the United States* (New York: Macmillan, 1913).

5. John P. Roche, "The Founding Fathers: A Reform Caucus in Action," *American Political Science Review 55* (1961): 816.

6. Congressional Quarterly, *Origins and Development of Congress,* 2d ed. (Washington, DC: Congressional Quarterly, 1982).

7. Ibid., 61.

8. Roche, 816.

9. James Madison, "Federalist 51," *The Federalist Papers*, Clinton Rossiter, ed. (New York: Mentor, 1961), 322.

10. Ibid., 323.

11. Joseph J. Keenan, *The Constitution of the United States: An Unfolding Story*, 2d ed. (Chicago: Dorsey Press, 1988), 27.

12. Patrick Henry, "Against the Federal Constitution: June 5, 1788," American Rhetorical Movements to 1900. Accessed online at http://www.wfu.edu on July 18, 2005.

13. James Madison, "Federalist 10," *The Federalist Papers*, Clinton Rossiter, ed. (New York: Mentor, 1961), 77–84.

14. Quoted in Keenan, 35.

15. Daniel Diller and Stephen H. Wirls, "Commander in Chief," in *Powers of the Presidency*, 2nd ed. (Washington, DC: CQ Press, 1997), 165.

16. Alexander Hamilton, "Federalist 78," *The Federalist Papers,* Clinton Rossiter, ed. (New York: Mentor, 1961), 467.

17. *Roe v. Wade*, 410 U.S. 113 (1975).

18. Frederick Jackson Turner, *The Frontier in American History* (New York: Holt, 1920).

19. Pub. L. 108–447, *Consolidated Appropriations Act*, 2005.

Chapter 3: Federalism: Citizenship and the Dispersal of Power

1. Mark Martin, "State's War on Warming: Governor Signs Measure to Cap Greenhouse Gas Emissions—Sweeping Changes Predicted in Industries and Life in Cities," *San Francisco Chronicle,* September 28, 2006.

2. Brett Rosenberg, "Mayors Implement Local Solutions to Global Climate Change," United States Conference of Mayors, May 22, 2006. Accessed online at http://www.usmayors.org on Dec. 1, 2006.

3. "The Warming Is Global but the Legislating, in the U.S., Is All Local," *New York Times,* Oct. 29, 2003.

4. U.S. Census Bureau Governments Integrated Directory. Accessed online at http://www.census.gov on February 4, 2005.

5. James Madison, "Federalist 51," *The Federalist Papers,* Clinton Rossiter, ed. (New York: Mentor, 1961), 232.

6. Steven Macedo, Yvetee Alex-Assensoh, Jeffrey M. Berry, Michael Brintnall, David E. Campbell, Luis Ricardo Fraga, Archon Fung, William A. Galston, Christopher F. Karpowitz, Margaret Levi, Meira Levinson, Keena Lipsitz, Richard G. Niemi, Robert D. Putnam, Wendy M. Rahn, Rob Reich, Robert R. Rogers, Todd

Swanstrom, and Katherine Cramer Walsh, *Democracy at Risk: How Political Choices Undermine Citizen Participation and What We Can Do About It* (Washington, DC: Brookings Institution, 2005), 68–73.

7. For an excellent discussion of the legacy of Jefferson's nullification movement and its contribution to factional strife leading to the Civil War, see Garry Wills, *A Necessary Evil: A History of American Distrust of Government* (New York: Simon and Schuster, 1999).

8. *McCulloch v. Maryland*, 4 Wheaton 316 (1819).

9. Ibid.

10. *Dred Scott v. Sandford,* 60 U.S. 393 (1857).

11. *Hammer v. Dagenhart*, 247 U.S. 251 (1918).

12. *U.S. v. E.C. Knight Co.,* 156 U.S. 1 (1895).

13. *Lochner v. U.S.,* 198 U.S. 25 (1905).

14. *Schechter Poultry Co. v. U.S.,* 295 U.S. 495 (1935).

15. *U.S. v. Butler,* 297 U.S. 1 (1936).

16. *Brown v. Board of Education of Topeka*, 347 U.S. 483 (1954).

17. *Roe v. Wade*, 401 U.S. 113 (1973).

18. See, for example, *Gideon v. Wainwright*, 372 U.S. 335 (1963).

19. *South Carolina v. Katzenbach*, 383 U.S. 301 (1966).

20. *United States v. Lopez,* 514 U.S. 549 (1995).

21. *Printz v. United States*, 521 U.S. 898 (1997).

22. *Kimel v. Florida Board of Regents*, 528 U.S. 62 (2000).

23. *Board of Trustees v. Garrett*, 531 U.S. 356 (2001).

24. Donald Boyd, "2006 Rockefeller Institute Reports on State and Local Government Finances," Rockefeller Institute for Government, May 2006.

25. Ben Canada, *Federal Grants to State and Local Government: A Brief History* (Washington, DC: Congressional Research Service, 2003).

26. Ben Canada, "Federal Grants to State and Local Governments: Overview and Characteristics, RS 20669," *CRS Report for Congress* (Washington, DC: Congressional Research Service, November 22, 2002), 3.

27. The first block grant, the Partnership for Public Health, was created by Congress in 1966. See Canada, 11.

28. Canada, 4.

29. Canada, 13.

30. Kenneth Finegold, Laura Wherry, and Stephanie Schardin, "Block Grants: Historic Overview and Lessons Learned," *New Federalism: Issues and Options for States,* Series A, No. A-63 (Washington, DC: Brookings Institution, 2004). Accessed online at http://www.urban.org on Feb. 5, 2005.

31. Congressional Budget Office, *CBO's Activities Under the Unfunded Mandates Reform Act, 1996–2000* (Washington, DC, May 2001).

32. National Council of State Legislatures, *Mandate Monitor*, vol. 1, no. 1 (March 31, 2004). Accessed online at http://www.ncsl.org on February 9, 2005.

33. David C. Nice and Patricia Fredericksen, *The Politics of Intergovernmental Relations*, 2d ed. (Chicago: Nelson-Hall, 1995), 35.

34. See, for example, Paul E. Peterson, "Federalism, Economic Development, and Redistribution," in *Public Values and Private Power in American Politics*, J. David Greenstone, ed. (Chicago: University of Chicago Press, 1982). Also see Grant McConnell, *Private Power and American Democracy* (New York: Knopf, 1966).

35. *National League of Cities v. Usery*, 426 U.S. 833 (1976).

36. *New York v. United States,* 505 U.S. 144 (1992).

37. *Printz v. United States*, 521 U.S. 898 (1997).

38. *Gonzales v. Raich*, 545 U.S. 1 (2005).

39. *Alden v. Maine,* 527 U.S. 706 (1999).

40. *Kimel v. Florida Board of Regents,* 528 U.S. 62 (2000).

41. *Tennessee v. Lane,* 541 U.S. 509 (2004).

42. Nice and Fredericksen, 122.

43. Robin Minietta, "Southern Hospitality," *Online Newshour* (October 14, 1996). Accessed online at http://www.pbs.org on February 5, 2005.

44. *New State Ice v. Liebmann,* 285 U.S. 262 (1932).

45. Jack L. Walker, "The Diffusion of Innovations Among the American States," *American Political Science Review* 63, no. 3 (1969): 880–899. For somewhat differing analyses and a discussion of the methodological problems involved in measuring innovation and diffusion, see Virginia Gray, "Innovation in the States: A Diffusion Study," *American Political Science Review* 67 (1973): 1174–1185; Jack L. Walker, "Comment: Problems in Research on the Diffusion of Policy Innovation, *American Political Science Review* 67 (1973): 1186–1191; John L. Foster, "Regionalism and Innovation in the American States," *Journal of Politics* 40:1 (1978): 179–187; David C. Nice, *Policy Innovation in the States* (Ames: Iowa State University Press, 1994).

46. Michael Mintrom, "Policy Entrepreneurs and the Diffusion of Innovation," *American Journal of Political Science* 41 no. 3 (1977): 738–770.

47. Susan Welch and Kay Thompson, "The Impact of Federal Incentives on State Policy Innovation," *American Journal of Political Science* 24:4 (1980): 715–729.

48. Daniel J. Elazar, *Federalism: A View from the States*, 3d ed. (New York: HarperCollins, 1984).

49. Macedo, et al., 72.

50. Alexis de Tocqueville, trans. George Lawrence, by J. P. Mayer, *Democracy In America* (New York: HarperCollins, 1969), 164.

Chapter 4: Civil Liberties: Expanding Citizens' Rights

1. Mark Walsh, "Testing the Limits of School Drug Tests," *Education Week* March 13, 2002. Accessed online at http://www.edweek.org.

2. Ibid., 3.

3. *Vernonia School District 475 v. Acton* (1995).

4. *Board of Education of Pottawatomie County v. Lindsay Earls* (2002). Accessed online at http://faculty.max.syr.edu.

5. Daniel J. Elazar, "How Present Conceptions of Human Rights Shape the Protection of Rights in the United States," in Robert A. Licht, ed. *Old Rights and New* (Washington DC: AEI Press, 1993), 39.

6. Daniel A. Farber and Suzanna Sherry, *A History of the American Constitution* (St. Paul, MN: West Publishing Company, 1990), 221–222.

7. Alexander Hamilton, John Jay, and James Madison, *The Federalist Papers,* Benjamin F. Wright, ed. (New York: Metro Books, 1961), 535.

8. Of the two that were rejected, one provided for the state to add a representative to the House each time their population grew by thirty thousand and the other called for an intervening congressional election before any pay raise for members of Congress could take effect. The latter became the Twenty-seventh Amendment nearly two hundred years later.

9. *Barron v. Baltimore* (1833).

10. Highlighting supplied by the authors.

11. *Farber and Sherry,* 122–123.

12. Although the establishment clause is mentioned first in the First Amendment, the free exercise clause is dealt with first because its interpretation is easier for students to understand.

13. Letter quoted in *Reynolds v. United States* (1879).

14. *Cantwell v. Connecticut* (1940).

15. *Reynolds v. United States* (1879) and *Employment Division, Department of Human Resources of Oregon v. Smith* (1990).

16. *Sherbert v. Verner* (1963).

17. *Wisconsin v. Yoder* (1972).

18. *Goldman v. Weinberger* (1986).

19. *City of Boerne v. Flores* (1997).

20. The Pew Forum on Religion & Public Life, "Comparative Religion-U.S. Religion Landscape Study," 2008. 21. See Michael J. Malbin, *Religion and Politics: The Intentions of the Authors of the First Amendment* (Washington, DC: American Enterprise Institute, 1978).

21. See Michael J. Malbin, *Religion and Politics: The Intentions of the Authors of the First Amendment* (Washington, DC: American Interprise Institute, 1978).

22. Lemon v. Kurtzman (1971).

23. *Walz v. Tax Commission of the City of New York* (1970).

24. *Epperson v. Arkansas* (1968).

25. *Edwards v. Aguillard* (1987).

26. *Widmar v. Vincent* (1981).

27. *Engle v. Vitale* (1962).

28. *School District of Abington Township v. Schempp* (1965).

29. Lee Epstein, Jeffrey A. Segal, Harold J. Spaeth, and Thomas G. Walker, *The Supreme Court Compendium: Data, Decisions, and Developments* (Washington, DC: Congressional Quarterly, 2003), Tables 8–23.

30. *Wallace v. Jaffree* (1985).

31. *Lee v. Weisman* (1992).

32. *Santa Fe Independent School District v. Doe* (2000).

33. The Pew Forum on Religion & Public Life, "Courts Not Silent On Moments of Silence," April 24, 2008, p. 4.

34. *Zobrest v. Catalina Foothills School District* (1993).

35. *Agostini v. Felton* (1997).

36. *Zelman v. Simmons-Harris* (2002).

37. *County of Allegheny v. A.C.L.U.* (1989).

38. *Lynch v. Donnelly* (1984).

39. *Van Orden v. Perry* (2005).

40. *McCreary County v. A.C.L.U. of Kentucky* (2005).

41. John Stuart Mill, *Essential Works of John Stuart Mill,* Max Lerner, ed. (New York: Bantam Books, 1961).

42. *Schenck v. United States* (1919).

43. *Whitney v. California* (1927).

44. *Gitlow v. New York* (1925).

45. *Brandenburg v. Ohio* (1969).

46. *Buckley v. Valeo* (1976).

47. *Virginia State Board of Pharmacy v. Virginia Citizens Consumer Council, Inc.* (1976).

48. *Bates v. State Bar of Arizona* (1977).

49. *United States v. O'Brien* (1968).

50. *Tinker v. Des Moines School District* (1969).

51. *Texas v. Johnson* (1989).

52. *United States v. Eichman* (1990).

53. *Jacobellis v. Ohio* (1964).

54. *Miller v. California* (1973).

55. Timothy C. Schiell, *Campus Hate Speech on Trial* (Lawrence, KS: University of Kansas Press, 1998), Chap. 1–3.

56. *Blackstone's Commentaries on the Laws of England,* vol. 4 (London, 1765–1769), 151–152.

57. *Smith v. Daily Mail Publishing Company* (1979).

58. *Nebraska Press Association v. Stuart* (1976).

59. *Miami Herald Publishing v. Tornillo* (1974).

60. *Branzburg v. Hayes* (1972).

61. *Houchins v. KQED* (1978).

62. *Wilson v. Layne* (1999).

63. *Gannett Company v. DePasquale* (1979).

64. *Edwards v. South Carolina* (1963).

65. *Cox v. Louisiana* (1965).

66. *Adderley v. Florida* (1966).

67. *Madsen v. Women's Health Center, Incorporated* (1994).

68. *Hill v. Colorado* (2000).

69. *NAACP v. Button* (1963).

70. *Board of Directors of Rotary International v. Rotary Club of Duarte* (1987).

71. *New York State Club Association v. City of New York* (1988).

72. *Hurley v. Irish-American Gay, Lesbian and Bisexual Group of Boston* (1995).

73. *Boy Scouts of America v. Dale* (2000).

74. Highlighting supplied by the authors.

75. *United States v. Miller* (1939).

76. *District of Columbia v. Heller* (2007).

77. The taking clause of the Fifth Amendment that guarantees a citizen the right to just compensation for property taken by the government is the only provision not related to the rights of the accused in the Fourth, Fifth, Sixth, and Eighth Amendments.

78. *Chimel v. California* (1969).

79. *United States v. Knights* (2001).

80. *Warden v. Hayden* (1967).

81. *Illinois v. Wardlow* (2000).

82. *Cupp v. Murphy* (1973).

83. Ibid.

84. *Ferguson v. City of Charleston* (2001).

85. *Hester v. United States* (1924).

86. *Florida v. Riley* (1988).

87. *Kyllo v. United States* (2001).

88. *City of Indianapolis v. Edmond* (2000).

89. *Weeks v. United States* (1914) and *Mapp v. Ohio* (1961).

90. *United States v. Leon* (1984).

91. *Dickerson v. United States* (2000).

92. *Powell v. Alabama* (1932).

93. *Gideon v. Wainwright* (1963).

94. *Argesinger v. Wainwright* (1972).

95. *Scott v. Illinois* (1979).

96. *Alabama v. Shelton* (2002).

97. *Strauder v. West Virginia* (1880) for African Americans and *Taylor v. Louisiana* (1975) for women.

98. *Batson v. Kentucky* (1986), *Georgia v. McCullum* (1992), and *J.E.B. v. Alabama ex rel. T.B.* (1994).

99. *Williams v. Florida* (1970).

100. *Johnson v. Louisiana* (1972) and *Apodaca v. Oregon* (1972).

101. *Furman v. Georgia* (1972).

102. *Gregg v. Georgia* (1976).

103. *Atkins v. Georgia* (2002).

104. *Roper v. Simmons* (2005).

105. *Baze v. Rees* (2007).

106. *Kennedy v. Louisiana* (2007).

107. *Griswold v. Connecticut* (1965).

108. By the time her case reached the Supreme Court, McCorvey had already given birth to the baby and put it up for adoption.

109. Charles S. Franklin and Liane Kosaki, "The Republican Schoolmaster: The Supreme Court, Public Opinion, and Abortion," *American Political Science Review* 83 (1989): 751–772.

110. *Akron, Ohio v. Akron Center for Reproductive Health* (1983).

111. *Webster v. Reproductive Health Services* (1989).

112. *Beal v. Doe* (1977) and *Harris v. McRae* (1980).

113. *Gonzales v. Carhart* (2006).

114. *Cruzan v. Director, Missouri Department of Health* (1990).

115. *Watchtower Bible and Tract Society v. Stratton* (2002).

116. Gregory A. Calderia and John R. Wright, "Organized Interests and Agenda Setting in the U.S. Supreme Court" *Political Science Review* 821109 (1988).

117. Adam Liptak, "A Liberal Case for the Individual Right to Own Guns Helps Sway the Federal Judiciary," *New York Times*, May 7, 2007.

118. Ibid., 1.

119. Ibid., 2.

Chapter 5: Civil Rights: Toward a More Equal Citizenry

1. Lisa Belkin, "She Says She Was Rejected by a College for Being White. Is She Paranoid, Racist, or Right?" *Glamour* (November 1998): 2.

2. Ibid., 1.

3. Ibid., 2.

4. For an excellent discussion of the difference between civil liberties and civil rights, see John C. Domino, *Civil Rights and Liberties in the 21st Century,* 2d ed. (New York: Longman Publishers, 2003), 1–5.

5. *Dred Scott v. Sanford* (1857).

6. "Jim Crow" was the stereotypical name given to African Americans in a nineteenth-century minstrel song.

7. See C. Vann Woodward, "The Case of the Louisiana Traveler," in John A. Garraty, ed., *Quarrels That Shaped the Constitution* (New York: Harper & Row: 1987), 157–174.

8. The grandfather clause denied the right to vote to anyone whose grandfather did not vote before the Reconstruction period.

9. For an excellent discussion of the NAACP's strategy, see Richard Kluger, *Simple Justice* (New York: Vintage Books, 1975).

10. The decision in *Missouri ex. Rel. Gaines v. Canada* (1938) led to the group's success in *Sweatt v. Painter* (1950).

11. *McLaurin v. Oklahoma* (1950).

12. *Brown v. Board of Education II* (1955).

13. *Swann v. Charlotte-Mecklenburg County Schools* (1971).

14. *Missouri v. Jenkins* (1995).

15. Southern Democrat Senator Strom Thurmond conducted an eight-week filibuster to hold up the voting on the bill. It is the longest filibuster in the history of the United States.

16. *Heart of Atlanta Motel v. United States* (1964).

17. *San Antonio Independent School District v. Rodriguez* (1973).

18. *United Steelworkers of America v. Weber* (1979).

19. *United States v. Paradise* (1987).

20. *Local 28 of the Sheet Metal Workers v. EEOC* (1986) and *Johnson v. Transportation Agency of Santa Clara County, California* (1987).

21. *Aderand Constructors v. Pena* (1995).

22. *New York Times,* February 2, 2003.

23. *Meredith v. Jefferson County Board of Education* (2007) and *Parents Involved in Community Schools v. Seattle School District No. 1* (2004).

24. For a criticism of affirmative action programs, see John David Skrentny, *The Ironies of Affirmative Action: Politics, Culture, and American Justice in America* (Chicago: The University of Chicago Press, 1996).

25. Harry Holzer and David Newmark, "Assessing Affirmative Action," *Journal of Economic Literature* 38 (2000): 245–269.

26. Rennard Strickland, "Native Americans," in Kermit Hall, ed., *The Oxford Companion to the Supreme Court of the United States* (New York: Oxford University Press, 1992), 557.

27. Dee Brown, *Bury My Heart at Wounded Knee* (New York: Holt, Rinehart, and Winston, 1971).

28. Joanne Nagel, *American Indian Ethnic Renewal: Red Power and the Resurgence of Identity and Culture* (New York: Oxford University Press, 1996).

29. David Pfeiffer, "Understanding Disability Policy," *Policy Studies Journal* (1996): 157–174.

30. *Cedar Rapids v. Garret F.* (1998).

31. *Bregdon v. Abbot* (1998).

32. *Sutton v. United Air Lines* (1999), *Albertsons v. Kirkinburg* (1999), and *Murphy v. United Parcel Service* (1999).

33. *O'Connor v. Consolidated Coil Casterers Corp.* (1996).

34. *Massachusetts Board of Retirement v. Murgia* (1976).

35. *Reeves v. Sanderson* (2000).

36. *Kimel v. Florida Board of Regents* (2000).

37. *CBOCS v. Humphries* (2007).

38. See Diane Helene Miller, *Freedom to Differ: The Shaping of the Gay and Lesbian Struggle for Civil Rights* (New York: New York University Press, 1998).

39. *Romer v. Evans* (1996).

40. *Bowers v. Hardwick* (1986).

41. *Boy Scouts of America v. Dale* (2000).

42. *Baehr v. Lewin* (1993).

43. *Baker v. Vermont* (1999).

44. See Judith A. Baer, *Equality Under the Constitution: Reclaiming the Fourteenth Amendment* (Ithaca, NY: Cornell University Press, 1983), 44–47.

45. See Nancy E. Glen and Karen O'Connor, *Women, Politics, and American Society,* 2d ed. (Upper Saddle River, NJ: Prentice Hall, 1998).

46. *Minor v. Happersett* (1875).

47. Robert Putnam sees this as one of the positive aspects of the Progressive Era in *Bowling Alone* (New York: Simon and Schuster, 2000), Chap. 23.

48. See Glen and O'Connor, 6–10.

49. *Hoyt v. Florida* (1961).

50. *Orr v. Orr* (1979).

51. *Mississippi University for Women v. Hogan* (1982).

52. *JEB v. Alabama ex rel.* (1996).

53. *Michael M. v. Superior Court of Sonoma County* (1981).

54. *Rotsker v. Goldberg* (1981).

55. Sara M. Evans and Barbara J. Nelson, *Wage Justice: Comparable Worth and the Paradox of Technocratic Reform* (Chicago: The University of Chicago Press, 1989).

56. *Meritor Savings v. Vinson* (1986).

57. *Burlington Industries v. Ellerth* (1998).

58. Charles Black, *The People and the Court* (New York: Macmillan, 1960).

Chapter 6: Public Opinion: Listening to Citizens

1. Steve Rosenfeld, "Yes, We Can: The Magic Behind Obama's Message," Alternet.org. Posted January 8, 2008 at http://www.alternet.org/story/73014/?page=entire.

2. Bonnie Azab Powell, "Framing the issues: UC Berkeley Professor George Lakoff tells how conservatives use language to dominate politics," *UC Berkeley News,* October 27, 2003.

3. Frank Luntz, *Words That Work: It's Not What You Say, It's What People Hear* (New York: Hyperion, 2007).

4. *V.O. Key, Jr.,* Public Opinion and American Democracy *(New York: Alfred Knopf, 1961), 14.*

5. Gabriel Almond and Sidney Verba, *The Civic Culture: Political Attitudes and Democracy in Five Nations* (Princeton: Princeton University Press, 1963). See also a series of critiques of the political culture thesis in Gabriel Almond and Sidney Verba, eds., *The Civic Culture Revisited* (Newbury Park, CA: Sage, 1989).

6. Herbert McClosky and John Zaller, *The American Ethos: Public Attitudes Toward Capitalism and Democracy* (Cambridge: Harvard University Press, 1984).

7. Alexander Hamilton, *The Federalist Papers, No. 71*, Clinton Rossiter, ed. (New York: Mentor, 1961), 432.

8. Forrest McDonald, *The American Presidency: An Intellectual History* (Lawrence: University of Kansas Press, 1994), 216.

9. Michael Schudson, *The Good Citizen: A History of American Civic Life* (New York: Free Press, 1998), 121.

10. Tom W. Smith, "The First Straw? A Study of the Origin of Election Polls," *The Public Opinion Quarterly* 54 no. 1 (1990): 27.

11. Bernard Hennessey, *Public Opinion,* 4th ed. (Monterey, CA: Brooks/Cole, 1981), 43.

12. See Fred I. Greenstein, *Children and Politics* (New Haven: Yale University Press, 1965); Robert D. Hess and Judith V. Torney, *The Development of Political Attitudes in Children* (Chicago: Aldine, 1967); and David Easton, *Children in the Political System: Origins of Political Legitimacy* (New York: McGraw-Hill, 1969).

13. David O. Sears, "Political Socialization," in Fred I. Greenstein and Nelson Polsby, eds. *Micropolitical Theory* (Reading, MA: Addison-Wesley, 1975), 93–153.

14. Ibid., 119.

15. M. Kent Jennings and Richard G. Niemi, "The Persistence of Political Orientations: An Over Time Analysis of Two Generations," *British Journal of Political Science* 8, no. 3 (1978): 333–363.

16. Richard G. Niemi and Jane Junn, *Civic Education: What Makes Students Learn?* (New Haven: Yale, 1998).

17. Sidney Verba, Kay Lehman Schlozman, and Henry E. Brady, *Voice and Equality: Civic Voluntarism in American Politics* (Cambridge: Harvard University Press, 1995), 422–426.

18. M. Kent Jennings, "Political Knowledge Across Time and Generations," *Public Opinion Quarterly* 60 (Summer): 228–252.

19. Nicole Speulda, *Pew Center Report: Youth and War* (Washington, DC: Pew Center for People and the Press, February 2006). Accessed online at http://pewresearch.org on April 20, 2007.

20. Paul Allen Beck, "The Role of Agents in Political Socialization," in Stanley Allen Renshon, ed., *Handbook of Political Socialization* (New York: Free Press, 1977), 117.

21. Lake, Snell, Perry, and Associates and the Tarrance Group, Inc., "Short-Term Impacts, Long-Term Opportunities: The Political and Civic Engagement of Young Adults in America," *Analysis and Report for the Center for Information and Research in Civic Learning & Engagement, The Center for Democracy and Citizenship, the Partnership for Trust in Government, and the Council for Excellence in Government*, March 2002. Accessed online at http://www.youngcitizensurvey.org on March 7, 2004.

22. Ibid.

23. Barry A. Kosmin and Egon Mayer, *American Religious Identification Survey* (New York: Graduate Center of the City University of New York). Accessed online at http://www.gc.cuny.edu on March 7, 2004.

24. Pew Center for the People and the Press, "Obama Weathers the Wright Storm, Clinton Faces Credibility Problem," March 27, 2008. Accessed at http://people-press.org/reports/display.php3?PageID=1276 on May 21, 2008.

25. Verba, Schlozman, and Brady, 228–268.

26. Peter Hart and Associates, "Making a Difference, Not a Statement: College Students and Politics, Volunteering, and an Agenda for America," *Panetta Institute Survey*, April 2001. Accessed online at http://www.panettainstitute.org on March 7, 2004.

27. Lake, Snell, Perry, and Associates and the Tarrance Group, Inc.

28. Alfonso Damico, M. Margaret Conway, and Sandra Bowman Damico, "Patterns of Political Trust and Mistrust: Three Moments in the Lives of Democratic Citizens," *Polity* 32 (2000): 333–356.

29. See Paul Lazerfeld, Bernard Berelson, and Hazel Gaudet, *The People's Choice* (New York: Columbia University Press, 1948); Bernard Berelson, Paul Lazerfeld, and William McPhee, *Voting* (Chicago: University of Chicago Press, 1954)

30. See Doris Graber, *Processing the News* (New York: Longman, 1988).

31. *What Americans Know: 1989–2007, Public Knowledge of Current Affairs Little Changed By News and Information Revolutions* (Washington, DC: Pew Center for People and Press, April 15, 2007).

32. Franklin D. Gilliam, Jr. and Shanto Iyengar, "Prime Suspects: The Influence of Local Television News on the Viewing Public," *American Journal of Political Science* 44:3 (2000): 560–573.

33. 1994 National Election Study. Some contend that the wording of NES questions on affirmative action exaggerate the differences between the races. See Lee Sigelman and Susan Welch, *Black Americans' View of Racial Inequality—The Dream Deferred* (Cambridge, England: Cambridge University Press).

34. Barbara A. Bardes and Robert W. Oldendick, *Public Opinion: Measuring the American Mind,* 2d ed. (Belmont, CA: Wadsworth/Thomson, 2003), 88.

35. Myriam Miedaian, *Boys Will Be Boys: The Link Between Masculinity and Violence* (New York: Doubleday, 1991).

36. Michael X. Delli-Carpini and Scott Keeter, *What Americans Know About Politics and Why It Matters* (New Haven: Yale University Press, 1996), 203–209.

37. Sidney Verba, Nancy Burns, and Kay Lehman Schlozman, "Knowing and Caring about Politics: Gender and Political Engagement," *The Journal of Politics* 59 (1997): 1055.

38. Gallup Organization, *Majority Still Extremely Proud to Be American*, July 3, 2006. Accessed online at http://www.galluppoll .com on September 5, 2007.

39. Daniel Elazar, *American Federalism: A View From the States,* 3d ed. (New York: Harper Collins, 1984).

40. Pew Center for the People and the Press. "The Impact of 'Cell-Onlys' on Public Opinion Polling," January 31, 2008. Accessed at http://people-press.org/reports/display.php3?PageID=1243 on May 21, 2008.

41. Herbert Asher, *Polling and the Public: What Every Citizen Should Know,* 6th ed. (Washington, DC: Congressional Quarterly Press, 2004), 28.

42. Delli-Carpini, and Keeter, 238.

43. Gallup Survey, *Americans Know Little About European Union* (June 16, 2004).

44. Markus Prior, "Political Knowledge After September 11," *PS: Politics and Society* (September 2002), 523–529.

45. Seymour Martin Lipset and William Schneider, *The Confidence Gap: Business, Labor, and Government in the Public Mind* (New York: The Free Press, 1983), 43.

46. Center for Democracy and Citizen Council for Excellence in Government, "Banners from a Nationwide Survey of 1,000 15–25 Year Olds," November 17–24, 2003. Accessed online at http:// www?.youngcitizensurvey.org on March 30, 2004.

47. Recent empirical evidence has confirmed this assessment. See Luke Keele, "Social Capital and the Dynamics of Trust in Government," *American Journal of Political Science* 51:2 (2007): 241–254.

48. See Pippa Norris, ed., *Critical Citizens: Global Support for Democratic Governments* (New York: Oxford Press, 1999); Ronald Inglehart, *Modernization and Postmodernization* (Princeton: Princeton University Press, 1997); Stein Ringen, "Wealth and Decay: Norway Funds a Massive Political Self-Examination and Finds Trouble for All," *Times Literary Supplement* (February 13, 2004), 3–5.

49. Angus Campbell, Gerald Gurin, and Warren E. Miller, *The Voter Decides* (New York: Harper and Row, 1954), 187.

50. See Samuel Stouffer, *Communism, Conformity and Civil Liberties* (New York: Doubleday, 1955); Herbert McClosky, "Consensus and Ideology in American Politics," *American Political Science Review* 58 (1964): 361–382.

51. John E. Meuller, "Trends in Political Tolerance," *Public Opinion Quarterly* 52 (1988): 1–25; John L. Sullivan, James E. Pierson, and George E. Marcus, *Political Tolerance and American Democracy* (Chicago: University of Chicago Press, 1982).

52. See Carol Pateman, *Participation and Democratic Theory* (New York: Cambridge University Press, 1970); Benjamin R. Barber, *Strong Democracy: Participatory Politics for a New Age* (Berkeley: University of California Press, 1984); and Jack L. Walker, "A Critique of the Elitist Theory of Democracy," *American Political Science Review* 60, (1966): 285–295.

53. Pew Center for the People and the Press, *Evenly Divided, Increasingly Polarized: 2004 Political Landscape* (Washington, DC: Pew Research Center, 2003), Table T-6.

54. Gallup, *Civil Liberties.* Accessed online at http://www .galluppoll.com on February 10, 2006.

55. Alan D. Monroe, "Public Opinion and Ideology," in *The Handbook of Political Behavior,* vol. 4, Samuel L. Long, ed. (New York: Plenum, 1981), 155–196.

56. See, for example, Gallup Organization, *Many Americans Use Multiple Labels to Describe Their Ideology* (December 6, 2006). Accessed online at http://www.galluppoll.com on September 6, 2007.

57. These figures are from the National Election Study, 2004.

58. Eileen Lorenzi McDonagh, "Constituency Influence on House Roll Call Votes in the Progressive Era, 1913–1915," *Legislative Studies Quarterly* XVIII:2 (May 1993), 185–210.

59. Benjamin I. Page and Robert Y. Shapiro, "Effects of Public Opinion on Policy," *The American Political Science Review* 77:1 (1983): 175–190.

60. See Alan D. Monroe, "Public Opinion and Public Policy, 1980–1993," *The Public Opinion Quarterly* 62:1 (1998): 6–28; Lawrence Jacobs and Robert Y. Shapiro, "Public Opinion, Institutions, and Policy Making," *PS: Political Science and Politics* 27:1 (1994): 9–17.

61. See, for example, John R. Hibbing and Elizabeth Theiss-Morse, *Stealth Democracy: Americans' Beliefs about How Government Should Work* (New York: Cambridge University Press, 2002).

62. Based on interview by Robin Gerrow, University of Rexas at Austin Online Newsletter, 2003. Accessed at http://www.utexas.edu/ features/archive/2003/polling.html, May 22, 2008.

63. Benamin I. Page and Robert Y. Shapiro. *The Rational Public: Fifty Years of Trends in Americans' Policy Preferences* (Chicago: University of Chicago Press, 1992), 389.

Chapter 7: Political Participation: Equal Opportunities and Unequal Voices

1. Personal communication. Quotes taken from personal Interview unless otherwise noted.

2. Marie Rice, "Student Runs for Mayor of California," *Calyou,* student portal of California University of Pennsylvania. Accessed on December 9, 2005 at http://calyou.cup.edu/daily_content/ view_article.php?article_id=1165180893&CALYOU=e3f2d926362 9b57605917453f0c877ce).

3. Sidney Verba, Kay Lehman Schlozman, and Henry E. Brady, *Voice and Equality: Civic Voluntarism in American Politics* (Cambridge: Harvard University Press, 1995), 115.

4. Alexis de Tocqueville, *Democracy in America,* trans. by George Lawrence and ed. by J. P. Mayer (New York: Perennial Classics, 1969), 520–521.

5. Verba, et al., 38.

6. This section roughly follows the "Civic Volunteerism Model" developed by Verba et al., 1995.

7. See Sidney Verba and Norman H. Nie, *Political Participation in America: Political Democracy and Social Equality* (New York: Harper & Row, 1972).

8. Steven J. Rosenstone and John Mark Hansen, *Mobilization, Participation and Democracy in America* (New York: Macmillan, 1993), 77.

9. Scott Keeter, Cliff Zukin, Molly Andolina, and Krista Jenkins, *The Civic and Political Health of the Nation: A Generational Portrait*, report prepared for the Center for Information and Research on Civic Learning and Engagement (September 19, 2002), 32.

10. Verba et al., 320–333.

11. Ibid., 255.

12. Frederick Solt, "Economic Inequality and Democratic Political Engagement," *American Journal of Political Science* 52 (January 2008): 48–60.

13. Verba et al., 345–348.

14. See Robert E. Lane, *Political Life: Why and How People Get Involved in Politics* (New York: Free Press, 1959).

15. Lake Snell Perry and Associates and the Tarrance Group, "Short-Term Impacts, Long-Term Opportunities: The Politics and Civic Engagement of Young Adults in America," report prepared for the Center for Information and Research on Civic Learning and Engagement, the Center for Democracy and Citizenship, the Partnership for Trust in Government, and the Council for Excellence in Government (March 2002), 31.

16. Francis Fox Piven and Richard A. Cloward, *Why Americans Don't Vote* (New York: Pantheon, 1989).

17. See discussion by Rosenstone and Hansen, 179–183.

18. See Samuel H. Barnes, Max Kaase, et al., *Political Action: Mass Participation in Five Western Democracies* (Beverly Hills: Sage, 1979), 541–542.

19. Verba et al., 115.

20. Pippa Norris, ed., *Critical Citizens: Global Support for Democratic Government* (New York: Oxford University Press, 1999).

21. Verba et al., 186–227.

22. See Theda Skocpol, *Diminished Democracy: From Membership to Management in American Civic Life* (Norman, OK: University of Oklahoma Press, 2004).

23. Keeter, et al., 20–22.

24. Stephen Shaffer, "Policy Differences Between Voters and Nonvoters in American Elections," *Western Political Quarterly* 35, no. 4 (1982), 496–510. Also see Verba, Schlozman, and Brady, 1995; Wolfinger and Rosenstone, 1980.

25. See also Stephen Earl Bennett and David Resnic, "The Implications of Nonvoting for Democracy in the United States," *American Journal of Political Science* 34, no. 3 (August 1990): 771–802.

26. Sidney Verba, "Would the Dream of Political Equality Turn Out to be a Nightmare?" *Perspectives on Politics* 1, no. 4 (2003): 671.

27. Solt, *AJPS*, 58.

28. *Verba*, 675.

29. This conforms to the views of many writers, see Thomas R. Dye and Harmon Zeigler, *The Irony of Democracy* (Pacific Grove, California: Brooks/Cole), 1990; Seymour Martin Lipset, *Political Man* (Garden City, NY: Doubleday, 1963); and William Kornhauser, *The Politics of Mass Society* (Glencoe, IL: Free Press, 1959).

30. Stephen Macedo, Yvette Alex-Assnsoh, Jeffrey M. Berry, Michael Britnall, David E. Campbell, Luis Ricardo Fraga, Archon Fug, William A. Galston, Christopher F. Karpowitz, Margaret Levi, Meira Levinson, Keena Lipsitz, Richard G. Niemi, Robert D. Putnam, Wendy M. Rahn, Rob Reich, Robert R. Rogers, Todd Swanstrom, and Katherine Cramer Walsh, *Democracy at Risk: How Political Choices Undermine Citizen Participation, and What We Can Do About It* (Washington, DC: Brookings Institution, 2005).

31. See Emily Hoban Kirby and Mark Hugo Lopez, *State Voter Registration and Election Day Laws*, paper prepared for the Center for Information and Research on Civic Learning and Engagement. Accessed online at http://www.civicyouth.org on June 24, 2006. Also see Raymond E. Wolfinger, Benjamin Highton, and Megan Mullin, "Mailed Ballots Might Increase Youth Vote," *Institute of Governmental Studies Public Affairs Report* 43, no. 4 (2002).

32. Martin Wattenberg, *Is Voting for Young People?* (New York: Pearson Education, 2007).

33. Macedo et al., 33.

34. Rosenstone and Hansen, 227.

Chapter 8: Interest Groups in America

1. This story draws heavily from S. Mitra Kalita, "Skilled Immigrants Turn to K Street," *Washington Post*, April 26, 2006; D01; and from Immigration Voice website, accessed at www.immigrationvoice.org on July 7, 2006.

2. The classic definition of an interest group offered by political scientist David Truman is "any group that, on the basis of one or more shared attitudes, makes certain claims upon other groups in the society for the establishment, maintenance, or enhancement of forms of behavior that are implied by the shared attitudes." David Truman, *The Governmental Process* (New York: Alfred Knopf, 1951), 33.

3. James Madison, *No. 10,* in Alexander Hamilton, James Madison, and John Jay, *Federalist Papers,* Clinton Rossiter, ed. (New York: New American Library, 1961), 78.

4. Sidney Verba, Kay Lehman Scholzman, and Henry E. Brady, *Voice and Equality: Civic Voluntarism in American Politics* (Cambridge, MA: Harvard University Press, 1995), 72–73. But see somewhat contradictory data from Steven J. Rosenstone and John Mark Hansen, *Mobilization, Participation, and Democracy in America* (New York: Macmillan, 1993), chap. 3. Skocpol (2003) argues that much of this activity is managed by Washington professionals. Theda Skocpol, *Diminished Democracy: From Membership to Management in American Civic Life* (Norman, OK: University of Oklahoma Press, 2003).

5. Arthur M. Schlesinger, "Biography of a Nation of Joiners," *The American Historical Review* 50 no. 1 (1944): 25.

6. Shirley J. Yee, *Black Women Abolitionists: A Study in Activism 1828–60* (Knoxville: University of Tennessee Press, 1992).

7. Matthew A. Crenson and Benjamin Ginsberg, *Downsizing Democracy* (Baltimore: The John Hopkins University Press, 2002), 107.

8. Robert D. Putnam, *Bowling Alone: The Collapse and Revival of American Community* (New York: Simon & Schuster, 2000), 80–92.

9. Michael Schudson, *The Good Citizen: A History of American Civic Life* (New York: Free Press, 1988), 245.

10. Michael Pertschuk, *Giant Killers* (New York: W. W. Norton, 1996).

11. Theda Skocpol, *Diminished Democracy.*

12. Kay Lehman Schlozman and John T. Tierney, *Organized Interests and American Democracy* (New York: Harper & Row, 1986), 66–68.

13. See, for example, Jack L. Walker, "The Origins and Maintenance of Interest Groups in America," *American Political Science Review* 77 (1983): 390–406.

14. Kay Lehman Schlozman, "What Accent the Heavenly Chorus? Political Equality and the American Pressure System," *Journal of Politics* 46 (1984): 1009.

15. Schlozman, 1022–1024.

16. Political scientist David Truman coined the term *latent interests* to refer to the ever-present possibility that new groups will to arise at any time to meet yet unforeseen challenges. See Truman, 1951.

17. James Q. Wilson, *Political Organizations* (New York: Basic Books, 1973).

18. Rosenstone and Hansen, 1993.

19. Mancur Olson, *The Logic of Collective Action* (Cambridge, MA: Harvard University Press, 1965).

20. Jack L. Walker, *Mobilizing Interest Groups in America* (Ann Arbor: University of Michigan Press, 1991), 87–89. This result is confirmed by the research of Verba, Schlozman, and Brady.

21. Verba, Schlozman, and Brady, 121–127.

22. Jonathan D. Salant, "The Lobbying Game Today," *Extensions: A Journal of the Carl Albert Congressional Research and Studies Center* (2006): 19.

23. Ibid., 17.

24. See Clyde Wilcox, "The Dynamics of Lobbying the Hill," in Paul S. Herrnson, Ronald G. Shaiko, and Clyde Wilcox, eds., *The Interest Group Connection* (Chatham, NJ: Chatham House Publishers, 1998), 89–90.

25. Norman J. Ornstein and Shirley Elder, *Interest Groups, Lobbying and Policymaking* (Washington, DC: Congressional Quarterly Press, 1978), 77–78.

26. Ibid., 86–87.

27. See John E. Chubb, *Interest Groups and the Bureaucracy* (Stanford: Stanford University Press, 1983) for a good discussion of the relationship of interest groups and the bureaucracy in the energy policy field.

28. Schlozman and Tierney, 333.

29. For an excellent discussion of research into "capture theory," see James Q. Wilson, *The Politics of Regulation* (New York: Basic Books, 1980).

30. Robert H. Salisbury, John Heinz, Robert L. Nelson, and Edward O. Laumann, "Triangles, Networks, and Hollow Cores: The Complex Geometry of Washington Interest Representation," in Mark Petracca, ed., *Interest Group Politics* (Washington, DC: Congressional Quarterly Press, 1995), 131.

31. See Walker, 125.

32. William T. Gromley, Jr., "Interest Group Interventions in the Administrative Process: Conspirators and Co-Conspirators," in Paul S. Herrnson, Ronald G. Shaiko, and Clyde Wilcox, eds., *The Interest Group Connection* (Chatham, NJ: Chatham House Publishers, 1998), 213–223.

33. "Open Secrets." Accessed at http://opensecrets.org on January 24, 2207.

34. James A. McCann and David Redlawsk, "As Voters Head to the Polls, Will They Perceive a 'Culture of Corruption'?" *PS: Political Science and Politics* 39 no. 4 (2006): 797–802.

35. Quoted in Larry Makinson, *Speaking Freely: Washington Insiders Talk About Money in Politics* (Washington, DC: Center for Responsive Politics, 2003), 85.

36. Schlozman and Tierney, 221.

37. *McConnell v. Federal Election Commission* 540 U.S. 93 (2003) and *FEC v. Wisconsin Right to Life* 551 U.S. (2007).

38. Salant, 17.

39. Center for Responsive Politics. Accessed online at http://www.opensecrets.org.

40. For an analysis of the general reliability of this finding, see Thomas Brunell, "The Relationship Between Political Parties and Interest Groups: Explaining Patterns of PAC Contributions to Candidates for Congress," *Political Research Quarterly* 58 no. 4 (2005): 681–688.

41. Center for Responsive Politics. Accessed online at http://www?.opensecrets.org.

42. Ibid.

43. *FEC v. Wisconsin Right to Life* 551 U.S. (2007).

44. Quoted in Schlozman and Tierney, 251.

45. Karen O'Connor, *Women's Organizations' Use of the Courts* (Lexington, MA: Lexington Books, 1980).

46. Stuart Scheingold, *The Politics of Rights* (New Haven: Yale University Press, 1974).

47. Karen O'Connor and Lee Epstein, "The Role of Interest Groups in Supreme Court Policymaking," in Robert Eyestone, ed., *Public Policy Formation* (Greenwich, CT: JAI Press, 1984) 63–81.

48. See Lucius J. Barker, "Third Parties in Litigation: A Systemic View of the Judicial Function," *Journal of Politics* 29 (1967): 41–69.

49. See Gregory A. Calderia and John R. Wright, "Organized Interests and Agenda Setting in the U.S. Supreme Court," *American Political Science Review* 82 (1988): 1109–1127.

50. James G. Gimpel, "Grassroots Organizations and Equilibrium Cycles in Group Mobilization and Access," in Paul S. Herrnson, Ronald G. Shaiko, and Clyde Wilcox, eds. *The Interest Group Connection* (Chatham, NJ: Chatham House Publishers, 1998), 100–115.

51. Kenneth M. Goldstein, *Interest Groups, Lobbying, and Participation in America* (New York: Cambridge University Press, 1999), 62.

52. Gimpel, 104.

53. See Kevin Hula, "Rounding Up the Usual Suspects: Forging Interest Group Coalitions in Washington," in Allan J. Cigler and Burdett A. Loomis, eds., *Interest Group Politics* (Washington, DC: Congressional Quarterly Press, 1995), 239–258.

54. Verba, Schlozman, and Brady, 189–191.

55. Crenson and Ginsberg, 151.

56. Skocpol, *Diminished Democracy*.

57. Crenson and Ginsberg, 194.

58. E. E. Schattschneider, *The Semisovereign People* (New York: Holt, Rinehart, and Winston, 1960), 35.

Chapter 9: Parties and Political Campaigns: Citizens and the Electoral Process

1. This discussion is drawn extensively from reporting by Kim Severson, "What's For Dinner? The Pollster Wants to Know," *The New York Times*, April 16, 2008.

2. Matt Bai, "The Multilevel Marketing of the President," *New York Times Magazine*, April 25, 2004, pp. 43–129.

3. Ibid.

4. Thomas B. Edsall and James V. Grimaldi, *Washington Post,* December 20, 2004, A01.

5. Severson, April 16, 2008.

6. Ibid.

7. Ibid.

8. V.O. Key, Jr., *Politics, Parties, and Pressure Groups, 5th Edition,* (New York: Crowell, 1964).

9. E.E. Schattsneider, *Party Government,* (New York: Holt, Rinehart and Winston, 1942).

10. Anthony Downs, *An Economic Theory of Democracy* (New York: Harper & Row, 1957), 25.

11. E. E. Schattschneider, "Intensity, Visibility, Direction, and Scope," *American Political Science Review* 51:4 (December 1957): 933–942.

12. See, for example, Morris Fiorina, "The Decline of Collective Responsibility in American Politics," *Daedalus* 109 (Summer 1980): 25–45. See also American Political Science Association, *Toward a More Responsible Two Party System* (New York: Rinehart, 1950).

13. Alexis de Tocqueville, 1848; *Democracy in America,* trans. George Lawrence, ed. J. P. Mayer). New York: Perennial Classics, 1969, 174.

14. Maurice Duverger, *Political Parties: Their Organization and Activity in the Modern State,* (New York: Wiley, 1954).

15. For a more thorough examination of other voting systems and their potential effects, see Joseph F. Zimmerman, "Alternative Voting Systems for Representative Democracy," *PS: Political Science and Politics* 27:4 (December 1994): 674–677.

16. Information available at The Reform Institute for Campaign and Election Issues, *Presidential Ballot Access,* http://reforminstitute. org/ (accessed September 7, 2007).

17. John H. Aldrich*, Why Parties? The Origins and Transformation of Political Parties in America* (Chicago: University of Chicago Press, 1995), 70–82.

18. Aldrich, 99.

19. See discussion in Frances Fox Piven and Richard A. Cloward, *Why Americans Don't Vote* (New York: Pantheon, 1989).

20. John C. Green, *The American Religious Landscape and Political Attitudes: A Baseline for 2004* (unpublished ms.).

21. See, for example, Susan J. Carroll, "Women's Autonomy and the Gender Gap: 1980 and 1982," in Carol M. Mueller, ed., *The Politics of the Gender Gap: The Social Construction of Political Influence* (Beverly Hills, CA: Sage Publications, 1988).

22. For a discussion of various factors associated with realignments, see Samuel Merrill III, Bernard Grofman, and Thomas L. Brunell, "Cycles in American National Electoral Politics: 1854–2006: Statistical Evidence and an Explanatory Model," *American Political Science Review* 102 (February 2008): 1–17.

23. V. O. Key, Jr., "A Theory of Critical Elections," *Journal of Politics* 17 (1955): 3–18; Walter Dean Burnham, *Critical Elections and the Mainsprings of American Politics* (New York: Norton, 1970); Paul Allen Beck, "A Socialization Theory of Partisan Realignment," in Richard Niemi, ed., *The Politics of Future Citizens* (San Francisco: Jossey-Bass, 1974).

24. A. James Reichley, "The Future of the American Two-Party System After 1996," in John C. Green and Daniel M. Shea, eds., *The State of the Parties: The Changing Role of Contemporary American Parties, 3rd Edition* (Lanham, MD: Rowman and Littlefield, 1999), 10–27.

25. See, for example, David R. Mayhew, *Electoral Realignments: A Critique of an American Genre* (New Haven, CT: Yale University Press, 2002).

26. See, for example, Martin P. Wattenberg, *The Decline of American Political Parties, 1952–1996* (Cambridge, MA: Harvard University Press, 1998); Paul Allen Beck, "The Changing American Party Coalitions," in John C. Green and Daniel M. Shea, eds., *The State of the Parties: The Changing Role of Contemporary American Parties, 3rd Edition* (Lanham, MD: Rowman and Littlefield, 1999), 28–49.

27. Some pollsters report that as many as a third of Americans identify themselves as independents. However, many political scientists claim that this independence is artificial since, when forced to make a choice, those who "lean" independent think and act like partisans who lean toward one or another party. See, for example, Abramowitz, 76. Others believe that independents are becoming a stable and truly independent lot, as evidenced by an increasing willingness to register as unaffiliated even when this means giving up the right to vote in primary contests. In Florida, for example, the number of registered "others" has quadrupled since 1987 and now accounts for 20 percent (1.8 million voters) of the state's electorate. See Rhodes Cook, "Moving On: More Voters Are Steering Away from Party Labels," *Washington Post* (Sunday, June 27, 2004), B1.

For a broader discussion of this issue, see Richard G. Niemi and Herbert F. Weisberg, eds., *Controversies in Voting Behavior, 2d ed.* (Washington, DC: Congressional Quarterly Press, 1984).

28. Wattenberg, 50–72.

29. Larry M. Bartels, "Partisanship and Voting Behavior, 1952–1996," *American Journal of Political Science* 44:1 (January 2000): 35–50.

30. James Q. Wilson, *Political Organizations* (Princeton, NJ: Princeton University Press, 1995), xiii.

31. Thomas E. Mann, "A Collapse of the Campaign Finance Regime?" *The Forum* 6:1. Available at: http://www.bepress.com/ forum/vol6/iss1/art1 (accessed June 1, 2008).

32. John F. Bibby, "Party Networks: National-State Integration, Allied Groups, and Issue Activists," in John C. Green and Daniel M. Shea, eds., *The State of the Parties: The Changing Role of Contemporary American Parties, 3d Edition* (Lanham, MD: Rowman and Littlefield, 1999), 69–85.

33. Center for Responsive Politics, "Leadership Secrets," http:// www.opensecrets.org/pacs/industry.asp?txt=Q03&cycle=2006 (accessed June 23, 2007).

34. Malcolm Jewell and David Olson, *American State Political Parties and Elections,* Rev. Ed. (Homewood, IL: Dorsey Press, 1982).

35. Third parties have been categorized in a number of ways. Key speaks of short-lived and doctrinal parties (Key, 1964). Orren lists principled, personalistic, and protest as third party types. See Gary R. Orren, "The Changing Styles of American Party Politics," in Joel L. Fleishman, ed., *The Future of American Political Parties,* (Englewood Cliffs, NJ: Prentice Hall, 1982). Here, we employ the categories splinter, ideological, and issue/candidate.

36. *Federal Election Commission v. Wisconsin Right to Life,* 551 U.S. (2007).

37. Stephen R. Weissman and Kara D. Ryan, "Soft Money in the 2006 Election and the Outlook for 2008: The Changing Nonprofits Landscape," Report from the Campaign Finance Institute, 2007. At http://www.cfinst.org/books_reports/pdf/NP_SoftMoney_0608.pdf (accessed on June 1, 2008).

38. Ibid.

39. Clyde Wilcox, "Internet Fundraising in 2008: A New Model?" *The Forum*: 6 :1. Available at http://www.bepress.com/forum/ vol6/iss1/art1 (accessed September 17, 2008); Also see Richard L. Hasen, "Political Equality, the Internet, and Campaign Finance Regulation, *The Forum*: Vol. 6 : Iss.1, Article 7. Available at http:// www.bepress.com/forum/vol6/iss1/art1; (accessed June 1, 2008).

40. *California Democratic Party v. Jones* 530, U.S. 567 (2000).

41. Wattenberg, p. 35.

42. Thomas E. Patterson, *The Vanishing Voter: Public Involvement in an Age of Uncertainty* (New York: Knopf, 2002), 99–127.

43. Gina M. Garramone, Charles K. Atkin, Bruce E. Pinkleton, and Richard T. Cole, "Effects of Negative Political Advertising on the Political Process," *Journal of Broadcasting and the Electronic Media* 34 (1990): 299–311.

44. Stephen Ansolabehere and Shanto Iyenger, *Going Negative: How Political Advertisements Shrink and Polarize the Electorate* (New York: Free Press, 1995).

45. Steven E. Finkel and John G. Geer, "A Spot Check: Casting Doubt on the Demobilizing Effect of Attack Advertising," *American Journal of Political Science* 42:2 (April 1998): 573–595.

46. Patterson, 51.

47. Richard R. Beeman, "Deference, Republicanism, and the Emergence of Popular Politics in Eighteenth Century America," *William and Mary Quarterly* 49:3 (July 1992): 417.

17. Andrew Gelman and Gary King, "Enhancing Democracy Through Legislative Redistricting," *American Political Science Review* 88 (1994): 541–559.

18. Alan Abramowitz, Brad Alexander, and Matthew Gunning, "Don't Blame Redistricting for Uncompetitive Elections," *PS: Politics and Society* 39 (2006): 87ff.

19. Public Policy Institute of California, "Voter Turnout in Majority Minority Districts," *Research Brief* 46 (June 2001).

20. See a full discussion of this matter in David Epstein and Sharyn O'Halloran, "Measuring the Electoral and Policy Impact of Majority-Minority Voting Districts," *American Journal of Political Science* 43:2 (1999): 367–395.

21. Richard Fenno, *Home Style: Members in their Districts* (Boston: Little Brown, 1978), 50ff.

22. Courtney Macavinta, "Congress Has Issue with E-Mail," C-Net News.com (February 25, 1998). Accessed online at http://news.com.com on December 10, 2004.

23. Robert S. Erikson and Gerald C. Wright, "Voters, Candidates, and Issues in Congressional Elections," in Lawrence C. Dodd and Bruce L. Oppenheimer, eds., *Congress Reconsidered,* 6th ed. (Washington, DC: Congressional Quarterly, 1997), 143.

24. David R. Mayhew, *Congress: The Electoral Connection* (New Haven: Yale University Press, 1974).

25. Support for Congress varies greatly ranging from a low of 18 percent in mid-2007 to a high of 84 percent just after the 9/11 attacks. (Gallup Organization at www.gallup.com, various years.)

26. G. William Whitehurst, "Lobbies and Political Action Committees: A Congressman's Perspective," in Lou Frey, Jr. and Michael T. Hayes, eds., *Inside the House: Former Members Reveal How Congress Really Works* (Lanham, MD: University Press of America, 2001), 210.

27. Ibid., 222.

28. Representative Ernest Istook (R-OK), then chair of the appropriations subcommittee with jurisdiction over the IRS, told the *New York Times* that the provision had been inserted in the bill without his knowledge. See David E. Rosenbaum, "Panel Chief Denies Knowing about Item on Inspecting Tax Returns," *New York Times,* November 23, 2004, 22A.

29. Barbara Sinclair, *The Transformation of the U.S. Senate* (Baltimore: Johns Hopkins University Press, 1989), 101.

30. Citizens Against Government Waste, "2008 Congressional 'Pig' Book Summary," accessed online at http://www.cagw.org/site/PageServer?pagename=reports_pigbook2008 on June 7, 2008.

31. Catharine Richert, "CQ Vote Studies: Party Unity, Together We Stand Opposed," *Congressional Quarterly Weekly*, Jan. 14, 143.

32. Sarah Binder, Thomas E. Mann, and Molly Reynolds, "Is the Broken Branch on the Mend? An Early Report on the 110th Congress," paper presented at forum sponsored by the Brookings Institution, September 4, 2007.

33. Gallup Organization, *Congress Approval at Twelve-Year Low*, April 17, 2006. Accessed online at http://poll.gallup.com on August 2, 2006.

34. See, for example, David Mayhew, *Divided We Govern* (New Haven, CT: Yale University Press, 1991); Charles O. Jones, *The Presidency in a Separated System* (Washington, DC: Brookings Institution Press, 1994).

35. See, for example, James L. Sundquist, *Constitutional Reform and Effective Government, rev.ed.* (Washington, DC: Brookings Institution Press, 1992); Samuel Kernell, "Facing an Opposition Congress: The President's Strategic Circumstance," in (Gary W.

Cox and Samuel Kernell, eds) The Politics of Divided Government (Boulder, CO: Westview Press, 1991).

36. George C. Edwards, III, Andrew Barrett, and Jeffrey Peake, "The Legislative Impact of Divided Government," *American Journal of Political Science* 41 (2), 1997 545–563.

37. Douglas B. Harris and Garrison Nelson, "Middlemen No More? Emergent Patterns in Congressional Leadership Selection," *PS: Political Science and Politics* 41 (January 2008), 49–55.

38. Lawrence A. Becker and Vincent G. Moscardelli, "Congressional Leadership on the Front Lines: Committee Chairs, Electoral Security, and Ideology, *PS: Political Science and Politics* 41 (January 2008), 77–82.

39. Robert S. Walker, "A Look at the Rules of the House," in Lou Frey, Jr. and Michael T. Hayes, eds., *Inside the House: Former Members Reveal How Congress Really Works* (Lanham, MD: University Press of America, 2001), 250.

40. *Origins and Development of Congress*, 261.

41. Hamilton, 55–56.

42. Barbara Sinclair, *Unorthodox Lawmaking: New Legislative Processes in the U.S. Congress* (Washington, DC: Congressional Quarterly Press, 1997).

43. Congressional Research Service, Report RL30172: *Instances of Use of United States Armed Forces Abroad, 1798–2001.*

44. This sentiment is traced to Roger Sherman. See *Origins and Development of Congress*, 62.

45. *Hamdan v. Rumsfeld*, 548 U.S. (2006).

46. Binder, Mann, and Reynolds, 15.

47. *Immigration and Naturalization Service v. Chadha*, 454 U.S. 812 (1983).

48. The War Powers Act includes a form of legislative veto.

49. Senate Historical Office, "Treaties." Online at http://www?.senate.gov on July 30, 2006.

50. John R. Hibbing and Elizabeth Theiss-Morse, *Congress as Public Enemy* (Cambridge: Cambridge University Press, 1995).

51. Gallup Organization, *Congress Approval Rating Matches Historic Low*, August 21, 2007. Accessed online at http://www.galluppoll.com on September 11, 2007.

52. Thomas Mann and Norman Ornstein, *The Broken Branch: How Congress is Failing America and How to Get It Back on Track* (New York: Oxford University Press, 2006).

53. Edward G. Carmines, Jessica C. Gerrity, and Michael W. Wagner, *How the American Public Views Congress: A Report Based on the Center on Congress at Indiana University's 2004 Public Opinion Survey* (Bloomington, IN: Indiana University Press, 2005).

54. Franklin D. Gilliam, Jr. "Influences on Voter Turnout for U.S. House Elections in Non-Presidential Election Years," *Legislative Studies Quarterly* 10:3 (1985): 339–351.

55. Steven E. Gottlieb, "Incumbents Rules," *The National Law Journal*, February 25, 2002, A21.

Chapter 12: The Presidency: Power and Paradox

1. *New York Times,* November 6, 2004, A1.

2. Gallup Organization, "Social Security." Accessed online at http://www.gallup.com on August 9, 2005.

3. George Edwards, *The Public Presidency* (New York: St. Martin's Press, 1983), 269.

4. Harold F. Bass, Jr., "The President and Political Parties," in *The President, the Public, and the Parties* (Washington, DC: Congressional Quarterly Press, 1997), 33.

5. D. Robert Dahl, "Myth of the Presidential Mandate," *Political Science Quarterly* 105 (1990): 359.

6. Ibid., 360.

7. Thomas E. Patterson, *The Vanishing Voter* (New York: Knopf, 2002), 169.

8. Darren Carlson, "Public Flunks Electoral College," November 2, 2004. Accessed online at http://www.galluppoll.com on March 16, 2007.

9. Quoted in James Pfiffner, *The Modern Presidency* (New York: St. Martin's Press, 1994), 54.

10. William G. Howell, *Power Without Persuasion: The Politics of Direct Presidential Action* (Princeton: Princeton University Press, 2003), Chap. 1.

11. Sidney M. Milkis and Michael Nelson, *The American Presidents: Origins and Development, 1776–1993* (Washington, DC: CQ Press, 1994), 77.

12. Lorraine H. Tong, " Senate Confirmation Process: An Overview" *CRS Report for Congress* (Washington, DC: Congressional Research Service, April 4, 2003).

13. Paul C. Light, *The President's Agenda: Domestic Policy Choice from Kennedy to Clinton* (Baltimore: Johns Hopkins Press, 1999), 230.

14. *Clinton v. City of New York* 524 U.S. (417) 1998.

15. National Commission on Terrorist Attacks upon the United States, *The 9–11 Commission Report* (Washington, DC: United States Printing Office, 2004).

16. W. Craig Bledsoe, Christopher J. Bosso, and Mark J. Rozell, "Chief Executive," in *Powers of the Presidency*, 2d ed. (Washington, DC: CQ Press, 1997), 41.

17. Milkis and Nelson, 45.

18. Daniel Diller and Stephen H. Wirls, "Commander in Chief," in *Powers of the Presidency,* 2d ed. (Washington, DC: CQ Press, 1997), 165.

19. Abraham Lincoln, "Letter to Albert Hodges," in John Nicolay and John Hay, eds., *The Complete Works of Abraham Lincoln* (New York: Francis Tandy, 1891), 10–66.

20. *Boumediene v. Bush*, 553 U.S. ___ (2008).

21. Daniel Diller and Stephen H. Wirls, "Chief Diplomat," in *Powers of the Presidency,* 2d ed. (Washington, DC: CQ Press, 1997), 140.

22. George Edwards, III, *At the Margins: Presidential Leadership in Congress* (New Haven: Yale University Press, 1989), 212.

23. Christopher J. Bosso, "Legislative Leader," in *Powers of the Presidency*, 2d ed. (Washington, DC: CQ Press, 1997), 86.

24. Samuel A. Alito, Jr., Office of Legal Counsel, U.S. Department of Justice, "Using Presidential Signing Statements to Make Fuller Use of the President's Constitutionally Assigned Role in the Process of Enacting Law," February 5, 1986, 1.

25. Center for Responsive Politics, "Embassy Row." Accessed online at http://www.capitaleye.org on August 15, 2005.

26. Jeremy D. Mayer and Lynn Kirby, "The Promise and Peril of Presidential Polling: Between Gallup's Dream and the Morris Nightmare," in Stephen J. Wayne, ed., *Is This Any Way to Run a Democratic Government?* (Washington, DC: Georgetown University Press, 2004), 103.

27. Lawrence R. Jacobs and Melinda S. Jackson, "Presidential Leadership and the Threat to Popular Sovereignty," in Michael A. Genovese and Matthew J. Streb, eds., *Polls and Politics: The Dilemmas of Democracy* (Albany, NY: State University of New York Press, 2004).

28. Diane J. Heith, "Continuing to Campaign: Public Opinion and the White House," in Michael A. Genovese and Matthew J. Streb, eds., *Polls and Politics: The Dilemmas of Democracy* (Albany, NY: State University of New York Press, 2004), 66.

29. Presidents sometimes elevate additional advisers to cabinet status as well. George W. Bush includes in his full cabinet the vice president, his chief of staff, the director of the Environmental Protection Agency, the director of the Office of Management and Budget, the U.S. trade representative, and the director of the Office of National Drug Control Policy.

30. These were the sentiments of Richard Nixon, who was included in cabinet deliberations. Quoted in Pfiffner, 12.

31. Bradley Patterson, Jr., *The White House Staff: Inside the West Wing and Beyond* (Washington, DC: The Brookings Institution, 2000), 11.

32. Dan Froomkin, "White House Briefing." Accessed online at http://www.washingtonpost.com on September 17, 2004.

33. B. Patterson, 62.

34. Karen M. Hult, "The Bush White House in Comparative Perspective," in Fred I. Greenstein, ed., *The George W. Bush Presidency: An Early Assessment* (Baltimore, MD: Johns Hopkins University Press, 2003), 64.

35. This model was advocated by advisers Clark Clifford and Richard Neustadt. See James Pfiffner, *The Strategic Presidency* (Chicago: Dorsey Press, 1988), 23–25.

36. Pfiffner, 67.

37. Gary Jacobson, *A Divider, Not a Uniter* (New York: Pearson, 2007), 74.

38. See, for example, Richard A. Clarke, *Against All Enemies: Inside America's War on Terror* (New York: Free Press, 2004); Paul O'Neill and Ron Suskind, *The Price of Loyalty: George W. Bush, the White House, and the Education of Paul O'Neill* (New York: Simon & Schuster, 2004). See also, account of interviews with cabinet members from the Bush White House in Bob Woodward, *Plan of Attack* (New York: Simon & Schuster, 2004).

39. James P. Pfiffner, "President George W. Bush and His War Cabinet," Paper presented at conference on *The Presidency, Congress, and the War on Terrorism*, University of Florida (February 7, 2003).

40. See, for example, Edward Hargrove, "What Manner of Man?" in James David Barber, ed., *Choosing the President* (New York: Prentice-Hall, 1974). Also see Thomas E. Cronin and Michael A. Genovese, *The Paradoxes of the American Presidency* (New York: Oxford, 1998), 33–38.

41. James David Barber, *The Presidential Character*, rev. ed. (New York: Prentice-Hall, 1992).

42. Arthur M. Schlesinger, Jr., *The Imperial Presidency* (Boston: Houghton Mifflin, 1973).

43. See, for example, Steven G. Calabresi and Christopher S. Yoo, "The Unitary Executive During the Second Half-Century," *Harvard Journal of Public Policy* 668 (2003).

44. Richard Neustadt, *Presidential Power and the Modern Presidents: The Politics of Leadership from Roosevelt to Reagan* (New York: Free Press, 1991).

45. Quoted in Cronin and Genovese, 317.

46. Thomas S. Langston, *With Reverence and Contempt: How Americans Think About Their President* (Baltimore: Johns Hopkins University Press 1995), xi.

Chapter 13: Bureaucracy: Citizens as Owners and Consumers

1. Evan Thomas, "What Went Wrong: Devastating a Swath of the South, Katrina Plunged New Orleans into Agony," *Newsweek*, September 12, 2005.

2. "Changes at the Top for FEMA," CBS News, September 12, 2005. Accessed online at http://www.cbsnews.com.

3. Joyce Appleby, "That's General Washington to You," *New York Times Book Review,* February 14, 1993, 11.

4. Herbert Kaufman, *Red Tape: Its Origins, Uses, and Abuses* (Washington, DC: The Brookings Institution, 1977), 11.

5. See David A. Stockman, *The Triumph of Politics: How the Reagan Revolution Failed* (New York: Harper and Row, 1986).

6. Mosher, 57.

7. James D. Richardson, *Messages and Papers of the Presidents*, Volume II (Washington, DC: Bureau of National Literature and Art, 1903), 438.

8. Robert C. Caldwell, *James A. Garfield* (Hamden, CT: Archon Books, 1965).

9. Matthew A. Crenson and Benjamin Ginsberg, *Downsizing Democracy* (Baltimore: Johns Hopkins University Press, 2002), 86.

10. David Osborne and Ted Gaebler, *Reinventing Government: How the Entrepreneurial Spirit Is Transforming the Public Sector* (Reading, MA: Addison-Wesley, 1992).

11. Mark Green and John Berry, *The Challenge of Hidden Profits: Reducing Corporate Bureaucracy and Waste* (New York: William Morrow, 1985).

12. See an interview in Ralph P. Hummel, *The Bureaucratized Experience* (New York: St. Martin's Press, 1977), 23.

13. Gerald E. Caiden, "What Is Maladministration?" *Public Administration Review*, 51: 6 (1991): 486–493.

14. Alexander Hamilton, James Madison, and John Jay, *The Federalist*, Benjamin F. Wright, ed. (New York: Metro Books, 2002), 451.

15. Hugh Helco, *A Government of Strangers: Executive Politics in Washington* (Washington, DC: Brookings Institution, 1997).

16. Postal workers have their own organization but are not allowed to strike. There are other federal workers like federal air traffic controllers who also are not allowed to strike. Political appointees, unlike career civil servants, serve at the pleasure of the president.

17. Robert Lineberry, *American Public Policy: What Government Does and What Difference It Makes* (New York: Harper & Row, 1977).

18. Theodore Lowi, *The End of Liberalism*, (New York: W. W. Norton, 1969).

19. See Cornelius M. Kerwin, *Rulemaking: How Government Agencies Write Law And Make Public Policy* (Washington, DC: CQ Press, 1994).

20. Ibid., 162.

21. Ibid., 194.

22. Ibid., 196.

23. Kerwin, 170–171.

24. Ibid., 170.

25. Ibid., 170.

26. *Humphrey's Executor v. United States* (1935).

27. Donald D. Kettl, *Government by Proxy: (Mis)Managing Federal Programs* (Washington, DC: The CQ Press, 1998).

28. Paul C. Light, *The True Size of Government* (Washington, DC: Brookings Institution, 1999).

29. Ibid., 9.

30. B. Dan Wood and Richard W. Waterman, *Bureaucratic Dynamics: The Role of Bureaucracy in a Democracy* (Boulder: Westview Press, 1994), 105.

31. See Patricia W. Ingraham and David H. Rosenbloom, *The Promise and Paradox of Civil Service Reform* (Pittsburgh: University of Pittsburgh Press, 1992), 4.

32. Wood and Waterman, 104.

33. John Brehm and Scott Gatew, *Working, Shirking, and Sabotage: Bureaucratic Response to a Democratic Public* (Ann Arbor: University of Michigan Press, 1997).

34. James Q. Wilson, *Bureaucracy: What Government Agencies Do and Why They Do It* (New York: Basic Books, 1989), 236

35. *McGrain v. Daugherty* (1972).

36. Johanna Neuman, "FAA's 'Culture of Coziness Targeted in Airline Safety Hearing," *Los Angeles Times*, April 4, 2008, 1.

37. See Clinton Rossiter, *The American Presidency* (New York: Harcourt, Brace, and World, 1960).

38. James G. March and Johan P. Olson, "Organizing Political Life: What Administrative Reorganization Tells Us About Government," *American Political Science Review* 77 (1983): 281–296.

39. Richard W. Waterman, *Presidential Influence and the Administrative State* (Knoxville: The University of Tennessee Press, 1989), 27.

40. Ibid., 30.

41. Gerald Ford, *A Time to Heal: The Autobiography of Gerald R. Ford* (New York: Harper & Row, 1979), 352.

42. Waterman, 37.

43. Ibid., 1–2.

Chapter 14: The Courts: Judicial Power in a Democratic Setting

1. The largest circuits, with over twenty judges, do not use every judge in the circuit for an *en banc* hearing.

2. Edward D. Re, *Stare Decisis* (Washington, DC: Federal Judicial Center, 1975), 2.

3. See Charles Rembar, *The Judicial Process* (New York: Oxford University Press, 1968), 12.

4. *Flast v. Cohen* (1968).

5. Ibid.

6. *Colegrove v. Green* (1946).

7. *Baker v. Carr* (1962).

8. Jethro K. Lieberman, *The Litigious Society* (New York: Basic Books, 1983), viii.

9. See Christopher E. Smith, *Courts, Politics, and the Judicial Process*, 2d ed. (Chicago: Nelson Hall, 1997), 330.

10. Howard Abadinsky, *Law and Justice: An Introduction to the American Legal System* (Chicago: Nelson Hall, 1995), 55.

11. Article III, Section 1 of the Constitution.

12. Alexander Hamilton, John Jay, and James Madison, *The Federalist Papers*, Benjamin F. Wright, ed. (New York: Metro Books, 1961), 490–491.

13. Bernard Schwartz, *A History of the Supreme Court* (New York: Oxford University Press, 1993), 15.

14. The number of justices on the Supreme Court is set by Congress because no set number was specified in the Constitution.

15. *Ex parte McCardle* (1869).

16. All the justices today have four clerks except Justice Stevens, who continues to have only three law clerks.

17. Quoted in H. W. Perry, *Deciding to Decide: Agenda Setting in the U.S. Supreme Court* (Cambridge, MA: Harvard University Press, 1992), 144.

18. Ibid., 222.

19. Ibid., 75.

20. See Lawrence Baum, *The Supreme Court*, 6th ed. (Washington, DC: CQ Press, 1998), 114.

21. Doris M. Provine, "Deciding What to Decide: How the Supreme Court Sets Its Agenda" *Judicature* 64, no. 7 (1981): 320.

22. See Lincoln Caplan, *The Tenth Justice: The Solicitor General and the Rule of Law* (New York: Vintage Books, 1987).

23. See Rebecca Mae Salokar, *The Solicitor General: The Politics of Law* (Philadelphia: Temple University Press, 1992), 3.

24. O'Brien, 294.

25. Ibid., 313.

26. Bob Woodward and Scott Armstrong, *The Brethren* (New York: Simon & Schuster, 1979), 136–139.

27. Charles A. Johnson and Bradley C. Canon, *Judicial Policies: Implementation and Impact,* 2d ed. (Washington, DC: Congressional Quarterly Press, 1999), Chap. 1.

28. See Richard L. Pacelle, Jr., and Lawrence Baum, "Supreme Court Authority in the Judiciary," *American Politics Quarterly* 20 (1992): 169–191.

29. J. W. Peltason, *Fifty-Eight Lonely Men: Southern Federal Judges and School Desegregation,* 2d ed. (Urbana: University of Illinois Press, 1971), 246.

30. *Employment Division, Department of Human Resources v. Smith* (1990).

31. *City of Boerne v. Flores* (1997).

32. *Atkins v. Virginia* (2002).

33. See Lee Epstein and Jack Knight, *The Choices Justices Make* (Washington, DC: CQ Press, 1998); Forest Maltzman, Paul J. Wahlbeck, and Jack Spriggs, *Crafting Law on the Supreme Court: The Collegial Game* (New York: Cambridge University Press, 2000); and Walter F. Murphy, *Elements of Judicial Strategy* (Chicago: University of Chicago Press, 1964).

34. Saul Brenner, "Fluidity on the Supreme Court, 1956–1967," *American Journal of Political Science* 90 (1996): 581.

35. Epstein and Knight, Chap. 3.

36. See Henry J. Abraham, *Justices and Presidents,* 2d ed. (New York: Oxford University Press, 1985).

37. See David O'Brien, *Storm Center* (New York: Norton, 1986).

38. Abraham, 191.

39. Alpheus T. Mason, *William Howard Taft: Chief Justice* (New York: Simon & Schuster, 1965), 215–216.

40. Philip Cooper and Howard Ball, *The United States Supreme Court: From the Inside Out* (Upper Saddle River, NJ: Prentice-Hall, 1996), 50.

41. Scigliano, 147–148.

42. Roger Taney was a Catholic who served on the Court from 1835 until 1864, but the tradition of a Catholic seat did not begin with him, because his replacement was not a Catholic.

43. Lawrence Baum, *American Courts,* 4th ed. (Boston: Houghton Mifflin, 1998), 106.

44. Michael Pertschuk and Wendy Schaetzel, *People Rising* (New York: Thunder's Mouth Press, 1989), 68.

45. See Karen O'Connor, "Lobbying the Justices for Justice," in Paul S. Herrnson, Ronald G. Shaido, and Clyde Wilcox, eds., *The Interest Group Connection* (Chatham, NJ: Chatham House, 1998), 273.

46. Baum, 112.

47. Lee Epstein, *Conservatives in Court* (Knoxville: University of Tennessee Press, 1985).

48. In *Newman v. Piggie Park Enterprises Inc.* (1968), the Supreme Court upheld the fee-splitting provision.

49. See Stephen C. Yeazell, *From Medieval Group Litigation to the Modern Class Action* (New Haven, CT: Yale University Press, 1987).

50. Samuel Issacharoff, "Goverance and Legitimacy in the Law of Class Actions," *Supreme Court Review* (1999): 337.

51. *Powell v. McCormack* (1969).

52. Matthew A. Crenson and Benjamin Ginsberg, *Downsizing Democracy: How America Sidelined Its Citizens and Privatized Its Public* (Baltimore: Johns Hopkins University Press, 2002), 154.

53. See Lucius J. Barker, "Third Parties in Litigation: A Systematic View of the Judicial Function," *The Journal of Politics,* 29, no. 1 (1967): 54–60.

Chapter 15: Public Policy: Responding to Citizens

1. John Leland, "Baltimore Finds Subprime Crisis Snags Women," *New York Times,* January 15, 2008. Facts in this paragraph are drawn from this story.

2. Mortgage Baners Association, "Delinquencies and Foreclosures Increase in Latest MBA National Delinquency Survey," June 5, 2008. Report accessed at http://www.mortgagebankers.org/NewsandMedia/PressCenter/62936.htm on June 21, 2008.

3. Thomas R. Dye, *Understanding Public Policy,* 10th ed. (Upper Saddle River, NJ: Prentice-Hall, 2002), 1.

4. This section draws heavily on the work of James Q. Wilson whose typology is described. See James Q. Wilson, *Political Organizations* (Princeton, NJ: Princeton University Press, 1995), 332–337.

5. Environmental Protection Agency, *Fiscal Year 2004 Annual Report* (Washington, DC: Government Printing Office, 2004).

6. Sholnn Freeman, "Carmakers Defeated on Emission Rule," *Washington Post,* September 13, 2007, D1.

7. Dye, 106.

8. U.S. Census Bureau, *Current Population Survey,* 2005. Accessed online at http://www.census.gov on May 28, 2007. See also Carmen DeNavas-Walt, Bernadette D. Proctor, and Robert J. Mills, *Income, Poverty, and Health Insurance Coverage in the United States: 2003* (Washington, DC: U.S. Census Bureau, August 2004).

9. Ceci Connolly, "OMB Says Medicare Drug Law Could Cost Still More," *Washington Post*, September 19, 2004, A04.

10. Urban Institute, *Assessing the New Federalism: Eight Years Later* (Washington, DC: Urban Institute, 2005).

11. Michael A. Fletcher, "Two Fronts in the War on Poverty: Bush Seeks More Aid for Church Groups; Others Face Uncertainty," *Washington Post*, May 17, 2005, A01.

12. Kaiser Family Foundation, *Health Coverage, and the Uninsured: Profile of the Uninsured.* Accessed online at http://www.kff.org on September 14, 2007.

13. Stephen Moore, ed., *Restoring the Dream: The Bold New Plan by House Republicans* (Washington, DC: Times Books, 1995), 156.

14. Dye, 152.

15. Benjamin I. Page and Robert Y. Shapiro, *The Rational Public* (Chicago: University of Chicago Press, 1992).

16. Katie Zezima, "In Boston, Residents Seek Face to Face Advice to Avoid Foreclosure," *New York Times,* March 30, 2008.

17. Deborah Yao, "Cities Help Residents Facing Foreclosure," Associated Press, Posted June 16, 2008, 20:07:19.

18. See, for example, The Center for Deliberative Democracy at Stanford University (accessed online at http://cdd.stanford.edu on May 25, 2005); the Deliberative Democracy Consortium (accessed online at http://www.deliberative-democracy.net on May 25, 2005); the Center for Deliberative Polling at the University of Texas Austin (accessed online at http://www.la.utexas.edu/research/delpol/cdpindex.html on May 25, 2005).

Chapter 16: Foreign and Defense Policy: Protecting American Interests in the World

1. George W. Bush, Remarks by the President on Iraq at Cincinnati Museum Center—Cincinnati Union Terminal, Cincinnati, Ohio. Online at http://www.whitehouse.gov/news/releases/2002/10/20021007-8.html (accessed December 28, 2007).

2. Tim Weiner, "Pssst: Some Hope for Spycraft," *New York Times,* December 9, 2007.

3. Ibid.

4. Alexis de Tocqueville, *Democracy in America,* trans. George Lawrence, ed. J. P. Mayer (New York: Harper and Row, 1969), 278.

5. Ibid., 227.

6. H. William Brands, *The United States in the World: A History of American Foreign Policy,* vol. 1 (Boston: Houghton Mifflin, 1994), 110.

7. George W. Bush, "President Bush Delivers Graduation Speech at West Point," White House website, http://www.whitehouse.gov/news/releases/2002/06/20020601-3.html (accessed April 29, 2005).

8. George W. Bush, "Remarks by the President at Whitehall Palace," White House website, http://www.whitehouse.gov/news/releases/2003/11/20031119-1.html (accessed May 17, 2005).

9. The Kissinger Telcons: Kissinger Telcons on Chile, National Security Archive Electronic Briefing Book No. 123, edited by Peter Kornbluh, posted May 26, 2004. This particular dialogue can be found at TELCON: September 16, 1973, 11:50 a.m. Kissinger Talking to Nixon. Accessed online November 26, 2006.

10. See, for example, Robert J. Lieber, *No Common Power: Understanding International Relations* (Boston: Scott Foresman, 1988).

11. See, for example, the excellent discussion of the school of realism in Bruce W. Jentleson, *American Foreign Policy: The Dynamics of Choice in the 21st Century,* 2d ed. (New York: W. W. Norton, 2004).

12. See, for example, Joseph Nye, *The Power to Lead: Soft, Hard, and Smart* (New York: Oxford University Press, 2008).

13. Francis Fukuyama, "After Neoconservatism," *New York Times,* February 19, 2006.

14. Richard A. Best, *CRS: Report for Congress: The National Intelligence Director and Intelligence Analysis* (Washington, D.C.: Congressional Research Service, 2004).

15. National Commission on Terrorist Attacks, The 9/11 Commission Report: Final Report of the Commission on Terrorist Attacks upon the United States *(New York: W. W. Norton, 2004).*

16. U.S. Department of State, *Mission Statement,* online at http://www.state.gov/m/rm/rls/dosstrat/2004/23503.htm (accessed May 1, 2005).

17. Jane Mayer, *The Dark Side: The Inside Story of How the War on Terror Turned into a War on American Ideals* (New York: Doubleday, 2008).

18. See, for example, Robert Higgs, "The Trillion-Dollar Defense Budget Is Already Here," The Independent Institute, online at http://www.independent.org/newsroom/article.asp?id=1941 (accessed January 26, 2008). See also War Resisters League, "Where Your Income Tax Money Really Goes," online at http://www.warresisters.org/piechart.htm (accessed January 26, 2008).

19. Ole R. Holsti, *Public Opinion and American Foreign Policy,* rev. ed. (Ann Arbor: University of Michigan Press, 2007), 55.

20. Gallup Organization, "Gallup's Pulse of Democracy: The War in Iraq," April 18–20, 2008, survey, online at http://www.gallup.com/poll/1633/Iraq.aspx (accessed July 6, 2008).

21. CIA World Factbook, online at https://www.cia.gov/library/publications/the-world-factbook/ (accessed January 27, 2008).

22. Curt Tarnoff and Larry Nowels, *Foreign Aid: An Introductory Overview of U.S. Programs and Policies* (Washington, DC: Congressional Research Service, April 15, 2004).

23. Ibid.

24. Joseph S. Nye, *Soft Power: The Means to Success in World Politics* (New York: Public Affairs, 2004), 4.

25. The Nuclear Information Project, Status of World Nuclear Forces, online at http://www.nukestrat.com/nukestatus.htm (accessed February 6, 2008).

26. United States Nuclear Regulatory Commission, *Fact Sheet on Dirty Bombs,* online at http://www.nrc.gov/reading-rm/doc-collections/fact-sheets/dirty-bombs.html (accessed February 9, 2008).

27. U.S. Census Bureau, *Foreign Trade Statistics,* online at http://www.census.gov/foreign-trade/balance/c5700.html#2007 (accessed February 9, 2008).

28. David Lague, "Beijing Increases Defense Spending," *International Herald Tribune,* March 4, 2007.

29. Wayne M. Morrison and Marc Labonte, "China's Holdings of U.S. Securities: Implications for the U.S. Economy," *Congressional Research Service Report for Congress,* January 9, 2008.

30. Nye, *Soft Power,* 5–11.

CREDITS

PHOTOS

Table of Contents "Why You Vote" 1: © Digital Vision; 2: © Stockbyte/Getty; 4: © BananaStock/JupiterImages; 5: © Stockbyte/Getty; p. iv: © Cory Ryan/Getty; p. vi left: © Joel Gordon; p. vi middle: © Joel Gordon; All other TOC photos are represented elsewhere in the credits

Chapter 1 Opener: © Martin H. Simon/Corbis; p. 2: Courtesy of Molly Kawahata; p. 4 © Neville Elder/Corbis; p. 5 top: © Ahmad Zaki/Reuters/Corbis; p. 5 bottom: © Nicholas Kamm/AFP/Getty; p. 7 top: © Dan Lamont/Corbis; p. 7 bottom: © Bettmann/Corbis; p. 9 top: © Stockbyte/PunchStock; p. 9 bottom: © Ryan McVay/Getty; p. 10: © Siqui Sanchez/The Image Bank/Getty; p. 11: © Ryan McVay/Getty; p. 12 top: © Wesley Bocxe/The Image Works; p. 12 bottom: © Photodisc/SuperStock; p. 13: © Stockbyte/Getty

Chapter 2 Opener: © Mandel Ngan/AFP/Getty; p. 18: © Copyright 2005 by Gregg Newton; p. 19 top: © Northwind Picture Archives/Northwind; p. 19 bottom: © Ingram Publishing/Alamy; p. 20: © The Granger Collection, NY; p. 21 top: © Kevin Fleming/Corbis; p. 21 bottom: © Northwind Picture Archives/Northwind; p. 22: © Northwind Picture Archives/Northwind; p. 23 top: © Bettmann/Corbis; p. 23 bottom: © Royalty-Free/Corbis; p. 24: © The Granger Collection, NY; p. 25: © Royalty-Free/Corbis; p. 26 left: © AP Photo/Pablo Martinez Monsivais; p. 26 middle: © Scott Olson/Getty; p. 26 right: © AP Photo/J. Scott Applewhite; p. 27: © Ron Sachs-Pool/Getty; p. 28: © Chuck Kennedy/NewsCom.com; p. 29: © Tim Pannell/Corbis; p. 31 top: © Katy Winn/Corbis; p. 31 middle: © Joe Raedle/Getty; p. 31 bottom: © Brand X Pictures; p. 32: © Digital Vision Ltd./SuperStock; p. 33: © AP Photo/J. Scott Applewhite; p. 34: James Leynse/Corbis; p. 35 bottom: © Bettmann/Corbis; p. 36: © Tim Boyle/Getty; p. 37: © Corbis

Chapter 3 Opener: © Ken James/Corbis; p. 42: © Abriel Bouys/AFP/Getty; p. 43: © AP Photo/Tim Graham Picture Library; p. 44 middle: © Royalty-Free/Corbis; p. 44 right: © Royalty-Free/Corbis; p. 45 top: © Robert E Daemmrich/Getty; p. 45 bottom left: © Omikron/Photo Researchers; p. 45 bottom right: © Burstein Collection/Corbis; p. 46 left: © The Granger Collection, New York; p. 46 right: © Northwind Picture Archives/Northwind; p. 47 top: © The Granger Collection, New York; p. 47 bottom: © Corbis; p. 48: © Underwood & Underwood/Corbis; p. 49 top: © Comstock/Corbis; p. 49 bottom: © Bettmann/Corbis; p. 50: © AP Photo; p. 51: © Reuters/Corbis; p. 52: © Tim Sloan/AFP/Getty; p. 53: © Kathy McLaughlin/The Image Works; p. 55: © Royalty-Free/Corbis; p. 56: © Shelly Katz/Time Life Pictures; p. 57: © Rebecca Cook/Reuters/Corbis; p. 58: © Will & Deni McIntyre/Corbis; p. 59: © Photodisc/SuperStock; p. 60: © Sandy Huffaker/Getty; p. 61: © BananaStock/JupiterImages

Chapter 4 Opener: © AP Photo/Nati Harnik; p. 66: © Jerry Laizure/Getty; p. 67: © moodboard/Corbis; p. 69: © 20th Century Fox/Photofest; p. 70: © Michael Schwarz/The Image Works; p. 71: © David Seawell/Alamy; p. 72 top: © Mandel Ngan/AFP/Getty; p. 72 bottom: © Jeff Greenberg/The Image Works; p. 75: © William Campbell/Sygma/Corbis; p. 77: © Amos Aikman/Getty; p. 78: © iStockphoto.com/Andres Peiro Palme; p. 79: © Robert Sullivan/AFP/Getty; p. 80: © Bettmann/Corbis; p. 81: © Kimberly White/Getty; p. 82: © AP Photo/Independent Florida Alligator, Andrew Stanfill, File; p. 84: © Visar Kryeziu/AP Photo; p. 86 top: © Reuters/Corbis; p. 87: © Look Twice/Alamy; p. 89: © Digital Vision Ltd./SuperStock; p. 90: © Comstock/Corbis

Chapter 5 Opener: © Robert W. Kelley/Time Life Pictures/Getty; p. 96: © AP Photo/Sandy Huffaker, Pool; p. 98: © Northwind Picture Archives/Northwind; p. 99 left: © Bettmann/Corbis; p. 99 right: © Corbis; p. 100: © Bruce Roberts/Photo Researchers, Inc.; p. 101: © Digital Vision/Getty; p. 102 top: © Bettmann/Corbis; p. 102 bottom: © Francis Miller//Time Life Pictures/Getty; p. 103: © Bettmann/Corbis; p. 105: © Brand X/SuperStock; p. 106: © C Squared Studios/Getty; p. 107: © Jim West/The Image Works; p. 109: © Photodisc/Getty; p. 110 top: © Photographer's Choice/Getty; p. 110 bottom left: © Rob Crandall/The Image Works; p. 110 bottom right: © AP Photo/Alex Brandon; p. 111 top: © Seattle Post-Intelligencer Collection; Museum of History and Industry/Corbis; p. 111 bottom: © Ryan McVay/Getty; p. 112: © Jim West/The Image Works; p. 113: © Stone/Getty; p. 114: © Liz Mangelsdorf/San Francisco Chronicle/Corbis; p. 115: © Hulton-Deutsch Collection/Corbis; p. 116 top: © Time Life Pictures/Timepix/Time Life Pictures/Getty; p. 116 bottom: © Bettmann/Corbis; p. 117 bottom: © Ryan McVay/Getty; p. 118 top: © Photonica/Getty; p. 118 bottom: © Corbis/Royalty Free; p. 119: © Peter Turnley/Corbis; p. 120: © Royalty-Free/Corbis

Chapter 6 Opener: © Robyn Beck/AFP/Getty; p. 126 left: © AP Photo/M. Spencer Green; p. 126 right: © Emmanuel L Dunand/AFP/Getty; p. 128: © Bob Daemmrich/The Image Works; p. 129: © Brand X Pictures/PunchStock; p. 130: © Steve Warmoski/Jacksonville Journal-Courier/The Image Works; p. 132: © Jason DeCrow/AP Photo; p. 135: © Digital Vision/Getty; p. 136: © Bettmann/Corbis; p. 137 top: © Photographers Choice RF/SuperStock; p. 137 bottom: © Ralf-Finn Hestoft/Corbis; p. 139: © Spencer Platt/Getty; p. 140 top: © Stockbyte; p. 140 bottom: © Kerry-Edwards 2004, Inc./Sharon Farmer, photographer; p. 142: © David McNew/Getty; p. 145: © Sgt Matthew Roe 10th Public Affairs Operations Center HANDOUT/epa/Corbis

Chapter 7 Opener: © Thiery Zoccolan/AFP/Getty; p. 150: Courtesy of Casey Durdines; p. 151: © Underwood & Underwood/Corbis; p. 152: © CMCD/Getty; p. 157 top: © Jeff Greenberg/The Image Works; p. 157 bottom: © John Gress/Reuters/Corbis; p. 158: © Ryan McVay/Getty; p. 160: © Yoshikazu Tsuno/AFP/Getty; p. 162: Courtesy of Mike Kostyo; p. 163: © Reuters/Jonathan Ernst; p. 164: © David McNew/Getty; p. 165: © William Whitehurst/Corbis; p. 167: © Jemal Countess/WireImage

Chapter 8 Opener: © David Bacon/The Image Works; p. 172: © Nicholas Kamm/AFP/Getty; p. 174: © Bettmann/Corbis; p. 176: Photo by Cliff Watts. Courtesy of TeachersCount and the National Education Association; p. 178: © JP Laffont/Sygma/Corbis; p. 179: © Editorial Image, LLC/Alamy; p. 180: © Jeff Fusco/Getty; p. 181: © Tetra images/Getty; p. 182: © Comstock/Alamy; p. 183: © Kevin Lamarque/Reuters/Corbis; p. 184: © AP Photo/Manuel Balce Ceneta; p. 185: © Peter Bono/Stock Illustration RF/Getty; p. 187: © Comstock Images/Alamy; p. 188 top: © Comstock/PictureQuest; p. 188 bottom: © Editorial Image, LLC/Alamy; p. 189: © Paul Gilligan/Photodisc/Getty; p. 190: © AP Photo/Paul Sakuma; p. 191: © Stockbyte/Getty

Chapter 9 Opener: © Stan Honda/AFP/Getty; p. 196: © Image Source/SuperStock; p. 198: © Bettmann/Corbis; p. 201: © Corbis; p. 204: © Spencer Platt/Getty; p. 208: © Martial Colomb/Getty; p. 209 top: © AP Photo; p. 209 bottom: © C Squared Studios/Getty; p. 210: © Elyse Eidelheit/The Image Works; p. 213: © AP Photo/Douglas C. Pizac; p. 214: Courtesy of the Brad Gideon; p. 215: © AP Photo/Doug Mills; p. 221: © Digital Vision/Getty

FIGURES/TEXT

idealism, **392–393**
ideological parties, **209**
ideologue, **142**
ideology, **7**, 55
impeachment, **279**–280
imperial presidency, **308**–**309**
implied powers, **43**
impoundment, **298**
Imus, Don, 234
incorporation, 68–69
incumbency factor, 259–260
incumbents, **258**
independent executive agencies, 328
independent regulatory agencies, 329
indirect mobilization, **157**
inflation, **376**
informational support, **135**
initiative, **6**
inner cabinet, **306**
inside strategy, **171, 173**
intelligence community, 395–396
intelligence Reform and Terrorism Protec-
    tion Act, 395
intelligent design, 73
intensity, **134–135**
interest groups, 170–191, **173**
    accessing the courts, 186–187
    coalition formation, 189
    current status, 190–191
    distinctive features, 173–174
    financing campaigns, 184–186
    grassroots mobilization, 187–189
    historical overview, 174–175
    lobbying, 181–184
    protests, 189–190
    tactics, 181
    what are they, 176–178
    why join?, 178–179
intergovernmental lobbies, 55
intermediate scrutiny test, **104**
internal political efficacy, **156–157**
internet, 240–241
interstate compacts, **56–57**
interstate relations, 56–59
Iraq intelligence fiasco, 385–386
iron triangle, **183**
issue networks, **183**

J

Jackson, Andrew, 47, 200, 256, 303, 320
Jay, John, 30
Jefferson, Thomas, 6, 22, 45, 70, 295
Jefferson, William, 184
Jim Crow laws, **99**
Johnson, Andrew, 279, 310
Johnson, Jim, 184
Johnson, Lyndon, 274, 311, 323, 351
joint committees, 271
Jones, Mary Harris (Mother Jones), 48
judicial activism, **352**
judicial restraint, **352**
judicial review, 34, **343**–344
judicial review in France/U.K., 343

judiciary. *See* Courts
jurisdiction, **344**
justiciability, **344**

K

Katrina, Hurricane, 318
Kawahata, Molly, 1, 2
Kennedy, John F., 116, 241, 309
Kennedy, Ted, 71
Kerry, John, 218
Kevorkian, Jack, 89
Key, V. O., Jr., 127
Keynes, John Maynard, 375
King, Martin Luther, Jr., 102, 103
Kissinger, Henry, 308, 392
Klaber, Andrew, 408
Koppel, Ted, 246
Korematsu v. United States, **111**
Kostyo, Mike, 162
Kyoto Protocol, 370

L

Lakoff, George, 125
Langston, Thomas, 312
lawmaking, 276–278
Lawrence v. Texas, 114
Leadership PACs, **187**
leading questions, **137**
Legal Defense and Educational Fund (LDF),
    106
legislative referendum, **6–7**
Legislative veto, **280**
Lemon **test,** 72–73
lesbians, 112–114
Libby, Lewis "Scooter," 299
libel, **78–79**
liberal democracy, **7**
liberalism, 141, **392–393**
libertarianism, **142**
Lieberman, Joe, 267
life cycle effects, **129**
Lincoln, Abraham, 290, 299, 347
Lindner, Carl, Jr., 212
line item veto, **298**
line organization, **328–329**
Literary Digest, 128
litigious, **346**
living room test, 239
lobbying, **174–175,** 181–184
Lobbying Disclosure Act, 184
Lochner v. New York, 48
Locke, John, 5, 7, 25
logrolling, **273**
Long, Huey P., 275
loss of evidence searches, 83
Luczak, Allison, 267
Luntz, Frank, 125–126

M

MAD, 389
Madison, James, 23, 25, 30, 44, 173
majority leader, **272–273**
majority opinion, **350**

majority rule, **4**
Mann, Christopher, 196
marble cake federalism, 50
Marbury v. Madison, 34, 343, 346
markup, **276–277**
Marshall, John, 46, 343, 350
Marshall, Thurgood, 351, 355
Marshall Plan, 392
Martin, Luther, 24
Mason, George, 24
mass media, **230**
McCain, John, 145, 292, 293, 294, 296, 304
McCain-Feingold bill, 185
McConnell v. Federal Election Commission,
    76
McCulloch v. Maryland, 46
McIntyre, Kue, 363
McKinley, William, 185
McReynolds, James C., 354
media, 224–249
    adversarial journalism, 235–236
    content regulation, 234–235
    covering Congress, 244–245
    covering the president, 242–244
    covering the Supreme Court, 245
    current status, 246–248
    election night coverage, 242
    entertainment, 235
    historical overview, 227–230
    Internet, 240–241
    narrowcasting, 232–233
    newspapers, 230–231
    ownership limits, 234
    penny press, 228
    personal lives, 241–242
    political bias, 236–237
    political campaigns, 237–242
    presidential debates, 238–239
    social networking sites, 232
    yellow journalism, 228–229
    young people, 231–232
Medicaid, 373
Medicare, 373
Medvedev, Dmitry, 404, 405
merit system, **321**
microtargeting, 195–196
Middle East, 405–406
midterm elections, 260
Miers, Harriet, 280, 339
Mill, John Stuart, 5
Miller test, **77**
minority groups. *See* Civil rights
minority leader, **272–273**
minority-majority district, **262**
minority rights, **4**
Miranda rights, **84**
Missouri Compromise, 98
Mitchell v. Helms, 74
mobilizing the grass tops, **186–187**
Mondale, Walter, 218
monetary policy, **378–379,** 378–380
Monroe, James, 387
Monroe Doctrine, 301, 387

Montesquieu, Baron de, 25
Mother Jones, 48
Mott, Lucretia, 114
muckraking, 229
Mugabe, Robert, 406
Murrow, Edward R., 229
mutually assured destruction (MAD),
    388–389

N

NAACP, 100–101
NAACP v. Alabama, 81
NAACP v. Button, 90
Nader, Ralph, 209, 210
NAFTA, 380
narrowcasting, **232–233**
National American Woman Suffrage As-
    sociation (NAWSA), 115–116
National Association for the Advancement
    of Colored People (NAACP), 100–101
National Consumers' League, 175
national convention, **206**
national interests, **391–392**
National League of Cities v. Usery, 55
National Organization for Women (NOW),
    117
National Performance Review (NPR),
    321–322
National Republican Congressional Com-
    mittee (NRCC), 206
National Republican Senatorial Committee
    (NRSC), 206
National Security Council, 308, 393
Native Americans, 108–109
NATO, 400–401
NAWSA, 115–116
Near v. Minnesota, 79
negative or attack advertising, **215**
negotiated rule making, 327
neoconservatism, **392–393**
New Deal, 48, 347
New Deal coalition, **201**
New State Ice Company v. Liebmann, 57
New York Times Company v. Sullivan, 78
New York Times v. Sullivan, 234
NGOs, 408
Nixon, Richard, 51, 299, 305, 306, 308, 310
No Child Left Behind Act, 52, 55
nominating convention, **294**
nonattitudes, **138**
nongovernmental organizations (NGOs),
    408
Norris, Pippa, 6
North American Free Trade Agreement
    (NAFTA), **380**
North Atlantic Treaty Organization (NATO),
    400–401
Norton, Eleanor Holmes, 18
NOW, 117
NRCC, 206
NRSC, 206
nuclear age, 388–390
nuclear threat, 404

nullification, **45**

O

O' Reilly, Leonora, 175
Obama, Barack, 12, 125, 131, 204, 219, 220,
    225, 291–294, 296, 304
Obscenity, 77, 78
O'Connor, Sandra Day, 339, 356, 357
Office of Management and Budget (OMB),
    308
Olson, Mancur, 179
OMB, 308
Open Door Policy, 388
open market operations, **379**
open primary, **213**
opinion, **350**
opposition research, **219**
original jurisdiction, **344**
Osborne, David, 322
Oslo Accords, 405
outside strategy, **172–173**
oversight, 280–281, **332–333**

P

PAC, 185
paid media, **215**
Palin, Sarah, 117, 294
Parks, Rosa, 102
party realignment, 202–203
Paterson, William, 23
patronage, **200–201,** 320–321
Pelosi, Nancy, 117, 273
Pendleton Act, 321
Penn, Mark, 196
penny press, 228
Pentagon Papers case, 79
per curiam opinion, **350–351**
Perkins, Frances, 324
Perot, Ross, 209
Peters, Douglas E., 334
Petraeus, David, 404
Phillips, David Graham, 229
platform, **206–207**
Plessy, Homer, 99
Plessy v. Ferguson, 101
pluralism, **4–5**
plurality, **198**
plurality opinion, **350–351**
pocket veto, **276–277**
police powers, 43
policy councils, 308
political action committee (PAC), **185**
political advertising in Scandinavia, 239
political appointees, 323
political campaign, 210–216
political culture, **127**
political cynicism, **138–139**
political disadvantage theory, **186–187**
political efficacy, **140–141**
political engagement, **155–156**
political entrepreneur, **179**
political ideology, 141–143
political information, **156–157**

political interest, **156–157**
political knowledge, 138–139
political machines, **200**
political mobilization, **156**–158
political movements, **173**
political participation, **8–9**
    150–169
    activities beyond voting, 162–164
    amount of information conveyed, 153
    current status, 165–166
    education, 154
    family wealth, 154
    gender, 155
    mobilization, 156–158
    opportunities, costs, benefits, 151–152
    political engagement, 155–156
    public policy, and, 165
    race, 155
    religious affiliation, 154–155
    voting, 158–161
    workplace, 155
political parties
    congressional/senatorial campaign com-
        mittees, 206–207
    current status, 219–220
    defined, **197**
    fundraising, 204–205
    historical overview, 200–202
    local party organizations, 208
    national committee, 203–206
    nature of parties, 197
    party realignment, 202–203
    precinct organizations, 208
    state committees, 207
    third parties, 208–210
    why two parties?, 198–199
political power, **4**
political questions, **344–345**
political socialization, **129**
political speech, 75
politico, **263**
politics, 3
Polk, James, 290
polls, 135–138
popular referendum, **6–7**
population, **136**
populists, **142**
pork barrel projects, **268–269**
poverty, 372–374
Powell, Colin, 385, 394
Powell v. Alabama, 85
prayer in school, 73–74
precedent, **342–343**
precinct, **208**
preemption, **391**
Presidency, 286–313
    chief diplomat, as, 302
    chief executive, as, 297–299
    commander in chief, as, 299–301
    current status, 312
    economic leader, as, 304–305
    Electoral College, **294–297**
    executive orders, **299**

[HOW YOU VOTED]

>> ELECTORAL MAP: 2008 PRESIDENTIAL ELECTION

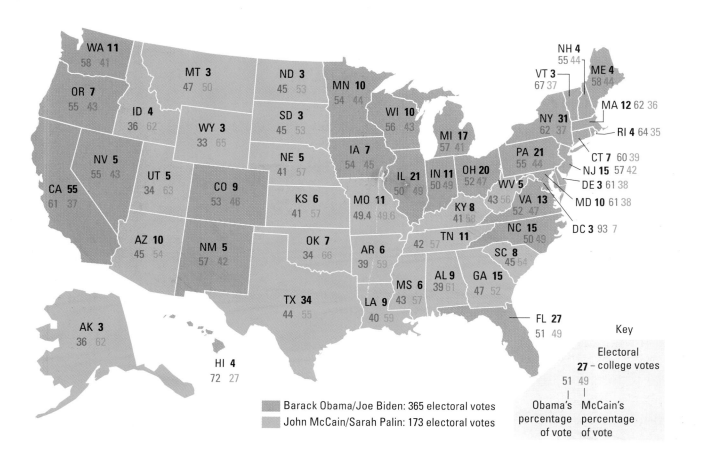

WA **11**
58 41

MT **3**
47 50

ND **3**
45 53

MN **10**
54 44

NH **4**
55 44

VT **3**
67 37

ME **4**
58 44

OR **7**
55 43

ID **4**
36 62

WY **3**
33 65

SD **3**
45 53

WI **10**
56 43

NY **31**
62 37

MA **12** 62 36

RI **4** 64 35

NV **5**
55 43

UT **5**
34 63

NE **5**
41 57

IA **7**
54 45

MI **17**
57 41

PA **21**
55 44

CT **7** 60 39

NJ **15** 57 42

CA **55**
61 37

CO **9**
53 46

KS **6**
41 57

IL **21**
50 49

IN **11**
50 49

OH **20**
52 47

WV **5**
43 56

VA **13**
52 47

DE **3** 61 38

MD **10** 61 38

DC **3** 93 7

AZ **10**
45 54

NM **5**
57 42

OK **7**
34 66

MO **11**
49.4 49.6

KY **8**
41 58

TN **11**
42 57

NC **15**
50 49

AR **6**
39 59

SC **8**
45 54

AK **3**
36 62

TX **34**
44 55

LA **9**
40 59

MS **6**
43 57

AL **9**
39 61

GA **15**
47 52

FL **27**
51 49

HI **4**
72 27

Key

Electoral
27 – college votes

51 | 49

Obama's | McCain's
percentage | percentage
of vote | of vote

Barack Obama/Joe Biden: 365 electoral votes
John McCain/Sarah Palin: 173 electoral votes